15th Edition

OCEAN SHIPS

15th Edition

OCEAN SHIPS

David Hornsby

Ian Allan
PUBLISHING

Contents

First published 1964
This edition 2009

ISBN 978 0 7110 3381 8

Published by Ian Allan Publishing

an imprint of Ian Allan Publishing Ltd, Hersham, Surrey KT12 4RG
Printed by Ian Allan Printing, Hersham, Surrey KT12 4RG

Code: 0905/B1

Visit the Ian Allan Publishing web site at:
www.ianallanpublishing.com

Front Cover: **Carnival Corp (Cunard).** QUEEN VICTORIA. *Getty Images*
Half title: **D'Amico Soc di Nav.** HIGH ENDEAVOUR. *C. Lous*
Title Page: **Carnival Corp (Ocean Village).** OCEAN VILLAGE TWO. *Mick Lindsay*
Back Cover, bottom: **Dockwise NV.** TARGET. *Hans Kraijenbosch*
Back Cover, top: **Martime GmbH.** CAP CASTILLO. *Hans Kraijenbosch*
Below: **A. P. Moller.** SKAGEN MAERSK. *Allan Ryszka Onions*

Preface

Welcome to this new enlarged edition of *Ocean Ships* with 100% colour illustrations and now including the web address and a brief 'thumb-nail' history of most companies. As with previous editions, the book provides details of the major cruise ships operating world-wide and the fleets of many shipping companies based in or operating deep-sea routes to British and northern European ports.

The three years, since the previous edition, have seen some remarkable changes in the world of international shipping, accentuated by the recent 'credit-crunch' as many economies slide into recession.

The cruise market currently remains one of the few buoyant sectors of the industry, but unsurprisingly, few orders for new ships have been placed in recent months. The large multi-brand operators are already shuffling cruise ships between their companies, no doubt in anticipation of large new cruise ships being delivered and possible changes in customer demands. This will again squeeze the margins for smaller operators, as will the availability of older-tonnage due to the Safety of Life at Sea (SOLAS) regulations. Later this year, yet another new record will be established with delivery of Royal Caribbean's new *Oasis of the Seas,* at 222,900 gross tons she will be over 40% larger than any previous passenger ship with many new innovative features.

Over 95% of the world's raw materials and manufactured goods are transported by sea and therefore it is no surprise that many cargo sectors are struggling in the current economic down-turn.

Until a year ago, container ships serving the Far East-Europe routes were 'full', despite the delivery of numerous new vessels carrying over 10,000 TEU (20-foot equivalent unit). Now, however, there are more than 400 container ships lying 'idle' around the world – equivalent to over 1,1 million TEU capacity -with numbers increasing each week. Ships are now operating at slower speeds, some services have been terminated and operators are combining their services to prevent gross over-supply. Some companies operating chartered vessels are also terminating charters at the earliest opportunity.

The bulk carrier market has also been badly hit, particularly the demand for large vessels transporting ore, coal and other raw materials. In mid-2008, the industry index for such vessels was at an all-time high, but within just a few months, the index had slumped to a record low. Today, hundreds of 'bulkers' are laid-up in ports and anchorages around the world 'awaiting orders' and many owners with newbuilding orders are seeking to delay delivery or even terminate contracts.

The specialist vehicle carrier sector has always been strong, but without export cars or plant and equipment to be transported, some older vessels have already headed for 'recycling' and market analysts suggest several hundred others could disappear before the end of the year, while there are already reports of newly delivered car carriers heading straight into lay-up.

Acts of piracy off the coasts of east Africa and more recently west Africa have escalated during the past year, culminating in the well-publicised seizure and ransom of *Sirius Star* late in 2008. Despite naval escorts, some cruise ships passing through the 'horn of Africa' have been forced to disembark passengers and container ships have imposed cargo surcharges or have been diverted via the Cape.

I again express my very grateful thanks to those who have provided their excellent photographs and to my many friends, acquaintances and correspondents for their interest, comments and information.

Finally, a great 'thank you' to my wife, who after nine editions of *Ocean Ships* is somehow resigned to the chaos and stress as each new edition reaches 'copy' deadline.

David Hornsby
Southampton, England
February 2009

Disclaimer

Glossary

The companies in each section are listed in alphabetical order under the main company name, followed by the country of origin. Individual 'one-ship' owning companies are not given, but in some cases subsidiary fleets are separately listed. Other variations in ownership, joint ownership, management or charter are generally covered by footnotes. Funnel and hull colours are those normally used by the companies, although these may vary when a vessel is operating on a particular service, or on charter to another operator.

Name	registered name
Eng	all vessels are single screw motorships unless indicated after the name as having more than one screw or other types of main propulsive machinery as follows

as	sail with auxiliary engines
me	diesel with electric drive
gm	combined gas turbine and diesel with electric drive
gt	gas turbine with electric drive
st	steam turbine
p	directional pod propulsion system

Flag

Ant	Netherlands Antilles	Chl	Chile	Irn	Iran	Phl	Philippines
Are	United Arab Emirates	Chn	China	Isr	Israel	Pmd	Madeira
		Cni	Canary Islands	Ita	Italy	Qat	Qatar
Arg	Argentina	Cym	Cayman Islands	Jpn	Japan	Rif	French International
Atf	Kerguelen Islands	Cyp	Cyprus	Kor	South Korea	Rom	Romania
Atg	Antigua and Barbuda	Deu	Germany	Kwt	Kuwait	Rus	Russia
		Dis	Danish International	Lbr	Liberia	Sau	Saudi Arabia
Aus	Australia	Dmk	Denmark	Lux	Luxembourg	Sgp	Singapore
Bel	Belgium	Egy	Egypt	Lva	Latvia	Swe	Sweden
Bgr	Bulgaria	Eth	Ethiopia	Mex	Mexico	Tha	Thailand
Bhr	Bahrain	Fin	Finland	Mhl	Marshall Islands	Twn	Taiwan
Bhs	Bahamas	Fra	France	Mlt	Malta	Usa	United States of America
Bmu	Bermuda	Gbr	United Kingdom	Mys	Malaysia		
Bra	Brazil	Gib	Gibralter	Nis	Norwegian International	Vct	St. Vincent and Grenadines
Brb	Barbados	Grc	Greece				
Brn	Brunei Darussalam	Hkg	Hong Kong (China)	Nld	Netherlands	Ven	Venezuela
Can	Canada	Hrv	Croatia	Nor	Norway	Zaf	South Africa
Che	Switzerland	Iom	Isle of Man (British)	Pan	Panama		

Year	year of completion — not necessarily of launching or commissioning.
GRT	gross registered tonnage — not weight, but volume of hull and enclosed space — one gross ton equals 100 cu. ft.
DWT	deadweight tonnes — maximum weight of cargo, stores, fuel etc — one tonne (1000 kg) equals 0.984 ton (British)
LOA	overall length (metres); (- -) length between perpendiculars
Bm	overall breadth of hull (metres) - some vessels have greater width to superstructure/bridge etc.
Kts	service speed in normal weather and at normal service draught — one knot equals 6,050ft per hour or 1.146 mph.
Type	general description of type of vessel

B	bulk carrier	Co	cargo/part container	R	refrigerated cargo
BC	bulk/container carrier	Cp	cargo-pitch carrier	Ro	roll-on, roll-off
Boh	bulk - open hatch	HL	heavy-lift vessel	ROI	roll-on, roll-off/icebreaker
Bp	bulk - pitch carrier	HLs	heavy-lift / semi-submersible	Rr	refrigerated with ro-ro
Bs	bulk refined sugar carrier	LC	lighter/container	T	tanker
Bu	bulk - self discharging	Lgc	liquefied gas carrier	Ta	tanker-asphalt
Bw	bulk woodchip carrier	Lng	liquefied natural gas	Tfj	tanker-fruit juice
C	general cargo	Lpg	liquefied petroleum gas	Tm	tanker-molten sulphur
Ca	cable layer	Lv	livestock carrier	V	vehicle carrier
CC	cellular container	O	ore carrier		
Ce	cement carrier	Obo	ore/bulk/oil carrier		

Pass	maximum number of passengers in lower and upper berths or (— —) in lower berths only
Remarks:	

conv	converted from other ship type (with date where known)
ex:	previous names followed by year of change to subsequent name
l/a	name at launch or 'float-out' prior to completion
l/dn	name allocated when laid-down at commencement of construction
pt:	part of ship
len	date hull lengthened
sht	date hull shortened
wid	date hull widened
NE	date re-engined
teu	twenty-foot equivalent unit (one teu equals about 14 tonnes deadweight)

PART ONE
Cruise Ships and Passenger Liners

Saga Group. SAGA RUBY. *N. Kemps*

Ambassadors International   USA

Windstar Cruises Ltd

Funnel: *White with turquoise symbol.* **Hull:** *White with turquoise band and blue boot-topping.* **History:** *Founded 1984 as Windstar Sail Cruises Ltd. Holland America acquired a 50% share in 1987 and the balance in 1988, before being taken over by Carnival Corp. Sold to Ambassadors International Inc in 2007.* **Web:** *www.windstarcruises.com*

Name		Flag	Year	GRT	Loa	Bm	Kts	Pass	Former names
Wind Spirit	(as/me)	Bhs	1988	5,736	134	16	11	150	
Wind Star	(as/me)	Bhs	1986	5,307	134	16	11	150	
Wind Surf	(as/me2)	Bhs	1989	14,745	187	20	15	453	ex Club Med 1-97, l/a La Fayette

Carnival Corporation   USA

Funnel: *Red forward, blue aft, separated by vertical curved white arc.* **Hull:** *White with narrow red band, blue boot-topping.* **History:** *Founded 1972 as Carnival Cruise Lines Inc until 1993. Betweem 1989 and 2001 acquired numerous other operators to become the largest cruising company with many brands aimed at different markets. The expansion continued with joint venture with TUI in 2006 and a joint venture with Iberojet in 2007, the same year as Swan Hellenic was closed down and Windstar Cruises was sold.* **Web:** *www.carnivalplc.com or www.carnivalcorp.com*

Name		Flag	Year	GRT	Loa	Bm	Kts	Pass	Former names
Carnival Conquest	(me2)	Pan	2002	110,239	290	36	19	3,700	
Carnival Destiny	(me2)	Bhs	1996	101,353	272	36	18	3,336	
Carnival Ecstasy	(me2)	Pan	1991	70,367	262	32	18	2,634	ex Ecstasy-07
Carnival Elation	(me2p)	Pan	1998	70,390	262	32	20	2,634	ex Elation-07
Carnival Fantasy	(me2)	Pan	1990	70,367	261	32	18	2,634	ex Fantasy-07
Carnival Fascination	(me2)	Bhs	1994	70,367	262	32	18	2,624	ex Fascination-07
Carnival Freedom	(me2)	Pan	2007	110,320	290	36	21	3,783	
Carnival Glory	(me2)	Pan	2003	110,239	290	36	22	3,700	
Carnival Imagination	(me2)	Bhs	1995	70,367	262	32	18	2,624	ex Imagination-07
Carnival Inspiration	(me2)	Bhs	1996	70,367	262	32	18	2,634	ex Inspiration-07
Carnival Legend	(me2p)	Pan	2002	85,942	293	32	22	2,680	
Carnival Liberty	(me2)	Pan	2005	110,320	285	32	22	3,700	
Carnival Miracle	(me2p)	Pan	2004	85,942	293	32	22	2,680	
Carnival Paradise	(me2p)	Pan	1998	70,390	262	32	21	2,634	ex Paradise-07
Carnival Pride	(me2p)	Pan	2001	85,920	293	32	22	2,680	
Carnival Sensation	(me2)	Bhs	1993	70,367	262	32	20	2,634	ex Sensation-07
Carnival Spirit	(me2p)	Pan	2001	85,920	293	32	22	2,680	
Carnival Splendor	(me2)	Pan	2008	112,000	290	36	22	3,540	
Carnival Triumph	(me2)	Bhs	1999	101,509	272	36	21	3,470	
Carnival Valor	(me2)	Pan	2004	110,239	290	36	22	3,710	
Carnival Victory	(me2)	Pan	2000	101,509	272	36	22	3,470	
Holiday	(2)	Bhs	1985	46,052	222	28	22	1,794	
newbuildings:									
Carnival Dream	(me2p)	Pan	2009	130,000	304	37	22	3,646	
Carnival Magic	(me2p)	Pan	2011	130,000	304	37	22	3,652	

Aida Cruises/Germany

Funnel: *White with 'AIDA' (letters in blue, red, yellow and green respectively).* **Hull:** *White with red 'lips' and 'eye' and blue wave symbols on bows.* **History:** *Originally founded 1999 as joint venture between by P&O and Arkona Touristik which merged with Seetours International in 2000.* **Web:** *www.aida.de*

Carnival Corp. CARNIVAL SPLENDOR. *N. Kemps*

Name		Flag	Year	GRT	Loa	Bm	Kts	Pass	Former names
AIDAaura	(me2)	Ita	2003	42,289	203	28	19	1,582	
AIDAbella	(me2)	Ita	2008	69,203	249	32	21	2,500	
AIDAcara	(2)	Ita	1996	38,557	193	28	18	1,230	ex Aida-01
AIDAdiva	(me2)	Ita	2007	69,203	252	32	21	2,500	
AIDAvita	(me2)	Ita	2002	42,289	203	28	19	1,582	
newbuildings:									
AIDAluna	(me2)	Ita	2009	68,500	252	32	21	(2,030)	
AIDAblu	(me2)	Ita	2010	71,000	252	32	21	(2,174)	
un-named cruise ship	(me2)	Ita	2011	71,000	252	32	21	(2,174)	
un-named cruise ship	(me2)	Ita	2012	71,000	249	32	21	(2,174)	

Costa Crociere SpA/Italy

Funnel: *Yellow with blue 'C' and black top.* **Hull:** *White with blue boot-topping.* **History:** *Founded 1924 and entered passenger shipping 1947. Acquired by Airtours and Carnival joint venture in 1997, Carnival acquiring complete control in 2001.*
Web: *www.costacruise.com or www.costacruises.co.uk*

Name		Flag	Year	GRT	Loa	Bm	Kts	Pass	Former names
Costa Allegre	(2)	Ita	1969	28,597	188	26	20	1,066	ex Alexandra-90, Regent Moon-88, Annie Johnson-86 (len/conv CC-92)
Costa Atlantica	(me2p)	Ita	2000	85,619	293	32	22	2,680	
Costa Classica	(2)	Ita	1991	52,926	221	31	19	1,766	
Costa Concordia	(me2)	Ita	2006	114,147	290	36	21	3,780	
Costa Europa	(2)	Ita	1986	54,763	243	29	19	1,773	ex Westerdam-02, Homeric-88 (len-90)
Costa Fortuna	(me2)	Ita	2003	102,587	272	36	20	3,470	
Costa Magica	(me2)	Ita	2004	102,587	272	36	20	3,470	
Costa Marina	(2)	Ita	1969	25,558	174	26	20	1,025	ex Italia-90, Regent Sun-86, Axel Johnson-86 (conv CC-90)
Costa Mediterranea	(me2p)	Ita	2003	85,619	293	32	22	2,680	
Costa Romantica	(2)	Ita	1993	53,049	221	31	19	1,782	
Costa Serena	(me2)	Ita	2007	114,147	290	36	21	3,780	
Costa Victoria	(me2)	Ita	1996	75,166	253	32	23	2,200	
newbuildings:									
Costa Pacifica	(me2)	Ita	2009	114,200	290	36	21	3,780	
Costa Luminosa	(me2p)	Ita	2009	92,700				2,828	
Costa Deliziosa	(me2p)	Ita	2010	92,700				2,828	
un-named cruise ship	(me2)	Ita	2011	114,200	290	36	21	3,780	
un-named cruise ship	(me2)	Ita	2012	114,200	290	36	21	3,780	

Carnival Corp (Aida Cruises). AIDAVITA. *Hans Kraijenbosch*

Name		Flag	Year	GRT	Loa	Bm	Kts	Pass	Former names

Cunard Line Ltd/UK

Funnel: *Red with two narrow black rings and black top.* **Hull:** *Charcoal grey with red boot-topping.* **History:** *Founded 1840 as British and North American RMSP Co by Samuel Cunard, becoming Cunard Steam-Ship Co Ltd in 1878. Merged with White Star Line in 1930's. Company acquired by Trafalgar House Investments in 1971 and acquired Norwegian America Cruises in 1983. Trafalgar acquired by Kvaerner in 1996 and Cunard sold to Carnival in 1998.* **Web:** *www.cunard.com or www.cunard.co.uk*

Name		Flag	Year	GRT	Loa	Bm	Kts	Pass	Former names
Queen Mary 2	(gme4p)	Gbr	2003	148,528	345	41	29	2,620	
Queen Victoria	(me2p)	Gbr	2007	90,049	294	32	23	2,014	
newbuilding:									
Queen Elizabeth	(me2p)	Gbr	2010	92,000	294	32	23	2,092	

Holland-America Line/Netherlands

Funnel: *White with black/white ship symbol within double black ring, narrow black top or vents.* **Hull:** *Black with red boot-topping.* **History:** *Founded 1873 as Nederlandsch Amerikaansche Stoomvaart Maatschappij. Later Holland America Cruises Inc until 1983 merger with Westours Inc to form Holland America Westours Inc to 2002. Acquired 50% share in Windstar Cruises in 1987 and acquired Home Lines in 1988. Acquired by Carnival in 1989.* **Web:** *www.hollandamerica.com*

Carnival Corp (Costa Crociere SpA). COSTA FORTUNA. *Hans Kraijenbosch*

Carnival Corp (Cunard Line). QUEEN MARY 2. *Hans Kraijenbosch*

Name		Flag	Year	GRT	Loa	Bm	Kts	Pass	Former names
Amsterdam	(me2p)	Nld	2000	60,874	238	32	21	1,738	
Eurodam	(me2p)	Nld	2008	86,273	285	32	22	2,104	
Maasdam	(me2)	Nld	1993	55,451	219	31	20	1,629	
Noordam	(gme2p)	Nld	2006	82,318	290	32	24	1,800	
Oosterdam	(gme2p)	Nld	2003	81,769	285	32	22	2,388	
Prinsendam	(2)	Nld	1988	37,983	204	29	21	837	ex Seabourn Sun-02, Royal Viking Sun-99
Rotterdam	(me2)	Nld	1997	59,652	238	32	22	1,620	
Ryndam	(me2)	Nld	1994	55,819	219	31	20	1,629	
Statendam	(me2)	Nld	1993	55,819	219	31	20	1,629	
Veendam	(me2)	Nld	1996	55,451	219	31	20	1,629	
Volendam	(me2)	Nld	1999	60,906	237	32	22	1,824	
Westerdam	(gme2p)	Nld	2004	81,811	285	32	22	1,800	
Zaandam	(me2)	Nld	2000	61,396	237	32	22	2,272	
Zuiderdam	(gme2p)	Nld	2002	81,769	285	32	22	1,848	
newbuilding:									
Nieuw Amsterdam	(me2p)	Nld	2010	86,000	290	32	24	(2,044)	

Iberojet Cruceros SL/Spain

Funnel: *Dark blue with yellow 5-pointed starfish.* **Hull:** *White.* **History:** *Subsidiary formed jointly with Spanish tour operator Orizonia Corp (25%).* **Web:** *www.cruceros.iberojet.es*

Name		Flag	Year	GRT	Loa	Bm	Kts	Pass	Former names
Grand Celebration	(2)	Pmd	1987	47,262	223	28	19	1,896	ex Celebration-08
Grand Mistral	(me2)	Mhl	1999	47,276	216	29	19	1,667	ex Mistral-05
Grand Voyager	(2)	Grc	2000	24,391	180	26	28	836	ex Voyager-06, Olympia Voyager-04, Olympic Voyager-01

Carnival Corp. (Holland-America Line). EURODAM. *Allan Ryszka Onions*

Carnival Corp. (Holland-America Line). PRINSENDAM. *C. Lous*

Name		Flag	Year	GRT	Loa	Bm	Kts	Pass	Former names

Ocean Village/UK

Funnel: *Pink with multi-coloured 'ocean village' on large white oval disc, black top..* **Hull:** *White with multi-coloured half-rings above waterline.* **History:** *Formed 2003 and to be closed-down at end of 2010.* **Web:** *www.oceanvillageholidays.co.uk*

Name		Flag	Year	GRT	Loa	Bm	Kts	Pass	Former names
Ocean Village **	(me2)	Gbr	1989	63,524	246	32	19	1,692	ex Arcadia-03, Star Princess-97, Sitmar Fairmajesty-89
Ocean Village Two *	(me2)	Ita	1990	70,310	245	32	19	1,900	ex AIDAblu-07, A'Rosa Blu-04, Crown Princess-02

** to P&O Australia at end of 2009 and renamed **Pacific Jewel** and ** to P&O Australia at end of 2010 and renamed **Pacific Pearl***

P&O Cruises Ltd/UK

Funnel: *Yellow.* **Hull:** *White with red boot-topping.* **History:** *Founded 1837 as Peninsulat Steam Navigation Co, becoming Peninsular & Oriental Steam Navigation Co in 1840. P&P-Orient Lines formed 1961 when remaining Orient Lines shares acquired. Princess Cruises acquired 1974. P&O Princess Cruises remerged from P&O in 2000. Acquired by Carnival in 2003.* **Web:** *www.pocruises.co.uk*

Name		Flag	Year	GRT	Loa	Bm	Kts	Pass	Former names
Arcadia	(me2p)	Gbr	2005	82,972	285	32	22	2,556	l/dn Queen Victoria
Artemis	(2)	Gbr	1984	44,348	231	29	21	1,260	ex Royal Princess-05
Aurora	(me2)	Gbr	2000	76,152	270	32	24	1,878	
Oceana	(me2)	Gbr	1999	77,499	261	32	21	2,272	ex Ocean Princess-02
Oriana	(2)	Gbr	1995	69,153	260	32	24	2,108	
Ventura	(me2)	Gbr	2008	116,000	290	36	22	3,100	
newbuilding									
Azura	(me2)	Gbr	2010	116,000	290	36	22	3,076	

P&O Cruises Australia Ltd/Australia

Funnel: *White with large yellow multi-pointed star above blue wave symbol, black top.* **Hull:** *White with broad blue above narrow yellow bands.* **History:** *Formed 1987 as P&O Resorts Pty Ltd to 1998, then as P&O Australian Resorts Pty Ltd to 2004* **Web:** *www.pocruises.com.au*

Name		Flag	Year	GRT	Loa	Bm	Kts	Pass	Former names
Pacific Dawn	(me2)	Bmu	1991	70,285	245	32	19	1,900	ex Regal Princess-07
Pacific Sun	(2)	Bhs	1986	47,262	225	28	19	1,800	ex Jubilee-04

Ocean Village cruise ships (see above) to be transferred over at end of 2009 and 2010.

Princess Cruises Inc/USA

Funnel: *White funnel with blue/white 'Princess' flowing hair insignia.* **Hull:** *White with green boot-topping.* **History:** *Founded 1965 and acquired by P&O in 1974. Acquired Sitmar in 1988. Demerged as P&O-Princess Cruises in 2000 and acquired by Carnival in 2003.* **Web:** *www.princesscruises.com*

Name		Flag	Year	GRT	Loa	Bm	Kts	Pass	Former names
Caribbean Princess *	(me2)	Bmu	2004	112,894	290	36	22	3,798	l/dn Crown Princess
Coral Princess	(gme2)	Bmu	2002	91,627	294	32	21	2,581	
Crown Princess	(me2)	Bmu	2006	113,561	290	36	22	3,599	
Dawn Princess	(me2)	Bmu	1997	77,441	261	32	21	1,950	
Diamond Princess *	(me2)	Bmu	2004	115,875	290	38	23	2,600	l/dn Sapphire Princess
Emerald Princess	(me2)	Bmu	2007	116,000	290	36	22	3,599	
Golden Princess	(me2)	Bmu	2001	108,865	290	36	22	3,300	
Grand Princess	(me2)	Bmu	1998	108,806	290	36	22	3,300	
Island Princess	(gme2)	Bmu	2003	91,627	294	32	24	2,581	
Pacific Princess	(me2)	Bmu	1999	30,277	181	25	18	688	ex R Three-02
Royal Princess	(me2)	Bmu	2001	30,277	181	25	18	777	ex Minerva II-07, R Eight-03
Ruby Princess	(me2)	Bmu	2008	113,561	290	36	22	3,599	

Carnival Corp (P&O Australia). PACIFIC DAWN. *David Hornsby*

Name		Flag	Year	GRT	Loa	Bm	Kts	Pass	Former names
Sapphire Princess *	(me2)	Bmu	2004	115,875	290	38	23	3,078	l/dn Diamond Princess
Sea Princess	(me2)	Bmu	1998	77,499	261	32	19	2,342	ex Adonia-05, Sea Princess-03
Star Princess	(me2)	Bmu	2002	108,977	290	36	22	3,211	
Sun Princess	(me2)	Bmu	1995	77,441	261	32	21	2,342	
Tahitian Princess **	(me2)	Bmu	1999	30,277	181	25	18	688	R Four-02

*owned by Princess Cruises Lines, Bermuda** to be renamed **Ocean Princess** late in 2009.

Seabourn Cruises Inc/USA

Funnel: White with three narrow white lines forming 'S' on blue shield and blue top. **Hull:** White with pale blue band and blue boot-topping. **History:** Founded 1987 by Norwegian industrialist. Carnival acquired 25% in 1991, a further 25% in 1996 and the balance in 1998. **Web:** www.seabourn.com

Name		Flag	Year	GRT	Loa	Bm	Kts	Pass	Former names
Seabourn Legend	(2)	Bhs	1992	9,961	135	19	16	212	ex Queen Odyssey-96, Royal Viking Queen-94, l/dn Seabourn Legend
Seabourn Pride	(2)	Bhs	1988	9,975	134	19	16	212	
Seabourn Spirit	(2)	Bhs	1989	9,975	134	19	16	212	
newbuildings:									
Seabourn Odyssey	(me2)	Bhs	2009	32,200	198	26	19	450	
Seabourn Sojourn	(me2)	Bhs	2010	32,200	198	26	19	450	
un-named cruise ship	(me2)	Bhs	2011	32,200	198	26	19	450	

Classic International Cruises Portugal

Funnel: White with white sailing ship symbol on dark blue disc, narrow black top. **Hull:** White with blue band, blue boot-topping.
History: Founded 1991 as subsidiary of Arcalia Shipping Co. Ltd., Portugal. **Web:** www.cic-cruises.cm

Name		Flag	Year	GRT	Loa	Bm	Kts	Pass	Former names
Arion	(2)	Pmd	1965	5,888	117	17	18	312	ex Nautilus 2000-99, Astra I-99, Astra-96, Istra-91
Athena *	(2)	Ita	1948	16,144	160	21	18	566	ex Caribe-05, Valtur Prima-03, Italia Prima-00, Italia I-93,Fridtjof Nansen-93, Volker-86, Volkerfreundschaft-85, Stockholm-60
Funchal	(2)	Pmd	1961	9,563	153	19	14	442	
Princess Danae	(2)	Pmd	1955	16,531	162	21	17	497	ex Baltica-96, Starlight Princess-94, Anar-92, Danae-92, Therisos Express-74, Port Melbourne-72
Princess Daphne	(2)	Prt	1955	15,833	162	21	17	500	ex Ocean Monarch-08, Ocean Odyssey-02, Switzerland-02, Daphne-96, Akrotiri Express-74, Port Sydney-72

* chartered until 2014 and managed for World Cruises Agency, Portugal
Vessels often chartered out to other operators.

Carnival Corp (Princess Cruises). EMERALD PRINCESS. *Mick Lindsay*

Peter Deilmann Cruises Germany

Funnel: *White with red 'D' outline containing insignia.* **Hull:** *White with red band.* **History:** *Founded 1973.* **Web:** *www.deilmann.co.uk*

| Deutschland | (2) | Deu | 1998 | 22,496 | 175 | 23 | 20 | 600 | |

Delphin Cruises GmbH Germany

Funnel: *White with light blue dolphin on dark blue disc interrupting three narrow dark blue bands.* **Hull:**.*White with red or blue boot-topping.* **Web:** *www.hansakreuzfahrten.de*

| Delphin | (2) | Mlt | 1975 | 16,214 | 156 | 22 | 21 | 554 | ex Kazakhstan II-96, Byelorussiya-93 |
| Delphin Voyager * | (2) | Jpn | 1990 | 21,884 | 174 | 24 | 21 | 626 | ex Cruise One-07, Orient Venus-05 |

*Operated by subsidiary Hansa Kreuzfahrten and * chartered from Enterprises Shipping & Trading, Greece.*

Disney Cruise Line USA

Funnel: *Red with white 'Mickey Mouse' symbol over three black waves, black top.* **Hull:** *Black with white band above red boot-topping.* **History:** *Founded 1995 as a subsidiary of Walt Disney World Corp.* **Web:** *www-disneycruise.com*

Disney Magic	(me2)	Bhs	1998	83,338	294	32	21	2,834	
Disney Wonder	(me2)	Bhs	1999	83,308	294	32	21	2,834	
newbuildings									
Disney Dream	(me2p)	Bhs	2011	124,000				4,000	
Disney Fantasy	(me2p)	Bhs	2012	124,000				4,000	

EasyCruise Ltd UK

Funnel: *Black with 'easycruis' symbol.* **Hull:** *Black with redtop band and 'easycruise' symbol.* **History:** *Founded 2004.* **Web:** *www.easycruise.com*

| easy Cruise Life | (2) | Mlt | 1981 | 12,711 | 135 | 21 | 20 | 650 | ex Farah-08, The Jasmine-06, Palmira-01, Natasha-98, Lev Tolstoy-98 |
| easyCruiseOne | (2) | Mlt | 1990 | 4,077 | 88 | 16 | 15 | 170 | ex The Neptune 2-05, The Neptune-04, Renaissance Two-98 |

Hebridean International Cruises Ltd UK

Funnel: *Red with narrow black top.* **Hull:** *Black with narrow white line above red boot-topping.* **History:** *Founded 1988 as Hebridean Island Cruises to 2006.* **Web:** *www.hebridean.co.uk*

| Hebridean Princess * | (2) | Gbr | 1964 | 2,112 | 72 | 14 | 14 | 49 | ex Columba-89 |
| Hebridean Spirit | (2) | Gbr | 1991 | 4,200 | 91 | 15 | 15 | 79 | ex Capri-01, MegaStar Capricorn-01, Sun Viva 2-00, Renaissance Six-98 |

* reported withdrawn and sold March 2009.

Hurtigruten Group Norway

Funnel: *Black with white 'H' symbol above white wave on red disc or black with broad white band edged with narrow red bands.* **Hull:** *Black with broad red band.* **History:** *Service commenced 1893 by Vesteraalens Dampskibs, alter being joined by Bergenske Dampskibs and Nordenfjeldske Dampskibs in 1894 and by Ofotens Dampskibs in 1936.* **Web:** *www.hurtigruten.co.uk*

Peter Deilmann Cruises. DEUTSCHLAND. *C. Lous*

Delphin Cruises. DELPHIN. *Phil Kempsey*

Delphin Cruises. DELPHIN VOYAGER. *Phil Kempsey*

Hurtigruten. MIDNATSOL. *Hans Kraijenbosch*

Name		Flag	Year	GRT	Loa	Bm	Kts	Pass	Former names
Finnmarken	(2)	Nor	2002	15,000	139	22	15	638	
Fram	(me2p)	Nor	2007	12,700	110	20	16	382	
Kong Harald	(2)	Nor	1993	11,200	122	19	15	490	
Lofoten		Nor	1964	2,621	87	13	16	147	
Midnatsol	(2)	Nor	2003	16,151	136	22	15	652	
Nordkapp	(2)	Nor	1996	11,386	123	20	15	464	
Nordlys	(2)	Nor	1994	11,200	122	19	15	482	
Nordnorge	(2)	Nor	1997	11,384	123	20	18	455	
Nordstjernen		Nor	1956	2,191	81	13	15	114	
Polar Star *	(me3)	Brb	1969	3,963	87	21	18	105	
Polarlys	(2)	Nor	1996	12,000	123	20	15	479	
Richard With	(2)	Nor	1993	11,205	122	19	15	483	
Trollfjord	(2)	Nor	2002	15,000	136	22	15	648	
Vesteralen	(2)	Nor	1983	6,261	109	17	15	316	

Operating Norwegian Coastal voyages and seasonal voyages to Alaska, Antarctica and Central America.
* owned by Karlson Shipping, Norway.

Louis Cruise Lines   Cyprus

Funnel: *White with red sun/wave symbol above dark blue 'L', black top.* **Hull:** *White with red or dark blue boot-topping.*
History: *Founded 1935 and commenced shipping owning in 1987.* **Web:** *www.louisgroup.com or www.louiscruises.com*

Name		Flag	Year	GRT	Loa	Bm	Kts	Pass	Former names
Aquamarine	(2)	Grc	1971	23,149	194	24	21	1,194	ex Arielle-08, Aquamarine-06, Carousel-05, Nordic Prince-95
Coral *	(2)	Grc	1971	14,194	148	22	24	912	ex Triton-05, Sunward II-91, Cunard Adventurer-77
Cristal	(2)	Grc	1980	25,611	159	25	21	1,452	ex Opera-07, Silja Opera-06, Superstar Taurus-02, Leeward-00, Sally Albatross-95, Viking Saga-86
Ivory	(st2)	Grc	1957	12,549	160	21	20	690	ex Aegean Two-08, Ivory-07, The Ausonia-06, Ausonia-06
Orient Queen	(2)	Grc	1968	15,781	160	23	20	928	ex Bolero-04, Starward-95
Sapphire *	(2)	Mhl	1967	12,263	149	21	16	562	ex Princesa Oceanica-96, Sea Prince V-95, Sea Prince-95, Ocean Princess-93, Italia-83
The Aegean Pearl *	(2)	Bhs	1971	16,710	163	23	21	750	ex Perla-08, Seawing-05, Southward-95
The Emerald	(st2)	Grc	1958	23,428	178	26	20	960	ex Regent Rainbow-96, Diamond Island-92, Santa Rosa-90

Managed by subsidiary Core Marine and * owned by Louis Hellenic Cruises subsidiary
See also Thomson Cruises (under TUI), Transocean Tours, Holland America (under Carnival Corp.) and Norwegian Cruise (under Star Cruise)

Majestic International Cruises Inc   Greece

Mediterranean Classic Cruises (formerly Monarch Classic Cruises)

Funnel: *White with blue swan symbol on yellow disc or charterers colours.* **Hull:** *White or dark blue with red boot-topping.*
History: *Founded 2002.* **Web:** *www.mccruises.gr*

Hurtigruten. NORDNORGE. *F. de Vries*

Majestic International Cruises. OCEAN COUNTESS. *Hans Kraijenbosch*

Majestic International Cruises. OCEAN MAJESTY. *C. Lous*

MSC Italian Cruises. MSC ARMONIA. *Hans Kraijenbosch*

Name		Flag	Year	GRT	Loa	Bm	Kts	Pass	Former names
Blue Monarch	(2)	Pmd	1966	11,429	150	21	18	536	ex Grand Victoria-07, World Renaissance-05, Awani Dream-98, World Renaissance-95, Homeric Renaissance-78, Renaissance-77
Ocean Countess	(2)	Pmd	1976	16,795	164	23	18	950	ex Ruby-08, Ocean Countess-07, Lili Marleen-06, Ocean Countess-05, Olympia Countess-04, Olympic Countess-01, Awani Dream 2-98, Cunard Countess-96
Ocean Majesty *	(2)	Prt	1966	10,417	131	19	20	613	ex Homeric-95, Ocean Majesty-95,Olympic-95, Ocean Majesty-94, Kypros Star-89, Sol Christiana-86, Juan March-85

* seasonally chartered to Page & Moy Holidays, UK until end of 2009.

Mitsui-OSK Lines KK   Japan

Funnel: *Light red.* **Hull:** *White.* **History:** *See cargo section.* **Web:** *www.mopas.co.jp*

Fuji Maru	(2)	Jpn	1989	23,235	167	27	20	603	
Nippon Maru	(2)	Jpn	1990	21,903	167	24	18	607	

MSC Italian Cruises   Italy

Funnel: *White with 'M' over 'SC'.* **Hull:** *White with narrow blue band, blue boot-topping.* **History:** *Formed 1986 as Mediterranean Shipping Cruises, a subsidiary of Mediterranean Shipping Co. (formed 1970) and renamed in 2002.* **Web:** *www.msccruises.co.uk*

Melody	(2)	Pan	1982	35,143	205	27	23	1,550	ex Starship Atlantic-97, Atlantic-88
MSC Armonia	(me2p)	Pan	2001	58,714	251	29	21	2,087	ex European Vision-04
MSC Fantasia	(me2)	Pan	2008	134,500	333	38	22	3,887	
MSC Lirica	(me2p)	Pan	2003	59,058	251	29	20	2,200	
MSC Musica	(me2p)	Pan	2006	92,409	294	32	22	3,013	
MSC Opera	(me2p)	Pan	2004	59,058	251	29	20	2,200	
MSC Orchestra	(me2p)	Pan	2007	92,409	294	32	22	3,013	
MSC Poesia	(me2p)	Pan	2008	92,409	294	32	22	3,013	
MSC Sinfonia	(me2p)	Pan	2002	58,714	251	29	21	2,087	ex European Stars-04, I/a European Dream
Rhapsody	(2)	Ita	1977	17,095	164	23	19	812	ex Cunard Princess-95, I/a Cunard Conquest
newbuildings									
MSC Splendida	(me2)	Pan	2009	133,500	333	38	22	3,887	I/dn as MSC Seranata
MSC Magnifica	(me2p)	Pan	2010	94,600	294	32	22	3,013	
MSC Meraviglia	(me2p)	Pan	2011	94,600	294	32	22	3,013	
MSC Favolosa	(me2p)	Pan	2012	94,600	294	32	22	3,013	

Nippon Yusen Kaisha   Japan

Crystal Cruises Inc/USA

Funnel: *Black, large white side panels with blue symbol.* **Hull:** *White with narrow blue band.* **History:** *Formed 1989 by NYK (founded 1885 – see cargo section).* **Web:** *www.crystalcruises.com*

Crystal Serenity	(me2p)	Bhs	2003	68,870	250	32	23	1080	
Crystal Symphony	(me2)	Bhs	1995	51,044	238	31	21	975	

Yusen Cruise/Japan

Funnel: *White with two red bands and black top.* **Hull:** *White with blue boot-topping.* **Web:** *www.asukacruise.co.jp*

Asuka II	(me2)	Bhs	1990	48,621	241	30	22	960	ex Crystal Harmony-06

Jointly owned by Asuka Ship Co., Japan

Oceania Cruises   USA

Funnel: *White with blue 'O' symbol.* **Hull:** *White.* **History:** *Founded 2002, the three original ships being chartered until purchased in 2006. Private equity firm acquired majority stake in 2007.* **Web:** *www.oceaniacruise.co.uk or www.oceaniacruises.com*

Insignia	(me2)	Mhl	1998	30,277	181	25	18	684	ex R One-03
Nautica	(me2)	Mhl	2000	30,277	181	25	18	684	ex Blue Star-05, R Five-04
Regatta	(me2)	Mhl	1998	30,277	181	25	18	684	ex Insignia-03, R Two-03
newbuildings:									
Marina	(me2)	Mhl	2010	65,000	252	32	20	1260	
un-named cruise ship	(me2)	Mhl	2011	65,000	252	32	20	1260	

Managed by V. Ships Leisure SAM, Monaco

Nippon Yusen Kaisha (Yusen Cruise). ASUKA II. *Mick Lindsay*

Nippon Yusen Kaisha (Crystal Cruises). CRYSTAL SYMPHONY. *C. Lous*

Fred Olsen Cruise Lines Ltd   UK

Funnel: *White with red oval and white/blue houseflag.* **Hull:** *White with green boot-topping.* **History:** Shipping company originally founded 1848 in Norway and UK cruise subsidiary formed in 1997. **Web:** *www.fredolsencruises.com*

Name			Flag	Year	GRT	Loa	Bm	Kts	Pass	Former names
Balmoral	(2)		Bhs	1988	43,537	218	32	22	1,340	ex Norwegian Crown-07, Crown Odyssey-03, Norwegian Crown-00, Crown Odyssey-96 (len-08)
Black Prince *	(2)		Bhs	1966	11,209	142	20	18	451	ex Black Prince/Venus-87
Black Watch	(2)		Bhs	1972	28,670	205	25	18	930	ex Star Odyssey-96, Westward-94, Royal Viking Star-91 (len-81, NE-05)
Boudicca	(2)		Pan	1973	28,388	205	25	18	1,022	ex Grand Latino-05, SuperStar Capricorn-04, Hyundai Kumgang-01, SuperStar Capricorn-98, Golden Princess-96, Sunward-93, Birka Queen-92, Sunward-92, Royal Viking Sky-91 (len-82, NE-05)
Braemar	(2)		Pan	1993	24,344	196	23	18	856	ex Crown Dynasty-01, Norwegian Dynasty-99, Crown Majesty-97, Crown Dynasty-97, Cunard Dynasty-97, Crown Dynasty-95 (len-08)

* scheduled to be withdrawn October 2009.

Phoenix Reisen   Germany

Funnel: *Turquoise with white seagull in flight over yellow sun.* **Hull:** *White with turquoise band, blue boot-topping.* **History:** *German tour operator.* **Web:** *www.phoenixreisen.com*

Name			Flag	Year	GRT	Loa	Bm	Kts	Pass	Former names
Albatros *	(2)		Bhs	1973	29,518	205	25	18	812	ex Crown-04, Norwegian Star I-02, Norwegian Star-01, Royal Odyssey-97, Royal Viking Sea-91 (len-83)
Amadea	(2)		Jpn	1991	28,856	190	25	21	604	ex Asuka-06

* chartered from Club Cruise, Netherlands.

Fred Olsen Cruise Lines. BOUDICCA. *Hans Kraijenbosch*

Regent Seven Seas Cruises Inc

USA

Funnel: White with purple 'Regent'. **Hull:** White with blue band and blue waterline above red boot-topping. **History:** Originally founded 1992 as Diamond Cruise Line, later becoming Radisson Seven Seas Cruises to 2006. Acquired by Apollo Management equity group in 2008. **Web:** www.rssc.com

Name		Flag	Year	GRT	Loa	Bm	Kts	Pass	Former names
Paul Gauguin *	(me2)	Bhs	1997	19,170	156	22	18	320	
Seven Seas Mariner	(me2p)	Wlf	2001	48,075	216	29	19	769	
Seven Seas Navigator	(2)	Bhs	1999	28,550	171	24	17	542	I/dn Akademik Nikolay Pilyugin (1991)
Seven Seas Voyager	(me2p)	Bhs	2003	41,500	207	29	20	769	

* chartered from Grand Circle Cruise Line, USA until 2010.

Royal Caribbean International

Norway

Funnel: White with blue crown and anchor symbol. **Hull:** White with blue band and blue boot-topping. **History:** Founded 1969 as Royal Caribbean Cruises Ltd by Norwegian shipowners Anders Wilhelmsen, I M Skaugen & Co and Gotaas-Larsen being renamed in 1997, when Celebrity Cruises was acquired. **Web:** www.royalcaribbean.com

Name		Flag	Year	GRT	Loa	Bm	Kts	Pass	Former names
Adventure of the Seas	(me3p)	Bhs	2001	137,276	311	39	23	3,840	
Brilliance of the Seas	(gt2p)	Bhs	2002	90,090	294	32	24	2,500	
Enchantment of the Seas	(me2)	Bhs	1997	82,910	301	32	22	2,730	(len-05)
Explorer of the Seas	(me3p)	Bhs	2000	137,308	311	39	23	3,840	
Freedom of the Seas	(me3p)	Bhs	2006	158,000	339	39	21	4,375	
Grandeur of the Seas	(me2)	Bhs	1996	73,817	279	32	22	2,440	
Independence of the Seas	(me3p)	Bhs	2008	158,000	339	39	22	4,328	

Phoenix Reisen. AMADEA. *Hans Kraijenbosch*

Royal Caribbean International. BRILLIANCE OF THE SEAS. *Tom Walker*

Name		Flag	Year	GRT	Loa	Bm	Kts	Pass	Former names
Jewel of the Seas	(gt2p)	Bhs	2004	90,090	293	32	24	2,500	
Legend of the Seas	(me2)	Bhs	1995	69,490	264	32	24	2,060	
Liberty of the Seas	(me3p)	Bhs	2007	158,000	339	39	22	4,328	
Majesty of the Seas	(2)	Nis	1992	73,937	268	32	20	2,744	
Mariner of the Seas	(me3p)	Bhs	2004	138,279	311	39	22	3,807	
Monarch of the Seas	(2)	Nis	1991	73,937	268	32	20	2,744	
Navigator of the Seas	(me3p)	Bhs	2003	138,279	311	39	22	3,807	
Radiance of the Seas	(gt2p)	Bhs	2001	90,090	293	32	24	2,500	
Rhapsody of the Seas	(me2)	Nis	1997	78,491	279	32	22	2,416	
Serenade of the Seas	(gt2p)	Bhs	2003	90,090	293	32	24	2,500	
Splendour of the Seas	(me2)	Nis	1996	69,130	264	32	24	2,066	
Vision of the Seas	(me2)	Bhs	1998	78,340	279	32	22	2,416	
Voyager of the Seas	(me3p)	Bhs	1999	137,276	311	39	22	3,840	
newbuildings.									
Oasis of the Seas	(me3p)	Bhs	2009	222,900	360	47	22	6,296	
Allure of the Seas	(me3p)	Bhs	2010	222,900	360	47	22	6,296	

Azamara Cruises/USA

Funnel: *White with brown diamond symbol.* **Hull:** *White with brown diamond symbol and 'AZAMARA' towards stern.*
History: *Subsidiary formed 2007.* **Web:** *www.azamaracruises.com*

Name		Flag	Year	GRT	Loa	Bm	Kts	Pass	Former names
Azamara Journey	(me2)	Mlt	2000	30,277	181	25	18	777	ex Blue Dream-07, R Six-05
Azamara Quest	(me2)	Mhl	2000	30,277	181	25	18	702	ex Blue Moon-07, Delphin Renaissance-06, R Seven-03

Celebrity Cruises/USA

Funnel: *Black or black/white horizontal striped with large white diagonal cross (edged yellow on later vessels).* **Hull:** *White with broad black bands at lifeboat level and waterline.* **History:** *Founded 1989 by Chandris and acquired 1997. Formed Celebrity Expeditions in 2004.* **Web:** *www.celebritycruises.com*

Name		Flag	Year	GRT	Loa	Bm	Kts	Pass	Former names
Celebrity Century	(2)	Bhs	1995	71,545	247	32	21	2,253	ex Century-08
Celebrity Constellation	(gt2p)	Mlt	2002	90,280	294	32	24	2,449	ex Constellation-07
Celebrity Galaxy *	(2)	Mlt	1996	76,522	264	32	21	1,896	ex Galaxy-08
Celebrity Infinity	(gt2p)	Mlt	2001	90,228	294	32	24	2,449	ex Infinity-07
Celebrity Mercury	(2)	Mlt	1997	76,522	264	32	21	1,896	ex Mercury-08
Celebrity Solstice	(me2p)	Bhs	2008	122,000	317	37	24	(2,850)	l/a Solstice
Celebrity Summit	(gt2p)	Bhs	2001	90,280	294	32	24	2,449	ex Summit-08
Millennium	(gt2p)	Bhs	2000	90,228	294	32	24	2,449	
Xpedition	Ecu	2001	2,842	89	14	13	96	ex Sun Bay-04	
newbuildings.									
Celebrity Equinox	(me2p)	Bhs	2009	122,000	317	37	24	(2,850)	
Celebrity Eclipse	(me2p)	Bhs	2010	122,000	317	37	24	(2,850)	
un-named cruise ship	(me2p)	Bhs	2011	122,000	317	37	24	(2,850)	
un-named cruise ship	(me2p)	Bhs	2012	122,000	315	37	24	(2,850)	

* scheduled to be transferred to TUI Cruises joint venture in 2009.

Pullmantur Cruises/Spain

Funnel: *Dark blue with red striped globe symbol on pale blue edged white disc.* **Hull:** *White with red 'pullmantur cruises'.*
History: *Formed 2000 by established Spanish travel company. Acquired by Royal Caribbean in 2006.*
Web: *www.pullmanturcruises.com*

Name		Flag	Year	GRT	Loa	Bm	Kts	Pass	Former names
Bleu de France *	(2)	Mlt	1981	37,301	200	29	21	758	ex Holiday Dream-08, SuperStar Aries-04, SuperStar Europe-99, Europa-99
Empress	(2)	Mlt	1990	48,563	211	31	19	2,020	ex Empress of the Seas-08, Nordic Empress-04
Ocean Dream	(2)	Mlt	1982	36,674	205	26	19	1,411	ex Pacific Star-08, Costa Tropicale-05, Tropicale-01
Oceanic	(st2)	Bhs	1965	38,772	238	29	20	1,562	ex Starship Oceanic-98, Royale Oceanic-85, Oceanic-85
Pacific	(2)	Bhs	1970	20,186	169	25	19	723	ex Pacific Princess-02, Sea Venture-75
Pacific Dream	(2)	Bhs	1990	46,811	208	29	19	1,798	ex Island Star-08, Horizon-05
Sky Wonder	(st2)	Mlt	1984	46,087	240	28	21	1,600	ex Pacific Sky-06, Sky Princess-00, Fairsky-88
Sovereign	(2)	Mlt	1987	73,192	268	32	21	2,524	ex Sovereign of the Seas-08
Zenith	(2)	Mlt	1992	47,255	208	29	21	1,774	

* operated by Croisieres de France, France (formed 2007)

Saga Group   UK

Funnel: *Yellow with narrow white band below narrow dark blue top.* **Hull:** *Dark blue with red boot-topping or white with black boot-topping (Spirit).* **History:** *Parent company founded in 1950's and entered shipping owning in 1997. Spirit of Adventure subsidiary formed 2005.* **Web:** *www.saga.co.uk/cruising*

Name		Flag	Year	GRT	Loa	Bm	Kts	Pass	Former names
Saga Pearl II	(2)	Bhs	1981	18,591	164	23	18	540	ex Astoria-09, Arkona-02, Astor-85

Royal Caribbean International. INDEPENDENCE OF THE SEAS. *Tom Walker*

Royal Caribbean International. NAVIGATOR OF THE SEAS. *David Walker*

Royal Caribbean (Azamara Cruises). AZAMARA JOURNEY. *N. Kemps*

Royal Caribbean (Celebrity Cruises). CELEBRITY SUMMIT. *Mick Lindsay*

Star Cruise (Norwegian Cruise Line). NORWEGIAN GEM. *Hans Kraijenbosch*

Star Cruise (Norwegian Cruise Line). NORWEGIAN JADE. *Phil Kempsey*

Name	Flag		Year	GRT	Loa	Bm	Kts	Pass	Former names
Saga Rose *	(2)	Bhs	1965	24,528	189	24	20	587	ex Gripsholm-97, Sagafjord-96
Saga Ruby	(2)	Gbr	1973	24,492	191	25	21	670	ex Caronia-05, Vistafjord-99
Spirit of Adventure	(2)	Bhs	1980	9,570	139	18	17	352	ex Orange Melody-06, Berlin-05, Princess Mahsuri-85, Berlin-82 (len-86)

* due to be withdrawn from service Autumn 2009.

Sea Cloud Cruises   Germany

Hull: White. **History:** Founded about 1994 by subsidiary of Hansa Treuhand Group. **Web:** www.seacloud.com

Name	Flag		Year	GRT	Loa	Bm	Kts	Pass	Former names
Sea Cloud	(as2)	Mlt	1931	2,532	110	15	12	68	ex Sea Cloud of Grand Cayman-87, Sea Cloud-80, Antarna-79, Patria-64, Angelita-61, Sea Cloud-52, Hussar-35
Sea Cloud II	(as2)	Mlt	2000	3,849	117	16	14	96	

Owned by Hansa Shipmanagement GmbH

Silversea Cruises   USA

Funnel: White with blue 'SS' symbol. **Hull:** White. **History:** Founded by former owners of Sitmar after 1988 sale to P&O. **Web:** www.silversea.com

Name	Flag		Year	GRT	Loa	Bm	Kts	Pass	Former names
Prince Albert II	(2)	Gbr	1969	6,072	108	16	15	140	ex World Discoverer-??, Dream 21-01, Delfin Star-97, Baltic Clipper-92, Sally Clipper-92, Delfin Clipper-90
Silver Cloud	(2)	Bhs	1994	16,927	156	21	17	314	
Silver Shadow	(2)	Bhs	2000	28,258	182	25	21	388	
Silver Whisper	(2)	Bhs	2001	28,258	182	25	21	388	I/dn Silver Mirage
Silver Wind	(2)	Bhs	1995	16,927	156	21	17	296	
newbuilding									
Silver Spirit	(2)	Bhs	2009	36,000				540	

Star Clippers Ltd   Monaco

Funnel: None. **Hull:** White. **History:** Founded 1991 as Star Clippers Inc to 2000. **Web:** www.starclippers.com

Name	Flag		Year	GRT	Loa	Bm	Kts	Pass	Former names
Royal Clipper	(as)	Lux	2000	4,425	133	16	13	224	I/a Gwarek
Star Clipper	(as)	Lux	1992	2,298	112	15	12	194	
Star Flyer	(as)	Lux	1991	2,298	112	15	12	194	I/a Star Clipper

Star Cruise AS Sendirian Berhad   Singapore

Funnel: Dark blue with yellow eight-pointed star on broad red band. **Hull:** White with red band and blue boot-topping. **History:** Formed 1993 and acquired Norwegian Cruise Line in 2000. **Web:** www.starcruises.com

Name	Flag		Year	GRT	Loa	Bm	Kts	Pass	Former names
MegaStar Aries	(2)	Pan	1991	3,264	82	14	16	82	ex Aurora II-94, I/a Lady Sarah
MegaStar Taurus	(2)	Pan	1991	3,341	82	14	16	82	ex Aurora I-94, Lady D-91, I/a Lady Diana
Star Pisces	(2)	Pan	1990	40,053	177	30	22	2,165	ex Kalypso-93
SuperStar Aquarius	(2)	Bhs	1993	51,309	230	29	18	2,100	ex Norwegian Wind-07, Windward-98 (len-98)
SuperStar Libra	(2)	Bhs	1988	42,276	216	32	20	1,798	ex Norwegian Sea-05, Seaward-97
SuperStar Virgo	(me2)	Pan	1999	75,338	269	32	24	2,975	

Norwegian Cruise Line/USA

Funnel: Dark blue with gold 'NCL' within gold square outline. **Hull:** White with red stripe (Norwegian Dawn with multi-coloured artwork; or dark blue, blue boot-topping. **History:** Founded in 1967 as Norwegian Caribbean Lines by Klosters Rederi, becoming Kloster Cruise AS in 1987 and Norwegian Cruise Line in 1996. Acquired Royal Viking Line in 1984 and Royal Cruise Line in 1989. **Web:** www.ncl.com

Name	Flag		Year	GRT	Loa	Bm	Kts	Pass	Former names
Norwegian Dawn	(me2)	Bhs	2002	92,250	292	32	25	2,500	I/dn SuperStar Sagittarius
Norwegian Dream	(2)	Bhs	1992	50,764	230	29	18	2,100	ex Dreamward-98 (len-98)
Norwegian Gem	(me2p)	Bhs	2007	93,000	294	32	24	2,384	
Norwegian Jade	(me2p)		2006	92,250	294	32	24	2,400	ex Pride of Hawaii-08
Norwegian Jewel	(me2p)	Bhs	2005	91,740	294	32	24	2,400	
Norwegian Majesty **	(2)	Bhs	1992	40,876	207	28	19	2,324	ex Royal Majesty-97 (len-99)
Norwegian Pearl	(me2)	Bhs	2006	93,500	294	32	24	2,400	
Norwegian Sky	(me2p)		1999	77,104	260	32	20	2,450	ex Pride of Aloha-08, Norwegian Sky-04, I/a Costa Olympia
Norwegian Spirit	(me2)	Bhs	1998	75,338	269	32	24	2,975	ex SuperStar Leo-04
Norwegian Star	(me2p)	Bhs	2001	91,740	294	32	24	2,500	I/dn SuperStar Libra
Norwegian Sun	(me2)	Bhs	2001	78,309	258	32	20	2,359	
Pride of America	(me2p)	Usa	2005	80,439	276	32	22	2,146	
newbuilding									
Norwegian Epic	(me2p)	Bhs	2010	166,000	325	40	-	4,200	

** owned by Louis Cruise and chartered until end of 2009.

Transocean Tours   Germany

Funnel: *White with blue 't' symbol inside blue ring interrupting pale blue over blue narrow bands.* **Hull:** *White with pale blue over blue bands.* **History:** *Tour operator formed in 1954.* **Web:** *www.transocean.de or www.transoceancruises.co.uk*

| Astor | (2) | Bhs | 1987 | 20,606 | 176 | 23 | 18 | 650 | ex Fedor Dostoevskiy-95, Astor-88 |
| Marco Polo | (2) | Bhs | 1965 | 22,080 | 176 | 24 | 20 | 850 | ex Aleksandr Pushkin-91 |

TUI AG   Germany

Hapag-Lloyd Cruises/Germany

Funnel: *Orange with blue 'HL'.* **Hull:** *White with orange/blue band, red boot-topping.* **History:** *Formed by 1970 merger of the long-established Hamburg America and Norddeutscher Lloyd lines. Control acquired by Preussag group in 1997 and Hapag-Lloyd acquired control of travel group TUI in 1998.* **Web:** *www.hl-cruises.com*

Bremen	(2)	Bhs	1990	6,752	112	17	16	184	ex Frontier Spirit-93
C. Columbus **	(2)	Bhs	1997	15,067	145	22	18	423	
Europa	(me2p)	Bhs	1999	28,437	199	24	21	408	
Hanseatic *	(2)	Bhs	1991	8,378	123	18	14	188	ex Society Adventurer-92

* chartered from Hanseatic Cruises GmbH until 2008 and ** chartered from NSB Niederelbe Schiffahrts. GmbH & Co. KG.

Quark Expeditions/USA

Funnel: *Chartered ships with various owners colours..* **Hull:** *Owners colours.* **History:** *TUI merged its expedition cruising subsidiaries in 2008, including Clipper Cruise Line (Founded 1982, sold to Kuoni in 1999 and acquired by First Choice in 2006), Peregrine Adventures (formed 1977 as part of First Choice), Quark Expeditions (formed 1991) and First Choice Expeditions.* **Web:** *www.quarkexpeditions.com*

Clipper Adventurer	(2)	Bhs	1975	4,376	100	16	17	116	ex Alla Tarasova-97
Clipper Odyssey	(2)	Bhs	1989	5,218	103	15	18	128	ex Oceanic Odyssey-98, Oceanic Grace-97
Lyubov Orlova	(2)	Mlt	1976	4,251	100	16	17	112	

*Also operates a number of smaller expedition ships including **Akademik Ioffe**, **Akademik Sergey Vavilov**, **Akademik Shokalskiy**, **Kapitan Khlebnikov**, **Ocean Nova** and **Quest** chartered from various owners and research organisations.*

Thomson Cruises/UK

Funnel: *Pale blue with red 'tui' logo.* **Hull:** *White with blue over yellow over red bands, blue or red boot-topping.* **History:** *Long established holiday operator acquired by TUI in 2000. Island Cruises subsidiary formed 2002 as joint venture between Royal Caribbean and First Choice (control acquired by TUI in 2007) was closed early in 2009.* **Web:** *www.thomson-cruises.co.uk*

| Island Escape | (2) | Bhs | 1982 | 40,132 | 185 | 27 | 18 | 1,863 | ex Viking Serenade-02, Stardancer-90, Scandinavia-85 |

TUI Group (Quark Expeditions). CLIPPER ADVENTURER. *Allan Ryszka Onions*

Name		Flag	Year	GRT	Loa	Bm	Kts	Pass	Former names
The Calypso	(2)	Bhs	1967	11,162	135	19	16	486	ex Calypso-05, Regent Jewel-94, Sun Fiesta-93, Ionian Harmony-90, Durr-89, Canguro Verde-81
Thomson Celebration *	(2)	Nld	1984	33,933	215	27	21	1,340	ex Noordam-05
Thomson Destiny	(2)	Cyp	1982	37,773	215	28	20	1,595	ex Sunbird-05, Song of America-99
Thomson Spirit	(2)	Bhs	1983	33,930	215	27	21	1,374	ex Spirit-03, Nieuw Amsterdam-02, Patriot-02, Nieuw Amsterdam-00

*Chartered from Louis Cruise Lines or * from Holland America Line (see under Carnival Corp.)*

TUI Group (Thomson Cruises). THE CALYPSO. *Hans Kraijenbosch*

TUI Group (Thomson Cruises). THOMSON DESTINY. *Mick Lindsay*

Name		Flag	Year	GRT	Loa	Bm	Kts	Pass	Former names

Voyages of Discovery   UK

Funnel: *White with narrow turquoise band below blue top.* **Hull:** *White with blue boot-topping.* **History:** *Commenced cruises in 1984 with chartered ships until acquiring vessel in 2004.* **Web:** *www.voyagesofdiscovery.com*

Name		Flag	Year	GRT	Loa	Bm	Kts	Pass	Former names
Discovery	(2)	Bmu	1972	20,216	169	25	18	689	ex Platinium-02, Hyundai Pungak-01, Island Princess-99, Island Venture-72

Swan Hellenic/UK

Funnel: *Dark blue with white swan symbol.* **Hull:** *Dark blue with red boot-topping.* **History:** *Founded in 1950's by Swan family, sold to P&O which was later acquired by Carnival. After closure in 2007, name acquired by Lord Sterling, who entered into agreement with Voyages parent.* **Web:** *www.swanhellenic.com*

Name		Flag	Year	GRT	Loa	Bm	Kts	Pass	Former names
Minerva *	(2)	Bhs	1996	12,331	133	20	16	428	ex Explorer II-08, Alexander von Humboldt-05, Explorer II-05, Saga Pearl-05, Minerva-03, I/a Okean

Other Cruise Ships

Adriatic Cruises, Croatia

Name		Flag	Year	GRT	Loa	Bm	Kts	Pass	Former names
Dalmacija	(2)	Hrv	1964	5,619	117	17	17	312	

Clipper Group, Denmark

Name		Flag	Year	GRT	Loa	Bm	Kts	Pass	Former names
Corinthian II *	(2)	Mlt	1991	4,200	91	15	15	114	ex Island Sun-05, Sun-04, Renai I-03, Renaissance Seven-01, Regina Renaissance-98, Renaissance Seven-92
Island Sky	(2)	Bhs	1992	4,200	90	15	15	114	ex Sky-04, Renai II-03, Renaissance Eight-01
Vision Star **	(2)	Pan	1992	19,093	164	23	19	940	ex SuperStar Gemini-09, Crown Jewel-95

*Managed by International Shipping Partners and chartered out to Noble Caledonia, * Travel Dynamics or ** Vision Cruises, Spain for joint venture with Modern Classic Cruises*

Compagnie des Isles du Ponant, France (CMA-CGM Group)

Name		Flag	Year	GRT	Loa	Bm	Kts	Pass	Former names
Le Diamant *	(2)	Wlf	1974	8,282	124	16	16	265	ex Song of Flower-04, Explorer Starship-89, Begonia-87, Fernhill-74
Le Levant	(2)	Wlf	1990	3,504	100	14	16	95	
newbuildings									
L'Austral			2010	10,600				264	
Le Boreal			2010	10,600				264	

** co-owned by Tapis Rouge Cruises, Spain. Also operates small sail-cruise vessels **La France** and **Le Ponant**.*

Elegant Cruises & Tours Inc, USA

Name		Flag	Year	GRT	Loa	Bm	Kts	Pass	Former names
Andrea		Lbr	1960	2,549	87	13	16	169	ex Harald Jarl-02

Currently operated seasonally by Noble Caledonia or Scantours Inc, USA

Ellevi Shipping Srl, Italy

Name		Flag	Year	GRT	Loa	Bm	Kts	Pass	Former names
Vistamar	(2)	Ita	1989	7,478	121	17	17	350	

operated by Plantours & Partner GmbH, Germany.

Golden Star Cruises, Greece

Name		Flag	Year	GRT	Loa	Bm	Kts	Pass	Former names
Aegean 1	(2)	Grc	1973	11,563	141	21	-	682	ex Aegean Dolphin-96, Dolphin-90, Aegean Dolphin-89, Alkyon-86, Narcis-85

Helios Shipping, Greece

Name		Flag	Year	GRT	Loa	Bm	Kts	Pass	Former names
Lauren L		Mlt	2002	2,842	89	14	13	96	ex Constellation-08, Corinthian-04, Sun Bay II-03

Institute for Shipboard Education Seawise Foundation, USA

Name		Flag	Year	GRT	Loa	Bm	Kts	Pass	Former names
Explorer	(2)	Bhs	2001	24,318	178	26	27	836	ex Olympia Explorer-04, I/a Olympic Explorer

Chartered from Stella Maritime, Bahamas for use as a floating University

Japan Cruise Line, Japan

Name		Flag	Year	GRT	Loa	Bm	Kts	Pass	Former names
Pacific Venus	(2)	Jpn	1998	26,518	183	25	20	720	

Name		Flag	Year	GRT	Loa	Bm	Kts	Pass	Former names
Kristina Cruises Ltd., Finland									
Kristina Regina		Fin	1960	4,295	100	15		353	ex Borea-87, Bore-77
Lindblad Expeditions, USA									
National Geographic Explorer	(2)	Bhs	1982	6,100	109	17	17	148	ex Lyngen-08, Midnatsol II-05, Midnatsol-03
National Geographic Endeavour		Bhs	1966	3,132	89	14	15	110	ex Endeavour-05, Caledonian Star-01, North Star-89, Lindmar-83, Marburg-82
National Geographic Polaris	(2)	Ecu	1960	2,138	72	13	14	82	ex Polaris-08, Lindblad Polaris-87, Oresund-81
Lindos Maritime, Greece									
Clelia II	(2)	Bhs	1990	4,077	88	15	15	84	ex Renaissance Four-96

Japan Cruise Line. PACIFIC VENUS. *N. Kemps*

Lindblad Expeditions. NATIONAL GEOGRAPHIC ENDEAVOUR. *Mike Lennon*

Name		Flag	Year	GRT	Loa	Bm	Kts	Pass	Former names

Marina Cruises, Monaco

Adriana III	(2)	Vct	1972	4,490	104	14	16	312	ex Adriana-08, Aquarius-87

The Peace Boat, Japan

Mona Lisa	(2)	Bhs	1966	28,891	210	27	21	720	ex Oceanic II-08, Mona Lisa-08, Victoria-03, Sea Princess-95, Kungsholm-79

operating world cruises on charter to non-governmental organisation as 'The Peace Boat'.

ResidenSea Ltd., Norway

The World	(2)	Bhs	2002	43,188	196	29	18	656	

operated by Silversea Cruises Ltd and with accommodation comprising 110 privately owned apartments and 88 guest suites

Salamis Lines (Hellas) Ltd., Cyprus

Salamis Glory	(2)	Cyp	1962	10,392	150	20	17	480	ex Regent Spirit-96, Morning Star-92, Constellation-92, Danaos-78, Anna Nery-78

SeaDream Yacht Club, Norway

SeaDream I	(2)	Bhs	1984	4,333	105	15	17	116	ex Seabourn Goddess I-01, Sea Goddess I-00
SeaDream II	(2)	Bhs	1985	4,333	105	15	17	116	ex Seabourn Goddess II-01, Sea Goddess II-00

Sete Yacht Management, Greece

Turama	(2)	Mlt	1990	8,343	116	17	17	330	ex Columbus Caravelle-08, Sally Caravelle-91, Delfin Caravelle-91

Societe Services et Transports, Monaco

Club Med 2	(as/me2)	Fra	1992	14,983	187	20	15	392	

Operated by Club Mediterranee and managed by V. Ships Leisure.

StarLine Cruises Ltd., Kenya

Royal Star	(2)	Bhs	1956	5,067	112	16	15	276	ex Ocean Islander-90, City of Andros-84, San Giorgio-76

operated by Africa Safari Club

ResidenSea. THE WORLD. *Allan Ryszka Onions*

PART TWO
Cargo Vessels and Tankers

OAO Sovcomflot. PETROPAVLOVSK. *Hans Kraijenbosch*

Christian F Ahrenkiel GmbH & Co Germany

Funnel: *Buff or buff with houseflag on blue band, or charterers colours.* **Hull:** *Black, dark blue, green or grey with red boot-topping.*
History: *Formed 1950 having previously being on the board of Hapag and his father having owned ships since 1910. Tankreederei Ahrenkiel founded in 1971, now United Chemical Transport (UCT) joint venture. Ahrenkiel Liner Services (ALS) formed 1982*
Web: *www.ahrenkiel.net*

Name	Flag	Year	GRT	DWT	LOA	Bm	Kts	Type	Former names
Anglia *	Lbr	1999	26,047	31,000	196	30	21	CC	ex Columbus Australia-05, Cherokee-03, Panthermax-02, CanMar Supreme-02, Panther Max-01
Aquitania *	Lbr	2000	26,044	31,000	196	30	21	CC	ex Maersk Aquitania-03, Corrado-03, Lion Max-02
AS Savonia *	Mhl	2000	17,167	21,150	169	27	20	CC	ex Bahamian Express-08
AS Scandia	Lbr	2000	19,131	24,973	189	27	22	CC	ex CMA CGM Puma-08, Scandia-03, P&O Nedlloyd Scandia-02, Scandia-02
Cardonia *	Lbr	2003	27,779	39,418	222	30	22	CC	ex CMA CGM Ukraine-06, Cardonia-03
Carpathia *	Lbr	2003	27,779	39,421	222	30	22	CC	ex CMA CGM Greece-06, Carpathia-04
Cimbria *	Lbr	2002	27,779	39,358	222	30	22	CC	
CMA CGM Galilee *	Lbr	2003	27,779	40,878	222	30	22	CC	ex Norasia Rigel-07, Carinthia-04
CMA CGM Oceano	Lbr	2006	27,100	34,496	210	30	22	CC	ex MOL Supremacy-08, Palatia-06
CMA CGM Orchid	Lbr	2006	28,592	39,426	222	30	22	CC	
CMA CGM Tulip *	Lbr	2006	28,592	39,374	222	30	22	CC	
Cordelia *	Lbr	2003	27,779	40,878	222	30	22	CC	
CSAV Rio Rapel *	Lbr	2000	26,047	28,337	195	30	21	CC	ex Asturia-04, Comanche-03, Ocelot Max-02
Danubia	Lbr	2004	38,975	68,524	229	32	15	T	ex Ocean Principal-05, Tavropos-04
Delmas Cameroun **	Lbr	1999	19,131	25,414	189	27	20	CC	ex Saxonia-06, P&O Nedlloyd San Francisco-05, Saxonia-99
Franconia	Lbr	1979	16,198	18,821	177	27	18	CC	ex Eagle Integrity-95, Sea Breeze-92, CMB Motion-91, European Senator-90, Franklin 1-87, TFL Franklin 86, Seatrain Bennington-80
Lobelia *	Lux	2001	23,232	37,263	183	27	14	T	ex Kersaint-08
Lombardia *	Lbr	2000	23,842	35,841	183	27	14	T	ex Silvia-08
Maersk Jakarta *	Lbr	2006	28.592	39,418	222	30	22	CC	ex Caria-06
Maersk Jeddah	Lbr	2006	28,592	39,418	222	30	22	CC	ex Catalania-06
Magpie *	Lbr	1999	23,843	35,930	183	27	14	T	
Masovia	Lbr	1995	17,285	22,183	175	29	20	CC	ex YM Izmir-08, Masovia-05, I/a Cape Negro
Melide *	Lbr	1999	23,843	35,841	183	27	14	T	
Montreux *	Lbr	1999	23,843	35,953	183	27	14	T	
Nordscot *	Lbr	2001	23,740	35,770	183	27	14	T	
Normannia	Lbr	1997	24,987	42,648	183	31	14	B	ex Batu-07
Patria I	Lbr	2006	27,100	34,600	210	30	22	CC	ex MOL Sunrise-08, Patria-06
Robin *	Lbr	1999	23,843	35,966	183	27	14	T	
Safmarine Illovo *	Lbr	2000	26,047	30,850	196	30	20	CC	ex Alicantia-05, Commander-03, Jaguar Max-02
Safmarine Mono *	Lbr	2001	26,047	30,703	196	30	20	CC	ex Andalusia-04, Centurion-03, Puma Max-02
Samaria	Deu	2000	19,131	25,360	189	27	20	CC	ex Calapadria-08, Samaria-04, P&O Nedlloyd Samaria-03, Samaria-00
Sevilla	Lbr	2008	21,019	25,884	180	28	20	CC	I/dn Manchester Strait
Sicilia	Lbr	2008	21,025	25,927	180	28	20	CC	
St. Katharinen *	Lbr	1999	25,202	43,760	182	30	14	T	
Turin Express	Lbr	2000	19,131	25,414	189	27	20	CC	ex Scotia-06, P&O Nedlloyd Scotia-02, Scotia-01

*newbuildings: eight 57,000 dwt, six 35,000 dwt bulk carriers for Suisse Outremer subsidiary, four 92,500 dwt bulk carriers for 2009-11 delivery. Managed by Ahrenkiel Shipmanagement GmbH & Co KG (founded 1991 as Constantia Schiffahrts GmbH to 1999) or * managed for FHH Fonds Haus Hamburg GmbH & Co KG or ** for HCI Capital AG*

Allocean Ltd UK

Funnel: *Charterers colours.* **Hull:** *Black with red boot-topping.* **History:** *Formed 1993 as Allco UK, subsidiary of Allco Finance Group (est 1979 in Australia), the ship-owning vehicle for Andreas Ugland & Sons. Renamed when UB Shipping acquired in 2002.*
Web: *www.allocean.co.uk*

Name	Flag	Year	GRT	DWT	LOA	Bm	Kts	Type	Former names
Algerian Express	Hkg	1995	15,095	18,294	169	27	17	CC	ex Syms Express I-08, Algerian Express-07, Young Liberty-05, Choyang Leader-01, Kuo Fah-95
Cap Arnauti ‡	Cyp	2004	18,334	23,579	175	27	20	CC	ex Philipp Schulte-04
Gem of Kilakarai	Sgp	2005	32,474	53,299	190	32	14	B	ex Lake Connie-07
MSC Acapulco ‡	Gbr	1996	10,730	14,148	163	22	17	CC	ex MOL Faithful-08, Sophie Schulte-05, Marfret Guyane-03, Sophie Schulte-03, CMA CGM Oyapock-02, X-press Annapurna-01, Sophie Schulte-00
MSC Amsterdam	Hkg	1995	28,892	41,624	203	31	20	CC	ex Trade Selene-03, MSC Amsterdam-02, Trade Selene-01

Name	Flag	Year	GRT	DWT	LOA	Bm	Kts	Type	Former names
MSC Belem	Hkg	1995	29,195	35,534	196	32	20	CC	ex Trade Harvest-02
MSC Greece	Hkg	1995	29,195	35,534	196	32	20	CC	ex Trade Maple-02, MSC Hamburg-02, Trade Maple-01
MSC Kiwi	Bhs	1999	24,836	14,367	217	27	25	CC	ex Ocean Producer-08, Perth-08, CP Master-06, Lykes Master-05, Perth-04, ADCL Sultana-01, Norasia Sultana-00
MSC Prospect ‡	Cyp	1994	14,619	20,275	166	25	19	CC	ex CMA CGM Papagayo-08, Bernhard Schulte-04, Tema Star II-00, Bernhard Schulte-99, Maersk Paita-98, TMM Tuxpan-97, Calapedra-96, Contship Tahiti-95, Bernhard Schulte-94
MSC Provider	Gbr	1999	24,836	14,169	217	27	25	CC	ex Ocean Provider-08, Hertford-08, Lykes Competitor-05, Hertford-04, ADCL Selina-01, Norasia Selina-00
MSC Zurich	Hkg	1995	28,892	41,553	203	31	20	CC	ex Trade Eternity-04, MSC London-02, Trade Eternity-01
Ocean Predator	Gbr	2002	27,656	48,635	190	32	14	B	ex Brilliant Star-07
Ocean Preface	Hkg	1993	37,550	70,255	225	32	13	B	ex Geeta-04, De Poterne-95
Ocean Prefect	Pan	2003	29,323	53,035	189	32	14	B	ex Scandinavian Express-06, Anni Selmer-04
Ocean Prelate	Gbr	2002	30,011	52,433	190	32	15	B	ex John Oldendorff-05
Ocean Prelude	Gbr	1995	36,097	68,541	225	32	14	B	ex Magnus Stove-03
Ocean President	Hkg	2001	28,647	50,913	190	32	14	B	ex Sea Angel-04
Ocean Promise ‡	Gbr	2001	26,718	33,871	210	30	22	CC	ex Henrika Schulte-07, P&O Nedlloyd Atacama-05, l/a Henrika Schulte
Ocean Prosper ‡	Sgp	1998	16,281	22,330	179	25	19	CC	ex Hans Schulte-07, CMA CGM Wallaby-06, Hans Schulte-02, Cabo Creus-01, Hans Schulte-98
Pac Antlia *	Sgp	2001	13,764	16,794	154	25	19	CC	ex H.H. Ruth-01
Pac Aquarius *	Sgp	2002	13,764	16,742	154	25	19	CC	ex Kota Mesra-08, Pac Aquarius-02
Priya	Gbr	1996	25,202	44,128	182	30	14	T	ex Jag Priya-03, Olympic Venture-01
Sanko Brave †	Sgp	2003	56,172	105,672	239	42	14	T	
Sanko Bright †	Sgp	2003	56,172	104,075	239	42	15	T	
TS Colombo	Hkg	1995	15,095	18,585	169	27	17	CC	ex Andalusian Express-08, Young Chance-02, Choyang Challenger-01

* managed by associated Allocean Maritime Ltd., UK (founded 2002) for subsidiary of Pacific Carriers Ltd, Singapore (Kuok Group).
† managed by Sanko Ship Management Co Ltd.or ‡ by Bernhard Schulte Shipmanagement companies.

Alpha Ship GmbH   Germany

Funnel: Green with wide light green and narrow light blue 'darts' on broad cream band or charterers colours. **Hull:** Green, brown or red with red boot-topping. **History:** Founded 1992 as Jan R Freese, later Reederei J Freese & Partner to 1994.
Web: www.alphaship.de

Name	Flag	Year	GRT	DWT	LOA	Bm	Kts	Type	Former names
AS Castor	Mhl	1997	14,241	18,445	159	24	19	CC	ex Cap Matatula-08, Castor-05, TMM Guadalajara-99, Castor-97
AS Mars	Mhl	1996	14,241	18,449	159	24	19	CC	ex Mars-07, Safmarine Emonti-01, Mars-00, Sea Viking-99, CMBT Mars-97, CGM La Bourdonnais-97, Mars-96
AS Pegasus	Mhl	1997	23,722	29,229	194	28	21	CC	ex Pegasus-07
AS Venus *	Mhl	1996	14,241	18,400	159	24	19	CC	ex Venus-07, DAL Karoo-02, Venus-00, CMBT Encounter-97, Venus-96
Astor **	Ant	1995	14,241	18,395	159	24	18	CC	ex APL Caracus-01, Astor-00, Infanta-97, l/a Astor
Cap Van Diemen	Mhl	1999	23,722	29,240	194	28	21	CC	ex Uranus-06, Alianca Antuerpia-03, Uranus-01
CMA CGM Castilla	Mhl	1998	23,722	29,240	194	28	21	CC	ex Cap Victor-06, Columbus Waikato-06, Taurus-02, Kota Perabu-01, Taurus-99
CMA CGM Cortes	Mhl	1998	23,722	29,240	194	28	21	CC	ex Cap Vincent-06, Neptun-02, Kota Perdana-00, Neptun-99
Condor **	Ant	1995	14,241	18,395	159	24	18	CC	ex TMM Chiapas-01, Condor-99, Recife-97, Condor-95
Delmas Anemone **	Ant	1996	14,241	18,400	159	24	18	CC	ex Saturn-06, TMM Leon-01, CMB Endurance-97, Saturn-96
Maersk Hong Kong *	Mhl	1997	21,199	25,039	178	28	21	CC	ex Nadir-98
Maersk Itajai	Mhl	2000	23,722	29,240	194	28	21	CC	ex Aries-01
Merkur **	Ant	1996	14,241	18,447	159	24	19	CC	ex APL Colon-01, Merkur-00, Sea Valiant-99, Merkur-97, CMBT Endeavour-97, Merkur-96
MOL Universe *	Mhl	1998	21,199	24,049	178	28	21	CC	ex Safmarine Amazon-08, Maersk Wellington-01, Zenit-98
Orion	Mhl	1997	21,199	25,107	178	28	21	CC	ex Maersk Lima-99, Orion-98, TNX Mercury-98, l/a Orion
Pluto	Mhl	1999	23,722	29,210	194	28	21	CC	
Pollux	Mhl	1997	14,241	18,400	159	24	18	CC	ex Lykes Pelican-01, Pollux-00
Safmarine Memling *	Mhl	1999	23,722	29,240	194	28	21	CC	ex SCL Memling-02, Poseidon-99

Name	Flag	Year	GRT	DWT	LOA	Bm	Kts	Type	Former names
Sirius *	Mhl	1998	21,199	25,107	183	28	21	CC	
Vega	Mhl	2000	23,722	29,240	194	28	21	CC	ex Maersk Valparaiso-08, Maersk Wellington-01, Maersk Itajai-01, Vega-00

Managed by Alpha Shipmanagement GmbH & Co KG
* managed for GHF Gesellschaft fur Handel und Finanz mbH or ** owned by HC companies and managed by Wallem GmbH & Co KG, Germany

Angelicoussis Shipping Group Ltd — Greece

Anangel Shipping Enterprises SA/Greece

Funnel: *White with green 'trefilli' between two narrow red bands beneath narrow black top.* **Hull**: *Light grey, dark grey or blue with red boot-topping.* **History**: *Company founded 1971, formerly trading since 1947 as A Angelicoussis and D Efthimiou, who had been shipowners since 1947.* **Web**: *www.agelef.co.uk .*

Name	Flag	Year	GRT	DWT	LOA	Bm	Kts	Type	Former names
Anangel Ambition	Grc	1994	81,120	161,587	280	44	13	B	
Anangel Destiny	Grc	1999	87,523	171,997	289	45	15	B	
Anangel Dynasty	Grc	1999	86,600	171,101	289	45	14	B	ex Yangtze Ore-02
Anangel Eternity	Grc	1999	86,600	171,176	289	45	14	B	ex Virginie Venture-02
Anangel Explorer	Grc	2007	87,582	171,927	289	45	14	B	
Anangel Fortune	Grc	2005	88,844	175,000	289	45	14	B	
Anangel Happiness	Grc	2008	89,565	177,720	292	45	14	B	
Anangel Innovation	Grc	2004	87,050	171,681	289	45	15	B	
Anangel Legend	Grc	1996	81,151	161,059	280	45	14	B	ex Bavang-03
Anangel Odyssey	Grc	2006	87,485	171,660	289	45	14	B	
Anangel Omonia	Grc	1996	38,859	73,519	225	32	14	B	
Anangel Pride	Grc	1993	81,569	161,643	280	45	13	B	
Anangel Prosperity	Grc	2006	88,853	174,240	289	45	14	B	
Anangel Sailor	Grc	2006	87,050	171,681	289	45	14	B	
Anangel Solidarity	Grc	1993	81,569	161,545	280	44	13	B	
Anangel Splendour	Grc	1993	81,120	161,643	280	45	13	B	
Anangel Vision	Grc	2007	87,485	171,810	289	45	14	B	
Pioneer	Grc	2004	87,050	171,681	289	45	15	B	

newbuildings: twelve 180,000 dwt, four 114,500 dwt and two 74,500 dwt bulk carriers for 2009-11 delivery.
managed by Anangel Maritime Services Inc. (founded 2001).

Kristen Navigation Inc/Greece

Funnel: *Light blue with yellow sun symbol on dark blue disc on broad light blue band.* **Hull**: *Black with red boot-topping.*
History: *Founded 1992.* **Web**: *www.kristennavigation.com*

Name	Flag	Year	GRT	DWT	LOA	Bm	Kts	Type	Former names
Andromeda Voyager *	Bhs	2005	160,808	320,472	332	58	15	T	
Gemini Voyager *	Bhs	1999	160,036	310,138	330	58	16	T	ex Richard H. Matzke-03
Regulus Voyager *	Bhs	2000	160,036	310,138	331	58	16	T	ex Chang-Lin Tien-03
Astro Altair	Grc	1997	53,074	98,805	248	43	15	T	
Astro Antares	Grc	1996	53,074	98,876	248	43	15	T	
Astro Arcturus	Grc	1997	53,074	98,805	248	43	15	T	
Astro Caesar	Grc	2009	161,500	318,010	333	60	15	T	
Astro Callisto	Grc	1999	157,833	299,167	332	58	15	T	ex Picardie-03
Astro Canopus	Grc	2007	158,970	320,472	333	60	15	T	
Astro Capella	Grc	1998	79,714	147,998	275	48	15	T	
Astro Capricorn	Grc	2008	158,970	320,513	333	60	15	T	
Astro Carina	Grc	2003	153,911	306,314	332	58	15	T	
Astro Cassiopeia	Grc	2003	83,000	159,000	274	48	15	T	
Astro Castor	Grc	2001	153,911	306,344	332	58	16	T	
Astro Centaurus	Grc	1995	156,565	300,294	332	58	15	T	ex Mindoro-00
Astro Challenge	Pan	2002	157,878	299,222	332	58	15	T	ex Maia-04, l/a Uvas
Astro Chloe	Grc	2009	161,500	318,010	333	60	15	T	
Astro Chorus	Grc	2001	159,016	305,704	332	58	16	T	ex Zeeland-03
Astro Corona	Grc	2003	153,911	305,870	332	58	16	T	
Astro Cygnus	Grc	2001	153,911	306,317	332	58	16	T	
Astro Leon	Grc	1992	153,427	285,771	328	57	15	T	ex Ambon-00
Astro Libra	Grc	1992	153,437	286,006	328	57	15	T	ex Irian-00
Astro Luna	Grc	1995	147,007	264,340	322	58	15	T	ex Tango-02, Diamond Iris-01
Astro Lupus	Grc	1989	137,893	257,589	321	57	15	T	ex Navix Seibu-00
Astro Lyra	Grc	1995	153,429	284,410	328	57	15	T	ex Flores-00
Astro Patroclus	Grc	2009	81,100	158,450	274	48	16	T	
Astro Pegasus	Grc	2009	81,100	158,450	274	48	16	T	
Astro Perseus	Grc	2004	80,620	158,982	274	48	15	T	
Astro Phaethon	Grc	2009	81,100	158,450	274	48	16	T	
Astro Phoenix	Grc	2004	85,000	159,000	274	48	15	T	
Astro Plato	Grc	2009	81,100	158,000	274	48	16	T	
Astro Polaris	Grc	2004	80,620	159,460	274	48	15	T	
Astro Pythia	Grc	2009	81,100	158,000	274	48	16	T	
Astro Saturn	Grc	2003	57,022	105,167	248	43		T	

Name	Flag	Year	GRT	DWT	LOA	Bm	Kts	Type	Former names
Astro Sculptor	Grc	2003	57,022	105,108	248	43	-	T	
Astro Sirius	Grc	1996	53,074	98,805	248	43	15	T	
Astro Taurus	Grc	1993	160,347	301,686	332	58	16	T	ex Eagle-07
Elizabeth I. Angelicoussi	Grc	2004	83,000	159,000	274	48	15	T	

CARDIFF
CAERDYDD

newbuildings: two further 158,000 dwt and seven 105,000 dwt tankers for 2009-11 delivery.
* managed by Chevron Shipping Co. LLC qv

Maran Gas Maritime Inc/Greece

Funnel: Blue with blue 'MG' and frame symbol inside blue ring on braod white band **Hull**: Brown with red boot-topping.
History: Founded 2003. **Web**: www.marangas.com

Name	Flag	Year	GRT	DWT	LOA	Bm	Kts	Type	Former names
Al Jassasiya (st)	Grc	2007	97,496	84,554	285	43	19	Lng	
Maran Gas Asclepius	Grc	2005	97,496	84,659	285	43	19	Lng	
Maran Gas Coronis	Grc	2007	97,491	84,623	285	43	19	Lng	
Maran Gas Knossos	Grc	2009	47,276	54,970	226	37	17	Lpg	l/dn Knossos Gas
Maran Gas Vergina	Grc	2008	47,276	55,251	226	37	17	Lpg	l/a Vergina Gas
Simaisma (st)	Grc	2006	97,496	84,500	285	43	19	Lng	
Umm Bab	Grc	2005	97,496	84,659	285	43	19	Lng	

newbuildings: one further 48,000 grt 54,000 dwt Lpg tanker for 2009 delivery.
Lng tankers up to 30% owned by Qatar Gas Transport Co and on 20-year charter to Ras Laffan Qatar-Mobil QM Gas project formed by subsidiaries of Qatar Petroleum and ExxonMobil.

Alpha Tankers & Freighters International Ltd/Greece

Funnel: White with black 'A' between narrow red bands below black top. **Hull**: Blue with red boot-topping. **History**: Related family company founded 1991. **Web**: www.alphatankers.com

Name	Flag	Year	GRT	DWT	LOA	Bm	Kts	Type	Former names
Alpha Action	Grc	1994	77,211	150,790	274	45	14	B	ex Action-02, World Action-02
Alpha Afovos	Grc	2001	39,941	74,428	225	32	15	B	ex Anangel Afovos-01
Alpha Century	Grc	2000	87,407	170,415	289	45	14	B	ex Anangel Century-02
Alpha Cosmos	Grc	2001	87,378	169,770	289	45	15	B	ex Mineral York-02, Mineral Trader-01
Alpha Effort	Grc	1999	38,564	72,844	225	32	15	B	
Alpha Era	Grc	2000	87,407	170,387	289	45	14	B	ex Mineral Sakura-02
Alpha Faith	Grc	2008	91,373	178,104	292	45	14	B	
Alpha Flame	Grc	1999	38,852	74,545	225	32	14	B	ex United Support-04
Alpha Friendship	Grc	1996	81,140	161,524	280	45	14	B	ex Anangel Friendship-02
Alpha Future	Grc	1999	38,564	72,893	225	32	15	B	
Alpha Glory	Grc	1999	37,715	72,270	225	32	14	B	ex Hebei Glory-06, Sea Lotus-04
Alpha Happiness	Grc	1999	38,564	72,800	225	32	15	B	
Alpha Harmony	Grc	2001	39,941	74,492	225	32	14	B	ex Alpha Harmony I-02, Alpha Harmony-01
Alpha Melody	Grc	2002	39,941	74,374	225	32	15	B	l/a Anangel Melody
Alpha Millennium	Grc	2000	87,407	170,415	280	45	15	B	ex Anangel Millennium-02
Alpha Prudence	Grc	2008	91,373	178,002	292	45	14	B	
Annoula	Grc	1997	36,559	70,281	225	32	14	B	
Antonis Angelicoussis	Grc	2007	91,373	177,855	292	45	14	B	
Maria A. Angelicoussi	Grc	2001	86,201	169,163	289	45	15	B	l/a Fabulous
Marvellous	Grc	2000	86,201	169,150	289	45	15	B	ex Mineral Marvel-04, Marvel-04

newbuildings: three further 177,000 dwt bulk carriers for 2010-12 delivery.

Angelicoussis Group (Anangel Shipping). ANANGEL ODYSSEY. N. Kemps

Atlanship SA Switzerland

Funnel: *White with narrow red diagonal line aft of blue triangle.* **Hull:** *Stone or white with red boot-topping.* **History:** *Founded 1987.*
Web: *none found.*

Name	Flag	Year	GRT	DWT	LOA	Bm	Kts	Type	Former names
Bebedouro	Lbr	1986	11,150	14,873	149	23	17	Tfj	
Orange Blossom	Lbr	1985	9,984	15,108	145	22	-	Tfj	
Orange Sky	Lbr	2000	22,063	26,863	172	27	14	Tfj	I/a May Oldendorff (conv B-02)
Orange Star	Lbr	1975	9,981	12,320	156	21	24	Tfj	ex Fife-86, Andalucia Star-84 (conv R-87)
Orange Sun	Lbr	2007	33,070	43,420	205	32	17	Tfj	
Orange Wave	Lbr	1993	13,444	16,700	157	26	18	Tfj	

Seereederei Baco-Liner GmbH Germany

Funnel: *Black with yellow/black 'bl' symbol on broad white band.* **Hull:** *Blue with white 'BACO-LINER', red boot-topping.*
History: *Founded 1979 and took over RMS Afrika Schiffahrts GmbH in 1992.* **Web:** *www.baco-liner.de*

Name	Flag	Year	GRT	DWT	LOA	Bm	Kts	Type	Former names
Baco-Liner 1	Lbr	1979	22,345	21,801	204	29	15	LC	
Baco-Liner 2	Lbr	1980	22,345	21,801	201	29	14	LC	
Baco-Liner 3	Lbr	1984	22,528	21,771	204	29	14	LC	

BBG-Bremer Bereederungs GmbH & Co KG Germany

Funnel: *White with blue 'BBG' on white diamond on blue band or charterers colours.* **Hull:** *Blue or black with red boot-topping.*
History: *Founded 1984 as Frigomaris Shipping GmbH, taking over Ganymed Schiffahrts in 1985, renamed Frigomaris Reefer Schiffahrt to 1990, then Ganymed Shipping GmbH to 2003.* **Web:** *www.bbg-shipmanagement.com*

Atlanship SA. ORANGE SUN. *Hans Kraijenbosch*

BBG-Bremer Bereederungs. CMA CGM AMERICA. *Allan Ryszka Onions*

Name	Flag	Year	GRT	DWT	LOA	Bm	Kts	Type	Former names
CMA CGM America **	Cyp	2006	42,382	52,683	268	32	25	CC	ex Laja-06, l/dn Conti Nantes
CMA CGM Sambhar **	Cyp	2006	42,382	51,870	268	32	25	CC	ex Longtue-06, Araya-04, l/dn Conti Nice
Conti Singa *	Deu	1996	42,336	41,460	242	32	22	CC	ex MSC Switzerland-05, Norasia Singa-02
Conti Shanghai *	Deu	1996	42,323	41,510	242	32	22	CC	ex Norasia Shanghai-02
Maersk Itaqui *	Lbr	1994	42,323	41,570	242	32	22	CC	ex P&O Nedlloyd Dammam-05, MSC Italy-05, Norasia Sharjah-02
Maersk Itea *	Lbr	1994	42,323	41,570	242	32	22	CC	ex P&O Nedlloyd Shanghai-05, MSC Munich-04, Norasia Hong Kong-02, MSC Houston-99, Norasia Hong Kong-98
MSC Boston	Mlt	1993	42,323	41,570	242	32	22	CC	ex Norasia Fribourg-97, l/dn Maritim Frankfurt
MSC New York	Lbr	1994	42,323	41,570	242	32	22	CC	ex Norasia Kiel-97, l/dn Maritim Kiel

*managed for Conti Reederei (Conti Holding GmbH) and ** by CMA CGM Ships.*

Belships ASA Norway

Funnel: *Blue with blue 'S' inside 'C' above blue anchor within narrow blue ring on white disc.* **Hull:** *Blue, dark grey or red with red boot-topping.* **History:** *Founded 1918 as Christen Smith & Co and 1926 as Skibs A/S Belships.* **Web:** *www.belships.biz*

Name	Flag	Year	GRT	DWT	LOA	Bm	Kts	Type	Former names
Belaia **	Pan	2007	28,799	48,673	180	32	15	B	
Belisland **	Pan	2003	39,727	76,662	225	32	15	B	
Bulk Avenir *	Nis	2002	27,989	50,399	190	32	14	B	ex Sun Master-07
Jaco Triumph *	Nis	1987	16,569	23.245	177	23	15	Co	ex Thor Triumph-07, Anny DP-03, Adamantios-00, Adamantia-98, Fremo Scorpius-95
Lake Harumi	Pan	2006	30,684	55,500	190	32		B	
Ondina	Pan	1996	26,449	47,639	190	31	14	B	ex Western Ondina-04
Stove Campbell	Nis	1999	26,966	46,223	186	31	14	Co	ex Western Onyx-01
Stove Trader	Nis	1999	26,966	46,223	186	31	14	Co	ex Western Obelisk-01
Stove Tradition	Nis	1998	26,966	46,223	186	31	14	Co	ex Western Opal-01
Stove Transport	Nis	1998	26,966	46,223	186	31	16	Co	ex Western Olivin-01
Super Adventure *	Pan	1996	17,977	28,630	172	27	14	B	ex IVS Super Adventure-03, Super Adventure-01
Super Challenge *	Pan	1996	17,977	28,581	172	27	14	B	ex IVS Super Challenge-03, Super Challenge-02
Triton Osprey	Pan	2007	42,702	81,448	225	32		B	
Virana	Nis	1979	41,905	42,424	183	32	14	V	ex G and C Parana-04, G and C Forest-01, Nosac Forest-94, Troll Forest-92, Skaubord-91

newbuildings: five 58,000 dwt bulk carriers for 2009-11 delivery.
*Managed by Belships Management Singapore Pte. Ltd., Singapore (www.belships.com.sg) or * by Belships Tianjin Shipmanagement.*
*** time-chartered until 2011/12*
Jointly owns Elkem Chartering operating 13 'handymax' bulkers on time charter. Also see Belchem Singapore Pte. Ltd. (formed jointly in 2004 with Chemikalien Seetransport GmbH q.v.)

Beluga Shipping GmbH Germany

Funnel: *White with white whale tail and water on blue rectangle or * buff with dark green 'G'.* **Hull:** *Dark blue with white 'BELUGA PROJECTS' or * dark green with white 'GREENFLEET', red boot-topping.* **History:** *Founded 1995 and acquired first ship in 1997. Acquired GenChart BV in 2003.* **Web:** *www.beluga-group.com*

Name	Flag	Year	GRT	DWT	LOA	Bm	Kts	Type	Former names
Maria Green *	Gib	1998	11,894	17,539	143	22	16	HL	ex BBC India-08, Maria Green-04
Marion Green *	Gib	1999	11,894	17,539	143	22	16	HL	ex BBC Malaysia-08, Marion Green-06
Beluga Constellation	Atg	2006	10,899	12,477	157	22	17	HL	
Beluga Constitution	Deu	2006	10,899	12,479	157	22	17	HL	
Beluga Generation	Atg	2008	11,894	17,110	143	22	16	HL	
Beluga Graduation	Atg	2008	11,894	17,110	143	22	16	HL	
Beluga Gratification	Atg	2008	11,894	17,110	143	22	16	HL	
Beluga Gravitation	Atg	2008	11,894	17,110	143	22	16	HL	
Beluga Indication	Atg	2000	11,434	13,289	162	20	17	HL	ex Nirint Iberia-07, Beluga Indication-06, CEC Apollon-04
Beluga Intonation	Atg	2000	11,434	13,426	162	20	17	HL	ex Nirint Atlas-07, Beluga Intonation-05, Nirint Atlas-04, TMC Atlas-03, Atlas-02, Industrial Atlas-02, CEC Atlas-01
Beluga Participation	Atg	2009	15,312	19,100	166	23	17	HL	
Beluga Persuasion	Atg	2009	15,312	19,100	166	23	17	HL	
Beluga Profession	Atg	2009	15,312	19,100	166	23	17	HL	
Beluga Promotion	Atg	2009	15,312	19,100	166	23	17	HL	
Margaretha Green *	Gib	1999	11,894	17,539	143	22	16	HL	ex Newpac Cumulus-05, Margaretha Green-04, Nirint Voyager-02, Coral Green-01, Margaretha Green-00

newbuildings: twenty 20,700 dwt multi-purpose with 800/1400 tonne heavy-lift capacity for 2010-11 delivery, also 18 smaller heavy-lift ships.
*managed by Beluga Fleet Management GmbH & Co KG * operated by Greenfleet subsidiary*
Multi-purpose ships with container/heavy-lift capacity for project cargo, also 44 other ships (9,800-12,000 dwt) lifting 80-500 tonnes.

Bergshav Shipholding AS   Norway

Funnel: *White with white 'B' symbol on broad red band, separated by narrow white band from black top.* **Hull:** *Brown with black 'BERGSHAV', red or grey boot-topping.* **History:** *Formed 1988 as Bergshav A/S and company now over 60% owned by Frontline.* **Web:** *www.bergshav.com*

Name	Flag	Year	GRT	DWT	LOA	Bm	Kts	Type	Former names
Bregen (2)	Nis	1994	10,012	13,941	150	21	13	T	
Cypress Pass	Lbr	1988	42,447	12,763	184	31	18	V	
Larvik	Bhs	2006	35,711	61,213	213	32	14	T	
Ocean Dignity †	Iom	2006	22,184	34,663	171	27	14	T	
Ocean Quest †	Iom	2000	22,181	34,999	171	27	14	T	ex Maersk Rochester-05
Ocean Spirit †	Iom	2005	22,184	34,603	171	27	14	T	
SPT Challenger	Bhs	2007	57,657	105,786	241	42	15	T	
SPT Champion	Bhs	2007	57,657	105,786	241	42	15	T	
SPT Conqueror	Bhs	2007	57,657	105,786	241	42	15	T	
SPT Crusader	Bhs	2007	57,657	105,850	241	42	15	T	
Vibeke (2)	Bhs	1996	16,940	23,025	169	24	17	Ro	ex Sochi-05
Vinni (2)	Mlt	1994	16,940	13,480	169	24	17	Ro	ex Novorossiysk-04
Xinyuan Hai *	Hkg	1988	95,291	186,876	290	47	16	B	ex Lowlands Sunrise-00,

* managed by COSCO Bulk Carrier Co Ltd, China. † bare-boat chartered to Roxana Shipping, Greece (to 2016)

BG Group plc   UK

Funnel: *Black with three narrow white bands.* **Hull:** *Black with white 'LNG' and red boot-topping.* **History:** *Formed 1997 after Centrica plc was demerged from British Gas plc, which was then renamed BG plc to 1999.* **Web:** *www.bg-group.com*

Name	Flag	Year	GRT	DWT	LOA	Bm	Kts	Type
Methane Alison Victoria	Bmu	2007	95,753	79,058	283	43	20	Lng
Methane Heather Sally	Bmu	2007	95,753	79,085	283	43	20	Lng
Methane Jane Elizabeth	Bmu	2006	95,753	78,984	283	43	20	Lng
Methane Kari Elin (st)	Bmu	2004	93,410	73,989	279	43	19	Lng
Methane Lydon Volney	Bmu	2006	95,753	78,957	283	43	20	Lng
Methane Nile Eagle *	Bmu	2007	95,753	79,006	283	43	20	Lng
Methane Rita Andrea	Bmu	2006	95,753	79,046	283	43	20	Lng
Methane Shirley Elisabeth	Bmu	2007	95,753	78,997	283	43	20	Lng

newbuildings: four 99,500 grt 170,000 m³ Lng tankers for 2010 delivery.
All (st) and owned or * managed by subsidiaries of Ceres LNG Services Ltd, Greece. Also charters vessels from Golar (see under Frontline)

Arne Blystad A/S   Norway

Funnel: *Yellow with red 'B' on broad white band edged with narrow blue bands, narrow black top.* **Hull:** *Black or red wih red boot-topping.* **History:** *Formed 1989 as Blystad Shipping (USA) Inc to 2003.* **Web:** *www.blystad.no*

Name	Flag	Year	GRT	DWT	LOA	Bm	Kts	Type	Former names
Sichem Jupiter **	Nis	2000	27,185	48,338	182	32	14	T	ex Team Jupiter-08
Sichem Neptun **	Nis	2000	27,185	48,309	182	32	14	T	ex Team Neptun-08
Songa Agnes *	Lbr	2000	157,831	299,089	332	58	15	T	ex Mars Glory-07, Great Polaris-05, Great Mars-05, Millennium Star-04
Songa Anette *	Lbr	1989	38,878	62,326	225	32	14	T	ex Anette-05, Nichian-00, World S-95, World Shanghai-95, l/a Cabo de Hornos
Songa Chelsea	Mhl	1995	156,802	298,432	332	58	15	T	ex Chelsea-07, Macoma-04
Songa Diamond **	Mhl	2008	11,259	17,543	144	23		T	
Songa Julie *	Mhl	2000	157,831	299,089	332	58	15	T	ex Venus Glory-07, Safinara I-00
Songa Nor *	Mhl	1996	26,449	47,369	190	31	14	B	ex Belnor-07
Songa Pearl *	Mhl	2008	11,259	17,539	144	23		T	
Songa Ruby *	Mhl	2008	11,259	17,604	144	23		T	
Songa Sapphire	Mhl	2008	11,259	17,539	144	23		T	
Team Anemonia *	Cyp	1995	22,633	40,296	176	32	14	T	ex Anemonia-00
Vega III *	Pan	1983	72,931	139,650	280	42	14	B	ex Great Polaris-05, Great Mars-05, Millennium Star-04, La Pampa-00, Venora-93, Snowdon-91, Cetra Sagitta-87

newbuildings: eight 25,000 dw, three 17,000 dwt tankers and a 170,000 dwt, four 91,800 dwt, sixteen 32,000 dwt bulk carriers due 2009-10
Managed by B Shipmanagement Ltd, UK (formed 1989 as Blystad Shipmanagement Ltd until 2006) or * by subsidiary Songa Shipping Pte Ltd, Singapore (founded 2008)
Norwegian subsidiary Team Tankers AS operating pool including vessels owned * by Consultores de Navegacion SA, Spain or ** by Chemikalien Seetransport GmbH, Germany q.v.
Songa vessels on charter to Eitzen Chemical (see under Eitzen Group); eight panamax bulk carriers chartered-in from various owners.

Aug Bolten Wm Miller's Nachfolger (GmbH & Co) KG   Germany

Funnel: *Black with black 'B' inside red rectangle outline and diagonal cross on white houseflag or (*) black 'L' on blue-edged white disc at centre of blue diagonal crossed and edged houseflag on broad white band.* **Hull:** *Black with red boot-topping.* **History:** *Parent originally founded 1801 and shipping company formed in 1906. Joint owners of Eurasia Shipping & Management with B Schulte to 1988.* **Web:** *www.aug-bolten.de*

Name	Flag	Year	GRT	DWT	LOA	Bm	Kts	Type	Former names
Arcadia *	Mhl	1995	25,190	41,455	186	30	14	B	ex Dimitra-07, Valiant-04, Multi-Purpose 3-03
Atlas Amelia	Lbr	1996	25,190	41,373	186	30	14	B	ex Lady Z-06, Santa Rosa-03
Dorothea	Cyp	1984	13,021	22,025	155	23	14	B	ex Garnet Star-94
Elisabeth Bolten	Lbr	2001	10,132	13,275	127	21	14	Co	
Lilly Bolten	Lbr	2009	19,000	30,760	179	28	14	B	
Lucia Bolten	Lbr	2009	30,000	54,000	190	32	14	B	
Marielle Bolten	Lbr	1997	19,354	29,534	181	26	14	Co	
Marietta Bolten	Lbr	2009	30,000	54,000	190	32	14	B	
Natalie Bolten	Lbr	2001	10,132	13,275	127	21	14	Co	
Naxos *	Mhl	1995	15,164	23,825	153	26	14	B	ex Hirosaki Cherry-04, Hirosaki Rainbow-01
Paros	Lbr	1997	14,397	23,984	154	26	14	B	ex Pacific Bridge-03
Santorin II *	Cyp	1984	14,147	23,899	160	24	14	B	ex Cynthia No. 5-93, Jovian Lark-90, Sanko Melody-85
Sigrun Bolten	Lbr	1997	19,354	29,534	181	26	14	Co	ex Cielo di Savona-01, Sigrun Bolten-97
Skyros *	Cyp	1998	14,781	24,128	154	26	14	B	ex Diamond Star-03
Sophie Bolten	Lbr	1996	16,041	27,609	169	26	14	B	ex Clipper Lis-08, Pacrose-04
Stavros P *	Mhl	1994	25,943	45,863	190	31	14	B	ex Matira-08, Minoan Pride-05, New Generation-04
Tinos	Lbr	1995	14,431	23,725	151	26	13	B	ex Bright Nextage-03
Western Wave	Lbr	2008	18.493	29,234	170	27	14	B	
William	Cyp	1995	15,164	23,829	153	26	14	B	ex Pacific Rainbow II-01

newbuildings: two 54,000 dwt, a 30,760 dwt (Laura Bolten) and two 24,000 dwt bulk carriers for 2009-10 delivery..
* owned by subsidiary Lydia Mar Shipping Co. SA, Greece (founded 1978 - www.lydiamar.gr)

BP Shipping Ltd UK

Funnel: *Red with green band on broad white band beneath black top.* **Hull:** *Black with red boot-topping.* **History:** *Subsidiary of BP plc formed 1909 as Anglo-Persian Oil Co Ltd (initially 97% owned by Burmah Oil) to 1935 and Anglo-Iranian Oil Co Ltd to 1954. UK government took majority shareholding in 1914, gradually reduced until ending in 1987. Acquired 25% of Standard Oil Co of Ohio in 1970, becoming majority owner in 1978 and taking total control in 1987. The British Petroleum Co plc and Amoco Corp (formed 1912 as Standard Oil Co Indiana to 1985) amalgamated in 1999 as BP Amoco plc. Merged 2000 with Atlantic Richfield Co (formed 1916 as Atlantic Refining Co to 1966 and amalgamated with Sinclair Oil Corp in 1969). Renamed BP plc in 2001.* **Web:** *www.bp.com*

Name	Flag	Year	GRT	DWT	LOA	Bm	Kts	Type	Former names
British Beech	Iom	2003	58,200	106,138	241	42	15	T	
British Chivalry	Iom	2005	29,335	46,803	183	32	15	T	
British Commerce	Iom	2006	48,772	54,478	230	37	17	Lpg	
British Confidence	Iom	2006	48,772	54,490	230	37	18	Lpg	
British Cormorant	Iom	2005	63,661	114,809	250	44	15	T	
British Councillor	Gbr	2007	48,772	54,478	230	37	18	Lpg	
British Courage	Iom	2006	48,772	54,490	230	37	18	Lpg	
British Courtesy	Iom	2005	28,000	46,080	183	32	14	T	
British Curlew	Iom	2004	63,562	114,809	250	44	15	T	
British Cygnet	Iom	2005	63,462	113,782	250	44	15	T	
British Diamond	Iom	2008	102,064	84,553	288	44	20	Lng	
British Eagle	Iom	2006	64,500	113,120	250	44	15	T	
British Emerald (me)	Iom	2007	102,064	84,303	282	44	20	Lng	
British Emissary **	Iom	2007	23,270	36,749	194	27	15	T	ex Aiolos-07, l/dn Alkividias
British Ensign **	Iom	2006	23,270	36,713	184	27	15	T	ex Atlantis-06
British Envoy **	Iom	2006	23,270	37,582	184	27	15	T	l/a Aktoras
British Esteem	Gbr	2003	23,235	37,220	183	27	15	T	
British Explorer	Gbr	2003	23,235	37,321	183	27	15	T	
British Falcon	Iom	2006	64,500	113,120	250	44	15	T	
British Fidelity	Iom	2004	29,335	46,803	183	32	14	T	
British Gannet	Iom	2005	63,661	114,809	250	44	15	T	
British Harmony	Iom	2005	29,335	46,803	183	32	14	T	
British Hawthorn *	Iom	2003	57,567	81,697	241	42	15	T	
British Hazel	Iom	2004	58,070	106,085	241	42	15	T	
British Holly	Iom	2004	58,070	106,085	241	42	15	T	
British Innovator (st)	Iom	2002	92,900	67,850	279	43	19	Lng	
British Integrity	Iom	2004	29,335	46,803	183	32	15	T	
British Kestrel	Iom	2006	64,500	113,120	250	44	15	T	
British Laurel *	Iom	2002	57,567	106,500	241	42	15	T	
British Liberty	Iom	2004	29,335	46,803	183	32	14	T	
British Loyalty	Iom	2004	29,335	46,803	183	32	14	T	
British Mallard	Iom	2005	63,661	114,809	250	44	15	T	
British Merchant (st)	Iom	2003	93,498	67,850	279	43	19	Lng	
British Merlin	Iom	2003	63,661	114,761	250	44	15	T	
British Oak *	Iom	2003	57,567	106,500	241	42	15	T	
British Osprey	Iom	2003	63,661	101,760	250	44	15	T	
British Pioneer	Iom	1999	160,216	306,397	334	58	15	T	
British Pride	Iom	2000	160,216	305,994	334	58	15	T	
British Progress	Iom	2000	160,216	306,497	334	58	15	T	

Name	Flag	Year	GRT	DWT	LOA	Bm	Kts	Type	Former names
British Purpose	Iom	2000	160,216	306,307	334	58	15	T	
British Robin	iom	2005	63,462	113,782	250	44	15	T	
British Ruby	Iom	2008	102,064	84,491	282	44	20	Lng	
British Sapphire	Iom	2008	102,064	84,455	282	44	20	Lng	
British Security	Iom	2004	29,335	46,803	183	32	14	T	
British Serenity	Iom	2005	28,000	46,080	183	32	14	T	
British Swift	Iom	2003	63,661	114,809	250	44	15	T	
British Tenacity	Iom	2004	28,000	46,080	183	32	14	T	
British Trader (st)	Iom	2003	93,498	75,109	279	43	19	Lng	
British Tranquility	Iom	2005	28,000	46,080	183	32	14	T	
British Unity	Iom	2004	28,000	46,080	183	32	14	T	
British Vine	Iom	2004	58,200	106,000	241	42	15	T	
British Willow *	Iom	2003	57,500	106,000	241	42	15	T	

* managed for Seaworld Management & Trading Inc or ** for Capital Maritime & Trading Corp, both Greece
Also see Alaska Tanker Co LLC, USA (formed 1999 jointly with Overseas Shipholding Group Inc and Keystone Shipping Group) under OSG

Briese Schiffahrts GmbH & Co KG Germany

Funnel: *Charterers colours.* **Hull:** *Blue or grey with green boot-topping.* **History:** *Founded 1983.* **Web:** *www.briese.de*

BBC Amazon *	Atg	2007	12,936	17,300	143	23	15	Co	I/a Hatzum
BBC Elbe *	Atg	2006	12,936	17,349	143	23	15	Co	ex Hornumersiel-06
BBC Ems *	Atg	2006	12,936	17,349	143	23	15	Co	ex Suderdamm-06
BBC Leer *	Lbr	1998	13,066	20,567	153	24	17	Co	ex NileDutch Privilege-08, Mellum-06, Libra Peru-02, CSAV Valencia-00, Cathrin Oldendorff-99

BP Shipping. BRITISH EXPLORER. *Hans Kraijenbosch*

BP Shipping. BRITISH MERLIN. *Allan Ryszka Onions*

Name	Flag	Year	GRT	DWT	LOA	Bm	Kts	Type	Former names
BBC Mississippi *	Atg	2006	12,936	17,349	143	23	15	Co	ex Greetsiel-07
BBC Ostfriesland *	Lbr	1998	13,066	20,567	153	24	17	Co	ex Delmas Nigeria-07, BBC Ostfriesland-06, Germana-06, BBC Argentina-04, Cielo di Caracas-02, Lily Oldendorff-01, Libra Chile-00, CSAV Genoa-00, Lily Oldendorff-99, Barrister-99, Lily Oldendorff-98
BBC Rheiderland *	Lbr	2000	13,066	20,500	153	24	17	Co	ex Delmas Ghana-07, BBC Rheiderland-06, Paul Oldendorff-02
BBC Weser *	Atg	2006	12,936	17,290	143	23	15	Co	ex Westerdamm-06
Borkum	Lbr	1994	11,264	18,355	148	23	14	B	ex Erna Oldendorff-05
Hooge	Gib	2005	15,633	16,921	161	25	19	CC	
Langenes	Gib	2006	15,633	16,921	161	25	19	CC	
Norderoog	Gib	2004	15,633	16,921	161	25	19	CC	ex Syms Peonia-08, Norderoog-04
Petkum	Deu	2008	15,633	16,921	161	25	19	CC	
Sjard	Atg	2007	12,936	17,300	143	23	15	Co	
Suderoog	Gib	2005	15,633	16,921	161	25	19	Co	
Wybelsum	Gib	2008	15,597	16,921	161	25	19	Co	

newbuildings: seven 17,300 dwt multi-purpose general cargo for 2009-10 delivery.
* operated by Briese Bischoff Chartering

Brostrom AB Sweden

Funnel: Blue with houseflag (blue 'AB' on white disc over red/blue horizontal bands) overlapping green rectangle on broad white band.
Hull: Blue or grey with red boot-topping. **History:** Brostrom AB formed 1934, orginally founded 1865 as A/B Tirfing to 1978, renamed Brostrom van Ommeren Shipping after merger in 1998. Brostrom Tankers SAS formed 1934 as Phs van Ommeren (France) SA (founded 1839), merged 1987 with Societe d'Armement Fluvial et Maritime (SOFLUMAR) as Soflumar Van Ommeren France SA to 1992, then Van Ommeren Tankers SA to 2000. Brostrom AB sold to Maersk Product Tankers AB in 2009.
Web: www.brostrom.se

Name	Flag	Year	GRT	DWT	LOA	Bm	Kts	Type	Former names
Bro Agnes §	Nld	2008	12,162	16,791	144	23		T	
Bro Albert *	Atf	1995	28,226	46,768	183	32	14	T	ex Port Albert-00
Bro Alexandre *	Atf	1995	28,226	46,738	183	32	14	T	ex Port Alexandre-00
Bro Alma §	Lbr	2008	12,162	17,000	144	23		T	
Bro Anna §	Lbr	2008	12,164	16,979	144	23		T	
Bro Anton	Swe	1999	11,375	16,376	144	23	15	T	ex United Anton-00
Bro Arthur *	Atf	1995	28,226	46,802	183	32	14	T	ex Port Arthur-00
Bro Atland	Swe	1999	11,377	16,326	144	23	15	T	ex United Atland-00, United Albert-99
Bro Axel	Swe	1998	11,324	16,389	144	23	13	T	ex United Axel-00
Bro Caroline *	Atf	1995	29,083	45,014	183	32	14	T	ex Port Caroline-00
Bro Catherine *	Atf	1997	29,083	44,922	180	32	14	T	ex Port Catherine-00
Bro Cecile *	Atf	1997	29,083	44,936	180	32	14	T	ex Port Cecile-00
Bro Charlotte *	Atf	1997	29,083	44,970	181	32	14	T	ex Port Charlotte-00
Bro Deliverer * (2me)	Swe	2006	11,344	14,766	147	22	13	T	
Bro Designer * (2me)	Swe	2006	11,344	14,846	147	22	13	T	
Bro Developer * (2)	Swe	2007	11,344	14,737	147	22	13	T	
Bro Distributor * (2me)	Swe	2006	11,344	14,907	147	22	13	T	
Bro Edward *	Atf	2005	26,659	37,300	184	30	14	T	
Bro Elizabeth *	Atf	2001	24,099	37,026	184	30	15	T	

Brostrom AB. BRO ANNA. *C. Lous*

Name	Flag	Year	GRT	DWT	LOA	Bm	Kts	Type	Former names
Bro Ellen *	Atf	2002	24,100	37,000	184	30	15	T	
Bro Elliot *	Atf	2005	26,659	37,300	184	30	14	T	
Bro Etienne *	Atf	2004	26,659	37,300	184	30	14	T	
Bro Premium	Swe	1999	29,289	45,790	183	32	15	T	ex Iver Exact-06
Bro Priority	Swe	2001	21,517	31,265	177	28	14	T	ex Iver Progress-05
Bro Promotion	Swe	1999	29,289	45,790	183	32	15	T	ex Iver Example-06
Bro Provider	Swe	2001	21,517	31,265	177	28	14	T	ex Iver Prosperity-06
Bro Sincero ‡	Swe	2002	11,855	16,008	146	22	14	T	
Cilaos †	Atf	1996	29,083	44,885	180	32	14	T	ex Port Christine-98
Evinco ‡ (me)	Swe	2005	13,769	19,999	156	24	14	T	
Excello ‡	Swe	2008	13,798	19,925	155	24		T	
Navigo ‡	Swe	1992	10,543	16,775	145	22	14	T	
Prospero ‡	Swe	2000	11.793	18,119	146	22	14	T	
Seto Eagle **	Pan	2004	26,902	47,040	183	32	15	T	ex Iver Eagle-05

*Owned by Brostrom Tankers AB (formed 1990 as United Tankers AB to 2000) and managed by Brostrom Ship Management AB (formed 1993) or
* owned by Brostrom Tankers France SAS, France or ** by Brostrom Tankers Norway AS (managed by Eagle Maritime Co Ltd, Japan)
† jointly owned with subsidiary of Societe d'Armement et de Transport (SOCATRA), France or ‡ with Rederi AB Donsotank, Sweden (founded
1952 – www.donsotank.se). § owned by Dunya Denizcilik ve Ticaret AS, Turkey.
Also see Rigel Schifahrts GmbH & Co KG*

Hermann Buss GmbH & Cie KG   Germany

Funnel: White with blue outlined 'H' interlinked with blue 'B' interupting narrow blue/red/blue band or charterers colours. **Hull:** Green
with red or black boot-topping or charterers colours. **History:** Family commenced ship-owning in 1838 and as Reederei Hermann
Buss from 1967 to 1988. Acquired 50% share in Schulte & Bruns in 2005. **Web:** www.buss-gruppe.de

Name	Flag	Year	GRT	DWT	LOA	Bm	Kts	Type	Former names
APL Colima	Atg	2007	14,000	18,480	166	25	19	CC	
APL Managua **	Atg	2006	15,375	18,291	166	25	19	CC	ex EWL Caribbean-07
Arkona Trader	Deu	1998	23,792	30,340	188	30	20	CC	ex CMA CGM Tucano-08, Arkona Trader-03, Cielo d'Italia-02, Arkona Trader-99
Arsos	Cyp	2007	14,500	18.480	166	25	19	CC	
Atlantic Trader	Atg	1996	16,165	22,250	168	27	19	CC	ex Calaparati-05, Atlantic Trader-04, CSAV Rauten-98, Sea Vista-97, Atlantic Trader -96
Clan Challenger	Atg	1999	25,361	34,017	207	30	21	CC	ex Baltrum Trader-07, P&O Nedlloyd Fremantle-00, Baltrum Trader-99
CMA CGM Corfu †	Atg	2007	15,375	18,318	166	25	19	CC	ex Warnow Whale-07
CSAV Hamburgo	Atg	1998	25,361	33,976	207	30	21	CC	ex Brasil Star-99, Borkum Trader-98
CSAV New York	Atg	1998	25,361	33,919	207	30	21	CC	ex Lykes Osprey-03, ECL Rotterdam-02, Maersk Sao Paulo-99, Helgoland Trader-99
Delmas Nacala	Atg	1996	16,165	22,525	168	27	19	CC	ex Pacific Trader-08, CSAV Recife-98, Maersk Sao Paulo-97, Pacific Trader-96
Elbe Trader	Atg	1994	15,895	22,525	168	27	21	CC	ex TS Manila-08, Elbe Trader-07, DAL Reunion-07, Elbe Trader-04, Zim Argentina III-04, CSAV Rauli-98, Elbe Trader-95
Ems Trader	Atg	2000	25,535	33,917	200	30	21	CC	ex Alemania Express-05, Sea Cheetah-02, I/a Ems Trader
Jade Trader	Atg	1995	11,987	14,700	157	24	20	CC	ex OOCL Accord-98, Jade Trader-96
Maersk Recife **	Cyp	2007	15,375	18,480	166	25	19	CC	

Brostrom AB. BRO DESIGNER. *C. Lous*

Name	Flag	Year	GRT	DWT	LOA	Bm	Kts	Type	Former names
Maruba Orion	Atg	1998	25,361	34,041	207	30	20	CC	ex Juist Trader-07, CP Canada-06, Cielo del Canada-05, Juist Trader-99
Medontario *	Cyp	2008	15,334	18,446	166	25	19	CC	
Michigan Trader *	Cyp	2008	15,334	18,414	166	25	19	CC	ex Medmichigan-08
MOL Achievement	Atg	1997	16,165	22,250	168	27	21	CC	ex Dollart Trader-06, Maruba Trader-06, Cap Serrat-05, Dollart Trader-04, Libra Genova-00, Repubblica de la Boca-99, Dollart Trader-98
MOL Agility	Atg	1996	16,165	22,250	168	27	21	CC	ex Warnow Trader-06, CMA CGM Springbok-06, Warnow Trader-03, Libra Valencia-99, Warnow Trader-96
MOL Honesty	Deu	1998	16,803	22,900	185	25	19	CC	ex CMA CGM Kiwi-08, Maruba Trader-04, l/a Szczecin Trader
MOL Sunshine	Atg	2000	25,535	33,934	200	30	22	CC	ex Leda Trader-07, Cap Castillo-05, l/a Leda Trader
Monteverde	Atg	1998	25,355	33,987	207	30	21	CC	l/a Jumme Trader
Mosel Trader	Atg	2009	28,048	37,950	215	30	21	CC	
Ocean Trader	Atg	1996	16,165	22,250	168	27	19	CC	ex Calapadria-03, Zim Brasil I-01, Atlantico-98, Ocean Trader-96
Oder Trader	Deu	1998	23,809	30,360	188	30	21	CC	ex Maruba Cathay-07, Oder Trader-05, Zim Lisbon I-03, Oder Trader-02, Cielo d'America-02, Maersk Rio Grande-99, Oder Trader-98
Trave Trader	Atg	1994	15,922	22,525	168	27	21	CC	ex CSAV Yokohama-04, Trave Trader-03, Zim Montevideo-98, Trave Trader-96
TS Qingdao	Atg	2008	28,048	37,950	215	30	21	CC	l/dn Main Trader
TS Xingang	Atg	2008	28,048	37,950	215	30	21	CC	ex Donau Trader-08
Vecht Trader **	Cyp	2007	15,375	18,350	166	25	19	CC	ex Medatlantic-08
Vliet Trader **	Cyp	2007	14,500	18,480	166	25	19	CC	ex Medpacific-08
Warnow Beluga *	Atg	2008	15,000	18,480	166	25	19	CC	
Warnow Dolphin †	Atg	2007	15,375	18,276	166	25	19	CC	
Warnow Porpoise	Atg	2008	15,000	18,480	166	25	19	CC	
Warnow Vaquita ***	Atg	2008	15,193	18,480	166	25	19	CC	

newbuildings: seven 30,500 dwt multi-purpose cargo, two 28,050 grt, two 22,000 grt and four 14,000 dwt container ships for 2009-10 delivery.
* owned or managed by 100% subsidiaries Medstar Shipmanagement Ltd, Cyprus, ** Reider Shipping BV, Netherlands (founded 1999 – www.reidershipping.com) or *** GB Shipping & Chartering GmbH & Co KG.
† managed by Marlow Ship Management Deutschland GmbH & Co KG (www.marlow-shipmanagement.de).

Carl Buttner-Bremen GmbH & Co KG Tankreederei   Germany

Funnel: Yellow with white 'CB' and four corner stars on red houseflag, narrow black top. **Hull:** Black with red boot-topping.
History: Formed 1856 as Carl Buttner GmbH to 2003. **Web:** www.carlbuettner.de

Name	Flag	Year	GRT	DWT	LOA	Bm	Kts	Type
Admiral	Gib	2002	16,914	23,998	168	26	15	T
Apatura	Gib	2004	16,901	24,064	168	26	15	T
Apollo	Gib	2003	16,914	24,028	169	26	15	T
Aurelia	Gib	2006	16,683	24,017	168	26	15	T
Aurora	Gib	2004	16,901	24,086	168	26	15	T
Avalon	Gib	2006	16,900	23,400	168	26	15	T

managed by Carl Buttner Shipmanagement GmbH.

Carl Buttner-Bremen GmbH. APOLLO. *N. Kemps*

BW Shipping Group

Norway

BW Gas ASA/Norway

Funnel: *Blue with white 'B' above white 'W'.* **Hull:** *Light green or red with white 'BW' on diagonal stripe, blue, red or grey boot-topping.* **History:** *Founded 1887 by Berge Bergesen and shipping company formed 1918 as Sigval Bergesen, then A/S Sig. Bergesen d.y. & Co to 1986, which merged in 1996 with A/S Havtor Management the gas tanker subsidiary of Kvaerner Shipping AS (formerly P Meyer to 1981 and Rederiet Helge R Meyer A/S to 1992 when merged with Irgens-Larsen A/S) as Bergesen dy ASA. In 2003 acquired by Sohmen family controlled World-Wide Shipping Group, Hong Kong (formed 1951), company being renamed Bergesen Worldwide Gas ASA from 2005 to 2007. Yara Gas fleet (formerly Norsk Hydro) taken over 2006.* **Web:** *www.bwgas.com*

Name	Flag	Year	GRT	DWT	LOA	Bm	Kts	Type	Former names
Berge Arzew (st)	Bhs	2004	90,844	77,410	277	43	19	Lng	
Berge Atlantic	Nis	1998	91,962	172,704	292	48	16	B	
Berge Bonde §	Pan	2005	104,727	206,312	300	50	15	B	
Berge Commander	Nis	1991	45,032	56,875	224	36	16	Lpg	
Berge Danuta **	Nis	2000	49,288	50,260	226	36	18	Lpg	
Berge Frost	Nis	1983	50,699	56,174	250	36	17	Lpg	ex Floreal-91
Berge Nantong ‡	Hkg	2006	47,012	58,757	225	37	16	Lpg	
Berge Ningbo ‡	Hkg	2006	47,012	58,899	225	37	16	Lpg	
Berge Pacific (2)	Nis	1986	118,491	231,850	315	56	13	B	ex Iron Pacific-98
Berge Racine	Nis	1985	49,130	63,254	228	36	14	Lpg	
Berge Shan	Nis	1986	100,070	200,692	300	50	13	O	ex Chiribetsu-00, Chiribetsu Maru-95
Berge Stahl	Nis	1986	175,720	364,767	343	64	13	O	
Berge Summit	Bhs	1990	44,690	50,748	230	37	15	Lpg	ex Sunny Hope-04
Berge Sword	Nis	1979	44,502	48,996	229	32	17	Lpg	ex Excaliber-88, Hoegh Sword-86
BW Amazon *	Pan	2006	43,815	76,565	229	32	15	T	ex Amazon-06
BW Ara	Bmu	1982	160,010	290,085	336	60	14	T	ex Tiara-08, Kazimah-06, Townsend-89, Kazimah-87
BW Arctic	Pan	2001	91,563	174,285	292	48		B	ex Berge Arctic-06
BW Atlas *	Pan	2008	90,092	180,180	289	45	15	B	
BW Austria	Nor	2009	48,000	60,000				Lpg	ex BW Duke-09
BW Bauhinia *	Hkg	2007	156,500	301,018	332	58		T	
BW Borg	Bhs	2001	47,156	54,000	230	36	16	Lpg	ex Formosagas Apollo-07
BW Boss	Bhs	2001	47,156	54,586	230	36	16	Lpg	ex Formosagas Bright-07
BW Bureya *	Pan	1993	153,506	293,238	332	57	15	B	ex BW Bandeira-07, Sebu-07, Seki-94 (conv T-07)
BW Captain	Nis	1991	45,032	56,945	224	36	16	Lpg	ex Berge Captain-06
BW Challenger	Nis	1992	45,032	56,885	224	36	16	Lpg	ex Berge Challenger-07
BW Clipper	Nis	1992	45,032	56,864	224	36	16	Lpg	ex Berge Clipper-07
BW Columbia	Pan	2007	43,815	76,604	229	32	15	T	
BW Danube *	Pan	2007	43,815	76,543	229	32	15	T	
BW Denali	Pan	1992	153,437	286,006	328	57	14	T	ex BW Noto-08, Noto-06, Argo Thetis-00 (to be conv to B-09)
BW Denise **	Rif	2001	49,292	56,745	226	36	18	Lpg	ex Berge Denise-06
BW Edelweiss *	Hkg	2008	158,569	301,021	332	58		T	
BW Fjord *	Pan	1986	159,534	310,698	332	57	13	O	ex Berge Fjord-06, Docefjord-00 (conv Obo-02)
BW Havfrost	Nis	1991	34,946	49,513	205	32	15	Lpg	ex Havfrost-07
BW Havlur	Sgp	1997	13,500	18,699	154	25	15	Lpg	ex Agri Viking-06
BW Havlys ‡	Lbr	1983	14,377	13,935	152	23	12	Lpg	ex Bussewitz-06
BW Havsol	Nis	1997	13,500	18,713	154	25	15	Lpg	ex Euro Viking-06

BW Shipping Group. BW BOSS. *Hans Kraijenbosch*

Name	Flag	Year	GRT	DWT	LOA	Bm	Kts	Type	Former names
BW Hebris	Nis	1983	15,397	20,566	158	24	17	Lpg	ex Hebris-08
BW Helios	Nis	1992	34,974	49,513	205	32	15	Lpg	ex Helios-07
BW Hemina	Nis	1979	34,577	43,386	220	29	16	Lpg	ex Hemina-07, Garala-87
BW Herdis ‡	Deu	2004	35,853	42,854	205	32	16	Lpg	ex Polar Viking-06
BW Hermes	Nis	1983	18,152	26,920	155	27	16	Lpg	ex Oscar Viking-06, Oscar Gas-96, Tielrode-90, l/a Petrogas II
BW Hesiod ‡	Deu	2005	25,852	42,937	205	32	16	Lpg	ex Pacific Viking-06
BW Hudson *	Pan	2007	43,737	76,574	229	32	15	T	
BW Hugin	Nis	2002	22,902	26,616	174	28	16	Lpg	ex Berge Hugin-07, Lancashire-05
BW Kibo *	Pan	1993	153,506	293,376	328	58	15	T	ex Sala-08
BW Lena *	Pan	2007	43,797	76,577	229	32	15	T	
BW Lord	Nis	2008	48,502	54,691	226	37	17	Lpg	ex Olympic Gas-08
BW Luna *	Hkg	2003	158,993	298,555	332	58	15	T	ex World Luna-08
BW Nantes **	Rif	2003	35,190	44,773	216	32	17	Lpg	ex Berge Nantes-07
BW Nice **	Rif	2003	35,346	44,639	216	32	17	Lpg	ex Berge Nice-07
BW Nile *	Hkg	1991	153,407	285,739	328	57	15	T	ex Nile-06, Argo Pallas-00
BW Odel	Pan	2007	104,721	206,312	300	50	15	B	
BW Odin	Nis	2005	25,994	29,000	180	29	16	Lpg	ex Berge Odin-07
BW Orinoco *	Pan	2008	43,797	76,580	229	32	15	T	
BW Phoenix *	Pan	1986	154,098	290,793	334	62	14	O	ex Berge Phoenix-06, Grand Phoenix-00 (conv Obo-04),
BW Pioneer	Bmu	1992	56,855	96,828	242	42	14	T	ex Sarasota-08, Tsunami-05, Minerva Concert-03, Stena Concert-99
BW Prince	Nis	2007	47,194	54,368	225	37		Lpg	
BW Princess	Nis	2008	47,194	53,500	225	37		Lpg	
BW Rachel	Nis	1984	49,130	63,296	228	36	14	Lpg	ex Berge Rachel-08
BW Ragnhild	Nis	1985	49,130	63,258	228	36	14	Lpg	ex Berge Ragnhild-08
BW Rhine *	Pan	2008	43,815	76,578	229	32	15	T	
BW Saga	Nis	1979	44,151	55,303	225	34	16	Lpg	ex Berge Saga-06
BW Seine *	Pan	2008	43,797	76,600	229	32	15	T	
BW Shinano *	Sgp	2008	43,797	76,594	229	32	15	T	
BW Sombeke	Bhs	2006	25,994	29,212	180	29	16	Lpg	ex Berge Sombeke-06
BW Stadt *	Rif	1994	160,467	306,951	332	58	16	T	ex Berge Stadt-07
BW Suez Boston (st)	Nis	2003	93,844	77,410	277	43	19	Lng	ex Berge Boston-07
BW Suez Brussels	Bmu	2009	105,000	80,000	295	43	19	Lng	
BW Suez Everett (st)	Nis	2003	93,844	77,410	277	43	19	Lng	ex Berge Everett-08
BW Suez Paris	Bmu	2009	105,000	80,000	295	43	19	Lng	
BW Sund	Nis	1981	43,849	55,303	225	34	16	Lpg	ex Berge Sund-06
BW Trader	Sgp	2006	50,625	53,151	225	36	17	Lpg	ex Berge Trader-07
BW Ulan *	Rif	2000	157,814	277,370	332	58	15	T	ex Ulan-06
BW Utah **	Rif	2001	157,814	299,498	332	58	15	T	ex Utah-08
BW Utik *	Hkg	2001	157,814	299,450	332	58	15	T	ex Utik-06
BW Vik	Pan	1987	159,534	310,686	332	57	13	O	ex Berge Vik-07, Tijuca-02 (conv Obo-04)
Havis	Nis	1993	34,951	49,513	205	32	15	Lpg	
Havkong	Nis	1978	34,577	43,386	220	29	17	Lpg	ex Galconda-87
Hedda	Nis	1993	22,521	30,815	170	27	18	Lpg	
Hekabe	Nis	1977	34,572	43,386	220	29	16	Lpg	ex Garinda-86
Helga	Nis	1994	22,521	30,800	170	27	16	Lpg	

BW Shipping Group. BW HAVSOL. *Hans Kraijenbosch*

Name	Flag	Year	GRT	DWT	LOA	Bm	Kts	Type	Former names
Herakles	Nis	1982	20,531	31,485	158	28	15	Lpg	ex Berge Fister-88
LNG Benue (st)	Bmu	2005	97,561	83,068	285	43	20	Lng	
LNG Enugu	Bmu	2005	97,561	83,068	285	43	20	Lng	
LNG Imo (st)	Bmu	2008	98,798	83,684	288	43	19	Lng	
LNG Kano (st)	Bmu	2007	98,798	83,961	288	43	19	Lng	
LNG Lokoja (st)	Bmu	2006	98,798	83.065	288	43	19	Lng	
LNG Ondo (st)	Bmu	2007	98,798	83,688	288	43	19	Lng	
LNG Oyo (st)	Bmu	2005	97,561	83,068	285	43	20	Lng	
LNG River Orashi (st)	Bmu	2004	97,561	83,068	285	43	20	Lng	
Nysa *	Sgp	2000	157,814	299,543	332	58	15	T	ex Argo Artemis-00
SG Enterprise †	Bhs	1997	108,083	211,485	312	51	14	B	ex Jedforest-00, SG Enterprise-98
SG Prosperity †	Bhs	1996	108,083	211,201	312	51	14	B	ex Lauderdale-00, SG Prosperity-98
Soro *	Pan	1993	156,539	299,718	332	58	15	T	
Suva *	Pan	1993	153,332	293,371	328	57	15	T	ex Argo Medea-00, Suva-98
Ubud *	Pan	1999	149,383	299,990	330	60	16	T	
Ural *	Pan	2000	149,383	299,990	330	60	16	T	
World Lake *	Hkg	2004	156,500	298,500	332	58	15	T	
World Lion *	Hkg	2004	158,557	298,563	332	58	15	T	
World Luck *	Hkg	2003	158,993	298,717	332	58	15	T	

newbuildings: four 380,000 dwt and one 206,000 dwt ore carriers, 48,000 grt Lpg tanker, two 320,000 dwt and three further 75,500 dwt tankers, also further 206,312 dwt bulker and six 83,000m3 Lpg tankers and two 162,400m3 Lng tankers for 2009-10 delivery.
* managed by BW Shipping Managers Pte. Ltd., Singapore or owned by subsidiary ** The Green Tankers AS, France (formed 1997)
† chartered out to Chinese steelmaker until 2012. ‡ managed by Reederei F Laeisz GmbH
‡ owned by Unique Shipping (HK) Ltd and managed by Anglo-Eastern Shipmanagement (S) Pte Ltd, Singapore
§ owned by subsidiary of Shoei Kisen Kaisha, Japan.

Neu Seeschiffahrt GmbH/Germany

Funnel: Blue/grey with blue 'NEU' on blue/white/blue horizontally striped flag on white rectangle. **Hull:** Black, dark grey or brown with red boot-topping. **History:** Formed 1958 as Krupp Seeschiffahrt GmbH to 1965, then other Krupp names until 1988, then Krupp-Lonrho GmbH Seeschiffahrt partnership to 1993, then Krupp Seeschiffahrt GmbH (part of ThyssenKrupp AG after 1997 merger) to 2001, when Bergesen acquired 51% control. **Web:** none found.

Name	Flag	Year	GRT	DWT	LOA	Bm	Kts	Type	Former names
Alfred N	Pan	1991	131,479	260,826	325	54	13	O	ex Lyra-02
Alster N	Lbr	1988	171,924	305,893	340	57	13	O	ex Alster Ore-03
Amy N	Pan	1997	155,051	322,457	332	58	13	O	ex Neckar Ore-01
Arthur N	Pan	1991	131,479	260,823	325	54	13	O	ex Athesis Ore-02
Bing N	Nis	1992	154,030	322,941	339	55	14	O	ex Bergeland-08
Edward N (2)	Pan	1979	112,947	225,162	313	50	17	O	ex Berge Athene-04, Pankar Theodoros-88, Konkar Theodoros-87
Eva N	Nis	1997	107,512	218,283	305	53	15	O	ex Berge Nord-08
Faith N	Pan	1990	131,479	260,783	325	54	13	O	ex Auriga-02
Grace N	Lbr	1983	113,342	224,222	312	50	13	B	ex Elbe Ore-05, Frontier Maru-96
Harriette N *	Sgp	2003	34,582	47,232	216	32	17	Lpg	ex Cantarell-00, l/a Petrogas II
Hugo N *	Pan	1980	34,582	46,486	216	32	-	Lpg	ex Ahkatun-99
Janice N	Lbr	1995	146,865	259,999	322	58	15	O	ex Diamond Hope-08 (conv T-08)
Julian N	Lbr	1993	77,090	149,394	270	43	13	B	ex Anja-05, Chou Shan-03
Karoline N	Lbr	2009	42,987	54,004	227	32		Lpg	
Margot N	Lbr	1989	142,488	255,028	322	56	14	O	ex Eastern Fortune-07, Honam Sapphire-97, Niels Maersk-91

BW Shipping Group. HEDDA. *Allan Ryszka Onions*

Name	Flag	Year	GRT	DWT	LOA	Bm	Kts	Type	Former names
Mosel N **	Lbr	1995	63,152	122,311	266	41	14	B	ex Mosel Ore-03
Patsy N *	Iom	1984	22,750	29,265	188	30	18	CC	ex Sea Pearl I-97, Patsy N-96, Lloyd Pacifico-95
Rebekka N	Lbr	1990	144,223	255,226	322	56	14	O	ex Azuma Enterprise-07, C. Voyager-01, Yukong Voyager-97 (conv T)
Regena N	Lbr	2006	90,091	180,277	289	45	15	O	
Renate N	Lbr	1992	154,644	285,933	328	58	15	T	ex New Frontier-08, Nuri-07, Argo Daphne-00
Ruhr N	Lbr	1987	171,924	305,863	340	57	13	O	ex Ruhr Ore-03
Saar N **	Lbr	1995	63,152	122,331	266	41	14	B	ex Saar Ore-03
Steven N *	Pan	1979	33,807	40,605	217	32	17	Lpg	ex Monterrey-99
Waterman N	Pan	1985	129,325	259,296	329	54	12	B	ex Hyundai Giant-03

newbuildings: seven 300,000 dwt, four 388,000 dwt ore carriers and six 36-47,000 grt Lpg tankers. for 2009-11 delivery
* owned by Blue Ocean Management Ltd subsidiaries of Maru Shipping Co Inc, USA.
** owned by Commerz Real Fonds Beteiligungsgellschaft and managed by Pronav Ship Management GmbH, Germany

Cardiff Marine Inc Greece

Funnel: *Black with broad blue band edged with narrow yellow bands or blue with black top.* **Hull:** *Black or grey with red boot-topping.*
History: *Formed 1992 as management subsidiary of DryShips Inc., 57% owned by Economou family.* **Web:** *www.cardiff.gr*

Name	Flag	Year	GRT	DWT	LOA	Bm	Kts	Type	Former names
Alameda *	Mlt	2001	86,743	170,726	290	45	14	B	ex Cape Araxos-05
Avoca *	Mlt	2004	39,736	76,629	225	32	14	B	ex Nord Mercury-08
Bargara *	Mlt	2001	40,437	74,500	225	32	14	B	ex Songa Hua-07, De Hua Hai-06
Bonita	Grc	2006	57,711	106,144	247	42		T	
Brisbane *	Mlt	1995	77,298	151,066	273	43	15	B	ex Spring Brave-07, Dyna Gemini-02
Capitola *	Mlt	2001	40,437	74,816	225	32	14	B	ex Songa Hui-07, De Hui Hai-06
Capri	Mlt	2001	87,390	172,529	289	45	15	B	ex Gran Trader-08
Carmel	Grc	2006	58,418	104,493	244	42	15	T	
Catalina *	Mlt	2005	40,485	74,432	225	32	14	B	
Coronado *	Mlt	2000	38,818	75,706	225	32	14	B	ex Seafarer II-05, Seafarer-04
Conquistador	Mlt	2000	38,802	75,607	225	32	14	B	ex Kookaburra-08
Delos	Lbr	1991	28,223	47,083	183	32	14	T	ex Innovator I-08, Victorious-07, Nagatino-04
Delray	Mlt	1994	37,629	71,862	225	32	14	B	ex Lacerta-08, Kiyoh-00
Ecola *	Mlt	2001	39,893	73,931	225	32	14	B	ex Zella Oldendorff-07, Trave River-01
Fernandina	Mlt	2006	88,853	174,204	289	45	14	B	
Flecha	Mlt	2004	87,440	170,012	289	45	14	B	ex Nightflight-08, Cape Kassos-07
Iguana	Mlt	1996	36,559	70,349	225	32	14	B	ex Pacific Carrier-04, Pacific Fortune-01
Juneau	Mlt	1990	77,096	149,495	270	43	13	B	ex Amazon-07, Bulk Atlanta-05, Cape Asia-00
La Jolla *	Mlt	1997	37,707	72,126	224	32	14	B	ex Konkar Maroula-05, World Refresh-03, l/a Valiant
Ligari *	Mlt	2004	38,851	75,845	225	32	14	B	ex Star of Emirates-06, l/a Hamburg Harmony
Lovina	Grc	2005	58,418	104,493	244	42	15	T	
Madeira	Mlt	2007	91,373	178,198	292	45	14	B	
Maganari *	Mlt	2001	39,126	75,941	225	32		B	ex Atacama-06, Semeli-05, Lowlands Kamsar-04
Majorca *	Mlt	2005	40,485	74,477	225	32	13	B	ex Maria G.O.-07
Malindi	Mlt	2008	91,373	177,987	292	45	14	B	
Manasota *	Mlt	2004	88,129	171,061	289	45	14	B	ex Katerina V-05
Marbella *	Mlt	2000	37,831	72,561	225	32	14	B	Restless-07, Ayrton II-06, Millennium Venture-05
Mendocino *	Mlt	2002	39,727	76,623	225	32	14	B	ex Conrad Oldendorff-06
Montego	Grc	2006	57,711	108,402	247	42		T	
Monterey	Grc	2007	58,418	105,009	244	42	15	T	
Morgiana	Pan	1988	93,710	186,001	292	48	14	B	ex Mugungwha-06
Mystic	Mlt	2008	89,510	170,102	291	45		B	ex Golden Nassim-08
Ocean Crystal *	Mlt	1999	38,372	73,688	225	32	14	B	ex Samsara-05, Ocean Crystal-05
Olinda	Mlt	1996	79,643	149,258	276	45	14	T	ex Tribute-04
Omaha	Grc	2008	91,373	177,986	292	45		B	
Oregon *	Mlt	2002	38,727	74,204	225	32	14	B	ex Athina Zafirakis-07, Jin Tai-04, Jin Hui-02
Oriental Green	Mlt	1998	56,955	99,991	244	42	14	T	
Pachino	Atg	2002	30,928	51,201	190	32	14	B	ex VOC Galaxy-08, Clipper Galaxy-03
Padre *	Mlt	2004	40,160	73,601	225	33	14	B	ex Belmonte-06
Petani	Mlt	2008	40,170	75,528	225	32	14	B	
Pink Sands	Mlt	1993	55,048	93,891	242	42	14	T	ex Angelo D'Amato-01, Sanko Protector-99
Pompano	Mlt	2006	88,853	174,240	289	45	14	B	
Positano	Mlt	2000	38,365	73,288	225	32	14	B	ex Nord Luna-08, Stefania L-06
Primera *	Mlt	1998	37,711	72,495	225	32	14	B	ex Sea Epoch-07
Primo Stealth	Grc	2005	58,418	105,034	235	42	15	T	
Redondo *	Mlt	2000	40,562	74,500	225	32	14	B	ex Liberty One-06, Alessandra d'Amato-06
Saldanha *	Mlt	2004	38,886	75,707	225	32	14	B	ex Shinyo Brilliance-07
Samatan *	Mlt	2001	40,437	74,823	225	32	14	B	ex Trans Atlantic-07, Yong Ler-05

Name	Flag	Year	GRT	DWT	LOA	Bm	Kts	Type	Former names
Samsara *	Mlt	1996	77,256	150,393	273	43	14	B	ex Cape Venture-07, Mineral Venture-04
Sarasota	Grc	2008	58,418	104,856	244	42		T	
Sidari	Mlt	2007	40,170	75,204	225	32	14	B	
Sivota	Mlt	2008	91,373	177,804	292	45		B	
Solana *	Lbr	1995	39,279	75,275	225	32	14	B	ex Linda Oldendorff-07
Sonoma *	Mlt	2001	40,437	74,786	225	32	14	B	ex Yong Kang-05
Sorrento	Mlt	2004	39,736	76,633	225	32	15	B	ex Federal Maple-08, Maple Ridge-07
Tamara	Mlt	1990	52,511	97,151	247	42	14	T	ex CSK Valiant-02
Tampa	Mlt	2008	91,373	177,987	292	45		B	
Tigani	Mlt	1991	52,603	97,114	247	42	14	T	ex Seafalcon-05
Tonga *	Mlt	1984	36,303	66,798	230	32	16	B	ex Stefanos-05, Ming Mercy-03
Toro *	Mlt	1995	38,567	73,034	225	32	14	B	ex Stalo-04
Toska	Grc	2009	83,545	167,554	275	48		T	
Universal Brave	Mlt	1997	156,692	301,242	331	58	15	T	
Universal Prime	Mlt	1997	156,692	299,985	331	58	15	T	
Venice	Grc	2004	61,764	109,637	245	42	15	T	ex Maersk Pristine-07
Ventura	Mlt	2006	88,930	174,316	289	45		B	
Waikiki *	Mlt	1995	39,385	75,473	225	32	14	B	ex Giuseppe D'Amato-05
Xanadu *	Mlt	1999	37,722	72,270	225	32	14	B	ex CMB Daisy-05, Sea Daisy-04
Zuma	Grc	2005	58,418	105,188	244	42	15	T	ex Corcovado-06

newbuildings: eleven 177-180,000 dwt and six 75-82,000 dwt bulk carriers, two 297,000 dwt, ten 156,000 dwt, eight 105,000 dwt and two 96,000 dwt* tankers due for 2009-11 delivery.
* managed on behalf of associated DryShips Inc (founded 2004 – www.dryships.com) or DryTank SA (founded 1987), both Greece.

Carisbrooke Shipping PLC   UK

Funnel: *Buff with buff 'CS' on blue rectangle.* **Hull:** *Light grey with green waterline over red boot-topping.* **History:** *Formed 1969, took over Soetermeer Fekkes BV in 1999 and Beck Scheepvaart BV in 2003.* **Web:** *www.carisbrookeshipping.com*

Name	Flag	Year	GRT	DWT	LOA	Bm	Kts	Type	Former names
Mark-C	Iom	2003	14,357	19,460	160	24	14	Co	ex Innogy Sprite-05, Dina-C-03

Champion Tankers AS   Norway

Funnel: *Dark blue with white 'CT'.* **Hull:** *Black with red boot-topping.* **History:** *Founded 2000.* **Web:** *www.champion-tankers.no*

Name	Flag	Year	GRT	DWT	LOA	Bm	Kts	Type	Former names
Champion *	Nis	1983	21,796	38,084	183	30	15	T	ex Team Tellus-01, Team Storviken-97
Champion Adriatic	Lbr	1981	21,963	37,658	171	30	15	T	ex Axios-04, Sacona-02, Mobil Endeavour-90
Champion Arctic	Nis	1986	28,292	48,375	202	30	14	T	ex Tervi-06
Champion Brali	Bhs	1985	31,248	49,273	183	32	14	T	ex Brali-06, Probo Brali-86 (conv Obo-86)
Champion Express	Lbr	1999	22,680	43,157	192	29	14	T	ex Isola Gialla-08
Champion Lion	Lbr	1985	26,113	45,979	172	32	14	T	ex Lion-07, Petrobulk Lion-96, Jahre Lion-86
Champion Pacific *	Nis	1982	21,777	33,886	183	30	15	T	ex Nicolas M-05, Carnac-01, Osco Stream-92
Champion Pioneer *	Nis	1990	22,572	40,525	176	32	14	T	ex Scottish Wizard-06, Stride-02, Osco Stripe-95
Champion Polar *	Nis	1986	28,292	47,750	200	30	14	T	ex Palva-06
Champion Spirit *	Nis	1991	28,256	45,998	183	32	14	T	ex Flamenco-06
Champion Star	Nis	1991	28,256	45,999	183	32	14	T	ex Fandango-06
Champion Trader	Gbr	1997	21,897	40,727	188	29	14	T	ex Isola Rossa-08

Managed by Genoa Maritime SA, Greece or by Thome Ship Management Pte Ltd, Singapore. * owned by Champion Shipping A/S, Norway.

Chandris Group   Greece

Funnel: *Dark blue with large white 'X'.* **Hull:** *Dark blue with red boot-topping.* **History:** *Founded 1911 as John D Chandris to 1942.* **Web:** *www.chandris-hellas.gr*

Name	Flag	Year	GRT	DWT	LOA	Bm	Kts	Type	Former names
Aktea	Grc	2005	60,007	107,091	248	43	15	T	
Al Nabila 4	Egy	1982	16,595	27,841	171	25	15	T	ex Gate-00, Sandgate-00, Ras al Barshah-87
Alexia	Egy	1982	54,537	91,740	245	40	15	T	ex Enalios Zephyros-02, Mexico-98, Esso Mexico-94
Alexia 2	Egy	1990	53,724	94,603	232	42	15	T	ex Meribel-08, Atalandi-04, Glory Central-97
Althea	Grc	1999	56,841	105,401	248	43	15	T	
Amira	Egy	2001	39,818	74,401	225	32	14	B	
Astrea	Grc	1999	56,841	84,999	248	43	15	T	
Athinea	Grc	2006	60,007	107,160	248	43	14	T	
Australis	Grc	2003	156,914	299,095	330	60	16	T	ex Saga-04, I/a Front Saga
Britanis	Grc	2002	157,581	304,732	332	58	16	T	
Chris	Egy	2006	39,736	76,629	225	32	14	B	
Ellinis	Grc	2007	157,844	306,507	332	58		T	
Louka	Egy	1989	38,792	68,159	243	32	15	T	ex Bregen-07
Maribella	Grc	2004	39,736	76,629	225	32	15	B	
Marichristina	Grc	2001	40,121	74,410	225	32	15	B	ex SA Warrior-03
Marietta	Grc	2004	40,135	73,880	225	32	15	B	ex World Prosperity-04
Marijeannie	Pan	2009	87,100	180,000	292	45		B	

Name	Flag	Year	GRT	DWT	LOA	Bm	Kts	Type	Former names
Mariloula	Pan	2008	87,100	180,000	292	45		B	
Marinicki	Grc	2005	39,738	76,629	225	32	15	B	
Myrto	Grc	2001	39,831	74,470	225	32	14	B	
Patris	Grc	2000	157,496	298,543	332	58	15	T	
Sharifa 3	Egy	1984	38,529	66,800	231	32	15	T	ex Elbe-04, Mantinia-89, Urania Coulouthros-89
Zeinat 2	Egy	1986	46,632	82,424	211	48	14	T	ex Ist-05

newbuildings: one 180,000 dwt bulk carrier, two 159,400 dwt and two 114,800 dwt tankers for 2009 delivery.
Operated by independent subsidiary Chandris (Hellas) Inc, Greece (founded 1988).
* managed by Ceres LNG Services Ltd, Greece. (www.ceresing.com)

Chemikalien Seetransport GmbH   Germany

Funnel: *Blue with white 'ST' inside large white outlined 'C' on blue square on broad white band.* **Hull:** *Black, blue or red with blue or red boot-topping.* **History:** *Formed 1989.* **Web:** *www.cst-hamburg.de*

Name	Flag	Year	GRT	DWT	LOA	Bm	Kts	Type	Former names
Athens Star	Lbr	2005	41,966	71,869	229	32	14	T	
Cancale Star	Lbr	2007	42,010	73,626	229	32	14	T	
Chemtrans Lyra	Lbr	1993	53,829	97,097	243	42	15	T	ex Eagle Lyra-03, Neptune Lyra-94, Athina II-94, Dalby-93, I/a Consensus Dalby
Chemtrans Moon	Lbr	2004	40,763	72,296	229	32	14	T	I/a Silver Dolphin
Chemtrans Petri *	Lbr	2000	28,534	47,228	183	32	14	T	ex St. Petri-07
Chemtrans Ray	Lbr	2000	40,516	71,637	227	32	15	T	ex Emerald Ray-03
Chemtrans Sea	Lbr	2004	40,764	72,365	229	32	14	T	ex Red Dolphin-04
Chemtrans Sky	Lbr	2000	37,033	63,381	229	32	14	T	ex Asopos-04
Chemtrans Star	Lbr	2000	37,033	63,331	229	32	15	T	ex Aliakmon-03
Chemtrans Sun	Lbr	1999	40,516	71,675	227	32	15	T	ex Emerald Sun-03
Gandhi	Lbr	2008	25,400	40,165	176	31		T	
Green Point	Lbr	2003	29,982	49,511	183	32	14	T	
Hamburg Star	Lbr	2005	40,000	73,400	229	32	14	T	
Hans Scholl *	Lbr	2004	25,399	40,250	176	31	15	T	
Isabella (st)	Lbr	1975	26,952	27,235	198	27	18	Lng	ex Kenai Multina-78, I/a Kentown
London Star	Lbr	2006	40,000	73,400	229	32	14	T	
Maersk Rhine	Lbr	1999	22,181	35,024	171	31	14	T	ex Ras Maersk-00
Maersk Riga	Lbr	2001	22,184	34,810	171	27	14	T	ex Roy Maersk-03
Maersk Rouen	Lbr	2000	22,181	34,860	171	27	15	T	ex Maersk Rye-03
Maersk Rugen	Lbr	2001	22,181	34,861	171	27	14	T	ex Maersk Ramsey-03
MS Simon	Lbr	2004	25,399	37,247	176	31	15	T	
MS Sophie	Lbr	2004	25,399	37,247	176	31	15	T	I/a Chemtrans Sophie
New York Star	Lbr	2006	41,966	73,869	229	32	14	T	
St. Jacobi *	Lbr	1999	25,202	43,760	182	30	14	T	
Tapatio †	Lbr	2003	26,914	46,764	183	32	14	T	
Trans Ocean *	Lbr	1983	44,910	75,568	244	32	15	Obo	ex Chemtrans Belocean-03, Belocean-94
Trans Pacific *	Lbr	2004	40,485	74,403	225	32	14	B	ex CMB Eline-05

* owned by subsidiary Chemtrans Overseas (Cyprus) Ltd and managed by Belchem Singapore Pte. Ltd. (formed 2004 jointly with Belships).
† managed for Laurin Tankers America Inc.
Partner in Star Tankers Pool with Heidmat Inc and in Baumarine Pool. Also see Team Tankers Pool under Blystad Shipmanagement Ltd.

Chandris Group. AKTEA. *N. Kemps*

Chevron Corp

USA

Chevron Shipping Co LLC/USA

Funnel: *White with three narrow blue bands, narrow black top.* **Hull:** *Black with red boot-topping.* **History:** *Formed 2005 as successor to ChevronTexaco Corp formed by 2001 by merger of Chevron Corp (founded 1906 as Standard Oil Co of California, merged 1926 with Pacific Oil Co (founded 1879) and acquired Gulf Oil Corp in 1984) and Texaco Inc (founded 1901 as The Texas Co to 1926, The Texas Corp to 1941 and The Texas Co to 1959). Subsidiary formed 1957 as California Shipping Co to 1965, then Chevron Shipping Co to 2001 and ChevronTexaco Shipping Co LLC to 2006.* **Web:** *www.chevron.com or www.chevrontexaco.com*

Name	Flag	Year	GRT	DWT	LOA	Bm	Kts	Type	Former names
Aberdeen §	Bhs	1996	47,274	87,055	222	37	14	T	
Antares Voyager †	Bhs	1998	160,036	309,995	333	58	16	T	ex Frank A. Shrontz-03
Antonis I. Angelicoussis	Bhs	2000	156,758	306,085	332	58	15	T	
Aquarius Voyager	Bhs	2006	161,331	300,000	333	60		T	
Aries Voyager	Bhs	2006	160,808	320,870	332	58	16	T	
Arizona Voyager (gt)	Usa	1977	22,664	39,836	199	29	16	T	ex Chevron Arizona-02
Capricorn Voyager ‡	Bhs	2007	58,442	104,610	244	42		T	
Castor Voyager	Bhs	2006	58,088	104,866	244	42		T	
Colorado Voyager (gt)	Usa	1976	22,735	39,842	199	29	15	T	ex Chevron Colorado-03
Dynamic Energy	Bhs	2002	46,506	53,556	227	36	17	Lpg	
Dynamic Vision	Bhs	2001	46,506	53,503	227	36	17	Lpg	
Kometik * (2)	Can	1997	76,216	126,646	272	46	14	T	
Maria A. Angelicoussis	Bhs	2000	156,505	300,000	332	58	15	T	
Neptune Voyager	Bhs	2003	58,156	104,875	244	42		T	
Northwest Swan (st)	Bmu	2004	96,165	73,676	280	43	19	Lng	
Orion Voyager	Bhs	1994	88,919	156,447	275	50	15	T	ex Chevron Employee Pride-02, Chevron Africa-94
Phoenix Voyager †	Bhs	1999	160,036	310,137	331	58	16	T	ex J. Bennet Johnston-03
Stellar Voyager	Bhs	2003	58,088	104,801	244	42		T	
Vega Voyager	Bhs	2003	58,088	104,864	244	42		T	
Washington Voyager (gt)	Usa	1976	22,761	39,795	199	29	15	T	ex Chevron Washington-03

newbuildings: 50,000 grt tanker and two 98,000 grt Lng tankers for 2009-10 delivery.
* jointly owned with Mobil Oil Corp (Exxon Mobil) and Murphy Oil Corp. managed by Canship Ugland Ltd, Canada.
† managed for Cambridge Petroleum Transport Corp, USA or ‡ for Mitsui Soko Co Ltd, Japan.
§ owned by Getty Maritime (managed by Northern Marine Management Ltd) and operated by Teekay Corp qv
See also Frontline Ltd and Angelicoussis Shipping Group Ltd.

China Ocean Shipping (Group) Co

China

Cosco Container Lines Co Ltd/China

Funnel: *Blue with white vertical line through white ring above white 'COSCO', broad yellow base and narrow black top.* **Hull:** *Grey or black with blue 'COSCO', green or red boot-topping.* **History:** *Parent founded 1961 as China Ocean Shipping Co to 1993. Container subsidiary formed 1997 by amalgamation with Shanghai Ocean Shipping Co.* **Web:** *www.coscon.com*

Name	Flag	Year	GRT	DWT	LOA	Bm	Kts	Type	Former names
Bing He	Chn	1985	23,542	33,389	201	28	15	CC	
Buyihe	Pan	1997	36,772	44,911	243	32	21	CC	
Chao He	Chn	1985	19,835	25,955	170	28	17	CC	
Chuanhe	Pan	1997	65,140	69,285	280	40	24	CC	
Cosco Africa	Pan	2008	114,394	110,038	349	46	25	CC	
Cosco America	Pan	2008	114,394	109,950	349	46	25	CC	

Chemikalien Seetransport GmbH. NEW YORK STAR. *J. M. Kakebeeke*

Name	Flag	Year	GRT	DWT	LOA	Bm	Kts	Type	Former names
Cosco Antwerp *	Hkg	2001	65,531	68,910	280	40	25	CC	
Cosco Asia	Pan	2007	114,394	109,968	349	46	25	CC	
Cosco Atlantic	Hkg	2009	115,776	111,385	349	46	25	CC	
Cosco Dalian	Pan	2005	66,380	67,209	279	40	25	CC	
Cosco Europe	Pan	2008	114,394	109,968	349	46	25	CC	
Cosco Felixstowe *	Gbr	2002	65,532	69,107	280	40	24	CC	
Cosco Hamburg *	Gbr	2001	65,531	69,193	280	40	24	CC	
Cosco Hong Kong *	Gbr	2002	65,531	68,895	280	40	24	CC	
Cosco Indian Ocean	Chn	2008	115,776	111,414	349	46	25	CC	
Cosco Oceania	Hkg	2008	115,776	111,385	349	46	25	CC	
Cosco Pacific	Hkg	2008	115,776	111,315	349	46	25	CC	
Cosco Qingdao	Pan	1997	65,140	69,285	280	40	24	CC	ex Yun He-01
Cosco Rotterdam *	Gbr	2002	65,531	69,224	280	40	25	CC	
Cosco Shanghai *	Gbr	2001	65,531	69,192	280	40	25	CC	
Cosco Singapore *	Gbr	2001	65,531	69,196	280	40	25	CC	
Cosco Tianjin	Pan	2005	66,380	67,209	279	40	24	CC	
Cosco Xiamen	Pan	2005	66,380	67,209	279	40	24	CC	
Da He	Chn	1994	49,375	51,950	275	32	25	CC	
Dong He	Chn	1990	37,143	47,625	236	32	19	CC	
Empress Dragon	Pan	1994	46,734	46,103	276	32	24	CC	
Empress Heaven	Pan	1993	46,734	46,099	276	32	24	CC	ex Ming Heaven-01, Empress Heaven-98
Empress Phoenix	Pan	1994	46,734	46,125	276	32	24	CC	
Empress Sea	Pan	1994	46,734	46,074	276	32	24	CC	
Fei He	Chn	1994	48,311	51,280	275	32	24	CC	
Fei Yun He	Chn	2000	20,569	25,723	180	28	20	CC	
Gao He	Chn	1990	37,143	47,625	236	32	19	CC	
Hanihe	Pan	1997	36,772	44,911	243	32	21	CC	
Jin He	Pan	1997	65,140	69,285	280	40	24	CC	
Jing Po He	Pan	1997	36,772	44,911	243	32	21	CC	
Ling Yun He	Chn	2000	20,569	25,723	180	28	20	CC	
Lu He	Pan	1997	65,140	69,285	280	40	24	CC	
Luo Ba He	Pan	1998	36,772	44,700	243	32	21	CC	
Min He	Chn	1989	37,143	47,625	236	32	19	CC	
Naxihe	Pan	1997	36,772	44,911	243	32	21	CC	
Pretty River	Pan	1993	22,746	33,650	188	28	18	CC	
Pu He	Chn	1990	35,963	46,136	236	32	19	CC	
Qing Yun He	Chn	2000	20,624	21,200	180	28	20	CC	
River Elegance	Pan	1994	48,161	49,945	277	32	24	CC	
River Wisdom	Pan	1994	48,161	49,955	277	32	24	CC	
Shan He	Chn	1994	49,375	51,985	275	32	24	CC	
Song He	Chn	1986	24,438	33,265	199	29	16	CC	
Tai He	Chn	1989	35,963	45,987	236	32	19	CC	
Teng He	Chn	1994	48,311	51,280	275	32	24	CC	
Teng Yun He	Chn	2000	20,569	25,723	180	28	20	CC	
Wanhe	Pan	1997	65,140	69,285	280	40	24	CC	
Xiang He	Chn	1985	24,043	30,939	200	28	17	CC	
Xibohe	Pan	1997	36,772	44,911	243	32	21	CC	
Ya He	Pan	1993	22,746	33,650	188	28	18	CC	ex Dainty River-08

China Ocean Shipping. COSCO ASIA. *N. Kemps*

Name	Flag	Year	GRT	DWT	LOA	Bm	Kts	Type	Former names
Yu He	Chn	1986	24,043	30,940	200	29	17	CC	
Yuan He	Chn	1994	48,311	51,280	275	32	24	CC	
Yue He	Pan	1997	65,140	69,285	280	40	24	CC	
Yuguhe	Pan	1997	65,140	69,285	280	40	24	CC	
Zhen He	Chn	1993	49,375	51,985	275	32	24	CC	
Zhong He	Chn	1993	48,311	51,280	264	32	23	CC	
Zhuang He	Chn	1985	24,438	33,240	199	29	17	CC	

newbuildings: numerous including eight 159,000 grt and ten 65,000 grt container ships for 2009-12 delivery.
Operated by Cosco Container Lines Co Ltd and Cosco Shanghai Ocean Shipping Co or * by subsidiary Cosco Maritime UK Ltd.

Cosco (HK) Shipping Co Ltd/Hong Kong (China)

Funnel: Blue with white 'CHS' and black top or * as main COSCO fleet. **Hull:** Grey with green boot-topping. **History:** Formed 1994 by amalgamation of Ocean Tramping Co Ltd and Yick Fung Shipping & Enterprises Co Ltd. **Web:** www.coscochs.com.hk

Name	Flag	Year	GRT	DWT	LOA	Bm	Kts	Type	Former names
Bai An Hai *	Chn	2008	90,685	177,000	292	45		B	
CHS Bright	Hkg	1995	77,255	151,053	273	43	14	B	ex Pantagruel-04, Royal Excelsior-02
CHS Cosmos	Hkg	2006	88,869	174,091	289	45		B	
CHS Creation	Hkg	2006	88,853	174,110	289	45	15	B	
CHS Harvest	Hkg	2006	89,659	173,624	289	45	15	B	ex Mariclia M-06
CHS Magnificence	Hkg	2006	89,659	173,541	289	45	15	B	
CHS Star	Pan	1991	75,675	150,149	269	43	13	B	ex Mercurian Virgo-05, Nord-Energy-01
CHS World	Hkg	2006	88,869	174,232	289	45	15	B	
Cospearl Lake	Pan	2008	156,915	298,195	330	60		T	
Huitai **	Pan	1996	75,722	149,228	266	43	14	B	ex Yukon-04, White Rose-97
RZS Fortune †	Mhl	1996	83,658	171,071	289	45	14	B	ex Sumihou-08, Asahisan-02
Sea Gloria **	Pan	1994	80,203	157,600	280	43	14	B	ex Sea Glory I-94
Sea Grace **	Pan	1994	80,203	157,600	280	43	14	B	
Sealink Majesty †	Pan	1982	92,308	177,754	300	48	14	B	ex Cape Maria-07, Harriet Maru-99, New Harriet-95, Harriet Maru-94
Sealink Prosperity †	Hkg	1984	85,504	160,993	280	47	14	B	ex Orient Fortune-07, Songa Arba-06, Daghild-05, Leviathan-03, Mindanao River 2-02
Star Xingang **	Pan	1985	78,625	148,140	284	47	14	B	ex Lowlands Yarra-04, Iron Newcastle-99
Star Yantai **	Pan	1986	78,625	148,140	284	47	14	B	ex Iron Kembla-05
Tian Bao Hai **	Chn	2004	88,856	174,505	289	45		B	
Tian Fu Hai *	Chn	1998	79,480	149,135	270	44	14	B	
Tian Li Hai *	Chn	1999	79,480	148.726	270	44	14	B	
Tian Lu Hai **	Chn	2005	88.856	174,398	289	45		B	
Tian Yang Hai	Pan	1997	85,676	169,999	289	45	17	B	
Tianronghai **	Pan	2000	87,625	171,877	289	45		B	
Tianshunhai **	Pan	2000	87,625	171,877	289	45		B	
Xinsheng Hai *	Hkg	1989	93,310	182,008	290	46	14	B	ex Topaz-01, Chita Maru-99

* owned by Cosco Bulk Carrier Co. Ltd, ** by Cosco Qingdao Ocean Shipping Co or † Cosco Shanghai Ship Management Co Ltd.
COSCO is one of the world's largest shipping groups with numerous subsidiaries owning over 660 vessels with more than 160 ships on order.
The above are just the largest container, bulk carriers and tanker currently operated by the main subsidiaries.
Also see Chinese-Polish Joint Stock Co. (Chinsko-Polskie Towarzystwo Okretowe SA) under Polish Ocean Line.

China Shipping (Group) Co

China

China Shipping Container Lines Co Ltd

Funnel: Blue with blue 'CIS' on broad white/yellow band. **Hull:** Green with white 'CHINA SHIPPING LINE', red boot-topping.
History: Government controlled company formed 1997 by merging of various government shipping Bureau and Administrations.
Web: www.cnshippingdev.com

Name	Flag	Year	GRT	DWT	LOA	Bm	Kts	Type	Former names
CSCL Africa **	Hkg	2005	90,645	101,612	334	43	25	CC	
CSCL Asia	Hkg	2004	90,645	101,612	334	43	25	CC	
CSCL Chiwan **	Hkg	2001	39,941	50,488	260	32	24	CC	
CSCL Dalian **	Hkg	2002	39,941	50,871	260	32	24	CC	
CSCL Felixstowe **	Hkg	2002	39,941	50,789	260	32	24	CC	
CSCL Hamburg **	Hkg	2001	39,941	50,500	260	32	24	CC	
CSCL Long Beach **	Hkg	2007	108,069	111,889	337	46	25	CC	
CSCL Melbourne **	Hkg	2005	39,941	50,796	263	32	24	CC	
CSCL Montevideo **	Hkg	2008	26,404	34,194	209	30	22	CC	
CSCL New York **	Hkg	2005	39,941	50,500	263	32	24	CC	
CSCL Ningbo **	Hkg	2002	39,941	50,789	260	32	24	CC	
CSCL Panama **	Hkg	2008	26,404	34,194	209	30	22	CC	
CSCL Qingdao †	Mlt	2001	39,941	50,953	260	32	24	CC	
CSCL Rotterdam †	Mlt	2002	39,500	50,863	260	32	24	CC	
CSCL Tianjin †	Mlt	2001	39,941	50,953	260	32	24	CC	
CSCL San Jose **	Hkg	2008	25.360	34,200	209	30	22	CC	
CSCL Santiago **	Hkg	2008	25.360	34,200	209	30	22	CC	
CSCL Sao Paulo **	Hkg	2008	26,404	34,194	209	30	22	CC	
CSCL Sydney **	Hkg	2005	39,941	50,869	260	32	24	CC	

Name	Flag	Year	GRT	DWT	LOA	Bm	Kts	Type	Former names
CSCL Vancouver **	Hkg	2005	39,941	50,500	263	32	24	CC	
CSCL Zeebrbrugge **	Hkg	2007	108,069	111,889	337	46	25	CC	
Xin Bei Lun	Chn	2005	41,482	52,000	263	32	24	CC	
Xin Beijing *	Hkg	2007	108,069	111,889	337	46	25	CC	ex Xin Hamburg-07
Xin Chang Sha	Chn	2005	41,482	52,000	263	32	24	CC	
Xin Chang Shu	Chn	2005	66,452	69,303	280	40	25	CC	
Xin Chi Wan	Chn	2004	66,452	69,271	280	40	25	CC	
Xin Chong Qing	Chn	2003	50,188	50,500	263	32	24	CC	
Xin Da Lian	Chn	2003	66,433	68,000	280	40	26	CC	
Xin Dan Dong	Chn	2006	41,482	52,000	263	32	24	CC	
Xin Fang Cheng	Chn	2005	41,482	52,000	263	32	24	CC	
Xin Fei Zhou	Chn	2008	90,757	102,400	335	43	25	CC	
Xin Fu Zhou	Chn	2004	66,452	69,303	280	40	26	CC	
Xin Hai Kou	Chn	2005	41,482	52,000	263	32	24	CC	
Xin Hong Kong *	Hkg	2007	108,069	111,746	337	46	25	CC	
Xin Huang Pu	Chn	2005	41,482	50,500	263	32	24	CC	
Xin Jin Zhou	Chn	1982	33,267	34,477	216	32	18	CC	ex Maple River-02, Tor Bay-93
Xin Lian Yun Gang	Chn	2003	66,433	69,023	280	40	26	CC	
Xin Los Angeles *	Hkg	2006	108,069	111,889	337	46	25	CC	
Xin Mei Zhou	Chn	2008	90,757	102,400	335	43	25	CC	
Xin Nan Sha	Chn	2005	41,482	52,000	263	32	24	CC	
Xin Nan Tong	Chn	2003	41,482	50,151	263	32	24	CC	
Xin Ning Bo	Chn	2003	66,433	69,303	280	40	26	CC	
Xin Ou Zhou	Chn	2007	90,757	102,460	335	43	25	CC	
Xin Pu Dong	Chn	2003	66,433	68,000	280	40	26	CC	
Xin Qin Huang Dao	Chn	2004	66,452	69,303	280	40	26	CC	
Xin Qing Dao	Chn	2003	66,433	69,423	280	40	26	CC	
Xin Quan Zhou	Chn	2005	41,482	50,500	263	32	24	CC	
Xin Ri Zhou	Chn	2005	41,482	52,000	263	32	24	CC	
Xin Shan Tou	Chn	2005	41,482	52,000	263	32	24	CC	
Xin Shanghai *	Hkg	2006	108,089	111,889	337	46	25	CC	
Xin She Kou	Chn	1983	33,267	34,477	216	32	18	CC	ex River Crystal-02, Providence Bay-93
Xin Su Zhou	Chn	2004	41,482	50,137	263	32	24	CC	
Xin Tai Cang	Chn	2008	41,482	52,000	263	32	24	CC	
Xin Tian Jin	Chn	2003	66,433	68,000	280	40	26	CC	
Xin Wei Hai	Chn	2006	41,482	52,219	263	32	24	CC	
Xin Wu Han	Chn	2009	41,482	52,233	263	32	24	CC	
Xin Xia Men	Chn	2004	66,433	69,259	280	40	25	CC	
Xin Ya Zhou	Chn	2007	90,757	102,395	335	43	25	CC	
Xin Yan Tai	Chn	2005	66,452	69,303	280	40	26	CC	
Xin Yan Tian	Chn	2004	66,433	68,023	280	40	26	CC	
Xin Yang Pu	Chn	2008	41,482	52,200	263	32	24	CC	
Xin Yang Shan	Chn	2005	41,482	52,242	263	32	24	CC	
Xin Yang Zhou	Chn	2004	41,482	50,137	263	32	24	CC	
Xin Ying Kou	Chn	2006	41,482	52,186	263	32	24	CC	
Xin Zhan Jiang	Chn	2006	41,482	52,279	263	32	24	CC	
Xin Zhang Zhou	Chn	2009	41,482	52,216	263	32	24	CC	

newbuildings: eight 159,000 grt, one 100,757 grt and ten 41,500 grt container ships plus over 80 bulk carriers for 2009-12 delivery.
* managed by subsidiary China International Ship Management.
** chartered from Seaspan Corp, Hong Kong (Seaspan International Ltd, Canadian subsidiary of Washington Corp, USA).
† chartered from KG Allgemeine Leasing GmbH & Co, Germany (founded 2003) and managed by V Ships (Germany) GmbH & Co KG.
In addition to the above, the company owns many smaller container ships, while other subsidiaries of China Shipping operate about 250 bulk
carriers and tankers between 10,000-158,000 grt. See other chartered vessels with 'CSCL' prefix in index.

Cido Shipping (HK) Co Ltd Hong Kong (China)

Funnel: *Charterers colours.* **Hull:** *Black or long-term charterers colours with red boot-topping.* **History:** *Founded 1993 as Cido Maritime Corp and Cido Shipping Co Ltd, which were merged in 2004.* **Web:** *www.cidoshipping.com*

Name	Flag	Year	GRT	DWT	LOA	Bm	Kts	Type
Alpine Mathilde	Hkg	2008	29,266	47,128	183	32	14	T
Atlantic Blue	Hkg	2007	29,266	47,128	183	32	14	T
Atlantic Breeze	Hkg	2007	29,266	47,128	183	32	14	T
Atlantic Crown	Hkg	2007	29,266	47,128	183	32	14	T
Atlantic Diana	Hkg	2007	29,266	47,128	183	32	14	T
Atlantic Eagle	Hkg	2007	29,266	47,128	183	32	14	T
Atlantic Frontier	Hkg	2007	29,266	47,128	183	32	14	T
Atlantic Gemini	Hkg	2008	29,266	47,128	183	32	14	T
Atlantic Grace	Hkg	2008	29,266	47,128	183	32	14	T
Atlantic Hope	Hkg	2008	29,266	47,128	183	32	14	T
Atlantic Leo	Hkg	2008	29,266	47,128	183	32	14	T
Atlantic Olive	Hkg	2008	29,266	47,128	183	32	14	T
Atlantic Rose	Hkg	2008	29,266	47,128	183	32	14	T

Name	Flag	Year	GRT	DWT	LOA	Bm	Kts	Type	Former names
Atlantic Star	Hkg	2008	29,266	47,128	183	32	14	T	
Bahia	Hkg	2004	40,014	76,801	225	32	14	B	
Beech Galaxy	Hkg	2007	11,623	19,998	146	24	14	T	
Belo Horizonte	Hkg	2004	40,014	76,801	225	32	14	B	
Betis	Hkg	2004	40,014	76,801	225	32	14	B	
Bow Rio	Hkg	2005	11,986	19,998	146	24	14	T	
Caribbean Emerald	Pan	1985	24,929	9,234	151	27	17	V	ex Bellflower-92
Charlotte Bulker	Hkg	2007	19,831	32,132	176	29	14	B	
Dream Angel	Pan	2006	41,662	15,089	177	28	19	V	
Dream Beauty	Pan	2006	41,662	15,119	177	28	19	V	
Dream Diamond	Pan	2007	41,662	15,069	186	28	20	V	
Dream Diva	Pan	2007	41,662	15,068	186	28	20	V	
Dream Jasmine	Pan	2008	41,662	15.068	186	28	20	V	
European Emerald	Pan	1984	37,996	13,208	175	29	18	V	ex Nissan Maru-92
Fortune Clover	Hkg	2006	40,080	77,430	225	32	14	B	
Fortune Ocean	Hkg	2006	40,040	76,600	225	32	14	B	
Fortune Princess	Hkg	2007	40,014	76,635	225	32	14	B	
Fortune Rainbow	Hkg	2008	42,665	82,372	225	32	14	B	
Fortune Spirit	Hkg	2005	21,227	33,562	180	28	15	B	
Fortune Sunny	Hkg	2008	42,665	82,338	225	32	14	B	
Forward Bright	Hkg	2007	59,164	115,577	244	42	15	T	
Grand Champion	Pan	2008	59,217	18,262	200	32	19	V	
Grand Choice	Pan	1999	50,309	16,669	179	32	19	V	
Grand Cosmo	Pan	2006	59,217	17,750	200	32	20	V	
Grand Diamond	Pan	2007	59,217	18,058	200	32	19	V	
Grand Duke	Pan	2005	59,217	18,315	200	32	20	V	
Grand Hero	Pan	2007	59,217	18,085	200	32	19	V	
Grand Mark	Pan	2000	50,310	16,681	179	32	19	V	
Grand Mercury	Pan	2002	58,947	19,121	200	32	20	V	
Grand Neptune	Pan	2006	59,217	17,550	200	32	20	V	
Grand Orion	Pan	2006	59,217	18,312	200	32	20	V	
Grand Pace	Pan	1999	50,309	16,714	179	32	19	V	
Grand Pavo **	Pan	2005	59,217	18,376	200	32	20	V	
Grand Pearl	Pan	2008	59,217	18,090	200	32	19	V	
Grand Phoenix **	Pan	2005	59,217	18,383	200	32	20	V	
Grand Pioneer	Pan	2002	58,947	19,120	200	32	20	V	
Grand Quest	Pan	2000	50,309	16,702	179	32	19	V	
Grand Race	Pan	2000	50,309	16,689	179	32	19	V	
Grand Ruby	Pan	2007	59,217	18,117	200	32	19	V	
Grand Sapphire	Pan	2007	59,217	18,099	200	32	19	V	
Grand Venus	Pan	2006	59,217	13,500	200	32	20	V	
Grand Victory	Pan	2008	59,217	18,299	200	32	19	V	
Great Challenger	Hkg	2005	88,594	176,279	289	45	15	B	
Great Chance	Hkg	2004	17,679	28,701	177	26	14	B	
Great Dream	Hkg	2004	19,829	33,745	169	28	14	B	
Great Leader	Hkg	2004	19,829	33,745	169	28	14	B	
Great Morning	Hkg	2004	17,679	28,310	177	26	14	B	
Great Navigator	Hkg	2006	88,594	176,303	289	45	15	B	
Great River	Hkg	2004	19,829	33,700	175	28	14	B	
Great Summit	Hkg	2005	19,829	33,745	169	28	14	B	
High Mars §	Hkg	2008	29,733	51,542	183	32	14	T	
High Saturn §	Hkg	2008	29,733	51,527	183	32	14	T	
Hoegh Dubai †	Pan	2004	58,947	19,121	200	32	19	V	ex Haul Dubai-06
Hoegh Durban †	Pan	2004	59,217	18,381	200	32	19	V	ex Haul Durban-07
Hoegh Oceania †	Pan	2003	58,947	19,121	200	32	19	V	ex Hual Oceania-05
Hyundai Harmony	Pan	2002	13,267	17,800	162	26	19	CC	
Ivy Galaxy	Hkg	2008	11,623	19,994	146	24		T	
Lowlands Ghent	Hkg	2004	40,014	76,801	225	32	14	B	
LR2 Pioneer ††	Pan	2008	59,172	115,273	244	42		T	
LR2 Polaris ††	Pan	2008	59,172	115,273	244	42		T	
LR2 Poseidon ††	Pan	2009	59,300	114,500	244	42		T	
Magic Sky	Pan	1982	21,574	10,642	166	22	17	V	ex Morning Sky-01, Magic Sky-00, Maersk Sky-97, Rich Seven-89
Magic Wind	Pan	1981	23,304	7,300	153	26	21	V	ex Maersk Wind-96
Marine Reliance	Mhl	1987	35,750	11,676	174	30	17	V	
Modern Chance	Lbr	1999	33,863	10,834	164	28	18	V	
Modern Express	Pan	2001	33,831	10,817	164	28	21	V	
Modern Link	Pan	2000	33,831	10,419	164	28	18	V	
Modern Peak	Pan	1999	33,831	10,817	164	28	18	V	
Morning Breeze	Pan	1977	24,278	8,545	169	26	16	V	ex Morning Grace-99, Puebla-95, Amoroso-93, North Blaze-90, Polar Ace-87

Name	Flag	Year	GRT	DWT	LOA	Bm	Kts	Type	Former names
Morning Ivy	Pan	1981	47,847	17,637	190	32	18	V	ex Princess Arrow-04, European Venture-90, l/a Automobile Venture
Morning Light	Pan	1978	30,070	10,601	180	28	17	V	ex Californian Star-95, Donaire-92, Young Splendour-90
Morning Power	Pan	1981	42,657	16,984	199	30	18	V	ex Vermilion Highway-02
Morning Prince	Pan	1979	45,423	13,910	190	32	19	V	ex Prince-95, Prince No.10-94, Prince Maru No.10-86
Morning Queen	Pan	1978	38,974	18,426	199	30	18	V	ex Hamburg Star-95, Golden Ace-91
Morning Saga	Lbr	1981	41,868	13,834	186	32	18	V	ex Viking Star-96, Viking Ace-92, Paramount Ace-90
Nord Rio	Hkg	2007	19,796	31,883	176	29	14	B	
Nord Singapore	Hkg	2008	19,831	32,114	176	29	14	B	
Pacific Amber	Pan	1993	146,527	264,512	322	58	15	T	ex Able Dolphin-05, Cosmo Delphinus-01
Pacific Apollo	Hkg	2007	59,164	115,577	244	42	15	T	
Pacific Beauty ‡	Pan	1992	146,762	258,096	322	58	15	T	ex Pacific Venus-02
Pacific Brave	Hkg	2007	59,164	115,677	244	42	15	T	
Pacific Condor	Hkg	2007	59,164	99,996	244	42	14	T	
Pacific Crystal ‡	Hkg	1994	147,005	264,158	322	58	15	T	ex Diamond Falcon-03
Pacific Delight	Hkg	2007	59,164	115,577	244	42	15	T	
Pacific Empire	Hkg	2008	59,164	115,577	244	42	15	T	
Pacific Fantasy	Hkg	2008	59,300	115,000	244	42	15	T	
Pacific Garnet ‡	Pan	1995	154,651	277,798	329	57	15	T	ex C.Navigator-07, Yukong Navigator-97
Pacific Oasis	Pan	2004	28,799	47,999	180	32	14	T	
Pacific Opal ‡‡	Pan	1995	154,651	278,157	329	57	15	T	ex C.Planner-07, Yukong Planner-97
Pacific Polaris	Pan	2004	28,799	47,999	180	32	14	T	
Pos Courage	Hkg	2004	40,014	76,810	225	32	14	B	
Pos Dignity	Hkg	2004	40,014	76,810	225	32	14	B	
Pos Eternity	Hkg	2004	39,964	76,295	225	32	14	B	
Pos Freedom	Hkg	2005	30,743	55,695	190	32	14	B	
Pos Glory	Hkg	2004	39,964	76,508	225	32	14	B	
Pos Harmony	Hkg	2005	30,743	55,700	190	32	14	B	
Pos Island	Hkg	2006	31,000	55,000	190	32	14	B	
Pos Jade	Hkg	2006	19,796	31,760	176	29	14	B	
Pos Knight	Hkg	2006	19,800	31,800	176	29	14	B	
Pos Leader	Hkg	2006	19,796	31,907	176	29	14	B	
Pro Emerald	Pan	2003	28,144	46,101	180	32	14	T	ex Pacific Honor-08
Salamanca	Hkg	2000	26,084	46,743	183	31	14	B	
Saracen Star	Pan	1984	26,758	11,554	158	28	17	V	ex Oscar Ace-92
Topaz Ace *	Pan	1995	48,210	14,696	180	32	18	V	
Trigger	Lbr	1976	25,909	9,993	188	23	18	V	ex Barcelona-92, Trigger-91, Nosac Trigger-88, Trigger-85, Hoegh Trigger-84

newbuildings: over 100 on order including 14 bulk carriers, 12 container ships, 54 tankers and 11 vehicle carriers for 2009-11 delivery.
* on charter to Mitsui OSK, ** to Kawasaki, † to Leif Hoegh & Co, †† to Torm LR2 Pool or to other owners including Eukor Car Carriers Inc. (see under Wallenius-Wilhelmsen).   ‡ managed by Univan Ship Management Ltd or ‡‡ by The Schulte Group

Clipper Group (Management) Ltd   Bahamas
Clipper Marine Services A/S/Denmark

Funnel: Black with white 'C' symbol. **Hull:** Black with white 'CLIPPER', red boot-topping. **History:** Formed 1972 and with subsidiaries currently operates some 240 vessels, 90 of which are owned or part-owned. **Web:** www.clipper-group.com

Name	Flag	Year	GRT	DWT	LOA	Bm	Kts	Type	Former names
Bossclip Trader ††	Bhs	2006	19,918	30,634	179	29	14	B	
CEC Star *	Iom	1993	10,546	12,184	149	23	18	CC	ex P&O Nedlloyd Wellington-05, OSS Kolkata-04, Ratana Sopa-03, Maersk San Jose-02, Dole Colombia-99, Ratana Sopa-98, l/a Merete
Clipper Glory	Hkg	2007	19.971	30,570	179	28	14	B	ex Clipper Transporter-08, Clipper Transport-07
Clipper Grace §	Hkg	2007	19,971	30,548	179	28	14	B	ex Clipper Treasure-08
Clipper Lake ††	Hkg	2001	16,953	28,492	169	27	14	B	ex Pacforest-04
Clipper Lancaster ‡	Bhs	1996	17,209	28,249	170	27	14	B	ex Paclogger-04, Sea Dream-99
Clipper Lancelot ‡	Lbr	1997	16,794	28,426	169	27	14	B	ex Pactrader-04, Sea Winner-99
Clipper Lasco ‡	Bhs	2004	16,954	28,200	169	27	14	B	
Clipper Melody †	Bhs	1997	16,405	25,069	172	25	14	B	ex Jan Zizka-99
Clipper Sterling §	Bhs	1999	14,118	20,730	158	23	15	Co	ex Changsha-06, Clipper Sterling-05, VOC Sterling-04, Clipper Sterling-00
Clipper Target ††	Bhs	2006	19,918	30,587	179	29	14	B	
Clipper Tenacious †	Bhs	2007	19,918	30,634	179	29	14	B	
Clipper Texan ††	Bhs	2007	19,918	30,618	179	29	14	B	
Clipper Tivoli ††	Bhs	2007	19,918	30,587	179	29	14	B	
Clipper Trust ††	Bhs	2007	19,918	30,611	179	29	14	B	
Clipper Valour ††	Bhs	2003	22,072	34,790	179	28	14	B	
Magdalena Green **	Nld	2001	11,894	17,520	141	22	15	Co	

Name	Flag	Year	GRT	DWT	LOA	Bm	Kts	Type	Former names
Makiri Green **	Nld	1999	11,894	17,539	143	22	16	Co	
Marinus Green **	Nld	2000	11,894	16,000	143	22	16	Co	
Marissa Green **	Nld	2000	11,894	16,000	143	22	16	Co	
Marlene Green **	Nld	2001	11,894	17,500	143	22	16	Co	

newbuildings: eleven 17-18,000 dwt multi-purpose cargo and seven 81,000 dwt, seven 37,000 dwt, two 31,900 dwt, twelve 30,000 dwt and seven 20,000 dwt bulk carriers for 2009-11 delivery.
* managed by CEC Shipmanagment A/S, Denmark (www.cecshipmanagement.com)
** owned by subsidiaries Holland Ship Service (formerly CEC Shipmanagement NL BV), Netherlands and managed by Clipper Elite Carriers A/S, Denmark, † by Clipper Denmark ApS (founded 1995), †† by Clipper Bulk (Portland) Inc, USA (formed 1963 as Lasco Shipping Co and acquired 2003), ‡ by Clipper Bulk (Singapore) Pte Ltd (founded 2007 – www.clipper-bulk.com) and managed by Roymar Ship Management, USA.
§ owned by Van Ommeren Clipper Shipping BV, Netherlands (Van Ommeren Shipping BV to 2000) and managed by Dockendale Shipping Co Ltd, Bahamas. § managed by Univan Ship Management Ltd, Hong Kong.

Dockendale Shipping Co Ltd/Bahamas

Funnel: *White with red 'D' and 'S' above points of black anchor.* **Hull:** *Black with white 'DOCKENDALE' or 'DOCKSHIP' red boot-topping.* **History:** *Associate company founded 1973, but became dormant in 1974 before re-entering shipping in 1985.*
Web: *www.dockendale.com*

Name	Flag	Year	GRT	DWT	LOA	Bm	Kts	Type	Former names
African Eagle	Bhs	2003	17,944	27,102	178	26	14	B	ex DS Mascot-03
African Falcon	Bhs	2003	17,944	27,101	178	26	14	B	ex Clipper Majestic-03
African Hawk	Bhs	2004	17,944	27,101	178	26	14	B	
Clipper Lagoon	Bhs	2004	16,954	28,200	169	27	14	B	
Clipper Mercury	Bhs	2004	17,944	27,082	178	26	14	B	
Clipper Mermaid	Bhs	2001	17,944	27,105	178	26	14	B	
Clipper Morning	Bhs	2002	17,944	27,141	178	26	14	B	
Clipper Talent	Bhs	2009	20,000	30,400	179	28	14	B	
Clipper Tango	Bhs	2009	20,000	30,400	179	28	14	B	
Clipper Tarpon	Bhs	2009	20,000	30,400	179	28	14	B	
Clipper Taurus	Bhs	2009	20,000	30,400	179	28	14	B	
Clipper Terminus	Bhs	2009	20,000	30,400	179	28	14	B	
Clipper Terra	Bhs	2009	20,000	30,400	179	28	14	B	
Clipper Tsuji	Bhs	2008	19.972	30,487	179	28	14	B	
Clipper Valour	Bhs	2003	22,072	34,790	179	28	14	B	
DS Manatee	Bhs	2002	17,944	27,128	178	26	14	B	
DS Mirage	Bhs	1997	16,405	25,096	172	25	14	B	ex Clipper Mirage-03, Prokop Holy-99
DS Montrose	Bhs	2001	17,944	27,028	178	26	14	B	
DS Vanguard	Bhs	2004	22,072	34,300	179	28	14	B	
Victory *	Bhs	2002	22,072	34,656	179	28	14	B	ex Leopold Oldendorff-06, IVS Victory-03

newbuildings: two further 30,000 dwt bulk carriers for 2009 delivery.
* managed by ASP Ship Management Ltd, UK (www.aspships.com)

CMA CGM Holding SA   France

Funnel: *Red 'CMA' and blue 'CGM' on white band between blue base and red top* **Hull:** *Blue with white 'CMA CGM', red boot-topping.* **History:** *Amalgamation in 1999 of Compagnie Maritime d'Affretement (founded 1978) and Compagnie Generale Transatlantique SA (founded 1854 and state-controlled from 1933), which itself was a 1977 merger of CGT and Compagnie des Messageries Maritimes (founded 1948). ANL name acquired 1998 (formed 1956 as Australian Coastal Shipping Commission, becoming Australian Shipping Commission in 1974 and Australian National Line in 1989. Cheng Lie Navigation Co Ltd acquired 2007 (founded 1971).* **Web:** *www.cma-cgm.com or www.anl.com.au*

Clipper Group (Dockendale Shipping). CLIPPER VALOUR. *Guido van Driessche*

Name	Flag	Year	GRT	DWT	LOA	Bm	Kts	Type	Former names
ANL Australia **	Bhs	1991	37,410	47,326	233	32	18	CC	ex OOCL Australia-02, Australian Endeavour-01
ANL Explorer	Bhs	1985	35,739	34,194	218	30	20	CC	ex CMA CGM Enterprise-02, Australian Enterprise-01, Asia Venus-97, California Venus-95, Med Kobe-95, California Venus-94
CMA CGM Alcazar *	Pan	2007	54,778	68,282	294	32	25	CC	
CMA CGM Amber *	Gbr	2008	49,810	50,200	282	32	24	CC	
CMA CGM Andromeda	Gbr	2009	135,000	128,760	363	46	24	CC	
CMA CGM Aristote	Gbr	2007	17,594	21,267	170	27	21	CC	
CMA CGM Bellini *	Bhs	2004	65,247	72,500	277	40	24	CC	
CMA CGM Berlioz *	Fra	2001	73,157	80,250	300	40	25	CC	
CMA CGM Bizet	Atf	2001	73,157	77,200	300	40	25	CC	
CMA CGM Blue Whale *	Gbr	2007	54,309	65,892	294	32	25	CC	
CMA CGM Camellia §	Hkg	2006	28,927	39,200	222	30	23	CC	
CMA CGM Capri	Pan	2007	54,778	68,235	294	32	25	CC	ex Cosco New York-08
CMA CGM Chateau d'If	Cyp	2007	54,778	67,600	294	32	25	CC	ex Cosco Norfolk-07
CMA CGM Chopin *	Fra	2004	69,022	72,500	277	40	24	CC	
CMA CGM Coral	Fra	2008	49,810	50,200	282	32	14	CC	
CMA CGM Debussy	Atf	2001	73,157	80,251	300	40	26	CC	
CMA CGM Dolphin *	Gbr	2007	54,309	65,992	294	32	25	CC	
CMA CGM Eiffel *	Bhs	2002	49,855	58,344	282	32	26	CC	
CMA CGM Fidelio	Bhs	2006	107,898	100,000	334	43	24	CC	l/a CMA CGM Othello
CMA CGM Florida	Gbr	2008	54,309	65,800	294	32	25	CC	
CMA CGM Fort St. Georges	Fra	2003	26,047	30,450	198	30	21	CC	
CMA CGM Fort St. Louis	Fra	2003	26,210	30,804	198	30	21	CC	
CMA CGM Fort St. Pierre	Atf	2003	26,047	30,450	198	30	21	CC	
CMA CGM Fort Ste. Marie	Fra	2003	26,210	30,450	198	30	21	CC	
CMA CGM Gardenia ‡	Mhl	1980	32,629	30,422	257	31	20	CC	ex Sea-Land Express-07
CMA CGM Georgia	Gbr	2008	54,309	65,890	294	32	25	CC	
CMA CGM Herodote	Gbr	2007	17,594	18,860	170	27	21	CC	
CMA CGM Homere	Gbr	2007	17,594	21,264	170	27	21	CC	
CMA CGM Impala	Gbr	1996	16,803	22,990	185	25	19	CC	ex Semira-03, P&O Nedlloyd Amado-03, Semira-02, CGM Seville-02, Semira-97
CMA CGM Junior S	Mlt	1994	9,600	12,582	150	22	18	CC	ex Active F-04, Perak-04, Sea Scandia-97, Maersk Miami-96, Fiona I-94
CMA CGM Kailas	Pan	2006	21,971	24,279	196	28	22	CC	
CMA CGM Kingfish *	Gbr	2007	54,309	65,974	294	32	25	CC	
CMA CGM La Tour *	Cyp	2001	26,050	30,500	196	30	22	CC	
CMA CGM La Traviata *	Atf	2006	91,410	101,779	334	43	25	CC	
CMA CGM Lilac §	Hkg	2005	28,927	39,262	222	30	23	CC	
CMA CGM Lys ‡	Mhl	1980	32,629	30,489	257	31	20	CC	ex Sea-Land Mariner-07
CMA CGM Manet *	Cyp	2001	26,050	30,442	196	30	21	CC	
CMA CGM Marlin *	Gbr	2007	54,309	65,949	294	32	25	CC	
CMA CGM Matisse *	Cyp	1999	25,777	32,274	196	30	21	CC	
CMA CGM Medea	Fra	2006	107,711	113,964	334	43	24	CC	
CMA CGM Mozart	Bhs	2004	69,247	72,500	277	40	24	CC	
CMA CGM Nabucco	Bhs	2006	91,410	101,879	334	43	24	CC	
CMA CGM New Jersey	Bhs	2008	53.675	65,890	294	32	25	CC	
CMA CGM Norma	Bhs	2006	107,711	113,909	334	43	24	CC	
CMA CGM North Africa 1	Mlt	1985	9,764	12,710	149	22	17	CC	ex Wilma-04, Coral Wilma-01, Wilma-00, Weserland-95, Sea Lake-93, Antartico-92, Red Sea Endeavour-89, Sudan Crown-87, Royal Eagle-85, Weserland-85
CMA CGM North Africa 2	Mlt	1984	9,764	12,816	149	22	17	CC	ex P&O Nedlloyd Christine-04, Christine Eberhardt-03, MSC Christine-01, Coral Christine-01, Christine Eberhardt-00, Horizon-00, Christine Eberhardt-99, Melbridge Christine-99, CGM de Lesseps-98, Christine Eberhardt-97, Maersk la Plata-97, Hannoverland-94, Sea Beach-93, Hannoverland-91, Columbus Oregon-91, ACT 9-90, Hannoverland-86, Lloyd Londres-86, Hannoverland-85
CMA CGM Okapi	Gbr	2000	16,803	22,900	185	25	19	CC	ex Mina K-03, CMA CGM Seville-03, Mina K-02, Alianca Hamburgo-01, l/a Mina K
CMA CGM Orca *	Gbr	2006	54,309	65,954	294	32	25	CC	
CMA CGM Otello	Bhs	2005	91,410	101,810	334	43	24	CC	l/a CMA CGM Fidelio
CMA CGM Platon	Gbr	2007	17,594	21,263	170	27	21	CC	
CMA CGM Potomac	Gbr	1980	31,154	28,955	215	31	21	CC	ex Douce France-03, Fort Saint Charles-95
CMA CGM Puccini	Fra	2004	69,022	73,234	277	40	24	CC	
CMA CGM Puget *	Bhs	2002	49,855	58,548	282	32	24	CC	

Name	Flag	Year	GRT	DWT	LOA	Bm	Kts	Type	Former names
CMA CGM Ravel	Atf	2001	73,059	79,465	300	40	25	CC	
CMA CGM Rigoletto	Bhs	2006	107,711	114,004	334	43	24	CC	
CMA CGM Rossini	Fra	2004	65,730	73,235	277	40	24	CC	
CMA CGM Scala	Pan	2007	54,778	68,241	294	32	25	CC	ex Cosco Boston-07
CMA CGM Simba	Gbr	1994	11,062	15,166	158	23	18	CC	ex TMM Durango-05, MSC Nigeria-04, P&O Nedlloyd San Pedro-01, Kent Merchant-99, Maersk Libreville-98, Antje-97, Lanka Amila-97, Antje-94
CMA CGM Straus *	Bhs	2004	65,247	73,235	277	40	24	CC	
CMA CGM Swordfish	Gbr	2007	54,309	65,987	294	32	25	CC	
CMA CGM Tarpon	Gbr	2007	54,309	65,903	294	32	25	CC	
CMA CGM Tosca	Bhs	2006	91,410	101,818	334	43	24	CC	
CMA CGM Utrillo *	Cyp	1999	25,777	32,274	196	30	21	CC	
CMA CGM Verdi *	Bhs	2004	65,247	73,235	277	40	24	CC	
CMA CGM Violet §	Hkg	2006	28,927	39,262	222	30	23	CC	
CMA CGM Virginia	Bhs	2008	54.309	65,890	294	32	25	CC	
CMA CGM Vivaldi *	Bhs	2004	90,745	101,661	334	43	24	CC	
CMA CGM Wagner *	Bhs	2004	65,247	73,235	277	40	24	CC	
CMA CGM White Shark *	Gbr	2007	54,309	53,790	294	32	25	CC	
Delmas Swala	Gbr	1994	11,062	15,166	158	23	18	CC	ex Macandrews Swala-08, CMA CGM Swala-06, Elbstrom-05, Cala Puebla-04, Elbstrom-02, P&O Nedlloyd Dakar-01, Urundi-99, Elbstrom-98, UB Lion-98, Lanka Ruwan-97, Elbstrom-95,

CMA CGM Holding. CMA CGM HERODOTE. *J. M. Kakebeeke*

CMA CGM Holding. CMA CGM ROSSINI. *Allan Ryszka Onions*

Name	Flag	Year	GRT	DWT	LOA	Bm	Kts	Type	Former names
Ville d'Aquarius	Cyp	1996	40,465	49,229	259	32	24	CC	ex Lykes Tiger-03, Ville d'Aquarius-02
Ville d'Orion	Cyp	1997	40,465	49,208	259	32	23	CC	ex ANL California-03, Ville d'Orion-03
Ville de Mars	Gbr	1990	37,235	43,714	242	32	22	CC	ex Australian Endurance-00, Lykes Challenger-99, CGM Pasteur-98, Nedlloyd Pasteur-98, CGM Pasteur-95, Ville de Virgo-91, CGM Pasteur-90

newbuildings: twelve 135,000 grt, eight 107,000 grt, seven 98,000 grt, four 76,100 grt, and ten 40,200 grt container ships for 2009-11 delivery.
* owned by subsidiaries CMA Ships UK Ltd (formed 1990 as Donrich Ltd, later CMA UK Ltd to 1999, then CMA CGM UK Ltd to 2003 and CMA CGM (UK) Shipping Ltd to 2007) or ** by ANL Container Line Pty Ltd, Australia. ‡ owned by Target Marine. § reported sold to Greek owner. Subsidiary Cheng Lie Navigation Co Ltd, Taiwan owns six 15,000 grt container ships operating in Far East.
See other vessels with 'CMA CGM' or 'ANL' prefixes in index

Delmas Armement/France

Funnel: Blue with white waterwheel device. **Hull:** Black with white 'DELMAS' or 'OTAL', red boot-topping. **History:** Formed 1864 as Societe Navale Delmas-Vieljeux until 1971. Acquired Navale et Commerciale Havraise Peninsulaire from CNN-Worms Group (1986), Chargeurs Reunis (1988) and amalgamated with L Martin & Cie in 1991. Later 1991 taken over by SCAC (Bollore Group) as SCAC-Delmas-Vieljeux. Acquired by CMA-CGM in 2005. **Web:** www.delmas.com

Name	Flag	Year	GRT	DWT	LOA	Bm	Kts	Type	Former names
Adeline Delmas **	Bhs	1985	23,275	33,520	176	30	14	BC	
Blandine Delmas **	Bhs	1986	23,275	33,611	176	30	14	BC	
Caroline Delmas	Atf	1986	23,275	33,611	176	30	14	BC	
CMA CGM Esmeraldas †	Mhl	2003	26,061	30,453	196	30	21	CC	ex Kaedi-06, Irma Delmas-02
Delmas Keta *	Cyp	2003	26,047	30,450	196	30	21	CC	ex MOL Rainbow-08. Louis Delmas-03
Delmas Kissama **	Bhs	1982	20,829	26,287	177	28	17	CC	ex MOL Horizon-07, Suzanne Delmas-03, Suzanne-99, Marfret Caraibes-98, Suzanne Delmas-97, Ville de Marseille-89, Suzanne Delmas-87
Delphine Delmas **	Bhs	1986	23,275	33,520	176	30	14	BC	
Elisa Delmas	Bhs	2002	16,916	20,979	169	27	20	CC	
Flora Delmas **	Bhs	2002	16,916	21,420	169	27	20	CC	
Julie Delmas	Cyp	2002	26,047	30,453	196	30	21	CC	
Kamina	Bhs	1982	20,829	26,288	177	28	18	CC	ex Renee Delmas-00, CGM Mascareignes-96, Renee Delmas-95, Nedlloyd Bordeaux-92, Ville de Rouen-91, Ibn Zaidoun-91, Ville de Rouen-90, Renee Delmas-87
Kumasi	Cyp	2001	26,061	30,450	196	30	21	CC	ex WAL Ubangi-04, Catherine Delmas-03
Laura Delmas **	Bhs	1979	35,748	22,564	197	32	20	Ro	ex Kintampo-02, Towada-98, Kintampo-97, Nedlloyd Rochester-96, Rochester-88, Nedlloyd Rochester-86
Lucie Delmas **	Bhs	1979	35,748	22,564	197	32	19	Ro	ex Kagoro-03, Nedlloyd Rotterdam-96, Rotterdam-88, Nedlloyd Rotterdam-86
Marie Delmas	Cyp	2001	26,061	30,450	196	30	21	CC	
Nala Delmas **	Bhs	2002	16,916	20,944	169	27	20	CC	ex Gaby Delmas-06
Nicolas Delmas	Bhs	2002	26,061	30,450	196	30	21	Co	
Patricia Delmas	Bhs	1982	20,424	26,287	177	28	18	CC	ex Patricia D-98, Patricia-98, Patricia Delmas-97
Roland Delmas **	Bhs	1980	30,774	24,223	187	32	17	Ro	ex Grand Bereby-94, Saint Roparzh-92, Hoegh Banniere-91, Woermann Banniere-90, Hoegh Banniere-89
Rosa Delmas *	Lbr	1985	32,951	27,577	185	32	16	Ro	ex Rosa Tucano-98, Calapoggio-95, Rosa Tucano-93
Saint Roch **	Bhs	1980	16,744	24,260	187	32	18	Ro	ex Hoegh Belle-81
Ursula Delmas	Bhs	1984	30,750	32,709	189	32	18	CC	ex MSC Ipanema-04, Ursula Delmas-03, Sherbro-94, Nedlloyd Zaandam-91, Ursula Delmas-90, Etienne Denis-89

newbuildings: four 33,000 grt 29,000 dwt ro-ro vessels for 2011 delivery.
* managed by CMA Ships UK Ltd or ** by Midocean (IOM) Ltd, Isle of Man. † owned by Salamon AG, Germany.

NV CMB SA   Belgium

Bocimar International NV/Belgium

Funnel: Blue with blue 'B' on broad cream band. **Hull:** Black or orange with blue or red boot-topping. **History:** Parent founded 1895 and formed from 1930 merger of Cie Belge Maritime du Congo SA and Lloyd Royal Belge SA. Armement Deppe (founded 1863) merged 1984. Acquired Merzario in 1989 and Woermann from Essberger (Deutsche Afrika-Linien) in 1990. Group taken over by Savery family in 1991. 43% share of Canmar (formed 1984) sold to CP Ships in 1993. Bocimar formed 1970. **Web:** www.cmb.be

Name	Flag	Year	GRT	DWT	LOA	Bm	Kts	Type	Former names
CMB Biwa	Bel	2002	29,963	53,505	190	32	15	B	ex Lake Biwa-06
Mineral Antwerpen ‡	Pan	2003	87,495	172,150	289	45	15	B	
Mineral Azalea †	Hkg	1999	85,386	171,199	281	45	14	B	ex Sea Azalea-03
Mineral Beijing	Bel	2004	88,930	173,880	289	45	15	B	
Mineral Belgium	Bel	2005	88,930	173,806	289	45	14	B	
Mineral Capeasia †	Hkg	2005	88,853	175,000	289	45	14	B	

Name	Flag	Year	GRT	DWT	LOA	Bm	Kts	Type	Former names
Mineral China	Bel	2003	88,292	171,448	289	45	14	B	I/a CIC Oslo
Mineral Hong Kong	Bel	2006	88,930	175,000	289	45	14	B	
Mineral Kyoto	Bel	2004	90,398	183,204	289	45	15	B	
Mineral Kyushu	Pan	2006	90,091	180,211	289	45	14	B	
Mineral Libin	Bel	2006	88,930	175,000	289	45	15	B	
Mineral London	Bel	2006	88,930	173,949	289	45	15	B	
Mineral Monaco	Hkg	2005	90,091	180,263	289	45	15	B	
Mineral Nippon	Pan	2007	101,933	203,275	300	50	14	B	
Mineral Noble	Bel	2004	88,179	170,649	289	45	15	B	ex Mineral Kiwi-04
Mineral Shikoku	Pan	2006	104,727	206,312	300	50	14	B	
Mineral Sines ‡	Pan	2002	87,495	172,319	289	45	15	B	
Mineral Tianjin	Bel	2004	88,930	173,691	289	45	15	B	
Mineral Viking	Bel	2001	87,363	172,964	289	45	15	B	ex Bagru-04
Mineral Water	Bel	1999	85,695	169,962	289	45	14	B	ex Ingenious-07

Partner in Cape International Pool formed jointly with Ofer (Zodiac), Belships, Moller, Torvald Klaveness and Overseas Shipholding Corp. Managed by Anglo-Eastern (Antwerp) NV or Anglo-Eastern Ship Management Ltd, Hong Kong.
† managed by 28% owned Wah Kwong Ship Management, Hong Kong or ‡ by Oak Maritime (Canada) Ltd., Canada.

Euronav NV/Belgium

Funnel: *Black, white flag with narrow red horizontal cross on broad white cross on blue disc or ** blue with gold overlapping 'GO'.* **Hull:** *Black with red boot-topping.* **History:** *Formed 1989 by Compagnie Nationale de Navigation (acquired 1986 by Worms Group from Elf Oil), France and Mercurius Group, Sweden. By 1995 jointly owned by CMB and CNN as Euronav Luxembourg SA. In 1998 CMB acquired 90% share of CNN, which was sold in 1999 and later demerged from CMB.* **Web:** *www.euronav.com*

Name	Flag	Year	GRT	DWT	LOA	Bm	Kts	Type	Former names
Algarve	Atf	1999	157,833	298,969	332	58	15	T	
Antartica	Grc	2009	160,991	291,180	333	60		T	
Artois	Atf	2001	159,456	298,330	334	60	16	T	
Bourgogne	Bel	1996	161,287	296,230	333	58	13	T	
Cap Charles *	Grc	2006	81,324	158,880	274	48		T	
Cap Diamant *	Grc	2001	94,729	160,044	277	53	14	T	
Cap Felix *	Bel	2008	81,324	158,765	274	48		T	
Cap Georges *	Grc	1998	81,148	147,443	274	48	14	T	
Cap Guillaume *	Grc	2006	81,324	158,889	274	48		T	
Cap Jean *	Grc	1998	81,148	146,439	274	48	14	T	
Cap Lara *	Grc	2007	81,324	158,826	274	48		T	
Cap Laurent *	Grc	1998	81,148	147,436	274	48	14	T	
Cap Leon *	Grc	2003	81,328	159,048	274	48	-	T	
Cap Philippe *	Grc	2006	81,324	158,880	274	48		T	
Cap Pierre *	Grc	2004	81,328	159,048	274	48	-	T	
Cap Romuald *	Grc	1998	81,148	146,639	274	48	14	T	
Cap Victor *	Grc	2007	81,324	158,880	274	48		T	
Famenne	Atf	2001	159,456	298,412	333	60	15	T	
Fantasy *	Grc	2002	57,683	106,560	241	42	-	T	
Fidelity *	Grc	2002	57,683	106,548	241	42	-	T	
Filikon *	Grc	2002	78,845	150,709	274	48	15	T	ex Paros-04
Finesse *	Grc	2003	78,845	150,709	274	48	15	T	ex Anafi-04
Flandre	Atf	2004	159,016	305,704	332	58	15	T	
Kalamata	Grc	2009	161,500	291,180	333	60		T	
Luxembourg	Atf	1999	157,833	298,997	332	58	15	T	
Namur	Atf	2000	159,397	298,628	333	60	15	T	ex Ichiban-03, Berge Ichiban-02
Pacific Lagoon	Bel	1999	163,346	305,839	333	58	15	T	
TI Asia	Bel	2001	234,006	441,893	380	68	16	T	ex Hellespont Alhanbra-04
TI Creation	Bel	1998	156,505	298,324	332	58	15	T	ex Crude Creation-05, World Creation-04
TI Europe	Bel	2002	234,006	442,000	380	68	16	T	ex Hellespont Tara-04
TI Hellas	Bel	2005	161,127	319,254	333	60	16	T	ex Chrysanthemium-05
TI Topaz	Bel	2002	161,135	318,934	333	60	16	T	ex Crude Topaz-05, Oriental Topaz-05

newbuildings: six 157-159,000 dwt tankers for 2009-11 delivery.
*managed by Euronav Ship Management SAS, France or * by Euronav Ship Management (Hellas) Ltd, Greece and operating mainly in Tankers International Pool (48 ULCC and VLCC tankers) formed jointly with Klaus Oldendorff, Sanko, Overseas Shipholding Group, Shinyo, Petronas, Oak Maritime, Wah Kwong and Essar Shipping.*

Exmar NV/Belgium

Funnel: *Blue with red 'E' on broad white band.* **Hull:** *Red with dark red boot-topping.* **History:** *Formed 1981 and now partly demerged from CMB Group.* **Web:** *www.exmar.be*

Name	Flag	Year	GRT	DWT	LOA	Bm	Kts	Type	Former names
Brugge Venture ‡	Hkg	1997	22,352	26,777	170	27	17	Lpg	
Brussels	Bel	1997	22,323	26,943	170	27	16	Lpg	ex Oxfordshire-05
Carli Bay	Bel	1998	17,527	20,613	155	26	17	Lpg	
Chaconia	Bel	1990	19,643	29,271	166	27	16	Lpg	
Courcheville	Bel	1989	19,719	29,171	166	27	16	Lpg	ex Nyhall-96
Donau	Bel	1985	23,508	32,339	183	30	15	Lpg	ex Gaz Nordsee-96, Donau-91
Eeklo	Bel	1995	23,519	28,993	179	27	16	Lpg	

Name	Flag	Year	GRT	DWT	LOA	Bm	Kts	Type	Former names
Elversele	Bel	1996	23,519	28,993	179	27	18	Lpg	
Excalibur (st)	Bel	2002	93,786	77,822	268	43	19	Lng	
Excel (st)	Bel	2003	93,786	77,774	277	43		Lng	I/a Peace River
Excelerate (st)	Bel	2006	93,786	77,822	277	43	19	Lng	
Excellence (st)	Bel	2005	93,937	77,348	277	43	19	Lng	
Excelsior (st)	Bel	2005	93,786	76,500	277	43		Lng	
Express	Bel	2009	114,987	76,500	277	43		Lng	
Explorer	Bel	2008	100,325	82,500	291	43		Lng	
Exquisite	Bel	2009	114,987	77,822	277	43		Lng	
Flanders Harmony	Bel	1992	47,597	64,220	228	36		Lpg	
Flanders Liberty	Bel	2007	48,456	55,056	226	37	15	Lpg	
Flanders Loyalty	Bel	2008	48,456	55,056	226	37	15	Lpg	
Flanders Tenacity ‡‡	Bel	1996	47,027	54,155	230	36	19	Lpg	
Gent	Bel	1985	18,155	26,820	155	27	16	Lpg	
Kemira Gas	Bel	1995	10,018	13,289	143	21	16	Lpg	
Libramont	Bel	2006	25,994	29,328	180	29	16	Lpg	
Methania (st)	Bel	1978	81,792	67,879	280	42	19	Lng	
Touraine ‡	Hkg	1996	25,337	30,309	196	29	19	Lpg	ex Antwerpen Venture-97
Valerie	Gib	2002	12,814	19,819	164	23		T	

newbuildings: two 95,800 grt Lng tankers for 2010 delivery.
Managed by subsidiary Exmar Shipmanagement NV, * for Sonatrach Gas Carrier, Belgium.
‡ jointly owned with or ‡‡ time chartered from Wah Kwong Shipping Agency Co. Ltd., Hong Kong (China)
Also operates LNG tankers in joint venture with Golar and Lpg tankers in Pool with Moller and BW Gas.

Cobelfret NV Belgium

Funnel: Yellow with red 'C' on white diamond on blue band. **Hull:** Black, grey or red with green or red boot-topping. **History:** Formed 1928. **Web:** www.cobelfret.com

Name	Flag	Year	GRT	DWT	LOA	Bm	Kts	Type	Former names
CSK Beilun *	Sgp	1999	87,522	172,561	289	45	14	B	ex Pierre LD-04
Lowlands Beilun *	Mlt	1999	85,906	170,162	289	45	14	B	
Lowlands Brilliance	Bel	2002	85,906	169,631	289	45	14	B	
Lowlands Camellia *	Pan	2006	40,040	76,807	225	32	14	B	
Lowlands Erica *	Pan	2007	89,603	176,862	289	45	16	B	
Lowlands Longevity	Bel	2001	86,848	173,000	289	45	15	B	
Lowlands Maine *	Pan	2005	40,039	76,600	225	32	14	B	
Lowlands Mimosa	Lux	2002	29,885	52,479	190	32	14	B	
Lowlands Nello *	Sgp	2004	40,040	76,830	225	32	14	B	
Lowlands Opal *	Pan	2007	30,678	55,381	190	32	14	B	
Lowlands Orchid *	Pan	2005	88,594	176,193	289	45	15	B	
Lowlands Patrasche *	Pan	2007	32,387	58,790	190	32		B	
Lowlands Phoenix *	Pan	2004	89,543	177,036	289	45	14	B	
Lowlands Prosperity	Bel	2001	86,201	169,229	289	45	14	B	ex Lowlands Prosperous-04
Lowlands Queen *	Pan	2008	39,737	76,585	225	32		B	
Lowlands Sumida *	Pan	1998	37,689	72,493	225	32	14	B	ex Federal Sumida-06
Lowlands Sunrise *	Pan	2003	88,594	176,298	289	45	15	B	

Operated by Cobelfret Bulk Carriers NV, Belgium.   * on time-charter from various Philippine, Singapore and Japanese owners.

NV CMB (Euronav). CAP FELIX. *Hans Kraijenbosch*

Compania SudAmericana de Vapores SA Chile

Funnel: Red with deep black top. **Hull:** Grey or white with red or green boot-topping. **History:** Founded 1872. **Web:** www.csav.com

Name	Flag	Year	GRT	DWT	LOA	Bm	Kts	Type	Former names
Braztrans I *	Bra	1980	22,011	38,186	194	28	15	B	ex Docemarte-99
Mapocho	Chl	1999	16,986	21,182	168	27	20	CC	ex Kribi-02, ANL Okapi-02, Fesco Endeavor-01, Kribi-00
Pacific Explorer	Mhl	1978	38,970	18,069	199	30	20	V	ex Asian Highway-93
Pacific Runner	Mhl	1977	38,754	18,099	199	30	20	V	ex Grand Lebanon-04, Pacific Runner-03, American Highway-92
Pacific Winner	Chl	1987	48,688	18,845	213	30	18	Ro	ex Republica di Pisa-03
Rio Blanco **	Chl	1981	41,208	18,142	199	30	17	V	ex Fuji Ace-98
Rio Enco	Chl	1978	19,867	7,426	139	26	18	V	ex Bright Ace-94, Singa Satu-83

newbuildings: four 158,000 grt container ships and one 58,000 dwt bulk carrier for 2010-11 delivery.
Managed by Southern Shipmanagement (Chile) Ltd (www.ssm.cl)
Owned * by subsidiary Cia. Libra de Navegacao (formed 1977 as Cia Maritima Nacional Ltda to 1999 – www.libra.com.br) or ** jointly with Mitsui OSK Lines and Grupo TMM SA de CV
Wholly owns Norasia Services SA, Switzerlandand has minority 27% interest in Navieros Group controlled Compania Chilena de Navegacion Interoceanica SA, Chile (CCNI) - see chartered vessels with 'CSAC', 'Norasia' and 'CCNI' prefixes in index

ConocoPhillips Inc USA

Funnel: Red with white 'globe' device. **Hull:** Black with red boot-topping. **History:** Founded as Continental Oil Co in 1875 on merger of Marland Oil Co and Continental Oil and Transportation Co until renamed Conoco Inc in 1979 and amalgamated with Phillips Petroleum Co in 2002. **Web:** www.conocophillips.com

Name	Flag	Year	GRT	DWT	LOA	Bm	Kts	Type	Former names
Constitution Spirit *	Mhl	1999	58,242	104,700	244	42	15	T	ex Constitution-08
Continental Spirit *	Lbr	1993	53,848	96,683	243	42	14	T	ex Continental-08
Guardian Spirit *	Bhs	1992	53,772	96,920	243	42	14	T	ex Guardian-08
Patriot Spirit *	Bhs	1992	53,772	96,920	248	42	14	T	ex Patriot-08
Pioneer Spirit *	Lbr	1993	53,858	96,724	248	42	14	T	ex Pioneer-08
Polar Adventure ** (2)	Usa	2004	85,387	141,739	273	46	16	T	
Polar Discovery ** (2)	Usa	2003	85,387	140,320	273	46	16	T	
Polar Endeavour ** (2)	Usa	2001	85,387	141,740	273	46	16	T	l/a Arco Endeavour
Polar Enterprise ** (2)	Usa	2005	85,387	141,739	273	46	16	T	
Polar Resolution ** (2)	Usa	2002	85,387	141,737	273	46	16	T	
Randgrid (me2)	Nor	1995	75,273	122,535	266	46	15	T	ex Heidrun-96
Sentinel Spirit	Pan	1999	58,242	104,700	244	42	15	T	ex Sentinel-08

Owned or managed by Conoco Shipping Co, USA. * managed by Teekay Shipping (USA) Inc or ** owned by subsidiary Polar Tankers Inc (formed 1980 as ARCO Marine Inc to 2000, when acquired by Phillips Petroleum), both USA

Costamare Shipping Co SA Greece

Funnel: Blue with black top or charterers colours. **Hull:** Grey or black with red boot-topping. **History:** Formed 1975. **Web:** None found.

Name	Flag	Year	GRT	DWT	LOA	Bm	Kts	Type	Former names
Britain Star *	Lbr	1978	14,050	15,270	157	25	18	CC	ex Zim Britain-04, MSC Chiwan-99, Ratana Pailin-97, ACX Jasmin-94, TSK Melody-91, Korean Senator-89, Democracy-88, Durga Felixstowe-87, TFL Democracy-86

Cobelfret NV. LOWLANDS ERICA. *C. Lous*

Name	Flag	Year	GRT	DWT	LOA	Bm	Kts	Type	Former names
Cap Akritas **	Hkg	1987	42,304	39,579	250	32	22	CC	ex Safmarine Igoli-07, APL Costa Rica-03, APL Pacific-01, MSC Pacific-01, Houston Express-99, Saturn-98, California Saturn-97
City of Glasgow **	Grc	1978	14,050	15,270	157	25	18	CC	ex Express-98, Choyang Express-98, Express-93, MSC Laura-90, Zim Guam-90, Express-88, Durga Osaka-87, Express-87, Nedlloyd Express-86, TFL Express-86, Alltrans Express-80
Cosco Beijing	Grc	2006	109,149	107,504	360	43	25	CC	
Cosco Guangzhou	Grc	2006	109,149	107,526	360	43	25	CC	
Cosco Hellas	Grc	2006	109,149	107,483	360	43	25	CC	
Cosco Ningbo	Grc	2006	109,149	107,493	360	43	25	CC	
Cosco Yantian	Grc	2006	109,149	107,498	360	43	25	CC	
Garden *	Lbr	1984	37,023	43,401	231	32	20	CC	ex Ever Garden-08
Gather *	Lbr	1984	37,023	43,401	231	32	20	CC	ex Ever Gather-08, LT Gather-04, Ever Gather-02, Cosco Durban-01, Ever Gather-00
Gem *	Lbr	1983	37,042	43,198	231	32	20	CC	ex LT Going-08, Ever Going-99
Gentle *	Lbr	1984	37,023	43,401	231	32	20	CC	ex Ever Gentle-08
Horizon **	Lbr	1991	15,783	14,764	167	27	18	CC	ex S. Caboto-05
Hyundai Challenger **	Grc	1986	39,678	37,915	233	32	21	CC	ex Navarino-04, Zim Shenzhen-02, California Zeus-98, Hidaka Maru-88
Liguria **	Grc	1978	14,050	15,451	157	25	18	CC	ex MSC Liguria-03, MSC Romania-02, MSC Busan-99, Captain George-97, Eagle Nova-96, ACX Orchid-95, Ratana Thevi-91, Pylos-91, Leon-91, Freedom-91, Zim Venezia-91, JSS Los Angeles-88, British Senator-88, Freedom-87, TFL Freedom-86
Maersk Kalamata	Grc	2003	74,656	81,094	304	40	25	CC	
Maersk Kawasaki	Grc	1997	81,488	90,456	318	43	25	CC	ex Kirsten Maersk-07
Maersk Kingston	Grc	2003	74,661	81,183	304	40	25	CC	ex Safmarine Antwerp-08, I/a Maersk Kobe
Maersk Kobe	Grc	2000	74,661	81,584	304	40	25	CC	ex Safmarine Himalaya-07, Sealand Virginia-03
Maersk Kokura	Grc	1997	81,488	84,900	318	43	25	CC	ex Katrine Maersk-08
Maersk Kolkata	Grc	2003	74,656	81,577	304	40	25	CC	
Maersk Kure	Grc	1996	81,488	82,135	318	43	25	CC	ex Regina Maersk-07
Maersk Mykonos	Grc	1988	52,191	60,639	294	32	23	CC	ex Marchen Maersk-05
Maersk Toyama	Grc	1984	40,238	48,600	256	32	24	CC	ex MSC Attica-04, Safmarine Victory-02, Maersk Toyama-01, Laust Maersk-98
MSC Alabama *	Grc	1996	37,518	42,966	243	32	23	CC	ex APL Italy-01, Chetumal-00, TMM Chetumal-97
MSC Antwerp	Grc	1976	34,382	37,852	223	31	21	CC	ex Maersk Bilbao-05, MSC Antwerp-03, Vancouver-98, Maersk Vancouver-98, Alva Maersk-95
MSC Austria *	Lbr	1977	38,991	40,624	241	32	21	CC	ex Houston Express-03, Rotterdam Express-00, Duesseldorf Express-97
MSC Germany *	Lbr	1978	38,991	40,849	240	32	21	CC	ex Genua Express-03, Nurnberg Express-00, Nurnberg Atlantic-93, Nurnberg Express-87
MSC Japan *	Grc	1996	37,518	42,938	243	32	23	CC	ex APL Panama-01, Manzanillo-00, TMM Manzanillo-97, Manzanillo-96, Carmen-96

Costamare Shipping Co SA. CAP AKRITAS (Oetker-HSDG charter). *Allan Ryszka Onions*

Name	Flag	Year	GRT	DWT	LOA	Bm	Kts	Type	Former names
MSC Korea *	Grc	1996	37,518	42,938	243	32	23	CC	ex APL Spain-01, Sinaloa-00, TMM Sinaloa-97, Sinaloa-96
MSC Kyoto	Grc	1981	43,325	53,540	270	32	23	CC	ex Maersk Tokyo-07, Lexa Maersk-97
MSC Mandraki	Grc	1988	52,191	60,639	294	32	23	CC	ex Maersk Mandraki-08, Marit Maersk-04
MSC Mexico *	Lbr	1978	38,991	40,849	241	32	22	CC	ex Koln Express-03, Koln Atlantic-93, Koln Express-87
MSC Namibia	Grc	1977	27,754	27,893	204	31	20	CC	ex Namibia-04, MSC Namibia-03, Cap Vilano-00, Laser Stream-96, Advisor-93, CGM Provence-90, Advisor-85, Asia Winds-84, Advisor-83
MSC Romania II *	Lbr	1979	16,471	19,261	179	25	18	CC	ex MSC Genova-02, Shanghai-98, MSC Shanghai-98, Heung-A Strait-97, Zim Genova-95, Zim Koper-91, Enterprise-88, TFL Enterprise-86, Eagle Faith-85, TFL Enterprise-85, Alltrans Enterprise-82, Incotrans Enterprise-82, TFL Enterprise-81, Alltrans Enterprise-79
MSC Sicily **	Grc	1978	20,676	24,382	186	28	20	CC	ex Carmen-01, MSC China-00, Prestige-98, California Express-93, Carmen-92, Asian Pearl-91
MSC Sierra	Grc	1977	27,970	23,020	204	31	20	CC	ex Sierra Express-08, Cordillera Epress-83
MSC Sudan	Grc	1976	27,971	27,795	204	31	21	CC	ex Caribia Express-03, Woermann Ulanga-91, ScanDutch Ledra-90, Caribia Express-87
MSC Toba	Grc	1982	43,325	53,690	270	32	24	CC	ex Maersk Toba-07, Leda Maersk-98
MSC Togo *	Nld	1980	30,175	23,678	206	31	21	CC	ex Vungtau-06, Maersk Vungtau-06, P&O Nedlloyd Los Angeles-05, Nedlloyd Zeelandia-98, Zeelandia-86, Java Winds-84, Nedlloyd Zeelandia-83, Benattow-82, Zeelandia-80
MSC Tuscany **	Grc	1978	20,676	24,383	186	24	14	CC	ex Mumbai-01, Indamex Mumbai-01, MSC Singapore-00, Nedlloyd Java-98, Asian Jade-91
MSC Venice *	Lbr	1978	16,471	19,261	179	25	18	CC	ex MSC Osaka-98, Osaka-97, Zim Osaka-96, Liberty-88, TFL Liberty-86
MSC Washington	Grc	1984	43,332	53,325	270	32	22	CC	ex Maersk Trondheim-05, Lars Maersk-99
MSC Yokohama	Grc	1979	30,249	27,738	203	31	21	CC	ex Romanos-97, Hyundai Vancouver-97, Gulf Speed-94, OOCL Brilliance-93, Gulf Speed-91, Incotrans Speed-86, China Winds-84, Incotrans Speed-83
New York Express	Grc	2000	54,437	66,818	294	32	24	CC	
Oakland Express	Grc	2000	54,437	66,781	294	32	24	CC	ex Kuala Lumpur Express-08
Reunion *	Lbr	1983	20,345	28,422	174	28	18	CC	ex DAL Reunion-02, Delmas Mascareignes-02, SEAL Ubena-00, Sea Merchant-97, Hongkong Senator-88, Ubena-87
Sealand Illinois	Grc	2000	74,661	81,584	304	40	25	CC	
Sealand Michigan	Grc	2000	74,583	81,584	304	40	25	CC	
Sealand New York	Grc	2000	74,661	81,584	304	40	25	CC	
Sealand Washington	Grc	2000	74,661	81,584	304	40	25	CC	
Singapore Express	Grc	2000	54,415	66,793	294	32	24	CC	
Sophia Britannia	Grc	1993	50,501	59,567	292	32	23	CC	ex Kirishima-99

Costamare Shipping Co SA. COSCO BEIJING (COSCO charter). *Allan Ryszka Onions*

Name	Flag	Year	GRT	DWT	LOA	Bm	Kts	Type	Former names
Westmed II *	Lbr	1978	16,471	19,621	179	25	17	CC	ex City of Dublin-98, Zim Yokohama-96, Independence-88, TFL Independence-86
Zim New York	Grc	2002	53,453	62,740	294	32	24	CC	ex China Sea-06, Zim New York-04
Zim Piraeus	Grc	2004	53,453	62,740	294	32	24	CC	ex Yangtze Star-06, Zim Piraeus-05
Zim Shanghai	Grc	2002	53,453	66,597	294	32	24	CC	

newbuildings: four 90,700 grt container ships for 2009-10 delivery.
* owned or managed by associated Ciel Shipmanagement SA, Greece (formed 2001) or ** by Shanghai Costamare Ship Management Co Ltd, China (founded 2005)

D'Amico Societa di Navigazione SpA — Italy

Funnel: Yellow with blue 8-pointed star. **Hull:** Grey or black with white or yellow 'd'AMICO', red boot-topping. **History:** Formed 1951.
Web: www.damicoship.com

Name	Flag	Year	GRT	DWT	LOA	Bm	Kts	Type	Former names
Cielo di Guangzhou	Lbr	2006	25,507	38,875	168	29	14	T	
Cielo di Londra	Lbr	2001	23,680	36,032	183	27	14	T	
Cielo di Milano *	Ita	2003	25,400	40,081	176	31	15	T	
Cielo di Monfalcone	Ita	2002	27,839	37,420	186	29	14	Co	
Cielo di Napoli	Ita	2003	25,400	40,081	176	31	15	T	
Cielo di Parigi	Lbr	2001	23,680	36,032	183	27	15	T	
Cielo di Roma *	Ita	2003	25,382	40,096	176	31	15	T	
Cielo di Salerno	Lbr	2002	23,680	36,023	183	27	15	T	
Cielo di Vaiano ††	Lbr	1998	19,712	31,962	172	27	16	B	ex Asteri J-05, Astro Ace-04
Cielo di Vancouver	Ita	2002	27,828	37,420	186	29	14	Co	
High Challenge	Lbr	1999	28,238	46,473	183	32	15	T	
High Consensus ††	Lbr	2005	28,059	45,896	180	32	15	T	
High Courage	Lbr	2005	30,048	46,991	183	32	14	T	
High Endeavour	Lbr	2004	30,028	46,991	183	32	14	T	ex High Star-04
High Endurance	Lbr	2004	30,028	46,991	183	32	14	T	ex High Pearl-04
High Energy ‡	Pan	2004	28,245	46,874	180	32	14	T	
High Harmony	Pan	2005	28,059	45,913	180	32	15	T	
High Light ‡	Pan	2005	28,245	46,843	180	32	15	T	
High Performance	Lbr	2005	30,081	51,303	183	32	15	T	
High Power ‡	Pan	2004	28,245	46,866	180	32	15	T	
High Presence †	Sgp	2005	28,245	48,040	180	32	15	T	
High Priority †	Sgp	2005	28,245	46,847	180	32	15	T	
High Progress †	Lbr	2005	30,081	51,302	183	32	15	T	
High Spirit	Lbr	1999	28,238	46,473	183	32	14	T	
High Valor	Lbr	2005	30,048	46,991	183	32	15	T	
High Venture	Lbr	2006	29,942	51,088	183	32	15	T	
High Wind	Lbr	1999	28,238	46,473	183	32	14	T	
Medi Cagliari	Ita	2004	38,877	75,772	225	32	14	B	ex Medi Vancouver-07
Medi Cork †	Pan	2004	29,952	53,552	190	32	14	B	ex Medi Melbourne-07
Medi Dubai	Ita	2001	29,367	52,523	190	32	14	B	ex Medi Monaco-05
Medi Nagasaki †	Lbr	2003	29,295	53,098	189	32	14	B	
Medi Sentosa §	Pan	2008	44,147	83,690	229	32	14	B	
Medi Tokyo	Ita	1999	38,835	74,356	225	32	14	B	
Rita D'Amato	Ita	2004	25,400	40,081	176	31	15	T	

newbuildings: 48,700 dwt tanker for 2009 delivery, also 11 bulk carriers for charter from various owners.
* managed for Perseveranza SpA di Nav, Italy subsidiary of Fratelli D'Amato SpA, Italy.
† owned by D'Amico Dry Ltd, Ireland (founded 2002) and †† managed by Ishima Pte Ltd., Singapore. ‡ chartered from Japanese finance houses. § jointly owned by Mitsui & Co Ltd and managed by Orient Marine Co Ltd, Japan.
Smaller tankers operate in 'Handytankers' Pool and 18 other bulk carriers (52-76,000 dwt) with 'Medi' prefix chartered from various owners.

A/S Thor Dahl Shipping — Norway

Funnel: Various operating company or charterers colours. **Hull:** Various including black with red boot-topping. **History:** Founded 1990. **Web:** www.thordahl.no or www.jdb.no

Name	Flag	Year	GRT	DWT	LOA	Bm	Kts	Type	Former names
Amasis	Cyp	1997	29,022	35,020	196	32	21	CC	ex ANL Empress-03, Ibex Empress-02, Amasis-97
MSC Parana	Nis	1987	23,761	34,380	202	28	17	CC	ex Cielo di Valencia-02, Lynx-00, Cast Lynx-99, Norasia Mubarak-94
MSC Peru	Nis	1987	23,761	34,380	202	28	17	CC	ex P&O Nedlloyd Falcon-03, Cielo di Livorno-01, Bear-00, Cast Bear-99, Norasia Al-Muntazah-94
MSC Tampa	Bhs	1984	43,332	53,325	270	32	24	CC	ex Maersk Tampa-07, Louis Maersk-99
Thorswave	Cyp	1996	29,022	35,021	196	32	21	CC	ex Eos I-08, Zim Mumbai-07, Eos I-06, Ming Dynasty-02, Hyundai Dynasty-98, Eos I-96

Operated by Thor Dahl Management AS (formed 1996 as Jahre Dahl Bergesen to 2005 and now owned by AS Thor Dahl Shipping (52.5%), Bulls Tankrederi AS (22.5%) and management) and managed by Jahre-Wallem AS (formed by JDB 50%, Wallem 40% and B. Skaugen 10%)

Danaos Shipping Co Ltd

Greece

Funnel: *Blue or charterers colours.* **Hull:** *Black with red boot-topping or charterers colours.* **History:** *Founded 1976 as successor to Roumeli Shipping formed in early 1970's when Dimitris Coustas bought out partners in joint venture (formed 1963).*
Web: *www.danaos.gr*

Name	Flag	Year	GRT	DWT	LOA	Bm	Kts	Type	Former names
Al Rayyan	Cyp	1989	46,697	44,851	275	32	22	CC	ex Norasia Hamburg-08, APL Arabia-04, ANL Hamburg-04, Norasia Hamburg-03, Cosco Bremerhaven-01, Honour-00, OOCL Honour-00, APL Arabia-97, OOCL Honour-96
APL Confidence	Cyp	1994	51,841	61,152	275	37	24	CC	ex MOL Confidence-08, Federal-04, Hyundai Federal-03
CMA CGM Elbe	Grc	1991	37,134	44,008	243	32	22	CC	ex Hanjin Bremen-03
CMA CGM Kalamata	Grc	1991	37,134	43,967	243	32	22	CC	ex Hanjin Singapore-03
CMA CGM Komodo	Grc	1991	37,134	43,966	243	32	22	CC	ex Hanjin Elizabeth-03
CMA CGM Lotus	Grc	1988	42,809	40,638	253	32	22	CC	ex Victory I-07, MOL Victory-03, Alligator Victory-01
CMA CGM Passiflore	Grc	1986	41,280	38,717	245	32	22	CC	ex Henry-07, APL Guatemala-05, Henry-04, APL Guatemala-04, Zim Xingang-01, Cape Henry-99
CMA CGM Vanille	Cyp	1986	41,413	38,624	248	32	22	CC	ex Independence-07, MOL Independence-03, Alligator Independence-01
CSCL Europe	Cyp	2004	90,645	101,612	334	43	25	CC	
CSCL Le Havre	Cyp	2006	108,069	111,790	337	46	26	CC	
CSCL Pusan	Cyp	2006	108,069	111,889	337	46	26	CC	
Hyundai Advance	Pan	1997	21,611	24,766	182	30	21	CC	
Hyundai Bridge	Pan	1998	21,611	24,766	182	30	21	CC	
Hyundai Commodore	Grc	1992	51,836	61,152	275	37	25	CC	
Hyundai Duke	Grc	1992	51,836	61,152	275	37	26	CC	
Hyundai Future	Pan	1997	21,611	24,799	182	30	21	CC	
Hyundai Highway	Pan	1998	21,611	24,799	182	30	21	CC	
Hyundai Progress	Pan	1997	21,611	24,766	182	30	22	CC	ex Wan Hai 252-00, Hyundai Progress-98
Hyundai Sprinter	Pan	1997	21,611	24,600	182	30	21	CC	
Hyundai Stride	Pan	1997	21,611	24,777	182	30	21	CC	
Hyundai Vladivostok	Pan	1997	21,611	24,766	182	30	21	CC	ex CMA Oakland-01, Hyundai Vladivostok-99
Maersk Derby	Cyp	2004	39,941	50,814	260	32	23	CC	ex P&O Nedlloyd Caracas-05
Maersk Deva	Cyp	2004	39,941	50,828	260	32	23	CC	ex Vancouver Express-08, Maersk Deva-06, P&O Nedlloyd Caribbean-06
Maersk Messologi	Pan	1991	52,181	60,350	294	32	23	CC	ex Mayview Maersk-06
Maersk Mytilini	Pan	1991	52,181	60,350	294	32	23	CC	ex Madison Maersk-06
Montreal Senator	Cyp	1984	30,500	35,472	240	30	20	CC	ex Pacific Bridge-08, MSC Fremantle-02, Pacific Bridge-98, Zim Mumbai-98, Hyundai Seattle-96, Pacific Bridge-94, Makalu-89, Pacific Bridge-86 (len-89)
MSC Baltic	Cyp	2004	90,645	101,612	334	43	25	CC	ex CSCL America-07
MSC Eagle	Bhs	1978	28,078	23,047	204	31	21	CC	ex Eagle Express-08, MSC Izmir-01, Eagle Quest-97, OOCL Beacon-95, Eagle Express-93, America Express-83
MSC Marathon	Pan	1991	52,181	60,350	294	32	23	CC	ex Maersk Marathon-08, Mc-Kinney Maersk-06
YM Milano	Grc	1988	41,786	45,036	248	32	21	CC	ex MSC Pegasus-03, Pegasus-02, Maersk Livorno-99, Pegasus-98, California Pegasus-98, Yamaaki Maru-92
YM Seattle	Cyp	2007	40,030	50,813	260	32	23	CC	
YM Singapore	Lbr	2004	41,855	53,611	264	32	24	CC	ex Norasia Atria-08, E.R. Wellington-04, l/a E.R. Auckland
YM Vancouver	Cyp	2007	40,030	50,632	260	32	23	CC	
YM Yantian	Cyp	1989	46,697	45,570	276	32	22	CC	ex Hope-03, OOCL Hope-00
Zim Rio Grande	Cyp	2008	40,030	50,842	260	32	23	CC	

newbuildings: five 125,000 grt, three 110,000 grt, five 90,500 grt, ten 75,000 grt, ten 35,000-39,900 grt containerships for 2009-11 delivery.

Dannebrog Rederi A/S

Denmark

Funnel: *Yellow with houseflag, white cross on red penant flag, on broad blue band.* **Hull:** *Grey with red boot-topping.*
History: *Formed 1883 as A/S Dannebrog to 1970.* **Web:** *www.dannebrog.com*

Name	Flag	Year	GRT	DWT	LOA	Bm	Kts	Type	Former names
Aalborg	Gib	1981	16,992	37,425	182	30	13	Co	ex Maya Princess-07, Taurus-05, Great Trans-01, Leopold Oldendorff-01, Great Trans-99, Infanta-94, Taurus-88
Amalienborg *	Dmk	2004	24,663	40,059	175	31	15	T	ex Southern Unity-08
Charlottenborg	Gib	1981	31,007	24,223	187	32	17	Ro	ex Romain Delmas-08, Charlottenborg-06, Romain Delmas-05, Kukawa-01, Romain Delmas-01, Saint Romain-94, Hoegh Biscay-83
Frederiksborg	Gib	1994	17,016	10,517	148	26	15	Ro	ex Global Africa-07

Name	Flag	Year	GRT	DWT	LOA	Bm	Kts	Type	Former names
Kronborg	Lbr	2007	25,400	40,208	176	31	15	T	
Marienborg	Gib	1979	32,875	27,980	188	32	17	Ro	ex Roxane Delmas-05, Robert-95, Grand Bassam-95, Sant Roland-92, Bullaren-84, Tarifa-83, Vindafjord-81, Bullaren-81
Naesborg	Lbr	1976	32,173	22,691	206	31	21	Ro	ex Rosario-06, Rosanne-04, Daisy-00, Euroshipping 2-97, Magnitogorsk-96
Nordborg	Lbr	1976	32,173	21,002	206	31	21	Ro	ex Roxanne-06, Nicole-00, Kotlini-97, Komsomolsk-95
Rosborg	Bhs	1978	15,992	22,986	166	27	16	C	ex Clipper Itajai-05, Orient Clipper-97, Clipper Itajai-96, African Sky-95, Minos-92, Cape Verde-92, Tendai Maru-91
Schackenborg	Cym	1979	14,805	10,470	161	24	15	Ro	ex Dana Caribia-84
Skanderborg	Cym	1979	14,805	10,470	161	24	15	Ro	ex Dana Arabia-84 (len-04)
Skodsborg	Cym	1979	14,805	10,470	161	24	15	Ro	ex Dana Africa-84

newbuildings: six 47,500 dwt tankers and twelve 12,840 dwt general cargo for 2009-11 delivery.
* managed by Weco Shipping, Denmark.

Herm Dauelsberg GmbH & Co KG   Germany

Funnel: White with black 'D' on cream band between narrow blue bands, or charterers colours. **Hull:** Black or grey with red boot-topping. **History:** Formed 1857 as shipbrokers and started shipowning in 1857. **Web:** www.dauelsberg.de

Name	Flag	Year	GRT	DWT	LOA	Bm	Kts	Type	Former names
ACX Jasmine	Lbr	1996	23,825	30,615	188	30	21	CC	ex Lindavia-06, Maersk Sydney-00, Lindavia-98, Sea Lindavia-98, Lindavia-96
Altavia	Lbr	1995	23,691	30,743	188	30	21	CC	ex Safmarine Tugela-07, Altavia-03, Safmarine Tugela-03, Maersk Nagoya-01, Maersk Santos-99, Choyang Fortune-97, Altavia-95
Bellavia	Mhl	2005	53,807	66,501	294	32	25	CC	
CMA CGM Oryx	Lbr	1995	23,691	30,743	188	30	21	CC	ex Bonavia-08, Cap Sunion-08, Bonavia-04, Safmarine Maluti-04, Maersk Algerciras-01, Contship Auckland-97, Bonavia-95
Fathulkhair	Lbr	2001	23,652	30,375	188	30	21	CC	ex Cala Pintada-08, Lobivia-04
Marivia	Lbr	2001	23,652	30,375	188	30	21	CC	
Melfi Iberia	Lbr	1995	14,968	20,176	167	25	19	CC	ex Cala Providencia-08, Novia-04, P&O Nedlloyd Slauerhoff-03, P&O Nedlloyd Mumbai-02, Novia-01, Sea Novia-97, Novia-95
Octavia	Mhl	2005	53,807	66,501	294	32	25	CC	
Olivia	Lbr	1995	14,968	20,176	167	25	19	CC	ex P&O Nedlloyd Mahe-02, Olivia-01
TS Incheon	Lbr	1996	23,825	30,743	188	30	21	CC	ex Magnavia-08, MOL Waratah-02, Alligator Unity-01, Maersk Oceania-00, Magnavia-97
YM Ningbo	Mhl	2005	40,952	55,490	261	32	24	CC	ex Cherokee Bridge-07, I/a Clivia
YM Taichung	Mhl	2005	40,952	55,497	261	32	24	CC	ex Chesapeake Bay Bridge-07, I/a Silvia

Del Monte Fresh Fruit International Inc   USA

Funnel: Dark green with white 'Del Monte' on yellow edged red fruit symbol. **Hull:** White with green above red boot-topping or grey with red boot-topping. **History:** Formed 1971 as West Indies Fruit Co, later Del Monte Banana Co. to 1986, then sold in 1989 by Nabisco to Polly Peck, becoming independent in 1992 when Polly Peck ceased trading. **Web:** www.freshdelmonte.com

Name	Flag	Year	GRT	DWT	LOA	Bm	Kts	Type	Former names
Alcazar Carrier	Bhs	1979	15,834	15,200	169	26	22	R	ex Winter Moon-99, Zenit Moon-87, Winter Moon-85
Alicante Carrier	Bhs	1979	15,834	15,200	169	26	22	R	ex Winter Star-99, Zenit Star-87, Winter Star-85
Cadiz Carrier	Bhs	1979	15,833	15,100	169	26	22	R	ex Winter Water-99, Zenit Water-87, Winter Water-85
Malaga Carrier	Bhs	1979	15,834	15,100	169	26	22	R	ex Winter Wave-99, Zenit Wave-87, Winter Wave-85
Segovia Carrier	Bhs	1980	15,834	15,200	169	26	22	R	ex Winter Sea-99, Zenit Sea-87, Winter Sea-85
Valencia Carrier	Bhs	1984	12,340	10,126	148	24	19	R	ex Spring Bride-02

Owned by subsidiary Network Shipping Ltd., USA (formed 1990) and managed by Norbulk Shipping UK Ltd (www.norbulkshipping.com).
Also owns 12 other smaller reefer vessels.

Horn-Linie (GmbH & Co)/Germany

Funnel: Grey with white 'H' on blue above red bands. **Hull:** White with red boot-topping. **History:** Founded 1864 and shipping company formed 1951 as Heinrich C Horn. **Web:** www.hornlinie.com

Name	Flag	Year	GRT	DWT	LOA	Bm	Kts	Type	Former names
Hornbay	Lbr	1990	12,887	9,069	154	23	20	Rr	
Horncap	Lbr	1991	12,887	9,069	154	23	20	Rr	
Horncliff	Lbr	1992	12,877	9,184	154	23	20	Rr	

Dockwise Shipping BV

Netherlands

Funnel: Dark blue with black 'D' on white disc on light blue square on white band. **Hull:** Black, orange or green with 'DOCKWISE', red boot-topping. **History:** Formed by 1994 merger of Wijsmuller Transport BV (formed 1914) with Dock Express Shipping BV (formed 1977) and owned by their respective parents Heerema (70%) and Royal Vopak (formerly Van Ommeren) (30%). Merged with Offshore Heavy Transport ASA, Norway (part owned by Wilh. Wilhelmsen and Dyvi) in 2001. Reported sold to equity group 3i in 2006.
Web: www.dockwise.com

Name	Flag	Year	GRT	DWT	LOA	Bm	Kts	Type	Former names
Black Marlin *	Ant	2000	37,938	57,021	218	42	14	HLs	
Blue Marlin *	Ant	2000	51,821	76,051	218	63	14	HLs	(wid-03)
Dock Express 10 (2) **	Nld	1979	13,110	12,928	154	27	15	HLs	ex Dock Express France-94, Dock Express 10-87
Dock Express 12 (2) **	Nld	1979	13,110	12,928	159	27	15	HLs	
Enterprise (2)	Ant	1984	17,395	8,727	158	29	12	LC	ex Smit Enterprise-03, Danube Express-98, Nikolay Markin-92
Explorer (2)	Ant	1984	19,453	8,638	159	31	13	LC	ex Smit Explorer-03, Pavel Antokolskiy-99
Mighty Servant 1 (me2)	Nld	1983	19,954	23,473	160	40	14	HLs	(len/wid-98)
Mighty Servant 3 (me2)	Nld	1984	22,391	27,720	181	40	14	HLs	sank 12/2006 reported to be rebuilt.
Super Servant 3 (2)	Ant	1982	10,224	14,138	140	32	13	HLs	
Super Servant 4 (2)	Ant	1982	12,642	17,600	140	32	13	HLs	
Swan	Ant	1981	22,788	30,060	181	32	16	HLs	ex Sea Swan-96, Swan H.L.-89, Dyvi Swan-88
Swift *	Ant	1983	22,835	32,187	183	32	15	HLS	ex Sea Swift-96, Swift H.L.-89, Dyvi Swift-88
Talisman *	Ant	1993	42,515	53,000	216	45	14	HLs	ex Front Comor-08, Comor-99 (conv/sht T-08)
Target *	Ant	1990	42,515	53,806	217	45	14	HLs	ex Front Target-07, Genmar Centaur-04, Crude Target-03, Nord-Jahre Target-00, Jahre Target-93 (conv/sht T-08)
Teal	Ant	1984	22,835	32,101	181	32	15	HLs	ex Sea Teal-96, Teal H.L.-89, Dyvi Teal-88
Tern	Ant	1982	22,788	30,060	181	32	16	HLs	ex Sea Tern-96, Tern H.L.-89, Dyvi Tern-88
Transporter	Ant	1992	42,609	53,806	217	45	14	HLs	ex Front Sunda-08, Sunda-99 (conv/sht T-08)
Transshelf (me2)	Ant	1987	26,547	34,030	173	40	15	HLs	
Treasure *	Ant	1990	42,515	53,818	217	45	14	HLs	ex Front Traveller-08, GenmarTraveller-04, Crude Traveller-03, Nord-Jahre Traveller-00, Jahre Traveller-93 (conv/sht T-08)
Triumph *	Ant	1992	42,515	53,818	269	45	14	HLs	ex Marble-08 (conv T-08)
Trustee *	Ant	1991	42,515	53,818	269	45	14	HLs	ex Front Granite-08, Granite-01 (conv T-08)
Yacht Express	Ant	2007	17,951	12,500	209	32	18	HLs	

* managed by Anglo-Eastern (UK) Ltd., UK (www.angloeasterngroup.com). ** reported sold to Chinese owners

Peter Döhle Schiffahrts-KG

Germany

Funnel: Black with black 'PD' on white diamond on broad red band bordered by narrow white bands, black with yellow 'ICL' above yellow wave inside yellow rectangular outline (Independent) or charterers colours. **Hull:** Grey or dark blue with red boot-topping.
History: Formed 1956 as Robert Bornhofen KG until 1962, then Peter Dohle to 1973. **Web:** www.doehle.de

Name	Flag	Year	GRT	DWT	LOA	Bm	Kts	Type	Former names
Aglaia	Mhl	2001	14,278	15,315	159	26	22	CC	l/a Sandy Rickmers
Amalthea	Mhl	2001	14,290	14,901	159	26	22	CC	
Amanda	Atg	2000	16,803	22,967	184	25	19	CC	ex YM Santos-08, MOL Americas-06, Amanda-04, Libra Livorno-03, l/a Amanda
Anna E	Lbr	1992	14,867	20,140	167	25	17	CC	ex Independent Action-07, Cielo di Colombia-99, Annabella D-98, CSAV Rupanco-97, Augusta-97, Brasil Express-94, Annabella D-92, l/a Auriga

Herm Dauelsberg GmbH. BELLAVIA. *Allan Ryszka Onions*

Name	Flag	Year	GRT	DWT	LOA	Bm	Kts	Type	Former names
Ariana	Lbr	2006	32,161	38,700	211	32	21	CC	ex Amerigo Vespucci-06
CCNI Antillanca *	Lbr	2005	35,645	41,850	220	32	22	CC	ex Demeter-06
CCNI Antofagasta	Lbr	2006	35,881	42,200	220	32	22	CC	l/dn Leto
CCNI Arica	Lbr	2006	35,881	41,748	220	32	22	CC	l/dn Daphne
Chacabuco †	Lbr	2006	65,600	67,970	276	40	25	CC	
Chaiten	Lbr	2006	66,280	67,970	276	40	25	CC	l/dn Anguila
CSAV Itajai	Lbr	2008	35,824	42,213	220	32	22	CC	
CSAV Moema	Atg	2002	35,645	42,200	220	32	22	CC	ex Norasia Makalu-06, APL Portugal-05, Antonia-02, l/a Chloe
Emirates Liberty	Lbr	2005	35,881	41,800	220	32	22	CC	ex Minna-06, Zeus-05
Glen Mooar ‡	Lbr	1998	25,537	46,570	183	31	14	B	ex Antuco-05
Glen Vine *	Mhl	1981	29,496	51,267	194	32	14	Ce	ex Big One-05, Cielo di Parma-04, Nebraska-97, Onda Chiara-94, Serafino Ferruzzi-90 (conv B-87, conv T-05)
Independent Accord	Lbr	2007	15,345	20,955	168	25	20	CC	
Independent Concept	Lbr	2007	15,345	20,994	168	25	20	CC	
Independent Pursuit	Lbr	2005	15,487	20,615	168	25	20	CC	ex Heide E-06
Independent Venture	Lbr	1993	14,849	20,540	167	25	19	CC	ex Sea Voyager-99, Nautique-98
Limari †	Lbr	2005	42,382	51,870	268	32	25	CC	
Lircay	Lbr	2006	42,300	51,870	268	32	25	CC	l/dn Ariba
Loa	Lbr	2005	42,382	51,870	268	32	25	CC	l/a Adda
Longavi †	Lbr	2006	42,300	51,870	268	32	25	CC	
Maersk Vera Cruz *	Iom	2004	17,188	22,513	179	28	21	CC	l/a Pyxis
Maersk Victoria *	Iom	2004	17,188	22,506	179	28	21	CC	l/a Palomar
Maruba Victory	Lbr	2008	32,161	39,000	211	32	21	CC	l/dn Arelia
MOL Ultimate	Deu	2000	16,803	22,968	184	25	20	CC	ex German Senator-08, Safmarine Mgeni-06, Altonia-04, Safmarine Buffalo-03, Maersk Felixstowe-01, CSAV Marsella-00, l/a Altonia
MSC Davos	Lbr	2006	32,161	39,600	212	32	21	CC	Vasco da Gama-06, Arosia-06, l/a Vasco da Gama
MSC Egypt	Lbr	2005	66,280	67,970	276	40	25	CC	ex Chillan-05, l/dn Arizona
MSC France	Lbr	2004	66,280	68,228	276	40	25	CC	ex Copiapo-06, Amazonia-04
MSC Malta	Lbr	2005	66,280	67,970	276	40	25	CC	ex Choapa-06
MSC Turchia	Lbr	2006	65,600	67,970	276	40	25	CC	ex Cholguan-06
Norasia Alya	Lbr	2004	35,881	41,748	220	32	22	CC	ex Renata-04
Norasia Balkans	Atg	2001	35,645	42,300	220	32	22	CC	ex Norasia Taurus-05, APL Mexico-04, l/a Katjana, l/dn Celine
Palena †	Lbr	2006	73,934	81,248	304	40	25	CC	
Pangal	Lbr	2006	73,934	81,236	304	40	25	CC	l/dn Alda
Petrohue	Lbr	2006	73,934	81,236	304	40	25	CC	

Dockwise NV. TARGET. *Hans Kraijenbosch*

Name	Flag	Year	GRT	DWT	LOA	Bm	Kts	Type	Former names
Postojna	Lbr	1998	25,537	46,570	183	31	14	B	ex Tristan-08, Glen Helen-08, Alicahue-04
Pucon †	Lbr	2006	73,934	81,099	304	40	25	CC	l/dn Paine
Puelche	Lbr	2007	73,934	81,243	304	40	25	CC	
Puelo †	Lbr	2006	73,934	81,250	304	40	25	CC	
Safmarine Mbashe	Mhl	2006	17,189	22,300	179	28	21	CC	ex Viona-06
TS Hochiminh	Lbr	2007	15,487	20,647	168	25	20	CC	
TS Hongkong **	Pan	2006	15,487	20,599	168	25	20	CC	
TS Keelung	Iom	2006	15,487	20,580	179	28	21	CC	l/a Adeline
TS Korea	Lbr	2008	26,358	34,439	209	30	22	CC	l/a Artemis
TS Shenzhen	Lbr	2006	15,487	20,615	168	25	20	CC	l/a Annaba
TS Singapore	Lbr	2008	25,320	34,282	209	30	22	CC	ex Apollon-08
TS Taipei **	Lbr	2006	15,487	20,615	168	25	20	CC	l/a Benita
Valbella	Deu	1998	28,148	46,376	185	32	15	Co	ex CCNI Atacama-08, l/a Valbella
Valdivia	Lbr	2006	17,189	22,308	179	28	21	CC	
Valentina	Mhl	2007	17,360	22,263	179	28	21	CC	
Violetta	Mhl	2007	17,189	22,267	179	28	21	CC	ex CMA CGM Providencia-08, MOL Drakensberg-07, l/a Violetta
Vipava	Lbr	1998	25,537	46,570	183	31	14	B	ex Isolde-08, Glen Maye-06, Allipen-05
YM Mersin	Lbr	1991	12,997	17,610	150	25	17	CC	ex Independent Trader-06, Carola E-97, Caroline-96, America-96, Carolina-91
YM Osaka	Lbr	1995	14,923	20,406	167	25	19	CC	ex Independent Endeavor-08, Astoria D-00, Libra New York-99, Libra Valencia-97, l/a Astoria
YM Portland	Lbr	2003	51,364	58,255	286	32	25	CC	ex Norasia Enterprise-07, Amaranta-03

Peter Dohle Schiffahrts. AGLAIA. *Allan Ryszka Onions*

Peter Dohle Schiffahrts. INDEPENDENT PURSUIT. *Guido van Driessche*

Name	Flag	Year	GRT	DWT	LOA	Bm	Kts	Type	Former names

newbuildings: sixteen 158,000 grt, six 74,900 grt, ten 42,600 grt, three 32,300 grt, eight 16-17,600 grt container ships, seven 57,000 dwt bulk carriers for 2009-12 delivery.
Also owns/manages a large number of smaller vessels and has a 13% minority interest in Navieros Group controlled Compania Chilena de Navegacion Interoceanica SA, Chile (CCNI)
* managed by Dohle IOM Ltd, UK (formed 1994 as Midocean Maritime Ltd to 2001 - www.doehle-iom.com) including ** for HCI Capital AG.
† managed by Southern Shipmanagement (Chile) Ltd, Chile (www.ssm.cl) or ‡ by Splosna Plovba, Slovenia.

Hammonia Reederei GmbH & Co KG/Germany

Funnel: Charterers colours. **Hull:** Red with red boot-topping. **History:** Founded 2003 jointly by Peter Dohle and HCI Hanseatische Capital AG. **Web:** www.hammonia.org

Name	Flag	Year	GRT	DWT	LOA	Bm	Kts	Type	Former names
Belgica	Deu	1997	25,608	34,015	208	30	21	CC	ex Cap Egmont-08, Cap Norte-06, Santos Express-03, Sea Ocelot-02, Transroll Argentina-00, Cap Norte-99, Impala-98, Brasil Star-98, Impala-97
CCNI Busan	Lbr	2007	25,320	34,191	209	30	22	CC	
CCNI Guayas	Deu	1998	25,608	34,015	208	30	21	CC	ex Alianca Hong Kong-06, Columbus Chile-04, Alianca Rotterdam-02, Lykes Traveler-01, CMA CGM Gaugain-01, CGM Gaugin-00, Charlotta-98
CCNI Ningbo	Lbr	2006	26,435	34,305	209	30	22	CC	l/dn Hammonia Palatium
CCNI Punta Arenas	Lbr	2005	30,047	35,741	208	32	22	CC	
CSAV Chicago	Cyp	1997	25,608	34,015	208	30	21	CC	ex Maersk Freeport-99, Liberta-99, Montebello-99, l/a Liberta
Emirates Freedom	Lbr	2005	35,881	42,157	220	32	22	CC	ex Letavia-06, Norasia Atlas-05, l/a Cosima
Emirates Kabir *	Lbr	2003	35,645	41,850	220	32	22	CC	ex APL Jakarta-06, Julia-03, Alessa-03, l/a Carmen
Emirates Marina	Lbr	2005	35,881	41,802	220	32	22	CC	ex CSAV Rio Trancura-06, Coletta-05
Hammonia Bavaria	Lbr	2009	26,435	34,000	209	30	22	CC	
Hammonia Berolina	Lbr	2007	26,435	34,236	209	30	22	CC	
Hammonia Calabria	Lbr	2009	39,941	50,418	209	30	22	CC	
Hammonia Fortuna	Lbr	2007	26,435	34,282	209	30	22	CC	
Hammonia Granada	Lbr	2009	39,941	50,418	209	30	22	CC	
Hammonia Pacificum	Lbr	2007	26,435	34,242	209	30	22	CC	
Hammonia Roma	Lbr	2009	25,320	33,800	209	30	22	CC	
Hyundai Qingdao	Lbr	2008	26,435	34,331	209	30	22	CC	ex Hammania Holsatia-08
Libra Copacabana	Lbr	2006	26,836	34,465	210	30	21	CC	l/a Hammonia Husum
Libra Ipanema	Lbr	2006	26,626	34,500	210	30	21	CC	ex Emden-06, l/a Hammonia Emden
Libra Rio	Atg	2003	35,645	41,850	221	32	22	CC	l/a Katharina, l/dn Albona
Maersk Karlskrona	Lbr	1996	81,488	82,135	318	43	25	CC	ex Karen Maersk-08
Maersk Kleven *	Lbr	1996	81,488	84,900	318	43	25	CC	ex Kate Maersk-08
Maersk Kotka *	Lbr	1996	81,488	84,900	318	43	25	CC	ex Knud Maersk-08
MOL Serenity	Lbr	2008	25,320	33,800	209	30	22	CC	ex Hammonia Teutonica-08
MSC Bilboa	Lbr	2006	89,941	97,400	334	43	25	CC	l/dn Hammonia Bremen
MSC Paris	Lbr	2006	88,600	97,430	334	43	25	CC	l/dn Hammonia Hamburg
MSC Valencia	Lbr	2006	89,941	97,400	334	43	25	CC	l/dn Hammonia Jork
TS Dubai *	Lbr	2003	35,645	42,062	220	32	22	CC	ex APL Shanghai-07, Azalea-03, l/a Clarissa
TS India	Lbr	2008	26,362	33,800	209	30	22	CC	ex Hammonia Massilia-08

Peter Dohle Schiffahrts. VALENTINA. *Allan Ryszka Onions*

Name	Flag	Year	GRT	DWT	LOA	Bm	Kts	Type	Former names

newbuildings: three 41,500 grt and three 26,400 grt container ships for 2009-10 delivery.
* owned by HCI Hammonia Shipping AG and ** managed by Ahrenkiel Shipmanagement GmbH & Co KG

Dole Food Co   Costa Rica

Funnel: Dark blue with with red 'Dole' symbol on white band or charterers colours. **Hull:** White or cream with red 'Dole' symbol above blue line, blue boot-topping. **History:** Founded 1851 and 1975 merged with Castle & Cook Inc to 1991. **Web:** www.dole.com

Name	Flag	Year	GRT	DWT	LOA	Bm	Kts	Type	Former names
Dole Africa	Bhs	1994	10,584	10,288	150	23	21	R	
Dole America	Bhs	1994	10,584	10,288	150	23	21	R	
Dole Asia	Bhs	1994	10,584	10,288	150	23	21	R	
Dole California	Ita	1989	16,488	11,800	179	27	20	CC	
Dole Chile	Bhs	1999	31,779	30,145	205	32	21	CC	
Dole Colombia	Bhs	1999	31,779	30,145	205	32	21	CC	
Dole Costarica	Ita	1991	16,488	11,800	179	27	20	CC	
Dole Ecuador	Ita	1989	16,488	11,800	179	27	20	CC	
Dole Europa	Bhs	1994	10,584	10,288	150	23	21	R	
Dole Honduras	Ita	1991	16,488	11,800	179	27	20	CC	
Tropical Mist *	Lbr	1986	9,749	11,998	149	22	20	R	
Tropical Morn	Lbr	1986	9,749	11,998	149	22	20	R	
Tropical Sky	Lbr	1986	9,749	11,998	149	22	20	R	
Tropical Star	Lbr	1986	9,749	11,998	149	22	20	R	

Managed by subsidiary Reefership Marine Services Ltd, Costa Rica (formed 1976 as Intercontinental Transportation Services Ltd to 1991 and Dole Fresh Fruit International Ltd to 2000) * chartered-out to Seatrade Groningen BV qv

DT-Bereederungs GmbH & Co KG   Germany

Funnel: Charteres colours. **Hull:** Dark blue or red with red boot-topping. **History:** Controlled by Danz (owners since 1870) and Tietjens (1824) families formed as Danz und Tietjens Schiffahrts KG in 1982, being renamed in 2003. **Web:** www.danz-tietjens.com

Name	Flag	Year	GRT	DWT	LOA	Bm	Kts	Type	Former names
Austria	Atg	1993	10,742	14,100	163	22	17	CC	ex Zim Houston III-08, Lukas-99, Kaedi-99, Kano-98, Lukas-98
Gloria	Atg	2001	16,803	22,967	185	25	20	CC	ex P&O Nedlloyd Pessoa-04, P&O Nedlloyd Lagos-02, I/a Gloria
Hamburg Goal *	Lbr	1983	22,112	38,110	188	28	15	B	ex Bulk Leader-08, Leader-07
Hamburg Pearl *	Lbr	1982	25,056	44,007	200	29	15	B	ex Elixir-07, Almerinda-94, Trinidad-91
Hamburg Team *	Lbr	1982	25,056	44,363	200	29	15	B	ex Heng Shun-07, Madredeus-05, Lucinda-94, Penbreizh-91, I/a tamarin
Hamburg Way *	Lbr	1982	24,864	44,415	200	29	15	B	ex Pasargad-07, Bao Jin Men-05, Cosmar-04, Garcia Lorca-91
Olympia	Atg	1986	10,287	12,500	148	23	18	CC	ex P&O Nedlloyd Cesme-05, Olympia-03, ACX Swallow-00, QC Mallard-00, Hansa Coral-99, Sea Eagle-92, Contship Australia-90, Ocean Australia-89, Fine Eagle-88
Xanadu *	Atg	1984	24,844	40,891	183	31	14	B	ex Maria-02, Cedrela-89, Western Jade-88, Dimitros Criticos-88, Kepbrave-86

newbuildings: two 80,500 dwt bulk carriers for 2010-11 delivery (to be named Burgia and Selandia)
owned or managed by associated BBC-Burger Bereederungs Contor GmbH, Germany or * managed for HBC Hamburg Bulk Carriers GmbH & Co KG (founded 1999 - www.hbc-hamburg.com)

Dyvi AS   Norway

Funnel: Black with blue 'D' between two narrow blue bands on broad white band. **Hull:** Grey with blue boot-topping. **History:** Formed 1957 as Jan-Erik Dyvi to 2003. **Web:** www.dyvi.no

Name	Flag	Year	GRT	DWT	LOA	Bm	Kts	Type	Former names
Dyvi Adriatic	Hkg	1988	39,187	9,772	183	30	18	V	ex Wolfsburg-03
Dyvi Baltic	Hkg	1989	39,043	9,772	183	30	17	V	ex Hannover-02
Dyvi Pamplona	Nis	1999	37,237	12,778	180	31	19	V	
Dyvi Puebla	Nis	1999	37,237	12,780	180	31	19	V	
Kassel	Pan	1999	51,204	17,297	180	32	19	V	

Eitzen Group   Norway

Funnel: Black with white 'E' inside blue 'C' on broad red band or * white with broad blue band beneath broad black top, some with 'ESO' below band. **Hull:** Black or red with white 'EITZEN' or 'EITZEN CHEMICAL', red boot-topping. **History:** Founded 1883 and traded as Tschudi & Eitzen from 1936 until joint venture terminated in 2003. Sichem Shipping merged with Blystad's Songa Shipholding in 2006 to form Eitzen Chemical, which acquired Mosvold Chemical AS in 2007. **Web:** www.eitzen-group.com or www.ems-shipmanagement.com

Name	Flag	Year	GRT	DWT	LOA	Bm	Kts	Type	Former names
Ballina	Bhs	1984	72,609	136,115	265	46	14	T	ex Nivosa-08
Difko Chaser *	Nis	1990	43,398	84,040	223	32	15	T	ex Northsea Chaser-01, Burwain Adriatic-95, Zafra-93
M3 Susanne *	Nis	1989	43,398	84,040	229	32	15	T	ex Difko Susanne-08, Northsea Bellows-01, Burwain Arctic-95, Zidona-94
Selandia	Iom	1996	30,928	58,139	200	31	14	B	ex Star Selandia -98, Selandia-96

Name	Flag	Year	GRT	DWT	LOA	Bm	Kts	Type	Former names
Sichem Arctic *	Mhl	1991	14,332	23,400	170	25	14	T	ex Songa Arctic-06, Dorsch-06
Sichem Defender	Pan	2006	11,660	19,999	144	24		T	
Sichem Eagle	Sgp	2008	17,789	25,421	170	26		T	
Sichem Eva	Sgp	1989	11,003	17,485	151	22	14	T	ex Songa Eva-06, Lake Eva-06, Jakov Sverdlov-03
Sichem Falcon	Sgp	2009	17,500	25,000	170	26		T	
Sichem Hawk	Sgp	2008	17,789	25,385	170	26		T	
Sichem Osprey	Sgp	2009	17,500	25,000	170	26		T	
Siteam Actinia *	Mlt	1993	22,633	40,296	176	32	14	T	ex Team Actinia-07, Actinia-00
Siteam Adventurer	Sgp	2007	26,751	46,190	183	32		T	
Siteam Anatas *	Mhl	1986	22,620	40,158	174	32	14	T	ex Team Anatas-07, Anatas-05, Maribel-04, Ferncourt-93, Antonio Dovali J-89, l/a Ferncourt
Siteam Aniara *	Lbr	1985	25,362	40,738	178	32	14	T	ex Team Aniara-07, Aniara-03, Levant-89, Avanti-88
Siteam Anja *	Mhl	1997	28,027	44,640	183	32	14	T	ex Team Anja-07, Simunye-05, Engen Simunye-00
Siteam Discoverer *	Mhl	2008	26,571	46,005	183	32		T	
Siteam Explorer *	Mhl	2007	27,199	46,190	183	32		T	
Siteam Leader *	Sgp	2009	27,139	46,190	183	32		T	
Siteam Leopard *	Mhl	1985	26,113	46,100	172	32	14	T	ex Team Leopard-07, Leopard-04, Petrobulk Leopard-96, Naess Leopard-86
Siteam Mars *	Mhl	1982	21,057	42,010	184	30	14	T	ex Team Mars-06, Team Troma-98, Troma-82
Siteam Ranger *	Sgp	2009	27,139	46,190	183	32		T	
Siteam Voyager	Sgp	2008	27,139	46,190	183	32		T	

newbuildings: eleven 60,000 dwt bulk carriers and * two further 46,190 dwt tankers for 2010 delivery.
* owned by Eitzen Chemical ASA and managed by EMS Ship Management, Denmark, Singapore or India.

Eletson Corp   Greece

Funnel: Buff base with red-edged blue five-pointed star on broad white band edged with narrow blue bands, beneath black top.
Hull: Black with red boot-topping. **History:** Formed 1966 as Eletson Maritime Services Inc to 1982. **Web:** www.eletson.com

Name	Flag	Year	GRT	DWT	LOA	Bm	Kts	Type
Agathonissos	Grc	2002	57,062	106,149	244	42	15	T
Alkyonis	Grc	1992	39,265	66,895	228	32	14	T
Alonissos	Grc	2004	57,062	106,290	244	42	15	T
Angistri	Grc	2000	39,283	76,019	213	37	15	T
Argironissos	Grc	1992	29,506	45,425	183	32	14	T
Dhonoussa	Grc	2005	40,038	69,180	228	32	15	T
Erikoussa	Grc	2003	41,679	70,142	228	32	15	T
Folegandros	Grc	1992	29,506	45,425	183	32	14	T
Halki	Grc	1989	27,793	46,538	183	32	14	T
Kandilousa	Grc	1995	28,507	46,700	183	32	14	T
Kastelorizo	Grc	1991	29,506	45,425	183	32	14	T
Makronissos	Grc	2002	57,062	106,149	244	42	15	T
Megalonissos	Grc	2004	57,062	106,290	244	42	15	T
Pelagos	Grc	1999	39,283	76,020	213	37	15	T
Polyaigos	Grc	2005	40,038	69,509	228	32	15	T
Psara	Grc	1989	27,793	46,538	183	32	14	T

Eletson Corp. AGATHONISSOS. *Phil Kempsey*

Name	Flag	Year	GRT	DWT	LOA	Bm	Kts	Type	Former names
Salamina	Grc	1991	29,506	45,425	183	32	14	T	
Serifopoulo	Grc	1995	28,507	46,700	183	32	14	T	
Serifos	Grc	1995	28,507	46,700	183	32	14	T	
Skiropoula	Grc	1995	38,792	68,232	242	32	14	T	
Skopelos	Grc	2003	41,679	70,142	228	32	15	T	
Sporades	Grc	1993	39,265	66,895	228	32	14	T	
Stavronisi	Grc	1996	38,667	68,232	243	32	14	T	
Strofades	Grc	2006	40,038	69,431	228	32	15	T	
Velopoula	Grc	1993	39,265	66,895	228	32	14	T	

newbuildings: eight 52,000 dwt tankers and four 23,500 grt Lpg tankers for 2009-11 delivery.

Enterprises Shipping & Trading SA — Greece

Funnel: Light grey with black top or * black with gold anchor on broad white band below narrow green band and black top or ** grey with narrow white band on broad blue band. **Hull:** Black or red with red boot-topping, * black with with yellow 'GOLDEN ENERGY' or ** brown with white 'SafOre'. **History:** Formed 1974 and part of Restis Group, who acquired bulk shipping interest of Safmarine (founded 1948) in 1999. **Web:** www.estsa.gr

Name	Flag	Year	GRT	DWT	LOA	Bm	Kts	Type	Former names
African Jaguar	Bhs	1996	16,041	26,477	169	26	14	B	ex Handy Roseland-05
African Lion	Bhs	1995	16,041	26,300	169	26	14	B	ex Handy Gunner-05
African Oryx	Bhs	1997	15,888	24,110	160	26	14	B	ex Gangga Nagara-05
African Puma	Bhs	1997	16,041	26,412	169	26	14	B	ex Pacific Selesa-05, I/a Selesa
African Wildcat	Bhs	1997	16,041	26,391	169	26	14	B	ex Marquisa-05
African Zebra	Bhs	1985	23,207	38,623	190	28	14	B	ex Handy Tiger-05, Brave Venture-94
Antwerp Max	Iom	1998	38,489	73,144	225	32	14	B	ex Bunga Saga Lima-05
Bay Ranger	Bhs	1995	24,550	43,125	185	31	14	B	ex Bunga Melor Dua-05
Bergen Max	Iom	1994	39,012	72,338	225	32	14	B	ex Bunga Saga Tiga-05
Bet Commander	Iom	1991	77,090	149,507	270	43	13	B	ex Celigny-08, Wah Shan-02, Donau Ore-96, Wah Shan-94
Bet Fighter	Iom	1992	90,991	171,800	298	46	13	B	ex Ferosa-07
Bet Intruder	Iom	1993	35,874	69,235	225	32	14	B	ex Tobata Max-08, Thanos F-06, Peruvian Express-04, Silver Regia-04, River Stream-03, Silver Star-00
Bet Prince	Iom	1995	82,830	163,554	284	45	14	B	ex Iron Prince-08, Lowlands Trassey-03
Bet Scouter **	Iom	1995	90,312	172,173	296	46	13	B	ex Saldanha-07
Bremen Max	Iom	1993	39,012	73,503	225	32	14	B	ex Bunga Saga Satu-05
Brugge Max	Iom	1998	38,489	73,056	225	32	14	B	ex Bunga Saga Enam-05
Channel Ranger	Bhs	1995	24,550	43,108	185	31	14	B	ex Bunga Melor Tiga-05
Constantia	Bhs	1996	83,658	171,039	289	45	14	B	ex Cape Mercury-00, First Mercury-99
Davakis G	Bhs	2008	30,937	53,800	190	32		B	
Delos Ranger	Bhs	2008	31,091	53,800	190	32		B	
Delphi Ranger	Bhs	2009	31,091	53,800	190	32		B	
Delta Ranger	Bhs	1995	24,550	43,108	185	31	14	B	ex Bunga Melor Empat-05
Elbe Max	Iom	1999	38,972	73,548	225	32	14	B	ex Bunga Saga 10-05
Energy Centaur	Iom	2008	42,298	74,995	228	32	14	T	
Energy Centaurion *	Iom	2008	42,998	74,471	228	32	14	T	
Energy Century	Iom	2003	41,397	70,470	228	32	14	T	
Energy Challenger	Iom	2005	42,011	70,675	228	32	14	T	
Energy Champion	Iom	2005	42,011	70,681	228	32	14	T	
Energy Chancellor	Iom	2005	42,011	70,558	228	32	14	T	
Energy Commander	Iom	2004	42,011	70,691	228	32	14	T	
Energy Conqueror	Iom	2004	42,011	70,616	228	32	14	T	
Energy Panther	Iom	2008	29,494	44,999	183	32	14	T	
Energy Patriot *	Iom	2008	28,500	46,583	183	32	14	T	
Energy Pioneer	Iom	2004	30,008	51,224	183	32	14	T	
Energy Power	Iom	2004	30,008	51,383	183	32	14	T	
Energy Pride **	Iom	2004	30,008	51,318	183	32	14	T	
Energy Progress *	Iom	2008	29,494	46,600	183	32	14	T	
Energy Protector **	Iom	2004	30,008	51,314	183	32	14	T	
Energy Puma	Iom	2008	29,494	49,549	183	32	14	T	
Energy Ranger	Iom	1996	26,330	45,950	190	32	14	B	ex Energy Saver-02, Cape Infanta-02
Energy Skier	Iom	2005	81,345	159,089	274	48	15	T	
Energy Sprinter	Iom	2005	81,345	159,089	274	48	15	T	
Force Ranger	Iom	1996	26,330	45,950	189	32	14	B	ex Cape Agulhas-02
Ghent Max	Iom	1998	38,489	73,220	225	32	14	B	ex Bunga Saga Tujuh-05
Glorius	Iom	2004	87,720	171,314	289	45	14	B	
Good Hope Max	Iom	2005	40,039	76,739	225	32	14	B	ex Georgios F-06, Ocean Lady-05
Hamburg Max	Iom	1994	39,012	72,338	225	32	14	B	ex Bunga Saga Empat-05
Iron Baron **	Iom	1999	88,385	169,981	289	45	14	B	ex Philippe LD-04
Iron King **	Iom	1996	81,155	161,167	280	45	14	B	ex Kalahari-02
Iron Queen **	Iom	1996	81,155	161,183	280	43	14	B	ex Karoo-02
Island Ranger	Bhs	1994	24,550	42,427	185	31	14	B	ex Bunga Melor Satu-05

Name	Flag	Year	GRT	DWT	LOA	Bm	Kts	Type	Former names
Louis Pasteur	Bhs	1996	9,330	9,000	138	22	21	R	ex Mont Blanc-96
Miden Max	Iom	1993	39,012	74,696	225	32	14	B	ex Bunga Saga Dua-05
Newcastle Max	Iom	1997	38,364	73,786	225	32	14	B	ex Nadia F-06, Agate-05, National Progress-04
Ntabeni	Pan	1984	25,005	37,425	183	30	15	Bp	ex Recife-96, Tellus-88
Olympius	Iom	2004	87,720	171,314	289	45	14	B	
Ostende Max	Iom	1998	38,489	73,207	225	32	14	B	ex Bunga Saga Lapan-05
Padova	Bhs	1983	7,983	8,471	148	20	18	R	ex Hectoras-02, Hellenic-96, Chiquita Hellenic-92, Kurashima Maru-91
Pierre Doux	Bhs	1995	9,438	9,357	138	22	20	R	
Power Ranger	Iom	1996	26,330	45,946	189	32	14	B	ex Cape Recife-02
SA Altius	Bhs	2001	87,542	171,480	289	45	14	B	
SA Fortius	Bhs	2001	87,542	171,509	289	45	14	B	
Steel Glory	Bhs	1984	23,536	39,345	181	31	14	B	ex Sea Mariner-02, Sanko Coral-91
Steel Might	Bhs	1985	22,132	39,132	181	31	15	B	ex Sea Trader-01, La Suerte-91
Storm Ranger	Bhs	1995	26,071	45,744	190	31	14	B	ex Lorenzina-03, Brilliance-00
Victorius	Iom	2004	87,720	171,314	289	45	14	B	

newbuildings: twelve 170,000 dwt, three 92,500 dwt and six 57,000 dwt bulk carriers for 2009-11 delivery.
* operated by subsidiaries Golden Energy Management SA, Greece (formed 2003) or ** South African Marine Corp, South Africa.
Also operates chartered bulk carriers as SwissMarine.

John T Essberger GmbH & Co KG　　　　　Germany

Funnel: Buff, narrow red band on black-edged broad white band and black top or buff with broad green band. **Hull:** Black with red boot-topping or light grey with blue 'DEUTSCHE AFRIKA-LINIEN'. **History:** Formed 1924 and now managed by third generation of Essberger/von Rantzau family. Acquired Deutsche Afrika Linien in 1941. **Web:** www.rantzau.de

Name	Flag	Year	GRT	DWT	LOA	Bm	Kts	Type	Former names
DAL Kalahari	Lbr	2005	50,736	62,994	266	37	24	CC	
Helvetia	Pan	1980	16,235	24,000	185	23	15	Ce	
Sanaga	Lbr	1997	17,784	28,215	169	27	14	B	ex Paclogger-98
Selinda *	Lbr	2001	17,784	28,107	169	27	14	B	
Swakop *	Lbr	2001	17,784	28,083	169	27	14	B	

* managed for Salamon AG, Germany.

The Ethiopian Shipping Lines　　　　　Ethiopia

Funnel: Green with yellow lion on brown eight-spoke wheel, red top. **Hull:** Green with red boot-topping. **History:** Formed 1966 **Web:** www.ethiopianshippinglines.com

Name	Flag	Year	GRT	DWT	LOA	Bm	Kts	Type	Former names
Abbay Wonz	Eth	1984	11,292	15,107	137	23	16	C	ex Mengistu H.M.-84
Abyot	Eth	1985	11,292	15,107	137	23	16	C	
Admas	Eth	1986	11,573	13,593	150	22	16	C	ex Spica-95, Warszawa II-93
Andinet	Eth	1985	11,731	14,897	137	23	15	C	
Netsanet	Eth	1985	11,731	14,894	137	23	15	C	
Shebelle	Eth	2006	20,471	27,391	179	27	15	Co	
Tekeze	Eth	1990	13,651	18,145	166	23	15	Co	ex Lim-99, Norviken-97, Moraca-95

Evergreen Marine Corp (Taiwan) Ltd　　　　　Taiwan

Funnel: Black with green eight-pointed star above 'EVERGREEN' within brown globe outline on broad white band or * green 'H' above 'HATSU' on globe outline. **Hull:** Black or dark green with white 'EVERGREEN', red or green boot-topping. **History:** Founded 1968. Formerly part-owned Uniglory Marine Corp merged 2002. **Web:** www.evergreen-marine.com or www.hatsu-marine.com

Name	Flag	Year	GRT	DWT	LOA	Bm	Kts	Type	Former names
Ever Dainty	Pan	1997	52,700	55,604	294	32	25	CC	
Ever Decent	Pan	1997	52,090	55,604	294	32	25	CC	
Ever Delight	Pan	1998	52,090	55,515	294	32	25	CC	
Ever Deluxe	Pan	1998	52,090	54,300	294	32	25	CC	
Ever Develop	Pan	1998	52,090	55,515	294	32	25	CC	
Ever Devote	Pan	1998	52,090	55,604	294	32	25	CC	
Ever Diadem	Pan	1998	52,090	55,604	294	32	25	CC	
Ever Diamond	Pan	1998	52,090	55,515	294	32	25	CC	
Ever Divine	Pan	1998	52,090	55,604	294	32	25	CC	
Ever Dynamic	Pan	1998	52,090	55,515	294	32	25	CC	
Ever Elite *	Gbr	2002	76,022	75,898	300	43	25	CC	ex Hatsu Elite-07
Ever Ethic *	Gbr	2002	76,067	75,898	300	43	24	CC	ex Hatsu Ethic-08
Ever Gaining	Pan	1987	46,410	53,240	270	32	20	CC	
Ever General	Pan	1987	46,410	53,240	270	32	20	CC	
Ever Genius	Twn	1984	37,023	43,401	231	32	20	CC	
Ever Gentry	Twn	1984	37,023	43,401	231	32	20	CC	
Ever Gifted	Twn	1984	37,023	43,401	231	32	20	CC	
Ever Given	Pan	1986	46,410	53,240	270	32	20	CC	
Ever Gleamy	Pan	1985	37,023	43,401	231	32	20	CC	ex LT Gleamy-04, Ever Gleamy-02, LT Gleamy-00, Ever Gleamy-00
Ever Golden	Twn	1985	37,023	43,401	231	32	20	CC	

Name	Flag	Year	GRT	DWT	LOA	Bm	Kts	Type	Former names
Ever Goods	Pan	1985	46,410	53,240	270	32	20	CC	
Ever Govern	Pan	1985	37,023	43,401	231	32	20	CC	
Ever Growth	Pan	1984	37,023	43,401	231	32	20	CC	
Ever Guest	Pan	1986	46,410	53,240	270	32	21	CC	
Ever Peace	Pan	2002	17,887	19,309	182	28	18	CC	ex LT Peace-04, l/a Ever Peace
Ever Pearl *	Pan	2002	17,887	19,309	182	28	18	CC	ex LT Pearl-04
Ever Power	Pan	2002	17,887	19,309	182	28	19	CC	ex LT Power-05, l/a Ever Power
Ever Pride *	Gbr	2003	17,887	19,309	182	28	19	CC	ex Hatsu Pride-08
Ever Racer	Pan	1994	53,359	57,904	294	32	23	CC	
Ever Radiant	Pan	1994	53,101	58,912	294	32	23	CC	ex Ever Renown-07
Ever Reach	Pan	1994	53,359	57,904	294	32	23	CC	
Ever Refine	Pan	1995	53,103	58,912	266	32	23	CC	
Ever Respect	Pan	1995	53,103	58,912	294	32	23	CC	ex Ever Repute-07
Ever Result	Pan	1994	53,103	58,912	294	32	23	CC	
Ever Reward	Pan	1994	53,103	58,912	294	32	23	CC	
Ever Safety	Pan	2007	75,246	78,618	300	43	25	CC	
Ever Salute	Pan	2008	75,246	78,733	300	43	25	CC	
Ever Shine *	Gbr	2005	75,246	78,693	300	43	25	CC	ex Hatsu Shine-08
Ever Sigma *	Gbr	2005	75,246	78,693	300	43	25	CC	ex Hatsu Sigma-08
Ever Steady	Pan	2006	75,246	78,664	300	43	25	CC	
Ever Strong	Pan	2007	75,246	78,715	300	43	25	CC	
Ever Summit	Pan	2007	75,246	78,612	300	43	25	CC	
Ever Superb	Pan	2006	75,246	78,661	300	43	25	CC	l/a Ever Spring
Ever Uberty	Pan	1999	69,246	63,216	285	40	25	CC	
Ever Ultra	Pan	1996	69,218	63,388	285	40	24	CC	
Ever Ulysses	Pan	2000	69,200	62,700	285	40	25	CC	ex LT Ulysses-05, Ever Ulysses-00
Ever Unicorn	Pan	2000	69,200	62,700	285	40	25	CC	ex LT Unicorn-05, l/a Ever Unicorn
Ever Unific	Pan	1999	69,246	63,216	285	40	25	CC	
Ever Union	Pan	1997	69,218	63,388	285	40	24	CC	
Ever Unique	Pan	1997	69,218	63,388	285	40	24	CC	
Ever Unison	Pan	1996	69,218	63,388	285	40	24	CC	
Ever United	Pan	1996	69,218	62,386	285	40	24	CC	ex LT United-03, Ever United-00
Ever Unity	Pan	1999	69,246	62,700	285	40	25	CC	ex LT Unity-04, Ever Unity-00
Ever Uranus	Pan	1999	69,246	63,216	285	40	24	CC	
Ever Urban	Pan	2000	69,246	63,216	285	40	24	CC	
Ever Ursula	Pan	1999	69,246	62,700	285	40	25	CC	ex LT Ursula-04, Ever Ursula-00
Ever Useful	Pan	1999	69,246	62,700	285	40	24	CC	
Ever Utile	Pan	2000	69,246	63,216	285	40	25	CC	ex LT Utile-05, Ever Utile-00
Hatsu Eagle *	Gbr	2001	76,022	75,898	300	43	25	CC	l/a Ever Eagle
Hatsu Envoy *	Gbr	2002	76,067	75,898	300	43	25	CC	l/a Ever Envoy
Hatsu Excel *	Gbr	2002	76,022	75,898	300	43	25	CC	
Hatsu Prima *	Gbr	2003	17,887	19,309	182	28	18	CC	
Hatsu Smart *	Gbr	2006	75,246	78,693	300	43	25	CC	
Hatsu Smile *	Gbr	2006	75,246	78,693	300	43	25	CC	

* owned by subsidiary Evergreen Marine (UK) Ltd, UK (formed 2002 as Hatsu Marine Ltd to 2007)
The company also operates 24 smaller container feeder ships (Ever-A, Uni-A and Uni-P classes) mainly in Far East services.

Evergreen Marine Corp. EVER SIGMA. *Hans Kraijenbosch*

Name	Flag	Year	GRT	DWT	LOA	Bm	Kts	Type	Former names

Italia Marittima SpA/Italy

Funnel: *Cream with blue 'LT' below narrow blue band, blue top.* **Hull:** *Blue with white 'ITALIA' or 'L TRIESTINO' and red boot-topping.*
History: *Founded in 1836 as Linee Triestine per l'Oriente SA di Nav Oriens, then Lloyd Austriaco to 1918 and formed as Lloyd Triestino di Navigazione SpA in 1937. Acquired from Italian state-owned Finmare in 1998 and renamed 2006.* **Web:** *www.italiamarittima.it*

Name	Flag	Year	GRT	DWT	LOA	Bm	Kts	Type	Former names
Ital Bianca	Ita	1983	13,420	19,440	162	23	14	CC	ex LT Bianca-08, Adria Bianca-05, Helga Wehr-01, P&O Nedlloyd Caracas-98, Helga Wehr-97, CMB Energy-96, Helga Wehr-93, Spirit of Amsterdam-93, City of Amsterdam-93, Kaduna-92, Helga Wehr-91, CMB Energy-90, Hartford Express-89, Helga Wehr-88, Asian Senator-87, Maersk Bella-87, Helga Wehr-86, Maersk Claudine-85, Helga Wehr-85, Norasia Helga-84, Helga Wehr-84
Ital Florida	Ita	2007	36,483	42,822	239	32	23	CC	
Ital Fortuna	Ita	2007	36,483	42,969	239	32	23	CC	
Ital Fulgida	Ita	2007	36,483	42,930	239	32	23	CC	
Ital Garland	Ita	1988	46,445	44,424	270	32	20	CC	ex LT Garland-06, Cosco Sao Paulo-01, LT Garland-01, Ever Garland-99
Ital Glamour	Ita	1987	46,445	53,240	270	32	20	CC	ex LT Glamour-07, Cosco Cape Town-03, LT Glamour-01, Ever Glamour-99
Ital Laguna **	Ita	2006	54,152	68,038	294	32	24	CC	
Ital Libera **	Ita	2007	54,152	67,986	294	32	24	CC	
Ital Lirica **	Ita	2007	54,152	68,138	294	32	24	CC	
Ital Lunare	Ita	2007	54,152	68,009	294	32	24	CC	
Ital Unica	Ita	2001	68,888	63,216	285	40	25	CC	ex LT Unica-08
Ital Universo	Ita	2001	68,888	63,216	285	40	25	CC	ex LT Universo-06
Ital Usodimare	Ita	2000	69,200	63,216	285	40	25	CC	ex LT Usodimare-08
LT Genova *	Ita	1993	38,395	41,500	234	32	21	CC	ex Nuova Genova-01
LT Lloydiana *	Ita	1989	35,629	40,196	231	32	20	CC	ex Nuova Lloydiana-00, LT Lloydiana-00, Nuova Lloydiana-99
LT Trieste *	Ita	1993	38,395	41,700	234	32	21	CC	ex Nuova Trieste-00

* formerly owned now on charter from Technomar Shipping Inc, Greece or ** managed for Niki Shipping Co Inc, Greece.

ExxonMobil Corp   USA

History: *Formed by 1999 amalgamation of Exxon Corp (formerly Standard Oil Co. of New Jersey to 1892 and Standard Oil Co until 1972) with Mobil Oil Corp (founded 1888 as Socony-Vacuum Oil to 1955 and Socony Mobil Oil Co until 1966)*
Web: *www.exxonmobil.com*

SeaRiver Maritime Inc/USA

Funnel: *Blue with white band separated from upper broad red band by further white band, narrow black top.* **Hull:** *Black with red or blue boot-topping.* **History:** *Founded 1920 as Humble Oil & Refining Co to 1973, later Exxon Shipping Co to 1993 and Exxon Co.*

Name	Flag	Year	GRT	DWT	LOA	Bm	Kts	Type	Former names
Kodiak (st)	Usa	1978	64,329	122,805	265	42	17	T	ex Tonsina-05
S/R American Progress	Usa	1997	26,092	45,435	183	32	14	T	ex American Progress-00
S/R Baytown	Usa	1984	32,136	59,625	238	32	15	T	ex Exxon Baytown-93
S/R Long Beach	Usa	1987	94,999	214,853	301	51	16	T	ex Exxon Long Beach-93
S/R Wilmington	Usa	1984	27,508	48,779	194	32	16	T	ex Exxon Wilmington-93
Sierra (st)	Usa	1979	64,329	125,091	265	42	17	T	ex Kenai-06

International Marine Transportation Ltd/UK

Funnel: *Black with white 'IMT' on blue rectangle on large white disc.* **Hull:** *Black or dark grey with red boot-topping.*
History: *Amalgamation in 1999 of Standard Marine Services Ltd (formerly Esso International Shipping to 1994) and Mobil Shipping Co Ltd (formerly Mobil Transportation Co Ltd to 1957)* **Web:** *None found.*

Name	Flag	Year	GRT	DWT	LOA	Bm	Kts	Type	Former names
Alrehab	Mhl	1999	160,279	301,620	335	58	15	T	
Osprey	Mhl	1999	160,279	284,893	335	58	16	T	

Also see Chevron Corp, USA

Fednav Ltd   Canada

Funnel: *White, red design incorporating part of maple leaf with interlinked 'F' and 'C', broad black top.* **Hull:** *Red or dark blue with red boot-topping.* **History:** *Founded 1946 as Federal Commerce & Navigation Ltd to 1984.* **Web:** *www.fednav.com*

Name	Flag	Year	GRT	DWT	LOA	Bm	Kts	Type	Former names
Arctic	Can	1978	20,236	28,418	221	23	15	Obo	
Federal Agno	Hkg	1985	17,821	29,643	183	23	14	BC	ex Federal Asahi-89
Federal Asahi	Hkg	1999	20,659	36,500	200	24	14	B	
Federal Baffin ‡	Pan	2007	30,721	55,309	190	32	14	B	
Federal Danube ††	Cyp	2004	23,100	35,000	200	24	14	B	
Federal Elbe ††	Cyp	2003	22,600	37,000	200	24	14	B	
Federal Ems ††	Cyp	2002	22,654	37,058	200	24	14	B	
Federal Franklin	Pan	2008	30,721	55,303	190	32	14	B	
Federal Hudson *	Hkg	2000	20,659	36,563	200	24	14	B	

Name	Flag	Year	GRT	DWT	LOA	Bm	Kts	Type	Former names
Federal Hunter *	Hkg	2001	20,659	36,563	200	24	14	B	
Federal Kivalina *	Hkg	2000	20,659	36,563	200	24	14	B	
Federal Kumano ‡	Hkg	2003	20,661	36,489	200	24	14	B	
Federal Kushiro ‡	Pan	2004	19,200	32,762	190	24	14	B	
Federal Leda ††	Cyp	2003	22,600	37,000	200	24	14	B	
Federal Maas	Brb	1997	20,837	34,372	200	24	14	B	
Federal Manitou †	Atg	2004	18,825	27,783	185	24	14	B	ex Lake Ontario-04
Federal Matane †	Atg	2004	18,825	27,780	185	24	14	B	ex Lake Erie-04
Federal Miramichi †	Lbr	2006	18,825	27,000	185	24	14	B	ex Lake St. Clair-05
Federal Nakagawa ‡	Hkg	2005	20,661	36,489	200	24	14	B	
Federal Oshima *	Hkg	1999	20,500	36,563	200	24	14	B	
Federal Patroller ††	Cyp	1999	12,993	17,451	143	23	15	Co	ex African Patroller-07, Atlantic Patroller-05, Forest Patroller-03, Atlantic Patroller-01
Federal Pioneer ††	Cyp	1999	12,993	17,451	143	23	15	Co	ex Seaboard Pioneer-07, Atlantic Pioneer-01
Federal Power ††	Cyp	2000	12,993	17,451	143	23	15	Co	ex Seaboard Power-07, Atlantic Power-01
Federal Pride ††	Cyp	2000	12,993	17,451	143	23	15	Co	ex Seaboard Chile II-07, Atlantic Pride-05, Seaboard Rover-02, Atlantic Pride-01
Federal Progress	Hkg	1989	21,469	36,445	177	30	14	B	
Federal Rhine	Brb	1997	20,837	34,372	200	23	14	B	
Federal Rideau *	Hkg	2000	20,500	36,563	200	24	14	B	
Federal Saguenay	Brb	1996	20,837	34,372	200	23	14	B	
Federal Schelde	Brb	1997	20,837	34,372	200	23	14	B	
Federal Seto ‡	Hkg	2004	20,861	36,300	200	23	14	B	
Federal Shimanto ‡	Pan	2001	19,125	32,787	190	24	14	B	

Fednav. FEDERAL RHINE. *Guido van Driessche*

Foster Yeoman. YEOMAN BRIDGE. *C. Lous*

Name	Flag	Year	GRT	DWT	LOA	Bm	Kts	Type	Former names
Federal St. Laurent	Brb	1996	20,837	34,372	200	23	14	B	
Federal Venture	Hkg	1989	21,469	36,445	177	30	14	B	ex Northern Venture-02
Federal Welland *	Hkg	2000	20,659	35,750	200	24	14	B	
Federal Weser ††	Cyp	2002	21,300	35,000	200	24	14	B	
Federal Yoshino ‡	Pan	2001	19,125	32,845	190	24	14	B	
Federal Yukon *	Hkg	2000	20,659	36,563	200	24	14	B	
Orsula ‡	Hrv	1996	20,837	34,198	200	24	14	B	ex Federal Calumet-97
Umiak I	Can	2006	22,462	31,992	189	27		B	

newbuildings: one 20,500 grt 35,300 dwt bulk carrier for 2012 delivery.
Owned ships and * ownd by subsidiary Fednav International Ltd, managed by Anglo-Eastern Ship Management Ltd. Hong Kong
(www.aesm.com.hk).
† chartered from Sunship Schiffahrts subsidiary of Reederei M Lauterjung KG, Germany or †† from Athena Marine Co Ltd, Cyprus.
‡ chartered from various other owners (nearly 20 others chartered without Federal prefix). See others with 'Federal' prefix in index.

Foster Yeoman Ltd
UK

Funnel: *Blue with blue 'y' on white rectangle above white 'YEOMAN', black top.* **Hull:** *Red or black with red boot-topping.*
History: *Founded 1923 as Foster Yeoman Ltd and acquired by Aggregate Industries UK Ltd in 2006.* **Web:** www.aggregate-uk.com

Name	Flag	Year	GRT	DWT	LOA	Bm	Kts	Type	Former names
Yeoman Bank	Lbr	1982	24,870	38,997	205	27	15	Bu	ex Salmonpool-90
Yeoman Bontrup	Bhs	1991	55,695	96,725	250	38	15	Bu	ex Western Bridge-02
Yeoman Bridge	Bhs	1991	55,695	96,772	250	38	15	Bu	ex Eastern Bridge-00

Frontline Ltd
Bermuda

Funnel: *White with light blue 'f' symbol on dark blue vertical rectangle above 'FRONTLINE'.* **Hull:** *Black, brown or light blue with red or dark blue boot-topping.* **History:** *Originally founded 1986 as Uddevalla Shipping AB by Swedish government, privatised 1989, controlling interest acquired in 1996 by John Fredriksen through Hemen Holdings and 1998 amalgamated with London & Overseas Freighters Ltd (founded 1949).* **Web:** www.frontmgt.no

Name	Flag	Year	GRT	DWT	LOA	Bm	Kts	Type	Former names
Altair Voyager †	Bhs	1993	80,914	135,829	259	48	15	T	ex Condoleezza Rice-01
Cygnus Voyager †	Bhs	1993	88,919	156,835	275	50	15	T	ex Samuel Ginn-03
Front Ace ‡	Lbr	1993	144,652	275,546	325	57	15	T	ex General Ace-00, Sea Princess-93
Front Ardenne ‡	Nis	1998	79,633	152,550	258	46	15	T	ex Ardenne-00
Front Brabant ‡	Nis	1998	79,633	152,550	269	46	15	T	ex Brabant-00
Front Breaker ‡	Nis	1991	89,004	169,146	285	45	14	B	(conv Obo)
Front Century ‡	Bhs	1998	157,976	311,189	334	58	15	T	
Front Champion ‡	Bhs	1998	157,976	311,286	334	58	15	T	
Front Circassia ‡	Mhl	1999	163,346	306,009	333	58	15	T	ex Omala-06, New Circassia-04, l/a Golden Circassia
Front Climber ‡	Sgp	1991	89,004	169,146	285	45	14	B	(conv Obo)
Front Comanche ‡	Atf	1999	159,423	300,133	333	60	15	T	ex Stena Comanche-01
Front Driver ‡	Nis	1991	89,004	169,146	285	45	14	B	(conv Obo)
Front Duchess ‡	Sgp	1993	149,997	284,480	322	56	14	T	ex Sea Duchess-96
Front Duke ‡	Sgp	1992	149,945	284,420	322	56	14	T	ex Sea Duke-96
Front Emperor	Mhl	2009	160,000	297,000	333	60	15	T	
Front Energy ‡	Cyp	2004	164,300	305,318	330	60	15	T	ex Sea Energy-05, l/a Mt. Pertamina 2
Front Falcon ‡	Bhs	2002	160,904	308,875	333	58		T	l/a Mosfalcon
Front Force ‡	Cyp	2004	156,873	305,442	330	60	15	T	ex Sea Force-05, l/a Mt. Pertamina 1
Front Glory ‡	Nis	1995	79,979	149,834	269	46	15	T	ex London Glory-97

Frontline Ltd. FRONT SCILLA. *N. Kemps*

Name	Flag	Year	GRT	DWT	LOA	Bm	Kts	Type	Former names
Front Guider ‡	Sgp	1991	89,004	169,146	285	45	14	B	(conv Obo)
Front Highness ‡	Sgp	1991	149,945	284,317	322	56	14	T	ex Sea Highness-96
Front Lady ‡	Sgp	1991	149,945	284,497	322	56	14	T	ex Sea Lady-96
Front Leader ‡	Sgp	1991	89,004	169,146	285	45	14	Obo	
Front Opalia ‡	Mhl	1999	159,756	302,193	333	60	15	T	ex Opalia-06
Front Page ‡	Lbr	2002	156,916	299,164	330	60	15	T	l/a Front Saga
Front President	Mhl	2009	160,000	297,000	333	60	15	T	
Front Pride ‡	Nis	1993	79,978	149,686	269	46	15	T	ex London Pride-98
Front Rider ‡	Sgp	1992	89,004	169,146	285	45	14	B	(conv Obo)
Front Sabang ‡	Sgp	1990	153,644	285,715	328	57	14	T	ex Sabang-00, Damar-94, Argo Dione-91
Front Scilla ‡	Iom	2000	160,805	302,561	333	60	16	T	ex Oscilla-05
Front Serenade ‡	Lbr	2002	157,000	298,300	333	60	16	T	
Front Shanghai	Hkg	2006	159,730	298,971	333	60	15	T	
Front Splendour ‡	Nis	1995	79,979	148,835	269	46	15	T	ex London Splendour-97
Front Striver ‡	Sgp	1992	89,004	169,204	285	45	14	B	(conv Obo)
Front Vanadis ‡	Sgp	1990	153,413	285,872	327	57	14	T	ex Vanadis-00
Front Vanguard ‡	Mhl	1998	159,423	300,058	333	60	14	T	ex New Vanguard-04
Front Viewer	Sgp	1992	89,004	169,146	285	45	14	B	(conv Obo)
Front Vista ‡	Mhl	1998	159,423	300,149	333	60	14	T	ex New Vista-04
Front Voyager	Bhs	1992	88,946	155,127	275	50	15	T	ex Virgo Voyager-06, William E. Crain-02
Mindanao ‡	Sgp	1998	81,265	147,447	274	48	15	T	
Sea Bay *	Hkg	2009	52,500	108,760	243	42	15	T	
Sea Cat *	Mhl	1985	50,272	89,636	244	40	15	T	ex GenMar Sun-05, Stavanger Sun-00, Glefi III-90, Atlantic Amity-90
Sea Hope *	Hkg	2009	52,500	108,701	243	42	15	T	
Sea Jaguar *	Mhl	1985	50,272	89,600	244	40	15	T	GenMar Boss-05, Stavanger Boss-00, Lithgow-90, Stellaris-90
Sirius Voyager †	Bhs	1994	88,919	156,382	275	50	15	T	ex Chevron Mariner-02

newbuildings: ten 297-320,000 dwt and eight 153-156,000 dwt tankers for 2009-12 delivery.
* owned by Seatankers Management Co. Ltd, Cyprus (64% controlled by Hemen Holdings) and ** managed by Thome Ship Management Pte Ltd, Singapore.
‡ chartered from Ship Finance International Ltd, Bermuda (originally forned as Frontline subsidiary in 2003) and managed by V. Ships (UK) Ltd, by Wallem Shipmanagement Ltd, Hong Kong, by V. Ships Norway AS or by International Tanker Management Holding Ltd, UAE.
§ owned by The OSM Group, Norway and managed by Wallem Shipmanagement Inc, USA.
† managed by Chevron Shipping Co LLC, USA.   Also see Euronav SA (under CMB) and other chartered ships with 'Front' prefix in index.

Golar LNG Ltd/Bermuda

Funnel: Blue with white swallowtail flag having blue 5-point star inside blue ring or * black with three narrow white bands. **Hull:** Black with white 'LNG', red boot-topping. **History:** Founded 1940 as T Gotaas & Co, renamed Gotaas-Larsen Shipping Corp in 1946. Golar Management (formed 1969) acquired by Singapore-based Osprey Maritime Ltd in !997, then purchased by World Shipholding (indirectly controlled by John Fredriksen) in 2001. **Web:** www.golar.com

Name	Flag	Year	GRT	DWT	LOA	Bm	Kts	Type	Former names
Gimi (st)	Gbr	1976	96,235	72,703	294	42	19	Lgc	
Golar Freeze (st)	Gbr	1977	95,879	66,200	288	43	20	Lng	
Golar Frost (st)	Lbr	2004	115,156	67,100	288	68	19	Lng	
Golar Mazo (st)	Lbr	2000	111,835	76,210	290	47	19	Lng	
Golar Spirit (st)	Gbr	1981	106,577	80,239	289	45	19	Lng	
Golar Winter (st)	Gbr	2004	93,899	80,810	277	43	19	Lng	
Gracilis (st)	Mhl	2005	93,899	80,810	280	43	19	Lng	ex Golar Viking-06
Granatina *	Mhl	2003	94,934	80,800	280	43	19	Lng	
Grandis	Iom	2006	97,491	84,894	277	43	19	Lng	
Granosa	Mhl	2006	97,491	84,823	277	43	19	Lng	
Hilli (st) *	Gbr	1975	96,235	72,703	293	42	19	Lgc	ex Golar Glacier-75
Khannur (st)	Gbr	1977	96,235	73,074	293	42	19	Lgc	
Methane Princess (st)	Gbr	2003	93,899	77,707	277	43	19	Lng	

Vessels managed by Golar Management (UK) Ltd, UK. Also operates LNG vessels in joint venture with Exmar q.v.
* managed by STASCO Ship Management, UK (see under Shell)

General Maritime Corp   USA

Funnel: Black with yellow 'G' inside yellow edged green diamond on yellow edged broad dark blue band or charterers colours. **Hull:** Black with red boot-topping. **History:** Formed 1997. Acquired Soponata SA in 2004 and merged with Arlington Tankers (27%) in 2008. **Web:** www.generalmaritimecorp.com

Name	Flag	Year	GRT	DWT	LOA	Bm	Kts	Type	Former names
GenMar Agamemnon	Lbr	1995	53,829	96,213	243	42	14	T	ex Emilie-98
GenMar Ajax	Lbr	1996	53,829	96,183	243	42	14	T	ex Julie-98
GenMar Alexandra	Mhl	1992	56,012	102,262	241	42	14	T	ex Nordpacific-00, Skaunord-00
GenMar Argus	Mhl	2000	81,151	159,901	274	48	15	T	ex Crude Tria-03
GenMar Constantine	Lbr	1992	56,021	102,262	241	42	14	T	ex Artois-98, Seahope D.Y.-96
GenMar Defiance	Lbr	2002	56,225	105,538	239	42	15	T	ex Peneda-04
GenMar George T	Mhl	2007	79,235	149,847	274	48	15	T	
GenMar Gulf	Mhl	1991	81,135	141,844	274	48	14	T	ex Crudegulf-03, landsort-97
GenMar Harriet G	Lbr	2006	79,325	150,205	274	48	15	T	

Name	Flag	Year	GRT	DWT	LOA	Bm	Kts	Type	Former names
GenMar Hope	Sgp	1999	81,526	159,539	274	48	15	T	ex Crude Hope-03, Nord Hope-00
GenMar Horn	Mhl	1999	81,526	159,474	274	48	15	T	ex Crude Horn-03, Nord Horn-00
GenMar Kara G	Lbr	2007	79,235	150,296	274	48	15	T	
GenMar Minotaur	Lbr	1995	53,829	96,213	243	42	14	T	ex Stephanie-98
GenMar Orion	Mhl	2002	81,381	159,992	274	48	-	T	ex Crude Okto-03, Antares-02
GenMar Phoenix	Mhl	1999	80,058	153,015	269	46	15	T	ex Crude Ena-03
GenMar Princess	Lbr	1991	52,164	96,765	228	42	14	T	ex Crude Princess-04, Genmar Princess-03, Crude Princess-03, Nord-Jahre Princess-00, Jahre Princess-93
GenMar Progress	Lbr	1991	52,164	96,765	228	42	14	T	ex Crude Progress-04, Genmar Progress-03, Crude Progress-03, Nord-Jahre Progress-00, Jahre Progress-93
GenMar Revenge	Lbr	1994	53,773	96,755	244	42	14	T	ex Sintra-04, Astro Perseus-00, Yuhsei Maru-99
GenMar Spyridon	Mhl	2000	81,151	159,959	274	48	15	T	ex Crude Dio-03
GenMar St. Nikolas	Mhl	2008	79,235	149,876	274	48	15	T	
GenMar Strength	Lbr	2003	56,225	105,674	239	42	15	T	ex Portel-04
Stena Companion **	Lbr	2004	41,589	72,637	229	32	15	T	
Stena Compatriot **	Lbr	2004	41,589	72,000	229	32	15	T	
Stena Concord **	Bmu	2004	27,357	47,171	183	32	14	T	
Stena Consul **	Bmu	2004	27,357	47,171	183	32	14	T	
Stena Victory **	Bmu	2001	163,761	312,679	335	70	16	T	
Stena Vision **	Bmu	2001	163,761	312,679	335	70	16	T	

newbuildings: 115,000 dwt tanker due for 2011 delivery.
Operated by subsidiaries General Maritime Management LLC, USA or General Maritime Management (Portugal) Lda (formerly Soponata SA to 2004)   ** time-chartered to Stena AB (18% owners of Arlington Tankers) or affiliate Concordia Maritime..

Green Reefers ASA   Norway

Funnel: *Dark green.* **Hull:** *Dark green with white 'GREEN REEFERS', red boot-topping.* **History:** *Founded 1989 as Nomadic Shipping ASA to 2003.* **Web:** *www.greenreefers.no*

Name	Flag	Year	GRT	DWT	LOA	Bm	Kts	Type	Former names
Green Autumn	Pan	1982	6,070	6,348	146	18	17	R	ex Thordis-06, Stork V-96, Suzuran-88
Green Brazil	Bhs	1994	7,743	7,721	131	20	19	R	ex Pittsburg-05, Pioneer-96, Crystal Pioneer-96
Green Chapeco	Mlt	1990	6,419	6,794	131	20	19	R	ex Cap Gris Nez-07, Minnesota-05, Blue Reefer-99, Blue Sky-94
Green Chile	Bhs	1992	7,743	7,726	131	20	19	R	ex Privilege-06, Crystal Privilege-03
Green Costa Rica	Bhs	1991	7,743	7,726	131	20	19	R	ex Prince-06, Crystal Prince-04
Green Guatemala	Bhs	1992	7,743	7,726	131	20	19	R	ex Primadonna-05, Crystal Primadonna-04
Green Honduras	Bhs	1992	7,743	7,721	131	20	19	R	ex Pride-06, Cyystal Pride-03
Green Iceland	Nld	1993	4,683	6,697	136	16	20	R	ex Caribic-06
Green Italia	Atg	1994	7,743	7,721	131	20	19	R	ex Pilgrim-06, Crystal Pilgrim-96
Green Magic	Bhs	1989	5,103	6,116	136	16	20	R	ex Magic-06
Green Magnific	Bhs	1992	5,103	6,116	136	16	20	R	ex Magnific-06
Green Majestic	Bhs	1988	5,089	6,105	136	16	20	R	ex Majestic-06
Green Maveric	Bhs	1993	5,103	6,105	136	16	20	R	ex Maveric-06
Green Music	Bhs	1990	5,103	6,116	136	16	20	R	ex Music-07

The company also operates a large number of smaller reefer vessels

Grimaldi Group   Italy

Funnel: *Yellow with red 'Gt' symbol or blue with either white 'I' or 'A' symbol or white 'S' within white ring.* **Hull:** *Yellow with black 'GRIMALDI LINES' on white upperworks, red boot-topping.* **History:** *Founded 1941 as Fratelli Grimaldi Armatori to 1993.* **Web:** *www.grimaldi.napoli.it*

Name	Flag	Year	GRT	DWT	LOA	Bm	Kts	Type
Gran Bretagna *	Ita	1999	51,714	18,461	181	32	18	Ro
Grand Benelux *	Ita	2001	37,712	12,594	176	31	20	Ro
Grande Amburgo †	Ita	2003	56,642	26,170	214	32	18	Ro
Grande America	Ita	1997	56,642	26,169	214	32	18	Ro
Grande Anversa	Ita	2004	38,651	12,353	177	31	20	Ro
Grande Atlantico	Ita	1999	56,640	26,170	214	32	18	Ro
Grande Buenos Aires	Ita	2004	56,642	26,169	214	32	18	Ro
Grande Colonia †	Ita	2007	38,651	12,292	177	31	20	Ro
Grande Ellade *	Ita	2001	52,000	18,440	181	32	18	Ro
Grande Europa *	Ita	1998	51,714	18,461	181	32	18	Ro
Grande Francia †	Ita	2002	56,642	26,170	214	32	18	Ro
Grande Italia *	Ita	2001	37,712	12,594	176	31	20	Ro
Grande Lagos	Ita	2004	44,408	13,740	196	31	19	Ro
Grande Mediterraneo *	Ita	1998	51,714	18,427	181	32	18	Ro
Grande Napoli	Ita	2003	42,600	14,900	201	31	20	Ro
Grande Nigeria †	Ita	2002	56,642	26,170	214	32	18	Ro
Grande Portogallo *	Ita	2002	37,712	12,594	176	31	20	Ro
Grande Roma	Ita	2003	42,600	14,900	201	31	20	Ro
Grande San Paolo	Ita	2003	56,642	26,170	214	32	18	Ro

Name	Flag	Year	GRT	DWT	LOA	Bm	Kts	Type	Former names
Grande Scandinavia *	Ita	2001	52,000	18,440	181	32	18	Ro	
Grande Spagna *	Ita	2002	37,712	12,594	176	31	20	Ro	
Repubblica Argentina	Ita	1998	51,925	23,882	206	30	20	Ro	
Repubblica del Brasile	Ita	1998	51,925	23,800	206	30	20	Ro	
Repubblica di Amalfi	Ita	1989	42,574	25,450	216	30	18	Ro	
Repubblica di Roma †	Ita	1992	42,001	19,287	184	30	19	Ro	
Repubblica di Venezia †	Ita	1987	48,622	18,730	213	30	18	Ro	

newbuildings: five 55,700 grt and five 50,000 grt ro-ro vessels for 2009-11 delivery
Ships owned by related Italian companies Grimaldi Compagnia di Navigazione SpA, * by Atlantica SpA di Navigazione or † by Industria Armamento Meridionale SpA,

ACL Shipmanagement AB/Sweden

Funnel: *White with blue 'ACL' over wavy line, black top.* **Hull:** *Black with white 'ACL' symbol.* **History:** *Originally formed 1965 as Atlantic Container Line by Wallenius, Swedish-America, Transatlantic and Holland-America, Cunard-Brocklebank and CGT added 1967. Consortium dissolved 1990 and ACL acquired by Transatlantic (Bilspedition subsidiary). Grimaldi acquired 44% share in 2000 and balance in 2001.* **Web:** *www.aclcargo.com*

Atlantic Cartier	Swe	1985	58,358	51,648	292	32	17	Ro	(len-87)
Atlantic Companion	Swe	1984	57,255	51,648	292	32	17	Ro	ex Companion Express-94, Atlantic Companion-87 (len-87)
Atlantic Compass	Swe	1984	57,255	51,648	292	32	17	Ro	(len-87)
Atlantic Concert	Swe	1984	57,255	51,648	292	32	17	Ro	ex Concert Express-94, Atlantic Concert-87 (len-87)
Atlantic Conveyor	Swe	1985	58,438	51,648	292	32	17	Ro	(len-87)
Grande Africa	Ita	1998	56,642	26,195	214	32	18	Ro	
Grande Argentina	Swe	2001	56,642	26,170	214	32	18	Ro	

Grimaldi Group. GRAND BENELUX. *Tom Walker*

Grimaldi Group. REPUBLICA DEL BRASILE. *Allan Ryszka Onions*

Name	Flag	Year	GRT	DWT	LOA	Bm	Kts	Type	Former names
Grande Brasile	Ita	2000	56,642	26,170	214	32	18	Ro	
Grande Detroit *	Ita	2005	38,651	12,353	176	31	20	Ro	
Grande Sicilia *	Ita	2006	41,900	14,900	179	31	20	Ro	

* owned by ACL Shipholding 2004 AB

Hanjin Shipping Co Ltd South Korea

Funnel: Orange with white 'H' inside white ring. **Hull:** Black with white 'HANJIN', red boot-topping. **History:** Formed 1988. Senator Lines GmbH (formed 1987 as Senator Linie, a subsidiary of Bremer Vulkan shipyard), later merged with former East German company Deutsche Seerederei Rostock and became 80% owned affiliate in 1997, before closing in early 2009. **Web:** www.hanjin.com

Name	Flag	Year	GRT	DWT	LOA	Bm	Kts	Type	Former names
Alexander Carl **	Pan	1993	110,627	208,189	312	50	13	B	
Empress **	Pan	1992	76,925	151,662	274	45	13	B	
Frontier **	Pan	1992	76,925	151,492	274	45	13	B	
Goodwill **	Pan	1992	75,277	149,401	269	43	14	B	
Hanjin Antwerp *	Kor	1996	16,252	27,367	167	26	14	B	
Hanjin Beijing *	Kor	1996	65,893	67,115	279	40	25	CC	
Hanjin Berlin *	Kor	1997	66,403	67,236	279	40	25	CC	
Hanjin Bombay	Kor	1994	16,252	27,029	167	26	14	B	
Hanjin Bremerhaven	Pan	2006	74,962	80,855	304	40	26	CC	
Hanjin Brisbane	Kor	1997	16,252	27,327	167	26	14	B	
Hanjin Budapest	Pan	2006	74,962	80,866	304	40	26	CC	
Hanjin Calcutta *	Kor	1997	16,270	27,365	167	26	14	B	
Hanjin Capetown	Pan	1993	76,954	147,631	274	45	13	B	
Hanjin Chongqing	Pan	2008	74,962	80,855	304	40	26	CC	
Hanjin Dampier	Kor	1989	110,541	207,346	309	50	13	B	
Hanjin Durban	Pan	2008	40,800	50,542	261	32	24	CC	
Hanjin Gladstone	Kor	1990	110,541	207,391	309	50	13	B	
Hanjin Haypoint	Kor	1990	77,650	151,431	274	45	13	B	
Hanjin Houston *	Kor	1995	16,232	27,209	167	26	14	B	
Hanjin Istanbul *	Kor	1997	16,270	27,369	167	26	14	B	
Hanjin Kaohsiung ‡	Cyp	1990	37,134	43,925	243	32	22	CC	
Hanjin Kingston	Pan	2008	40,487	51,733	261	32	24	CC	
Hanjin London	Kor	1996	66,687	67,298	279	40	26	CC	
Hanjin Los Angeles	Kor	1997	51,754	62,700	290	32	24	CC	
Hanjin Madras	Kor	1990	77,650	150,431	274	45	13	B	
Hanjin Malta	Kor	1993	51,299	62,649	290	32	24	CC	
Hanjin Marseilles	Kor	1993	51,299	62,681	290	32	24	CC	
Hanjin Melbourne	Kor	1987	93,643	186,260	292	48	13	B	ex Westin Seven-89
Hanjin Mumbai	Pan	2007	74,962	85,250	304	40	26	CC	
Hanjin Muscat (st)	Pan	1999	93,765	75,463	280	43	20	Lng	
Hanjin Nagoya	Pan	1998	51,754	62,500	290	32	24	CC	
Hanjin New Orleans	Kor	1994	37,550	70,337	225	32	13	B	
Hanjin Norfolk	Pan	2008	40,487	51,752	261	32	24	CC	
Hanjin Oslo	Pan	1998	65,469	68,993	279	40	25	CC	
Hanjin Paris	Kor	1997	66,687	68,500	279	40	25	CC	
Hanjin Penang *	Kor	1997	16,270	27,369	167	26	14	B	
Hanjin Piraeus	Pan	2008	40,800	50,542	261	32	24	CC	
Hanjin Pittsburg	Kor	1990	25,461	38,393	186	28	15	B	ex Pittsburg-93
Hanjin Port Kelang	Pan	2006	75,061	80,811	304	40	26	CC	
Hanjin Port Kembla	Kor	1993	68,243	126,267	264	41	13	B	
Hanjin Pyeong Taek (st)	Pan	1995	90,004	71,041	269	43	19	Lng	
Hanjin Ras Laffan (st)	Pan	2000	93,769	75,079	280	43	20	Lng	
Hanjin Richards Bay	Kor	1997	75,752	149,322	269	43	14	B	
Hanjin Rio de Janiero	Pan	2008	40,487	51,648	261	32	24	CC	
Hanjin Roberts Bank	Kor	1994	73,706	135,069	268	43	14	B	
Hanjin Rome	Pan	1998	65,469	68,955	280	40	25	CC	
Hanjin San Francisco *	Kor	1996	50,792	62,681	290	32	24	CC	
Hanjin Shanghai	Kor	1995	50,792	62,799	290	32	24	CC	
Hanjin Shenzhen	Pan	2008	74,962	80,855	304	40	26	CC	
Hanjin Sur (st)	Pan	2000	93,769	75,193	280	43	20	Lng	
Hanjin Tacoma	Kor	1994	37,550	70,347	225	32	13	B	
Hanjin Tianjin	Pan	2007	74,962	80,855	294	40	26	CC	
Hanjin Valencia	Kor	1998	51,754	62,799	290	32	24	CC	
Hanjin Vancouver ‡	Cyp	1990	35,745	44,764	241	32	20	CC	ex Hanjin Hamburg-90
Hanjin Washington	Kor	1997	65,643	67,272	279	40	25	CC	
Hanjin Wilmington	Kor	1997	50,792	62,799	290	32	24	CC	
Hanjin Xiamen	Pan	2007	74,962	80,855	304	40	26	CC	
Innovator **	Pan	1993	75,277	149,298	269	43	14	B	
Keoyang Majesty **	Pan	1997	43,181	48,618	221	32	15	Bw	
Keoyang Noble **	Pan	1997	43,181	51,662	221	32	15	Bw	
Keoyang Orient **	Pan	1997	75,752	149,322	269	43	14	B	

Name	Flag	Year	GRT	DWT	LOA	Bm	Kts	Type	Former names
Pos Ambition **	Pan	1992	75,277	149,330	269	43	14	B	
Pos Bravery **	Kor	1992	110,593	207,096	309	50	13	B	
Pos Challenger **	Pan	1992	75,277	140,302	269	43	13	B	
Pos Dedicator **	Kor	1993	110,627	208,393	312	50	13	B	
Pos Harvester **	Pan	1992	75,277	140,302	269	43	13	B	

newbuildings: two 318,000 dwt tankers, two 312,000 dwt, ten 179,400 dwt and two 82,300 dwt bulk carriers, four 100,000 grt, five 91,650 grt, one 89,000 grt and three further 39,900 grt container ships for 2009-12 delivery.
* owned by Korea French Banking Corp. (formed jointly with Societe Generale SA) and by subsidary ** Keoyang Shipping Co. Ltd (formed 1990).
‡ formerly owned now chartered from Samartzis Maritime Enterprises Co. SA, Greece

Hansa Hamburg Shg International GmbH & Co KG   Germany

Funnel: *White with blue houseflag or charterers colours.* **Hull:** *Dark blue, red or black with black or red boot-topping.*
History: *Formed 1999.* **Web:** *www.hansahamburg.de*

Barmbek	Deu	2005	16,324	15,955	169	27	21	CC	
CSAV Venezuela *	Lbr	2007	18,480	23,745	177	27	20	CC	ex G.W. Lessing=07
Eilbek	Deu	2005	16,324	15,952	169	27	21	CC	ex Cast Prosperity-06, Eilbek-05
Flottbek	Deu	2005	16,324	15,952	169	27	21	CC	
Reinbek	Deu	2005	16,324	15,952	169	27	21	CC	ex Cast Prestige-06, Reinbek-05
RHL Agilitas *	Lbr	2007	18,480	23,664	175	27	20	CC	ex Wilhelm Busch-07

newbuildings: two 54,000 grt and three 49,000 grt container ships for 2009-11 delivery.
Managed by Wappen Reederei GmbH & Co KG, Germany. * owned by associated Reederei Hamburger Lloyd GmbH & Co KG.
See also vessels managed by Ernst Jacob GmbH, Leonhardt & Blumberg Reederei GmbH and Reederei Karl Schluter GmbH.

Hansa Treuhand Schiffsbeteiligungs AG & Co KG   Germany

Funnel: *White with blue houseflag or charterers colours.* **Hull:** *Dark blue, red or black with black or red boot-topping.*
History: *Founded 1983.* **Web:** *www.hansatreuhand.de*

Alianca Gavea ‡	Lbr	2000	25,369	33,899	207	30	21	CC	ex Cala Palos-08, CSCL Xiamen-07, Hansa Victory-00
APL Australia ‡	Lbr	2002	50,243	58,486	282	32	24	CC	ex MSC Lausanne-04, HS Explorer-02, I/a Hansa Explorer
APL Italy ‡	Lbr	2002	50,243	58,213	282	32	24	CC	ex MSC Arizona-05, HS Voyager-03, I/a Hansa Voyager
Cap Azul	Lbr	2002	18,334	23,493	175	27	19	CC	ex P&O Nedlloyd Nelson-04, Hansa Nordburg-02
CMA CGM Newton	Lbr	2007	32,968	38,547	213	32	23	CC	ex HS Scott-07
CSCL Seattle *	Lbr	2001	65,131	68,100	275	40	26	CC	I/a HS Columbia, I/dn Hansa Columbia
Hansa Aalesund †	Lbr	2001	15,988	20,461	170	25	16	CC	ex Al Yamamah-08, Hansa Aalesund-04, MSC New Plymouth-04 Hansa Aalesund-02
Hansa Africa †	Lbr	1997	37,398	43,378	243	32	22	CC	ex ANL Excellence-03, Ville de Venus-02, Ibn Zaidoun-00, Hansa Africa-97
Hansa Arendal †	Lbr	2001	15,988	20,700	170	25	16	CC	ex TMM Chiapas-05, Hansa Arendal-02
Hansa Berlin †	Lbr	1993	9,609	12,582	150	22	17	CC	ex P&O Nedlloyd Orinoco-05, APL Manaus-05, MB Caribe-04, Melbridge Berlin-03, EWL Venezuela-99, Hansa Berlin-98, Eagle Wisdom-95, Hansa Berlin-93
Hansa Bremen ††	Lbr	1989	10,842	12,942	157	23	21	R	

Hansa Hamburg Shipping. FLOTTBEK. *J. M. Kakebeeke*

Name	Flag	Year	GRT	DWT	LOA	Bm	Kts	Type	Former names
Hansa Caledonia †	Deu	1998	16,927	21,563	168	27	19	CC	ex Maersk Malaga-07, Hansa Caledonia-03, CSAV Suape-98, Hansa Caledonia-98
Hansa Calypso †	Lbr	1998	16,915	21,480	168	27	19	CC	ex Maersk Pireaus-07, Hansa Calypso-00, CMA Hakata-00, Hansa Calypso-99
Hansa Castella †	Lbr	1998	16,915	21,480	168	27	19	CC	ex Damaskus-06, CMA Mersin-00, Hansa Castella-99
Hansa Catalina †	Lbr	1997	16,915	21,519	168	27	19	CC	ex Cap Lobos-06, Hansa Catalina-03, CMA Xiamen-00, P&O Nedlloyd Abidjan-99, Hansa Catalina-97
Hansa Centaur †	Lbr	1998	16,927	20,860	168	27	19	CC	ex Pacific Merchant-01, CMA Qingdao-00, P&O Nedlloyd Luanda-99, I/a Hansa Centaur
Hansa Centurion †	Lbr	1998	16,915	21,473	168	27	19	CC	ex Maersk Athens-07, Hansa Centurion-00, CMA Kobe-00, Hansa Centurion-99
Hansa Century ‡	Lbr	1997	31,730	34,954	193	32	22	CC	ex Kota Perdana-04, Zim Pusan I-02, Hansa Century-98, Ibn Duraid-98, Hansa Century-97
Hansa Commodore †	Lbr	1997	16,915	21,470	168	27	19	CC	
Hansa India †	Deu	1994	37,563	43,600	243	32	22	CC	ex NYK Prestige-07, Hansa India-04, P&O Nedlloyd Yantian-02, Largs Bay-99
Hansa Lauenburg †	Lbr	2006	18,327	23,482	175	27	19	CC	
Hansa Liberty ‡	Lbr	2000	25,369	33,912	207	30	21	CC	ex CSCL Yantian-07, Hansa Liberty-00
Hansa London †	Lbr	1992	9,608	12,575	150	22	17	CC	ex Marfret Normandie-99, Maersk Zambezi-98, Gouritz-97, Hansa London-96, Maersk Santiago-96, Hansa London-92
Hansa Lubeck ††	Lbr	1990	10,842	12,942	157	23	21	R	
Hansa Narvik †	Lbr	1998	15,988	20,630	170	25	20	CC	ex Kota Serikat-03, Hansa Narvik-02, Direct Eagle-00, Hansa Narvik-99
Hansa Oldenburg †	Lbr	2002	18,334	23,493	175	27	19	CC	ex Delmas Kerguelen-07, Hansa Oldenburg-02
Hansa Riga †	Lbr	1994	16,927	21,480	168	27	19	CC	ex Maersk Marseille-07, CMA Inchon-00, P&O Nedlloyd Accra-99, Nedlloyd River Plate-97, Hansa Riga-94
Hansa Rostock †	Lbr	1994	9,606	12,575	150	23	18	CC	
Hansa Sonderburg †	Lbr	2000	18,037	23,579	175	27	18	CC	ex CP Kestrel-06, Direct Kestrel-05, Hansa Sonderburg-01
Hansa Stockholm ††	Lbr	1991	10,842	12,942	157	23	21	R	
Hansa Trondheim †	Lbr	1998	15,988	20,840	170	25	20	CC	ex Al Shamiah-08, Hansa Trondheim-04, MSC Thailand-03, Hansa Trondheim-02, Direct Hawk-01, Hansa Trondheim-01, Direct Jabiru-00, Maersk Reunion-99, Hansa Trondheim-98
Hansa Visby ††	Lbr	1989	10,842	12,942	157	23	21	R	
HS Alcina *	Lbr	2001	83,723	160,183	274	48	14	T	ex Somjin-06
HS Bach *	Lbr	2007	38,320	44,985	247	32	23	CC	
HS Berlioz *	Lbr	2007	38,320	46,288	247	32	23	CC	
HS Bizet *	Lbr	2007	38,320	46,312	247	32	23	CC	
HS Bruckner *	Lbr	2009	35,600	42,100	231	32	23	CC	
HS Carmen *	Lbr	2003	62,254	113,033	250	44	23	T	ex Avor-06
HS Challenger ‡	Lbr	2004	30,123	35,600	207	32	22	CC	ex Hansa Challenger-04
HS Chopin *	Lbr	2007	38,320	46,345	247	32	23	CC	
HS Debussy *	Lbr	2009	35,900	42,100	231	32	23	CC	

Hansa Treuhand Schiffs. HANSA INDIA in Leonhardt & Blumberg colours. *Allan Ryszka Onions*

Name	Flag	Year	GRT	DWT	LOA	Bm	Kts	Type	Former names
HS Discoverer ‡	Lbr	2003	30,123	35,600	207	32	22	CC	ex Zim Charleston-07, HS Discoverer-06, Hansa Discoverer-04
HS Elektra *	Dis	1998	57,009	105,994	244	42	13	T	ex Nordasia-07
HS Haydn *	Lbr	2009	35,600	42,100	231	32	23	CC	
HS Medea *	Lbr	2003	62,254	113,033	250	44		T	ex Sinova-06
HS Puccini ‡	Lbr	2007	16,162	17,350	161	25	19	CC	
HS Tosca §	Lbr	2004	62,796	115,630	250	44	15	T	
Ital Oceano	Lbr	2006	32,968	38,686	214	32	23	CC	ex HS Cook-06
Ital Onesta	Lbr	2007	32,968	38,617	214	32	23	CC	I/a HS Magellan
Ital Onore ‡	Lbr	2006	32,968	38,609	214	32	23	CC	ex HS Amundsen-06
Maersk Dampier ‡	Lbr	2002	50,242	57,600	280	32	24	CC	ex CMA CGM Neptune-06, I/a HS Colon-02, I/dn Hansa Colon
Maersk Darmstadt ‡	Mlt	2004	54,271	68,187	294	32	23	CC	ex HS Livingstone-04, I/dn Maersk Dunkirk
Maersk Dortmund ‡	Mlt	2004	54,271	66,672	294	32	23	CC	ex HS Humboldt-04
Maersk Drammen ‡	Lbr	2002	50,242	58,512	280	32	24	CC	ex CMA CGM Mercure-06, HS Caribe-02, I/a Hansa Caribe
Maersk Dresden †	Deu	1996	50,644	62,399	292	32	24	CC	ex Dagmar Maersk-04, Hansa Atlantic-96
Maersk Duisburg †	Deu	1996	50,644	62,400	277	32	24	CC	ex Dorthe Maersk-04, Hansa Pacific-96
Maruba America *	Lbr	2008	36,007	42,100	231	32	23	CC	ex HS Wagner-08
Norasia Alps †	Deu	1997	31,730	34,954	193	32	22	CC	ex Hansa Constitution-05, MSC Florida-03, Hansa Constitution-98, Ibn Al Akfani-98, Hansa Constitution-97
Tiger Jade †	Lbr	2003	18,334	23,493	175	27	19	CC	ex Maersk Auckland-07, Hansa Brandenburg-03
Zim Kingston I †	Lbr	1993	9,606	12,575	150	22	18	CC	ex Hansa Wismar-08, EWL Antilles-07, Nedlloyd Curacao-97, Sea-Land Panama-95, Maya Star-94, Hansa Wismar-93
Zim Santos †	Lbr	2001	15,988	20,700	170	25	16	CC	ex MOL Focus-08, Hansa Kristiansand-07, Kota Machan-03, Hansa Kristiansand-02

newbuildings: two 41,500 grt container ships for 2011 delivery.
* owned by subsidiary Hansa Shipping GmbH & Co KG. † managed by Leonhardt & Blumberg Schiffahrts GmbH & Co KG, Germany and ††
chartered out to Seatrade Groningen BV, ‡ managed by Hansa Shipping GmbH & Co KG or § Wallem GmbH & Co KG
See also Norddeutsche Reederei H Schuldt GmbH, KG Projex-Schiffahrts GmbH & Co, F A Vinnen & Co and Oskar Wehr KG.

Hanseatic Lloyd AG Switzerland

Funnel: Black with red dot over blue wave on broad white band or charterers colours. **Hull:** Blue or light grey with red boot-topping.
History: Formed 2003. **Web:** www.hanseatic-lloyd.com

Name	Flag	Year	GRT	DWT	LOA	Bm	Kts	Type	Former names
APL Atlanta	Atg	2008	43,071	55,482	267	32	25	CC	
APL Costa Rica	Atg	1995	50,698	62,441	292	32	24	CC	ex Maersk Dublin-07, Dragor Maersk-02
APL Denver	Atg	2008	43,071	55,612	267	32	25	CC	
APL Los Angeles	Atg	2008	43,071	55,387	267	32	25	CC	
APL Oakland	Atg	2008	43,071	55,476	267	32	25	CC	
APL Peru	Atg	2002	41,834	53,554	266	32	25	CC	ex Delaware Bridge-05, HLL Atlantic-02
MCT Alioth	Lbr	1999	12,358	19,996	149	24	15	T	ex Alioth-04
MCT Almak	Lbr	1999	12,358	17,561	149	24	15	T	ex Almak-03
MCT Altair	Lbr	1999	12,358	17,553	149	24	15	T	ex Altair-03
MCT Amazon	Lbr	2009	12,000	19,800	164	27	15	T	

Hanseatic Lloyd. MCT MONTE ROSA. *C. Lous*

Name	Flag	Year	GRT	DWT	LOA	Bm	Kts	Type	Former names
MCT Arcturus	Lbr	1999	12,358	17,563	149	24	15	T	ex Arcturus-03
MCT Breithorn *	Che	2007	12,776	19,950	164	27	15	T	
MCT Matterhorn *	Che	2006	14,000	19,980	164	23	15	T	I/a HLL Arctic
MCT Mississippi	Lbr	2008	12,000	19,800	164	27	15	T	
MCT Monte Rosa *	Che	2007	12,776	19,953	164	27	15	T	
MCT Rhine	Lbr	2008	12,000	19,953	164	27	15	T	
MCT Stockhorn *	Che	2008	12,776	19,844	164	23	15	T	
MCT Yangtze	Lbr	2008	12,000	19,800	164	27	15	T	

Owned by subsidiaries of Hanseatic Lloyd Schiffahrt GmbH & Co KG, Germany. * managed by Mega Chemicals Schiffahrts AG, Switzerland.

Hansa Mare Reederei GmbH & Co KG/Germany

Funnel: Black with red dot over blue wave on broad white band or charterers colours. **Hull:** Blue or light grey with red boot-topping.
History: Formed 1991 and jointly owned by Hanseatic Lloyd Reederei and Schlussel Reederei KG (founded 1950).
Web: www.hansamare.de

Name	Flag	Year	GRT	DWT	LOA	Bm	Kts	Type	Former names
APL Argentina	Atg	2000	40,306	52,250	261	32	22	CC	ex YM Savannah-04, Trade Hallie-03, Mare Caribicum-01
APL Chile	Atg	2000	40,306	52,250	261	32	22	CC	ex Mare Arcticum-04, YM New York-04, Trade Tesia-03, Mare Arcticum-01
APL Kaohsiung	Atg	2000	40,306	52,250	261	32	22	CC	ex APL Panama-06, APL Britannicum-04, YM Wilmington-04, Trade Freda-03, I/a Mare Britannicum
CMA CGM Beirut	Atg	1995	29,383	34,625	196	32	21	CC	ex Maersk Portland-07, Mare Caspium-04, ANL China-02, NYK Minerva-01, Mare Caspium-00
Kota Ekspres	Atg	1997	29,383	34,670	196	32	22	CC	ex Mare Africum-02
Kota Mawar *	Atg	1994	16,266	22,494	168	25	19	CC	ex Ibuki-07, Mare Ibericum-04, Indamex Impala-03, ANL Impala-01, Mare Ibericum-01, Carina Challenger-01, Mare Ibericum-97, CSAV Ranco-97, Mare Ibericum-94
Libra Mexico	Atg	1999	40,306	47,660	261	32	24	CC	ex Mumbai Express-07, Mare Lycium-06, P&O Nedlloyd Cobra-05, Mare Lycium-03, Mosel Bridge-02, I/a Mare Lycium
Maersk Dulles	Atg	1998	40,306	52,357	261	32	25	CC	ex Maersk Tangier-06, P&O Nedlloyd Tiger-05, Weser Bridge-04, I/a Mare Siculum
Maersk Peterhead	Atg	1997	29,750	34,800	196	32	21	CC	ex OOCL Harmony-04, Mare Ionium-00
Maersk Tirana	Atg	1998	40,306	52,329	261	32	24	CC	ex Dalian Express-07, Maersk Tirana-06, P&O Nedlloyd Cartagena-05, Elbe Bridge-04, Mare Superum-98
Mare Adriaticum	Atg	1993	9,581	12,721	150	23	17	CC	ex Mekong Stream-03, Mare Adriaticum-03, ACX Wagle-02, Mare Adriaticum-00, Rotterdam Stad-98, Mare Adriaticum-97, Sea Nordic-95, Independent Trader-94, Mare Adriaticum-94
Mare Balticum	Atg	1993	9,584	12,712	150	23	17	CC	ex X-Press Konkan-02, Mare Balticum-01, Saudi Dammam-99, Mare Balticum-99, Maersk Euro Octavo-94, Mare Balticum-93
Mare Internum	Atg	1997	29,383	34,705	196	32	22	CC	ex Maersk Pittsburg-07, Mare Internum-04
Mare Phoenicium	Atg	1999	40,306	52,330	261	32	24	CC	ex Ems Bridge-01, I/a Mare Phoenicium
Mare Thracium	Atg	1997	29,383	34,705	196	32	22	CC	ex Maersk Petersburg-07, Mare Thracium-04, MSC Oregon-01, Mare Thracium-00
MSC Belize	Atg	1995	9,590	12,705	150	22	17	CC	ex Mare Doricum-07, ACX Falcon-02, Mare Doricum-00, Breda Stad-98, Mare Doricum-97, Sea Nordic-95, Mare Doricum-95
MSC Scandinavia	Atg	2000	40,306	52,250	261	32	24	CC	ex Donau Bridge-04, Mare Atlanticum-01
YM Hiroshima	Deu	1996	29,383	34,671	196	32	22	CC	ex Mare Gallicum Ipex Emperor-02, OOCL Haven-01, Mare Gallicum-00, Acapulco-98, TMM Acapulco-97, Mare Gallicum-96

* managed by Uniteam Marine Shipping, Germany

Hapag-Lloyd AG   Germany

Funnel: Orange with blue 'HL' symbol. **Hull:** Black or red with white 'Hapag-Lloyd' and red boot-topping. **History:** Formed in 1970 by amalgamation of Hamburg-Amerika Linie (founded 1847) and Norddeutscher Lloyd (founded 1857). Rickmers Linie became wholly owned subsidiary in 1987 (part-owned since 1974), later being resold to Rickmers family. Control of Hapag acquired by Preussag AG in 1997 and Hapag acquired control of TUI Group in 1998, Preussag (now TUI) acquiring remaining shares in 2002 and in 2005 TUI acquired CP Ships (originally founded 1883 as Canadian Pacific Railway Co, first ship chartered 1886, later Canadian Pacific Steamships (founded 1922) and Canadian Pacific Ltd from 1981. Canada Maritime founded 1987, jointly with CMB (43%) whose share was acquired 1993. Later acquired Cast (1983) Ltd in 1995, Lykes Bros Steamship Co (founded 1900) and Contship in 1997, Ivaran Lines and ANZDL in 1998, TMM and CCAL in 2000 and Italia Line in 2002). Terms agreed for sale by TUI to 'Albert Ballin consortium' late in 2008, but delayed due to EU approval and funding. **Web:** www.hapag-lloyd.com

Name	Flag	Year	GRT	DWT	LOA	Bm	Kts	Type	Former names
Altamira Express *	Bmu	1987	40,436	40,845	270	32	20	CC	ex CP Ambassador-06, Lykes Ambassador-05, Ming Plenty-01
Antwerpen Express	Deu	2000	54,437	67,145	294	32	24	CC	ex Tokyo Express-99

Name	Flag	Year	GRT	DWT	LOA	Bm	Kts	Type	Former names
Barcelona Express *	Bmu	1987	40,439	40,744	270	32	20	CC	ex CP Sinaloa-06, TMM Sinaloa-05, Ming Promotion-01
Berlin Express	Deu	2003	88,493	100,019	320	43	26	CC	
Bonn Express	Deu	1989	35,919	45,977	236	32	20	CC	
Bremen Express	Deu	2008	93,750	103,567	335	43	25	CC	
Canberra Express	Deu	2000	23,652	29,841	188	30	20	CC	ex CP Eagle-06, Lykes Eagle-05, Clivia-00
Charleston Express †	Usa	2002	40,146	36,644	243	32	20	CC	ex CP Everglades-07, Lykes Ranger-05
Chicago Express	Deu	2006	93,811	103,691	336	43	25	CC	
Colombo Express	Deu	2005	93,750	103,800	335	43	25	CC	
Copenhagen Express *	Bmu	1987	39,132	44,966	259	32	21	CC	ex CP Explorer-06, Lykes Explorer-05, Genevieve Lykes-98, President Arthur-96, I/a Doctor Lykes
Dresden Express	Deu	1991	53,883	67,680	294	32	23	CC	
Dublin Express	Deu	2002	46,009	54,157	281	32	25	CC	ex Maersk Dale-08, CP Australis-06, Contship Australis-05
Duesseldorf Express	Deu	1998	53,523	66,525	294	32	23	CC	
Dubai Express ‡	Hkg	2006	39,941	50,500	260	32	24	CC	ex CP Corbett-06, I/a CP Guerrero, I/dn TMM Guerrero
Endurance **	Bmu	1983	32,152	32,424	222	32	22	CC	ex CP Endurance-06, CanMar Endurance-05, Cast Performance-03, Contship Endeavour-99, CanMar Endeavour-98, Alligator Joy-95, Tokyo Maru-90
Essen Express	Deu	1993	53,815	67,680	294	32	23	CC	
Fremantle Express *	Gbr	1995	23,540	30,645	187	30	19	CC	ex CP Voyager-06, Lykes Voyager-05, P&O Nedlloyd Bandar Abbas-01, P&O Nedlloyd Yafo-99, Pax-98, CMBT Melbourne-97, Contship Melbourne-97, I/a Pax
Genoa Express	Bmu	1988	40,436	40,845	270	32	20	CC	ex CP Jalisco-06, TMM Jalisco-05, Ming Progress-01
Glasgow Express	Deu	2002	46,009	54,221	281	32	25	CC	ex Maersk Dayton-08, CP Borealis-06, Contship Borealis-05
Glory *	Bmu	1979	16,145	18,964	177	27	22	CC	ex CP Glory-06, CanMar Glory-05, Sea Falcon-94, CMB Monarch-91, CMB Mover-90, Asian Senator-90, Jefferson-88, TFL Jefferson-86, Seatrain Saratoga-80
Gothenburg Express *	Bmu	1987	39,132	44,966	259	32	21	CC	ex CP Liberator-06, Lykes Liberator-05, Stella Lykes-97, President Garfield-96, Tillie Lykes-87
Hamburg Express	Deu	2001	88,493	100,006	320	43	26	CC	
Hanover Express	Deu	2007	93,750	103,760	336	43	25	CC	
Heidelburg Express	Deu	1989	35,919	45,977	236	32	20	CC	ex Ville De Verseau-91, Heidelberg Express-91
Helsinki Express *	Bmu	1987	39,132	44,966	259	32	21	CC	ex CP Discoverer-06, Lykes Discoverer-05, Margaret Lykes-97, President Harding-96, I/a James Lykes
Hero	Bmu	1986	41,023	40,009	243	32	22	CC	ex CP Hero-06, Lykes Hero-05, Cast Progress-03, Alligator Reliance-01, Astro Prosperity-96

Hapag-Lloyd. BERLIN EXPRESS. *Tom Walker*

Name	Flag	Year	GRT	DWT	LOA	Bm	Kts	Type	Former names
Hoechst Express	Deu	1991	53,833	67,680	294	32	23	CC	
Hong Kong Express	Deu	2002	88,493	100,016	320	43	26	CC	ex Berlin Express-02
Humboldt Express **	Sgp	1984	32,444	34,037	200	32	16	CC	
Jakarta Express ‡	Hkg	2006	39,600	50,500	260	32	24	CC	ex CP Dartmoor-06, CP Banyan-06, l/dn Contship Banyan
Kiel Express	Deu	1991	53,783	67,680	294	32	23	CC	ex Hannover Express-07
Kobe Express	Deu	1998	53,523	67,537	294	32	23	CC	ex Shanghai Express-02
Kuala Lumpur Express	Deu	2008	93,811	103,538	336	43	25	CC	
Kyoto Express	Deu	2005	93,750	103,890	335	43	25	CC	
Lahore Express ‡	Hkg	2006	39,941	50,000	260	32	24	CC	ex CP Morelos-06
Leverkusen Express	Deu	1991	53,783	67,680	294	32	23	CC	
Lisbon Express	Bmu	1995	33,735	34,330	216	32	20	CC	ex CP Prospect-06, Cast Prospect-05, CanMar Fortune-03
Liverpool Express	Deu	2002	46,009	54,156	281	32	25	CC	ex Maersk Dexter-07, CP Aurora-06, Contship Aurora-05
Livorno Express	Bmu	1991	37,474	43,084	242	32	21	CC	ex Lykes Motivator-06, Jupiter-01, Ville de Jupiter-01, CGM Pascal-00, Nedlloyd Pascal-98, CGM Pascal-95
London Express	Deu	1998	53,523	66,577	294	32	23	CC	
Ludwigshafen Express	Deu	1992	53,833	67,680	294	32	23	CC	
Madrid Express	Bmu	1986	40,447	40,744	270	32	20	CC	ex CP Hermosillo-06, TMM Hermosillo-05, Ming Propitious-01
Manila Express ‡	Hkg	2007	39,941	50,813	261	32	23	CC	

Hapag-Lloyd. GOTHENBURG EXPRESS. *Allan Ryszka Onions*

Hapag-Lloyd. HONG KONG EXPRESS. *Mick Lindsay*

Name	Flag	Year	GRT	DWT	LOA	Bm	Kts	Type	Former names
Milan Express *	Bmu	1996	33,663	33,659	216	32	20	CC	ex CP Los Angeles-06, Cielo di Los Angeles-05, Cast Premier-05, OOCL Canada-03
Mississauga Express *	Bmu	1998	39,174	40,881	245	32	21	CC	ex CP Pride-06, CanMar Pride-05
Montreal Express	Gbr	2003	55,994	62,300	294	32	22	CC	ex CP Spiri-06, CanMar Spirit-05
New Delhi Express ‡	Hkg	2005	39,941	50,813	260	32	24	CC	ex CP Kanha-06, I/a CP Charger, I/dn Lykes Charger
New Orleans Express *	Gbr	1989	35,958	42,976	240	32	21	CC	ex CP Campeche-06, TMM Campeche-05, Choyang Park-01
Norfolk Express	Deu	1995	36,606	45,362	245	32	24	CC	ex OOCL Atlantic-03, Norfolk Express-02, Hong Kong Express-02, Northern Majesty-96
Osaka Express	Deu	2007	93,750	103,662	336	43	25	CC	
Oslo Express	Bmu	1987	39,132	44,966	259	32	21	CC	ex CP Navigator-07, Lykes Navigator-05, Almeria Lykes-98, President Buchanan-96, I/a Almeria Lykes
Ottawa Express *	Bmu	1998	39,174	40,120	245	32	21	CC	ex CP Honour-06, CanMar Honour-05
Paris Express	Deu	1994	53,815	67,613	294	32	23	CC	ex Hamburg Express-01
Philadelphia Express †	Usa	2003	40,146	40,478	243	32	22	CC	ex CP Yosemite-06, TMM Yucatan-05
Power *	Bmu	1982	31,570	32,207	223	32	22	CC	ex CP Power-06, Montreal Senator-05, Cast Power-03, Contship Success-99, CanMar Success-98, Alligator Excellence-95, America Maru-90
Rio de Janeiro Express ‡	Hkg	2007	39,941	50,500	260	32	24	CC	ex CP Nuevo Leon-07, TMM Nuevo Leon-05
Rio Grande Express ‡	Hkg	2006	39,941	50,500	260	32	24	CC	ex CP Margosa-06

Hapag-Lloyd. LISBON EXPRESS. *Allan Ryszka Onions*

Hapag-Lloyd. MONTREAL EXPRESS. *Allan Ryszka Onions*

Name	Flag	Year	GRT	DWT	LOA	Bm	Kts	Type	Former names
Rome Express *	Bmu	1986	40,464	40,744	270	32	20	CC	ex CP Challenger-06, Lykes Challenger-05, Ming Peace-01
Rotterdam Express	Deu	2000	54,400	66,975	294	32	24	CC	
Saigon Express ‡	Hkg	2006	39,600	50,500	260	32	24	CC	ex CP Jasper-06, CP Trader-06, l/dn Lykes Trader
Santiago Express **	Sgp	1984	32,444	33,997	206	32	18	CC	ex Isla de la Plata-96, Cordillera Express-84
Santos Express ‡	Hkg	2006	39,941	50,000	260	32	24	CC	ex CP Victor-06, l/dn Lykes Victor
Seoul Express	Deu	2000	54,465	66,981	294	32	24	CC	ex Bremen Express-07
Shanghai Express	Deu	2002	88,493	100,003	320	43	26	CC	l/a Berlin Express
St. Louis Express †	Usa	2002	40,146	35,200	244	32	22	CC	ex CP Yellowstone-06, TMM Guanajuato-05
Stuttgart Express	Deu	1993	53,815	67,640	294	32	23	CC	
Sydney Express *	Gbr	1994	23,540	30,621	187	30	19	CC	ex CP Dynasty-06, CanMar Dynasty-05, TMM Guadalajara-03, P&O Nedlloyd Melbourne-01, Coral Seatel-98, Contship Sydney-98, Coral Seatel-94
Tokyo Express	Deu	2000	54,437	54,766	294	32	24	CC	
Toronto Express *	Gbr	2003	55,994	62,300	294	32	-	CC	ex CP Venture-06, CanMar Venture-05
Triumph *	Bmu	1978	16,289	18,606	177	27	19	CC	ex CP Triumph-06, CanMar Triumph-05, CMB Marque-90, American Senator-89, Dart Americana-87, Seapac Independence-81, Seatrain Independence-81
Tsingtao Express	Deu	2007	93,750	103,760	336	43	25	CC	
Valencia Express	Bmu	1996	33,735	34,330	216	32	20	CC	ex CP Performer-06, Lykes Performance-05, Cast Prominence-05, CanMar Courage-03

Hapag-Lloyd. NEW ORLEANS EXPRESS. *Allan Ryszka Onions*

Hapag-Lloyd. WASHINGTON EXPRESS. *Phil Kempsey*

Name	Flag	Year	GRT	DWT	LOA	Bm	Kts	Type	Former names
Veracruz Express *	Bmu	1987	40,439	40,870	270	32	20	CC	ex CP Achiever-06, Lykes Achiever-05, Ming Pleasure-01
Victory	Bmu	1979	16,289	18,381	177	27	18	CC	ex CP Victory-06, CanMar Victory-05, American Senator-90, Singapore Senator-89, Dart Atlantica-87, Seapac Chesapeake-81, Seatrain Chesapeake-81
Washington Express †	Gbr	2003	40,146	40,478	243	32	22	CC	ex CP Denali-06, Lykes Flyer-05
Wellington Express	Deu	2001	23,652	29,894	188	30	21	CC	ex CP Tabasco-06, TMM Tabasco-05, Silvia-01
Yorktown Express †	Usa	2002	40,146	40,478	243	32	21	CC	ex CP Shenandoah-07, TMM Colima-05, Contship Tenacity-02

newbuildings: twelve 93,750 grt 8759 teu container ships for 2010-11 delivery.
* owned by subsidiary Hapag-Lloyd Ships Ltd, UK and managed by Anglo-Eastern Ship Management Ltd., Hong Kong (China).
† owned by Hapag-Lloyd USA LLC and managed by Marine Transport Management, USA or ‡ chartered from Seaspan Corp, Hong Kong (Seaspan International Ltd, Canadian subsidiary of Washington Corp, USA).
See other chartered ships with 'Express' suffix under Costamare Shipping Co SA, Norddeutsche Vermogensanlage GmbH & Co KG, NSB Niederelbe Schiffahrts GmbH & Co KG and Ofer Brothers (Zodiac Maritime Agencies).

Harren & Partner Schiffahrts GmbH   Germany

Funnel: *Cream with two dark sails above three waves.* **Hull:** *Light grey with red boot-topping.* **History:** *Formed 1989.*
Web: *www.harren-partner.de*

Name	Flag	Year	GRT	DWT	LOA	Bm	Kts	Type	Former names
Blue Giant (2)	Atg	2008	18,169	10,480	169	25	15	HL	ex Combi Dock II-08
Clipper Gemini **	Atg	2003	30,928	51,187	192	32	14	B	ex VOC Gemini-06, Clipper Gemini-03
Combi Dock I (2)	Atg	2008	17,341	10,480	169	25	15	HL	
Combi Dock III (2)	Atg	2008	18,169	10,480	169	25	15	HL	
Maersk Naantali	Cyp	2005	11,935	16,400	144	23	14	T	ex Patricia-05
Maersk Nairn	Cyp	2006	11,935	16,400	144	23	14	T	l/a Patagona
Maersk Newport	Mlt	2005	11,935	16,664	144	23	14	T	ex Patalya-05
Maersk Nordenham	Cyp	2005	11,935	16,716	144	23	14	T	ex Patrona-05
Marida Boreas *	Cyp	2007	10,549	15,212	149	22	15	T	
Marida Patea	Mlt	2008	11,935	16,651	144	23	14	T	
Marida Paterna	Cyp	2006	11,935	16,748	149	22	15	T	
Marida Patnos	Cyp	2006	11,935	16,714	149	22	14	T	
Paiute	Atg	1995	36,615	70,273	225	32	14	B	
Patani	Cyp	2008	11,000	16,500	144	23	14	T	
Peoria	Atg	1996	36,615	70,231	225	32	14	B	
Pochard †	Atg	2003	22,655	37,384	199	24	14	B	l/a Panarea
Puffin	Atg	2003	22,654	37,641	199	24	14	B	
Sibulk Premier	Atg	2003	29,985	53,609	190	32	14	B	ex Sibulk Pioneer-03
VOC Gallant **	Bhs	2002	30,928	51,215	190	32	14	B	ex DS Gallant-04

newbuildings: five further 15,000 dwt tankers on order for 2009 delivery.
Owned or managed by Harren & Partners Ship Management GmbH & Co KG or * by Marlow Ship Management Deutschland GmbH & Co KG.
† managed for H&H Schiffahrts GmbH or ** on charter to Van Ommeren Clipper Holdings (Clipper Group)

Emil Hartmann   Germany

Funnel: *Yellow with red 'GT' on white segments of white/blue diagonally quartered flag, narrow black top.* **Hull:** *Black with red boot-topping.* **History:** *Appears to have been founded about 1998.* **Web:** *www.german-tanker.de*

Name	Flag	Year	GRT	DWT	LOA	Bm	Kts	Type
Seabass	Deu	2001	21,353	32,480	178	28	14	T
Seaconger	Deu	2005	21,329	32,200	178	28	16	T
Seahake	Deu	2003	21,329	32,480	178	28	16	T
Sealing	Deu	2003	21,356	32,480	178	28	16	T
Seamarlin	Deu	2007	26,548	40,550	188	32	15	T
Seamullet	Deu	2001	21,353	32,230	178	28	15	T
Searay	Deu	2004	21,353	32,310	178	28	16	T
Seashark	Deu	2004	21,329	32,310	178	28	16	T
Seasprat	Deu	2007	26,548	40,597	188	32	16	T
Seatrout	Deu	2006	26,548	40,600	188	32	15	T
Seaturbot	Deu	2000	21,353	32,230	178	28	14	T

newbuildings: one 43,000 dwt tanker on order for 2009 delivery
Managed by German Tanker Shipping GmbH & Co KG (founded 1998)

Hartmann Schiffahrts GmbH & Co KG   Germany

Funnel: *White with blue 'h' symbol or charterers colours.* **Hull:** *Blue or red, some with white 'UCC', red boot-topping.* **History:** *Formed 1981.* **Web:** *www.hartmann-reederei.de*

Name	Flag	Year	GRT	DWT	LOA	Bm	Kts	Type	Former names
Cap Doukato	Lbr	2004	25,406	33,847	207	30	21	CC	l/a Frisia Kiel
Cap Saray	Deu	2004	25,406	33,784	207	30	21	CC	l/a Frisia Rotterdam
Cosco Karachi	Deu	2005	27,915	37,900	215	30	21	CC	ex Frisia Kopenhagen-05
CSAV Rio Lontue	Lbr	2004	25,406	27,400	207	30	21	CC	l/a Frisia Wismar
CSAV Santos	Lbr	2004	25,406	33,900	207	30	21	CC	l/a Frisia Rostock

Name	Flag	Year	GRT	DWT	LOA	Bm	Kts	Type	Former names
Daewoo Brave	Lbr	2008	31,094	53,408	190	32	14	B	
Daewoo Challenge	Lbr	2008	31,094	53,571	190	32	14	B	
Federal Patriot *	Cyp	2003	12,993	17,471	143	23	15	Co	ex BBC Russia-08, Atlantic Progress-03
Federal Pendant *	Cyp	2003	12,993	17,477	143	23	15	Co	ex BBC Korea-08, Atlantic Pendant-05
Federal Katsura *	Pan	2005	19,165	32,594	190	24	14	B	
Federal Sakura *	Pan	2005	19,165	32,583	190	24	14	B	
Frisia Lissabon	Lbr	2004	25,406	33,829	207	30	22	CC	ex Cap Flinders-08, Cabo Prior-06, I/a Frisia Lissabon
Frisia Lubeck	Lbr	2004	25,406	33,781	207	30	22	CC	ex Libra Santa Catarina-09, Frisia Lubeck-04
Itajai Express	Lbr	2006	25,406	33,743	207	30	22	CC	ex Frisia Hannover-06
Ital Ordine	Lbr	2006	27,779	38,345	222	30	23	CC	
Ital Oriente	Lbr	2007	27,779	39,269	222	30	23	CC	
Ital Ottima	Lbr	2007	27,779	39,332	222	30	23	CC	
Paranagua Express	Lbr	2005	25,406	33,900	207	30	22	CC	ex Frisia Loga-06
Tango	Lbr	2008	78,809	150,096	274	48		T	
UBC Santa Marta *	Cyp	2008	19,748	31,582	172	27	14	B	
UBC Stavanger *	Cyp	2004	19,748	31,751	172	27	14	B	
UBC Tampico *	Cyp	2004	24,140	37,821	182	29	14	B	
UBC Tokyo *	Cyp	2005	24,140	37,865	182	29	14	B	
Waltz	Lbr	2008	78,809	150,393	274	48		T	

*newbuildings: seven 118,000 dwt, * three 38,000 dwt and * three 32,000 dwt open-hatch bulk carriers, five 25,000 dwt general cargo, two 35,000 grt and eight 22,000 grt container ships for 2009-10 delivery.*
*Owned by associated * Intership Navigation Co. Ltd (formed 1988 - www.intership-cyprus.com), Cyprus.*
'Frisia' vessels operate in United Container Carrier (UCC) pool formed in 2004. The company also operates smaller container ships in the Mini-Container Pool (MCP). The two large tankers operate in the Heidmar Inc controlled Blue Fin Pool. Also see United Product Tanker (UPT) pool under Schoeller Holdings Ltd

Leif Hoegh & Co Ltd Norway

Funnel: *White with blue/grey top and houseflag interrupting white band or ** dark blue/grey 'A' on broad white band between blue/grey bands above white base.* **Hull:** *Dark grey with dark blue 'HOEGH AUTOLINERS' on white superstructure, red boot-topping.*
History: *Founded 1927 as Leif Hoegh & Co. to 1938, Leif Hoegh & Co ASA to 2003 and Leif Hoegh & Co AS to 2006. Formed Hoegh-Ugland Auto Liners (HUAL) in 1968 jointly with Ugland International, but took complete control in 2000 and renamed as Hoegh Autoliners in 2005. Tanker and OBO vessels demerged into Bona Shipping AS in 1992. Acquired Cool Carriers in 1994, renamed Unicool in 1997 as joint venture with Safmarine, who withdrew in 1999, Cool Carriers subsequently sold to Lauritzen in 2001. Open-hatch activities transferred to Saga Forest Carriers and liner business sold in 2001. Moller-Maersk acquired 37.5% share in Hoegh Autoliners in 2008.* **Web:** *www.hoegh.no*

Name	Flag	Year	GRT	DWT	LOA	Bm	Kts	Type	Former names
Alliance New York **	Usa	2005	57,280	15,990	200	32	20	V	ex Hoegh New York-05, Hual New York-05
Alliance Norfolk	Usa	2007	57,280	21,500	200	32	20	V	
Alliance St Louis	Usa	2005	57,280	15,880	200	32	20	V	ex Hoegh Paris-08, Hual Paris-07
Arctic Lady (st) ‡	Nis	2006	121,597	74,400	288	49	19	Lng	
Arctic Princess ‡	Nis	2006	121,597	74,400	288	49	19	Lng	
City of Mumbai *	Sgp	1987	27,887	7,894	158	27	19	V	ex Hoegh Mumbai-08, Maersk Sun-08
Gandria (st) ‡	Nis	1977	96,011	71,630	288	43	19	Lng	ex Hoegh Gandria-08
Hoegh Asia	Bhs	2000	66,374	21,484	229	32	19	V	ex Hual Asia-06 (len-08)
Hoegh Bangkok ***	Nis	2007	55,775	16,632	200	32	20	V	
Hoegh Berlin	Nis	2005	66,364	16,006	229	32	20	V	(len-08)

Hartmann Schiffahrts. FRISIA LISSABON. *J. M. Kakebeeke*

Name	Flag	Year	GRT	DWT	LOA	Bm	Kts	Type	Former names
Hoegh Brasilia ****	Pan	2007	51,731	17,252	180	32	19	V	
Hoegh Chennai	Sgp	1987	27,887	7,902	158	27	19	V	ex Maersk Sea-08
Hoegh Chiba	Sgp	2006	52,691	21,500	199	32	19	V	ex Maersk Welkin-08
Hoegh Cochin	Sgp	1983	30,588	11,164	167	28	17	V	ex Maersk Cloud-08, Rich Victoria-89
Hoegh Delhi ***	Nis	2007	55,775	16,890	200	32	20	V	
Hoegh Detroit	Nis	2006	67,364	15,921	229	32	20	V	(len-08)
Hoegh Inchon	Sgp	1997	44,219	12,490	179	32	19	V	ex Maersk Tide -08
Hoegh Kobe	Sgp	2006	52,691	21,500	199	32	19	V	ex Maersk Wizard-08
Hoegh Kyoto	Sgp	2005	52,691	21,500	199	32	19	V	ex Maersk Willow-08
Hoegh Kunsan *	Sgp	1996	44,219	13,778	179	32	19	V	ex Maersk Taiyo-08
Hoegh London	Nis	2008	57,280	15,880	199	32	20	V	
Hoegh Manila	Nis	2007	51,964	17,252	180	32	19	V	
Hoegh Masan *	Sgp	1998	44,219	12,490	179	32	19	V	ex Maersk Teal-08
Hoegh Oslo	Nis	2008	51,964	17,252	180	32	19	V	
Hoegh Pusan *	Sgp	1998	44,219	13,695	179	32	19	V	ex Maersk Taiki-08
Hoegh Shanghai	Nis	2007	57,280	15,880	200	32	20	V	
Hoegh Sydney ****	Jpn	2007	51.731	17,311	180	32	19	V	
Hoegh Tokyo	Nis	2004	67,364	21,500	229	32	20	V	ex Hual Tokyo-06 (len-08)
Hoegh Tracer	Nis	1981	33,236	12,961	180	29	18	V	ex Hual Tracer-06, Tracer-95, Hual Tracer-94
Hoegh Trader	Bhs	1998	56,816	16,393	200	32	20	V	ex Hual Trader-06
Hoegh Tramper	Bhs	1980	33,369	12,169	180	29	17	V	ex Hual Tramper-06, Hual Rolita-00, ex Rolita-82
Hoegh Transit	Nis	1981	45,573	17,650	190	32	19	V	ex Hual Transit-05, Hual Transita-00, Kyushu-96, Kyushu Maru-88

Leif Hoegh & Co. HOEGH SHANGHAI. *C. Lous*

Leif Hoegh & Co. HOEGH SYDNEY. *Hans Kraijenbosch*

Name	Flag	Year	GRT	DWT	LOA	Bm	Kts	Type	Former names
Hoegh Transporter	Bhs	1999	57,757	21,300	200	32	20	V	ex Hual Transporter-06
Hoegh Trapeze	Nis	1983	41,871	15,500	180	31	17	V	ex Hual Trapeze-06, Hual Carmencita-00
Hoegh Trapper	Nis	1981	33,236	12,961	180	29	18	V	ex Hual Trapper-06
Hoegh Traveller	Nis	1983	35,022	15,370	180	29	18	V	ex Hual Traveller-05
Hoegh Treasure *	Bhs	1999	58,684	21,199	200	32	19	V	ex Hual Treasure-06, Hual Carolita-00
Hoegh Trekker	Nis	1981	33,374	11,977	180	29	17	V	ex Hual Trekker-06, Hual Angelita-00, Angelita-82
Hoegh Trident	Bhs	1995	56,164	21,423	200	32	20	V	ex Hual Trident—06
Hoegh Trinity	Nis	1981	45,365	17,938	190	32	19	V	ex Hual Trinity-05, Hual Trinita-00, Yokohama-95, Yokohama Maru-88
Hoegh Trooper	Bhs	1995	56,164	21,414	200	32	20	V	ex Hual Trooper-05
Hoegh Tropicana	Nis	1980	33,359	12,003	180	32	17	V	ex Hual Tropicana-05, Hual Lisita-00, Lisita-82
Hoegh Trotter	Nis	1983	35,022	15,370	180	29	18	V	ex Hual Trotter-05
Hoegh Trove	Bhs	2000	57,200	21,200	200	32	19	V	ex Hual Trove-05, Hual Maritita-00
Hoegh Trubadour	Nis	1980	33,369	12,165	180	29	17	V	ex Hual Trubadour-05, Hual Ingrita-00, Ingrita-82
Hual Seoul	Nis	2004	57,280	16,006	200	32	20	V	
Kiwi Auckland	Nis	1985	37,841	13,295	175	29	18	V	ex Cosmo Spirit-05, Excelsior-99, Young Skipper-91
Kiwi Breeze †	Pan	1978	20,961	8,494	157	25	18	V	ex Marico-99, Northern Highway-95
Maersk Wave	Sgp	2000	51,770	12,473	180	32	20	V	
Maersk Wind	Sgp	2000	51,720	12,473	180	32	20	V	
Morning Mercator	Bhs	1988	52,422	23,096	200	32	18	V	ex Hual Tricorn-04, Hual Champ-00, Auto Champ-00
Morning Meridian	Bhs	1988	52,422	23,052	200	32	18	V	ex Hual Triton-04, Auto Diana-00, l/a Auto Daewoo
Morning Rose	Nis	1980	45,007	15,603	194	32	18	V	ex Hual Trailer-04, Hual Karinita-00, Karinita-82
Norman Lady (st) ‡	Nis	1973	71,469	50,922	250	40	18	Lgc	

newbuildings: four 60,000 grt and two 57,000 grt vehicle carriers plus two 98,000 grt Lng tankers for 2009-11 delivery.
Managed by Hoegh Fleet Services AS, Norway (formed 1995), * by IUM Shipmanagement AS (www.ium.no), both Norway, ** by Liberty Maritime Corp, USA or † by Pacific Basin Ship Management Ltd, Hong Kong. ‡ jointly owned with Mitsui OSK Lines Ltd., Japan q.v.
*** managed for P D Gram & Co AS, Norway (founded 1982 – www.pdgram.com) **** owned by subsidiary of Tsuneishi Holdings Corp, Japan and managed by Astro Shipmanagement Inc, Philippines. See also Cido Shipping.

Hyundai Merchant Marine Co Ltd South Korea

Funnel: White with yellow edged green triangle. **Hull:** Blue with white 'HYUNDAI', red or pink boot-topping. **History:** Founded 1976 as subsidiary of Hyundai Corporation. **Web:** www.hmm21.com or www.hyundaicorp.com

Name	Flag	Year	GRT	DWT	LOA	Bm	Kts	Type	Former names
APL General	Kor	1996	64,054	68,378	275	40	25	CC	ex Hyundai General-07
Asian Jade	Pan	2005	57,164	106,062	244	42	14	T	ex KWK Jade-05
CMA CGM Courage **	Pan	2008	94,511	99,100	340	46	27	CC	ex Hyundai Courage-08
CMA CGM Force **	Pan	2008	94,511	99,000	340	46	27	CC	ex Hyundai Force-08
Global Victory *	Pan	1996	76,068	149,155	270	43	14	B	
Global Winner *	Pan	1997	81,152	161,121	280	45	14	B	
Hyundai Aquapia (st)	Pan	2000	113,998	77,564	289	48	20	Lng	
Hyundai Atlas	Kor	1995	76,068	149,310	270	43	13	B	
Hyundai Bangkok	Pan	2007	74,651	80,108	304	40	26	CC	
Hyundai Banner	Kor	1996	151,977	281,074	330	58	15	T	
Hyundai Brave **	Pan	2008	94,511	99,123	340	46	27	CC	
Hyundai Colombo	Pan	2007	74,651	80,108	340	40	26	CC	
Hyundai Confidence	Pan	2003	64,845	68,114	275	40	25	CC	
Hyundai Continental	Kor	1988	101,466	200,269	309	50	13	B	
Hyundai Cosmopia (st)	Pan	2000	113,998	77,591	289	48	20	Lng	
Hyundai Cosmos	Kor	1986	85,678	163,256	290	45	13	B	
Hyundai Dynasty	Pan	2008	52,581	63,254	294	32	25	CC	
Hyundai Ecopia	Kor	2008	99,600	83,959	288	44		Lng	
Hyundai Faith **	Pan	2008	94,511	98,967	340	46	27	CC	
Hyundai Forward **	Pan	2007	52,581	63,439	294	32	25	CC	
Hyundai Freedom	Pan	1996	64,054	68,363	275	40	25	CC	
Hyundai Glory	Pan	2004	53,352	63,404	294	32	25	CC	
Hyundai Goodwill	Pan	2008	52,581	63,439	294	32	25	CC	
Hyundai Grace **	Pan	2007	52,581	63,439	294	32	25	CC	
Hyundai Greenpia (st)	Pan	1996	103,764	71,684	274	47	19	Lng	
Hyundai Highness	Kor	1996	64,054	68,379	275	40	25	CC	
Hyundai Integal	Kor	2008	52,581	63,439	294	32	25	CC	
Hyundai Island	Kor	1986	67,897	127,852	274	43	12	B	
Hyundai Jakarta	Pan	2007	74,651	80.108	304	40	26	CC	
Hyundai Oceanpia (st)	Pan	2000	113,998	77,000	288	48	20	Lng	
Hyundai Olympia	Kor	1987	93,005	186,330	292	46	13	B	
Hyundai Power	Pan	1998	76,068	149,322	269	43	14	B	

Name	Flag	Year	GRT	DWT	LOA	Bm	Kts	Type	Former names
Hyundai Prosperity	Kor	1990	77,650	151,257	274	45	13	B	
Hyundai Spirit	Kor	1993	68,093	126,051	263	41	18	B	
Hyundai Star	Kor	1995	151,592	281,199	330	58	15	T	
Hyundai Sun	Pan	1998	156,692	301,178	330	58	15	T	
Hyundai Technopia (st)	Pan	1999	113,998	77,584	289	48	20	Lng	
Hyundai Unity **	Pan	2007	52,581	63,439	294	32	25	CC	
Hyundai Universal	Kor	1990	101,604	200,052	309	50	13	B	
Hyundai Utopia (st)	Kor	1994	103,764	71,909	274	47	18	Lng	
Hyundai Voyager	Pan	2008	52,581	64,220	294	32	25	CC	
Oriental Emerald *	Pan	2005	30,971	50,379	189	32	15	T	ex Ocean Globe-05
Oriental Ruby *	Pan	2005	30,971	50,375	189	32	15	T	ex Ocean Jupiter-05
Pacific Champ *	Pan	1996	25,503	43,229	185	31	14	B	
Pacific Courage *	Pan	1992	145,403	258,096	338	58	15	T	ex Stena Comfort-00, Wisteria-97
Pacific Royal *	Pan	1997	25,503	43,210	185	31	14	B	
Pacific Success	Kor	1989	24,790	38,412	186	28	14	B	
Pacific Superior *	Pan	1994	146,849	269,605	338	58	15	T	ex Apollo Akama-04
Universal Crown *	Pan	2005	163,465	309,316	333	60	15	T	
Universal Hope *	Pan	1993	158,475	299,700	344	56	14	T	ex Eugen Maersk-04, British Vigilance-02, Emma Maersk-97
Universal Peace **	Pan	1995	158,475	299,700	344	56	14	T	ex Emma Maersk-04, Ellen Maersk-97
Universal Queen *	Pan	2005	163,465	309,373	333	60	15	T	
VL Malibu †	Pan	1989	137,024	248,976	324	58	15	T	ex Nichioh-03

newbuildings: two 180,000 dwt bulk carriers, 61,000 grt vehicle carrier and 55,000 grt containr ship for 2009-11 delivery.
* managed by subsidiary Haeyoung Maritime Services Co. Ltd., South Korea, ** for Korea Ship Finance Co Ltd or † for Stealth Maritime Corp SA (Brave Maritime Corp Inc), Greece. See also Eukor Car Carriers Inc (under Wallenius Wilhelmsen)

International Shipholding Corporation USA

Central Gulf Lines Inc/USA
Funnel: White with blue symbol within blue ring, narrow black top or buff with 8-pointed white star on white edged broad red band or green with two broad white bands. **Hull:** Black with red boot-topping. **History:** Founded 1947 as Central Gulf SS Corp to 1974.
Web: www.intship.com www.waterman-steamship.com

Name	Flag	Year	GRT	DWT	LOA	Bm	Kts	Type	Former names
Asian Emperor **	Pan	1999	55,729	21,479	228	32	20	V	(len-06)
Asian King ‡	Pan	1998	55,729	21,511	200	32	19	V	
Bali Sea (2)	Sgp	1982	24,201	22,268	175	36	13	HLs	ex Super Servant 5-95, Dan Lifter-85 (len-95)
Banda Sea (2)	Sgp	1982	24,201	13,282	175	36	13	HLs	ex Super Servant 6-95, Dan Mover-85 (len-95)
Energy Enterprise (st)	Usa	1983	28,250	33,373	203	29	15	Bu	ex Energy Independence-96
Green Cove	Usa	1994	50,308	16,178	179	32	19	V	ex Shohjin-00
Green Bay *	Usa	2007	59,217	18,090	200	32	19	V	
Green Dale	Usa	1999	50,087	15,894	179	32	19	V	ex Altair Leader-99
Green Lake	Usa	1998	57,623	22,799	200	32	19	V	ex Cygnus Leader-01
Green Point	Usa	1994	51,819	14,930	180	32	19	V	ex Triton Diamond-98
Green Ridge	Usa	1998	57,449	21,523	200	32	19	V	ex Hercules Leader-05
Intra Bhum	Mhl	1984	23,790	29,730	183	31	17	CC	ex Buenos Aires-08, P&O Nedlloyd Buenos Aires-06, Nedlloyd van Noort-98

managed by LMS Shipmanagement Inc (founded 1997 as Lash Marine Services Inc) including for ISC subsidiaries * Waterman Steamship Corp (founded 1920) and ** LCI Shiphoilding Inc (founded 1997).

Interorient Navigation Co Ltd Cyprus

Funnel: Buff with blue 'IN' symbol inside blue ring. **Hull:** Black or light grey with red boot-topping. **History:** Formed 1977.
Web: www.interorient.com

Name	Flag	Year	GRT	DWT	LOA	Bm	Kts	Type	Former names
Arctic Bay *	Mlt	2006	30,053	50,921	183	32	14	T	ex West Point-06
Arctic Blizzard *	Mlt	2006	30,053	50,922	183	32	14	T	ex Baltic Point-06
Arctic Breeze *	Mlt	2006	30,053	50,922	183	32	14	T	ex Ice Point-06
Arctic Bridge *	Mlt	2005	30,053	50,930	183	32	14	T	ex Ice Point-06
Arctic Point *	Cyp	2003	23,235	37,197	183	27	14	T	l/a Baltic Adonia
Arya Payam	Cyp	2005	32,474	53,565	190	32	14	B	ex Bulk Voyager-05, Paracan-05
Arya Payk	Cyp	2006	32,474	53,565	190	32	14	B	ex Bulk Navigator-06
Atlantic Spirit	Cyp	2008	62,775	113,091	250	44	15	T	
Baltic Advance	Cyp	2006	23,240	37,332	183	27	14	T	
Baltic Ambition	Cyp	2006	23,240	37,343	183	27	14	T	
Baltic Captain I	Cyp	2000	23,235	37,389	183	27	14	T	ex Baltic Captain-02, l/a Androcles
Baltic Champion **	Mlt	2003	23,240	37,333	183	27	14	T	ex British Experience-07, Baltic Champion-05
Baltic Chief I	Cyp	2000	23,235	37,389	183	27	14	T	ex Baltic Chief-01, Baltic Carrier-01, l/a Armodius
Baltic Commander I *	Cyp	2000	23,235	37,418	183	27	14	T	ex Baltic Commander-02, l/a Antifon
Baltic Commodore **	Mlt	2003	23,240	37,343	183	27	14	T	ex British Engineer-07, Baltic Commodore-05
Baltic Faith	Cyp	2006	23,337	37,067	183	27	14	T	
Baltic Favour	Cyp	2006	23,337	37,106	183	27	14	T	

Name	Flag	Year	GRT	DWT	LOA	Bm	Kts	Type	Former names
Baltic Force	Cyp	2006	23,337	37,039	183	27	14	T	
Baltic Freedom	Cyp	2006	23,337	37,048	183	27	14	T	
Baltic Front	Cyp	2006	23,337	37,340	183	27	14	T	
Baltic Mariner	Cyp	2006	23,240	37,304	183	27	14	T	
Baltic Marshall	Cyp	2006	23,240	37,304	183	27	14	T	
Baltic Merchant	Cyp	2006	23,240	37,304	183	27	14	T	
Baltic Monarch	Cyp	2006	23,240	37,273	183	27	14	T	
Baltic Sky I *	Mlt	2001	23,235	37,272	183	27	14	T	ex Flores-06, Flores I-01
Baltic Soul *	Mlt	2001	23,235	37,244	183	27	14	T	ex Sicilia-06
Baltic Sun II *	Mlt	2005	23,235	37,305	183	27	15	T	ex Baltic Sun-05
Baltic Wave *	Mlt	2003	23,235	37,300	183	27	15	T	ex Prostar-05, Ice Point-03
Baltic Wind *	Mlt	2003	23,235	37,296	183	27	15	T	ex Prosky-05
Champion	Deu	1997	31,207	38,400	210	32	22	CC	ex CMA CGM Dardanelles-08, Indamex Delaware-04, Champion-03, Contship Champion-02, I/a Telendos
CMA CGM Maasai *	Gib	1995	14,961	20,406	167	25	19	CC	ex Sea Navigator-08, Indamex Mississippi-01, Sea Navigator-00, Nauplius-99, TNX Sprint-98, Zim Brasil-98, Energy-97, Nauplius-95
Conti Harmony *	Cyp	1997	31,207	38,400	210	32	22	CC	ex Contship Innovator-02, Contship Harmony-99, Conti Harmony-97, I/a Timarchos
Giannutri *	Mlt	2004	23,235	37,272	183	27	14	T	
Glacier Point *	Cyp	2003	23,235	37,389	183	27	15	T	ex Baltic Sea-03
Ice Base	Cyp	2008	38,899	63,605	228	32	15	T	
Ice Beam	Cyp	2008	38,899	63,495	228	32	15	T	
Ice Blade	Cyp	2008	38,899	63,599	228	32	15	T	
Kerel **	Mlt	2002	23,235	37,272	183	27	14	T	
Leander	Pan	1999	159,187	308,491	333	58	15	T	ex Elisabeth Maersk-06
Nautic	Cyp	1996	31,207	38,400	210	32	22	CC	ex Norasia Telamon-07, Telamon-04, Contship Ambition-03, Telamon-96
Norasia Tegesos **	Cyp	1996	31,207	38,400	210	32	22	CC	ex Tegesos-04, Contship Action-03, Tegesus-97
Nordamerika *	Mhl	2000	23,740	35,775	183	27	14	T	
Norient Saturn *	Cyp	2007	25,864	40,435	180	32	15	T	I/a Nordic Saturn
Norient Scorpius *	Mlt	2009	25,814	40,400	180	32	15	T	
Norient Solar *	Mlt	2008	25,864	40,429	180	32	15	T	
Norient Star *	Mlt	2008	25,814	40,400	180	32	15	T	
Pacific Spirit	Cyp	2008	62,775	113,010	250	44	15	T	
Peterpaul ‡	Cyp	1998	19,257	35,994	175	30	15	T	ex Formosa Nine-07
Polar †	Pan	2005	40,690	72,825	229	32	15	T	

newbuildings: eight 115,000 dwt and sixteen 30,500 dwt bulk carriers, four 156,000 dwt, four 114,000 dwt, three 62,000 dwt, six 46,600 dwt and four 37,250 dwt tankers for 2009-11 delivery.
Managed by Interorient Marine Services Ltd, Cyprus, except * owned or managed by subsidiary Interorient Navigation (Germany) GmbH & Co KG, Germany (formed 1995 as Interorient Navigation Hamburg GmbH to 2000 and INC Interorient Navigation Hamburg GmbH & Co KG to 2007).
** managed for Gebab Conzeptions-und Emissions GmbH, Germany or ‡ for Locat Locazione Attrezzature SpA, Italy
† managed by Paradise Navigation SA, Greece. See also Konig & Cir GmbH & Co KG.

Islamic Republic of Iran Shipping Lines   Iran

Funnel: Red base with broad white band below green top. **Hull:** Light grey or black with black or white 'IRISL' and red boot-topping.
History: Founded 1967 as Arya National Shipping Lines to 1980, then Iran National Shipping Lines to 1981. **Web:** wwwirisl.net

Name	Flag	Year	GRT	DWT	LOA	Bm	Kts	Type	Former names
Accurate	Hkg	1986	25,770	43,365	190	30	14	B	ex Drifter-09, Iran Abozar-08
Adventist	Hkg	1985	25,768	43,345	190	30	14	B	ex Iran Madani-08
Ajax	Hkg	1985	25,768	43,442	190	30	14	B	ex Dynasty-08, Iran Ghazi-08
Alameda	Hkg	1986	25,770	43,480	190	30	14	B	ex Dolphin-09, Iran Ghodousi-08
Angel	Hkg	1985	25,768	43,342	190	30	14	B	ex Dapper-09, Iran Ashrafi-08
Anil	Hkg	1986	25,768	40,345	191	30	14	B	ex Dandy-09, Iran Eghbal-08
Anoosh	Irn	1979	20,672	35,839	180	28	15	B	ex Iran Azadi-09, Oinoussian Friendship-81
Apollo	Hkg	1986	25,768	43,342	190	30	14	B	ex Destiny-09, Iran Navab-08
Aquarian	Irn	1985	25,768	43,309	190	30	14	B	ex Dignified-09, Iran Chamran-08
Assa	Irn	1978	20,811	35,896	180	28	15	B	ex Iran Entekhab-08, Oinoussian Prestige 81
Azim	Mlt	2008	31,117	53,100	190	32	14	B	ex Iran Azim-09
Barsam	Irn	1983	25,168	44,468	200	29	15	B	ex Iran Shariat-09, Thorlock-84
Daffodil *	Mlt	2000	36,014	41,962	240	32	22	CC	ex Eleventh Ocean-08, Iran Hormozgan-07
Dais	Hkg	1985	25,768	40,422	190	30	14	B	ex Iran Shariati-08
Dandelion	Mlt	2000	36,014	41,937	240	32	22	CC	ex New State-08, Iran Tehran-08
Dandle *	Mlt	2000	36,014	41,971	240	32	22	CC	ex Twelfth Ocean-08, Iran Isfahan-07
Decker	Mlt	2008	75,595	81,112	304	40	25	CC	ex Fifth Ocean-09, Iran Atrak-08
Decorous	Irn	1985	25,768	43,369	190	30	14	B	ex Iran Ghafari-08
Decretive	Mlt	2008	75,395	79,030	304	40	25	CC	ex Sixth Ocean-08, Iran Tajan-08
Delegate	Hkg	1985	25,768	43,265	190	30	14	B	ex Iran Sadr-08
Delight	Irn	1985	25,768	40,422	190	30	14	B	ex Iran Jamal-08

Name	Flag	Year	GRT	DWT	LOA	Bm	Kts	Type	Former names
Developer	Hkg	1985	25,768	43,309	190	30	14	B	ex Iran Taleghani-08
Devotee	Hkg	1984	25,768	43,309	190	30	14	B	ex Iran Kashani-08
Devotional	Hkg	1985	25,768	43,369	190	30	14	B	ex Iran Eshraghi-08
Diamond	Hkg	1984	25,768	43,369	190	30	14	B	ex Iran Dastghayb-08
Dinna	Irn	1978	13,917	17,970	170	23	18	C	ex Iran Broojerdi-08, Arastou-93, Merbabu-86, Rheinbels-83, Strathelgin-82
Diplomat	Hkg	1985	25,768	43,262	190	30	14	B	ex Iran Mufateh-08
Dreamland	Hkg	1986	25,768	43,369	190	30	14	B	ex Iran Saeidi-08
Dynamize	Hkg	1985	25,768	43,369	190	30	14	B	ex Iran Sadoughi-08
Eighth Ocean *	Mlt	1998	15,670	22,882	168	26	16	Co	ex Iran Baakeri-07
First Ocean *	Mlt	2008	74,175	85,896	299	40		CC	
Fourth Ocean *	Mlt	2008	74,200	82,200	299	40		CC	
Gabion *	Mlt	1998	15,670	22,882	168	26	16	Co	ex Seventh Ocean-08, Iran Sattari-07
Galax *	Mlt	1998	15,670	22,882	168	26	16	Co	ex Ninth Ocean-09, Iran Hesabi-07
Garland	Mlt	1999	15,670	22,882	168	26	16	Co	ex Lucky Man-08, Iran Shahryar-08
Gladiolus *	Mlt	1998	15,670	22,882	168	26	16	Co	ex Tenth Ocean-08, Iran Baabael-07
Glory	Mlt	2008	41,226	76,500	225	32		B	
Goldenrod	Mlt	1998	15,670	22,621	168	26	16	Co	ex Lucky Lily-09, Iran Tabataei-08
Graceful	Mlt	2008	41,226	76,500	225	32		B	
Haadi	Mlt	2008	32,474	53,442	190	32		B	
Iran Adi	Irn	1983	22,027	37,537	186	28	15	B	ex World Fraternity-84
Iran Afzal	Irn	1983	22,027	37,588	186	28	15	B	ex Manila Faith-84, Primelock-83
Iran Akhavan	Irn	1984	20,576	34,859	198	24	15	B	ex Philippine Success-84
Iran Amanat	Irn	1983	20,576	34,859	198	24	15	B	ex Manila Pride-84
Iran Ardebil	Irn	2004	25,369	37,875	207	30	22	CC	
Iran Azarbayjan	Irn	2000	39,424	72,642	225	32	14	B	
Iran Baghaei	Irn	1979	12,775	17,970	170	23	18	C	ex Ydra-93, Almas-92, Tannenbels-86, Stratherrol-82
Iran Bam	Mlt	2006	40,166	73,664	225	32	14	B	
Iran Beheshti	Irn	1979	22,048	39,026	205	26	15	T	ex Selma-82
Iran Birjand	Mlt	2006	40,166	73,664	225	32	14	B	
Iran Bojnoord	Mlt	2005	40,166	73,518	225	32	14	B	
Iran Esteghial	Irn	1978	20,811	35,839	180	28	15	B	ex Oinoussian Virtue-81
Iran Fars	Irn	2004	25,391	33,702	207	30	22	CC	
Iran Gilan	Mlt	2000	39,424	63,400	225	32	14	B	
Iran Golestan	Irn	2001	39,517	72,162	225	32	14	B	
Iran Hamedan	Irn	2001	39,517	72,162	225	32	14	B	
Iran Hamzeh	Irn	1986	25,770	43,288	190	30	14	B	
Iran Ilam	Irn	2004	25,369	37,600	207	30	22	CC	
Iran Jomhuri	Irn	1978	20,811	35,830	180	28	15	B	ex Oinoussian Leadership-81
Iran Kashan	Irn	2007	23,200	29,870	207	30	22	CC	
Iran Kermanshah	Cyp	2001	40,609	75,249	225	32	14	B	ex Cape Tenaron-03
Iran Khorasan	Irn	2000	39,424	72,622	225	32	14	B	
Iran Mahallati	Irn	1978	13,914	16,905	170	23	18	C	ex Lindenbels-88, Strathewe-82
Iran Matin	Irn	1996	16,621	22,948	174	26	16	Co	
Iran Mazandaran	Irn	2000	39,424	72,642	225	32	14	B	
Iran Modares	Irn	1977	20,049	33,667	182	27	15	B	ex Gentle River-83, Treana-78
Iran Sarbaz	Irn	1984	20,576	34,859	198	24	15	B	
Iran Sepah	Irn	1976	19,701	33,856	186	26	14	B	ex Ocean Cosmos-84
Iran Teyfouri	Irn	1979	16,173	23,720	159	25	16	Co	ex Simba-84
Iran Yasooj	Irn	2004	25,369	33,850	207	30	20	CC	
Iran Yazd	Cyp	2001	40,609	72,642	225	32	14	B	ex Cape Race-03
Karim	Mlt	2008	31,117	63,100	190	32	14	B	ex Iran Karim-08
Lantana	Mlt	1999	16,694	23,176	174	26	16	Co	ex Ocean Candle-09, Iran Lorestan-08
Lavender	Mlt	1999	16,694	23,116	174	26	16	Co	ex Pretty Sea-08, Iran Khuzestan-08
Lilied	Mlt	1999	16,694	23,116	174	26	16	Co	ex Sea State-08, Iran Kordestan-08
Limnetic	Mlt	1999	16,694	23,176	174	26	16	Co	ex Sea Flower-08, Iran Seestan-08
Lodestar	Mlt	2000	16,694	22,600	174	26	16	Co	ex Sea Bloom-08, Iran Baluchestan-08
Margrave	Mlt	1997	16,621	24,065	174	26	17	Co	ex Brave-08, Iran Makin-08
Marigold	Mlt	1996	16,621	22,982	174	26	16	Co	ex Brightness-08, Iran Mobin-08
Markarid	Irn	1983	25,168	44,468	200	29	15	B	ex Iran Deyanat-08, Odinlock-84
Mulberry	Mlt	1996	16,621	22,967	174	26	17	Co	ex Brilliance-08, Iran Yamin-08
Ragga	Irn	1983	21,959	40,325	176	32	14	T	ex Iran Bahonar-09, Cleon-83
Rahim	Mlt	2008	31,117	53,100	190	32	14	B	ex Iran Rahim-08
Raika	Irn	1983	22,097	40,367	176	32	14	T	ex Iran Rajai-09, Ferncraig-83
Sabalan	Mlt	2008	53,453	66,900	294	32		CC	l/a Iran Sabalan
Sahand	Mlt	2008	53,453	66,900	294	32		CC	l/a Iran Sahand
Sakas	Irn	2003	25,369	33,853	207	30	22	CC	ex Iran Piroozi-08
Second Ocean *	Mlt	2009	74,200	82,200	299	40		CC	
Sepitam	Irn	2004	27,681	37,600	222	30	22	CC	ex Iran Ilam-09
Shaafi	Mlt	2008	32,474	53,000	190	32	14	B	

Name	Flag	Year	GRT	DWT	LOA	Bm	Kts	Type	Former names
Shere	Mlt	2005	40,166	73,586	225	32	14	B	ex Iran Tabas-08
Silver Craft	Mlt	2000	36,014	41,978	240	32	22	CC	ex Iran Kerman-09
Silver Zone	Mlt	2004	23,285	30,146	207	30	20	CC	ex Iran Bushehr-08
Third Ocean *	Mlt	2009	74,200	82,200	299	40		CC	
Tuchal	Mlt	2008	54,851	66,441	294	32		CC	
Vaafi	Mlt	2008	32,474	53,000	190	32	14	B	
Visea	Irn	2003	25,391	33,757	207	30	22	CC	ex Iran Zanjan-09
Vobster	Mlt	2006	40,160	73,664	225	32	14	B	ex Persian Gulf-08
Zagros	Mlt	2009	53,453	54,340	294	32		CC	I/a Iran Sabalan
Zaven	Irn	1978	16,173	23,720	159	25	16	Co	ex Iran Takhti-09, Sargodha-84

newbuildings: seven 75,000 dwt, fourteen 53,500 dwt and nine 35,000 dwt bulk carriers, ten 37,500 dwt tankers, eight 28,000 dwt general cargo, five 23,200 grt container ships for 2009-11 delivery.
* managed for subsidiary IRISL Europe GmbH, Germany.

Irano-Hind Shipping Co Ltd/Iran

Funnel: *Black with green/brown diagonally quartered flag with white 'I' and 'H' in upper and lower quarters respectively or * blue.*
Hull: *Black with red boot-topping.* **History:** *Formed 1974 with The Shipping Corp of India Ltd (49%).* **Web:** *www.iranohind.com*

Name	Flag	Year	GRT	DWT	LOA	Bm	Kts	Type	Former names
Attar	Mlt	1994	25,885	43,706	186	30	14	B	ex Parisian Trader-00
ISI Olive *	Mlt	1992	81,135	141,861	274	48	14	T	ex Mastera-02
Sattar	Mlt	1992	24,155	43,419	185	31	14	B	ex Belstar-01
Teen	Mlt	1995	26,828	43,671	190	31	14	B	ex Oriental Dream-03, Eun Ji-97
Tour *	Mlt	2007	81,295	158,817	274	48	14	T	

newbuildings: two 159,000 dwt tankers for 2010 delivery.
* managed by International Tanker Management Holding Ltd, UAE (www.tankermanager.com)

Ernst Jacob GmbH & Co KG   Germany

Funnel: *Black, white diagonal cross on broad blue band with blue 'J' on white centre diamond or charterers colours.* **Hull:** *Grey or red with red boot-topping or white with blue boot-topping.* **History:** *Founded 1955.* **Web:** *www.ernstjacob.de*

Name	Flag	Year	GRT	DWT	LOA	Bm	Kts	Type	Former names
Ariadne Jacob *	Cym	2007	42,403	74,875	228	32	14	T	
Chaleur Bay *	Cym	2000	40,705	71,345	229	32	14	T	
Chinook *	Mhl	2001	24,252	38,695	189	28	14	T	ex Glasgow-01, I/a Calinesti
Colin Jacob *	Cym	2007	42,403	74,896	228	32	14	T	
Four Schooner *	Cym	2000	40,037	73,083	229	32	15	T	
Four Smile *	Cym	2001	81,236	160,573	274	48	14	T	
Four Sun *	Cym	2003	81,236	160,292	274	48	14	T	
Ice Blizzard	Cyp	2008	38,899	63,589	228	32	14	T	
Jill Jacob *	Cym	2003	40,037	72,909	229	32	15	T	ex Four Clipper-04
Johann Jacob *	Cym	2000	40,037	73,001	229	32	15	T	ex Four Brig-04
Kim Jacob *	Lbr	1998	81,265	159,211	274	48	15	T	ex Celebes-98
Los Roques *	Cym	2000	40,705	61,130	229	32	15	T	
Margara *	Cym	1999	40,705	60,913	229	32	14	T	
Max Jacob *	Deu	2000	81,565	157,449	274	48	14	T	ex Soyang-01
Oliver Jacob **	Lbr	1999	81,565	157,326	274	48	14	T	ex Columbia-02
Santa Ana *	Cym	2002	24,252	39,768	190	28	14	T	ex Greenock-02, I/a Diamant
Tanya Jacob *	Cym	2003	40,037	73,004	229	32	15	T	ex Four Ketch-07
Urals Princess †	Lbr	2006	63,619	114,847	254	44		T	
Urals Star †	Lbr	2006	63,619	114,847	254	44		T	

* managed for Hansa Hamburg Shipping International GmbH & Co KG, ** for Salamon AG or † for Hamburg Tankers GmbH, all Germany.

Kristian Gerhard Jebsen Skipsrederi AS   Norway

Funnel: *Black with white pennant flag on blue band.* **Hull:** *Black with red boot-topping.* **History:** *Formed 1967.* **Web:** *www.kgjs.no*

Name	Flag	Year	GRT	DWT	LOA	Bm	Kts	Type	Former names
Avocet Arrow	Bhs	1985	27,470	39,239	199	30	15	Boh	ex City of Alberni-98, Belwood-93
Barbet Arrow	Bhs	1985	27,470	39,260	199	30	15	Boh	ex City of New Westminster-98, Belforest-93
CHL Innovator †	Sgp	1976	19,426	26,931	175	26	15	B	ex Rodney-86, Cape Rodney-85
CHL Progressor †	Sgp	1985	32,333	48,251	189	32	-	B	ex Therassia-89
Cotinga Arrow *	Bhs	1987	28,805	45,252	200	31	15	Boh	ex Westwood Anette-07
Cozumel Cement	Bhs	1984	18,102	27,145	195	23	14	Ce	ex Dania Portland-04, Sea Prosperity-86
Gannet Arrow	Bhs	1985	27,470	39,260	199	30	15	Boh	ex City of Nanaimo-98, Beltimber-93
Jaeger Arrow	Bhs	2001	29,103	24,101	171	25	18	Cp	
Pipit Arrow	Bhs	1974	25,931	38,636	182	29	14	Boh	ex Toki-05, Toki Arrow-99
Swan Arrow *	Bhs	1987	28,805	45,295	200	31	15	Boh	ex Norsul America-04, Westwood Jago-03
Tinamou Arrow *	Bhs	1986	28,805	45,295	200	31	15	Boh	ex Westwood Marianne-07
Tsuru Arrow *	Bhs	1987	28,805	45,295	200	31	15	Boh	ex Norsul Vancouver-04, Westwood Cleo-02

newbuildings: four 82,000 grt 159,000 dwt tankers and one 13,100 grt bitumen tanker (Sunbird Arrow) on order for 2006-7 delivery.
* managed by Bernhard Schulte Shipmanagement (Cyprus) Ltd.
† managed for CHL Shipping BV, Netherlands (subsidiary of TNT Shipping & Development Ltd., Australia)

Name	Flag	Year	GRT	DWT	LOA	Bm	Kts	Type	Former names

Gearbulk Holding Ltd/Bermuda

Funnel: *Black with large white 'G'.* **Hull:** *Black with white 'GEARBULK', red boot-topping.* **History:** *Associated company founded 1968 as Gearbulk Ltd to 1991 and 40% owned by Mitsui OSK. Acquired Borgestad Shipping AS in 2006.* **Web:** *www.gearbulk.com*

Name	Flag	Year	GRT	DWT	LOA	Bm	Kts	Type	Former names
Alouette Arrow	Bhs	1980	12,688	14,602	159	21	16	Cp	ex Chimo-94, Finnarctis-91
Apalis Arrow	Bhs	1983	30,767	42,149	208	32	14	Boh	ex Emerald Coast-98, Star Everwin-87, Everwin-83
Aracari Arrow	Nis	1992	29,369	46,956	199	31	15	Boh	ex Bridge Arrow-08, Westwood Bridge-05, Saga River-03, Sea River-92
Aspen Arrow	Bhs	1985	18,993	28,030	170	28	14	Co	ex Sharpnes-05
Auk Arrow	Bhs	1984	27,962	43,952	188	29	13	Boh	ex Heina-91
Bergen Arrow	Bhs	1984	25,063	38,800	182	29	14	Boh	ex Bergen Thistle-86
Canelo Arrow	Bhs	1997	32,520	48,077	187	31	14	Boh	
Cedar Arrow	Bhs	2001	32,458	47,818	190	31	14	Boh	
Condor Arrow	Bhs	1979	25,846	38,618	182	29	15	Boh	ex Molda-81
Cormorant Arrow	Bhs	1986	28,005	43,074	188	29	13	Boh	
Crane Arrow	Bhs	1984	27,818	42,913	188	29	14	Boh	ex Chelsfield-89
Dunlin Arrow	Bhs	1986	27,012	38,760	183	29	13	Boh	ex Aris-04, Rio Acre-93
Eagle Arrow	Bhs	1977	30,719	45,063	201	31	15	Boh	ex Norsul Bahia-04, Cielo d'Europa-01, Star Europa-96, Cielo d'Europa-91, Star Mallard-89, Hoegh Mallard-87
Emu Arrow	Bhs	1997	36,008	51,419	200	32	14	Boh	
Falcon Arrow ***	Bhs	1986	28,805	45,295	200	31	15	Boh	ex Norsul Europa-04, Westwood Belinda-03
Finch Arrow	Bhs	1984	26,130	39,273	183	29	13	Boh	ex Francois LD-90

Kristian Gerhard Jebsen (Gearbulk). JAEGER ARROW. *C. Lous*

Kristian Gerhard Jebsen (Gearbulk). WEAVER ARROW. *Allan Ryszka Onions*

Name	Flag	Year	GRT	DWT	LOA	Bm	Kts	Type	Former names
Grebe Arrow	Bhs	1997	35,998	51,633	200	32	16	Boh	
Grouse Arrow	Bhs	1991	44,398	42,276	185	30	15	Boh	
Gull Arrow	Bhs	1982	25,846	38,787	182	29	16	Boh	ex Horda-91
Harefield	Bhs	1985	27,818	41,651	188	29	13	Boh	
Hawk Arrow	Bhs	1985	28,092	40,269	188	29	14	Boh	
Hornbill Arrow	Bhs	1980	21,139	31,247	180	28	15	Boh	ex Star Bettina-05, Alberni Dawn-03
Ibis Arrow	Bhs	1986	28,239	42,497	188	29	14	Boh	ex Singapore Express-91, Ibis Arrow-91
Jacamar Arrow *	Nis	1992	29,369	46,998	199	31	15	Boh	ex Borg Arrow-06, Westwood Borg-04, Spero-98, Saga Ocean-95
Kestrel Arrow	Bhs	1983	30,767	42,149	208	32	15	Boh	ex Jade Forest-98, Star Everace-87, Everace-83
Kite Arrow	Bhs	1997	36,008	51,800	200	32	16	Boh	
Kiwi Arrow	Bhs	1981	27,069	38,695	182	29	14	Boh	
Mandarin Arrow *	Bhs	1996	35,998	51,733	200	32	16	Boh	
Merlin Arrow	Bhs	1999	36,008	51,459	200	32	15	Boh	ex Tolten-04
Mozu Arrow	Bhs	1992	44,398	42,276	185	30	15	Boh	
Nandu Arrow	Bhs	1978	25,063	38,618	182	29	14	Boh	
Osprey Arrow	Bhs	1985	27,938	42,596	188	29	13	Boh	
Pelican Arrow	Bhs	1982	25,846	38,787	182	29	16	Boh	ex Folga-91
Penguin Arrow	Bhs	1997	36,008	51,738	200	32	16	Boh	
Petersfield	Bhs	1985	27,818	41,646	188	29	13	Boh	
Petrel Arrow	Bhs	1985	27,824	42,964	188	29	14	Boh	ex Alain LD-90
Pine Arrow	Bhs	1996	32,520	48,041	190	31	14	Boh	
Plover Arrow	Bhs	1997	36,008	51,880	200	32	14	Boh	
Poplar Arrow	Bhs	2005	35,250	47,818	190	31	14	Boh	
Puffin Arrow	Bhs	1981	27,069	38,695	183	29	13	Boh	ex Brierfield-89, La Sierra-83
Quetzal Arrow	Nis	1992	29,369	46,908	199	31	15	Boh	ex Breeze Arrow-08, Westwood Breeze-03, Saga Breeze-98
Raven Arrow	Bhs	1981	24,855	38,771	182	29	14	Boh	
Rhein	Bhs	1979	26,948	38,596	183	29	14	Boh	ex Maya-89, Sun Maya-86, Charles LD-83
Rhone	Bhs	1978	26,204	38,542	182	29	16	Boh	ex Rokko-89, Sun Rokko-86, La Cordillera-83
Siskin Arrow	Bhs	1985	26,130	39,151	183	29	14	Boh	ex Monique LD-90
Spruce Arrow	Bhs	2002	32,458	47,818	190	31	14	Boh	
Sun Suma	Bhs	1978	26,204	38,542	182	29	16	Boh	ex La Costa-84
Sunbird Arrow	Bhs	2005	12,959	15,002	144	24	14	Ta	
Swift Arrow	Bhs	1992	44,398	42,276	185	30	15	Boh	
Tawa Arrow	Pan	2008	31,600	53,560	190	32		Boh	
Teal Arrow	Bhs	1984	27,962	43,002	188	29	13	Boh	ex Lista-91
Tern Arrow	Bhs	1986	28,239	42,570	188	29	14	Boh	
Toki Arrow	Bhs	1980	21,139	31,247	180	28	17	Boh	ex Harmac Dawn-04
Toucan Arrow	Bhs	1996	35,998	51,880	200	32	16	Boh	
Weaver Arrow	Bhs	1997	36,008	51,364	200	32	14	Boh	
Westfield	Bhs	1985	27,818	41,619	188	29	13	Boh	
Windfield	Bhs	1980	26,942	38,715	183	29	14	Boh	ex Pierre LD-86
Wren Arrow	Bhs	1985	27,824	41,637	188	29	13	Boh	ex Charles LD-90

newbuildings: four 71,220 dwt and four 55,500 dwt open-hatch bulk carriers for 2010-12 delivery.
Vessels owned by Gearbulk Shipowning Ltd, Norway or * by Gearbulk Shipping AS, Norway and ** managed by Borgestad Shipmanagement AS, Norway or *** by Bernhard Schulte Shipmanagement (Cyprus) Ltd.

SKS OBO Holding Ltd & SKS Tankers Ltd/Bermuda

Funnel: *Pale green with white 'SKS' on broad red band, narrow black top.* **Hull:** *Red with green boot-topping.* **History:** *Founded 1996 jointly with Nordship AS subsidiary of CSAV to 2004.* **Web:** www.sksobo.com

Name	Flag	Year	GRT	DWT	LOA	Bm	Kts	Type	Former names
SKS Mersey	Nis	2003	70,933	120,499	250	44	15	Obo	
SKS Mosel	Nis	2003	70,933	121,000	250	44	15	Obo	
SKS Saluda *	Nis	2003	81,270	159,438	274	50	15	T	
SKS Satilla	Nis	2006	81,380	158,842	274	48	15	T	
SKS Segura	Nis	2007	81,380	158,784	274	48	15	T	
SKS Senne *	Mhl	2003	81,270	159,385	274	48	15	T	
SKS Sinni *	Nis	2003	81,270	159,385	274	48	15	T	
SKS Sira *	Mhl	2002	81,270	159,453	274	48	15	T	
SKS Skeena	Nis	2006	81,380	158,943	274	48	15	T	
SKS Spey	Nis	2007	81,380	158,842	274	48	15	T	
SKS Tagus	Nis	1997	63,515	109,933	244	42	15	Obo	
SKS Tana	Nis	1996	63,515	109,906	244	42	14	Obo	
SKS Tanaro	Nis	1999	63,515	109,787	244	42	14	Obo	
SKS Tiete	Nis	1999	63,515	109,773	244	42	14	Obo	
SKS Torrens	Nis	1999	63,515	109,846	244	42	14	Obo	
SKS Trent	Nis	1997	63,515	109,832	244	42	15	Obo	
SKS Trinity	Nis	1999	63,515	109,798	244	42	14	Obo	
SKS Tugela	Nis	1997	63,515	109,913	244	42	15	Obo	
SKS Tweed	Nis	1996	63,515	109,832	244	42	15	Obo	

Name	Flag	Year	GRT	DWT	LOA	Bm	Kts	Type	Former names
SKS Tyne	Nis	1996	63,515	109,891	244	42	14	Obo	

newbuildings: eight 119,950 dwt tankers for 2009-11 delivery.
managed by V.Ships Norway A/S or by Columbia Shipmanagement (Deutschland) GmbH.
* 40% owned by subsidiaries of Konig & Cie GmbH & Co KG (managed by Columbia Shipmanagement (Deutschland) GmbH)

Jungerhans Maritime Services GmbH & Co KG   Germany

Funnel: *White with pale blue 'J' inside pale blue diamond outline between two narrow pale blue bands or charterers colours.*
Hull: *Black or grey with red boot-topping.* **History:** *Founded 1983 as Reederei Heinrich Jungerhans to 1995, then Jungerhans & Co Reedereiverwaltung OHG to 2003.* **Web:** *www.juengerhans.de*

Name	Flag	Year	GRT	DWT	LOA	Bm	Kts	Type	Former names
ACX Plumeria	Deu	1997	18,233	26,260	177	28	20	CC	ex City of Stuttgart-05, Klaus J-02, Irma Delmas-02, Maersk San Antonio-99, TNX Express-98, Aldebaren-97, l/a Klaus J
CMA CGM Montenegro	Atg	1997	18,233	26,260	178	28	20	CC	ex Helene J-07, Clan Praetorian-07, Helene J-05, ANL Oryx-03, Helene J-02, Fesco Express-00, Maersk Manzanillo-99, TNX Sprint-98, Antares-97, Helene J-97
Delmas Lisboa	Atg	2002	14,062	18,832	156	25	19	CC	ex Maersk Rostock-07, l/a Taurus J-03
Libra J	Atg	1998	12,004	14,174	149	23	19	CC	ex Tausala Samoa-05, l/a Libra J
Maersk Ravenna	Atg	2001	14,062	18,400	156	25	18	CC	l/a Auriga J
Maersk Rio Grande	Atg	2002	16,129	16,794	161	25	19	CC	ex Corona J-02
Maersk Rosario	Atg	2003	16,129	16,824	161	25	19	CC	ex Crux J-03
Maersk Rotterdam	Atg	2002	14,062	18,400	156	25	18	CC	l/a Antares J

Kristian Gerhard Jebsen (SKS OBO). SKS TIETE. *J. M. Kakebeeke*

Kahn Scheepvaart. JUMBO JAVELIN. *Hans Kraijenbosch*

Kahn Scheepvaart BV   Netherlands

Funnel: *White with red elephant and red/blue eight-pointed star between narrow green bands.* **Hull:** *Dark blue with white web address, red boot-topping.* **History:** *Founded 1956 and subsidiary Jumbo Shipping Co formed 1969.* **Web:** *www.jumboshipping.nl*

Name	Flag	Year	GRT	DWT	LOA	Bm	Kts	Type	Former names
Fairpartner	Ant	2004	15,071	11,350	143	27	17	HL	
Finnplayer	Ant	2008	15,027	13,278	145	27	17	HL	
Jumbo Javelin	Ant	2004	15,022	12,870	143	27	17	HL	
Jumbo Jubilee	Nld	2008	15,022	12,870	145	27	17	HL	

Also owns ten smaller heavy-lift vessels.

Kawasaki Kisen KK ('K' Line)   Japan

Funnel: *Bright red with white 'K', above grey base.* **Hull:** *Grey with red boot-topping.* **History:** *Formed 1919 as Kawasaki Kisen Kaisha and merged 1964 with Iino Kisen Kaisha (formed 1918). Taiyo Nippon Kisen subsidiary formed 2000 by merger of Taiyo Kaiun KK with Kobe Nippon KK (founded 1917).* **Web:** *www.kline.co.jp*

Name	Flag	Year	GRT	DWT	LOA	Bm	Kts	Type	Former names
Adriatic Highway	Pan	2008	58,990	18,869	200	32	20	V	
Aegean Highway	Pan	2008	60,320	18,867	200	32	20	V	
Akashi Bridge	Pan	1993	48,237	47,425	277	32	24	CC	
Akinada Bridge	Pan	2001	68,687	71,366	285	40	25	CC	
American Highway	Pan	2000	49,212	16,750	179	32	20	V	
Arcadia Highway	Pan	1994	49,012	15,507	180	32	20	V	
Athens Highway	Pan	2008	59,440	18,809	200	32	20	V	
Atlantic Highway	Pan	2002	55,493	17,232	200	32	20	V	
Atlas Highway	Lbr	1987	45,742	14,487	180	32	20	V	
Baltic Highway	Pan	2001	42,238	17,828	179	32	20	V	
Bauhinia Bridge	Hkg	1993	48,342	47,425	277	32	24	CC	ex Seto Bridge-04
Bay Bridge	Lbr	1985	34,467	35,396	227	32	20	CC	
Bremen Bridge †	Pan	2001	66,332	67,170	279	40	25	CC	ex YM Bridge-06, Bremen Bridge-04
Californian Highway	Pan	1983	43,407	16,519	183	32	18	V	
Cape Acacia	Pan	2005	104,732	206,237	300	50	15	B	
Cape Alliance	Pan	2007	104,732	206,190	300	50	15	B	
Cape Apricot	Pan	2004	90,091	180,310	289	45	14	B	
Cape Awoba	Pan	1996	87,803	171,978	289	45	14	B	ex Cape Acacia-05
Cape Azalea	Pan	1996	87,799	171,846	289	45	14	B	
Cape Camellia	Pan	2000	87,322	172,502	289	45	14	B	ex Cape Daisy-04
Cape Dover *	Pan	2006	92,993	185,805	290	47	14	B	
Cape Enterprise	Pan	2003	92,993	185,909	290	47	14	B	
Cape Flora	Pan	2000	83,056	164,361	280	47	14	B	
Cape Future	Pan	2002	92,993	185,820	290	47	14	B	
Cape Glory	Pan	2003	89,529	177,173	289	45	14	B	
Cape Jacaranda	Pan	1995	93,698	183,863	290	46	14	B	
Cape Liberty	Pan	2005	92,993	185,897	290	47	14	B	
Cape Lotus	Pan	2000	83,849	170,780	289	45	16	B	
Cape Med *	Pan	2006	93,003	185,827	290	47	14	B	
Cape Olive	Pan	1996	85,663	169,963	290	46	14	B	
Cape Orchid **	Pan	2001	87,322	172,569	289	45	14	B	
Cape Provence	Pan	2005	89,651	177,022	289	45	14	B	
Cape Riviera *	Pan	2005	93,006	185.879	290	47	14	B	

Kawasaki Kisen KK (K Line). CAPE ORCHID. *C. Lous*

Name	Flag	Year	GRT	DWT	LOA	Bm	Kts	Type	Former names
Cape Rosa	Pan	2005	101,911	203,163	300	50	15	B	
Cape Salvia	Pan	2002	87,341	172,559	289	45	14	B	
Cape Sophia	Pan	2005	55,285	99,047	250	43	14	B	
Cape Triumph	Pan	2004	88,594	176,343	289	45	15	B	
Cape Vanguard	Pan	2006	104,732	206,180	300	50	14	B	
Cape Victory	Pan	2003	89,492	177,359	289	45	14	B	
Cape Wakaba	Pan	1996	87,803	171,978	289	45	14	B	ex Cape Maple-05
Cape Wisteria	Pan	1997	87,322	172,846	289	45	14	B	ex Cape Rosa-04
Caribbean Highway	Pan	2002	42,238	17,866	179	32	20	V	
Century Highway No. 1	Pan	1984	43,198	15,363	186	32	18	V	
Century Highway No. 2	Pan	1985	44,616	15,509	186	32	18	V	
Century Highway No. 3	Pan	1986	46,186	14,304	186	32	18	V	
Century Highway No. 5	Pan	1986	44,969	15,380	190	32	18	V	
Chang Jiang Bridge	Pan	1992	48,237	47,425	277	32	24	CC	ex Brooklyn Bridge-01
Chicago Bridge	Pan	2001	66,332	67,170	279	40	25	CC	ex YM Chicago-06, Chicago Bridge-04
Chiswick Bridge	Pan	2001	68,687	68,280	285	40	25	CC	
Clifton Bridge	Jpn	1988	48,305	47,539	277	32	24	CC	ex Humber Bridge-06
Colorado Highway	Pan	2005	44,382	12,806	183	30	20	V	
Concord Bridge	Pan	1998	47,541	51,805	275	32	23	CC	
Continental Highway	Pan	2001	55,493	17,201	200	32	20	V	
Cooper River Bridge	Jpn	1987	42,407	40,934	241	32	22	CC	ex Henry Hudson Bridge-08
Coral Highway	Pan	1987	49,439	14,597	180	32	20	V	ex Michigan Highway-95
Eastern Highway **	Pan	2006	39,422	12,991	188	28	20	V	
Emden	Pan	1987	38,062	13,898	178	29	17	V	
European Highway	Pan	1999	48,039	15,057	180	32	20	V	
Florida Highway †	Pan	2008	59,493	18,930	200	32	20	V	
Fujikawa	Pan	2004	159,929	299,984	333	60	15	T	
Genoa Bridge	Pan	2002	66,292	67,197	279	40	25	CC	
George Washington Bridge	Pan	2006	68,687	71,000	285	40	25	CC	
Georgia Highway **	Jpn	2007	56,973	17,685	200	32	20	V	
Glen Canyon Bridge	Pan	2006	68,687	71,000	285	40	25	CC	
Global Highway	Pan	1982	51,087	15,148	200	32	18	V	
Golden Gate Bridge	Pan	2001	68,687	71,376	285	40	25	CC	
Grande Progresso	Pan	2008	145,000	297,351	327	55	14	O	
Greenwich Bridge	Pan	2006	68,687	71,000	285	40	25	CC	
Guang Dong Bridge	Pan	2006	68,687	71,000	285	40	25	CC	
Guangzhou Highway	Pan	2006	48,927	15,301	180	32	20	V	
Hannover Bridge	Pan	2006	98,747	99,214	336	46	25	CC	
Hercules Highway	Jpn	1987	46,875	14,977	180	32	18	V	
Humber Bridge	Pan	2006	98,800	87,000	336	46	24	CC	
Hume Highway	Pan	1985	51,235	16,169	200	32	18	V	
Indiana Highway **	Jpn	2003	55,457	17,442	200	32	20	V	
Isuzugawa	Pan	2004	159,929	299,984	333	60	15	T	
James River Bridge	Pan	2001	68,687	71,336	285	40	25	CC	
Kentucky Highway	Jpn	1987	50,320	15,587	180	32	19	V	
Kumanogawa	Lbr	2001	159,566	299,988	333	60	15	T	
La Paloma	Pan	1990	77,332	149,571	270	43	14	B	
Lions Gate Bridge	Pan	2001	68,687	71,395	285	40	25	CC	
London Highway	Pan	2006	55,600	17,765	200	32	20	V	
Long Beach Bridge	Pan	2001	66,332	68,280	279	40	25	CC	
Mackinac Bridge	Jpn	1986	42,414	40,982	241	32	22	CC	
Manhatten Bridge	Pan	1987	42,394	40,934	241	32	22	CC	
Marble Highway	Pan	1984	33,131	11,907	173	28	18	V	
Mediterranean Highway *	Pan	2002	55,493	17,228	200	32	20	V	
Melbourne Highway	Pan	1983	43,259	16,483	183	32	18	V	
Michigan Highway **	Jpn	2008	56,951	17,673	200	32	20	V	
Mogamigawa	Jpn	2001	160,229	299,999	333	60	15	T	
Morning Noble	Pan	1984	45,699	13,687	180	32	18	V	ex Tokyo Highway-05
Morning Sapphire	Jpn	1985	45,706	13,684	180	32	18	V	ex New York Highway-05
Newport Bridge	Pan	1993	48,220	47,384	277	32	25	CC	
Nippon Highway	Pan	1999	49,212	16,827	179	32	20	V	
Normandie Bridge	Lbr	1989	48,235	47,351	277	32	23	CC	ex YM Tacoma-05, Normandie Bridge-02
Ocean Highway	Pan	2000	49,212	16,733	179	32	20	V	
Olympian Highway *	Pan	1995	47,077	14,226	180	32	20	V	
Oregon Highway **	Pan	2007	57,147	17,699	200	32	20	V	
Oriental Highway	Lbr	1980	28,997	12,434	175	27	17	V	
Orion Highway	Lbr	1984	44,576	14,384	179	32	19	V	
Pacific Highway	Pan	2000	48,039	15,127	180	32	20	V	
Pegasus Highway	Pan	1994	49,012	15,553	180	32	18	V	
Princes Highway	Pan	1986	51,233	16,191	200	32	18	V	

Name	Flag	Year	GRT	DWT	LOA	Bm	Kts	Type	Former names
Rhein Bridge	Pan	1989	48,235	46,200	277	32	24	CC	
Rotterdam Bridge †	Pan	2001	66,332	68,280	285	40	25	CC	ex YM Rotterdam-06, Rotterdam Bridge-04
Sapphire Highway	Pan	1986	49,098	14,683	179	32	19	V	ex London Highway-94
Scandinavian Highway	Pan	1986	48,014	14,569	190	32	18	V	ex European Highway-96
Seven Seas Highway **	Pan	2001	55,493	17,232	200	32	20	V	
Shanghai Bridge	Pan	2001	68,687	68,280	285	40	25	CC	
Shanghai Highway	Pan	2005	48,927	15,413	180	32	20	V	
Shenandoah Highway	Pan	1992	47,368	12,308	180	32	18	V	
Sierra Nevada Highway **	Pan	2007	44,364	12,851	183	30	20	V	
Sinfonia	Pan	1991	93,788	184,403	290	46	13	B	ex Mikasa-98
Sirius Highway	Pan	1984	44,576	14,301	179	32	18	V	
Southern Highway **	Pan	2008	39,422	12,892	188	28	20	V	
Suez Canal Bridge	Pan	2002	68,687	71,359	285	40	25	CC	
Tamagawa	Pan	2007	160,231	314,237	333	60	15	T	
Texas Highway **	Jpn	2003	55,458	17,481	200	32	20	V	
Tianjing Highway	Pan	2005	48,927	15,410	180	32	19	V	
Tower Bridge	Sgp	1985	34,487	34,775	227	32	20	CC	
Triton Highway	Jpn	1987	45,783	14,484	180	32	18	V	
Tsing Ma Bridge	Pan	2002	68,687	68,280	285	40	25	CC	
Valencia Bridge	Pan	2004	54,519	65,006	294	32	23	CC	
Vancouver Bridge	Pan	2005	54,519	65,002	294	32	23	CC	
Vecchio Bridge	Pan	2005	54,519	64,983	294	32	23	CC	
Venice Bridge	Pan	2005	54,519	64,989	294	32	23	CC	
Verrazano Bridge	Pan	2004	54,519	65,038	294	32	23	CC	
Victoria Bridge	Pan	2005	54,519	64,986	294	32	23	CC	
Vincent Thomas Bridge	Pan	2005	54,519	65,023	294	32	23	CC	
Virginia Bridge	Pan	2004	54,519	64,990	294	32	23	CC	
Washington Highway **	Jpn	1986	50,334	14,081	190	32	19	V	
Western Highway **	Pan	2007	39,422	12,980	188	28	19	V	
Williamsburg Bridge	Pan	1998	47,541	51,759	275	32	23	CC	ex Victoria Bridge-05
Yamato	Pan	1991	93,699	184,349	290	46	13	B	
Yamatogawa	Pan	2006	160,231	302,488	333	60	15	T	

newbuilldings: over 80 on order including five 89,000 grt container ships, two 315,000 dwt tankers, and vehicle, Lpg and bulk carriers.
*Managed by 'K' Line Ship Management Co Ltd, Japan or by subsidiaries * Stargate Shipmanagement GmbH, Germany or ** Taiyo Nippon Kisen*
(founded 1944 as Kobe Nippon KK and merged 2000 with Taiyo Kaiun KK - www.nipponkisen.co.jp) † owned by Shoei Kisen Kaisha, Japan.
The company and its many subsidiaries own or manage over 210 vessels, only the larger container ships, tankers, bulk carriers and vehicle
carriers being listed. The owned and managed fleet also includes over 35 'panamax' or 'handy' bulk carriers, 10 wood-chip carriers, 10 product
and Lpg tankers, 23 Lng tankers and several smaller vehicle carriers.
Also see Cido Shipping and various chartered container ships with 'Bridge' suffix in index.

Klaveness Maritime Logistics AS   Norway

Funnel: Yellow with blue 'K' on white disc and blue edged narrow white band. **Hull:** Grey or orange with red boot-topping.
History: Founded 1946 as Gorrissen & Klaveness A/S to 1958 and as Torvald Klaveness & Co AS to 2005. **Web:** www.tk-group.com or
www.klaveness.com

Name	Flag	Year	GRT	DWT	LOA	Bm	Kts	Type	Former names
Al Mansour	Mhl	2002	38,889	72,562	225	32	14	Bu	
Bakkedal	Mhl	2007	38,883	72,450	225	32	14	B	
Balder	Mhl	2002	30,739	48,184	190	32	14	B	

Kawasaki Kisen KK (K Line). WESTERN HIGHWAY. *Allan Ryszka Onions*

Name	Flag	Year	GRT	DWT	LOA	Bm	Kts	Type	Former names
Ballangen	Mhl	1987	24,621	41,734	184	31	14	Bu	ex Yamburg-92, Oinoussian Fighter-89
Banasol	Mhl	2001	38,889	72,562	225	32	14	Bu	
Banastar	Mhl	2001	38,889	72,700	225	32	16	Bu	
Baniyas	Nis	2001	38,889	72,562	225	32	14	B	
Bantry	Mhl	2005	38,883	72,562	225	32	14	Bu	
Baru	Mhl	1986	43,733	83,970	229	32	14	T	ex ex Arius-08, Citius-06, Carlisle-04, Loucas-00, Nordtramp-97
Barkald	Mhl	2002	28,912	49,900	190	32	14	Bu	
Bauta	Mhl	1987	24,621	41,756	184	31	14	Bu	ex Yasnaya Polyana-92, Oinoussian Prudence-89
KCL Bardu	Lbr	1979	21,630	33,684	177	27	15	B	ex Bardu-05, Swan Cliff-99, Bardu-95
Trans Bay ††	Mhl	1996	37,550	70,120	225	32	13	Bu	ex Balsfjord-07, Sumava-98
Trans Emirates ††	Mhl	1993	37,550	70,456	225	32	13	Bu	ex Bakra-07, Bakar-99, Beskydy-98
Trans Gulf †	Lbr	1982	46,996	81,659	259	32	15	B	ex Bandar-07, Bulkgulf-03

*owned by subsidiary American Bulker KS (formed 2002) and managed by Dockendale Shipping Co. Ltd or Clipper Bulk (Portland) Inc (Clipper Group). † formerly owned, now chartered by Bulk Transloading AS to 2012 (†† to 2022) from Norwegian KS company managed by Pioneer Ship Management, UAE.
Also operates time-chartered vessels in Bulkhandling and Baumarine Pools (currently about 21 and 56 vessels respectively in pools)

Knutsen OAS Shipping AS   Norway

Funnel: Black with two red bands. **Hull**: Orange (larger vessels with white 'KNUTSEN O.A.S.'), red boot-topping. **History**: Founded 1896 as Knut Knutsen OAS until 1982. **Web**: www.knutsenoas.com

Name	Flag	Year	GRT	DWT	LOA	Bm	Kts	Type
Anna Knutsen (2)	Nis	1987	69,313	129,154	257	46	14	T
Anneleen Knutsen	Nis	2002	24,242	35,140	183	27	15	T
Betty Knutsen	Nis	1999	24,185	35,807	183	27	14	T

Knutsen OAS Shipping. KAREN KNUTSEN. *David Hornsby*

Knutsen OAS Shipping. TOVE KNUTSEN. *Allan Ryszka Onions*

Name	Flag	Year	GRT	DWT	LOA	Bm	Kts	Type	Former names
Bilbao Knutsen (st)	Cni	2004	90,920	68,530	284	43	19	Lng	
Cadiz Knutsen (st)	Cni	2003	90,835	68,411	284	43	19	Lng	
Catherine Knutsen §	Nis	1992	77,352	141,200	277	43	14	T	ex Tanana-99, Wilomi Tanana-98, Tanana-98, Wilomi Tanana-97
Elisabeth Knutsen (me2)	Nor	1997	71,880	124,788	265	43	14	T	
Ellen Knutsen	Nis	1991	11,433	17,071	142	23	13	T	
Evi Knutsen	Nis	1989	72,120	126,352	260	46	14	T	ex Evita-06
Gerd Knutsen	Iom	1996	79,244	134,510	277	44	14	T	ex Knock An-03
Gijon Knutsen	Gbr	2006	24,242	35,309	187	27	15	T	
Hanne Knutsen (2) **	Gbr	2000	72,245	123,851	265	43	15	T	
Heather Knutsen §	Can	2005	80,918	148,644	277	46	14	T	I/a Rose Knutsen
Helene Knutsen ‡	Nis	1992	11,737	14,848	142	23	13	T	
Hilda Knutsen	Nis	1989	11,425	14,910	142	23	13	T	
Iberica Knutsen (st)	Nis	2006	93,915	77,541	277	43		Lng	
Isabel Knutsen	Gbr	2001	13,753	22,377	160	23	15	T	ex Chembulk Savannah-00
Jasmine Knutsen §	Nis	2005	80,918	148,706	277	46	14	T	
Jorunn Knutsen (2)	Nor	2000	72,651	125,772	265	43	15	T	ex Asgard C-05, Jorunn Knutsen-00
Karen Knutsen (2)	Iom	1999	87,827	154,390	276	50	14	T	ex Knock Whillan-03
Kristin Knutsen	Nis	1998	12,184	19,152	148	23	15	T	
Maria Knutsen	Gbr	2001	13,753	22,377	160	23	15	T	I/a Chembulk Barcelona
Nancy Knutsen	Nis	1993	51,161	91,263	242	40	14	T	ex Natura-06
Pascale Knutsen	Gbr	1993	11,688	14,848	142	23	13	T	
Rita Knutsen (2) *	Nor	1986	70,434	124,472	252	46	14	T	ex Nordic Sarita-05, Sarita-98
Sallie Knutsen (2)	Iom	1999	87,827	154,390	276	50	14	T	ex Knock Sallie-03
Sestao Knutsen (st)	Cni	2007	90,583	68,530	284	43	19	Lng	
Sidsel Knutsen	Nis	1993	15,806	22,625	163	23	13	T	
Siri Knutsen	Gbr	2004	24,242	35,309	187	27	15	T	
Synnove Knutsen	Nis	1992	11,433	17,071	142	23	13	T	
Tordis Knutsen	Nor	1993	66,671	123,848	265	43	14	T	
Torill Knutsen	Nis	1990	11,425	14,910	142	23	13	T	ex Vinga Knutsen-90
Tove Knutsen	Nis	1989	60,719	112,508	243	43	14	T	
Turid Knutsen	Nis	1993	15,689	22,617	142	23	13	T	
Vigdis Knutsen	Nor	1993	66,671	123,423	265	43	14	T	
Windsor Knutsen	Nis	2007	87,146	162,000	281	50		T	

newbuildings: 159,000 dwt, three 105,000 dwt and four 16,400 dwt tankers, also four 110,000 grt Lng tankers for 2008-11 delivery
* managed by Teekay Corp, ** by Bluewater Energy BV, ‡ by AS Norske Shell or § by Canship Ugland Ltd (formed jointly by A/S Ugland Rederi and Canship Ltd), Canada (www.canship.com). Also see Teekay Corp, Canada.

Ernst Komrowski Reederei KG (GmbH & Co)   Germany

Funnel: White with white diamond at centre of blue/red diagonally quartered flag or charterers colours. **Hull:** Black or grey with red boot-topping. **History:** Formed 1923 as Ernst Komrowski Reederei GmbH to 1938. **Web:** www.komrowski.net

Name	Flag	Year	GRT	DWT	LOA	Bm	Kts	Type	Former names
Adrian	Lbr	1997	16,793	22,994	185	25	19	CC	ex TMM Hidalgo-06, Delmas Tourville-03, Adrian-03, Ivory Star-02, TMM Manzanillo-01, Adrian-01, CSAV Barcelona-01, Adrian-99, Santa Paula-98, Adrian-97, Jan Ritscher-97
Balkan **	Mlt	2007	15,633	17,005	161	25	19	CC	ex CSAV Caribe-08
Bonanza	Ant	2004	40,160	73,513	225	32	14	B	
Heluan	Mlt	2007	15,633	16,960	161	25	19	CC	
Kota Manis	Lbr	1994	16,191	22,426	179	25	19	CC	ex Dorian-07, DAL Karoo-02, Dorian-01, Karawa-00, Dorian-99, Sea Bold-98, Dorian-98, Sea Bold-97, Maersk Charleston-97, TSL Bold-96, Dorian-94
Merian	Deu	2000	40,562	74,717	225	32	14	B	ex Cinzia d'Amato-08
MOL Springbok	Lux	1996	16,800	22,982	185	25	19	CC	ex Vulkan-06, Marfret Caraibes-05, CMA CGM Karukera-04, Vulkan-01, CMA CGM Karukera-01, Vulkan-01, Cap York-00, Vulkan-99, CSAV Rengo-99, Vulkan-06
Providence *	Mlt	1995	16,252	23,334	179	25	19	CC	ex Nordcloud-96
Taipan	Deu	2007	10,965	12,612	141	23	19	Co	
WEC Vermeer	Deu	2007	10,965	12,600	141	23	19	Co	ex Tongan-08

* managed for Montan Capital GmbH & Co KG, Germany or ** for New World Shipping Co NV, Netherlands Antilles

Konig & Cie GmbH & Co KG   Germany

Funnel: Operator or charterers colours. **Hull:** Operator or charterers colours. **History:** Investment organisation founded 1999 and 40% owned by Schoeller Holdings Ltd. **Web:** www.emissionshaus.com

Name	Flag	Year	GRT	DWT	LOA	Bm	Kts	Type	Former names
Cosco Dammam †	Mhl	2005	27,786	37,825	222	30	22	CC	ex Cape Moreton-05
Cosco Melbourne †	Mhl	2005	27,786	37,883	222	30	22	CC	
Cosco Sydney ‡	Lbr	2004	27,915	37,978	215	30	21	CC	I/a Frisia Leipzig

Name	Flag	Year	GRT	DWT	LOA	Bm	Kts	Type	Former names
CSAV Tubul	Cyp	2007	28,007	37,570	222	30	22	CC	ex Cape Mayor-07, I/a King Andrew
King Alfred	Mhl	2007	28,007	37,938	222	39	22	CC	ex CMA CGM Kepler-08, King Alfred-07
King Basil	Mlt	2008	17,964	24,092	183	25	19	CC	
King Brian	Lbr	2008	17,964	24,150	182	25	19	CC	
King Bruce	Mlt	2008	17,964	24,150	183	25	19	CC	
King Byron	Mlt	2007	17,964	24,161	183	25	20	CC	
King Daniel *	Mhl	2008	42,010	73,720	229	32	14	T	
King Darius *	Mhl	2007	42,010	73,634	229	32	14	T	
King Darwin *	Mhl	2007	42,010	73,604	229	32	14	T	
King Dorian *	Mhl	2007	42,010	73,611	229	32	14	T	ex King David-08
King Douglas *	Mhl	2008	42,010	73,666	229	32	14	T	
King Duncan *	Mhl	2008	42,010	73,720	229	32	14	T	
King Edward *	Mhl	2004	23,240	37,384	183	27	14	T	ex Ruby-06, Baltic Admiral-04
King Edwin *	Mhl	2000	23,740	35,775	183	27	14	T	ex Nordeuropa-07
King Eric *	Mhl	2001	23,217	37,270	183	27	14	T	ex Ashley-07
King Ernest *	Mhl	2004	23,246	37,106	183	28	14	T	ex Ganges-07
King Everest *	Mhl	2001	23,217	37,230	183	27	14	T	ex Marne-06, I/a Ruby Star
Mare Action **	Mhl	2005	23,240	37,467	183	27	14	T	ex Baltic Action-07
Mare Ambassador **	Mhl	2005	23,240	37,371	183	27	14	T	ex Baltic Ambassador-07
Mare Atlantic **	Mlt	2001	39,085	68,467	229	32	14	T	ex Latgale-07, Inca-01
Mare Caribbean **	Mhl	2004	29,327	46,718	183	32	14	T	ex Cape Bauld-07
Mare Pacific **	Mlt	2001	39,085	68,467	229	32	14	T	ex Zemgale-07, Maya-01
Montania ‡‡	Lbr	1996	17,287	22,148	175	27	20	CC	ex YM Jakarta-06, Montania-04
SC Laura	Sgp	2001	61,764	110,000	245	42	15	T	ex Maersk Pointer-07
SC Sara §	Lbr	2001	56,346	105,322	239	42	15	T	ex Nordatlantic-07

newbuildings: four 57,000 dwt bulk carriers for 2009-10 delivery.
* managed by subsidiaries Scorship Tankers GmbH & Co KG, Germany (formed jointly with Scorpio Ship Management SAM, Monaco) or **
Marenave Schiffahrts AG, Germany (managed by Columbia Shipmanagement (Deutschland) GmbH)
† managed by Martime GmbH, ‡ by V.Ships (Gemany) GmbH & Co KG, ‡‡ by Ahrenkiel Ship Managemenet or § by H Clarkson.
See other vessels managed by Columbia Shipmanagement (Deutschland) GmbH (under Schoeller Holdings Ltd), SKS OBO Holding Ltd (under
Kristian Gerhard Jebsen Skipsrederi AS), Thien & Heyenga GmbH and Oskar Wehr KG (GmbH & Co).
Also see United Product Tanker (UPT) pool under Schoeller Holdings Ltd

Kuwait Oil Tanker Co (SAK)   Kuwait

Funnel: Red with gold Arabic characters on green oval disc on broad white band beneath black top. **Hull:** Black with red or grey boot-topping. **History:** Founded 1957 as subsidiary of Kuwait Petroleum Corp. **Web:** www.kotc.com.kw

Name	Flag	Year	GRT	DWT	LOA	Bm	Kts	Type	Former names
Al Awdah	Kwt	1991	149,647	284,533	322	56	14	T	
Al Badiyah	Kwt	1989	26,356	35,643	183	32	13	T	
Al Deerah	Kwt	1989	26,356	35,643	183	32	13	T	
Al Jabriyah II	Kwt	2007	161,113	317,250	333	60		T	
Al Kuwaitiah	Kwt	1988	26,351	35,643	183	32	13	T	
Al Maqwa	Kwt	1983	43,970	66,652	241	32	15	T	ex West Kirby-88, Umm Al Jathathel-87
Al Sabiyah	Kwt	1988	26,356	35,644	183	32	13	T	
Al Salam II	Kwt	2007	42,798	69,790	228	32		T	
Al Salheia	Kwt	1998	158,503	310,453	334	58	15	T	

Konig & Cie GmbH. MARE AMBASSADOR. *N. Kemps*

Name	Flag	Year	GRT	DWT	LOA	Bm	Kts	Type	Former names
Al Samidoon	Kwt	1992	149,719	284,889	322	57	14	T	
Al Shegaya	Kwt	1998	158,503	310,433	334	58	15	T	
Al Shuhadaa	Kwt	1992	149,719	285,116	322	57	14	T	
Al Soor II	Kwt	2007	42,798	69,835	228	32		T	
Al Tahreer	Kwt	1991	149,719	284,532	322	56	14	T	
Arabiyah	Kwt	1988	75,029	121,109	250	43	13	T	
Gas Al Burgan	Kwt	1979	42,904	47,471	230	35	21	Lpg	ex Gas King-89, Gas Al Burgan-87
Gas Al-Gurain	Kwt	1993	44,868	49,874	230	37	16	Lpg	
Gas Al Kuwait II	Kwy	2007	48,104	57,738	225	37		Lpg	
Gas Al Mutlaa	Kwt	1993	44,868	49,874	230	37	16	Lpg	
Gas Al Negeh	Kwt	2007	48,104	57,748	225	37		Lpg	
Hadiyah	Kwt	1988	75,029	121,109	250	43	13	T	
Kazimah II	Kwt	2006	161,113	317,250	333	60	15	T	
Keefan	Kwt	1982	43,970	66,652	241	32	15	T	ex Hoylake-88, Umm Al Roos-87
Wafrah	Kwt	2007	63,440	113,849	250	44		T	
Warbah	Kwt	1982	43,970	66,652	241	32	15	T	ex Helsby-88, Umm Ruwaisat-87

Reederei F Laeisz GmbH & Co KG   Germany

Funnel: *Yellow or charterers colours.* **Hull:** *Black with red boot-topping or white with blue boot-topping.* **History:** *Founded 1824 as F Laeisz until 1982 and F Laeisz Schiffahrts GmbH to 1993. Fleet merged in 1993 with privatised East German state fleet of Deutsche Seereederei Rostock as joint venture with Hamburg business associate until 1999, when fully taken-over.* **Web:** *www.laeiszline.de*

Name	Flag	Year	GRT	DWT	LOA	Bm	Kts	Type	Former names
Babitonga ‡	Lbr	1997	38,215	73,726	225	32	15	B	ex William Oldendorff-06, Wiltrader-03, Win Trader-02
Chrismir	Lbr	1997	81,329	159,829	280	45	14	B	
Cific ‡	Lbr	1992	34,231	45,696	216	32	19	CC	ex Zim Texas-06, Pacific Senator-06, DSR-Pacific-97
CMA CGM Copernic	Lbr	2007	27,968	37,570	222	30	22	CC	ex Pona-07
CSAV Appennini	Deu	1997	53,334	62,200	294	32	23	CC	ex Pugwash Senator-07
CSAV Jura	Deu	1998	53,324	63,645	294	32	23	CC	ex CMA CGM Asia-08, Portugal Senator-06
CSAV Pyrennes	Deu	1998	53,334	63,537	294	32	23	CC	ex Pohang Senator-08
Gulf Bridge ‡	Lbr	2006	28,270	33,000	213	32	22	CC	I/a Pontremoli
Hanjin Colombo ‡	Pan	1994	50,792	62,850	290	32	24	CC	
Hanjin Osaka ‡	Pan	1992	51,754	62,681	290	32	24	CC	ex Ville de Shanghai-99, Hanjin Osaka-98
Hanjin Philadephia ‡	Lbr	2002	50,242	58,810	282	32	24	CC	
Hanjin Phoenix ‡	Lbr	2002	50,242	58,423	282	32	24	CC	
Hanjin Portland ‡	Lbr	1993	50,792	62,716	290	32	24	CC	
Hanjin Praha *	Lbr	2001	50,242	58,423	280	32	24	CC	I/a Praha
Hanjin Pretoria *	Lbr	2002	50,242	58,768	282	32	24	CC	

Reederei F Laeisz GmbH. OOCL BREMEN. *Allan Ryszka Onions*

Name	Flag	Year	GRT	DWT	LOA	Bm	Kts	Type	Former names
Kota Pahlawan	Lbr	1997	25,499	33,950	200	30	21	CC	ex CMA CGM Emerald-04, Pembroke Senator-03, P&O Nedlloyd Fos-01, ECL Europa-99, Pembroke Senator-99
Kota Permas ‡	Lbr	2008	28,270	32,949	213	32	22	CC	ex Pontresina-08
Kota Pelangi ‡	Lbr	1996	31,131	38,650	210	32	22	CC	ex Potsdam-02, Ipex Emperor-99, Sea Elegance-97, Potsdam-96
Kota Pusaka ‡	Lbr	1996	31,131	38,650	210	32	22	CC	ex Pommern-02, P&O Nedlloyd Unity-01, Pommern-97, Sea Excellence-97, Pommern-96
Luise Oldendorff ‡	Lbr	1994	38,513	72,873	225	32	14	B	
Matilde	Mhl	1997	81,329	160,013	280	45	14	B	
MSC Basel ‡	Lbr	1992	34,231	45,696	216	32	19	CC	ex Shanghai Senator-04, DSR-Atlantic-97
MSC Chile	Lbr	1997	28,701	32,500	202	31	20	CC	ex Priwall-04, MSC Chile-04, Priwall-02, Sea Panther-01, Priwall-97
MSC Kenya	Deu	1997	53,324	63,584	294	32	23	CC	ex Pusan Senator07
MSC Palermo ‡	Lbr	1992	34,231	45,696	216	32	19	CC	ex Palermo Senator-03, DSR-Baltic-96
MSC Tanzania	Deu	1997	53,324	62,057	294	32	23	CC	ex Pudong Senator-07
MSC Uganda	Deu	1997	53,324	63,645	294	32	23	CC	ex Punjab Senator-07
OOCL Bremen ‡	Lbr	2007	27,968	37,570	222	30	22	CC	ex Posen-07
Paradise N ***	Lbr	1997	155,051	322,398	332	58	13	B	ex Peene Ore-02
Patmos II	Lbr	1992	34,231	45,696	216	32	19	CC	ex Atmos-08, Zim Alabama-07, Patmos-06, Patmos Senator-06, DSR-Europe-97
Peking Senator **	Deu	1997	53,324	63,527	294	32	23	CC	ex Cho Yang Ark-00
Penang Senator	Deu	1997	53,324	63,533	294	32	23	CC	ex Cho Yang Atlas-01
Pequot	Lbr	1996	36,615	70,165	225	32	15	B	
Port Said	Lbr	1994	19,819	22,300	174	27	19	CC	ex Port Said Senator-05, DSR-Port Said-00, Northern Pleasure-94
Portland Senator **	Deu	1997	53,324	63,645	294	32	23	CC	ex Cho Yang Alpha-01
Powhatan ‡	Lbr	1995	36,615	69,045	225	32	15	B	

newbuildings: six 28,000 grt container ships for 2009-10 delivery.
Owned or managed by Reederei F. Laeisz GmbH or ‡ by associated Hamburgische Seehandlung GmbH
* managed for Dr. Peters KG fund, ** for Norddeutsche Vermogensanlage GmbH & Co or *** for Gebab GmbH & Co KG, all Germany.
Also see managed vessels under BW Gas and NSB Niederelbe Schiffahrt GmbH.

Latvian Shipping Company

Latvia

Funnel: *Dark brown with dark brown 'Lat' symbol on broad white band or blue with white 'L+C' overlapping broad red band.*
Hull: *Black or red with red boot-topping.* **History:** *Government controlled and formed 1940.* **Web:** *www.lk.lv or www.lscsm.lv*

Abava	Mlt	1992	7,057	6,366	140	19	16	R	ex Chiquita Abava-93
Ainazi	Mhl	2008	30,641	52,606	195	32	14	T	
Amata	Mlt	1991	7,392	6,231	140	19	16	R	ex Chiquita Amata-93, Amata-91, Mazoiusze-91
Ance	Mhl	2006	30,641	52,622	195	32	14	T	
Asari	Lbr	1984	18,526	28,750	179	25	15	T	ex Georgiy Kholostyakov-92
Bulduri	Lbr	1983	18,625	28,750	179	25	15	T	ex Dmitriy Medvedyev-91
Dzintari	Lbr	1985	10,944	16,341	152	22	15	T	ex Moris Bishop-91
Estere	Lbr	1989	18,625	28,610	178	25	14	T	ex Esther-94
Indra	Lbr	1994	21,183	28,840	179	25	14	T	ex Puikovo-94
Inga	Lbr	1990	18,625	28,610	179	25	14	T	

Latvian Shipping Co. KULDIGA. *J. M. Kakebeeke*

Name	Flag	Year	GRT	DWT	LOA	Bm	Kts	Type	Former names
Jurkalne	Mhl	2006	30,641	52,622	195	32	14	T	
Kaltene	Mhl	2003	23,217	37,000	183	27	14	T	ex Pink Star-04
Kandava	Mhl	2007	23,315	37,258	183	27	14	T	
Kazdanga	Mhl	2007	23,315	37,312	183	27	14	T	
Kemeri	Lbr	1985	10,944	17,610	152	22	15	T	ex Yuliy Danishevshiy-91
Kolka	Mhl	2003	23,217	37,211	183	27	14	T	ex Purple Star-04
Kraslava	Mhl	2007	23,315	37,258	183	27	14	T	
Krisjanis Valdemars	Mhl	2007	23,315	37,266	183	27	14	T	
Kuldiga	Mhl	2003	23,217	37,237	183	27	14	T	ex Coral Star-04
Kurzeme	Lva	1997	18,503	23,100	160	26	15	Lpg	
Mar	Lbr	1990	18,625	28,610	178	25	14	T	
Ojars Vacietis	Lbr	1985	10,944	16,341	152	22	15	T	ex Oyar Vatsietis-91
Piltene	Mhl	2007	30,641	52,648	195	32	14	T	
Pumpuri	Lbr	1987	18,526	28,750	179	25	14	T	ex Mikhail Gromov-92
Puze	Mhl	2006	30,641	52,622	195	32	14	T	
Riga	Lva	2001	39,085	68,467	229	32	14	T	ex Aztec-01
Rundale	Rus	1977	13,704	17,025	160	23	15	T	ex Leninsk Kuznetskiy-91
Salacgriva	Mhl	2008	30,641	52,600	195	32	14	T	
Samburga	Rus	1976	13,704	17,200	160	23	15	T	ex Samburg-92
Targale	Mhl	2007	30,641	52,622	195	32	14	T	
Ugale	Mhl	2007	30,641	52,642	195	32	14	T	
Usma	Mhl	2007	30,641	52,684	195	32	14	T	
Uzava	Mhl	2008	30,541	52,650	195	32	14	T	
Vidzeme	Lbr	1997	18,503	23,100	160	26	15	Lpg	
Zanis Griva	Lbr	1985	10,944	16,341	152	22	15	T	ex Zhan Griva-91
Zoja I	Lbr	1988	18,625	28,610	179	25	14	T	ex Don-89
Zoja II	Lva	1989	18,625	28,610	178	25	14	T	ex Kmir-90

newbuildings: four 52,000 dwt tankers for 2011-12 delivery.
managed by LSC Shipmanagement Sia, Latvia (formed 1999) except * by Columbia Shipmanagement Ltd., Cyprus,

J Lauritzen A/S   Denmark

Funnel: *Red with ivory 'J' above 'L' separated by narrow cream band.* **Hull:** *Red or white with red boot-topping.* **History:** *Founded 1884. Reefer operations sold to joint venture partner NYK in 2007.* **Web:** *www j-lauritzen.com*

Chilean Reefer	Dis	1992	7,944	11,095	141	20	22	R	ex Carelian Reefer-97
Ditlev Lauritzen	Dis	1990	14,406	16,950	164	24	20	R	
Ivar Lauritzen	Dis	1990	14,406	16,950	165	24	19	R	
Jorgen Lauritzen **	Dis	1991	14,406	16,950	164	24	19	R	
Knud Lauritzen	Dis	1991	14,406	16,950	164	24	19	R	
Peruvian Reefer	Dis	1992	7,944	11,092	141	20	22	R	ex Savonian Reefer-97
Scandinavian Reefer	Dis	1992	7,944	11,054	141	20	22	R	

Chartered out to NYKCool AB qv

Lauritzen Bulkers A/S

Funnel: *As above or red upper part with white 'LB', white lower part with red over blue 'ivs' logo or black with red over blue 'ivs' logo on white square.* **Hull:** *Red, black or grey with white 'Lauritzen-IVS Bulk', red boot-topping.* **History:** *Subsidiary formed in 1997 to re-enter the bulk carrier trade. Operates mainly chartered vessels, including a 'Handysize' joint venture with South African-based Island View Shipping (acquired by Grindrod Group in 1999).* **Web:** *www.lauritzenbulkers.com*

J Lauritzen. JORGEN LAURITZEN. *Hans Kraijenbosch*

Name	Flag	Year	GRT	DWT	LOA	Bm	Kts	Type	Former names
Amine Bulker	Mlt	2007	17,663	28,700	177	26	14	B	
IVS Hunter *	Pan	2001	19,712	31,812	177	29	14	B	
IVS Kanda *	Hkg	2004	19,885	32,621	177	28	14	B	
IVS Kawana *	Pan	2005	19,885	32,642	177	28	14	B	
IVS Kenso *	Pan	2005	19,885	32,642	177	28	14	B	
IVS Kestrel *	Hkg	2002	19,872	32,537	177	28	14	B	
IVS Kingbird *	Pan	2007	19,885	32,561	177	28	14	B	
IVS Kite *	Pan	2002	19,885	32,556	177	28	14	B	
IVS Kittiwake *	Pan	2007	19,885	32,555	177	28	14	B	
IVS Kwaito *	Pan	2004	19,885	32,573	177	28	14	B	
IVS Kwela *	Pan	2002	19,872	32,474	177	28	14	B	
IVS Lavender *	Hkg	2004	18,020	29,727	171	27	14	B	
IVS Nightingale *	Pan	2005	20,283	32,316	173	29	14	Co	
IVS Nightjar *	Pan	2004	20,283	32,328	173	29	14	Co	
IVS Swift *	Pan	2003	21,185	32,662	178	28	14	B	
Sendai Bulker	Pan	2000	17,852	28,378	172	27	14	B	
Sofie Bulker	Mlt	2007	17,663	28,682	177	26	14	B	
Tilda Bulker	Mlt	2003	16,966	28,481	169	27	14	B	ex Triton Seagull-06

newbuildings: four 179,600 dwt, four 58,500 dwt, four 31,900 dwt bulk carriers for 2009-11 delivery, plus 20 others for charter.
*managed by New Century Overseas Management Inc, Philippines or * owned/managed by Island View Shipping.*
Currently operates over 60 other bulk carriers chartered from various owners/managers, many with 'Bulker' suffix.

Lauritzen Tankers A/S

Funnel: *Red with white 'J' above and 'L' below ivory band.* **Hull:** *Red with white 'LAURITZEN TANKERS, red boot-topping.*
History: *Subsidiary formed in 2004 to re-enter the tanker trade.* **Web:** *www.lauritzentankers.com*

Name	Flag	Year	GRT	DWT	LOA	Bm	Kts	Type	Former names
Dan Eagle	Dmk	1999	28,448	46,185	183	32	14	T	ex Freja Pacific-08, Soundless-06, Hellas Serenity-05
Freja Atlantic	Dis	2004	30,004	45,967	183	32	14	T	ex Crozon-04
Freja Baltic *	Pan	2008	26,897	47,538	183	32	14	T	
Freja Breeze *	Pan	1996	28,433	47,172	183	32	15	T	I/a Asia Prosperity
Freja Dania *	Lbr	2007	31,500	53,755	186	32	14	T	
Freja Fionia *	Pan	2007	31,433	53,714	186	32	14	T	
Freja Hafnia *	Pan	2006	31,433	53,712	186	32	14	T	
Freja Polaris	Dis	2004	23,244	37,217	186	27	14	T	ex Kermaria-07
Freja Selandia *	Pan	2007	31,433	53,712	186	32	14	T	
Freja Spring *	Pan	1999	28,546	47,110	183	32	14	T	

newbuildings: eight 50,500 dwt chemical tankers and two 69,000 dwt shuttle tankers for 2010-11 delivery.
** chartered from various owners.*

C M Lemos & Co Ltd   UK

Funnel: *Yellow with blue 'L' on white houseflag, black top.* **Hull:** *Black or grey with red boot-topping.* **History:** *Parent founded 1950 and subsidiary formed 1967.* **Web:** *none located.*

Name	Flag	Year	GRT	DWT	LOA	Bm	Kts	Type
Authentic	Grc	2004	78,922	150,249	274	48	15	T
Cosmic	Grc	2000	78,918	150,284	274	48	15	T
Emerald	Grc	1986	27,535	46,793	189	32	14	B
Gloric	Grc	2006	156,933	298,495	330	60	15	T

J Lauritzen Tankers. FREJA SELANDIA. *F. de Vries*

Name	Flag	Year	GRT	DWT	LOA	Bm	Kts	Type	Former names
Majestic	Grc	2000	78,918	150,284	274	48	15	T	
North Star	Grc	1996	79,832	148,561	269	46	15	T	
Poetic	Grc	2003	78,922	150,103	274	48	15	T	
Romantic	Grc	2004	78,922	150,247	274	48	15	T	
Symphonic	Grc	2006	156,933	298,522	330	60	15	T	
Topaz	Grc	1985	27,535	46,874	189	32	14	B	

Operated by subsidiary Nereus Shipping SA, Greece.

Leonhardt & Blumberg Schiffahrts GmbH & Co KG   Germany

Funnel: Black with red 'x' and black '+' combined on broad white band, * black with blue single wave on white rectangle with white 'Maltese Cross' on dark blue square in top corner or charterers colours. Hull: Dark grey, blue or black with red boot-topping or white with blue boot-topping. **History:** *Founded 1903 by Adolf Leonhardt and Arthur Blumberg to succeed Leonhardt & Heeckt (formed 1899) and now in third generation of family.* **Web:** *www.leonhardt-blumberg.com*

Name	Flag	Year	GRT	DWT	LOA	Bm	Kts	Type	Former names
H Fyn †	Deu	2003	16,145	20,367	170	27	19	CC	ex Maersk Vaasa-07, I/a H. Fyn
H Kirkenes *	Lbr	2002	15,988	20,463	175	27	18	CC	I/a Hansa Kirkenes
Hansa Augsburg	Lbr	2008	18,327	23,400	176	27	18	CC	ex NileDutch Tianjin-09, Hansa Augsburg-08
Hansa Augustenburg *	Lbr	2003	18,335	23,606	175	27	18	CC	ex Maersk Vilnius-07, Hansa Augustenburg-03
Hansa Bergen	Lbr	1997	15,988	20,887	170	25	20	CC	ex Columbus Bondi-01, Hansa Bergen-00, Maersk Windhoek-99, Maersk Gothenburg-98, Hansa Bergen-98
Hansa Flensburg *	Lbr	2000	18,335	23,579	175	27	18	CC	ex Melbourne Express-06, CP Condor-06, Direct Condor-05, Hansa Flensburg-00
Hansa Greifswald *	Mlt	1996	9,605	12,559	150	22	17	CC	ex EWL West Indies-04, Hansa Greifswald-96
Hansa Limburg	Lbr	2008	18,327	23,447	175	27	18	CC	
Hansa Ravensburg	Lbr	2008	18,327	23,500	176	27	18	CC	
Hansa Rendsburg *	Lbr	2000	18,335	23,600	175	27	18	CC	ex CP Jabiru-06, Direct Jabiru-05, Hansa Rendsburg-01
Hansa Stavanger	Deu	1997	15,988	20,526	170	25	18	CC	ex Lykes Trader-05, Cap Pasado-04, Hansa Stavanger-03, Direct Condor-00, Maersk Gauteng-99, Maersk Izmir-98, Hansa Stavanger-98
Hansa Stralsund *	Lbr	1993	9,603	12,577	150	22	17	CC	ex Chile Star-98, Hansa Stralsund-97, Eagle Wave-96, Hansa Stralsund-93
Maersk Volos *	Lbr	2003	18,334	17,600	175	27	19	CC	I/a H.Freyburg, I/dn Hansa Freyburg
Maersk Voshod ††	Deu	2003	18,334	23,600	175	27	18	CC	ex Cap Aguilar-05, Hansa Augustenburg-03
Maruba Aldebaran	Lbr	2007	18,327	23,400	176	27	18	CC	I/a Hansa Papenburg
Maruba Parana †	Lbr	2004	18,334	17,600	175	27	19	CC	ex Maersk Ventspils-07, I/a H. Ronneburg
MOL Accord †	Lbr	2003	16,145	20,700	170	25	19	CC	ex H. Langeland-06, CSAV Ilha Bela-05, Cap Pilar-04, H. Langeland-03
NileDutch Asia	Lbr	2007	18,327	23,452	176	27	18	CC	ex Hansa Coburg-07
NileDutch Hong Kong	Lbr	2007	18,327	23,419	176	27	18	CC	ex Hansa Meersburg-07
NileDutch Singapore	Lbr	2007	18,327	23,396	176	27	18	CC	

newbuildings: four 42,000 grt and nine 18,327 grt container ships for 2010-11 delivery.
* owned by Leonhardt & Blumberg Reederei GmbH † managed for Hansa Hamburg Shipping International GmbH & Co KG (founded 1999 – www.hansahamburg.de) or †† for its subsidiary HHSI Flottenfonds GmbH & Co KG (founded 2003)

Livanos Group   Greece

Funnel: Black with red 'L' between 'greek key' borders on broad white band. Hull: Black or grey with red boot-topping.
History: *Formed 1920.* **Web:** *none located*

Name	Flag	Year	GRT	DWT	LOA	Bm	Kts	Type	Former names
Achilleus	Grc	1983	22,587	39,731	174	32	15	T	ex Sylvan Arrow-02, Mobil Challenge-92
Aliakmon	Grc	2006	30,020	46,792	183	32	14	T	
Amazon Beauty	Grc	2003	43,075	72,909	228	40	15	T	
Amazon Brilliance	Grc	2005	43,075	72,910	228	40	15	T	
Amazon Explorer	Grc	2002	43,075	72,826	228	40	15	T	
Amazon Gladiator	Grc	2001	43,075	72,910	228	40	15	T	
Amazon Guardian	Grc	1999	43,075	72,910	228	40	15	T	
Artemis	Grc	1983	22,587	39,776	174	32	15	T	ex Royal Arrow-01, Mobil Courage-91
Atlantic Hawk	Bhs	2002	38,727	74,204	225	32	14	B	ex Jin Kang-04
Axios	Grc	2006	30,020	46,792	183	32	14	T	
Chios	Grc	1993	157,213	301,824	327	58	14	T	
Christina	Grc	1999	158,110	309,344	335	58	16	T	
Evros	Grc	2005	30,020	47,120	183	32	14	T	
Ioannis Zafirakis	Bhs	2004	38,700	74,000	225	32	14	B	
Meandros	Grc	2000	157,883	309,498	335	58	15	T	
Strymon	Grc	2005	30,020	47,120	183	32	14	T	

newbuildings: two 158,000 dwt tankers for 2010-11 delivery.
Operated by subsidiary Sun Enterprises Ltd, Greece

Louis Dreyfus Armateurs SAS

France

Funnel: *Black with blue 'LD & C' on white band between two narrow red bands.* **Hull:** *Black.* **History:** *Founded 1851 as Louis-Dreyfus et Cie to 1972 taking the current company name in 1995.* **Web:** *www.lda.fr*

Name	Flag	Year	GRT	DWT	LOA	Bm	Kts	Type	Former names
Jean LD	Atf	2005	89,076	171,908	289	45	14	B	
Pierre LD	Atf	2006	89,100	173,000	289	45	14	B	

Joint Stock Co LUKoil

Russia

Murmansk Shipping Co/Russia

Funnel: *Blue with white polar bear, (or white with polar bear on broad blue band) and black top.* **Hull:** *Grey, black or red with red boot-topping.* **History:** *Established in 1939 and controlled by LUKoil (founded 1997 and controlled by Russian government) since 1998.* **Web:** *www.msco.ru*

Name	Flag	Year	GRT	DWT	LOA	Bm	Kts	Type	Former names
Admiral Ushakov	Rus	1979	16,257	19,885	162	23	14	BC	
Aleksandr Nevskiy	Rus	1978	14,141	19,885	162	23	14	BC	
Aleksandr Sledzyuk	Rus	1975	13,153	17,200	160	23	16	T	ex Urengoy-02
Aleksandr Suvorov	Rus	1979	14,141	19,885	162	23	14	BC	
Anatoliy Lyapidevskiy *	Cyp	1984	14,141	19,252	162	23	15	BC	
Arctic Trader *	Mlt	1994	28,420	48,170	192	32	15	B	ex Goldstar-94
Arctic Voyager *	Mlt	1994	28,420	48,131	192	32	15	B	ex Silverstar-94
Arkhangelsk *	Cyp	1983	18,627	23,128	174	25	17	Ro	
Dmitriy Pozharskiy	Rus	1978	16,257	19,885	162	23	14	BC	
Fifth	Mhl	1977	14,141	19,885	162	23	14	BC	ex Dmitriy Donskoy-09
Grumant	Rus	2006	15,868	22,945	181	23	14	B	
Indiga	Rus	1976	11,290	16,420	164	22	14	T	ex Lunni-03
Ivan Papanin	Rus	1990	14,400	10,105	166	23	17	Ro	
Ivan Susanin	Rus	1981	16,257	19,885	162	23	14	BC	
Kandalaksha	Rus	1984	18,627	19,943	177	25	17	ROl	
Kapitan Bochek *	Cyp	1982	14,141	19,252	162	23	14	BC	
Kapitan Chukhchin	Rus	1981	14,141	19,240	162	23	14	BC	
Kapitan Danilkin	Rus	1987	18,574	19,763	174	25	17	Ro	
Kapitan Kudlay *	Cyp	1983	14,009	19,252	162	23	15	BC	
Kapitan Nazarev *	Cyp	1984	14,141	19,252	162	23	15	BC	
Kapitan Sviridov	Rus	1982	14,141	19,240	162	23	14	BC	
Kapitan Vakula *	Cyp	1983	14,141	19,252	162	23	15	BC	
Kapitan Vodenko *	Cyp	1982	14,141	19,240	162	23	15	BC	
Khatanga	Rus	1987	14,937	23,050	158	26	15	T	ex Bauska-04, Nord Skagerrak-87
Kola	Rus	1983	18,627	19,943	177	25	17	ROl	
Kuzma Minin	Rus	1980	16,257	19,885	162	23	14	BC	
Mikhail Kutuzov	Rus	1979	16,257	19,885	162	23	14	BC	
Mikhail Strekalovskiy	Rus	1981	16,253	19,250	162	23	14	BC	
Monchegorsk *	Cyp	1983	18,672	19,943	177	25	17	ROl	
Nataly	Rus	1993	77,470	142,498	274	43	14	T	ex Velez-Blanco-05
Nadezhda *	Rus	1993	77,477	143,396	274	43	14	T	ex Almudaina-07
Norilsk *	Cyp	1982	18,627	19,942	174	25	17	ROl	

LUKoil (Murmansk Shipping). ANATOLIY LYAPIDEVSKIY . *Allan Ryszka Onions*

Name	Flag	Year	GRT	DWT	LOA	Bm	Kts	Type	Former names
Pavel Vavilov	Rus	1981	14,141	19,240	162	23	15	BC	
Pomorye	Rus	2007	15,868	23,645	181	23	14	B	
Pyotr Velikiy	Rus	1978	16,257	19,885	162	23	14	BC	
Sevmorput	Rus	1988	38,226	33,980	260	32	14	C	
Tim Buck *	Cyp	1983	14,009	19,240	162	23	14	BC	
Varzuga	Rus	1977	11,290	15,954	164	22	14	T	ex Uikku-03
Viktor Tkachyov	Rus	1981	14,141	19,240	162	23	15	BC	
Yuriy Arshenevskiy	Rus	1986	18,574	19,724	177	25	17	ROl	
Yuriy Dolorukiy	Rus	1980	14,141	19,885	162	22	15	BC	
Zapolyarye	Rus	2008	15,868	23,645	181	23	14	B	

newbuildings: six 75,000 dwt bulk carriers for 2009-10 delivery.
* owned by subsidiaries NB Shipping (managed by NB Maritime Management (Cyprus) Ltd.).

Lundqvist Rederierna AB Finland

Funnel: *White with yellow diamond interrupting thin blue band on blue edged broader yellow band.* **Hull:** *Brown or black with red boot-topping.* **History:** *Founded 1917 as Hugo Lundqvist to 1937, Arthur Karlsson to 1955 and Fraenk Lundqvist to 1959.*
Web: *www.lundqvist.aland.fi*

Alfa Britannia	Bhs	1998	56,115	99,280	248	43	14	T	
Alfa Germania	Bhs	1998	56,115	99,193	248	43	14	T	
Alfa Italia	Bhs	2002	59,719	105,588	249	43	15	T	
Hildegaard	Bhs	1999	56,115	99,122	248	43	14	T	
Katja	Bhs	1995	52,067	97,220	232	42	15	T	
Penelop	Bhs	2006	62,448	115,091	254	44	15	T	
Sarpen	Bhs	2002	59,719	105,655	248	43	15	T	
Thornbury	Bhs	2001	56,115	99,220	248	43	15	T	

MACS - Maritime Carrier AG Switzerland

Funnel: *Blue with white 'macs'.* **Hull:** *Black with white rhinoceros symbol and 'macs', some with white band above red boot-topping.*
History: *Formed 1987.* **Web:** *www.macship.com*

Name	Flag	Year	GRT	DWT	LOA	Bm	Kts	Type	Former names
Algoa Bay	Mhl	1978	18,600	26,901	173	24	16	BC	ex St. Blaize-93, Rosebank-91, Virgo-89, Victory-86
Amber Lagoon	Mhl	1997	23,401	31,916	187	27	17	Co	
Blue Master *	Sgp	1971	20,578	28,876	179	26	16	Co	ex Nahoda Biru-86, Blue Master-84
Diamond Land	Mhl	1981	21,826	28,042	177	27	18	Ro	ex Columbine-94, Conti Bavaria-89, Genova-86, Conti Bavaria-85, Costa Ligure-84
Green Cape	Mhl	1981	21,826	28,052	177	27	18	Ro	ex Natal-94, Bandama-92, Conti Hammonia-91, Als Dedication-89, Conti Hammonia-87, Manhattan-86, Conti Hammonia-85, Costa Arabica-84
Grey Fox	Lbr	1998	23,401	33,684	192	27	16	Co	
Purple Beach	Lbr	1998	23,401	31,916	187	27	17	Co	
Silverfjord *	Sgp	1972	20,584	28,876	179	26	15	Co	ex Chung Shing-87, Silverfjord-83
Stellenbosch	Vct	1978	18,600	26,847	173	24	15	BC	ex Vidal-93, Rowanbank-91, Vento-89, Venture-86

MACS - Maritime Carrier AG. ALGOA BAY. *Hans Kraijenbosch*

Name	Flag	Year	GRT	DWT	LOA	Bm	Kts	Type	Former names
Viborg *	Sgp	1971	20,578	28,876	179	26	15	Co	ex Golden Isle-98, Tropical Isle-87, Arica-85, Taurus-81, Norbeth-78

Operated by MACS - Maritime Carrier Shipping GmbH & Co, Germany
* owned by Choosan Shipping Pte. Ltd (Singapore subsidiary of Tailwind AS, Norway).

Marconsult Schiffahrt (GmbH & Co) KG Germany

Funnel: *Charterers colours.* **Hull:** *Black or grey with red boot-topping.* **History:** *Founded 2003 following end of merger between Marconsult Gesellschaft fur Reedereiberatung (formed 1991) and Johs Thode GmbH (founded 1890).* **Web:** *www.mc-schiffahrt.de*

Name	Flag	Year	GRT	DWT	LOA	Bm	Kts	Type	Former names
CCNI Rotterdam	Atg	1993	16,282	23,465	164	28	19	CC	ex Marcalabria-08, CMA CGM La Bourdonnais-05, CMA La Bourdonnais-00, CMBT Serengeti-98, Contship Pacific-97
Delmas Leixoes	Atg	1996	14,473	18,323	159	24	18	CC	ex Steindeich-07, Guatemala-06, P&O Nedlloyd Mobasa-01, Steindeich-98
Lydia Oldendorff	Atg	1998	13,066	20,526	153	24	17	Co	
Marcatania	Atg	1994	16,259	23,465	165	28	18	CC	ex Pride of Delhi-05, Conti Singapore-04, Maersk Bangkok-00, Contship Singapore-98
Marcommander	Atg	1983	10,544	14,180	151	23	16	CC	ex P&O Nedlloyd Chekka-05, Marcommander-04, MSC Suffolk-03, EWL Costa Rica-02, Marcommander-00, Magallanes-98, CTE Magallanes-98, Magallanes-95, CCNI Magallanes-94, Zim Uruguay-92, Doria-91, Westermarsch-90, Woermann Ulanga-90, Westermarsch-86, Zim Melbourne-86, l/a Westermarsch
Marcompetition	Atg	1994	16,269	23,465	165	28	19	CC	ex Shanghai Star I-06, Buxsund-04, Maersk Shimizu-02, Contship Europe-98
NileDutch Kuito *	Atg	2000	13,066	20,140	153	24	17	Co	ex MSC Toulouse-07, Trina Oldendorff-04, Cielo del Caribe-03, Trina Oldendorff-01
NileDutch Prestige	Atg	1999	13,066	20,567	153	24	17	Co	ex MSC Maracaibo-06, Georg Oldendorff-03, Libra Ecuador-02, CSAV Estambul-00, Georg Oldendorff-00
NileDutch Shanghai ***	Atg	1994	16,282	23,276	163	28	18	CC	ex Marcampania-08, Lina-06, Rejane Delmas-04, Contship New Zealand-97
Ocean **	Atg	1996	12,029	14,587	157	24	19	CC	ex Cala Providencia-04, Ocean-02, Urundi-01, Ocean-99, Ankara-98, Ocean-97
Tasman Challenger	Lbr	1992	17,726	24,190	177	27	18	CC	ex Margret Oldendorff-04, NDS Proteus-03, MSC Damas-03, Margret Oldendorff-02, CCNI Austral-99

MACS - Maritime Carrier AG. PURPLE BEACH. *Allan Ryszka Onions*

Name	Flag	Year	GRT	DWT	LOA	Bm	Kts	Type	Former names

*managed for subsidiary of HCI Capital AG, ** for Viamare Schiffahrts subsidiary of Walther Moller & Co, or *** for Ownership Emissionshaus GmbH, all Germany.*

Compagnie Maritime Marfret   France

Funnel: *Blue with red 'MF', black top.* **Hull:** *Black or light grey with red or pink boot-topping.* **History:** *Formed 1957 as Armement Marseille-Fret SA until 1989.* **Web:** *www.marfret.fr*

Name	Flag	Year	GRT	DWT	LOA	Bm	Kts	Type	Former names
Marfret Douce France	Fra	2004	14,067	17,145	155	25	18	CC	ex Sima Prime-04
Marfret Durande	Fra	2003	18,334	23,579	175	27	18	CC	ex Delmas Forbin-06, Durande-03, I/a Hansa Sonderburg
Marfret Guyane	Fra	2007	17,594	18,860	170	27	21	CC	
Marfret Marajo	Rif	2008	17,594	21,260	170	27	21	CC	
Sormiou	Lux	2001	27,093	33,220	210	30	22	CC	ex Rodin-07, CMA CGM Rodin-06, I/a Ansgaritor

Martime-Gesellschaft fur Maritime Diens GmbH   Germany

Funnel: *Large blue 'M' or charterers colours.* **Hull:** *Grey with red boot-topping.* **History:** *Formed 1994.* **Web:** *www.martime.de*

Name	Flag	Year	GRT	DWT	LOA	Bm	Kts	Type	Former names
Alianca Andes **	Deu	1996	16,211	20,976	168	28	21	CC	ex Cap Reinga-06, Columbus Coromandel-04, I/a Hispania
Alianca Patagonia **	Lbr	1997	16,211	20,983	168	27	21	CC	ex Cap Cortes-06, Fresena-03, Cabo Creus-03, Monte Rosa-01, Azteca-00, Columbus la Plata-99, Fresena-98

Marconsult Schiffahrt. NILEDUTCH PRESTIGE. *Guido van Driessche*

Compagnie Maritime Marfret. MARFRET DOUCE FRANCE. *Hans Kraijenbosch*

Name	Flag	Year	GRT	DWT	LOA	Bm	Kts	Type	Former names
Alianca Shanghai **	Lbr	1998	25,499	34,116	200	30	21	CC	ex P&O Nedlloyd Eagle-03, Columbus Texas-01, Gallia-98
Americas Bridge	Lbr	2007	28,050	38,096	215	30	21	CC	I/a Olivia
ANL Binburra **	Lbr	2002	25,587	33,940	201	30	21	CC	ex Cap Spencer-08, Alianca Bahia-07, Kassandra-02
Cap Bonavista **	Lbr	1999	25,535	33,917	200	30	21	CC	ex P&O Nedlloyd La Spezia-02, I/a Cap Bonavista
Cap Campbell	Lbr	2007	28,050	38,013	215	30	21	CC	ex Olympia-07
Cap Castillo	Lbr	2008	28,097	37,763	215	30	21	CC	
Cap Delgado **	Lbr	2000	25,535	34,026	200	30	21	CC	ex P&O Nedlloyd Salerno-02, Cap Delgado-00
Cap Ortegal **	Lbr	1998	25,500	34,362	199	30	21	CC	ex CMA CGM Delacroix-02, Cap Ortegal-00, Gemini-98
Cap Reinga **	Lbr	2001	25,535	33,917	200	30	21	CC	ex CSCL Longkou-07, Juturna-01
Cap Stewart **	Lbr	2001	25,535	33,894	200	30	21	CC	ex CSCL Yantai-08, I/a Jasmin
Cape Molloni †	Mhl	2006	27,786	37,800	222	30	22	CC	ex CMA CGM Jefferson-08, Cape Molloni-06
Conti Emden *	Lbr	2006	27,915	37,900	215	30	21	CC	ex Medusa-06, Zim Norfolk-07, Conti Emden-06
Cosco Brisbane	Lbr	2005	27,915	38,121	215	30	21	CC	
Cosco Panama	Lbr	2005	27,915	37,900	215	30	21	CC	
CSAV Romeral	Lbr	2008	36,087	42,600	229	32	24	CC	ex Quadriga-08
CSAV Rungue	Lbr	2008	36,087	42,600	229	32	24	CC	
DAL Reunion	Mhl	2006	27,786	37,854	222	30	22	CC	ex YM Mondego-07, Cape Mondego-06
Dolores **	Lbr	1987	20,344	29,358	181	29	20	CC	ex CSAV Rio Amazonas-04, Dolores-03, P&O Nedlloyd Nina-02, Dolores-01, Kota Sempena-01, Zim Chicago-00, Dolores-99, City of Haifa-99, Dolores-98, Nelson Bay-98, Dolores-94, OOCL Breeze-93, Dolores-91, ScanDutch Gallia-90, Dolores-87
Elisabeth	Lbr	1994	21,034	29,931	182	28	19	CC	ex CSAV Colombia-08, X-Press Resolute-07, CCNI Valparaiso-05, Kota Permasan-04, Elisabeth-99, Cielo di Los Angeles-99, Elisabeth-94
Europa Bridge	Lbr	2007	27,915	38,131	215	30	21	CC	ex Najade-07
Eyrene **	Lbr	1993	21,034	29,931	182	28	19	CC	ex Clan Tribune-07, Eyrene-05, Norasia Seoul-03, CSAV Seattle-00, P&O Nedlloyd San Jose-00, Nedlloyd San Jose-98, Eyrene-94
Fiducia **	Deu	1997	16,211	21,008	168	27	21	CC	ex TS Kobe-08, Columbus Florida-06, Fiducia-97
Helvetia **	Lbr	1996	15,859	20,084	167	27	19	CC	ex TS Shanghai-08, Helvetia-05, Columbus Pacific-03, Sea Amazon-97, Helvetia-96, Columbus Olinda-96, Helvetia-96
MOL Symphony **	Lbr	2001	25,535	35,976	200	30	21	CC	ex CSCL Lianyungang-08, Katharina-01
MSC Wellington	Atg	1980	16,868	21,569	164	29	18	CC	ex Barbarossa-06, Nuova Australia-98, Zura Bhum-96, Barbarossa-94, Alum Bay-94, Sea Progress-92, Hoechst Express-91, JSS Britannia-88, JSS Los Angeles I-86, JSS Los Angeles-86, Barbarossa-86, Ibn Al-Akfani-83, I/a Barbarossa
Nona **	Lbr	2006	27,915	37,900	215	30	21	CC	
Tiger Shark **	Lbr	1994	22,738	34,500	188	28	19	CC	ex Sea Bright-06, Med Kaohsiung-95, Ming Bright-95

* managed for Conti Holdings GmbH & Co KG, ** for Gebab GmbH or † for Salamon AG. See also Konig & Cie GmbH

Mediterranean Shipping Co SA   Switzerland

Funnel: Cream with cream 'MSC' on black disc, narrow black band below black top. **Hull:** Black with cream 'MSC', red boot-topping.
History: Formed 1970. **Web:** www.mscgva.ch

Name	Flag	Year	GRT	DWT	LOA	Bm	Kts	Type	Former names
Cosco Chiwan *	Pan	1986	39,892	43,567	244	32	21	CC	ex Hyundai Innovator-06, Sydney Star 1-03, Hyundai Innovator-02
Cosco Lianyungang *	Pan	1986	39,892	43,567	244	32	21	CC	ex Hyundai Frontier-06, MSC Pretoria-04, Hyundai Frontier-02, Lalandia-92, Hyundai Frontier-88
Cosco Shekou *	Pan	1986	39,892	43,567	244	32	21	CC	ex Hyundai Explorer-06, P&O Nedlloyd Pusan-03, Hyundai Explorer-02

Name	Flag	Year	GRT	DWT	LOA	Bm	Kts	Type	Former names
MSC Accra ***	Mhl	1985	22,667	33,857	188	28	18	CC	ex Nautic-07, Hellas Macedonia-03, MSC Africa-03, Hellas Macedonia-02, MSC Recife-02, P&O Nedlloyd Peru-01, MSC Caracas-00, Hellas Macedonia-99, Canmar Pride-96, Canmar Fortune -95, Sea Macedonia-94, Hellas Macedonia-94, Hellas Senator-92, Bremen Senator-92, ScanDutch Honshu-88, Modern Trader-87, Alameda-86, World Success-85 (conv C)
MSC Adele	Pan	1986	21,633	31,205	187	28	17	CC	ex Norasia Sharjah-94
MSC Adriana	Pan	1998	25,219	18,779	216	27	25	CC	ex MSC Malaysia-04, Warwick-03, ADCL Sheba-02, Norasia Sheba-00
MSC Africa §	Mlt	1987	16,250	23,465	163	28	18	CC	ex Tiger Sea-07, Scio Star-03, Merkur River-03, Venezuela-01, Merkur River-01, MSC Diego-99, Merkur River-98, CMB Antwerp-97, Antwerp-94, Red Sea Enterprise-93, Ville de Saturne-91
MSC Agata *	Pan	1982	20,345	28,422	174	28	18	CC	ex DAL Madagascar-03, SEAL Usaramo-00, Sea Trade-97, Usaramo-87
MSC Alexa	Pan	1996	42,307	51,111	244	32	22	CC	
MSC Alexandra	Pan	1987	31,340	41,771	199	32	18	BC	ex MSC Orinoco-99, Toluca-99, MSC Nicole-99, Toluca-98
MSC Alpana *	Pan	1978	28,060	28,153	204	31	20	CC	ex Indfex SCI-02, Angela-01, Zim Beijing-01, Angela-99, Oregon Star-98, Angela-97, Uruguay Express-96, Alemania Express-92
MSC Alyssa	Pan	2001	43,575	61,487	274	32	23	CC	
MSC America *	Pan	1993	34,231	45,696	216	32	19	CC	ex American Senator-04, DSR-America-00
MSC Amy *	Pan	1992	11,872	14,342	157	23	17	CC	ex Pellini-04, Esteclipper-04, MSC Ukraine-03, Esteclipper-01, Melbridge Pride-99, Cielo del Venezuela-98, Esteclipper-97, Nedlloyd Catarina-97, Aurora-95, Esteclipper-92, I/a Kalamazoo
MSC Anafi ***	Lbr	1994	30,526	34,079	205	32	19	CC	ex Anafi-08, Ajama-07, CP Pathfinder-06, Lykes Pathfinder-05, DAL East London-04, Ajama-02, Sea Star-99, Choyang Grace-97, Delaware Bay-95, Sea Musketeer-94, Ajama-94, I/a Charles de Foucauld
MSC Anahita *	Pan	1985	34,285	36,377	224	32	20	CC	ex CMC Pearl-04, Harbour Bridge-02
MSC Anastasia	Pan	1970	16,670	21,307	181	28	20	CC	ex POL Baltic-95, Leverkusen Express-90, CGM Lorraine-86, Leverkusen Express-85, pt.ex Leverkusen-78 (len/wid-78)
MSC Ancona #	Hkg	1989	52,191	60,640	294	32	23	CC	ex Maersk Moncton-08, Mathilde Maersk-06
MSC Angela	Pan	2008	41,225	50,568	265	32	24	CC	
MSC Aniello	Pan	2000	40,631	56,916	260	32	23	CC	
MSC Annamaria	Pan	1987	21,633	31,205	187	28	17	CC	ex Norasia Al-Mansoorah-94
MSC Annick *	Pan	1988	13,315	16,768	159	23	15	CC	ex Promotor N-04, Contship Asia-03, NDS Benguela-02, Contship Asia-02, Tiger Wave-98, Jurong Express-96, Columbus Ohio-96
MSC Ans	Pan	2004	53,500	67,800	294	32	24	CC	
MSC Antonia	Pan	1985	22,667	33,864	188	28	18	CC	ex Mixteco-94, Birthe Oldendorff-93, Ville de Castor-92, DSR Oakland-92, London Senator-91, ScanDutch Hispania-89, Commander-87, Astoria-86, World Champion-85
MSC Arabia ***	Mlt	1972	14,453	21,834	171	23	16	CC	Zim Odessa I-04, Heung-A Carmen-98, Leeward-96, Lizard-85, Neckar Express-84, Freienfels-80, Aristarchos-75
MSC Asli	Pan	2000	24,836	14,150	217	27	25	CC	ex Lincoln-04, ADCL Salwa-02, Norasia Salwa-00
MSC Astrid *	Pan	2004	35,954	42,186	231	32	22	CC	ex MSC Delhi-07, Northern Distinction-04
MSC Asya	Pan	2008	107,849	112,063	337	46	26	CC	
MSC Atlantic ‡‡	Pan	1991	37,071	46,975	237	32	21	CC	ex Rostock Senator-02, DSR-Rostock-00
MSC Augusta	Pan	1986	21,648	31,205	187	28	17	CC	ex Norasia Pearl-94
MSC Aurelie *	Pan	1979	37,238	39,766	251	32	25	CC	ex OOCL Envoy-07, China Container-91 (len-82)
MSC Aurora *	Pan	1971	13,276	18,534	175	23	19	CC	ex Aurora-94, Acadia-86, Atlantica Genova-76, Gruenfels-71 (len-73)
MSC Ayala *	Pan	1985	36,124	35,382	215	32	20	CC	ex Alen-04, Oasis Altair-03, Ligwa-03, Great Rizal-96, Oasis Altair-90
MSC Baleares ††	Mhl	1962	17,618	15,417	202	24	18	CC	ex Pacer-07, Sea-Land Pacer-06, San Juan-78 (rblt-78)
MSC Bali †††	Mhl	1980	32,629	30,298	257	31	20	CC	ex Sea-Land Explorer-07
MSC Banu *	Pan	2004	35,964	42,141	231	32	22	CC	ex MSC Queensland-07, I/a Northern Devotion

Name	Flag	Year	GRT	DWT	LOA	Bm	Kts	Type	Former names
MSC Barbara	Pan	2002	73,819	85,250	304	40	25	CC	
MSC Beatrice	Pan	2009	135,000	165,000	380	51	25	CC	
MSC Belgium #	Cyp	2004	90,645	101,810	334	43	25	CC	ex CSCL Oceania-07
MSC Benedetta ø	Sgp	2006	54,214	68,126	294	32	23	CC	
MSC Borneo †	Pan	1985	18,145	25,088	180	27	17	CC	ex Mamitsa-06, Ghana Star-02, Arkona-00, MSC Argentina-99, MSC Nicole-98, Arkona-97, CGM Colbert-95, Arkona-95, Kaduna-93, CGM La Perouse-93, CMB Merzario-92, Lyme Bay-90, Red Sea Excellence-89, Arkona-88
MSC Brianna *	Pan	1986	40,177	43,288	244	32	19	CC	ex Neptune Jade-97
MSC Brooke	Pan	1992	12,997	17,610	150	25	17	CC	ex MOL Rise-08, YM Hai Phong-07, Holnis-04, Lagos Star II-01, Elise Schulte-98, Maersk Banjul-98, Elise Schulte-97, CCNI Antartico-95, Elise Schulte-92
MSC Bulgaria ##	Lbr	1988	30,824	25,684	202	31	17	CC	ex Kestrel I-07, Pelican I-03, Zim Antwerp I-02, Asia Opal-02, LT Mediterranea-99, Nuova Mediterranea-99, Genova-96, Erna Oldendorff-81, H. Cegielski-91
MSC Caitlin	Pan	1998	25,219	18,779	216	27	25	CC	ex Oxford-05, ADCL Shamsaa-01, Norasia Shamsaa-00, Norasia Salome-99
MSC Calcutta §§	Cyp	1979	17,682	18,782	201	24	18	CC	ex Hanjin Busan-07
MSC Camille	Pan	2009	135,000	165,000	380	51	25	CC	
MSC Canberra	Pan	1995	29,181	41,583	203	31	19	CC	ex Joseph-01, TMM Puebla-01, Joseph-00, Zim Venezia I-98, Med Fos-97, Joseph Lykes-96
MSC Candice	Pan	2007	107,849	111,749	337	46	26	CC	
MSC Carina *	Pan	1986	42,260	45,725	241	32	22	CC	ex MSC Europe-03, Rainbow Bridge-02
MSC Carla *	Pan	1986	35,953	43,300	241	32	20	CC	ex Hanjin Longbeach-01
MSC Carmen *	Pan	2008	50,963	63,359	275	32	23	CC	
MSC Carole *	Pan	1980	16,600	21,936	179	23	15	Co	ex Vega-03, Seaboard Santiago-02, Vega-02, Pamina-83, CP Hunter-81, Pamina-80
MSC Carolina	Pan	2005	65,483	72,000	275	40	26	CC	
MSC Chelsea *	Pan	1983	17,468	25,412	166	29	18	CC	ex Concordia-04, Hyundai Inchon-95, Concordia-95, Nedlloyd Seoul-95, Red Sea Eureka-93, Concordia-92, Incotrans Pacific-90, Concordia-87, JSS Los Angeles-86, Concordia-86, ScanDutch Concordia-85, Concordia-83
MSC Chiara	Pan	1988	31,430	41,828	199	32	18	BC	ex TMM Morelos-01, Morelos-00
MSC Chitra *	Pan	1980	33,113	38,485	231	32	23	CC	ex Crystal I-04, APL Crystal-01, NOL Crystal-00, Neptune Crystal-96
MSC Christina *	Cyp	1998	37,579	56,902	243	32	23	CC	ex P&O Nedlloyd Chicago-04
MSC Clorinda	Pan	1981	32,238	30,714	222	32	23	CC	ex Ace Concord-94, Neptune Accord-86, Kawana-84, Ace Concord-82
MSC Corinna	Pan	1984	32,703	38,466	207	32	20	CC	ex Med Singapore-97, Ville de Sirius-94, Rhein Express-91, Verhaeren-84
MSC Corsica ††	Mhl	1980	27,994	27,631	204	31	20	CC	ex Safmarine Infant-02, SCL Infanta-00, Author-99, Benarmin-82, Author-81
MSC Cristiana *	Pan	1984	17,700	20,221	184	25	18	Co	ex Absalon-03, Kota Maha-01, Absalon-00, Kenya Star I-00, Absalon-99, Presidente Sarmiento-98, Lanka Abhaya-87, Andalusia-85, Euro Star-84
MSC Damla ‡	Pan	1980	32,629	30,379	257	31	20	CC	ex Sea-Land Defender-07
MSC Daniela	Pan	2008	151,559	165,000	380	51	25	CC	
MSC Debra Ø	Mhl	2006	54,214	68,080	294	32	23	CC	ex MSC Deborah-06
MSC Deila *	Pan	1979	20,391	21,457	186	27	21	Ro	ex Nuova Piave-93, Da Mosto-89 (conv Ro-89)
MSC Denisse *	Pan	1977	28,176	23,058	204	31	21	CC	ex CanMar Force-01, Caraibe-00
MSC Didem *	Pan	1987	35,598	43,108	241	32	21	CC	ex Savannah-05, SCI Asha-03, Savannah-02, Hanjin Savannah-01
MSC Diego	Pan	1999	40,631	56,889	260	32	23	CC	
MSC Don Giovanni *	Pan	1996	29,181	41,583	203	31	19	CC	ex Jean-96, I/a Jean Lykes
MSC Donata *	Lbr	2002	40,108	52,806	258	32	24	CC	
MSC Dymphna	Pan	1988	36,420	43,224	241	32	22	CC	ex Hanjin Rotterdam-98
MSC Edith	Pan	1998	25,219	18,779	216	27	25	CC	ex Lykes Crusader-05, Ayrshire-04, Safmarine Prime-04, Ayrshire-03, ADCL Samantha-01, Norasia Samantha-00
MSC Edna	Pan	1977	35,599	38,686	252	31	23	CC	ex OOCL Educator-96, Oriental Educator-88, Seapac Lexington-83, Oriental Researcher-81, I/a Oriental Chevalier
MSC Ela	Pan	2004	54,304	67,800	294	32	24	CC	
MSC Elena *	Pan	1994	30,971	36,887	202	32	21	CC	ex TMM Sonora-04, Houston Express-00, Sonora -99
MSC Eleni	Pan	2004	54,881	67,800	294	32	24	CC	

Name	Flag	Year	GRT	DWT	LOA	Bm	Kts	Type	Former names
MSC Eleonora *	Pan	1994	28,892	41,667	203	31	20	CC	ex MSC Beijing-03, Trade Cosmos-02, Sea Excellence-96, Trade Cosmos-95
MSC Eliana *	Pan	1970	13,875	14,258	187	23	18	CC	ex Ming Hope-90, Ho Ming-77, Hai Mou-73 (len-79)
MSC Eloise *	Pan	1991	37,902	44,541	241	32	18	CC	ex Maersk Niigata-07, Arafura-06
MSC Emma	Pan	2003	53,500	67,800	294	32	24	CC	
MSC Endurance ††	Mhl	1980	32,629	30,224	257	31	20	CC	ex Sea-Land Endurance-07
MSC Erminia *	Pan	1979	17,304	14,520	170	25	19	CC	ex MSC Provence-04, City of Liverpool-03, Zim Liverpool I-00, Mor Canada-99, Nikolay Golovanov-94
MSC Esthi	Lbr	2006	107,849	110,838	337	46	26	CC	
MSC Eugenia	Pan	1992	53,521	61,428	275	37	24	CC	ex Bunga Pelangi-07
MSC Eyra *	Pan	1982	21,586	21,370	203	25	20	CC	ex Pelineo-04, Miden Agan-02, Maersk Toronto-00, Miden Agan-97, CMA Le Cap-95, Kapitan Kozlovskiy-95 (len-89)
MSC Fabienne	Pan	2004	54,774	66,825	294	32	24	CC	
MSC Federica * (2)	Cyp	1974	21,296	21,101	209	27	18	CC	ex MSC Gina-99, Gina-94, Water Gina-91, Gina S-90, Australia-86, Malmros Monsoon-84
MSC Fiammetta	Pan	2008	66,242	73,355	277	40	24	CC	
MSC Finland ***	Lbr	1986	42,000	40,928	243	32	22	CC	ex West Gate Bridge-07, George Washington Bridge-05
MSC Florentina	Pan	2003	75,590	85,000	304	40	25	CC	
MSC Floriana	Pan	1986	21,648	31,205	187	28	17	CC	ex Princess-95, Norasia Princess-94
MSC Francesca	Pan	2009	120,000	145,000	366	46	25	CC	
MSC Freedom ††	Mhl	1980	32,629	30,416	257	31	20	CC	ex Sea-Land Freedom-07
MSC Gabriella *	Pan	1983	13,038	17,330	158	23	15	Co	ex Pearl Merchant-01, New Hailong-95, Ciudad de Buenaventura-93, Webber's Post-88, Nedlloyd Cristobal-86, Giahara-86, Woermann Wangoni-85, Family Irini-84
MSC Gianna *	Pan	1983	27,758	42,077	209	30	15	BC	ex Hellen C-03, Jolly Ebano-01, Hellen C-00, Ellen Hudig-97
MSC Gina	Pan	1999	40,631	56,889	260	32	23	CC	
MSC Giorgia	Pan	1985	22,667	33,823	188	28	18	CC	ex Maya-94, DSR Yokohama-93, Tokyo Senator-91, ScanDutch Massilia-88, Azuma-87, Pacific Pride-86
MSC Giovanna	Pan	1987	27,103	25,904	178	32	18	CC	ex MSC Provence-99, Dubrovnik Express-99, Koper Express-96
MSC Giulia	Pan	1970	16,670	21,185	181	28	21	CC	ex POL Gulf-93, Ludwigshafen-90, Ludwigshafen Express-90, pt ex Ludwigshafen-79 (len/wid-79)
MSC Grace *	Pan	1991	13,861	17,298	155	23	16	Co	ex Putney Bridge-02, Melanesian Chief-00, Putney Bridge-99, Mikhail Tsarev-97, Zim Rio-96, Mikhail Tsarev-94, Contship Columbus-93, Mikhail Tsarev-93
MSC Hailey *	Pan	1994	38,395	46,967	236	32	21	CC	ex Alva Star-05, Norasia Malta-01, MSC Jasmine-98, Norasia Malta-96
MSC Hanne *	Pan	1989	32,630	33,310	206	32	19	CC	ex Energy I-08, ANL Energy-06, CMA CG< Energy-06, Cristoforo Colombo-04, Zim Antwerp-01, Cristoforo Colombo-99

Mediterranean Shipping Co. MSC INES. *Hans Kraijenbosch*

Name	Flag	Year	GRT	DWT	LOA	Bm	Kts	Type	Former names
MSC Heidi	Pan	2006	95,000	107,850	332	43	25	CC	
MSC Himalaya ***	Mlt	1978	27,297	33,621	228	29	19	CC	ex Himalaya-02, MSC Himalaya-02, Evge-01, Smart River-99, YS Prosperity-92, Oriental Premier-86, Oriental Expert-83 (len-83)
MSC Hina *	Pan	1984	21,585	21,370	203	25	20	CC	ex Leixoes-03, MSC Melbourne-01, Leixoes-98, Tikhon Kiselyev-95
MSC Ibiza ≠	Hkg	1993	9,602	12,577	150	23	17	CC	ex Judith Schulte-08, P&O Nedlloyd Curacao-05, Judith Schulte-98, Maersk Conakry-98, Fas Lattaquie-96, Judith Schulte-96, Libra Barcelona-95, Judith Schulte-95, TSL Gallant-94, Judith Schulte-94
MSC Ilaria *	Pan	1977	20,408	16,167	181	27	18	CC	ex Antigoni-00, Norasia Toronto-00, Antigoni-99, MSC Granada-99, Antigoni-98, UB Tiger-98, Malacca Glory-98, Alkistis-96, Eastern Trader-95, Golfo de Chiriqui-95, Ciudad de Quito-84
MSC Imma *	Pan	1983	27,758	42,077	209	30	17	BC	ex Princess Stefanie-04, Jolly Avorio-01, Princess Stefanie-00, Prince Nicolas-00, Cornelis Verolme-97
MSC Immacolata *	Pan	1979	17,304	14,719	170	25	20	CC	ex Immacolata-04, Sumatra-04, MSC Sumatra-03, Essex-02, Mor UK-00, Nadezhda Obukhova-94
MSC India *	Pan	1991	13,258	17,298	155	23	16	Co	ex Albert Bridge-02, Kiribati Chief-01, Niugini Chief-01, Chekiang-99, Albert Bridge-98, Nedlloyd Everest-97, Aleksandr Marinesko-95, Orient Shreyas-95, Aleksandr Marinesko-93
MSC Ines	Lbr	2006	107,551	108,461	337	46	25	CC	
MSC Ingrid *	Pan	1999	53,208	67,678	294	32	25	CC	ex Saudi Jeddah-02
MSC Iris *	Pan	1982	21,586	21,370	203	25	20	CC	ex Pelat-04, MSC Eyra-04, Pelat-04, Lisboa-02, P&O Nedlloyd Ottawa-00, Sea-Land Canada-99, Lisboa-97, Kapitan Gavrilov-95 (len-89)
MSC Ivana	Pan	2009	135,000	165,000	380	51	25	CC	
MSC Jade *	Pan	1986	36,514	43,293	241	32	20	CC	ex Hanjin Yokohama-01
MSC Jasmine	Pan	1988	31,430	41,828	199	32	18	BC	ex TMM Oaxaca-00, Contship Houston-97, Oaxaca-96
MSC Jeanne *	Pan	1979	33,113	38,492	233	32	23	CC	ex CMC Diamond-04, APL Diamond-02, NOL Diamond-98, Neptune Diamond-96
MSC Jemima ‡‡	Pan	1994	30,971	36,887	202	32	20	CC	ex Nuevo Leon-05, TMM Nuevo Leon-03, Nuevo Leon-00
MSC Jenny *	Pan	1988	39,990	43,537	245	32	21	CC	ex Hyundai Commander-04, NYK Pride-04, Hyundai Commander-00
MSC Jessica *	Pan	1980	23,291	23,930	202	30	19	CC	ex Columbus Olivos-01, Alianca Hamburgo-98, Columbus Olivos-97, Monte Pascoal-96, Columbus Olivos-95, Monte Pascoal-90, Dunedin-86
MSC Jilhan *	Pan	1986	14,068	19,560	162	25	18	CC	ex Kapitan Kurov-04, Contship Italy-93, Red Sea Europa-91, CGM Roussillon-90, Sandra K-88, Sea Merchant-88, JSS Scandinavia-88, l/a Sandra K
MSC Joanna	Lbr	2006	107,849	107,850	337	46	25	CC	
MSC Jordan	Lbr	1993	37,071	47,120	237	32	21	CC	ex Sovcomflot Senator-03
MSC Judith	Pan	2006	90,300	101,000	325	43	25	CC	
MSC Katherine Ann *	Pan	1985	17,700	20,169	184	25	18	CC	ex Alter Ego-04, Kota Mutiara-01, Alter Ego-00, Dr. Juan B. Alberdi-98, Lanka Amitha-87, Aquitania-85, l/a Eurosun
MSC Kerry	Pan	1995	37,323	45,530	240	32	22	CC	ex Ville de Norma-98
MSC Kim	Pan	2008	41,225	50,547	265	32	24	CC	
MSC Krystal	Pan	2008	66,242	72,900	277	40	24	CC	
MSC Lana *	Pan	1983	31,403	32,631	218	32	21	CC	ex Pacific Quest-08, Richmond Bridge-98, Hyundai Portland-97, Maersk Rotterdam-94, Richmond Bridge-93
MSC Lara *	Pan	1994	28,892	38,270	203	31	20	CC	ex MSC Bruxelles-04, Trade Apollo-02, Jadroplov Trader-95, Chesapeake Bay-95, Sea Excellence-94, Trade Sol-94
MSC Laura	Pan	2002	75,590	85,928	300	40	24	CC	
MSC Lauren	Pan	1982	32,238	30,790	222	32	25	CC	ex OOCL Charisma-93, Oriental Patriot-91
MSC Laurence	Pan	1977	32,341	30,937	222	32	23	CC	ex Dragon Komodo-97, NOL Coral-96, Neptune Coral-96
MSC Lea	Pan	2000	24,836	14,150	217	27	25	CC	ex Shropshire-04, ADCL Sabrina-01, l/a Norasia Sabrina
MSC Leader ††	Mhl	1962	17,618	15,417	202	24	18	CC	ex Sea Leader-08, Sea-Land Leader-89,

Name	Flag	Year	GRT	DWT	LOA	Bm	Kts	Type	Former names
MSC Leanne *	Pan	1983	17,702	20,128	184	25	18	Co	Elizabethport-78 (rblt-78) ex Honour-03, MSC Leanne-03, Honour-03, Kota Molek-01, Delmas Surville-00, Honour-99, Ocean Sirius-95, Lanka Asitha-89, Laredo-84
MSC Leigh	Pan	2006	50,963	63,411	275	32	23	CC	
MSC Leila *	Pan	1987	13,315	16,804	159	23	16	CC	ex Tiger Cloud-05, Heluan-03, Dubai Confidence-98, Heluan-96, Columbus Olinda-96
MSC Levina	Pan	1989	36,420	43,140	241	32	21	CC	ex Hanjin Le Havre-98
MSC Lieselotte *	Pan	1983	21,586	21,370	203	25	20	CC	ex Aveiro-03, Tiger Sea-02, Aveiro-02, Nikolay Tikhonov-95 (len-89)
MSC Linzie	Pan	2003	54,881	68,209	294	32	23	CC	
MSC Lisa	Pan	2004	54,304	68,577	294	32	24	CC	
MSC Lorena	Pan	2006	50,000	54,450	261	32	24	CC	
MSC Loretta	Pan	2002	73,819	85,801	304	40	25	CC	
MSC Lucia *	Pan	1978	14,953	20,239	187	25	17	CC	ex Tiger Star-04, Hanjin Cheju-00, Ever Voyager-83
MSC Lucy	Pan	2005	89,954	101,661	325	43	25	CC	
MSC Ludovica	Pan	2003	75,590	85,882	304	40	25	CC	
MSC Lugano	Pan	1988	35,958	42,795	241	32	21	CC	ex CSCL Bremen-04, Choyang Success-01
MSC Luisa	Pan	2002	75,590	84,920	304	40	25	CC	
MSC Madeleine	Lbr	2006	107,551	108,637	337	46	25	CC	ex Ambika-06
MSC Maeva	Pan	2005	89,954	101,661	325	43	25	CC	
MSC Magali *	Pan	1980	33,113	38,485	231	32	23	CC	ex Amber I-03, APL Amber-01, NOL Amber-00, Neptune Amber-96
MSC Malin *	Pan	1982	21,586	21,370	203	25	20	CC	ex Pelado-04, Tavira-03, Maersk Montreal-00, Tavira-97, Kapitan Kanlevskiy -95 (len-89)
MSC Mandy	Pan	1993	37,071	47,120	237	32	21	CC	ex SCI Vaibhav-04, Bremen Senator-03
MSC Manila §§	Cyp	1979	17,933	18,798	201	24	17	CC	ex Hanjin Pohang-07
MSC Manu (2)	Pan	1978	52,682	49,217	259	32	22	CC	ex Kalahari-05, DAL Kalahari-05, Maersk Hamburg-95, Aberdeen Bay-93, Ortelius-92, London Express-92, Ortelius-91, London Express-90, Nuptse-88, Ortelius 86
MSC Mara Ø	Pan	2006	54,214	68,165	294	32	23	CC	
MSC Maria *	Pan	1985	21,586	21,370	203	26	20	CC	ex Delphic Spirit-03, Zim Seoul-99, Delphic Spirit-99, MSC Uruguay-98, Miden River-98, Spevde Vradeos-97, Algoa Bay-95, Professor Tovstykh-95
MSC Maria Elena	Pan	2006	107,849	108,200	337	46	25	CC	ex MSC Fiorenza-06
MSC Maria Laura	Pan	1988	36,343	42,513	229	32	20	CC	ex Sea Cheetah-00, Cap Verde-00, CGM La Perouse-98, Ville de la Fontaine-93, La Fontaine-92, CGM La Perouse-91
MSC Maria Pia	Pan	1997	29,115	40,117	196	32	22	CC	ex MSC Bremen-04, Lykes Innovator-03, Safmarine Erebus-02, CMBT Erebus-01, Northern Vision-97
MSC Marianna	Pan	2002	73,819	85,250	304	40	25	CC	ex MSC Loraine-02
MSC Marina	Pan	2003	73,819	85,806	304	40	25	CC	

Mediterranean Shipping Co. MSC LORENA. *Hans Kraijenbosch*

Name	Flag	Year	GRT	DWT	LOA	Bm	Kts	Type	Former names
MSC Marta	Pan	2005	65,483	72,000	275	40	26	CC	
MSC Martina	Pan	1993	37,398	43,378	243	32	22	CC	ex Maersk Hong Kong-97, Hansa America-93
MSC Marylena	Pan	1998	25,219	18,779	216	27	25	CC	ex Cheshire-05, ADCL Savannah-01, Norasia Savannah-00
MSC Matilde *	Pan	1999	53,208	67,615	294	32	25	CC	ex Saudi Jubail-02
MSC Maureen	Pan	2003	75,590	85,832	304	40	25	CC	
MSC Maya	Pan	1988	35,598	43,184	242	32	21	CC	ex Maersk Levant-04, MSC Jamie-02, Hanjin Seattle-98
MSC Mediterranean	Pan	1995	29,181	41,583	203	31	19	CC	ex Nautic II-04, CMA CGM Monet-02, James-00, James Lykes-96
MSC Mee May	Pan	1970	16,670	21,185	181	29	21	CC	ex Mee May-94, Erlangen Express-86, Incotrans Progress-82, Erlangen Express-81, Erlangen-79 (len/wid-79)
MSC Mekong ***	Mlt	1978	11,314	13,101	153	23	16	CC	ex Beauty-07, Sea Lotus-01, World Tiger-89
MSC Melissa	Pan	2002	73,819	85,250	304	40	25	CC	
MSC Mia Summer	Pan	1999	25,219	18,779	216	27	25	CC	ex Buckinghamshire-05, ADCL Scarlet-01, Norasia Scarlet-00
MSC Michaela	Pan	2002	73,819	85,797	304	40	25	CC	
MSC Michele	Pan	1971	16,670	21,185	181	29	21	CC	ex Michele-94, Incotrans Pacific-86, Hoechst Express-84, Incotrans Promise-83, Hoechst Express-81, Hoechst-79 (len/wid-79)
MSC Mirella *	Pan	1989	27,103	25,904	178	32	18	CC	ex Zagreb Express-99,
MSC Monica	Pan	1993	37,398	43,378	243	32	22	CC	ex Ville d'Aquila-97, Hansa Asia-93
MSC Natalia *	Pan	1986	40,177	43,403	244	32	21	CC	ex MSC California-01, Vision-99, Choyang Vision-98, Neptune Garnet-96

Mediterranean Shipping Co. MSC MARIA ELENA. *J. M. Kakebeeke*

Mediterranean Shipping Co. MSC MARTA. *Hans Kraijenbosch*

Name	Flag	Year	GRT	DWT	LOA	Bm	Kts	Type	Former names
MSC Nederland	Pan	1992	37,071	47,120	237	32	21	CC	ex Vladivostok Mariner-03, Vladivostok Senator-02
MSC Nerissa	Pan	2004	54,881	67,800	294	32	24	CC	
MSC Nicole	Pan	1989	31,430	41,828	199	32	18	BC	ex Contship America-00, Monterrey-00, MSC Lima-98, Nedlloyd Montevideo-98, Monterrey-97
MSC Nikita	Pan	1980	32,629	30,374	257	31	20	CC	ex Sea-Land Independence-07
MSC Nilgun	Pan	1994	30,971	36,887	202	32	20	CC	ex P&O Nedlloyd Pinta-05, Contship Inspiration-02, TMM Yucatan-01, Yucatan-00
MSC Noa *	Pan	1986	35,953	43,270	241	32	20	CC	ex Hanjin Newyork-02
MSC Normandie	Pan	1983	20,345	28,422	174	28	18	CC	ex New Challenge-02, DAL Reunion-02, Catherine Delmas-00, Sea Commerce-97, Usambara-87, Victoria Bay-86, Usambara-84
MSC Nuria	Pan	2008	50,963	63,377	275	32	23	CC	
MSC Olga Ø	Sgp	2006	54,214	68,135	294	32	23	CC	
MSC Oriane	Pan	2008	66,399	72,900	277	40	24	CC	
MSC Ornella	Pan	2004	54,304	67,800	294	32	24	CC	
MSC Oslo *	Pan	1989	32,630	33,310	206	32	19	CC	ex SCI Tej-07, CMA CGM Force-06, Amerigo Vespucci-04, Zim Hamburg-01, Amerigo Vespucci-99
MSC Pamela	Pan	2005	107,849	110,592	337	46	26	CC	
MSC Paola *	Pan	1978	20,295	19,974	202	26	22	CC	ex Safmarine Nomzi-01, Nomzi-00, Boringia-95
MSC Patricia *	Pan	1990	13,651	18,150	166	24	14	Co	ex Torm America-02, Tisno-98, Torm America-97, Vardar Delmas-92, Vardar-91
MSC Peggy	Pan	1984	32,696	38,981	207	32	20	CC	ex Atlantic Bridge-98, CMBT Maeterlinck-97, Med Barcelona-96, Ville de Canopus-94, ScanDutch Helvetia-91, Maeterlinck-89
MSC Perle *	Pan	1983	17,414	25,329	166	29	18	CC	ex Corona-03, Nautic I-02, City of Dublin-00, City of Antwerp-98, City of London-97, Pacific Span-93, Incotrans Pacific-90, ScanDutch Arcadia-90, Korean Senator-88, Corona-87, Atlantic Corona-85, Corona-84, ScanDutch Corona-84, Corona-83
MSC Pilar *	Pan	1984	30,751	30,458	189	32	17	CC	ex Rigena-04, MSC Pilar-04, Rigena-04, Argolikos-03, Morgane Delmas-03, MSC Bogota-01, Argolikos-98, Nedlloyd Pernambuco-97, Deppe Texas-95, Yolande Delmas-95
MSC Pina	Pan	2007	107,849	108,200	337	46	25	CC	
MSC Pioneer ††	Gib	1978	17,618	20,719	202	24	18	CC	ex Sea Pioneer-08, Sea-Land Pioneer-89, Los Angeles-78 (rblt 78)
MSC Poh Lin	Pan	2004	54,774	66,786	294	32	24	CC	
MSC Rachele	Pan	2005	91,038	101,898	335	43	25	CC	
MSC Rafaela	Pan	1996	42,307	51,210	243	32	22	CC	
MSC Rania	Pan	2006	94,489	107,898	332	43	25	CC	
MSC Rebecca *	Pan	1997	37,879	42,926	243	32	22	CC	ex Grand Concord-97
MSC Regina	Pan	1999	40,631	56,890	260	32	23	CC	
MSC Rhone †	Pan	1979	36,133	29,701	216	32	21	CC	ex Arcadian-04, Hakuba Maru-03

Mediterranean Shipping Co. MSC ORIANE. *J. M. Kakebeeke*

Name	Flag	Year	GRT	DWT	LOA	Bm	Kts	Type	Former names
MSC Rimini §	Bhs	1990	10,868	15,174	158	23	18	CC	ex Maersk Rimini-07, Estestar-04, Safmarine Shebeli-03, Estestar-02, P&O Nedlloyd Kowie-01, Estestar-00, Kent Scout-00, Ulf Ritscher-98
MSC Rita	Pan	2005	89,954	101,661	325	43	25	CC	
MSC Roberta *	Pan	1986	39,892	43,567	244	32	21	CC	ex Hyundai Challenger-05, P&O Nedlloyd Panama-04, Hyundai Challenger-03
MSC Ronit *	Pan	1990	18,000	26,288	177	28	18	CC	ex Conti Arabian-08, YM Cairo I-04, Conti Arabian-04, Delmas Mascareignes-03, Kaedi-02, Conti Arabian-00, Maruba Challenger-00, Conti Arabian-97, Arabian Senator-97
MSC Rosa M *	Cyp	1978	20,418	20,185	186	27	23	CC	ex Rosa M-94, D'Albertis-87 (con Ro-97)
MSC Rosaria	Pan	2007	50,963	63,427	275	32	23	CC	
MSC Rossella	Pan	1993	37,396	43,878	243	32	22	CC	ex Ville de Carina-97, Hansa Europe-93
MSC Sabrina	Pan	1989	35,598	43,078	243	32	21	CC	ex Hanjin Oakland-98
MSC Samantha *	Pan	1982	30,955	34,098	210	32	18	CC	ex Pacific Sky-04, Safmarine Vaal-02, S.A. Vaal-00, Vaal-96, S.A. Vaal-87
MSC Sandra	Pan	2001	43,575	61,468	274	32	23	CC	
MSC Santhya ‡	Pan	1991	37,071	46,600	237	32	21	CC	ex Baykal Senator-04, DSR Senator-00, Vladivostok-91
MSC Sarah *	Lbr	1999	53,208	67,795	294	32	24	CC	ex Saudi Yanbu-02
MSC Sariska *	Pan	1971	13,276	18,836	175	23	18	CC	ex MSC Alexa-96, Alexa-94, Carmen Mare-87, Ville de Zenith-86, Carmen Mare-86, Passero-85, Ruhr Express-85, Geyerfels-80, Seatrain Bremen-80, Geyerfels-79, Seatrain Valley Forge-78, Atlantic Livorno-77, I/a Geyerfels (len-74)
MSC Scotland ***	Lbr	1992	37,071	47,120	237	32	21	CC	ex Bengal Sea-06, SCI Gaurav-04, German Senator-02, Choyang Volga-98
MSC Seine	Grc	1990	37,193	43,940	243	32	21	CC	ex CMA CGM Seine-08, Hanjin Hamburg-03, I/a Hanjin Vancouver
MSC Selin *	Pan	1981	22,131	17,993	173	32	17	Ro	ex Puerto Cortes-04, Kota Eagle-89, Contender Argent-87, Cavara-86, Contender Argent-84
MSC Sena *	Pan	1986	39,892	43,567	244	32	21	CC	ex Hyundai Pioneer-06, MSC Pioneer-04, Hyundai Pioneer-04, P&O Nedlloyd Miami-03, Hyundai Pioneer-02
MSC Seoul §§	Cyp	1979	17,675	18,835	201	24	17	CC	ex Hanjin Seoul-97
MSC Serena *	Pan	1977	38,991	40,624	241	32	21	CC	ex Zim Eilat I-02, New York Express-98, Maersk Algeciras-96, Stuttgart Express-92 (len-85)
MSC Shannon ‡	Pan	1991	37,071	47,120	237	32	21	CC	ex Berlin Senator-04
MSC Shaula *	Pan	1977	20,295	19,974	202	26	21	CC	ex MSC Mbashi-00, Mbashi-99, CMBT America-96, Fionia-95
MSC Sheila ‡	Pan	1999	12,396	16,211	150	23	14	CC	ex Atlantik Trader-05
MSC Silvana	Pan	2006	94,489	107,500	332	43	25	CC	
MSC Sindy	Pan	2007	107,849	111,894	337	46	26	CC	
MSC Socotra ***	Lbr	1980	35,065	43,070	246	32	23	CC	ex Astoria Bridge-03, Transworld Bridge-99
MSC Sola	Pan	2008	120,000	145,000	366	46	25	CC	
MSC Sophie	Pan	1993	37,398	43,294	243	32	22	CC	ex Maersk Colombo-97, Hansa Australia-93
MSC Soraya	Pan	2008	66,399	73,262	277	40	24	CC	
MSC Stefania	Pan	1969	23,881	24,245	213	30	23	CC	ex Stefania-94, Shireen-88, Crescent-88, Hakozaki Maru-81
MSC Stella	Pan	2004	73,819	85,680	304	40	24	CC	
MSC Suez ‡	Pan	1993	37,071	47,120	237	32	21	CC	ex Hamburg Senator-02
MSC Sukaiyna *	Pan	1987	22,746	24,362	198	28	18	CC	ex La Boheme-04, Antares-98, Isla Gran Malvina-98
MSC Susanna	Pan	2005	107,849	109,600	337	46	25	CC	
MSC Sweden #	Hkg	1989	52,191	60,639	294	32	23	CC	ex Maersk Merritt-07, Mette Maersk-06
MSC Tasmania *	Pan	1993	34,231	45,696	216	32	19	CC	ex Japan Senator-04, Choyang Elite-98, DSR-Asia-96
MSC Tia	Pan	1984	47,667	44,751	261	32	21	CC	ex Sea-Land Value-07, Kim D-88, American Utah-87
MSC Tina *	Pan	1986	42,259	45,721	249	32	22	CC	ex Ambassador Bridge-04
MSC Tomoko	Pan	2006	94,489	107,915	332	43	25	CC	
MSC Ukraine ##	Lbr	1989	30,824	26,132	202	31	17	CC	ex White Swan-07, Zim Hamburg I-02, Asia Jade-02, LT Nipponica-99, Nuova Nipponica-99, Trieste-96, T. Wenda-91
MSC Vanessa	Pan	2003	75,590	85,844	300	40	25	CC	
MSC Venezia	Deu	2001	65,131	68,045	275	40	25	CC	ex Hanjin Venezia-08, Cosco Busan-08, Hanjin Cairo-06
MSC Veronique	Pan	1976	32,341	30,934	222	32	23	CC	ex NOL Pearl-97, Neptune Pearl-96
MSC Vittoria	Pan	2006	89,954	105,101	325	43	25	CC	
MSC Viviana	Pan	2003	73,819	85,250	304	40	25	CC	

126

Name	Flag	Year	GRT	DWT	LOA	Bm	Kts	Type	Former names
MSC Volos §	Gbr	1985	10,282	13,346	147	23	18	CC	ex Brave Eagle-02, MSC Santos-98, Brave Eagle-97, Independent Endeavour-97, Contship Brave-94, Brave Eagle-88
MSC Voyager ††	Mhl	1980	32,629	30,390	257	31	20	CC	ex Sea-Land Voyager-07
MSC Zanzibar †††	Pan	1985	22,667	33,857	188	28	18	CC	ex Mediterranean Express-07, MSC Paraguay-04, Contship America-98, Buxsea-96, Contship America-96, Canmar Intrepid-95, Arabian Sea-94, New York Senator-93, ScanDutch Luzon-88, Andra I-87, Arosia-86, World Peace-85 (conv C)

newbuildings: numerous large container ships on order.
* managed by MSC Ship Management (Hong Kong) Ltd., Hong Kong or ** owned by Mediterranean Shipping Co. SrL, Italy.
‡ managed by Dobson Fleet Management Ltd., Cyprus or ‡‡ by DFM Ltd, Poland
† chartered from Technomar Shipping Inc, Greece, †† from Target Marine SA, Greece, ††† from Conbulk Shipping, Greece, *** from Goldenport, § from Dania International, §§ from Varship, # from Seaspan Corp, Hong Kong (Seaspan International Ltd, Canadian subsidiary of Washington Corp, USA), ## from Cosmoship, ≠ from ID Shipping, Denmark or Ø from Seacastle, Singapore (Fortress Investments, USA) until 2011 managed by Bernhard Schulte Shipmanagement (Singapore) Pte Ltd.
World's second largest container carrier (by vessels and capacity) - see other chartered ships in index with 'MSC' prefix

Mibau Holding GmbH   Germany

Funnel: *Blue with yellow 'mibau+stema', red boot-topping.* **Hull:** *White with yellow 'H' over yellow wave on blue square, narrow black top.* **History:** *Formed 2003.* **Web:** *www.mibau.de*

Sandnes	Atg	2005	17,357	28,000	167	25	15	Bu	
Splittnes (2)	Pan	1994	9,855	16,073	148	21	14	B	ex Kari Arnhild-02
Stones	Atg	2001	17,357	28,115	166	25	14	Bu	

Jointly owned by Heidelberg Zement GmbH and Hans-Jurgen Hartmann, operated by Mibau & Stema and managed by HJH Shipmanagement

Minerva Marine Inc   Greece

Funnel: *White with light blue over dark blue trianges.* **Hull:** *Black or dark grey with blue 'MINERVA' or red with red boot-topping.*
History: *Formed 1996 and associated with Thenamaris (Ships Management) Inc.* **Web:** *wwwminervatank.gr*

Amalthea	Grc	2006	60,007	107,115	248	43	14	T	
Andromeda	Grc	2008	162,198	321,300	333	60		T	I/a Mars Glory
Atalandi	Grc	2004	59,781	105,306	244	42	14	T	ex Valpiave-04
Minerva Alexandra	Grc	2000	58,125	104,643	244	42	14	T	
Minerva Anna	Grc	2005	30,053	50,939	183	32	14	T	
Minerva Astra	Grc	2001	59,693	105,830	248	43	15	T	I/a Stromness
Minerva Clara	Grc	2006	58,156	104,500	244	42	14	T	
Minerva Concert	Grc	2003	56,477	105,817	241	42	15	T	
Minerva Doxa	Grc	2007	83,722	159,438	277	50	15	T	
Minerva Eleonora	Grc	2004	58,156	104,875	244	42	14	T	
Minerva Ellie	Grc	2005	58,156	103,194	244	42	14	T	
Minerva Georgia	Grc	2008	84,914	163,417	274	50		T	
Minerva Grace	Grc	2005	30,053	50,922	183	32	14	T	
Minerva Helen	Grc	2004	58,156	104,875	244	42	14	T	
Minerva Iris	Grc	2004	58,156	103,124	244	42	14	T	
Minerva Julie	Grc	2008	28,960	50,922	183	32	14	T	
Minerva Libra	Grc	1999	58,156	105,344	244	42	15	T	I/a Al Bizzia

Minerva Marine. MINERVA ELLIE. *N. Kemps*

Name	Flag	Year	GRT	DWT	LOA	Bm	Kts	Type	Former names
Minerva Lisa	Grc	2004	58,156	103,622	244	42	14	T	
Minerva Maya	Grc	2002	57,508	105,709	244	42	14	T	
Minerva Nike	Grc	2004	57,301	105,330	244	42	14	T	
Minerva Rita	Mlt	2005	30,050	50,922	183	32	14	T	
Minerva Roxanne	Grc	2004	58,156	103,622	244	42	14	T	
Minerva Symphony	Grc	2006	83,722	159,450	277	50	14	T	
Minerva Vaso	Grc	2006	28,960	50,921	183	32	14	T	
Minerva Virgo	Grc	2006	28,960	50,921	183	32	14	T	
Minerva Xanthe	Grc	2006	28,960	50,921	183	32	14	T	
Minerva Zenia	Grc	2002	59,693	105,946	248	43	15	T	ex Torness-02, l/a Wrabness
Minerva Zoe	Grc	2004	57,000	105,000	244	42	14	T	
Parapola	Mlt	2008	88,500	177,000	292	45		T	
Sapienza	Mlt	2008	88,500	177,000	292	45		T	
Surfer Rosa	Mlt	2004	29,327	46,719	183	32	14	T	ex Kazbek-04

Associated with Thenamaris (Ships Management) Inc.

MISC Berhad   Malaysia

Funnel: *Blue, broad red band divided by white band with 14-pointed yellow star.* **Hull:** *Black or red with white 'MISC' or 'MISC MALAYSIA', red or grey boot-topping.* **History:** *Founded 1968 as Malaysian International Shipping Corporation Berhad to 1995, then Malaysia International Shipping Corp Berhad to 2005. Government's majority share sold in 1997 to national oil company Petronas Group (Petroleum Nasional Berhad) founded 1974.* **Web:** *www.misc.com.my*

Name	Flag	Year	GRT	DWT	LOA	Bm	Kts	Type	Former names
Bunga Bidara	Mys	1990	17,215	23,518	177	27	18	CC	
Bunga Delima	Mys	1990	17,215	23,518	177	27	18	CC	
Bunga Kantan Dua **	Sgp	2005	11,590	19,766	144	24	14	T	
Bunga Kantan Satu **	Sgp	2005	11,590	19,774	144	24	14	T	
Bunga Kantan Tiga **	Sgp	2005	11,590	19,734	144	24	14	T	
Bunga Kasturi Empat *	Mys	2007	156,967	300,325	330	60	17	T	
Bunga Kasturi Enam *	Mys	2008	157,209	299,319	330	60	15	T	
Bunga Kasturi Lima *	Mys	2007	157,209	300,246	330	60	17	T	
Bunga Kasturi Tiga *	Mys	2006	156,967	300,398	330	60	17	T	
Bunga Kenari	Mys	1991	17,215	23,574	177	27	18	CC	
Bunga Melati Dua	Mys	1997	22,254	32,169	177	30	14	T	
Bunga Melati Satu	Mys	1997	22,254	32,127	177	30	14	T	
Bunga Melati 3	Mys	1999	22,116	31,967	177	30	14	T	
Bunga Melati 4	Mys	1999	22,116	30,000	177	30	15	T	
Bunga Melati 5	Mys	1999	22,116	31,986	177	30	15	T	
Bunga Melati 6	Mys	2000	22,116	31,980	177	30	15	T	
Bunga Melati 7	Mys	2000	22,116	31,972	177	30	15	T	
Bunga Pelangi Dua	Mys	1995	53,521	61,777	275	32	24	CC	
Bunga Raya Dua	Mys	1998	39,582	48,244	258	32	24	CC	
Bunga Raya Satu	Mys	1998	39,582	48,304	258	32	24	CC	
Bunga Saga 9	Mys	1999	38,972	73,127	225	32	14	B	
Bunga Seroja Dua	Mys	2007	89,776	103,773	318	43	25	CC	
Bunga Seroja Satu	Mys	2006	89,776	97,000	318	43	25	CC	
Bunga Terasek	Mys	1991	17,215	20,000	177	27	19	CC	
Bunga Teratai	Mys	1998	21,339	24,612	184	27	19	CC	ex Bunga Teratai Satu-01
Bunga Teratai Dua	Mys	1998	21,339	24,554	184	27	19	CC	

MISC Berhad. BUNGA KANTAN SATU. *Hans Kraijenbosch*

Name	Flag	Year	GRT	DWT	LOA	Bm	Kts	Type	Former names
Bunga Teratai 3	Mys	1998	21,339	24,554	184	27	19	CC	
Bunga Teratai 4	Mys	1998	21,339	24,561	184	27	19	CC	ex Bunga Teratai Empat-05
Kvarven	Mys	1991	18,453	29,980	172	26	14	T	ex Bunga Tanjung-06
Puteri Delima (st)	Mys	1995	86,205	73,519	274	43	21	Lng	
Puteri Delima Satu (st) †	Mys	2002	93,038	76,190	276	43	21	Lng	
Puteri Firus (st)	Mys	1997	86,205	73,519	274	43	21	Lng	
Puteri Firus Satu †	Mys	2004	94,446	76,197	276	43	21	Lng	
Puteri Intan (st)	Mys	1994	86,205	73,519	274	43	21	Lng	
Puteri Intan Satu (st) †	Mys	2002	93.038	76,110	276	43	19	Lng	
Puteri Mutiara Satu †	Mys	2005	94,446	76,229	276	43	21	Lng	
Puteri Nilam (st)	Mys	1995	86,211	73,519	274	43	21	Lng	
Puteri Nilam Satu (st)	Mys	2003	94,446	76,110	276	43	21	Lng	
Puteri Zamrud (st)	Mys	1996	86,205	73,519	274	43	21	Lng	
Puteri Zamrud Satu (st)	Mys	2003	94,446	76,144	276	43	21	Lng	
Seri Alam (st)	Mys	2005	95,729	73,351	283	43	19	Lng	l/a Puteri Intan Dua
Seri Amanah (st)	Mys	2006	95,729	83,400	283	43	19	Lng	
Seri Anggun (st) †	Mys	2006	95,729	83,395	283	43	19	Lng	
Seri Angkasa (st) †	Mys	2006	95,729	71,500	283	43	19	Lng	
Seri Ayu (st)	Mys	2007	95,729	83,365	283	43	19	Lng	
Seri Bakti (st) †	Mys	2007	105,335	89,000	290	47	19	Lng	
Seri Begawan (st) †	Mys	2007	105,335	89,953	290	47	19	Lng	
Seri Bijaksana (st) †	Mys	2008	104,881	89,953	290	47	19	Lng	
Skarven **	Mys	1989	18,453	29,928	172	26	15	T	ex Bunga Cenderawasih-06
Stolzen	Mys	1990	18,453	29,974	172	26	15	T	ex Bunga Mawar-06
Tenaga Dua (st) †	Mys	1981	80,510	70,949	281	42	20	Lng	
Tenaga Empat (st)†	Mys	1981	80,510	71,555	281	42	20	Lng	
Tenaga Lima (st) †	Mys	1981	80,510	72.319	281	42	20	Lng	
Tenaga Satu (st) †	Mys	1982	80,510	72,083	281	42	20	Lng	
Tenaga Tiga (st) †	Mys	1981	80,510	70,949	281	42	20	Lng	
Varden	Mys	1989	18,453	29,995	172	26	15	T	ex Bunga Anggerik-06

newbuildings: two 110,000 grt Lng tankers, eight 45,000 dwt and eight 38,000 dwt tankers for 2009-10 delivery,
* managed by subsidiary AET Inc, ** by MSI Ship Management Pte Ltd, Singapore or † by parent Petronas Tankers Sdn Bhd, Malaysia

AET Inc Ltd/Bermuda

Funnel: White with grey eagle-head symbol on grey edged blue disc. **Hull:** Orange with red boot-topping. **History:** Subsidiary of MISC founded 1994 as American Eagle Tankers by Neptune Orient Lines and acquired in 2003. **Web:** www.aetweb.com

Name	Flag	Year	GRT	DWT	LOA	Bm	Kts	Type
C.S. Stealth †	Mhl	2006	58,418	104,500	244	42	14	T
C.V. Stealth †	Mhl	2005	58,418	104,499	244	42	14	T
Bunga Kasturi	Mys	2003	156,967	299,999	330	60	15	T
Bunga Kasturi Dua	Mys	2005	157,008	300,542	330	60	15	T
Bunga Kekaras	Mys	1995	20,378	29,990	178	30	14	T
Bunga Kelana Dua **	Mys	1997	57,017	105,575	244	42	14	T
Bunga Kelana Satu	Mys	1997	57,017	105,575	244	42	14	T
Bunga Kelana 3	Mys	1998	57,017	105,784	244	42	14	T
Bunga Kelana 4	Mys	1999	57,017	105,815	244	42	14	T
Bunga Kelana 5	Mys	1999	57,017	105,811	244	42	14	T
Bunga Kelana 6	Mys	1999	57,017	105,400	244	42	14	T

MISC Berhad. BUNGA TERATAI. *Hans Kraijenbosch*

Name	Flag	Year	GRT	DWT	LOA	Bm	Kts	Type	Former names
Bunga Kelana 7	Mys	2004	58,194	105,193	244	42	14	T	
Bunga Kelana 8	Mys	2004	58,194	105,193	244	42	14	T	
Bunga Kelana 9	Mys	2004	58,194	105,200	244	42	14	T	
Bunga Kenanga	Mys	2000	40,037	73,083	229	32	15	T	ex Four Cutter-00
Bunga Kerayong	Mys	1994	12,994	18,130	160	26	13	T	
Eagle Albany	Sgp	1998	57,929	107,160	247	42	14	T	
Eagle Anaheim	Sgp	1999	57,929	107,160	247	42	14	T	
Eagle Atlanta *	Sgp	1999	57,929	107,160	247	42	14	T	
Eagle Augusta	Sgp	1999	58,156	105,345	244	42	14	T	
Eagle Auriga	Sgp	1993	55,962	102,352	241	42	14	T	ex Neptune Auriga-94
Eagle Austin	Sgp	1998	58,156	105,000	244	42	14	T	
Eagle Baltimore	Sgp	1996	57,456	99,405	253	44	14	T	
Eagle Beaumont	Sgp	1996	57,456	99,448	253	44	14	T	
Eagle Birmingham	Sgp	1997	57,456	99,343	253	44	14	T	
Eagle Boston	Sgp	1996	57,456	99,328	253	44	14	T	
Eagle Carina	Sgp	1993	52,504	95,639	247	42	14	T	ex Neptune Carina-94
Eagle Centaurus	Sgp	1992	52,504	95,644	247	42	14	T	ex Neptune Centaurus-94
Eagle Charlotte *	Sgp	1997	57,949	107,169	247	42	14	T	
Eagle Columbus	Sgp	1997	57,949	107,166	247	42	14	T	
Eagle Corona	Sgp	1993	52,504	79,993	235	42	14	T	ex Neptune Corona-94
Eagle Milwaukee	Sgp	1987	53,483	104,385	236	43	13	T	ex Neptune Phoenix-95
Eagle Otome	Sgp	1994	52,504	95,663	247	42	14	T	ex Neptune Otome-00
Eagle Phoenix	Sgp	1998	56,346	105,500	241	42	14	T	ex Paola I-01
Eagle Seville	Grc	1999	58,125	105,000	244	42	14	T	ex Minerva Emma-08
Eagle Stealth	Mhl	2001	56,346	105,300	239	42	14	T	ex Nord Stealth-07
Eagle Subaru *	Sgp	1994	52,504	95,675	247	42	14	T	ex Neptune Subaru-99
Eagle Tacoma	Sgp	2002	57,950	107,123	247	42	14	T	
Eagle Tampa	Sgp	2003	58,166	107,123	247	42	14	T	
Eagle Toledo	Sgp	2002	58,166	107,092	247	42	14	T	
Eagle Torrance	Sgp	2007	58,168	107,123	247	42	14	T	
Eagle Trenton	Sgp	2003	58,166	107,123	247	42	14	T	
Eagle Tucson	Sgp	2003	58,166	107,123	247	42	14	T	
Eagle Turin	Sgp	2008	58,168	107,123	247	42	14	T	
Eagle Valencia	Sgp	2005	160,046	306,999	333	58	15	T	
Eagle Venice	Mys	2005	160,046	309,164	333	58	15	T	
Eagle Vermont	Sgp	2002	161,233	318,338	333	60	16	T	
Eagle Vienna	Sgp	2004	161,233	306,999	333	60	15	T	
Eagle Virginia	Sgp	2002	161,233	318,338	333	60	16	T	

newbuildings: eight 107,500 dwt tankers for 2009-11 delivery.
*Managed by AET Shipmanagement subsidiaries in Malaysia, Singapore and UK, * by V.Ships (Asia) Pte Ltd, Singapore or ** by Anglo-Eastern Shipmanagement (S) Pte Ltd, Singapore. † managed for Stealth Maritime Corp SA (Brave Maritime Corp Inc), Greece.*

Mitsui OSK Lines   Japan

Funnel: *Bright red.* **Hull:** *Light blue with white 'MOL' or grey with green waterline and red boot-topping.* **History:** *Formed 1884 as Osaka Shosen Kaisha, merged in 1964 with Mitsui Senpaku KK to form Mitsui OSK. Merged 1999 with Navix Line which had been formed by 1989 merger of Japan Line (founded 1930 and 1964 merger of Nitto Shosen KK with Daido Kaiun KK) and Yamashita-Shinnihon Steamship Co (founded 1903 and 1964 merger of Yamashita Kisen KK with Shinnihon Kisen KK).* **Web:** *www.mol.co.jp*

Amethyst Ace	Cym	2008	60,143	18,700	200	32	20	V	

MISC (AET Inc). EAGLE TURIN. *N. Kemps*

Name	Flag	Year	GRT	DWT	LOA	Bm	Kts	Type	Former names
APL Chiwan *	Pan	1995	59,622	63,440	299	37	24	CC	ex MOL Tyne-02, Tyne-01
APL Dubai *	Pan	1995	60,133	62,905	300	37	24	CC	ex MOL Rhine-02, Rhine-01
APL Earnest	Pan	2007	54,098	56,100	294	32	24	CC	ex MOL Earnest-08
APL Expeditor *	Pan	2003	53,822	62,800	294	32	24	CC	ex MOL Expeditor-08
APL Experience	Pan	2007	54,098	62,953	294	32	23	CC	ex MOL Experience-08
APL Finland	Pan	2008	88,059	90,400	320	46	25	CC	
APL France	Bhs	2008	86,692	90,649	316	46	25	CC	ex MOL Celebration-07
APL Ningpo *	Pan	1995	58,531	61,470	300	37	24	CC	ex MOL Loire-02, La Loire-01
APL Poland	Bhs	2008	86,692	90,634	316	46	25	CC	
APL Russia *	Bhs	2008	86,692	90,613	316	46	25	CC	
Aquamarine Ace	Cym	2008	60,143	18,772	200	32	20	V	
Aquarius Ace *	Pan	1998	36,615	14,353	175	29	15	V	
Asian Spirit †	Lbr	1988	53,578	21,835	200	32	18	V	ex Hual Tribute-04
Astral Ace	Pan	2000	36,615	14,280	175	29	18	V	
Atagosan Maru	Jpn	1989	94,068	179,658	390	46	13	B	
Atlantic Spirit †	Lbr	1987	47,287	16,165	190	32	18	V	ex Honmoku Maru-97
Atlixco	Pan	1982	41,697	18,217	199	30	18	V	ex Clover Ace-99
Azul Cielo	Pan	2005	101,933	203,195	300	50	14	B	
Azul Fortuna	Pan	2005	101,933	203,095	300	50	14	B	
Bravery Ace *	Pan	2000	52,276	17,686	189	32	20	V	
Brilliant Ace	Pan	1987	47,505	14,189	180	32	17	V	
Camellia Ace *	Pan	1994	55,336	18,938	200	32	18	V	
Cape Maple	Pan	2005	104,932	206,204	300	50	14	B	
Cape Sentosa	Sgp	2003	89,545	177,346	289	45	14	B	
Cattleya Ace *	Vut	1988	56,823	18,762	199	32	21	V	
Celestial Wing *	Pan	2005	44,146	15,438	180	30	19	V	
Clover Ace *	Bhs	2008	60,065	17,100	200	32	20	V	
Comet Ace	Pan	2000	36,615	14,283	175	29	18	V	
Cosmos Ace *	Pan	1998	46,346	15,439	182	31	19	V	
Cosmos Venture *	Lbr	1986	46,051	17,750	188	31	18	V	
Courageous Ace *	Pan	2003	56,439	19,927	198	32	20	V	
Crystal Ace *	Pan	1983	27,566	10,538	161	27	16	V	
Dyna Auk ‡	Hkg	1990	77,336	151,220	273	43	14	B	ex New Honor-03, Hosei-01, Hosei Maru-94
Eminent Ace *	Pan	2005	58,616	18,947	200	32	20	V	
Eternal Ace *	Pan	1988	55,380	18,701	200	32	19	V	
Euphony Ace *	Pan	2005	58,631	18,944	200	32	20	V	
Euro Spirit *	Lbr	1998	46,346	15,483	188	31	19	V	
Favorite Ace *	Pan	2006	60,118	17,709	200	32	20	V	
Felicity Ace *	Pan	2006	60,118	17,738	200	32	20	V	
Firmament Ace *	Pan	2006	60,118	17,713	200	32	20	V	
Freedom Ace *	Pan	2005	60,175	19,093	200	32	20	V	
Frontier Ace *	Pan	2000	52,276	17,693	189	32	20	V	
Frontier Express ***	Pan	1993	40,721	68,520	229	32	14	T	
Galaxy Ace	Hkg	1986	33,733	13,418	168	30	19	V	ex Nosac Galaxy-96, Galaxy Ace-95
Global Spirit †	Lbr	1987	47,500	16,493	191	32	19	V	ex Tochigi-99, Tochigi Maru-96
Glorious Ace *	Pan	1981	46,047	17,743	190	32	18	V	
Harmony Ace *	Pan	1992	47,819	14,256	180	32	19	V	
Heroic Ace *	Pan	2002	56,439	19,879	198	32	20	V	
Iris Ace *	Pan	1983	33,521	16,461	190	32	19	V	ex Rainbow Ace-93
Japan Linden	Pan	1985	102,395	196,800	305	50	13	B	
Japan Platanus	Pan	1987	77,871	149,986	284	47	13	B	
Lambert Maru	Pan	1986	98,661	197,981	300	50	13	B	
Lavender Ace *	Bhs	2008	59,800	17,100	200	32	20	V	
Liberty Ace *	Pan	2004	60,175	19,106	200	32	20	V	
London Courage	Mhl	2007	104,721	206,366	300	50	14	B	
Maple Ace II *	Lbr	1992	38,349	15,361	188	28	18	V	
Martorell	Pan	2003	57,789	19,531	200	32	20	V	
Marvelous Ace	Pan	2006	59,422	18,900	200	32	20	V	
Mercury Ace	Pan	1985	44,979	16,603	176	29	17	V	
Miraculous Ace	Cym	2006	59,422	19,381	200	32	20	V	
MOL Advantage	Pan	2001	66,332	66,532	279	40	25	CC	
MOL Bravery	Pan	1995	41,114	39,788	245	32	23	CC	ex Alligator Bravery-01
MOL Columbus	Pan	1991	41,144	40,331	245	32	21	CC	ex Alligator Columbus-00
MOL Competence	Pan	2008	86,692	90,613	316	46	25	CC	
MOL Cosmos	Pan	2008	88,089	90,466	320	46	25	CC	
MOL Creation	Bhs	2007	86,692	90,678	316	46	25	CC	
MOL Discovery	Pan	1991	42,812	40,499	253	32	22	CC	ex Alligator Discovery-01, OOCL Shanghai-98, Alligator Discovery-96
MOL Efficiency	Pan	2002	53,822	63,160	294	32	24	CC	
MOL Elbe	Jpn	1990	50,352	58,112	292	32	23	CC	ex Elbe-01
MOL Encore	Pan	2003	53,096	61,441	294	32	24	CC	

Name	Flag	Year	GRT	DWT	LOA	Bm	Kts	Type	Former names
MOL Endeavor	Pan	2003	53,096	61,441	294	32	24	CC	
MOL Endowment	Pan	2007	54,098	62,949	294	32	24	CC	
MOL Endurance	Pan	2003	53,096	61,441	294	32	24	CC	
MOL Enterprise	Pan	2004	53,600	49,600	294	32	24	CC	
MOL Eternity	Jpn	1985	35,234	33,637	205	32	19	CC	ex Southern Cross Maru-01
MOL Excellence	Pan	2003	53,822	63,096	294	32	24	CC	
MOL Explorer	Pan	2007	53,822	62,958	294	32	24	CC	
MOL Express *	Pan	2003	53,400	62,800	294	32	24	CC	
MOL Fortune	Lbr	1986	40,354	41,513	226	32	20	CC	ex Alligator Fortune-01
MOL Glory	Lbr	1986	39,283	40,817	226	32	20	CC	ex Aligator Glory-01
MOL Golden Wattle	Lbr	1986	40,354	41,474	226	32	19	CC	ex Alligator Hope-01
MOL Integrity	Pan	2001	66,332	66,800	279	40	25	CC	
MOL Ingenuity *	Pan	1992	50,204	58,986	292	32	24	CC	ex MOL Danube-02, Danube-01
MOL Initiative *	Pan	1988	50,030	59,488	290	32	23	CC	ex La Seine-02
MOL Liberty *	Pan	1986	42,117	38,512	246	32	22	CC	ex Alligator Liberty-02
MOL Maas *	Lbr	1995	60,133	62,905	300	37	23	CC	ex Maas-01
MOL Miracle	Pan	1991	41,495	40,330	245	32	21	CC	ex Alligator Miracle-02, Alligator America-99
MOL Mosel	Pan	1995	58,923	61,489	300	37	23	CC	ex APL Qingdao-08, MOL Mosel-02, Mosel-00
MOL Pace	Pan	2006	71,902	72,968	293	40	25	CC	
MOL Paradise	Pan	2005	71,902	72,968	293	40	25	CC	
MOL Paramount	Pan	2005	71,892	72,968	293	40	25	CC	
MOL Partner	Pan	2005	71,902	72,968	293	40	25	CC	
MOL Performance *	Pan	2001	74,071	74,453	294	40	27	CC	
MOL Precision	Pan	2002	71,902	72,300	293	40	25	CC	
MOL Pride *	Lbr	1988	41,126	40,192	245	32	21	CC	ex Alligator Pride-01
MOL Priority *	Pan	2002	74,071	74,453	294	40	26	CC	
MOL Progress *	Pan	2002	71,902	74,453	293	40	25	CC	
MOL Promise	Pan	2002	71,902	73,063	293	40	25	CC	
MOL Solution	Pan	2001	71,902	72,300	293	40	25	CC	
MOL Thames *	Pan	1990	50,628	59,056	290	32	23	CC	ex Thames-00
MOL Triumph	Lbr	1988	43,082	40,540	253	32	22	CC	ex Alligator Triumph-01
MOL Wellington	Pan	1979	32,163	29,888	216	32	22	CC	ex Wellington Maru-01, Canberra Maru-87
MOL Wisdom	Pan	1995	41,114	59,814	245	32	23	CC	ex Alligator Wisdom-01
Mona Century *	Pan	2000	87,523	172,036	289	45	15	B	
Mona Liberty	Sgp	1992	77,195	151,533	273	43	14	B	ex Kohju-01
Mona Linden *	Pan	2000	84,507	170,473	289	45	14	B	
Neptune Ace *	Pan	1985	44,979	16,560	176	29	17	V	
New Brisk ‡	Pan	1995	85,629	168,421	290	46	14	B	ex Bungo-01, Bungo Maru-99
Niitaka Maru	Jpn	1988	93,131	180,972	290	46	14	B	
Nordic Spirit †	Nis	1988	53,578	20,885	200	32	18	V	ex Hual Triumph-07, Hual Margarita-00
Ocean Ace	Pan	1983	43,684	16,149	184	32	18	V	ex Meiho Maru-88
Ocean Spirit †	Lbr	1985	47,561	16,770	191	32	19	V	ex San Laurel-97, Nissan Laurel-95
Orchid Ace	Jpn	2008	59,262	17,289	200	32	20	V	
Oriental Phoenix *	Lbr	1985	27,658	11,824	159	28	17	V	
Pacific Glory	Pan	2004	118,249	233,694	317	55	14	O	(conv Obo)
Pacific Spirit †	Nis	1987	53,578	20,885	200	32	18	V	ex Hual Trophy-05, Hual Favorita-01
Paradise Ace	Pan	2004	60,175	19,080	200	32	20	V	
Pearl Ace *	Pan	1994	45,796	15,194	188	31	18	V	

Mitsui OSK Lines. MOL PARADISE. *Allan Ryszka Onions*

Name	Flag	Year	GRT	DWT	LOA	Bm	Kts	Type	Former names
Pegasus Ace *	Pan	1998	36,615	14,348	175	29	19	V	
Planet Ace *	Pan	1992	38,349	15,327	188	28	18	V	
Polaris Ace *	Pan	1997	46,346	15,522	182	31	19	V	
Primrose Ace	Cym	2007	59,952	17,339	200	32	20	V	
Progress Ace	Pan	2003	57,789	19,512	200	32	20	V	
Prominent Ace	Pan	2004	57,789	13,500	200	32	20	V	
Rainbow Wing *	Pan	1986	41,643	15,199	190	32	19	V	ex Salvia Ace-00, Continental Wing-97
Rubin Artemis	Pan	1997	77,065	151,982	273	43	14	B	
Rubin Hope ‡	Pan	1999	83,833	170,409	289	45	14	B	
Rubin Phoenix	Pan	1997	83,658	171,080	289	45	14	B	
Ruby Express ***	Pan	2004	57,468	106,516	241	42	14	T	
Salvia Ace	Cym	2008	42,401	15,013	186	28		V	
Sapphire Ace	Pan	1993	45,796	15,204	188	31	18	V	
Shinzan Maru	Jpn	1987	115,741	200,999	320	53	13	O	
Solar Wing *	Lbr	1988	41,604	13,224	187	32	19	V	
Splendid Ace *	Pan	2003	56,439	19,893	198	32		V	
Sun Ace *	Pan	1981	29,973	13,051	179	27	17	V	
Swallow Ace *	Bhs	2007	58,685	18,864	200	32	20	V	
Swan Ace *	Bhs	2008	58,685	18,867	200	32	20	V	
Swift Ace *	Bhs	2008	58,685	18,865	200	32	20	V	
Tachibana	Pan	2000	83,528	154,324	275	47	14	B	
Triumph Ace *	Pan	2000	55,880	20,131	194	32	20	V	
Tsunomine	Pan	2000	83,496	152,400	275	47	14	B	
Universal Spirit †	Lbr	1985	39,948	13,025	173	30	19	V	ex Sanwa-98, Sanwa Maru-91
Utopia Ace	Pan	2004	60,175	19,086	200	32	20	V	
Victory Ace *	Pan	1985	36,026	16,068	200	28	18	V	(len-87)
Wisteria Ace	Cym	2007	59,952	17,325	200	32	20	V	
World Spirit †	Lbr	1998	37,949	14,101	175	29	19	V	

newbuildings: Over 100 on order including container ships (16), vehicle carriers (16), tankers (23), Lng carriers (6), bulk and ore carriers (32).
* owned or managed by MO Ship Management Co. Ltd., Japan, ** by Jahre-Wallem AS, Norway or *** by Thome Ship Management, Singapore.
† owned by World Car Carriers and managed by MOLShip.
‡ owned by subsidiary of Solar Japan Co Ltd (formed jointly by subsidiary Asahi Tanker Co and vanguard Enterpries Co Ltd)

MOL Tankship Management Ltd/Japan

Name	Flag	Year	GRT	DWT	LOA	Bm	Kts	Type	Former names
African Ruby *	Pan	1994	81,803	147,638	278	45	15	T	
Al Deebel (st)	Bhs	2005	95,824	78,594	283	43	20	Lng	
Altair Trader **	Pan	2005	160,216	299,985	333	60	15	T	
Asian Progress II **	Sgp	2000	160,079	314,026	333	60	15	T	
Asian Progress III **	Sgp	2004	159,875	306,352	333	60	14	T	
Asian Progress IV **	Bhs	2006	160,292	313,992	333	60	15	T	
Atlantic Hero *	Pan	1992	51,984	96,687	232	42	13	T	ex Stena Concertina-99
Atlantic Liberty *	Pan	1995	164,373	311,625	330	58	15	T	
Atlantic Prosperity *	Pan	1996	164,373	310,000	330	58	15	T	
Bandaisan *	Pan	2000	149,282	281,037	330	60	15	T	
Diamond Jasmine	Pan	1999	152,041	281,050	330	60	16	T	
Duom *	Pan	2008	160,300	309,200	333	60	15	T	
Glen Maye *	Pan	1992	79,595	140,991	272	46	14	T	
Grand Sea †	Hkg	2008	160,216	310,444	333	60	15	T	
Ibukisan	Pan	2000	160,079	299,999	330	60	15	T	
Ikomasan	Pan	2000	160,079	299,986	333	60	15	T	
Iwatesan **	Pan	2003	159,912	300,667	333	60	16	T	
Kaimon II	Pan	2002	160,079	314,014	333	60	15	T	
Kaminesan **	Pan	2003	159,813	303,896	333	60	16	T	
Kasagisen **	Bhs	2006	160,216	302,478	333	60	15	T	
Katori **	Pan	1995	146,510	259,999	324	56	15	T	
Kashimasan	Bhs	2007	159,873	306,033	333	60	15	T	
Katsuragisan **	Pan	2005	160,292	311,620	333	60	15	T	
Millennium Explorer *	Pan	2000	56,695	100,063	241	42	15	T	
Navix Azalea **	Pan	1995	146,745	269,141	333	58	15	T	
Ohminesan	Pan	1996	151,039	259,984	333	60	15	T	
Oriental Jade **	Pan	2004	159,875	306,352	333	60	14	T	
Orion Trader	Pan	1998	151,039	267,736	333	60	15	T	
Otowasan	Pan	2005	160,292	302,477	333	60	15	T	
Pacific Alliance *	Pan	2004	57,226	105,941	244	42	14	T	
Pacific Partner	Pan	2004	57,226	105,946	244	42	14	T	
Perseus Trader *	Pan	2003	160,066	299,992	333	60	15	T	
Phoenix Vanguard **	Sgp	2007	157,844	306,506	333	60	15	T	
Rokkosan	Pan	2003	160,066	300,257	333	60	15	T	
Ryuohsan **	Pan	2000	149,282	281,050	330	60	16	T	
Selene Trader	Pan	2003	159,912	299,991	333	60	15	T	

Name	Flag	Year	GRT	DWT	LOA	Bm	Kts	Type	Former names
Takase	Pan	1999	160,220	259,993	333	60	15	T	
Vega Trader	Pan	2003	159,813	299,985	333	60	15	T	
Washusan	Pan	2000	152,041	281,050	330	60	16	T	
Yohteisan	Pan	2000	149,282	281,050	330	60	16	T	
Yufusan **	Pan	2005	160,216	311,389	330	60	15	T	

* owned or managed by subsidiaries MOL Tankship Management (Europe) Ltd, UK (founded 1992 as MOL Tankship Management Ltd to 2006) or
** by MOL Tankship Management (Asia) Pte Ltd, Singapore (formerly International Energy Transport Co Ltd to 2006), including † jointly owned by
Sinotrans, China.

One of the world's largest shipping groups with many subsidiaries owning or managing over 520 vessels. Only the largest container, tanker, bulk
carrier and vehicle carriers are listed, in addition to which there are many other bulk carriers, wood-chip carriers, product tankers and Lng
carriers.

A P Moller Denmark

A P Moller-Maersk A/S/Denmark

Funnel: Black with white seven-pointed star on broad light blue band. **Hull:** Light blue with black 'Maersk Line' or 'MAERSK
SEALAND', red boot-topping. **History:** Formed 2003 by merger of A/S Dampskibs Svendborg (founded 1904) and Dampskibs af 1912
A/S (founded 1912). Acquired liner services of Chargeurs Reunis and CMB (both 1987), also Torm (2002) and the container lines of
Sea-Land and Safmarine (both 1999) and P&O Nedlloyd (2005). Brostron AB acquired 2009. **Web:** www.maersk.com or
www.maerskline.com

Name	Flag	Year	GRT	DWT	LOA	Bm	Kts	Type	Former names
A. P. Moller	Dis	2000	91,560	104,750	347	43	25	CC	
Adrian Maersk	Dis	2004	93,496	109,000	353	43	25	CC	
Albert Maersk	Dis	2004	93,496	105,750	352	43	25	CC	
Alexander Maersk	Dis	1998	14,120	17,375	155	25	18	CC	ex Adrian Maersk-04
Anna Maersk	Dis	2003	93,496	109,000	352	43	25	CC	
Argonaut † (st)	Usa	1979	17,902	16,401	186	24	20	CC	
Arnold Maersk	Dis	2003	93,496	109,000	352	43	25	CC	
Arthur Maersk	Dis	2003	93,496	105,750	352	43	25	CC	
Axel Maersk	Dis	2003	93,496	109,000	352	43	25	CC	
Brigit Maersk	Dis	2006	19,758	29,017	175	29	14	T	
Britta Maersk	Dis	2007	19,758	29,017	175	29	14	T	
Caribe	Ven	2000	17,980	20,815	159	26	18	Lpg	ex Maersk Holyhead-06
Caroline Maersk	Dis	2000	91,560	104,750	347	43	25	CC	
Carsten Maersk	Dis	2000	91,560	104,750	347	43	25	CC	
Cecilie Maersk	Dis	1994	20,842	28,550	190	28	18	CC	
Charlotte Maersk	Dis	2002	91,000	104,000	347	43	25	CC	
Chastine Maersk	Dis	2001	91,560	104,750	347	43	25	CC	
Claes Maersk	Dis	1994	20,842	28,550	190	28	18	CC	
Clara Maersk	Dis	1992	18,979	25,275	176	28	18	CC	
Clementine Maersk	Dis	2002	91,921	104,750	347	43	25	CC	
Clifford Maersk	Dis	1999	91,560	104,700	348	43	25	CC	
Columbine Maersk	Dis	2002	91,921	110,000	347	43	25	CC	
Cornelia Maersk	Dis	2002	91,921	104,750	347	43	25	CC	
Cornelius Maersk	Dis	2000	91,560	104,700	347	43	25	CC	
Dirch Maersk	Dis	1996	50,698	62,418	292	32	24	CC	
Ebba Maersk	Dis	2007	170,794	156,900	398	56	25	CC	
Edith Maersk	Dis	2007	170,794	156,907	398	56	25	CC	
Eleonora Maersk	Dis	2007	170,794	156,900	398	56	25	CC	
Eli Maersk	Dis	2000	159,187	308,491	333	58	16	T	
Elly Maersk	Dis	2007	170,794	156,907	398	56	25	CC	
Emma Maersk	Dis	2006	170,794	156,907	398	56	25	CC	
Estelle Maersk	Dis	2006	170,794	156,907	398	56	25	CC	
Eugen Maersk	Dis	2008	170,794	156,907	398	56	25	CC	
Evelyn Maersk	Dis	2007	170,794	156,907	398	56	25	CC	
Georg Maersk	Dis	2006	97,900	115,700	367	43	25	CC	
Gerd Maersk	Dis	2006	97,900	115,700	367	43	25	CC	
Gjertrud Maersk	Dis	2005	97,933	115,700	367	43	25	CC	
Glasgow Maersk	Gbr	1999	50,698	62,400	292	32	24	CC	
Grasmere Maersk	Gbr	2000	50,698	62,007	292	32	24	CC	
Greenwich Maersk	Gbr	2000	50,698	62,228	292	32	24	CC	
Grete Maersk	Dis	2005	97,933	115,700	367	43	25	CC	
Gudrun Maersk	Dis	2005	97,933	115,700	367	43	25	CC	
Gunvor Maersk	Dis	2005	97,900	115,700	367	43	25	CC	
Jens Maersk	Dis	2001	30,166	27,300	216	32	23	CC	
Jepperson Maersk	Dis	2001	30,166	35,097	216	32	22	CC	
Johannes Maersk	Dis	2001	30,166	27,300	216	32	23	CC	
Josephine Maersk	Dis	2002	30,166	27,300	216	32	23	CC	
Lars Maersk	Dis	2004	50,657	62,994	267	37	24	CC	
Laura Maersk	Dis	2001	50,721	63,200	266	37	24	CC	
Laust Maersk	Dis	2001	50,721	63,000	266	37	24	CC	

Name	Flag	Year	GRT	DWT	LOA	Bm	Kts	Type	Former names
Leda Maersk	Dis	2001	50,721	63,200	266	37	24	CC	
Lexa Maersk	Dis	2001	50,721	63,400	266	37	24	CC	
Lica Maersk	Dis	2001	50,721	63,400	266	37	24	CC	
Luna Maersk	Dis	2002	50,721	63,400	266	37	25	CC	
Maersk Aberdeen #	Sgp	1999	14,130	17,720	155	25	18	CC	
Maersk Ahram ***	Egy	1998	14,063	17,728	155	25	18	CC	
Maersk Antwerp #	Sgp	1999	14,063	17,720	155	25	18	CC	
Maersk Arun #	Gbr	1999	14,063	14,175	155	25	18	CC	
Maersk Arwa	Mhl	2008	104.169	82,187	286	43		Lng	
Maersk Atlantic #	Sgp	1999	14,063	17,720	155	25	18	CC	ex Swan River Bridge-00, Maersk Atlantic-99
Maersk Avon #	Gbr	1999	14,063	17,728	155	25	18	CC	
Maersk Gairloch	Gbr	2002	50,698	62,242	292	32	24	CC	
Maersk Garonne	Atf	2003	50,698	62,007	282	32	24	CC	
Maersk Gateshead	Gbr	2002	50,686	62,242	292	32	24	CC	
Maersk Gironde	Atf	2002	50,757	62,007	292	32	24	CC	
Maersk Houston ‡‡	Vct	1993	18,360	23,257	160	26	16	Lpg	ex Hans Maersk-06
Maersk Innoshima **	Nld	2008	35,491	41,337	232	32	22	CC	
Maersk Inverness **	Nld	2008	35,491	41,350	232	32	22	CC	
Maersk Izmir **	Nld	2008	35,491	41,238	232	32	22	CC	
Maersk Kalmar *	Nld	1998	80,942	82,700	300	43	24	CC	ex P&O Nedlloyd Rotterdam-06
Maersk Kampala	Nld	2001	80,654	88,967	300	43	24	CC	ex P&O Nedlloyd Houtman-06
Maersk Karachi *	Gbr	1998	80,600	82,700	300	43	24	CC	ex P&O Nedlloyd Kobe-06
Maersk Kelso	Gbr	2007	74,642	84,000	300	43	24	CC	

A. P. Moller. ARTHUR MAERSK. *Phil Kempsey*

A. P. Moller. ELEONORA MAERSK . *Hans Kraijenbosch*

Name	Flag	Year	GRT	DWT	LOA	Bm	Kts	Type	Former names
Maersk Kendal	Gbr	2007	74,642	84,771	300	43	24	CC	
Maersk Kensington	Gbr	2007	74,642	84,000	300	43	24	CC	
Maersk Kiel *	Gbr	1998	80,942	82,702	300	43	24	CC	ex P&O Nedlloyd Southampton-06
Maersk Kimi *	Nld	1998	80,600	82,700	300	43	24	CC	ex P&O Nedlloyd Kowloon-06
Maersk Kinloss	Gbr	2008	74,642	84,835	299	40	24	CC	
Maersk Kithira *	Gbr	2001	80,654	83,370	300	43	24	CC	ex P&O Nedlloyd Cook-06
Maersk Klaipeda *	Nld	2001	80,654	87,343	300	43	24	CC	ex Maersk Kingston-07, P&O Nedlloyd Stuyvesant-06
Maersk Kyrenia *	Gbr	2001	80,654	87,343	300	43	24	CC	ex P&O Nedlloyd Shackleton-06
Maersk Madrid	Gbr	1989	50,538	59,285	290	32	23	CC	ex Peninsular Bay-06
Maersk Marib (st)	Mhl	2008	104,169	82,114	285	43		Lng	
Maersk Matane ‡	Dis	1989	52,191	60,639	294	32	23	CC	ex Margrethe Maersk-06
Maersk Montreal *	Gbr	1989	50,538	59,285	291	32	23	CC	ex Oriental Bay-06
Maersk Nottingham ††	Lbr	2004	26,833	34,000	210	32	21	CC	ex P&O Nedlloyd Regina-06, l/dn Regina Star
Maersk Palermo *	Nld	1999	31,207	38,400	210	32	22	CC	ex P&O Nedlloyd Auckland-06
Maersk Patras *	Gbr	1998	31,333	37,845	210	32	19	CC	ex P&O Nedlloyd Marseille-06
Maersk Pembroke *	Nld	1998	31,333	38,400	210	32	22	CC	ex P&O Nedlloyd Sydney-06
Maersk Penang *	Nld	1998	31,333	38,170	210	32	22	CC	ex P&O Nedlloyd Jakarta-06
Maersk Phuket	Mhl	1998	31,333	37,845	210	32	22	CC	ex P&O Nedlloyd Genoa-06
Maersk Qatar (st)	Dis	2006	96,508	77,803	279	43	20	Lng	
Maersk Ras Laffan (st)	Dis	2004	93,226	73,705	279	43	20	Lng	
Maersk Saigon ††	Lbr	2006	94,483	108,251	332	43	24	CC	
Maersk Salalah *	Nld	2008	94,127	102,311	334	46	25	CC	

A. P. Moller. MARIT MAERSK. *David Hornsby*

A. P. Moller. NEDLLOYD MARITA. *Phil Kempsey*

Name	Flag	Year	GRT	DWT	LOA	Bm	Kts	Type	Former names
Maersk Salina *	Nld	2008	91,427	101,550	334	43	25	CC	
Maersk Sana ††	Lbr	2004	94,724	94,724	335	43	24	CC	ex P&O Nedlloyd Mondriaan-06, Mondriaan Star-04
Maersk Savannah *	Sgp	2008	94,127	102,367	334	46	25	CC	
Maersk Seoul ††	Lbr	2006	94,483	108,344	332	43	24	CC	
Maersk Sofia *	Lbr	2007	94,724	97,549	332	43	24	CC	
Maersk Stepnica	Nld	2008	91,427	102,367	334	46	25	CC	
Maersk Stockholm *	Nld	2008	91,400	102,000	334	42	25	CC	
Maersk Stralsund ††	Lbr	2005	94,483	101,500	332	43	24	CC	ex P&O Nedlloyd Marilyn-05
Maersk Sydney ††	Lbr	2005	94,724	94,724	335	43	24	CC	ex P&O Nedlloyd Miro-06, Miro Star-05
Maersk Tangier ≠	Lbr	1990	17,700	21,238	161	28	18	CC	ex Torben Maersk-07
Maersk Tarragona ≠	Lbr	1990	17,700	21,229	161	28	18	CC	ex Tobias Maersk-07, TRSL Antares-96, Tobias Maersk-95
Maersk Torino ≠	Lbr	1990	17,700	21,229	161	28	18	CC	ex Trein Maersk-07, TRSL Arcturus-97, Trein Maersk-95
Maersk Trapani ≠	Lbr	1990	17,700	21,238	161	28	18	CC	ex Thorkil Maersk-07, CMA CGM Hispaniola-06, Marienborg-04, Thorkil Maersk-01
Magleby Maersk	Dis	1990	52,181	60,350	294	32	23	CC	
Majestic Maersk	Dis	1990	52,181	60,639	294	32	23	CC	
Marchen Maersk	Dis	2008	98,268	115,993	367	43		CC	
Maren Maersk	Dis	2009	98,268	116,100	367	43		CC	
Margrethe Maersk	Dis	2008	98,268	115,993	367	43		CC	
Marie Maersk	Dis	1990	52,181	60,350	294	32	23	CC	
Marit Maersk	Dis	2009	98,268	110,000	367	43		CC	
Mathilde Maersk	Dis	2009	98,268	110,000	367	43		CC	
Mercosul Manuas	Nld	1983	23,930	30,040	183	31	17	CC	ex P&O Nedlloyd Houston-06, Nedlloyd van Neck-98
Mette Maersk	Dis	2009	98,268	116,100	367	43		CC	
MSC Everest **	Nld	1996	49,985	59,964	292	32	24	CC	ex Sea-Land Racer-07
Nakskov Maersk	Dis	2007	12,105	16,427	144	23	14	T	
Nedlloyd Adriana ††	Lbr	2003	26,833	34,567	210	30	21	CC	ex P&O Nedlloyd Adriana-06, Adriana Star-03
Nedlloyd Barentsz †	Nld	2000	66,526	67,785	278	40	25	CC	ex P&O Nedlloyd Barentsz-05
Nedlloyd de Liefde *	Lbr	1995	10,917	13,700	151	24	18	CC	ex P&O Nedlloyd de Liefde-06, Milena-05, Sigrid Wehr-04, Washington Express-01, Sigrid Wehr-00, Independent Venture-98, Sigrid Wehr-96, Cape Scott-95
Nedlloyd Drake †	Gbr	2000	66,590	67,500	278	40	25	CC	ex P&O Nedlloyd Drake-06
Nedlloyd Hudson †	Nld	2000	66,526	67,900	278	40	24	CC	ex P&O Nedlloyd Houston-06
Nedlloyd Juliana ††	Lbr	2003	26,833	34,315	210	30	22	CC	ex P&O Nedlloyd Juliana-06, Juliana Star-03
Nedlloyd Marita ††	Lbr	2003	26,833	34,296	210	30	21	CC	ex P&O Nedlloyd Marita-05, Marita Star-04
Nedlloyd Mercator †	Nld	2000	66,526	67,785	278	40	25	CC	ex P&O Nedlloyd Mercator-06
Nedlloyd Tasman †	Gbr	1999	66,526	67,900	278	40	24	CC	ex P&O Nedlloyd Tasman-06
Nedlloyd Valentina †	Lbr	2004	26,833	32,000	210	32	19	CC	ex P&O Nedlloyd Valentina-06, l/dn Valentina Star
Nele Maersk	Dis	2000	27,733	30,194	199	30	21	CC	
Nex□ Maersk	Dis	2001	27,733	30,420	199	30	21	CC	
Nibe Maersk	Dis	2007	12,105	16,533	144	23	14	T	
Nicolai Maersk	Dis	2000	27,733	30,420	199	30	21	CC	
Nicoline Maersk	Dis	2000	27,733	30,191	199	30	21	CC	
Nissum Maersk	Dis	2008	12,105	16,400	144	23	14	T	
Nora Maersk	Dis	2000	27,733	30,194	199	30	21	CC	
Nordby Maersk	Dis	2007	12,105	16,511	144	23	14	T	
Nuuk Maersk	Dis	2008	12,105	16,631	144	23	14	T	
Nyborg Maersk	Dis	2007	12,105	16,564	144	23	14	T	
Nysted Maersk	Dis	2001	27,733	30,194	197	30	21	CC	
Olga Maersk	Dis	2003	34,202	41,028	237	32	24	CC	
Olivia Maersk	Dis	2003	34,202	41,097	237	32	24	CC	
Oluf Maersk	Dis	2003	34,202	41,028	237	32	24	CC	
Ras Maersk	Dis	2003	22,181	34,999	171	27	14	T	
Ribe Maersk	Dis	2004	22,181	35,000	171	27	14	T	
Richard Maersk	Dis	2001	22,184	34,909	171	27	14	T	
Rita Maersk	Dis	2004	22,184	35,199	171	27	14	T	
Robert Maersk	Dis	2003	22,181	34,801	171	27	14	T	
Romo Maersk	Dis	2003	22,161	34,808	171	27	14	T	
Rosa Maersk	Dis	2005	22,184	35,192	171	27	14	T	
Roy Maersk	Dis	2005	22,184	35,190	171	27	14	T	
Sally Maersk	Dis	1998	91,560	104,696	348	43	25	CC	
Sea-Land Eagle #	Hkg	1997	49,985	59,961	292	32	24	CC	
Sea-Land Liberator	Mhl	1980	32,629	30,250	227	31	20	CC	
Sea-Land Mercury #	Hkg	1995	49,985	59,840	292	32	24	CC	
Sine Maersk	Dis	1998	91,560	104,696	348	43	25	CC	

Name	Flag	Year	GRT	DWT	LOA	Bm	Kts	Type	Former names
Skagen Maersk	Dis	1999	91,500	104,700	348	43	25	CC	
Sofie Maersk	Dis	1999	91,500	104,696	348	43	25	CC	
Sorø Maersk	Dis	1999	91,500	104,696	348	43	25	CC	
Sovereign Maersk	Dis	1997	91,560	104,886	348	43	25	CC	
Susan Maersk	Dis	1997	91,560	104,886	348	43	25	CC	
Svend Maersk	Dis	1999	91,500	104,696	348	43	25	CC	
Svendborg Maersk	Dis	1998	91,560	104,696	348	43	25	CC	
Tâsinge Maersk	Dis	1994	20,842	28,550	190	28	18	CC	ex Maersk California-02, Caroline Maersk-97
Thies Maersk	Dis	1992	16,982	21,825	162	28	18	CC	ex Cornelia Maersk-01
Thomas Maersk	Dis	1994	18,859	25,368	176	28	18	CC	ex Maersk Tennesse-02, Thomas Maersk-97
Thur Maersk	Dis	1991	16,982	21,825	162	28	18	CC	ex Chastine Maersk-01
Tigris Leader	Sgp	1983	30,572	11,430	167	28	18	V	ex Maersk Crest-06, Rich Queen-89
Tinglev Maersk	Dis	1994	18,859	25,431	176	28	18	CC	ex Maersk Texas-02, Tinglev Maersk-97
Tove Maersk	Dis	1992	16,982	21,825	162	28	18	CC	ex Charlotte Maersk-01
Troense Maersk	Dis	1992	16,982	21,825	162	28	18	CC	ex Maersk Colorado-03, Clifford Maersk-97

newbuildings: two 93,750 grt, eight 34,500 grt and four 21,000 grt container ships, two 308,800 dwt and seven 39,000 dwt tankers, four 95-98,000 grt Lng tankers, three 18,000 grt Lpg tankers, two 90,000 dwt bulk carriers for 2008-11 delivery.
Vessels are owned or managed by subsidiaries * Maersk Ship Management BV or P&O Nedlloyd BV, ** by Nedlloyd BV, both Netherlands, *** by Maersk Egypt SAE, Egypt, † by Reederei Blue Star GmbH, Germany including †† managed for Commerz Real Fonds Beteiligungsgesellschaft, # by Maersk Shipping Hong Kong Ltd.
§ managed for Zodiac Maritime Agencies Ltd., UK (see Ofer Bros.) ‡ owned by Seaspan Corp, Hong Kong (Seaspan International Ltd, Canadian subsidiary of Washington Corp, USA), ≠ owned/managed by Eastwind Group or ‡‡ by MC Shipping See also MPC Munchmeyer Petersen & Co. World's largest container carrier (by vessels and capacity) - see other chartered ships with 'Maersk' prefix or suffix in index.

A. P. Moller. NORDBY MAERSK. *J. M. Kakebeeke*

A. P. Moller. SKAGEN MAERSK. *Allan Ryszka Onions*

Name	Flag	Year	GRT	DWT	LOA	Bm	Kts	Type	Former names

A P Moller Singapore Pte Ltd/Singapore

Funnel: Black with white seven-pointed star on broad light blue band. **History:** Formed 1978 as Maersk Co (Singapore) Pte Ltd to 1989. **Web:** www.apmsingapore.com.sg

Name	Flag	Year	GRT	DWT	LOA	Bm	Kts	Type	Former names
Effie Maersk	Sgp	2000	159,187	307,190	333	58	16	T	
Maersk Alfirk	Sgp	2008	108,393	110,401	338	46	25	CC	
Maersk Algol	Sgp	2008	108,393	110,228	338	46	25	CC	
Maersk Altair	Sgp	2007	108,393	110,295	338	46	25	CC	
Maersk Antares	Sgp	2007	108,393	110,271	338	46	25	CC	
Maersk Batam	Sgp	2008	35,835	43,133	224	32	22	CC	
Maersk Bering	Sgp	2005	19,758	29,057	176	29	14	T	
Maersk Bintan	Sgp	2008	35,835	43,097	224	32	22	CC	
Maersk Borneo	Sgp	2007	19,758	29,013	176	29	14	T	
Maersk Buton	Sgp	2008	35,835	43,123	224	32	22	CC	
Maersk Jade	Sgp	2006	25,994	29,300	180	29	15	Lpg	
Maersk Jewel	Sgp	2006	25,994	29,190	180	29	16	Lpg	
Maersk Kalea	Sgp	2004	25,507	38,850	168	29	14	T	ex Meriom Pride-08
Maersk Kowloon	Sgp	2006	74,642	84,676	299	40	25	CC	
Maersk Kuantan	Sgp	2007	74,642	84,775	299	40	25	CC	
Maersk Kushiro	Sgp	2007	74,642	84,704	299	40	25	CC	
Maersk Kwangyang	Sgp	2007	74,642	84,676	299	40	25	CC	
Maersk Methane (me)	Sgp	2008	104,169	82,115	285	43		Lng	
Maersk Nautica	Sgp	2008	156,000	307,284	333	58	16	T	
Maersk Nautilus	Sgp	2006	159,911	307,284	333	58	16	T	

A. P. Moller. MAERSK BORNEO. *Allan Ryszka Onions*

A. P. Moller. MAERSK KUANTAN. *Allan Ryszka Onions*

Name	Flag	Year	GRT	DWT	LOA	Bm	Kts	Type	Former names
Maersk Navarin	Sgp	2007	159,911	307,284	333	58	16	T	
Maersk Nectar	Sgp	2008	159,911	307,284	333	58	16	T	
Maersk Neptune	Sgp	2007	159,911	307,284	333	58	16	T	
Maersk Nova	Sgp	2008	163,539	307,284	333	58	16	T	
Maersk Nucleus	Sgp	2007	159,911	307,284	333	58	16	T	
Maersk Pearl	Sgp	2005	61,764	109,570	245	42	14	T	
Maersk Pelican	Sgp	2007	61,724	109,647	245	42	14	T	
Maersk Penguin	Sgp	2007	61,724	109,647	245	42	14	T	
Maersk Phoenix	Sgp	2005	61,764	109,571	245	42	15	T	
Maersk Princess	Sgp	2005	61,724	109,637	245	42	14	T	
Maersk Priority*	Sgp	2004	59,843	105,636	248	43	15	T	ex Unique Priority-07
Maersk Privilege *	Sgp	2003	56,285	105,483	248	43	15	T	ex Unique Privilege-07
Maersk Producer	Sgp	2006	61,724	109,647	248	43	15	T	
Maersk Progress	Sgp	2005	61,764	109,181	248	43	15	T	
Maersk Promise	Sgp	2006	61,724	109,647	248	43	15	T	
Maersk Radiant	Sgp	2004	22,184	34,806	171	27	14	T	
Maersk Sebarok	Sgp	2007	79,702	87,534	318	40	25	CC	
Maersk Seletar	Sgp	2007	79,702	87,545	318	40	25	CC	
Maersk Semakau	Sgp	2007	79,702	87,621	318	40	25	CC	
Maersk Sembawang	Sgp	2007	79,702	87,534	318	40	25	CC	
Maersk Senang	Sgp	2007	79,702	87,608	318	40	25	CC	
Maersk Sentosa	Sgp	2007	79,702	87,618	318	40	25	CC	
Maersk Serangoon	Sgp	2007	79,702	87,624	318	40	25	CC	
Maersk Taikung	Sgp	2007	94,193	107,329	332	43	24	CC	
Maersk Tanjong	Sgp	2007	94,193	107,500	332	43	24	CC	
Maersk Taurus	Sgp	2008	94,193	107,500	332	43	24	CC	
Maersk Tukang	Sgp	2008	94,193	107,404	332	43	24	CC	
Maersk Value	Sgp	2008	47,386	59,423	225	37	16	Lpg	
Maersk Venture	Sgp	2008	47,386	58,159	225	37	16	Lpg	
Maersk Virtue	Sgp	2007	47,386	58,123	225	37	16	Lpg	
Maersk Visual	Sgp	2007	47,386	58,063	225	37	16	Lpg	
MISC Merlion	Sgp	1990	49,874	55,971	294	32	24	CC	ex Maersk Merlion-07, Marstal Maersk-03, Arosia-93
MSC Malacca	Sgp	1990	49,779	56,049	294	32	24	CC	ex Maersk Malacca-08, Munkebo Maersk-03, Alsia-93
Sea-Land Integrity	Mhl	1984	57,075	58,869	290	32	19	CC	ex Virginia-88, Jacqueline-88, American Virginia-87
Sea-Land Patriot	Mhl	1980	32,629	30,225	257	31	20	CC	

* managed by Anglo-Eastern Shipmanagement (S) Pte Ltd, Singapore
Also see Shell-Royal Dutch Group.

The Maersk Co Ltd/UK

History: *Formed 1972.* **Web:** *www.maersk.co.uk*

Name	Flag	Year	GRT	DWT	LOA	Bm	Kts	Type
Gosport Maersk	Gbr	2000	50,698	51,100	292	32	24	CC
Loch Rannoch * (2)	Gbr	1998	75,526	130,031	270	46	14	T
Maersk Baltimore	Gbr	2006	48,853	53,634	294	32	29	CC
Maersk Barry	Gbr	2006	19,758	29,000	176	29	14	T

A. P. Moller. MAERSK BEAUMONT . *Hans Kraijenbosch*

Name	Flag	Year	GRT	DWT	LOA	Bm	Kts	Type	Former names
Maersk Beaufort	Gbr	2006	19,758	29,015	175	29	14	T	
Maersk Beaumont	Gbr	2007	48,853	53,890	294	32	29	CC	
Maersk Belfast	Gbr	2005	19,758	29,031	175	29	14	T	
Maersk Bentonville	Gbr	2006	48,853	53,201	294	32	29	CC	
Maersk Boston	Gbr	2006	48,808	53,701	294	32	29	CC	
Maersk Bristol	Gbr	2005	19,758	29,051	176	29	14	T	
Maersk Brooklyn	Gbr	2007	48,853	53,201	294	32	29	CC	
Maersk Brownsville	Gbr	2007	45,000	53,807	294	32	29	CC	
Maersk Buffalo	Gbr	2007	48,853	53,701	294	32	29	CC	
Maersk Humber	Iom	1998	17,980	20,815	159	26	18	Lpg	ex Burgos-05, Maersk Humber-00
Maersk Kelso	Gbr	2007	74,642	84,783	299	40	25	CC	
Maersk Kendal	Gbr	2007	74,642	84,771	299	40	25	CC	
Maersk Maryland	Gbr	1991	23,953	31,829	181	31	18	CC	ex Endurance-06, Ibn Jubayr-97, I/a CMB Dolphin
Maersk Rapier	Iom	2000	22,181	35,000	171	27	15	T	ex Robert Maersk-00
Maersk Remlin **	Gbr	2003	22,181	34,548	171	27	14	T	ex Maersk Regent-06
Maersk Riesa **	Bhs	2003	22,181	34,558	171	27	14	T	ex Maersk Richmond-06
Maersk Rosyth	Gbr	2003	22,184	34,811	171	27	14	T	
Sea-Land Champion	Nld	1995	49,985	59,840	292	32	24	CC	
Sea-Land Developer	Mhl	1980	32,629	30,296	257	31	20	CC	
Sea-Land Innovator	Mhl	1980	32,629	30,341	257	31	20	CC	

newbuildings: five 26,050 grt container ships for 2009 delivery
* managed by BP Shipping Ltd., UK or ** owned by KG Allgemeine Leasing GmbH & Co, Germany.

Maersk Line Ltd/USA

Funnel: Black with white seven-pointed star on broad light blue band. **History:** *Formed 1947.* **Web:** *www.maersklinelimited.com*

Name	Flag	Year	GRT	DWT	LOA	Bm	Kts	Type	Former names
Georgia	Usa	1998	50,698	62,400	292	32	24	CC	ex Maersk Georgia-07, Gudrun Maersk-02
Maersk Alabama	Usa	1998	14,120	17,375	155	25	18	CC	ex Alva Maersk-04
Maersk Arizona	Dis	1998	14,120	17,375	155	25	18	CC	ex Agnete Maersk-08
Maersk Arkansas	Usa	1998	14,120	17,375	155	28	18	CC	ex Angelica Maersk-04, Albert Maersk-04
Maersk California	Usa	1992	18,979	25,375	176	28	18	CC	ex Christian Maersk-08
Maersk Carolina	Usa	1998	50,698	62,229	292	32	24	CC	ex Grete Maersk-02
Maersk Constellation	Usa	1980	20,529	21,213	182	27	18	Ro	ex Elisabeth Maersk-88, C.R. Marseille-88, Elisabeth Maersk-87
Maersk Iowa	Usa	2006	50,686	61,454	292	32	24	CC	ex Maersk Greenock-07
Maersk Missouri	Usa	1998	50,698	62,226	292	32	24	CC	ex Gerd Maersk-02
Maersk Montana	Usa	2006	50,686	50,416	292	32	24	CC	ex Maersk Guernsey-07
Maersk Maine **	Gbr	1992	23,953	31,829	181	31	18	CC	ex Enterprise-06, Ibn Zuhr-97, CMB Dawn-92
Maersk Nebraska *	Usa	1985	31,920	36,003	206	32	18	CC	ex Chesapeake Bay-06, Tillie Lykes-99, Chesapeake Bay-90, American Georgia-87
Maersk Nevada *	Usa	1985	31,920	40,621	206	32	18	CC	ex Deleware Bay-06, Tyson Lykes-99, Deleware Bay-90, American Ohio-87
Maersk Vermont **	Gbr	1991	23,953	31,829	181	31	18	CC	ex Endeavor-06, Ibn Khaldoun-97, China Sea-94, CMB Drive-91
Maersk Ohio	Usa	2006	50,686	61,454	292	32	24	CC	ex Maersk Gosforth-07
Maersk Rhode Island	Usa	2002	22,161	34,801	171	27	14	T	I/a Maersk Ramsey
Maersk Utah	Usa	2006	50,686	62,000	292	32	25	CC	ex Maersk Gloucester-09
Maersk Virginia	Usa	2002	50,686	62,009	292	32	24	CC	ex Maersk Geelong-03
Sea-Land Achiever	Usa	1984	57,075	59,869	290	32	18	CC	ex Galveston Bay-02, Sea-Land Achiever-94, Leyla A-88, American Alabama-87
Sea-Land Atlantic	Usa	1985	57,075	58,943	290	32	19	CC	ex Karen H-88, American Oklahoma-87
Sea-Land Charger	Usa	1997	49,985	59,961	292	32	24	CC	
Sea-Land Comet	Usa	1995	49,985	59,840	292	32	24	CC	
Sea-Land Commitment	Usa	1985	57,075	58,869	290	32	19	Cc	ex OOCL Inspiration-00, CGM Ile de France-93, Sea-Land Commitment-91, Marguerite-88, American California-87
Sea-Land Florida	Usa	1984	57,075	58,943	290	32	19	CC	ex Nedlloyd Holland-00, Catherine K-88, American New York-87
Sea-Land Intrepid	Usa	1997	49,985	59,000	292	32	24	CC	
Sea-Land Lightning	Usa	1996	49,985	59,938	292	32	24	CC	
Sea-Land Meteor	Usa	1996	49,985	59,938	292	32	24	CC	
Sea-Land Motivator	Usa	1984	47,667	46,987	261	32	21	CC	ex Raleigh Bay-94, Elizabeth L-88, American New Jersey-87
Sea-Land Performance	Usa	1985	57,075	58,869	290	32	19	CC	ex Ruth W-88, American Washington-87
Sea-Land Pride	Usa	1985	47,667	47,171	261	32	21	CC	ex Galveston Bay-94, Mary Anne-88, American Kentucky-87
Sea-Land Quality	Usa	1985	57,075	58,869	290	32	19	CC	ex Patricia M-88, American Illinois-87

* owned by Farrell Lines Inc, USA (founded 1925 as American South African Lines to 1947) and managed by E-Ships Inc, USA or ** managed by The Maersk Co Ltd, UK. Also owns twelve other vessels long-term chartered to US military fleet

Safmarine Container Lines/Belgium

Funnel: *Blue with 'Safmarine' houseflag (white with orange cross) on large white disc* **Hull:** *White with blue 'Safmarine', red or green boot-topping.* **History:** *Container subsidiary founded 1996 as Safmarine & CMBT Lines NV to 1998 and acquired 1999.* **Web:** *www.safmarine.com*

Name	Flag	Year	GRT	DWT	LOA	Bm	Kts	Type	Former names
Safmarine Asia **	Iom	1985	21,887	31,290	189	28	17	CC	ex CMBT Asia-00, Norasia Samantha-84 (len-89)
Safmarine Basilea *	Che	2005	9,990	12,680	140	22	17	Co	ex SCL Basilea-05
Safmarine Cameroun	Bel	2004	24,488	28,936	196	32	20	CC	
Safmarine Concord	Nld	1988	18,037	26,152	177	28	17	CC	ex Zoe Delmas-00, Concord-99, CMBT Concord-97, Hansa Concord-95, POL East-93, Ville de Mars-92
Safmarine Cotonou	Nld	1986	21,054	29,800	182	29	18	CC	ex Maersk Cotonou-00, Nomaza-98, Mediterraneo-98, Zim Australia-96, Nedlloyd van Linschoten-94, ScanDutch Edo-89, Santa Catarina-86
Safmarine Europe **	Iom	1985	21,887	31,290	189	28	17	CC	ex CMBT Europe-00, Norasia Susan-94 (len-89)
Safmarine Kariba	Gbr	2008	74,642	84,626	299	40	25	CC	
Safmarine Komati	Gbr	2008	74,642	84,688	299	40	25	CC	
Safmarine Kuramo	Bel	2004	24,488	28,844	196	32	20	CC	
Safmarine Leman *	Che	2005	9,990	12,680	140	22	17	Co	ex SCL Leman-05
Safmarine Mafadi	Gbr	2007	50,698	61,433	292	32	25	CC	
Safmarine Makutu	Gbr	2007	50,698	61,407	292	32	25	CC	
Safmarine Meru	Gbr	2006	50,686	61,392	292	32	25	CC	
Safmarine Mulanje	Gbr	2007	50,686	61,447	292	32	25	CC	
Safmarine Nakuru	Gbr	2008	25,904	35,137	211	30	21	CC	
Safmarine Ngami	Bel	2008	25,904	35,119	211	30	21	CC	
Safmarine Nile	Gbr	2008	25,904	35,181	211	30	21	CC	
Safmarine Nimba	Bel	2004	24,488	28,897	196	32	20	CC	
Safmarine Nokwanda	Gbr	2005	50,657	62,994	266	37	24	CC	
Safmarine Nomazwe	Gbr	2004	50,657	62,994	266	37	25	CC	
Safmarine Nuba	Gbr	2008	25,904	35,144	211	30	21	CC	
Safmarine Nyassa	Gbr	2008	25,800	35,292	211	30	21	CC	
Safmarine Oranje	Zaf	1991	27,103	29,651	178	32	18	CC	ex Oranje-05, Safmarine Oranje-04, S.A. Oranje-00, Oranje-96

*Managed by Safmarine (Pty) Ltd, South Africa. * chartered from Enzian Shipping AG, Switzerland or ** from Eastwind Group.*
Also see other chartered vessels with 'Safmarine' prefix in index.

A/S J Ludwig Mowinckels Rederi Norway

Funnel: *Cream with narrow blue band on white band on broad red band beneath black top.* **Hull:** *Black, grey or brown with red boot-topping.* **History:** *Originally founded 1898 and split into separate family operating subsidiaries Viken and Vista in 2002.* **Web:** *www.jlmr.no*

Name	Flag	Year	GRT	DWT	LOA	Bm	Kts	Type	
Goya	Hkg	2008	42,785	75,500	225	32	14	B	
Grena	Bhs	2003	80,691	148,553	278	46	14	T	
Lista (2)	Nor	1995	17,751	27,892	170	24	14	T	
Molda	Nis	1994	52,157	96,347	238	42	14	T	
Ogna	Hkg	2009	40,500	75,000	225	32	14	B	

A. P. Moller (Safmarine). SAFMARINE NAKURU. *Hans Kraijenbosch*

Name	Flag	Year	GRT	DWT	LOA	Bm	Kts	Type	Former names

newbuilding: 75,000 dwt bulk carrier for 2009 delivery (Golden Strength)
Operated by Mowinckel Ship Management AS (formerly Vista Ship Management to 2008)

MPC Munchmeyer Petersen & Co GmbH — Germany

Funnel: Black with houseflag (red/black diagonally divided with white 'MPC') or charterers colours. **Hull:** Grey with red boot-topping.
History: Parent founded 1998 and subsidiary MPC Capital AG in 2000 (holds 40% interest in HCI Capital). **Web:** www.mpc-marine.com or www.mpc-steamship.de

Name	Flag	Year	GRT	DWT	LOA	Bm	Kts	Type	Former names
Austin Angol ††	Mhl	1998	28,148	46,376	185	32	15	Co	ex CCNI Angol-08, I/a Valdivia
Cap Valiente	Deu	2003	25,703	33,795	208	30	21	CC	ex Cabo Creus-07, Rio Valiente-03
Cap Verde	Deu	2003	25,703	33,741	208	29	21	CC	ex Alianca Sao Paulo-07, Rio Verde-03
CCNI Ancud ††	Mhl	1998	28,148	44,596	185	32	15	Co	ex CSAV Valencia-03, CCNI Ancud-01
CMA CGM Auckland	Lbr	2006	27,322	34,200	212	30	22	CC	ex Rio Ardeche-06
CMA CGM Comoe	Lbr	2008	23,633	27,155	191	29	20	CC	ex CMA CGM Rio San Francisco-08
CMA CGM Ebony	Lbr	2006	28,000	28,325	191	29	20	CC	ex TS Mumbai-08, OM Tridium-08, Rio Susa-08
CMA CGM Iguacu	Lbr	2006	27,322	34,200	212	30	22	CC	ex Rio Adour-06
CMA CGM Togo	Lbr	2007	23,666	28,325	191	29	20	CC	ex Rio Stora-07
CSAV Lonquen	Lbr	2008	40,807	55,301	261	32	24	CC	ex Rio Cadiz-08
CSAV Lonquimay	Lbr	2008	40,807	55,313	261	32	24	CC	ex Rio Charleston-8
Ella	Lbr	1999	13,066	20,567	153	24	17	Co	ex NileDutch Portugal-08, MSC Canada-07, Rio Rubio-06, Maruba Fitzroy-05, Rio Rubio-05, Johann Oldendorff-02
Hamburgo ‡	Mhl	1996	24,046	32,482	174	31	19	CC	ex CCNI Busan-07, Ghana Star I-04, Hamburgo-02, P&O Nedlloyd Ottawa-01, Superba Bridge-00, CCNI Aysen-00, Maersk Montevideo-98, CCNI Aysen-96
Maersk Delmont *	Gbr	1995	50,350	59,093	292	32	22	CC	ex Colombo Bay-06
Maersk Miami *	Nld	1994	56,248	55,238	279	38	23	CC	ex Nedlloyd Hongkong-06
Maersk Naples	Lbr	2004	27,059	34,415	212	30	22	CC	
Maersk Narvik	Lbr	2005	27,059	34,444	212	30	22	CC	I/a Rio Eider
Maersk Nolanville *	Lbr	2004	26,833	34,287	210	30	21	CC	ex P&O Nedlloyd Susana-05, I/a Rio Taku
Maersk Santana *	Lbr	2005	94,724	94,724	335	43	24	CC	ex P&O Nedlloyd Manet-06, Manet Star-05
Maersk Sarnia *	Lbr	2005	94,724	94,724	335	43	24	CC	ex P&O Nedlloyd Michelangelo-06, Michelangelo Star-05
Maersk Seville *	Deu	2006	94,724	97,552	335	43	24	CC	ex Mahler Star-06, P&O Nedlloyd Mahler-05
Maersk Sheerness *	Lbr	2006	94,724	97,536	335	43	24	CC	ex P&O Nedlloyd Mendelssohn-06
Maersk Singapore *	Lbr	2007	94,724	97,552	335	43	24	CC	
MISC Darlington *	Gbr	1993	50,350	59,093	292	32	22	CC	ex Maersk Darlington-07, Newport Bay-06
MSC Almeria *	Gbr	1992	50,235	59,093	292	32	22	CC	ex Jervis Bay-08
MSC Dalton *	Gbr	1992	50,350	59,093	292	32	22	CC	ex Maersk Dalton-08, Repulse Bay-06
MSC Dartford *	Gbr	1993	50,350	59,093	292	32	23	CC	ex Maersk Dartford-08, Singapore Bay-06
MSC Hong Kong	Lbr	2001	65,059	68,122	275	40	26	CC	ex CSCL Hong Kong-08
MSC Malaysia *	Gbr	1994	50,350	59,093	292	32	22	CC	ex Maersk Dauphin-07, Providence Bay-06, Shenzen Bay-94
MSC Salerno *	Gbr	1994	50,350	59,093	292	32	22	CC	ex Maersk Delano-08, Shenzen Bay-06
MSC Shenzen	Lbr	2000	65,059	68,122	275	40	26	CC	ex CSCL Shanghai-08
Nedlloyd Africa *	Nld	1992	48,508	50,792	266	32	21	CC	
Nedlloyd America *	Nld	1992	48,508	50,620	266	32	21	CC	
Nedlloyd Asia *	Nld	1991	48,508	50,620	266	32	21	CC	
Nedlloyd Europa *	Nld	1991	48,508	50,792	266	32	21	CC	
Nedlloyd Evita *	Lbr	2004	26,833	34,567	210	30	22	CC	ex P&O Nedlloyd Evita-06
Nedlloyd Honshu *	Nld	1995	56,248	55,238	279	38	24	CC	
Nedlloyd Maxima *	Lbr	2004	26,833	34,567	210	30	22	CC	ex P&O Nedlloyd Maxima-05
Nedlloyd Oceania *	Nld	1992	48,508	50,620	266	32	21	CC	
Nedlloyd Teslin *	Lbr	2004	26,833	34,567	210	30	22	CC	ex P&O Nedlloyd Teslin-05, I/dn Rio Teslin
NileDutch Benguela	Lbr	1998	13,066	20,567	153	24	17	Co	ex Rio Grande-07, Friedrich Oldendorff-03, Cielo del Peru-01, Friedrich Oldendorff-01
NileDutch Brazil	Lbr	1999	13,066	20,567	153	24	17	Co	ex MSC Angola-07, Rio Negro-06, Maruba Huascan-05, Rio Negro-05, Hermann Oldendorff-03
Pearl River	Lbr	1998	25,791	44,144	199	30	14	B	ex Hugo Oldendorff-06
Rio Genoa ‡	Lbr	2007	83,722	159,395	277	50	14	B	
Rio Rhine	Lbr	2009	22,000	34,000				B	
Rio Rhone	Lbr	2009	22,000	34,000				B	
Yangtze River	Lbr	1998	25,791	44,114	199	30	15	B	ex Gerdt Oldendorff-05

newbuildings: nine 142,000 grt, six 39,100 grt, five 36,600 grt and two 25,000 grt container ships and five 34,000 dwt bulkers for 2009-12 delivery.
* managed by Reederei Blue Star GmbH (A P Moller-Maersk), † by Bernard Schulte Shipmanagement (Deutschland) GmbH, †† by Uniteam Marine Shipping GmbH or ‡ by Rickmers Reederei GmbH & Cie KG
Also other ships under Reederei Claus-Peter Offen GmbH & Co and Seatrade Groningen BV (Triton Schiffahrts GmbH))

The National Shipping Company of Saudi Arabia   Saudi Arabia

Funnel: *White with yellow palm tree above crossed swords between two narrow green bands, narrow black top.* **Hull:** *Green or red some with yellow 'NSCSA', red or blue boot-topping.* **History:** *Formed 1981 as Saudi National Shipping Co. with 25% owned by Saudi government.* **Web:** *www.nscsa.sa*

Name	Flag	Year	GRT	DWT	LOA	Bm	Kts	Type	Former names
Abqaiq	Bhs	2002	159,990	302,986	333	58	16	T	
Dancing Brave ‡	Sgp	2009	17,000	16,800	154	26		Lpg	
Desert Orchid ‡	Sgp	2009	17,000	16,800	154	26		Lpg	
Ghawar	Bhs	1996	163,882	300,361	340	56	15	T	
Habari	Bhs	2008	160,782	317,693	333	60	15	T	
Harad	Bhs	2001	159,990	303,115	333	58	17	T	I/a Hellespont Burnside
Jana	Bhs	2007	160,782	318,000	333	60	15	T	
Layla	Bhs	2007	160,782	317,788	333	60	15	T	
Marjan	Bhs	2002	159,990	303,115	333	58	17	T	
Maori Venture ‡‡	Sgp	1985	47,289	51,232	220	38	16	Lpg	ex Hourai Maru-07
Mill House ‡‡	Sgp	2008	47,197	58,564	225	37	16	Lpg	
Mill Reef ‡‡	Sgp	2008	47,197	58,564	225	37	16	Lpg	
Nashwan ‡	Bmu	2008	17,852	16,800	154	26		Lpg	
NCC Abha *	Pan	2006	29,575	45,958	183	32	14	T	
NCC Arar *	Nis	1982	14,627	23,016	159	23	14	T	ex Austanger-90
NCC Asir *	Nis	1982	14,627	23,016	159	23	16	T	ex Bow Explorer-90, Grenanger-90
NCC Baha *	Nis	1985	15,817	24,728	172	28	14	T	ex Bow Falcon-90, Fjellanger-90, Northern Falcon-89, Portela-88
NCC Dammam *	Pan	2008	29,575	45,965	183	32	14	T	
NCC Haiel *	Pan	2008	29,575	45,953	183	32	14	T	
NCC Hijaz *	Pan	2005	29,575	46,000	183	32	14	T	
NCC Jubail **	Nis	1996	23,197	37,449	183	32	16	T	
NCC Mekka **	Nis	1995	23,197	37,272	183	32	16	T	
NCC Najd *	Pan	2005	29,575	45,998	183	32	14	T	
NCC Qassim *	Pan	2008	29,575	46,038	183	32	14	T	
NCC Rabigh	Sau	2006	29,575	46,038	183	32	14	T	
NCC Riyad **	Nis	1994	23,197	37,252	183	32	16	T	
NCC Sudair	Pan	2007	29,575	46,012	183	32	14	T	
NCC Tabuk	Pan	2006	29,575	45,963	183	32	14	T	
NCC Tihama	Pan	2005	29,575	45,948	183	32	14	T	
Njinsky ‡	Sgp	2008	16,804	16,800	154	26		Lpg	
Ramlah	Bhs	1996	163,882	300,361	340	56	15	T	
Safaniyah	Bhs	1997	163,882	300,361	340	56	15	T	
Safwa	Bhs	2002	159,990	302,977	333	58	16	T	
Saudi Abha	Sau	1983	44,171	42,600	249	32	18	Ro	
Saudi Diriyah	Sau	1983	44,171	42,600	249	32	18	Ro	
Saudi Hofuf	Sau	1983	44,171	42,600	249	32	18	Ro	
Saudi Tabuk	Sau	1983	44,171	42,600	249	32	18	Ro	
TI Hawtah	Bhs	1996	163,882	300,361	340	56	15	T	ex Hawtah-07
TI Watban	Bhs	1996	163,882	300,361	340	56	15	T	ex Watban-07
Wafrah	Bhs	2007	160,782	317,788	333	60	15	T	

newbuildings: six further 318,000 dwt and sixteen 45,000 dwt tankers for 2009-11 delivery.
Managed by Mideast Ship Management Ltd, UAE (formed 1996 jointly by NSCSA and V.Ships (UK) Ltd - www.msml.com)
* owned by National Chemical Carriers Ltd (formed 1990) with ** managed by Odfjell SE, Norway (www.odfjell.com) on bareboat charter to 2019.
‡ owned by 30% owned Petredec Ltd, Bemuda or Petredec Services UK Ltd and managed by Bernhard Schulte Shipmanagement (Singapore) Pte Ltd or ‡‡ by Anglo-Eastern Shipmanagement Pte Ltd, Singapore.

Navalmar (UK) Ltd   UK

Funnel: *Black.* **Hull:** *Black or grey with red boot-topping.* **History:** *Founded 1990.* **Web:** *www.navalmar.co.uk*

Name	Flag	Year	GRT	DWT	LOA	Bm	Kts	Type	Former names
Bio Bio	Pan	1979	26,078	38,542	182	29	14	Boh	ex Bio Bio I-95, Bio Bio-93, Grebe Arrow-92, Mannar-90, Sun Maiko-86, La Primavera-85
Carrara Castle	Mlt	1984	30,163	44,959	211	31	15	Boh	ex Star Evanger-08, Celestine-90, Birdie-89, Lily Star-87
Clifford Castle †	Pan	1978	27,735	43,051	183	31	15	Boh	ex Star Drottanger-07, Star Magnate-92
Dover Castle	Cym	1982	28,964	41,800	187	30	15	Boh	ex Waardrecht-01, Westwood Fuji-98, Waardrecht-94, Med Sky-94, Puebla-93, Med Sky-92, Waardrecht-89, Westwood Magellan-86, Waardrecht-85, Willine Tokyo-85, Waardrecht-84, Ibn al Kadi-83, I/a Waardrecht
Fjordstone	Vct	1978	21,193	31,945	162	27	15	BC	ex Dryso-98
Humboldt Current	Vct	1981	16,992	24,432	193	23	16	Co	ex Torm S.P.-93, Simo Matavulj-91, Konkar Thetis-87
Leeds Castle	Cym	1982	26,964	41,880	187	30	16	Boh	ex CSAV Barcelona-01, Leeds Castle-01, Wieldrecht-01, Westwood Halla-99, Star Livorno-95, Yucatan-93, Star Livorno-92, Wieldrecht-90

Name	Flag	Year	GRT	DWT	LOA	Bm	Kts	Type	Former names
Luni Castle	Mlt	1982	20,919	31,960	183	28	15	B	ex Lokris-04, Bunga Kenanga-99
Malaspina Castle	Pan	1981	21,173	32,587	183	28	15	BC	ex Adventure-05, Venture Star-94
Norwich Castle †	Pan	1978	27,735	43,052	183	31	15	Boh	ex Star Drivanger-07, Star Hong Kong-92
Olinda Castle *	Vct	1981	21,284	32,680	183	28	15	BC	ex Timberland-03, Ljubljana-02, Cielo di Firenze-98, Ljubljana-93, Ioannis Zafirakis-88, Brazil Venture-86
Oxford Castle †	Pan	1978	27,125	43,793	183	31	15	Boh	ex Star Davanger-07, Star Denver-89, Star Enterprise-85
Portland Castle	Mlt	1985	29,660	46,650	196	32	17	BC	ex Highgate-07, Colima-96
Richmond Castle †	Pan	1978	27,743	43,051	183	31	15	Boh	ex Star Djervanger-07, Star World-89
Rossel Current	Vct	1981	16,992	24,491	193	23	16	Co	ex Juraj Dalmatinac-93, Konkar Doris-87
Valpolicella	Vct	1983	20,627	32,243	183	28	15	B	ex Swordfish-04, Packing-03
Van Dyck *	Vct	1976	16,166	26,681	171	25	14	B	ex Eliki-98, Pacbaron-93
Vulturnus	Pan	1978	18,374	29,121	172	28	14	B	ex Autumn-06, Ming Autumn-93
Windsor Castle	Cym	1982	26,964	41,820	187	30	16	Boh	ex Wennsdrecht-01, Nedlloyd Abidjan-97, Star Lorraine-95, Altamira-93, Star Lorraine-92, Woensdrecht-90
York Castle	Mlt	1985	29,660	46,650	196	32	17	Boh	ex Maria-03, Mitla-99

*Managed by B Navi Shipmanagement Srl. Italy (www.bnavi.it) and * owned by subsidiaries Navalmar Transportes Maritimos Ltda, Madeira or ** Navalmar Lanka (Pvt) Ltd., Sri Lanka. † managed by Masterbulk Pte Ltd.*

Navigation Maritime Bulgare   Bulgaria

Funnel: *Yellow with broad red band, narrow black top.* **Hull:** *Black with red boot-topping.* **History:** *Founded 1892 and Government controlled, but with 43% owned since 2000 by British Orient Holdings.* **Web:** *www.navbul.com*

Name	Flag	Year	GRT	DWT	LOA	Bm	Kts	Type	Former names
Adalbert Antonov	Bgr	1979	23,363	38,510	202	28	14	B	
Aleko Konstantinov	Bgr	1985	12,554	15,442	159	23	17	CC	
Alexander Dimitrov	Bgr	1985	23,609	38,524	199	28	15	B	
Balgarka	Mlt	2004	25,065	41,425	186	30	14	B	ex Dolly-03
Balkan	Bgr	1975	15,865	24,386	185	23	14	B	
Dimitrovsky Komsomol	Bgr	1985	23,444	38,545	201	28	15	B	
Geo Milev	Bgr	1985	12,174	14,814	159	23	18	C	
Georgi Grigorov	Mlt	1986	23,540	38,518	199	28	15	B	
Hemus	Mlt	2008	25,327	42,704	186	30	14	B	
Kamenitza	Bgr	1980	16,188	24,150	185	23	14	B	
Kapitan Georgi Georgiev	Bgr	1980	16,188	24,150	185	23	14	B	
Koznitsa	Bgr	1984	16,502	24,100	185	23	14	B	
Liliana Dimitrova	Bgr	1982	23,779	38,135	202	28	16	B	
Malyovitza	Bgr	1983	16,188	24,456	184	23	14	B	
Midjur	Bgr	1992	13,834	21,537	168	25	13	B	
Milin Kamak	Bgr	1979	16,166	24,596	185	23	14	B	
Okoitchitza	Bgr	1982	16,188	24,148	184	23	14	B	
Petimata OT RMS	Bgr	1978	23,363	38,400	202	28	14	B	
Peyo Yavorov	Bgr	1984	12,554	15,104	159	23	18	C	
Pirin	Mlt	2007	13,965	21,211	169	25	14	B	
Plana	Mlt	1991	13,834	19,985	169	25	13	B	
Plovdiv	Mlt	1989	11,982	14,101	157	23	16	Co	ex Nedlloyd Marne-97, Armada Sprinter-97, Nedlloyd Marne-96, Waterdrager-91

Navigation Maritime Bulgare. SVILEN RUSSEV. *Allan Ryszka Onions*

Name	Flag	Year	GRT	DWT	LOA	Bm	Kts	Type	Former names
Rodina	Bgr	1978	30,596	52,975	215	32	14	B	
Rodopi	Bgr	1978	16,166	24,708	185	23	14	B	
Rojen	Bgr	1978	16,166	24,500	185	23	14	B	ex Sakar-78
Rousse	Bgr	1989	11,982	14,101	157	23	16	CC	ex Nedlloyd Musi-97, Wateraids-91, Kariba-91, Wateraids-91, CMB Effort-90, Wateraids-89
Sakar	Mlt	1995	13,957	21,591	168	25	13	B	
Shipka	Bgr	1979	16,166	24,285	185	23	14	B	
Slavianka	Bgr	1978	16,166	24,685	185	23	14	B	
Sofia	Bgr	1988	11,977	13,800	157	23	16	CC	ex Nedlloyd Maas-96, Waterkoning-91, Contship Singapore-90, Waterkoning-89, AEL America-89, Waterkoning-88
Svilen Russev	Bgr	1982	23,779	38,142	202	28	14	B	
Trapezitsa	Bgr	2003	13,967	21,250	169	25		B	
Tzarevetz	Mlt	1998	13,965	21,470	169	25		B	
Verila	Bgr	1996	14,431	23,723	151	26		B	
Vitosha	Bgr	1977	16,166	25,864	185	23	14	B	
Vola 1	Mlt	1992	13,834	20,620	168	25	13	B	ex Vola-03
Yordan Lutibrodski	Bgr	1986	23,589	38,519	198	28	15	B	
Yordanka Nikolova	Bgr	1979	23,363	38,400	202	28	14	B	

newbuildings: two 21,200 dwt bulk carriers for 2009-10 delivery.

Neptune Orient Lines Ltd   Singapore

Funnel: *Blue with horizontal blue and diagonal green triple wave design on broad white band, narrow black top or blue with white 'eagle' symbol on red band (APL).* **Hull:** *Light grey with blue 'NOL' or black with white 'APL' with red or dark grey boot-topping.*
History: *Singapore government controlled and founded 1969. American President Lines (founded 1896 and 1973 amalgamation with American Mail Lines) acquired 1997.* **Web:** *www.nol.com.sg or www.apl.com*

Name	Flag	Year	GRT	DWT	LOA	Bm	Kts	Type	Former names
APL Alexandrite	Sgp	1992	49,716	59,603	288	32	25	CC	ex MOL Ideal-02, APL Alexandrite-02, Neptune Alexandrite-01
APL Almandine	Sgp	1993	49,716	59,560	288	32	23	CC	ex Tokyo Bay-98, Neptune Almandine-96
APL Amazonite	Sgp	1993	49,716	59,603	288	32	24	CC	ex APL Sweden-01, NOL Amazonite-00, Osaka Bay-97, NOL Amazonite-96, Neptune Amazonite-95
APL Beijing	Lbr	2004	54,605	67,022	294	32	25	CC	
APL Belgium	Sgp	2002	65,792	67,500	277	40	24	CC	
APL Cairo	Sgp	2001	25,305	34,133	207	30	21	CC	
APL China *	Usa	1995	64,502	67,432	276	40	24	CC	
APL Coral	Sgp	1998	65,475	64,145	275	40	24	CC	ex NOL Coral-01
APL Cyprine	Sgp	1997	65,475	64,156	272	40	24	CC	ex NOL Cyprine-00
APL Dalian	Sgp	2002	25,305	34,133	207	30	21	CC	ex Indamex Dalian-04, APL Dalian-03
APL England	Sgp	2001	65,792	67,967	277	40	24	CC	
APL Florida	Lbr	2008	71,787	72,300	293	40	25	CC	
APL Germany **	Lbr	2003	66,462	67,109	281	40	25	CC	
APL Holland	Sgp	2001	65,792	67,500	277	40	24	CC	
APL Hong Kong **	Lbr	2002	66,573	67,009	280	40	25	CC	
APL Iolite	Sgp	1997	63,900	62,693	272	40	26	CC	ex MSC Hudson-04, APL Iolite-03, NOL Iolite-00
APL Ireland **	Lbr	2002	66,462	67,009	280	40	25	CC	

Neptune Orient Lines. APL IRELAND. *Mick Lindsay*

Name	Flag	Year	GRT	DWT	LOA	Bm	Kts	Type	Former names
APL Iris	Sgp	1998	63,900	62,693	272	40	24	CC	ex NOL Iris-01
APL Jade	Sgp	1995	53,519	66,647	294	32	24	CC	ex Hyundai Grace-05, APL Jade-04, NOL Sheratan-98, l/a Neptune Sheratan
APL Jeddah	Sgp	2001	25,305	34,122	207	30	21	CC	ex Indamex Malabar-04, APL Jeddah-03
APL Korea *	Usa	1995	64,502	66,370	276	40	24	CC	
APL Minnesota	Lbr	2008	71,787	72,912	295	40	26	CC	
APL New Jersey	Lbr	2008	71,787	72,912	295	40	26	CC	
APL Norway **	Lbr	2007	71,867	72,807	295	40	26	CC	
APL Orchid	Sgp	1984	13,488	18,437	161	25	17	CC	ex Eagle Orion-99, Dragon Nias-97, Neptune Jasper-96, Anro Adelaide-93, Neptune Jasper-89
APL Pearl	Sgp	1998	65,475	64,050	275	40	24	CC	ex NOL Pearl-99
APL Pusan	Sgp	2002	25,305	34,122	207	30	21	CC	ex Indamex Chesapeake-04, APL Pusan-02
APL Philippines *	Usa	1996	64,502	66,370	276	40	24	CC	
APL Ruby	Sgp	1988	47,893	51,437	276	32	24	CC	ex President Grant-06, NOL Ruby-98, Neptune Ruby-96
APL Scotland	Sgp	2001	65,792	67,500	277	40	24	CC	
APL Singapore *	Usa	1995	64,502	66,370	276	40	24	CC	
APL Spain **	Lbr	2004	66,300	66,100	281	40	25	CC	
APL Thailand *	Usa	1995	64,502	66,370	276	40	24	CC	
APL Topaz	Sgp	1989	47,893	51,534	276	32	24	CC	ex MOL Commitment-05, APL Topaz-04, America-01, President Hoover-99, NOL Topaz-98, Neptune Topaz-96
APL Tulip	Sgp	1984	13,488	18,437	161	25	17	CC	ex NOL Beryl-99, Neptune Beryl-97, Anro Fremantle-93, Neptune Beryl-89
APL Turquoise	Sgp	1996	52,086	60,323	294	32	24	CC	ex NOL Turquoise-98
APL Vietnam	Lbr	2005	54,605	67,025	294	32	25	CC	
APL Zircon	Sgp	1989	47,893	51,534	276	32	24	CC	ex President Wilson-06, NOL Zircon-98, Neptune Zircon-96
Hyundai Garnet	Sgp	1995	53,519	66,565	294	32	24	CC	ex APL Garnet-05, MOL Vigor-05, MSC Louisiana-03, APL Garnet-02, NOL Seginus-98, l/a Neptune Seginus
Hyundai Japan	Sgp	1995	64,502	66,520	276	40	24	CC	ex APL Japan-07
Hyundai Kennedy	Sgp	1988	61,926	54,665	275	39	24	CC	ex APL Kennedy-07, President Kennedy-03
MOL Freedom	Sgp	1997	65,475	63,693	272	40	24	CC	ex APL Agate-08, NOL Agate-00
MOL Innovation	Sgp	1995	52,086	60,323	294	32	24	CC	ex APL Tourmaline-04, MOL Innovation-04, MOL Tourmaline-03, APL Tourmaline-02, NOL Tourmaline-98
MOL Velocity	Sgp	1996	53,519	66,511	294	32	24	CC	ex APL Spinel-05, MOL Velocity-04, APL Spinel-03, MOL Velocity-03, APL Spinel-02, NOL Spinel-98
MOL Vision	Sgp	1995	53,519	65,598	294	32	24	CC	ex MSC Maryland-03, APL Sardonyx-02, NOL Sardonyx-98, Neptune Sardonyx-96
New Dynamic	Sgp	2001	13,764	16,400	154	25	19	CC	
President Adams *	Usa	1988	61,296	53,613	275	39	24	CC	
President Jackson *	Usa	1988	61,296	53,613	275	39	24	CC	
President Polk *	Usa	1988	61,296	53,613	275	39	24	CC	
President Truman *	Usa	1988	61,296	53,613	275	39	24	CC	

newbuildings: eight 114,000 grt container ships for 2011 delivery.
managed by Neptune Shipmanagement Services (Pte) Ltd, Singapore, except * owned by subsidiary APL Maritime Ltd, USA (founded 1984 as American Automar Inc to 2005) and managed by American Ship Management LLC, USA ** chartered from Japanese owners or banks.

Neste Oil Corporation   Finland

Funnel: Black with diamond divided green over blue. **Hull:** Black or dark blue, some with pale green or white 'NESTESHIP', red or pink boot-topping. **History:** Subsidiary of Fortum Oyj founded 1948 as government controlled Neste Oil to 1999, then Fortum Oil Oy until 2005. **Web:** www.nesteoil.com

Name	Flag	Year	GRT	DWT	LOA	Bm	Kts	Type	Former names
Futura	Fin	2004	15,980	25,084	170	24	14	T	
Jurmo	Fin	2004	15,980	25,049	169	24	14	T	
Mastera (me2)	Fin	2003	64,259	106,208	252	44	14	T	
Neste	Fin	2004	15,980	25,117	170	24	14	T	
Palva *	Fin	2007	42,810	74,940	229	32	14	T	l/a Neste Polaris
Purha	Fin	2003	15,980	25,000	170	24	14	T	
Stena Arctica *	Fin	2005	65,293	117,099	250	44	14	T	
Stena Poseidon *	Fin	2006	42,810	74,927	229	32	14	T	l/a Stena Polaris
Tempera (me2)	Fin	2002	64,259	106,034	252	44	14	T	

* owned jointly with Concordia Maritime AB (see under Stena AB)

NileDutch Africa Line

Netherlands

Funnel: *Blue base below broad white band with orange flash above blue 'NileDutch', deep orange top.* **Hull:** *Black, dark grey or blue with red or black boot-topping.* **History:** *Founded 1988.* **Web:** *www.niledutch.com*

Name	Flag	Year	GRT	DWT	LOA	Bm	Kts	Type	Former names
NDS Prodigy *	Cyp	1985	22,211	17,773	182	28	20	Ro	ex Silkeborg-98, Hudson-97, Yuriy Maksaryov-96
NileDutch Atlantic	Ant	1980	32,498	22,138	213	30		Ro	ex Sangwin-07, Sangwin I-07, Sassandra-06, Atlantic Arrow-01, CGM Ronsard-97, Ronsard-87
NileDutch Prominence	Cyp	1982	22,211	17,773	181	28	20	Ro	ex Atlantic Herald-03, NDS Prominence-03, Atlantic Herald-97, Georgiy Pyasetskiy-95
NileDutch Prospector	Atg	1981	32,068	22,447	204	31	22	Ro	ex Laura-04, Laura Delmas-02, Jolly Celeste-00, Katsina-99, Anatoily Vasilyev-97

*Managed or * owned by Bernhard Schulte Shipmanagement (Cyprus) Ltd*
See other vessels in index with NDS or NileDutch prefixes.

Nippon Yusen Kaisha (NYK)

Japan

Funnel: *Black with two narrow red bands on broad white band.* **Hull:** *Black or dark blue (vehicle carriers) with white/grey/pale blue diagonal stripes and white 'NYK LINE' with red boot-topping.* **History:** *Founded 1870 as Tsukumo Shokai being renamed Mitsukawa Shokai in 1872, Mitsubishi Shokai in 1873, Mitsubishi Kisen then Mitsubishi Mail Steamship Co in 1875. Merged in 1885 with Kyodo Unyu Kaisha to form NYK. Became joint-stock corporation in 1893 and name changed to Nippon Yusen Kabushiki Kaisha. Acquired Dai-ni Tokyo Kisen Kaisha in 1926 and Kinkai Yusen Kaisha in 1939. Merged with Mitsubishi Shipping in 1964 and Showa Line in 1998.* **Web:** *www.nykline.com*

Neste Oil Corporation. PURHA. *Phil Kempsey*

Neste Oil Corporation. STENA POSEIDON. *C. Lous*

Name	Flag	Year	GRT	DWT	LOA	Bm	Kts	Type	Former names
Aegean Leader	Pan	1993	47,171	13,157	180	32	18	V	ex Ocean Beluga-99, Mercury Diamond-96
Alioth Leader *	Pan	1998	51,790	14,909	180	32	19	V	
Andromeda Leader *	Pan	2004	62,195	21,443	200	32	20	V	
Anna **	Nis	1978	39,710	17,224	196	30	19	V	ex Hojin Maru-89
Apollon Leader *	Pan	2008	60,213	18,573	200	32	20	V	
Aquarius Leader *	Pan	1998	57,623	22,815	200	32	19	V	
Baltic Leader	Pan	1982	27,424	10,449	161	27	16	V	ex Brava-99, Jinyo Maru-87
Bellona	Pan	1985	45,495	15,160	184	32	18	V	ex Centry Leader No. 2-94
Bijin	Pan	1988	47,521	14,126	180	32	17	V	
Blue Hawk	Lbr	1978	40,711	14,407	186	32	18	V	
Bujin *	Pan	1993	41,931	17,189	196	29	18	V	
California Jupiter *	Lbr	1986	41,668	38,438	248	32	22	CC	
California Mercury	Jpn	1987	41,442	38,538	248	32	22	CC	
Cape Charles *	Pan	1986	41,843	38,449	249	32	22	CC	
Cape May	Jpn	1986	42,145	38,217	248	32	22	CC	ex Yamataka Maru-91
Capricornus Leader	Pan	2004	61,854	20,120	200	32	20	V	
Cassiopeia Leader	Pan	1999	57,455	21,547	200	32	19	V	
Centaurus Leader	Pan	2004	62,195	21,471	200	32	20	V	
Century Leader No.1 *	Pan	1984	45,422	11,772	180	32	18	V	
Century Leader No.3	Jpn	1986	44,830	14,154	179	32	18	V	
Century Leader No.5	Jpn	1986	50,867	15,293	200	32	18	V	
Cepheus Leader *	Pan	2006	62,571	21,402	200	32	20	V	
Cetus Leader	Pan	2005	62,195	21,466	200	32	20	V	
Champion Peace	Pan	1999	56,249	106,042	241	42	15	T	
Champion Pleasure	Pan	2008	56,362	105,852	241	42	15	T	
Champion Pride	Pan	1998	58,141	99,997	244	42	13	T	
Columbia Leader	Pan	1987	38,659	13,491	182	30	18	V	ex Green Bay-01
Delphinus Leader	Pan	1998	57,391	21,514	200	32	19	V	
Eijin	Pan	1982	41,195	14,361	180	32	18	V	ex Eijin Maru-85
Equuleus Leader *	Pan	2005	61,804	20,141	200	32	20	V	
Eufonia **	Pan	1981	27,163	10,480	165	28	18	V	ex Yujin-92, Yujin Maru-85
Fanta	Pan	1983	36,437	13,732	190	29	16	V	ex Evviva-98, Madonna-93, Aso Maru-90
Festa	Pan	1983	36,439	13,656	190	29	16	V	ex Amagi Maru-90
Fuji *	Lbr	1984	47,751	16,204	190	32	18	V	ex Fuji Maru-90
Ganta	Pan	1978	25,431	11,311	165	27	17	V	ex Beach-90, Pioneer Racer-90
Grand Pacific	Pan	1994	147,580	263,097	333	60	15	T	
Hakone	Pan	1983	35,309	29,733	212	32	21	CC	ex Hakone Maru-99
Heijin *	Pan	1989	47,521	14,366	180	32	18	V	
Hojin *	Vut	1990	55,470	18,273	200	32	19	V	
Hudson Leader	Pan	1987	47,707	14,104	180	32	18	V	ex Green Lake-01
Jingu Maru *	Jpn	1992	42,164	17,216	196	32	18	V	
Jinsei Maru	Jpn	1990	55,489	17,914	199	32	19	V	
Jupiter Diamond	Sgp	1978	45,998	14,687	214	29	18	V	
Kaga	Jpn	1988	51,047	59,188	289	32	23	CC	
Kaijin *	Pan	1994	41,931	17,183	196	29	18	V	
Kamakura *	Pan	1988	50,462	59,441	290	32	23	CC	
Katsuragi *	Pan	1990	50,437	59,418	292	32	23	CC	ex Kowloon Bay-98, Katsuragi-96
Kitano	Jpn	1990	50,618	59,804	288	32	23	CC	
Koh Jin	Vut	1981	49,844	19,712	199	32	18	V	
Kou-Ei	Pan	1999	149,371	279,999	330	60	15	T	
Leo Leader	Pan	1999	57,566	22,733	200	32	19	V	
Linden Pride *	Pan	2001	46,021	49,999	230	37	16	Lpg	
Lyra Leader	Pan	2005	62,510	21,453	200	32	20	V	
Morning Melody	Pan	1988	47,068	13,162	180	32	18	V	ex Phoenix Diamond-04
Nada V *	Pan	1984	43,101	14,820	186	32	18	V	
New Nada *	Pan	1992	47,519	14,180	180	32	19	V	
Nippon *	Pan	2002	159,613	298,399	333	60	18	T	
NYK Andromeda *	Pan	1998	75,637	81,819	300	40	23	CC	
NYK Antares *	Pan	1997	75,637	81,819	300	40	23	CC	
NYK Aphrodite *	Pan	2003	75,484	81,171	300	40	25	CC	
NYK Apollo *	Pan	2002	75,484	81,171	300	40	25	CC	
NYK Aquarius *	Pan	2003	75,484	81,171	300	40	25	CC	
NYK Argus *	Pan	2004	75,484	81,000	300	40	25	CC	
NYK Artemis *	Pan	2003	75,484	81,171	300	40	25	CC	
NYK Athena *	Pan	2003	75,484	81,171	300	40	25	CC	
NYK Atlas *	Pan	2004	75,519	81,171	300	40	25	CC	
NYK Canopus *	Pan	1998	76,847	82,275	300	40	23	CC	
NYK Castor *	Pan	1998	76,847	82,275	300	40	23	CC	
NYK Clara	Sgp	2008	27,051	34,578	210	30	23	CC	
NYK Daedalus	Pan	2007	55,534	65,867	294	32	25	CC	
NYK Daniella	Sgp	2008	27,051	34,536	210	30	23	CC	

Name	Flag	Year	GRT	DWT	LOA	Bm	Kts	Type	Former names
NYK Delphinus *	Pan	2007	55,534	65,950	294	32	25	CC	
NYK Demeter	Pan	2008	55,534	65,965	294	32	25	CC	
NYK Deneb *	Pan	2008	55,534	65,953	294	32	25	CC	
NYK Diana	Pan	2008	55,534	65,976	294	32	25	CC	
NYK Kai *	Pan	1993	50,606	59,658	288	32	24	CC	ex Kai-95
NYK Leo *	Pan	2002	75,201	77,900	300	40	27	CC	
NYK Libra	Pan	2002	75,201	77,900	300	40	26	CC	
NYK Loadstar *	Pan	2001	75,201	77,900	300	40	27	CC	
NYK Lynx	Pan	2002	75,201	77,950	300	40	26	CC	
NYK Lyra *	Pan	2002	75,201	78,000	300	40	26	CC	
NYK Oceanus	Pan	2007	98,799	99,563	336	46	25	CC	
NYK Olympus	Pan	2008	98,799	99,563	336	40	25	CC	
NYK Orion	Pan	2008	98,799	99,563	336	40	25	CC	
NYK Orpheus	Jpn	2008	99,543	99,563	336	40	25	CC	
NYK Pegasus *	Pan	2003	76,199	80,270	300	40	25	CC	
NYK Phoenix *	Pan	2003	76,199	80,270	300	40	25	CC	
NYK Procyon †	Pan	1995	60,117	63,179	300	37	22	CC	
NYK Sirius	Pan	1998	76,847	82,271	300	40	23	CC	
NYK Springtide *	Pan	1992	43,213	39,394	253	32	23	CC	
NYK Starlight *	Pan	1991	43,327	39,015	251	32	23	CC	
NYK Terra	Pan	2008	76,928	80,282	300	40	25	CC	
NYK Themis	Pan	2008	76,928	80,282	300	40	25	CC	
NYK Theseus	Pan	2008	79,280	79,030	300	40	25	CC	

Nippon Yusen Kaisha. NYK ANTARES. *N. Kemps*

Nippon Yusen Kaisha . OCEAN CERES. *Hans Kraijenbosch*

Name	Flag	Year	GRT	DWT	LOA	Bm	Kts	Type	Former names
NYK Triton	Pan	2008	76,000	79,280	300	40	25	CC	
NYK Vega *	Pan	2006	97,825	103,310	338	46	25	CC	
NYK Venus	Pan	2007	97,825	100,900	338	46	25	CC	
NYK Vesta	Pan	2007	97,825	103,260	338	46	26	CC	
NYK Virgo	Pan	2007	97,825	103,284	338	46	25	CC	
Ocean Ceres	Sgp	1999	88,385	171,850	289	45	14	B	ex Charles LD-04
Ocean Champion	Jpn	1985	101,222	198,906	300	50	13	B	ex Onga Maru-01
Ocean Cygnus	Pan	2006	89,603	178,996	289	45	15	B	
Orion Diamond	Vut	1982	53,251	15,396	214	32	18	V	
Orion Leader	Pan	1999	57,513	21,526	200	32	19	V	
Pacific Leader	Pan	1983	47,129	16,138	184	32	17	V	ex Prospero-99, Jinkai Maru-90
Pegasus Diamond	Jpn	1986	47,164	13,068	180	32	18	V	
Pegasus Leader	Pan	1999	57,566	22,747	200	32	19	V	
Perseus Leader	Pan	1999	57,449	21,503	200	32	19	V	
Phoenix Leader *	Pan	2004	61,804	20,146	200	32	20	V	
Pioneer Leader **	Pan	1980	41,116	17,859	200	32	17	V	
Poseidon Leader *	Jpn	2007	63,001	21,449	200	32	20	V	
Procyon Leader	Pan	2000	51,259	17,361	180	32	19	V	
Prometheus Leader	Sgp	2008	41,886	14,382	190	28	20	V	
Pyxis Leader	Pan	2004	62,195	21,466	200	32	20	V	
Queen Ace	Pan	1988	55,423	18,777	200	32	19	V	
Rhine Ore	Jpn	1990	116,427	233,016	315	54	14	O	ex Once Maru-01
Ryujin	Pan	1993	47,737	14,080	180	32	19	V	
Sagittaurus Leader	Pan	2005	61,801	20,098	200	32	20	V	
Shin Onoe	Pan	2004	101,953	203,248	300	50	15	B	
Sirius Leader	Pan	2000	51,496	16,451	180	32	19	V	
Sky Wing	Pan	2002	154,369	299,997	333	60	15	T	
Taga *	Pan	2004	160,007	303,430	333	60	15	T	
Taizan	Pan	2002	160,084	300,405	333	60	15	T	
Tajima	Pan	1996	148,330	258,096	333	60	16	T	
Takachiho II	Pan	1998	149,376	280,889	330	60	16	T	
Takahashi	Pan	2007	160,295	314,020	333	60	15	T	
Takamine	Pan	2004	150,084	306,206	333	60	15	T	
Takasago Maru	Jpn	1999	149,376	281,050	330	60	15	T	
Takasaki	Pan	2005	159,939	300,390	333	60	15	T	
Takasuzu *	Pan	2000	152,139	279,989	330	60	15	T	
Takayama	Jpn	1993	150,053	264,457	332	58	15	T	
Tateyama	Pan	2002	160,072	300,373	333	60	15	T	
Tenki *	Pan	2007	160,295	316,021	333	60	15	T	
Tenryu	Lbr	1999	152,139	281,050	330	60	16	T	
Tenyo	Lbr	2000	152,139	281,050	330	60	15	T	
Tenzan	Pan	2000	152,139	281,050	330	60	15	T	
Toba	Pan	2004	160,068	299,980	333	60	15	T	
Tohdoh	Pan	1991	149,356	261,212	330	59	15	T	
Tohshi	Pan	2007	159,939	300,363	333	60	15	T	
Tokachi *	Pan	1999	149,376	280,973	330	60	16	T	
Tokio	Pan	2005	159,953	306,206	333	60	15	T	
Tosa	Pan	2008	159,927	302,150	333	60	15	T	

Nippon Yusen Kaisha. SIRIUS LEADER. *David Walker*

Name	Flag	Year	GRT	DWT	LOA	Bm	Kts	Type	Former names
Towada	Pan	2006	159,982	305,801	333	60	15	T	
Toyo *	Pan	2005	160,096	310,309	333	60	15	T	
Tsurumi *	Pan	2003	159,960	300,838	333	60	15	T	
Vega Leader	Pan	2000	51,496	16,396	180	32	19	V	
Virgo Leader *	Pan	2004	61,854	20,111	200	32	20	V	
Volans Leader *	Pan	2007	61,775	20.168	200	32	20	V	

newbuildings: more than 130 on order including four 300,000 dwt tankers, sixteen 176-300,000 dwt bulk carriers, over thirty container ships up to 98,800 grt and several vehicle carriers and Lng tankers..
* managed by NYK Ship Management Co. Ltd, Singapore (formed 2001) or ** NYK Ship Management, Hong Kong (formed 1989).
† ownwd by Goldenport Shipmanagement Ltd, Greece
The company and its numerous subsidiaries own or manage over 410 vessels with many others on charter. Only the largest container ships, bulk carriers, vehicle carriers and tankers are listed. Tthe company also owns, manages or operates 22 large Lng tankers, 46 wood-chip carriers, many other bulk carriers, tankers and smaller container ships and vehicle carriers. See also Ray Shipping, Stolt-Nielsen, Torm and Vroon.

NYKCool AB/Sweden

Funnel: *Deep red base and broad blue top with blue and red arcs on broad white central band.* **Hull:** *Red, cream or white with red/blue 'NYKCool', red or blue boot-topping.* **History:** *Formed 2007, when the reefer operations of LauritzenCool AB (formed 2001 following acquisition of Cool Carriers AB (formed 1984) from Leif Hoegh) were acquired having previously been a joint venture since 2005.* **Web:** www.lauritzencool.com

Name	Flag	Year	GRT	DWT	LOA	Bm	Kts	Type	Former names
Atlantik Frigo	Hrv	1989	10,366	11,000	143	23	19	R	
Autumn Wind †	Bhs	1993	13,077	13,981	158	24	22	R	ex St. Lucia-08, Geest St. Lucia-97
Belgian Reefer	Bhs	1983	12,383	14,786	145	24	18	R	ex Anne B-92
Brazilian Reefer	Bhs	1984	12,383	14,786	145	24	16	R	ex Betty B-92
Chaiten **	Lbr	1988	13,312	12,838	152	24	18	R	
Chiquita Belgie §	Bhs	1992	13,049	13,930	158	24	22	R	
Chiquita Bremen **	Bhs	1992	10,842	12,890	157	23	21	R	
Chiquita Deutschland §	Bhs	1991	13,049	13,930	158	24	22	R	
Chiquita Italia §	Bhs	1992	13,049	13,930	158	24	22	R	
Chiquita Nederland §	Bhs	1991	13,049	13,930	158	24	21	R	
Chiquita Rostock **	Bhs	1993	10,842	12,850	157	24	21	R	
Chiquita Scandinavia §	Bhs	1992	13,049	13,930	159	24	21	R	
Chiquita Schweiz §	Bhs	1992	13,049	13,930	158	24	22	R	
Crown Emerald *	Pan	1996	10,519	10,351	152	23	18	R	
Crown Garnet *	Pan	1996	10,519	10,322	152	23	21	R	
Crown Jade *	Pan	1997	10,519	10,332	152	23	21	R	
Crown Opal *	Pan	1997	10,519	10,332	152	23	21	R	
Crown Ruby *	Pan	1997	10,519	10,338	152	23	21	R	
Crown Sapphire *	Pan	1997	10,519	10,334	152	23	21	R	
Crown Topaz	Pan	1999	10,527	10,318	152	23	21	R	
Cygnus Reefer *	Lbr	1990	8,818	9,679	144	22	20	R	
Dominica †	Bhs	1993	13,077	13,981	158	24	22	R	ex Geest Dominica-97
Galaxy Harvest *	Pan	1988	8,519	8,800	142	21	19	R	ex Gallant Harvest-93
Global Harvest	Pan	1993	8,520	8,752	144	21	19	R	
Glorious Harvest *	Pan	1989	8,519	8,830	142	21	19	R	ex Glorious Express-93
Ice River	Cym	1985	12,408	14,519	145	24	18	R	ex American Reefer-96
Ice Runner	Cym	1984	12,411	14,519	145	24	18	R	ex Rauma Reefer-06, Australian Reefer-00
Ivory Ace	Vut	1990	10,394	10,713	150	23	20	R	
Ivory Dawn	Bhs	1991	10,412	10,600	150	23	20	R	
Ivory Girl	Vut	1996	11,438	10,432	154	24	21	R	

Nippon Yusen Kaisha (NYKCool). AUTUMN WIND. *J. M. Kakebeeke*

Name	Flag	Year	GRT	DWT	LOA	Bm	Kts	Type	Former names
Lady Korcula	Mhl	2000	11,443	12,913	155	23	20	R	
Lady Racisce	Hrv	2000	11,443	12,913	155	23	20	R	
Orion Reefer *	Pan	1989	8,818	9,643	144	22	20	R	
Southern Harvest *	Sgp	1990	8,483	8,946	141	23	19	R	ex Serene Harvest-00
Splendid Harvest *	Lbr	1988	8,483	8,955	141	21	19	R	
Summer Bay **	Bhs	1985	12,660	13,613	169	24	24	R	ex Summer Breeze-00, Chiquita Baracoa-96, Ellen D-90
Summer Flower **	Bhs	1984	12,659	13,556	169	24	22	R	ex Chiquita Baru-96, Vivian M-90
Summer Meadow **	Bhs	1985	12,659	13,584	169	24	20	R	ex Chiquita Bocas-96, Irma M-90
Summer Wind **	Bhs	1985	12,660	13,636	169	24	24	R	ex Chiquita Burica-96, Edyth L-90
Supreme Harvest *	Vut	1988	8,483	8,937	141	21	19	R	
Triton Reefer *	Lbr	1990	8,818	9,683	144	22	18	R	
Wild Cosmos **	Pan	1998	9,859	10,097	150	22	20	R	
Wild Heather	Pan	1998	9,859	10,114	150	22	20	R	
Wild Jasmine	Pan	1998	9,859	10,110	150	22	20	R	
Wild Lotus	Pan	1998	9,859	10,139	150	22	20	R	
Wild Peony **	Pan	1998	9,859	10,110	150	22	20	R	

* managed by Wallem Shipmanagement Ltd, Hong Kong.
chartered from various owners/managers including ** from Chartworld Shipping Corp., Greece (www.chartworld.gr), † from Geest PLC (FII Fyffes Ltd), ‡ from DFM, Poland and § from Diamond Ship Management NV, Belgium (www.diamondship.be).
See also vessels chartered from J Lauritzen A/S and Leonhardt & Blumberg Reederei.

Nordcapital Holding GmbH & Cie KG   Germany
ER Schiffahrt GmbH & Cie KG
Funnel: Black with white 'ER' on broad blue band edged with narroe white bands of charterers colours. **Hull:** Dark blue with pink boot-topping or charterers colours. **History:** Both companies formed 1998. **Web:** www.nordcapital.com or www.er-ship.com

Name	Flag	Year	GRT	DWT	LOA	Bm	Kts	Type	Former names
Aenne Rickmers †	Lbr	1998	26,131	30,781	196	30	19	CC	ex CP Rome-06, Contship Rome-05, l/a Aenne Rickmers
Albert Rickmers †	Lbr	1998	26,131	30,721	196	30	20	CC	ex CP Tui-06, Direct Tui-05, Contship Washington-02, l/a Albert Rickmers
Alexandra Rickmers †	Lbr	1997	26,131	30,781	195	30	20	CC	ex CP London-06, Contship London-05, Alexandra Rickmers-97
Alice Rickmers †	Lbr	1998	26,131	30,726	196	30	20	CC	ex Direct Kea-04, CMA CGM Cezanne-01, CGM Cezanne-99, l/a Alice Rickmers
Andreas †	Lbr	1998	26,131	30,723	196	30	20	CC	ex CGM Renoir-01, l/a Andreas Rickmers
Anna Rickmers ‡	Lbr	1997	28,148	45,070	185	32	15	Co	ex CCNI Chagres-07, Anna Rickmers-98
APL Canada	Lbr	2001	65,792	68,025	277	40	26	CC	ex E.R. Canada-01
APL Denmark	Lbr	2002	65,792	67,935	277	40	26	CC	ex E.R. Denmark-02
APL India	Lbr	2002	65,792	68,025	277	40	26	CC	ex E.R. India-02
APL Sweden	Lbr	2002	65,792	68,025	277	40	26	CC	ex E.R. Sweden-02
CCNI Manzanillo	Lbr	2003	27,322	33,800	212	30	22	CC	ex Maersk Norfolk-07, E.R. Bremen-03
China Star	Lbr	1996	30,280	35,962	202	32	22	CC	ex E.R. Darwin-02, Ganges-02, Hanjin Genoa-00
CMA CGM Aegean	Lbr	1996	30,280	35,966	202	32	22	CC	ex E.R. Brisbane-03, Pan Crystal-02, Zim Trieste-99, Pan Crystal-98, Hyundai Emerald-98, Zim Trieste-96
CMA CGM Anemone	Lbr	2007	27,779	39,200	222	30	23	CC	ex E.R. Martinique-07

Nordcapital Holding (ER Schiffahrt). ALBERT RICKMERS . *Hans Kraijenbosch*

Name	Flag	Year	GRT	DWT	LOA	Bm	Kts	Type	Former names
CMA CGM Carmen	Lbr	2006	91,649	100,680	334	43	25	CC	l/a E.R. Tokyo
CMA CGM Don Carlos	Lbr	2006	91,649	100,680	334	43	25	CC	l/a E.R. Toulouse
CMA CGM Don Giovanni	Lbr	2006	91,649	100,680	334	43	25	CC	ex E.R. Toronto-06
CMA CGM Jaguar	Lbr	2004	26,836	34,289	210	30	21	CC	ex E.R. Caen-04
CMA CGM Kingston	Lbr	2003	39,941	50,900	264	32	24	CC	ex E.R. Kingston-04, CMA CGM Kingston-03, l/a E.R. Kingston
CMA CGM La Boussole	Lbr	2005	26,836	34,263	210	30	21	CC	ex E.R. Cannes-05
CMA CGM L'Astrolabe	Lbr	2005	26,718	34,567	210	30	21	CC	
CMA CGM Lavender	Lbr	2006	27,779	39,418	222	30	23	CC	ex E.R. Montpellier-06
CMA CGM Mimosa	Lbr	2006	27,779	39,200	222	30	23	CC	ex E.R. Monaco-06
CMA CGM Nilgai	Lbr	2003	39,941	50,900	264	32	24	CC	ex ANL Pacific-04, CMA CGM New York-04, l/a E.R. New York
CMA CGM Parsifal	Lbr	2006	95,000	101,505	335	43	25	CC	l/a E.R. Toulon
CMA CGM Yantian	Lbr	2003	39,941	53,000	264	32	24	CC	l/a E.R. Yantian
Cosco China	Lbr	2005	91,649	101,570	335	43	25	CC	l/a E.R. Tianan
Cosco Germany	Lbr	2006	91,649	101,532	335	43	25	CC	l/a E.R. Tianshan
Cosco Long Beach	Lbr	2004	83,133	93,572	300	43	25	CC	
Cosco Napoli	Lbr	2006	91,649	101,491	335	43	25	CC	l/a E.R. Tianping
Cosco Seattle	Lbr	2004	83,133	93,728	300	43	25	CC	
Cosco Shenzen	Lbr	2004	83,133	93,643	300	43	25	CC	l/dn E.R. Shenzen
Cosco Vancouver	Lbr	2004	83,133	93,638	300	43	25	CC	
Cosco Yokohama	Lbr	2004	83,133	93,659	300	43	25	CC	
CSCL Fuzhou	Lbr	2000	25,500	33,855	207	30	21	CC	ex E.R. Lubeck-01, E.R. Fuzhou-01
CSCL Kobe	Lbr	2001	66,289	68,196	277	40	26	CC	l/a E.R. Kobe
CSCL Los Angeles	Lbr	2001	66,289	68,131	277	40	26	CC	l/a E.R. Los Angeles
Delmas Joliba †	Lbr	1998	16,801	23,027	184	25	19	CC	ex Dorothea Rickmers-07, WAL Ulanga-03, Dorothea Rickmers-01
E.R. Albany	Lbr	1996	30,280	35,966	202	32	22	CC	ex MacAndrews America-07, CMA CGM Egypt-06, E.R. Albany-04, Rhein-02, Zim Sydney-00
E.R. Canberra	Lbr	1996	30,280	35,962	202	32	22	CC	ex CMA CGM Power-09, CMA CGM Virginia-05, Indamex Mumbai-04, E.R. Canberra-03, Donau-02, Hanjin Dalian-00
E.R. Durban	Lbr	1999	16,803	23,075	185	26	19	CC	ex Maersk Verona-06, E.R. Durban-04, Direct Falcon-03, Griffin Clio-99, l/a E.R. Durban
E.R. Elsfleth	Lbr	2003	26,200	33,800	212	30	22	CC	ex Andes Bridge-08, Maersk Newcastle-07, E.R. Elsfleth-03
E.R. Fremantle	Lbr	1998	30,280	35,848	202	32	22	CC	ex CMA CGM Turkey-08, CSCL Indus-03, Indus-02, Hyundai Infinity-01
E.R. Hamburg	Lbr	1998	26,125	30,721	196	30	19	CC	ex CSAV Shanghai-07, Las Americas Bridge-03, Aconcagua-99, CSAV Shanghai-01, l/a E.R. Hamburg
E.R. Perth	Lbr	1998	30,280	35,798	202	32	22	CC	ex CMA CGM Marmara-07, CSCL Nile-03, Nile-02, Hyundai Nobility-01
E.R. Santiago	Lbr	1998	26,125	30,720	196	30	19	CC	ex CSAV Ningbo-07, Copiapo-04, l/a E.R. Santiago
E.R. Sydney	Deu	1998	36,603	45,400	232	32	23	CC	ex YM Napoli-04, Amazonas-02, Choyang Zenith-01, l/a Zenith Globe

Nordcapital Holding (ER Schiffahrt). CMA CGM CARMEN. *Phil Kempsey*

Name	Flag	Year	GRT	DWT	LOA	Bm	Kts	Type	Former names
E.R. Wilhelmshaven	Lbr	2002	27,322	33,800	212	30	22	CC	ex Maersk New Orleans-07, E.R. Wilhelmshaven-02
Indamex Cauvery	Lbr	1998	36,603	45,383	232	32	23	CC	ex CMA CGM Constellation-04, Safmarine Vinson-03, E.R. Melbourne-02, Congo-02, Choyang Honour-01
Ital Massima *	Lbr	2007	42,020	53,728	264	32	23	CC	
Ital Mattina *	Lbr	2007	42,020	53,644	264	32	23	CC	
Ital Melodia *	Lbr	2007	42,020	53,697	264	32	23	CC	
Ital Milione *	Lbr	2008	42,020	53,641	264	32	24	CC	
Ital Moderna *	Lbr	2009	42,020	53,685	264	32	24	CC	l/a E.R. Bounty
Kota Permai	Lbr	2005	27,779	39,200	222	30	23	CC	ex E.R. Malmo-05
Lara Rickmers ‡	Lbr	1997	28,148	45,070	185	32	15	Co	ex CCNI Potrerillos-07, l/a Lara Rickmers
Lissy Schulte **	Lbr	1995	16,800	23,001	185	25	20	CC	ex P&O Nedlloyd Takoradi-04, Lissy Schulte-01, CSAV Rubens-98, Lissy Schulte-95
Maersk Dallas	Lbr	2004	54,592	67,170	294	32	25	CC	ex E.R. Dallas-04
Maersk Denver	Lbr	2004	54,592	67,170	294	32	25	CC	ex E.R. Denver-04
Maersk Napier	Deu	1999	25,630	33,855	207	30	21	CC	ex E.R. Stralsund-05, Indamex Tuticorin-04, E.R. Stralsund-03, Maersk Mendoza-02, l/a E.R. Stralsund
Maersk Newark	Lbr	2002	26,200	33,800	212	30	22	CC	ex E.R. Cuxhaven-02
Maersk Valencia	Lbr	1999	25,630	33,855	207	30	21	CC	ex E.R. Copenhagen-99
MSC Antares	Deu	2000	66,289	67,557	277	40	26	CC	ex E.R. Amsterdam-08, P&O Nedlloyd Magellan-05, l/a E.R. Amsterdam
MSC Bengal	Lbr	2006	91,649	100,680	334	42	25	CC	
MSC Gemma	Deu	2000	66,289	67,566	277	40	26	CC	ex E.R. London-09, P&O Nedlloyd Vespucci-05, l/a E.R. London
MSC Hobart	Lbr	1994	22,736	33,523	188	28	18	CC	ex E.R. Hobart-04, Mosel-02, Zim Koper-98, Hyundai Longview-96
MSC Mira	Lbr	2000	66,289	67,500	277	40	26	CC	ex E.R. Felixstowe-08, P&O Nedlloyd Torres-06, l/a E.R. Felixstowe
MSC Xian *	Lbr	2007	91,649	101,477	334	42	25	CC	
Nordstrand ††	Cyp	1993	30,526	34,079	205	32	19	CC	ex ACX Lavender-07, Nordstrand-06, Nautic-00, Nordstrand-99, Byron Bay-98, Nordstrand-97, Med Marseilles-96, Saint Corentin-94
OOCL France	Lbr	2001	66,289	67,591	277	40	26	CC	ex E.R. Paris-01
OOCL Germany	Lbr	2000	66,289	67,660	277	40	26	CC	ex E.R. Berlin-01
OOCL Los Angeles	Deu	2000	66,289	67,737	277	40	26	CC	l/a E.R. Pusan
OOCL Malaysia	Lbr	2000	66,289	66,298	277	40	26	CC	ex E.R. Seoul-00
OOCL New York	Lbr	1999	66,289	67,660	277	40	26	CC	l/a E.R. Hong Kong
OOCL Shanghai	Lbr	1999	66,289	67,473	277	40	26	CC	l/a E.R. Shanghai
Pacific Mariner	Lbr	1995	16,175	22,900	185	26	19	CC	ex E.R. Cape Town-08, Panatlantic-04, Quadrant Express-99
Safmarine Cunene	Lbr	2002	27,332	33,800	212	30	22	CC	ex E.R. Bremerhaven-02
Safmarine Zambezi	Lbr	2002	27,322	34,608	212	30	22	CC	ex E.R. Helgoland-02
YM Colombo §	Lbr	2004	41,855	53,610	264	32	24	CC	ex Norasia Integra-07, E.R. Auckland-04, l/a E.R. Wellington
Zim Beijing	Lbr	2005	54,626	66,939	294	32	25	CC	

Nordcapital Holding (ER Schiffahrt). MAERSK DALLAS. *Allan Ryszka Onions*

Name	Flag	Year	GRT	DWT	LOA	Bm	Kts	Type	Former names
Zim Savannah	Lbr	2004	54,626	67,170	294	32	25	CC	ex E.R. Savannah-04

newbuildings: eight 135,000 grt container ships, ten 180,000 dwt and fourteen 56,000 dwt bulk carriers for 2010-11 delivery.
Shipping subsidiary of Erck Rickmers' investment group Nordcapital Ges. Fur Unternehmensbeteiligungen mbH & Cie.
* managed by subsidiary Katharinen SchiffahrtsGmbH & Cie KG (formed 2007)
† managed by Rickmers Reederei GmbH, ** by Berrnhard Schulte Shipmanagement (Deutschland) GmbH, †† by Reederei 'Nord' Klaus E Oldendorff, ‡ by Uniteam Marine Shipping GmbH, Germany or § Danaos Shipping Co Ltd, Greece.

Norddeutsche Vermogensanlage GmbH & Co KG   Germany

Norddeutsche Reederei H Schuldt GmbH & Co KG/Germany

Funnel: *White with red 'S' on white triange on blue square or c harterers colours.* **Hull:** *Black or red with red boot-topping.*
History: *Parent founded 1984 and subsidiary 2002 following merger of 'NRG' Norddeutsche Reederei Beteiligungs GmbH with H Schuldt OHG (founded 1868) and Engineering Consulting & Management GmbH which had merged in 1989.*
Web: *www.norddeutsche.de*

Name	Flag	Year	GRT	DWT	LOA	Bm	Kts	Type	Former names
APL Arabia	Lbr	2000	54,415	66,895	294	32	24	CC	ex MOL Vigilance-03, Vantage-03, MOL Vantage-02, APL Arabia-02, I/a Northern Grace
APL Egypt	Lbr	2000	54,415	66,922	294	32	24	CC	ex MOL Virtue-03, APL Egypt-02
APL Malaysia	Lbr	2000	54,415	66,910	294	32	24	CC	ex MOL Value-03, APL Malaysia-02, I/a Northern Glance
APL Yokohama	Lbr	2006	27,437	37,800	222	30		CC	ex Northern Volition-06, Sinotrans Dalian-06, I/a Northern Volition
Bangkok Express	Deu	2003	75,590	85,400	300	40	25	CC	ex Northern Magnitude-04
Busan Express	Deu	2004	75,590	85,400	300	40	25	CC	
Cap Frio	Lbr	2001	25,713	33,900	208	30	21	CC	ex Northern Endeavour-03, Andhika Loreto-01

Norddeutsche Reederei. NORTHERN DIVINITY (in MISC colours). *J. M. Kakebeeke*

Norddeutsche Reederei. SAVANNAH EXPRESS. *Phil Kempsey*

Name	Flag	Year	GRT	DWT	LOA	Bm	Kts	Type	Former names
Cap Gabriel	Lbr	2008	41,835	53,870	264	32	24	CC	I/dn Northern General
Cap George	Lbr	2008	41,835	53,800	264	32	24	CC	I/dn Northern Genius
Cap Gilbert	Lbr	2008	41,835	53,800	264	32	24	CC	I/dn Northern Gleam
Cap Graham	Lbr	2008	41,835	53,800	264	32	24	CC	I/dn Northern Guard
Cap Gregory	Lbr	2008	41,835	53,800	264	32	24	CC	I/dn Northern Guild
CMA CGM Qingdao	Lbr	2005	27,437	37,800	222	30	22	CC	ex Sinotrans Qingdao-09
CSAV Cantabrian	Lbr	1998	53,324	63,615	294	32	23	CC	ex ANL Hong Kong-08, Yokohama Senator-06, Cho Yang Ace-01
CSAV Rahue	Lbr	2007	35,975	42,183	231	32	23	CC	
CSAV Ranquil	Lbr	2008	36,007	42,002	231	32	23	CC	
CSAV Rauten	Lbr	2008	35,975	41,977	231	32	23	CC	
CSAV Renaico	Lbr	2007	35,975	42,121	231	32	23	CC	
CSAV Rupanco	Lbr	2008	36,007	42,011	231	32	23	CC	
Duburg	Lbr	1990	18,000	26,288	177	28	18	CC	ex Kota Perkasa-02, Japan Senator-98
Houston Express	Deu	2005	94,483	108,106	332	43	25	CC	I/dn Northern Jade
Indamex Godavari	Lbr	1997	36,606	45,131	245	32	23	CC	ex MSC Bursa-04, P&O Nedlloyd Barcelona-02, Northern Diversity-98
Los Angeles Express	Lbr	2003	75,590	85,400	300	40	25	CC	I/a Northern Magnum
Luetjenburg	Deu	1995	37,323	45,530	239	32	23	CC	ex Garden Bridge-03, Heaven River-00, Lutjenburg-98
MSC Prague	Lbr	2003	41,078	48,874	260	32	23	CC	ex Barcelona Bridge-06, I/a Northern Delicacy
MSC Vienna	Lbr	2003	41,078	48,923	260	32	23	CC	ex Potomac Bridge-06, I/a Northern Decency
Northern Democrat	Lbr	2009	35,954	42,000	231	32	23	CC	
Northern Diamond	Lbr	2009	35,954	42,000	231	32	23	CC	
Northern Diplomat	Lbr	2009	35,954	42,000	231	32	23	CC	
Northern Discovery	Lbr	2008	35,954	42,000	231	32	23	CC	
Northern Divinity	Lbr	1997	36,606	44,117	245	32	23	CC	ex P&O Nedlloyd Damietta-05, OOCL Europe-02, P&O Nedlloyd Damietta-01, Northern Divinity-97
Northern Endurance	Lbr	2001	25,713	33,900	208	30	21	CC	ex Cap Matapan-08, Alianca Singapore-07, Cap Matapan-04, Northern Endurance-03, Andhika Fatima-01
Northern Enterprise	Lbr	2001	25,713	33,836	208	30	21	CC	ex Cap Salinas-08, NYK Freesia-05, Cap Salinas-04, Northern Enterprise-03, Andhika Lourdes-02
San Francisco Express	Deu	2004	75,590	85,400	300	40	25	CC	
Savannah Express	Deu	2005	94,483	101,500	332	43	25	CC	I/dn Northern Julie
Sinotrans Shanghai	Lbr	2005	27,437	37,800	222	30	22	CC	I/a Northern Valence
Sinotrans Tianjin	Lbr	2005	27,437	37,800	222	30	22	CC	I/a Northern Vivacity
Tiger Sky	Lbr	1991	16,236	23,596	163	28	17	CC	ex Mildburg-02, Direct Condor-99, Mildburg-96, Contship Australia-95
Troyburg	Lbr	1988	18,037	26,070	177	28	17	CC	ex MSC Callao-02, Troyburg-98, NOL Koi-98, Deppe Florida-96, Troyburg-94, Ville de Venus-93

newbuildings: ten 107,000 dwt (Northern J class) and six 58,400 dwt (Northern P class) container ships for 2009-11 delivery.
* managed for Conti Holding GmbH & Co KG. Also see vessels managed by F. Laeisz Schiffahrts GmbH

Dampskibsselskabet 'Norden' A/S   Denmark

Funnel: *Black with narrow red band on broad white band.* **Hull:** *Black or dark blue with red boot-topping.* **History:** Formed 1871 and now 32% owned by A/S Dampskibsselskabet Torm. **Web:** www.ds-norden.com

Name	Flag	Year	GRT	DWT	LOA	Bm	Kts	Type	Former names
Dawn Voyager	Pan	1994	38,267	70,003	225	32	14	B	ex Endurance II-08, Estepona-07, Bulk Patriot-06, CIC Horizon-06
Freyja Divine	Pan	1994	38,267	70,029	225	32	14	B	ex Endeavour II-08, Delray-07, Bulk Phoenix-06, SD Triumph-06
Ice Dreamer	Pan	1998	37,978	69,146	225	32	14	B	ex Navigator II-08, Foremost-07
Izara Princess	Pan	1995	27,078	43,706	190	31	14	B	ex Ice Power II-08, Baffin-08, Federal Baffin-05
Moon Dancer	Pan	1995	27,078	43,706	190	31	14	B	ex Ice Trader II-08, Franklin-08, Federal Franklin-05
Nord Bell	Dis	2007	24,048	38,461	183	27	14	T	
Nord Butterfly	Dis	2008	24,048	38,431	183	27	14	T	
Nord Empathy *	Sgp	2006	30,822	55,803	190	32	14	B	
Nord-Kraft	Dis	2000	85,379	171,199	289	45	14	B	
Nord Maru	Sgp	2006	30,684	55,745	190	32	14	B	
Nord Mermaid	Dis	2007	24,048	38,461	183	27	14	T	
Nord Nightingale *	Dis	2008	24,048	38,461	183	27	14	T	
Nord Ocean	Dis	2003	30,058	52,441	190	32	14	B	
Nord Princess	Dis	2007	24,048	38,500	183	27	14	T	
Nord Snow Queen	Dis	2008	24,066	38,500	183	27	14	T	
Nord Spirit	Pan	2008	29,987	53,482	190	32	14	B	
Nord Thumbelina	Dis	2006	24,048	38,461	183	27	14	T	

Name	Flag	Year	GRT	DWT	LOA	Bm	Kts	Type	Former names
Nord Whale	Dis	2004	27,989	50,354	190	32	14	B	
Norden	Sgp	2005	31,263	56,032	190	32	14	B	
Nordflex	Dis	2002	30,085	52,344	190	32	14	B	
Nordholt *	Sgp	2005	30,688	55,697	190	32	14	B	
Nordkap	Dis	2002	40,066	77,229	225	32	14	B	
Nordpol`	Dis	2002	40,066	77,195	225	32	14	B	

newbuildings: four 115,000 dwt, 56,000 dwt and six 31,800 dwt bulk carriers, three 50,500 dwt and three 38,500 dwt tankers for 2009-11 delivery.
* owned by subsidiary Norden Shipping (Singapore) Pte Ltd.
Including charters, the Company currently operates 186 dry bulk and 29 tankers, including the Norden MR and Handysize bulk carrier pools (formed 2005 with Interorient Navigation Co Ltd) and a tanker Pool (formed 2008 with Interorient).

Nordic American Tanker Shipping Ltd   Bermuda

Funnel: White with blue and red coloured/striped rectangle, black top. **Hull:** Blue with white 'NAVION' towards stern, red boot-topping. **History:** Formed 1995 as Navion ASA to 2003, when it was acquired from Statoil ASA. **Web:** www.nat.bm

Name	Flag	Year	GRT	DWT	LOA	Bm	Kts	Type	Former names
Gulf Scandic **	Iom	1997	80,187	151,459	274	46	14	T	ex British Harrier-04
Nordic Apollo	Mhl	2003	81,310	159,988	274	48	14	T	ex Glyfada Spirit-06, Euro Spirit-03
Nordic Cosmos	Mhl	2003	81,310	159,999	274	48	14	T	ex Calm Sea-06, Euro Sea-03
Nordic Discovery	Nis	1998	79,669	153,328	269	46	14	T	ex Front Hunter-05
Nordic Fighter	Nis	1998	79,669	153,328	269	46	14	T	ex Front Fighter-05
Nordic Freedom	Bhs	2005	83,594	159,331	274	48	14	T	ex Santiago Spirit-05
Nordic Hawk	Iom	1997	80,187	151,400	274	46	14	T	ex British Hawk-04
Nordic Hunter *	Bhs	1997	80,100	151,400	274	46	14	T	ex British Hunter-04
Nordic Jupiter	Mhl	1998	81,565	157,411	274	48	14	T	ex Sacramento-06
Nordic Moon	Mhl	2002	81,310	160,200	274	48	14	T	ex Summer Sky-06, Euro Sky-03
Nordic Saturn	Mhl	1998	81,565	157,331	274	48	14	T	ex Sabine-05
Nordic Voyager *	Nis	1996	79,494	149,775	270	45	15	T	ex Wilma Yangtze-07

newbuildings: two 163,000 dwt tankers for 2009/10 delivery,
managed by V.Ships Norway AS, except * by Teekay Marine Services AS, Norway and ** by Gulf Navigation Ship Management, UAE.

NSB Niederelbe Schiffahrts GmbH & Co KG   Germany

Funnel: Blue with blue 'NSB' on white diamond or blue 'N' on square on broad white band or charterers colours. **Hull:** Black, dark blue or dark grey with red boot-topping. **History:** Formed 1982 and associated with W Harms GmbH & Co KG and Conti Holding GmbH & Co KG. **Web:** www.reederei-nsb.com

Name	Flag	Year	GRT	DWT	LOA	Bm	Kts	Type	Former names
Al Fujairah	Deu	1994	34,617	45,025	216	32	21	CC	ex California Senator-06, Sea Initiative-95, Chesapeake Bay-94, California Senator-94
ANL Esprit **	Deu	1998	25,713	33,995	206	30	21	CC	ex CMA CGM Falcon-04, CSCL Nantong-03, Sea Leopard-01, Buxhansa-98
Buxfavourite **	Deu	1997	25,713	34,083	206	30	21	CC	ex CSCL Yingkou-03, Sea Puma-01, Buxfavourite-98
Buxhill	Deu	1995	16,259	23,465	163	30	18	CC	ex CSAV Santos-04, Buxhill-03, Indamex Malabar-03, Buxhill-02, Contship Ticino-98
Buxlagoon	Deu	1994	16,270	23,130	163	28	17	CC	ex YM Surabaya-04, Indamex New Delhi-03, Kota Perwira-00, Contship Italy-98
Buxlink	Deu	2002	25,375	33,817	207	30	23	CC	ex APL Jebel Ali-08, Buxlink-06, P&O Nedlloyd Hunter Valley-05
Buxmaster	Lbr	1986	16,250	23,465	163	28	18	CC	ex Delmas Ango-05, WAL Ulangi-04, Buxmaster-04, Cotonou Star-02, Buxmaster-01, WEC Rotterdam-01, Buxmaster-98, CMB Melody-96, Red Sea Endurance-92, Ville de Pluton-91
Buxmoon	Deu	1995	16,270	23,130	163	28	18	CC	ex Melbourne Star I-06, YM Kwang Yang-04, Buxmoon-03, Maersk Osaka-02, Contship Lavagna-98
Buxsailor	Deu	1993	16,282	23,465	163	28	19	CC	ex Marfret Caraibes-06, Buxsailor-05, City of York-03, Buxsailor-01, CSAV Salerno-00, Libra Houston-00, CMBT Amboseli-98, Contship Atlantic-97
Buxstar	Deu	1997	40,465	49,238	259	32	23	CC	ex ANL Georgia-06, Ville de Mimosa-04
CMA CGM Alabama	Deu	1997	31,730	34,731	193	32	22	CC	ex Indamex Alabama-04, Conti Wellington-03, Contship Vision-03, I/a Conti Wellington
CMA CGM Balzac	Deu	2001	73,172	77,941	300	40	26	CC	ex Conti Paris-01
CMA CGM Baudelaire	Deu	2001	73,172	77,946	300	40	26	CC	ex Conti Lyon-01
CMA CGM Capella	Deu	1995	35,595	42,673	240	32	22	CC	ex Ville de Capella-02, Northern Honour-95
CMA CGM Esperanza	Lbr	2007	22,801	31,200	204	28	21	CC	
CMA CGM Fortuna *	Lbr	2007	22,801	31,200	204	28	21	CC	
CMA CGM Galaxy *	Deu	2006	41,899	53,704	264	32	23	CC	ex NYK Galaxy-08
CMA CGM Hugo *	Deu	2004	90,745	101,662	334	43	25	CC	
CMA CGM Hydra *	Deu	2009	128,600	107,500	347	46	24	CC	

Name	Flag	Year	GRT	DWT	LOA	Bm	Kts	Type	Former names
CMA CGM Jamaica *	Deu	2006	41,899	53,663	264	32	23	CC	
CMA CGM Musca *	Deu	2009	128,600	107,500	347	46	24	CC	
CMA CGM Pacifico	Deu	2002	25,375	33,864	207	30	21	CC	ex APL Osaka-08, Cap Ferrato-06
CMA CGM Thalassa *	Deu	2008	128,600	107,500	347	46	24	CC	
CMA CGM Vela	Lbr	2008	128,600	107,500	347	46	24	CC	
CMA CGM Verlaine **	Deu	2001	72,760	77,900	300	40	26	CC	I/a Buxcliff
CMA CGM Vernet	Deu	1994	35,595	42,673	240	32	22	CC	ex Northern Pioneer-02, Ville de Sagitta-01, I/a Northern Pioneer
CMA CGM Voltaire **	Deu	2001	72,760	77,900	300	40	26	CC	I/a Buxcoast
Conti Asia	Lbr	1993	16,282	23,596	163	28	18	CC	ex Contship Asia-98
Conti Barcelona	Mhl	1991	16,236	23,596	164	28	17	CC	ex Tiger Speed-01, Conti Barcelona-01, Maersk Barcelona-01, Conti Barcelona-99, New York Express-98, Conti Barcelona-97, Contship Barcelona-96
Conti Esperance	Deu	1996	31,730	34,800	193	32	22	CC	ex Contship Romance-03, I/a Conti Esperance
Conti Germany	Lbr	1992	16,236	23,596	164	28	17	CC	ex MSC Victoria-01, Contship Germany-98
Conti Hong Kong	Mhl	1989	18,000	26,288	177	28	19	CC	ex YM Pearl River I-07, Conti Hong Kong-03, MSC Guayaquil-01, Conti Hong Kong-99, MSC Guayaquil-98, Nedlloyd Zaandam-97, Buxmerchant-95, Choyang Star-94, Hongkong Senator-91
Conti Jork *	Lbr	1990	16,236	23,596	163	28	17	CC	ex Kota Permas-00, Conti Jork-99, Contship Jork-97
Conti Salome	Lbr	2007	22,801	30,573	204	28	21	CC	
Conti Sydney	Deu	1990	16,236	23,596	163	28	17	CC	ex MSC Sydney-04, Conti Sydney-03, MSC Senegal-01, Conti Sydney-99, Direct Currawong-98, Contship Ipswich-95, I/a Contship Sydney
Conti Valencia	Deu	1998	25,713	34,051	206	30	21	CC	ex MSC Spain-05, Conti Valencia-03, Lykes Hunter-01, Ivaran Hunter-99, Sea Tiger-98, Conti Valencia-98
Delmas Libreville	Deu	1997	24,053	27,100	205	27	20	CC	ex Tiger Bay-07, APL Melbourne-06, Vancouver-04, Ivory Star 1-03, Conti Seattle-02, CCNI Antartico-02, Sea Lynx-00, Conti Seattle-97
Emirates Spring	Deu	1997	31,730	34,790	193	32	22	CC	ex Conti Albany-06, ANL Albany-03, Conti Albany-03, Contship Optimism-02, I/a Conti Albany
Ever Champion *	Deu	2005	90,449	100,949	334	43	25	CC	
Ever Charming *	Deu	2005	90,465	98,700	334	43	25	CC	
Ever Chilvary *	Deu	2006	90,465	98,700	334	43	25	CC	
Ever Conquest *	Deu	2006	90,465	98,700	334	43	25	CC	
Frontier	Lbr	1987	10,811	13,464	147	23	15	CC	ex Doria-08, ANL Pioneer-04, MSC Kiwi-02, Everett Express-01, Doria-00, OOCL Admiral-98, Doria-97, Sea-Land Mexico-94, Doria-94, Contship Asia-91, Ocean Asia-88, Doria-88
Hanjin Amsterdam	Deu	1999	66,278	67,900	279	40	26	CC	I/a Conti Canberra
Hanjin Athens	Deu	2000	66,278	67,900	279	40	26	CC	ex YM Athens-05, Hanjin Athens-03, Conti Fremantle-00
Hanjin Baltimore *	Deu	2005	83,133	92,964	300	43	24	CC	
Hanjin Basel	Deu	2003	65,918	68,200	279	40	26	CC	ex Hanjin Lisbon-03
Hanjin Boston *	Deu	2005	83,133	92,964	300	43	24	CC	
Hanjin Brussels *	Deu	2000	66,278	67,900	279	40	26	CC	
Hanjin Chicago **	Deu	2003	65,918	68,037	278	40	26	CC	
Hanjin Copenhagen	Deu	1999	66,278	68,996	279	40	26	CC	ex Conti Darwin-99
Hanjin Dallas *	Deu	2005	83,133	92,964	300	43	24	CC	
Hanjin Geneva *	Deu	2000	65,918	68,263	279	40	26	CC	ex Cosco Tianjin-05, Hanjin Geneva-03, Conti Porto-00
Hanjin Gothenburg	Deu	2002	65,131	68,045	275	40	25	CC	I/a Conti Goteborg
Hanjin Helsinki *	Deu	2002	65,131	68,045	275	40	25	CC	
Hanjin Lisbon **	Deu	2003	65,918	67,979	279	40	26	CC	
Hanjin Madrid *	Deu	2003	65,918	67,979	279	40	26	CC	
Hanjin Miami *	Deu	2005	83,133	92,964	300	43	24	CC	
Hanjin Ottawa *	Deu	2000	66,278	68,834	278	40	26	CC	ex Conti Melbourne-00
Hanjin Taipei *	Deu	2001	65,131	68,086	275	40	25	CC	
Hanjin Vienna *	Deu	2000	65,918	68,263	279	40	26	CC	ex Conti Lissabon-00
Hanjin Yantian *	Deu	2005	82,794	92,964	300	43	24	CC	
Hatsu Courage *	Deu	2005	90,465	98,700	334	43	25	CC	
Hatsu Crystal *	Deu	2006	90,465	98,700	334	43	25	CC	
Hongkong Senator	Deu	1995	34,617	45,470	216	32	21	CC	

Name	Flag	Year	GRT	DWT	LOA	Bm	Kts	Type	Former names
Ibn Sina	Deu	1993	34,454	45,470	216	32	24	CC	ex Tokyo Senator-97, Sea Progress-96, Tokyo Senator-94
Ital Contessa *	Deu	2006	90,465	101,007	334	43	25	CC	l/a LT Contessa
Jilfar *	Deu	1996	37,549	44,765	241	32	24	CC	ex Yellow Sea-06, City of Edinburgh-03, Humen Bridge-02, Sea-Land Victory-00, Yellow Sea-96
London Senator	Deu	1994	34,454	45,696	216	32	24	CC	ex Sea Endeavour-95, Delaware Bay-94, London Senator-94
LT Cortesia *	Deu	2005	90,449	100,863	334	43	25	CC	
Maruba Africa	Lbr	2007	22,801	30,607	204	28	21	CC	
Maruba Asia *	Lbr	2007	22,801	30,580	204	28	21	CC	
Maruba Europa *	Deu	2007	28,050	37,950	215	30	22	CC	ex Buxharmony-07
Maruba Maxima **	Deu	2008	28,050	38,093	215	30	22	CC	ex Buxmelody-08
MOL Splendor	Deu	1997	25,713	34,083	205	27	20	CC	ex Cap Pilar-07, Conti Cartagena-05, CMA CGM Eagle-04, Conti Cartagena-03, MSC Provence-01, Sea-Land Argentina -00, l/a Conti Cartagena
MOL Wish	Deu	1996	37,549	44,731	241	32	24	CC	ex Caribbean Sea-06, MSC Madrid-03, Sea-Land Endeavour-01, Sea Endeavour-96, Caribbean Sea-96
MSC Alessia	Deu	2001	75,590	84,920	304	40	25	CC	
MSC Carouge	Deu	2007	50,963	63,428	275	32	24	CC	
MSC Cordoba	Lbr	2008	50,963	63,428	275	32	24	CC	
MSC Flaminia	Deu	2001	75,590	84,920	304	40	24	CC	l/a Buxclipper
MSC Geneva	Deu	2006	50,963	63,505	275	32	24	CC	l/a Buxsong

NSB Niederelbe Schiffahrts. HATSU CRYSTAL. *Hans Kraijenbosch*

NSB Niederelbe Schiffahrts. JILFAR. *Hans Kraijenbosch*

Name	Flag	Year	GRT	DWT	LOA	Bm	Kts	Type	Former names
MSC Ilona	Deu	2001	75,590	84,920	304	40	25	CC	I/a Buxcomet
MSC Lausanne **	Deu	2005	50,963	63,300	275	32	24	CC	I/a Buxhai
MSC Malaga *	Deu	1998	25,713	24,083	205	27	20	CC	ex Conti Malaga-08, MSC Chile-02, Sea-Land Uruguay-01, Conti Malaga-98
MSC Monterey	Deu	2007	50,963	63,300	275	32	24	CC	
MSC Texas *	Deu	2004	90,745	101,898	334	43	25	CC	
Northern Delight	Lbr	1994	19,819	22,246	174	27	19	CC	ex P&O Nedlloyd Rumba-05, Kairo-05, P&O Nedlloyd Dubai-03, Kairo-03, Northern Delight-03, Zim Chicago II-01, Kota Sejati-00, Northern Delight-99, P&O Nedlloyd Dubai-99, Dubai Bay-98, Nedlloyd Sao Paulo-96, Northern Delight-94
Northern Faith	Deu	1994	35,595	42,673	240	32	22	CC	ex Indamex Mumbai-05, Contship Innovator-04, Northern Faith-02, Ville de Libra-02
Northern Felicity	Lbr	1994	19,819	22,246	174	27	19	CC	ex P&O Nedlloyd Beirut-05, Northern Felicity-03, CMA Los Angeles-00, Northern Felicity-99, P&O Nedlloyd Dammam-99, Dammam Bay-98, Nedlloyd Salvador-96, Northern Felicity-94
Northern Happiness	Lbr	1994	19,819	22,273	174	27	19	CC	ex Cap Velas-04, Northern Happiness-03, Kairo-00, DNOL Kairo-99, Kairo-98, Northern Happiness-94
Northern Reliance	Deu	1994	35,595	42,085	240	32	22	CC	ex Indamex New York-05, Contship Champion-04, Northern Reliance-02, Ville de Vela-02
Northern Joy	Deu	1992	30,567	31,160	203	31	19	CC	ex Canada Senator-08, Northern Joy-01, CMA Xingang-01, Contship Mexico-99, Northern Joy-98, Sea Vigor-97, Hyundai Tacoma-96, Sea Hawk-94, Northern Joy-93
OEL Mumbai *	Lbr	1990	16,236	23,596	163	28	17	CC	ex Aka Bhum-08, Conti La Spezia-04, MSC Amazonia-01, Buxlady-99, Contship La Spezia-95
Pacific Link *	Deu	2004	90,745	101,661	334	43	25	CC	
Queen Zenobia	Lbr	2002	16,770	19,621	156	25		Lpg	
Rialto Bridge *	Deu	1996	37,549	44,647	241	32	24	CC	ex Safmarine Kimley-03, Sea-Land Mistral-02, I/a White Sea
San Pedro Bridge	Deu	1996	37,549	44,690	241	32	24	CC	ex Sea-Land Initiative-00, Sea Initiative-96, Sargasso Sea-96
Tiger Speed	Deu	1997	25,713	34,083	206	30	22	CC	ex Kota Pertama-07, CMA CGM Albatross-04, Conti Bilbao-03, Brasilia-02, Sea-Land Brasil-99, I/a Conti Bilbao
Ville de Taurus	Deu	1997	40,400	49,238	259	32	23	CC	
Washington Senator	Deu	1994	34,454	45,455	216	32	20	CC	ex Tabuk-08, Washington Senator-06, Maersk Antwerp-95, Tor Bay-94, Washington Senator-94
X-Press Kailash	Lbr	1989	18,000	26,288	177	28	17	CC	ex Buxcrown-08, Kota Pertama-01, Buxcrown-98, Singapore Senator 95
YM Anping *	Deu	2006	41,899	53,000	264	32	23	CC	ex YM Chiwan-06
YM Ibiza	Deu	1997	31,730	34,894	193	32	22	CC	ex P&O Nedlloyd Newark-05, Contship Nobility-03, Conti Brisbane-97
YM Tianjin *	Deu	2006	41,899	53,727	264	32	23	CC	

newbuildings: one 50,963 grt, eight 39,900 grt, six 35,000 grt container ships for 2010 delivery and * two 92,500 dwt, twelve 75,300 dwt, sixteen 57,000 dwt bulk carriers, two 105,200 dwt tankers for 2009-11 delivery.
* managed for associated Conti Reederei (Conti Holding GmbH & Co KG – www.conti-gruppe.de) or ** for Gebab Konzeptions-und Emissions GmbH. Also see United Product Tanker (UPT) pool (under Schoeller Holdings), BBG-Bremer GmbH & Co KG and Maritime—Gesellschaft GmbH

NSC Schiffahrts GmbH & Cie KG Germany

Funnel: White with white 'NSC' on a dark blue/grey houseflag or charterers colours. **Hull:** Blue or grey with red boot-topping.
History: Formed 2004. **Web:** www.nsc-ship.com

Name	Flag	Year	GRT	DWT	LOA	Bm	Kts	Type	Former names
Albert	Lbr	2008	35,881	41,850	220	32	22	CC	
Algarrobo	Lbr	2009	32,900	34,700	224	31	21	CC	
Andino	Deu	2008	40,628	12,303	176	31	19	V	
Angeles	Lbr	2009	32,900	34,700	224	31	21	CC	
Angol	Lbr	2009	32,900	34,700	224	31	21	CC	
Anthea	Lbr	1996	34,885	49,370	196	32	15	B	ex Skauboard-06
APL Bahrain	Lbr	2009	39,900	51,400	260	32	24	CC	
APL Brisbane **	Lbr	2006	35,573	44,133	223	32	22	CC	ex Cape Ray-07
APL Chicago	Lbr	2007	35,573	44,234	223	32	22	CC	ex Cape Rupert-08
APL Doha	Lbr	2009	39,900	51,400	260	32	24	CC	
APL Guangzhou **	Lbr	2007	35,573	44,165	223	32	22	CC	ex Cape Rosa-07
APL New York **	Lbr	2005	54,592	66,633	294	32	25	CC	I/a E.R. Savannah
APL Riyadh	Lbr	2009	39,900	51,400	260	32	24	CC	
APL Seattle	Lbr	2007	35,573	44,239	223	32	22	CC	ex Cape Rexton-07

Name	Flag	Year	GRT	DWT	LOA	Bm	Kts	Type	Former names
APL Seoul	Lbr	2009	39,900	51,400	260	32	24	CC	
APL Virginia **	Lbr	2005	54,592	66,644	294	32	25	CC	
Beagle Sea	Lbr	2009	34,800	49,800	196	32	15	BC	
Bodega Sea	Lbr	2008	34,800	49,800	196	32	15	BC	
Botany Sea	Lbr	2009	34,800	49,800	196	32	15	BC	
Cap Norte †	Lbr	2007	35,824	41,850	220	32	22	CC	ex Alegra-07
Cap Prior **	Lbr	2007	35,824	41,850	220	32	22	CC	ex Almathea-07
Cape Darnley **	Mhl	2003	23,132	30,345	193	28	19	Co	
Cape Delfaro **	Mhl	2004	23,132	30,343	193	28	19	Co/hl	
Cape Delgardo	Mhl	2003	23,132	30,000	193	28	19	Co/hl	
Cape Donington **	Mhl	2003	23,132	30,490	193	28	19	Co/hl	ex Golden Isle-04, Cape Donington-03
Hyundai Jumbo **	Mhl	2002	23,132	30,586	193	28	15	Co/hl	ex CCNI Magallanes-07, Cape Dyer-03
Hyundai Rhino **	Mhl	2002	23,132	30,490	193	28	15	Co/hl	ex CCNI Antartico-08, CSAV Genova-04, Cape Dorchester-03
Johannesburg *	Lbr	2006	35,574	44,174	223	32	22	CC	ex MOL Will-08, Johannesburg-06
Maersk Damietta	Lbr	2008	54,675	68,463	294	32	24	CC	
Maersk Danang	Lbr	2008	54,675	68,411	294	32	24	CC	
Maersk Denpasar	Lbr	2008	54,675	68,463	294	32	24	CC	
Maersk Dhahran	Lbr	2008	54,675	67,410	294	32	24	CC	
Maersk Jakobstad *	Lbr	2007	32,901	34,700	225	31	21	CC	ex Arica-07
Maersk Jambi	Lbr	2008	32,901	35,556	224	31	21	CC	ex Austral-08
Maersk Jefferson	Lbr	2008	32,901	35,391	225	31	21	CC	ex Andino-08
Maersk Jena	Lbr	2007	32,901	34,345	225	31	21	CC	ex Andes-07
Maersk Jennings	Lbr	2008	32,901	35,534	225	31	21	CC	ex Antofagasta-08
Maersk Narbonne *	Lbr	2005	27,059	34,426	212	30	22	CC	l/a Caroline E, l/dn Coral Bay
Maersk Nashville *	Lbr	2005	27,059	34,200	212	30	22	CC	l/a Andres E, l/dn Crystal Bay
Monte Carlo	Lbr	2009	40,500	12,300	176	31	19	V	
Montreal	Lbr	2008	40,500	12,300	176	31	19	V	
Silver Bay *	Lbr	1998	17,295	22,800	175	27	20	CC	ex YM Genova II-07, Cape North-04, Tiger Pearl-03, Cape North-01, Maersk Skagen-99, l/a Cape North
Sunset Bay *	Lbr	1998	17,295	22,339	175	29	20	CC	ex Ningbo Star-05, Cape Nati-03, Tiger Island-02, Cape Nati-02, Sea-Land Mediterranean-99

newbuildings: eight 135,999 grt, two 39,900 dwt, five 35,900 grt container ships, four 50,000 dwt cargo ships, one 49,800 dwt open-hatch and six 92,500 dwt bulk carriers for 2009-11 delivery.
** managed for FHH Fonds Haus Hamburg GmbH & Co KG or ** for Lloyd Fonds AG. † managed by Columbia Shipmanagement.*

Odfjell ASA   Norway

Funnel: *White with blue diagonal chain link symbol, black top.* **Hull:** *Orange with blue 'ODFJELL SEACHEM', red or black boot-topping.* **History:** *Formed 1914 as Storli ASA to 1998; Seachem merged 1989 and Ceres Hellenic merged 2000. Acquired 50% of Flumar Brazil in 1999 and remainder in 2008 from Kristian Gerhard Jebsen Skips.* **Web:** *www.odfjell.com*

Name	Flag	Year	GRT	DWT	LOA	Bm	Kts	Type	Former names
Bow Americas ‡	Pan	2004	11,924	19,707	146	24	13	T	
Bow Architect ‡	Pan	2005	18,405	30,058	170	26	14	T	
Bow Atlantic	Sgp	1995	10,369	17,480	142	23	14	T	ex Brage Atlantic-07
Bow Cape	Pan	2008	11,722	19,975	144	24	14	T	
Bow Cardinal **	Nis	1997	23,196	37,479	183	32	16	T	
Bow Cecil **	Nis	1998	23,206	37,545	183	32	16	T	
Bow Cedar	Nis	1996	23,196	37,455	183	32	16	T	
Bow Century	Nis	2000	23,206	37,438	183	32	16	T	
Bow Chain	Nis	2002	23,190	37,518	183	32	16	T	
Bow Cheetah *	Sgp	1988	22,637	40,257	171	32	14	T	ex Santa Anna-00, Falkanger-91, Fort Cheetah-89, Northern Cheetah-88
Bow Clipper	Nis	1995	23,197	37,221	183	32	16	T	
Bow Eagle	Nis	1985	15,829	24,728	172	28	14	T	ex Northern Eagle-89, Mangueira-88
Bow Europe ‡	Pan	2005	11,690	19,728	144	24	14	T	ex North Contender-05
Bow Fagus	Nis	1995	23,197	37,221	183	32	16	T	
Bow Faith	Nis	1997	23,196	37,479	183	32	16	T	
Bow Favour	Nis	2001	23,190	37,467	183	32	16	T	
Bow Fertility *	Sgp	1987	27,963	39,611	177	32	14	T	ex Fertility L-04
Bow Fighter	Nis	1982	20,478	35,100	174	32	15	T	
Bow Firda	Nis	2003	23,190	37,000	183	32	16	T	
Bow Flora	Nis	1998	23,206	37,369	183	32	16	T	
Bow Flower	Nis	1994	23,197	37,221	183	32	16	T	
Bow Fortune	Nis	1999	23,206	37,395	183	32	16	T	
Bow Fraternity *	Sgp	1987	27,262	45,593	177	32	14	T	ex Fraternity L-04
Bow Hector §	Phl	2009	21,000	32,000	174	28		T	
Bow Heron §	Phl	2008	20,145	33,707	174	28		T	
Bow Hunter	Sgp	1983	14,627	23,002	158	23	15	T	
Bow Kiso	Pan	2008	19,420	33,641	170	27		T	
Bow Leopard *	Sgp	1988	22,637	40,257	171	32	14	T	ex Fort Leopard-89, Northern Leopard-88

Name	Flag	Year	GRT	DWT	LOA	Bm	Kts	Type	Former names
Bow Lion *	Sgp	1987	22,637	40,272	171	32	14	T	ex Fort Lion-89, Northern Lion-88
Bow Maasslot *	Sgp	1982	24,794	38,039	172	32	15	T	ex Maasslot L-04, Maasslot-93
Bow Maasstroom *	Sgp	1983	24,794	38,039	172	32	15	T	ex Maasstroom L-04, Maasstroom-93
Bow Oceanic	Sgp	1997	10,369	16,094	142	23	14	T	ex Brage Pacific-07
Bow Octavia §	Phl	2007	11,570	19,993	146	24	14	T	
Bow Olivia §	Phl	2007	11,570	19,980	146	24	14	T	
Bow Omaria §	Phl	2007	11,570	19,980	146	24	14	T	
Bow Ophelia §	Phl	2006	11,561	19,993	146	24	14	T	
Bow Orania §	Phl	2006	11,561	19,993	146	24	14	T	ex Orania-06
Bow Orelia §	Phl	2008	11,570	19,971	146	24	14	T	
Bow Pacifico †	Chl	1982	12,198	15,200	161	23	15	T	ex Bow Saphir-01
Bow Panther *	Sgp	1986	22,714	40,263	171	32	14	T	ex Northern Panther-89
Bow Peace *	Sgp	1987	28,001	45,655	177	32	14	T	ex Peaceventure L-00
Bow Pioneer	Sgp	1982	14,627	23,016	158	23	15	T	
Bow Power *	Sgp	1987	28,001	39,571	177	32	14	T	ex Powerventure L-00
Bow Pride *	Sgp	1987	28,001	39,586	177	32	14	T	ex Pridevenure L-00
Bow Prima *	Sgp	1987	28,001	45,655	177	32	14	T	ex Primaventure L-00
Bow Prosper *	Sgp	1987	28,008	39,574	177	32	14	T	ex Prosperventure L-00
Bow Puma *	Sgp	1986	22,714	40,091	171	32	14	T	ex Santa Maria-91, Finnanger-91, Fort Puma-89, Northern Puma-86
Bow Saga **	Nis	2007	29,965	40,085	183	32	15	T	
Bow Santos *	Pan	2004	11,986	19,997	148	24	14	T	
Bow Sea	Sgp	2006	29,965	40,036	183	32	14	T	
Bow Sirius	Nis	2006	29,965	40,048	183	32	14	T	
Bow Sky	Sgp	2005	29,965	40,005	183	32	15	T	
Bow Spring	Nis	2004	29,965	39,942	183	32	15	T	
Bow Star	Nis	2004	29,971	39,832	183	32	15	T	
Bow Summer	Sgp	2005	29,965	40,036	183	32	15	T	
Bow Sun	Sgp	2003	29,965	39,942	183	32	15	T	l/a Multicarrier
Bow Viking	Sgp	1981	19,639	33,695	183	30	16	T	ex Mauranger-90, Kaupanger-81

Majority owned or managed by Odfjell SE, Norway (formed 2007), * by Odfjell Asia II Pte Ltd, Singapore (formed 2000) or ** Odfjell (UK) Ltd (formed 2002). † jointly owned by Compania SudAmericana de Vapores SA, managed by Southern Shipmanagement (Chile) Ltd (www.ssm.cl). § owned by Nisshin Kaiun KK and managed by Victoria Ship Management Inc, Philippines or ‡ chartered from other owners. Also see chartered vessels under The National Shipping Company of Saudi Arabia.

J O Odfjell A/S   Norway

JO Tankers AS/Norway

Funnel: *Blue with white interlinked 'JO' symbol.* **Hull:** *Orange some with blue 'JO TANKERS', red boot-topping.* **History:** *Parent founded 1977, Dutch subsidiary JO Tankers BV in 1981 as Winterport Tankers to 1990 and JO Management BV to 1996, Norwegian subsidiary JO Tankers AS in 1989 as JO Management A/S to 1996.* **Web:** *www.jotankers.com*

Jo Acer *	Nis	2004	18,703	29,709	170	26	14	T	
Jo Ask	Nis	1997	12,317	19,087	148	23	16	T	
Jo Betula *	Nis	2003	15,992	25,032	159	25	15	T	
Jo Birk	Nis	1982	22,772	39,293	175	32	16	T	
Jo Brevik	Nis	1986	19,685	33,490	183	30	15	T	
Jo Cedar	Nld	1994	22,415	36,733	182	32	15	T	

Odfjell ASA. BOW SUMMER. *C. Lous*

Name	Flag	Year	GRT	DWT	LOA	Bm	Kts	Type	Former names
Jo Eik	Nis	1998	12,249	19,234	148	23	16	T	
Jo Kashi	Pan	2003	15,895	25,148	159	26	14	T	
Jo Kiri	Pan	2003	11,769	19,508	145	24	14	T	
Jo Lonn	Nis	1982	22,772	39,273	175	32	16	T	
Jo Oak	Nis	1983	22,772	39,270	175	32	16	T	
Jo Selje	Nld	1993	22,380	36,800	182	32	15	T	
Jo Sequoia *	Nis	2003	23,129	37,622	183	32	15	T	
Jo Spruce	Nld	1993	22,415	36,778	182	32	15	T	
Jo Sycamore	Nis	2000	23,200	37,500	183	32	15	T	
Jo Sypress	Nld	1998	22,415	36,752	182	32	15	T	

* managed by JO Tankers UK Ltd (formed 2003)   Also see A/S Borgestad ASA and Knutsen O.A.S. Shipping A/S, both Norway.

Rudolf A Oetker   Germany
Hamburg-Sudamerikanische Dampfschiffahrts-ges (HSDG)

Funnel: *White with red top or yellow 'CCL' on blue/red diagonally divided with black top.* **Hull:** *Red with white 'HAMBURG SUD' or 'COSTA CONTAINER LINES', red boot-topping.* **History:** *HSDG founded 1871. Dr August Oetker acquired an interest in 1934 and Rudolf A Oetker (founded 1951) took control in 1952, amalgamating the companies in 1973. Acquired 50% of Ybarra Cia Sudamericaa in 1989, Furness-Withy (Shipping) Ltd from CY Tung (OOCL) in 1990, Laser Lines from Nordstjernan (Johnson Line) in 1991, Alianca in 1998, Transroll in 1999, Ellerman in 2003, the balance of Ybarra in 2005 and Costa Container Lines (formed 1947) in 2007.*
Web: *www.hamburgsud.com*

Name	Flag	Year	GRT	DWT	LOA	Bm	Kts	Type	Former names
Alianca Maua	Deu	2005	69,132	64,730	272	40	23	CC	ex Monte Verde-05
Bahia Blanca	Deu	2007	41,483	53,094	254	32	21	CC	
Bahia Castillo	Deu	2007	41,483	53,100	254	32	21	CC	
Bahia Grande	Deu	2007	41,483	53,176	254	32	21	CC	
Bahia Laura	Deu	2007	41,483	53,139	254	32	21	CC	
Cala Ponente *	Ita	2002	16,661	23,051	185	25	19	CC	
Cala Portofino *	Ita	2002	16,600	22,967	185	25	19	CC	
Cala Positano *	Ita	1996	16,803	22,965	184	25	19	CC	
Cap Blanche **	Cyp	2006	28,371	37,883	222	30	22	CC	ex Fesco Baykal-06
Cap Carmel	Lbr	2003	25,705	33,600	207	30	22	CC	
Cap Melville	Lbr	2003	25,705	33,836	207	30	22	CC	
Cap Nelson	Lbr	2004	25,709	33,925	207	30	22	CC	ex Santos Express-05, Cap Nelson-04
Cap Palmas	Lbr	2003	25,709	33,795	208	30	21	CC	ex NYK Fantasia-05, Cap Palmas-03
Cap Pasado **	Cyp	2006	27,786	37,883	222	30	22	CC	ex Fesco Bratsk-06
Cap Polonia	Deu	1990	29,739	33,221	200	32	18	CC	
Cap San Antonio	Lbr	2001	40,085	51,060	257	32	23	CC	
Cap San Augustin	Lbr	2001	40,085	51,087	257	32	23	CC	
Cap San Lorenzo	Lbr	2001	40,085	51,045	257	32	23	CC	
Cap San Marco	Lbr	2001	40,085	51,087	257	32	23	CC	
Cap San Nicolas	Lbr	2001	40,085	51,101	257	32	22	CC	
Cap San Raphael	Lbr	2002	40,085	51,059	257	32	22	CC	
Cap Vilano **	Cyp	2006	27,786	37,883	222	30	22	CC	ex Fesco Barguzin-06
CCNI Shenzhen	Deu	2007	41,483	53,142	254	32	21	CC	ex Bahia Negra-08
Monte Aconcagua	Deu	2009	69,000	71,200	272	40	23	CC	
Monte Alegre	Deu	2008	69,132	71,273	272	40	23	CC	

Rudolf A. Oetker (HSDG). MONTE TAMARO. *Allan Ryszka Onions*

Name	Flag	Year	GRT	DWT	LOA	Bm	Kts	Type	Former names
Monte Azul	Deu	2008	69,132	65,066	272	40	23	CC	
Monte Cervantes	Deu	2004	69,132	64,730	272	40	23	CC	ex P&O Nedlloyd Salsa-06, Monte Cervantes-05
Monte Olivia	Deu	2004	69,132	64,730	272	40	23	CC	
Monte Pascoal	Deu	2004	69,132	65,066	272	40	23	CC	ex P&O Nedlloyd Lambada-06, Monte Pascoal-05
Monte Rosa	Deu	2004	69,132	64,888	272	40	23	CC	
Monte Sarmiento	Deu	2004	69,132	65,028	272	40	23	CC	
Monte Tamaro	Deu	2007	69,000	64,800	272	40	23	CC	
Rio de Janeiro	Deu	2008	73,899	80,398	287	40	23	CC	
Rio de la Plata	Deu	2008	73,899	80,455	287	40	23	CC	
Rio Negro	Deu	2008	73,900	80,450	287	40	23	CC	

newbuildings: six 74,000 grt and five 69,000 grt container ships for 2009-10 delivery.
managed by Columbus Shipmanagement GmbH (formed 1998)
* operated by subsidiary Costa Container Lines SpA, Italy and managed by Seatrade Groningen BV.
** chartered by HSDG until 2012 from Premium Capital Emissionshaus GmbH & Co KG (founded 2004) and managed by Reederei Alnwick Harmstorf & Co GmbH & Co KG, Germany (formed 1950 as A F Harmstorf & Co GmbH to 2000 - www.harmstorf-co.com)

Alianca Navegacao e Logistica Ltda/Brazil

Funnel: *Yellow with broad white over red bands beneath black top, black triangular 'A' on white band or HSDG colours.* **Hull:** *Blue with white 'ALIANCA', red boot-topping.* **History:** *Founded 1950 as Alianca Transportes Maritimos SA to 2000.* **Web:** *www.alianca.com.br*

Alianca Brasil	Bra	1994	28,397	32,984	200	32	18	CC	
Alianca Europa	Bra	1994	28,397	32,984	200	32	18	CC	
Copacabana	Bra	1984	20,995	26,848	179	31	18	CC	
Flamengo	Bra	1985	20,994	26,868	179	31	18	CC	

Maritime Services Aleuropa GmbH/Germany

Funnel: *White with red half-circle on broad blue top above broad green band.* **Hull:** *White.* **History:** *Formed 1980.* **Web:** *None found.*

Carlos Fischer *	Lbr	2002	33,005	43,067	204	32	20	Tfj	
Ouro do Brasil *	Lbr	1993	15,218	19,519	173	26	20	Tfj	
Premium do Brasil	Lbr	2003	33,005	43,002	205	32	20	Tfj	
Sol do Brasil *	Lbr	1994	15,218	19,563	173	26	20	Tfj	

* managed for Group Fischer, Brazil (founded 1932)

Ofer Brothers (Holdings) Ltd   Israel

Funnel: *Blue or charterers colours.* **Hull:** *Various colours.* **History:** *Founded 1957 as Mediterranean Seaways Ltd to 1967 and Mediterranean Lines Ltd to 1970.* **Web:** *www.oferbrothers.com*

Name	Flag	Year	GRT	DWT	LOA	Bm	Kts	Type	Former names
Blue Diamond *	Lbr	2006	32,572	53,000	190	32	14	B	
Cap Blanco	Mlt	1984	32,150	37,042	203	32	15	CC	ex CGM Magellan-97, Andes-94
Cap Domingo	Mlt	1984	31,446	34,680	201	32	19	CC	ex Alianca Mexico-99, Cap Corrientes-98, Laser Pacific-96, Bo Johnson-93
Cap Finisterre *	Lbr	1991	29,841	32,675	200	32	18	CC	
Cap Roca *	Lbr	1990	35,303	42,221	234	32	21	CC	ex New York Express-96, Berlin Express-93, POL Jos-92, Berlin Express-91
Cap Trafalgar *	Lbr	1990	29,739	33,222	200	32	19	CC	ex CMA CGM Pasteur-06, CGM Pasteur-01, Cap Trafalgar-99
Cape Carmel	Bmu	1996	92,194	179,869	290	46	14	B	ex Pytchley-05, SGC Capital-98
Cape Tavor	Lbr	1999	87,363	172,515	289	45	15	B	ex Cape Lowlands-06, La Selva-04
Car Bridge I	Lbr	1981	41,368	17,344	199	30	17	V	ex Zimcar 1-01, Delborg-00, Primavera-96, Jinto Maru-89
Car Star 1 *	Cyp	1981	41,363	17,427	199	30	17	V	ex Thonborg-99, Margherita-96, Jinmu Maru-90
Caribbean Sea *	Lbr	1992	37,071	46,975	237	32	21	CC	ex Zim Florida-05, St. Petersburg Mariner-03, St. Petersburg Senator-02
Carmel Bio-Top	Bmu	2004	18,931	15,052	186	25	20	CC	l/a Rio Yarkon
Carmel Eco-Fresh	Bmu	2003	18,931	15,052	186	25	20	CC	l/a Rio Alexandre
Dafnis	Mlt	1981	13,586	16,728	160	24	15	Co	ex Bonny-98, Zagreb-95
Durban Star III	Mlt	1982	15,611	22,918	166	27	16	Co	ex Hillary-99, Earnest Venture-96
Lorraine	Lbr	2006	27,786	37,800	222	30	22	CC	ex Cape Mayor-06
Marmara Sea *	Cyp	1990	36,584	44,025	241	32	23	CC	ex Zim Dalian-05, Choyang Victory-98
Marseille Star	Mlt	1981	31,694	28,615	222	31	21	CC	ex Zim Marseille-06, Azov Sea-01, Asia Crown-01, APL Monterrey-01, Asia Crown-00, Zim Osaka-98, Asia Crown-96, California Ceres-96, Shin-Kashu Maru-81
MSC Andalucia II	Mlt	1978	20,408	21,857	181	27	17	CC	ex Lora-02, MSC Andalucia-02, Lora-00, Norasia Alexandria-00, Lora-99, Diana-96, Asean Unity-94, Ciudad de Pasto-93 (con C-95)
MSC Black Sea *	Mlt	1990	36,584	44,014	240	32	22	CC	ex Black Sea-08, Zim Ravenna I-05, Choyang Glory-98

Name	Flag	Year	GRT	DWT	LOA	Bm	Kts	Type	Former names
MSC Krittika	Gbr	1994	30,971	36,999	202	32	21	CC	ex Lykes Commander-05, TMM Mexico-01, Sea Guardian-96, Mexico-94
MSC Mahima	Mlt	1985	37,814	53,726	243	32	19	CC	ex SCI Mahima-07, Zim Chicago-04, Zim Venezia II-02, Alma A-01, Houston-00, Houston Express-97, Sea Premier-94, CGM Paris-94, Maersk Tacoma-88, C.R. Paris-87
North Sea *	Lbr	1992	37,071	47,120	237	32	21	CC	ex Zim Singapore-04, Korea Star-03, Moscow Mariner-02, Moscow Senator-02, Choyang Moscow-98
Ori A	Pan	1978	14,741	21,513	163	24	14	T	ex Marina-94, Terutoku Maru-93
Pearl River I	Lbr	2007	39,906	50,532	261	32	24	CC	ex Zim Vancouver-07
Philippine Star	Mlt	1986	22,667	33,852	188	28	19	CC	ex Zim Mumbai 1-02, MSC Cameroon-01, Zim Shanghai-01, Vesta-95, Ville de Vesta-94, Japan Sea-93, Ville de Vesta-89, Pacific Prosperity-88
Qingdao Star	Mlt	1985	22,667	32,934	188	28	18	CC	ex CSCL Huangpu-02, Zim India-00, Zim Singapore-98, Vega-95, Ville de Vega-94, Pacific Progress-88
Zim California	Isr	2002	53,453	62,740	294	32	24	CC	
Zim Genova	Lbr	2007	39,906	50,532	261	32	24	CC	
Zim Livorno	Lbr	2006	39,906	50,689	261	32	24	CC	
Zim Mediterranean	Isr	2002	53,453	62,686	294	32	24	CC	
Zim Shekou	Lbr	2007	39,906	50,629	260	32	24	CC	

newbuildings: 46,000 grt Lpg tanker for 2011 delivery.
Owned by Ofer (Ships Holding) Ltd (formed 2001) except * by subsidiary Kotani Shipmanagement Ltd, Cyprus (founded jointly with Zodiac Maritime Agencies Ltd in 1999)

Zodiac Maritime Agencies Ltd/UK

Funnel: Blue with blue 'Z' on white disc with globe outline.some with black top or charterers colours. **Hull:** Black, grey, red or white with red boot-topping. **History:** Formed 1976, acquired 50% P&O share of Associated Bulk Carriers in 2000 and balance in 2003. **Web:** www.zodiac-maritime.com

Name	Flag	Year	GRT	DWT	LOA	Bm	Kts	Type	Former names
APL Liberty	Gbr	1996	64,054	68,539	275	40	25	CC	ex Hyundai Liberty-07
APL London	Gbr	2008	71,786	72,982	293	40	25	CC	
Asian Beauty	Gbr	1994	44,481	13,308	185	31	18	V	
Asian Glory	Gbr	1994	44,818	13,363	184	31	18	V	
Asian Trader	Lbr	1991	16,731	22,735	175	28	19	CC	ex Asian Pollux-03
Bavaria Express	Gbr	2003	39,941	50,811	260	32	24	CC	ex CP Indigo-06, Contship Indigo-05, APL Panama-04
Brazil Star	Lbr	1983	100,912	201,227	299	50	12	B	ex Tsukuba Maru-94
Broadgate	Lbr	1984	20,986	35,287	176	28	14	B	ex Marine Royal-95, Unyo Maru-88
Brother Glory	Gbr	1998	27,105	46,211	190	31	13	B	
Buccleuch #	Bmu	1993	90,820	182,675	284	47	13	B	
Cape Eagle	Gbr	1993	81,589	161,475	280	45	14	B	
Cape Falcon	Gbr	1993	81,589	149,480	280	45	14	B	
Cape Flamingo	Gbr	2005	90,092	180,201	290	45	14	B	
Cape Hawk	Gbr	1995	81,589	161,425	280	45	14	B	
Cape Kestrel	Gbr	1993	81,589	161,475	280	45	14	B	
Cape Merlin	Gbr	1994	77,503	150,966	273	43	13	B	ex Universal Spirit-01

Ofer Brothers (Zodiac Marine). APL LONDON. *David Hornsby*

Name	Flag	Year	GRT	DWT	LOA	Bm	Kts	Type	Former names
Cape Osprey	Gbr	1996	81,589	161,448	280	45	14	B	ex Sanko Oriole-03
Cape Stork	Gbr	1996	83,658	171,039	278	45	14	B	ex Lowlands Rose-04
Captain Aysuna	Lbr	1986	16,080	26,914	168	27	13	B	ex New Venus-97, Helm Star-92, Liberty Star-88
Carrera	Gbr	2008	46,800	12,315	183	32	20	V	
Castlegate ‡	Gbr	2008	29,923	53,503	190	32		B	
CMA CGM Sapphire	Lbr	1991	36,627	44,013	240	32	22	CC	ex Grand Vision-03, Choyang Giant-01
Cotswold	Bmu	1986	80,578	151,016	289	45	14	B	
CSAV Rio Aysen	Gbr	2007	46,800	12,315	183	32	20	V	
CSAV Rio Grande	Gbr	2007	46,800	12,260	183	32	20	V	
CSAV Rio Imperial	Gbr	2006	46,800	12,235	183	32	20	V	
CSAV Rio Nevado	Gbr	2007	46,800	12,315	183	32	20	V	
Cumbria	Lbr	1990	13,455	13,453	146	23	14	Lpg	ex Victoire-04, Kelvin-96
Duhallow	Bmu	1993	63,240	122,774	266	41	14	B	
Eastgate	Lbr	1990	17,066	27,877	177	26	14	B	ex Japan Rainbow II-01
Eridge	Bmu	1993	63,153	122,792	266	41	14	B	
Fernie #	Bmu	1996	63,153	122,292	266	41	14	B	
Golden Jewel	Lbr	1994	147,580	264,932	333	60	15	O	ex Han-Ei-07 (conv T-08)
Grafton #	Bmu	1996	63,153	122,301	266	41	14	B	
Grand View	Lbr	1991	36,627	44,006	242	32	22	CC	ex P&O Nedlloyd Xiamen-04, Choyang World-01
Hammonia Express	Gbr	2003	39,941	50,759	260	32	24	CC	ex CP Aguascalientes-06, TMM Aguascalientes-05
Heythrop	Bmu	1996	85,364	165,729	288	44	13	B	
Holsatia Express	Gbr	2003	39,941	50,913	260	32	24	CC	ex CP Provider-06, Lykes Provider-05
Hyundai Admiral	Gbr	1992	51,836	61,152	275	37	24	CC	
Hyundai Baron	Gbr	1992	51,836	61,152	275	37	24	CC	
Hyundai Busan	Gbr	2006	74,651	80,120	304	40	27	CC	
Hyundai Discovery	Gbr	1996	64,054	51,120	275	40	25	CC	
Hyundai Emperor	Gbr	1992	51,836	61,152	275	37	26	CC	ex APL Emperor-08, Hyundai Emperor-07
Hyundai Global	Lbr	2009	93,750	101,550	340	46	27	CC	
Hyundai Hongkong	Gbr	2006	74,651	80,120	304	40	27	CC	
Hyundai Independence	Gbr	1996	64,054	68,537	275	40	25	CC	
Hyundai Loyalty	Lbr	2009	93,750	101,550	340	46	27	CC	
Hyundai Mercury	Lbr	2009	93,750	101,550	340	46	27	CC	
Hyundai No. 106	Lbr	1987	42,469	12,939	184	31	18	V	
Hyundai No. 107	Lbr	1987	42,469	12,989	184	31	18	V	
Hyundai No. 108	Lbr	1987	30,024	9,783	174	28	18	V	
Hyundai No. 109	Lbr	1987	31,367	9,694	174	28	19	V	ex Toronto-99, Hyundai No.109-97
Hyundai Shanghai	Gbr	2006	74,651	80,120	304	40	26	CC	
Hyundai Singapore	Gbr	2006	74,651	80,120	304	40	26	CC	
Hyundai Tokyo	Gbr	2006	74,651	80,120	304	40	26	CC	
Irfon #	Bmu	1996	84,921	165,628	288	44	13	B	
Irongate	Lbr	1982	92,614	179,618	299	48	13	B	ex Kinokawa-96, Kinokawa Maru-93
Kent §	Lbr	2007	22,914	26,438	174	28		Lpg	
Kildare	Bmu	1996	108,083	211,320	312	50	14	B	ex SGC Express-98
Kyoto Tower	Gbr	2007	17,229	21,975	172	28	19	CC	
Kyushu Star	Lbr	1982	73,657	142,936	270	43	14	B	ex Kitaura Maru-95
London Tower	Lbr	1994	17,651	23,884	183	28	19	CC	ex Nantai Queen-99

Ofer Brothers (Zodiac Marine). HYUNDAI HONGKONG. *J. M. Kakebeeke*

Name	Flag	Year	GRT	DWT	LOA	Bm	Kts	Type	Former names
Lucky Transporter	Lbr	1984	15,763	26,650	167	26	14	B	ex Prime Unity-96, Maersk Pine-92, Mercury Island-90
Meynell	Bmu	1997	93,629	185,767	292	48	15	B	ex SG Universe-98
Millenia Tower	Gbr	1990	16,731	22,734	185	28	19	CC	ex Sinar Toba-08, Kota Perabu-05, Millenia Tower-03, ACX Rose-00
Moorgate	Lbr	1990	25,965	45,875	190	31	13	B	ex Federal Kumano-97
Morning Cloud	Lbr	1983	36,304	66,755	230	32	15	B	ex Morning Camellia-90, Panamax Neptune-86
Morning Midas	Gbr	2006	46,800	12,672	183	32	20	V	
Morning Miracle	Gbr	2006	46,800	12,600	183	32	20	V	
MSC Catania	Gbr	1994	60,117	63,163	300	37	23	CC	ex Sandra Azul-07, NYK Altair-01
MSC Colombia	Gbr	1996	51,931	60,348	294	32	23	CC	ex Maersk Doha-07, P&O Nedlloyd Caribbean-03, Germany-02, APL Germany-02, OOCL Germany-98
MSC Darwin	Gbr	1996	51,938	60,348	294	32	23	CC	ex Maersk Darwin-08, ANL Indonesia-03, Indonesia-02, APL Indonesia-01
MSC Messina	Gbr	1995	60,117	63,014	300	37	23	CC	ex Sandra Blanca-07, NYK Vega-01
MSC Venezuela	Gbr	1996	51,931	60,348	294	32	23	CC	ex Maersk Dundee-07, France-03, APL France-01, OOCL France-98
Newforest	Bmu	1996	93,629	185,688	292	48	15	B	ex SGC Foundation-98
Noa	Lbr	1985	26,014	43,590	186	30	14	B	ex Soarer Adonis-97
Norasia Bellatrix	Lbr	2002	50,242	58,814	282	32	24	CC	ex Hanjin Pennsylvania-04
Northgate	Lbr	1984	93,049	179,422	299	48	13	B	ex Kii Maru-97
Northumberland	Gbr	1990	11,822	16,137	158	21	15	Lpg	ex Nelly Maersk-03, Reinanger-98, Anne-Laure-97, Sloka-93
Ormond	Bmu	1986	96,794	187,025	300	47	13	B	
Quorn	Bmu	1996	92,194	179,869	290	46	14	B	ex SG China-98
Recife	Lbr	1991	17,156	22,219	186	28	18	CC	ex YM Hongkong II-07, Tiger Shark-04, Recife-01, Pacific Vista-98, Tokyo Bridge-98,
Rutland	Bmu	1997	85,848	170,013	292	46	14	B	ex SG Fortune-98
Santa Barbara	Gbr	1992	43,213	39,402	253	32	23	CC	ex NYK Surfwind-99
Santa Cruz	Gbr	1991	43,209	38,970	252	32	23	CC	ex NYK Sunrise-99
Santa Monica	Lbr	1991	43,213	39,376	253	32	23	CC	ex NYK Seabreeze-99
Saxonia Express	Gbr	2003	39,941	50,841	260	32	24	CC	ex CP Monterrey-06, TMM Monterrey-05
Seagate	Gbr	1989	17,590	28,836	170	27	14	C	ex Alabama Rainbow-01
Seoul Tower	Gbr	2008	26,688	34,500	212	30		CC	
Shagang Giant	Lbr	1993	155,359	308,902	332	60	14	O	ex Starlight Jewel-08, Front Tartar-01, Tartar-00 (conv T-93)
Shetland	Iom	1981	14,102	18,270	153	25	17	Lpg	ex Maersk Shetland-01, Svendborg Maersk-94
Silvergate	Lbr	1987	37,025	68,158	225	32	14	B	ex Glory Hope-97
Snowdon	Bmu	1998	85,848	170,013	292	46	14	B	l/a SG Creation
Somerset	Gbr	1981	14,046	18,270	153	25	17	Lpg	ex Maersk Somerset-01, Sally Maersk-93
Southgate	Lbr	1982	15,274	25,417	161	25	14	B	ex Menina Elisa-93, Oriental Swan-89
Springwood	Lbr	1984	22,009	37,694	188	28	14	B	ex Spring Hawk-93, Sanko Hawk-86
Stafford	Gbr	1984	14,102	18,270	153	25	17	Lpg	ex Maersk Stafford-01, Sine Maersk-93, Olga Maersk-92
Stanley Park	Gbr	2008	11,590	19,994	146	24	14	T	
Stonegate	Lbr	1984	107,083	187,011	305	51	13	B	ex Sunny Ocean-98, River Star-97

Ofer Brothers (Zodiac Marine). MORNING MIDAS. *Hans Kraijenbosch*

Name	Flag	Year	GRT	DWT	LOA	Bm	Kts	Type	Former names
Suffolk	Gbr	1984	14,102	18,270	153	25	17	Lpg	ex Maersk Suffolk-01, Sofie Maersk-93, Oluf Maersk-92
Surrey	Gbr	1982	14,102	18,270	153	25	17	Lpg	ex Maersk Surrey-01, Svend Maersk-93
Sussex	Gbr	1981	14,102	18,270	153	25	17	Lpg	ex Maersk Sussex-01, Susan Maersk-92
Taunton	Bmu	1986	95,835	186,324	300	47	13	B	ex Marine Crusader-89
Thuringia Express	Gbr	2003	39,941	50,785	260	32	24	CC	ex CP Tamarind-06, Contship Tamarind-05, APL Honduras-04
Tokyo Tower †	Gbr	2007	17,229	21,975	172	28	19	CC	
Triumph	Gbr	2008	46,800	12,300	183	32	20	V	
Vine	Bmu	1990	63,106	114,975	266	42	14	B	
Waterford	Bmu	1990	77,113	149,513	270	43	12	B	
Westfalia Express	Gbr	2003	39,941	50,886	260	32	24	CC	ex CP Deliverer-06, Lykes Deliverer-05
Wugang Asia	Lbr	1992	150,203	264,484	322	58	15	O	ex Asian Jewel-08, Helios Breeze-04 (conv T)
Wugang Atlantic	Lbr	1995	154,277	281,226	328	57		O	ex Atlantic Jewel-08, C. Trust-07, C. Achiever-03, Yukong Achiever-97 (conv T)
Wugang Orient	Lbr	1991	144,631	275,628	326	57	14	O	ex Orient Jewel-08, Nichiyo-03, Goho-94, I/a Sea Duchess (conv T)
YM Hamburg	Gbr	1997	40,268	49,238	259	32	23	CC	ex Ville de Virgo-04
YM Kaohsiung	Gbr	1998	40,068	50,059	259	32	23	CC	ex Ville de Tanya-05
YM Moji	Lbr	1994	16,708	24,444	183	28	19	CC	ex Tiger Bridge-04, Libra Australia II-02, Libra Australia-00
YM Shanghai	Gbr	1997	40,268	49,225	259	32	23	CC	ex Ville d'Antares-04
York	Bmu	1990	77,113	149,513	270	43	13	B	
Zenith Leader	Gbr	2007	62,080	22,602	200	32	20	V	
Zetland	Bmu	1985	74,003	145,905	267	43	13	B	ex Mosbulk-90
Zim India	Gbr	2007	39.912	50,607	261	32	24	CC	
Zim Panama	Gbr	2002	53,453	55,000	294	32	24	CC	
Zim Pusan	Gbr	2004	53,453	62,740	294	32	24	CC	
Zim Shenzhen	Gbr	2004	53,453	62,740	294	32	24	CC	
Zim Xiamen	Gbr	2006	39,906	50,689	261	32	24	CC	

newbuildings: five 115,800 dwt, four 95,810 dwt, six 72,665 dwt and two 34,500 dwt container ships, four 298,000 dwt ore carriers, a 53,400 dwt and four 28,000 dwt bulk carriers, three 19,800 dwt chemical tankers, one 26,200 dw, three 52,650 dwt, three 18,000 grt LPG tankers, and four vehicle carriers for 2009-11 delivery.
* owned by subsidiary Kotani Shipmanagement Ltd, Cyprus (founded jointly by Ofer Bros and Zodiac Maritime Agencies Ltd in 1999)
† manged for Iino Kaiun Kaisha, ‡ for Itochi Corp or § for Mizuho Sangyo Co Ltd, all Japan or # for Unique Shipping (HK) Ltd, Hong Kong (China)

Tanker Pacific Management (Singapore) Pte Ltd/Singapopre

Funnel: *Blue with yellow band.* **Hull:** *Black with red boot-topping.* **History:** *Subsidiary founded 1989.* **Web:** *www.tanker.com.sg*

	Flag	Year	GRT	DWT	LOA	Bm	Kts	Type	Former names
Adriatic Sea	Lbr	1992	55,790	98,680	243	38	14	T	ex Genmar Champ-06, Genmar Champion-03, SCF Champion-01, SKS Champion-95 (conv Obo)
Alaskan Sea	Lbr	1992	57,082	96,027	243	38	14	Obo	ex Genmar Star-06, SCF Star-01, SKS Star-95
Amoy	Lbr	1992	25,800	41,476	182	30	14	T	ex Agility-01, Minas Leo-97
Arafura Sea	Sgp	2000	57,680	105,856	244	43	15	T	
Aral Sea	Sgp	1999	58,129	104,884	244	42	14	T	ex Bali Sea-04
Baltic Sea	Sgp	1993	53,833	97,046	243	42	14	T	ex Colby-00, I/a Consensus Colby
Barents Sea	Sgp	2000	57,680	105,588	248	43	15	T	

Ofer Brothers (Zodiac Marine). WATERFORD. *Allan Ryszka Onions*

Name	Flag	Year	GRT	DWT	LOA	Bm	Kts	Type	Former names
Batavia	Lbr	1992	25,825	41,430	182	30	14	T	ex Navix Erica-00
Beaufort Sea	Sgp	1992	55,790	98,929	243	38	14	T	ex Genmar Hector-06, SC Horizon-00, SKS Horizon-95, Scanobo Horizon-92 (conv Obo)
Bering Sea	Sgp	1996	53,639	96,124	243	42	14	T	
Black Sea	Sgp	1999	58,129	104,943	244	42	14	T	
Brilliant Jewel	Sgp	1989	140,818	247,471	324	58	15	T	ex Takachiho-04
Calm Sea	Lbr	1992	55,790	98,929	243	38	14	T	ex Genmar Spirit-06, SCF Spirit-01, SKS Spirit-95, Scanobo Spirit-92 (conv Obo)
Centennial Jewel	Lbr	1997	163,720	300,955	340	56	15	T	ex Courtenay Bay-07, Irving Galloway-02
Ceram Sea	Sgp	2004	57,680	105,666	248	43	15	T	
Ceylon	Sgp	2002	28,099	46,001	180	32	15	T	ex Akebono-04
Coral Sea	Sgp	2003	57,680	105,665	244	43	15	T	
Cosmic Jewel	Lbr	1997	163,720	300,955	340	56	15	T	ex Tantramar-07, Irving Primrose-02
Eastway	Mhl	1989	79,553	149,999	267	46	14	T	ex Genmar Kestrel-05, Crudemed-03, Ioannis-98, Golar Beatrice-93
Emerald Isle	Lbr	1989	39,415	68,337	229	32	13	T	ex Prestige-99
Emerald Sky	Lbr	1988	39,285	70,894	225	32	11	T	ex Hoyo-93, Hoyo Maru-92
Flores Sea	Lbr	1992	55,790	98,885	243	38	14	Obo	ex Genmar Trust-06, SCF Trust-01, SKS Trust-95, Scanobo Trust-92
Gateway	Nis	1988	79,544	152,385	267	46	14	T	ex Kronviken-04, Eurus-97, Golar Jane-91
Headway	Sgp	1989	79,544	152,385	267	46	14	T	ex Solviken-04, Corus-97, Golar Colleen-91
Ionian Sea	Sgp	1992	55,790	98,827	243	38	14	T	ex Genmar Pericles-06, SC Breeze-00, SKS Breeze-95, Scanobo Breeze-92 (conv Obo)
Irish Sea	Lbr	1991	55,790	98,786	243	38	14	T	ex Genmar Challenger-06, SCF Challenger-01, SKS Challenger-95 (conv Obo)
Java Sea	Lbr	1991	55,790	99,016	243	38	14	T	ex Genmar Endurance-06, SCF Endurance-01, SKS Endurance-95 (conv Obo)
Kingsway	Lbr	1992	84,488	159,719	271	49	14	T	ex Genmar Honour-05, Erati-04
Kyoto	Sgp	1992	25,800	41,461	182	30	14	T	ex Dignity-00, MinasLibra-97
Laiwu Steel Harmonious *	Sgp	1989	150,454	270,857	337	58	16	T	ex Eastern Jewel-08, T.S. Asclepius-02
Maritime Jewel	Lbr	2000	157,833	299,364	332	58	15	T	ex Limburg-03
Montara Venture	Lbr	1990	76,992	148,251	274	43	14	T	ex Freeway-07, Genmar Alta-05, Alta-01, Wilomi Alta-97
Nara	Sgp	1996	28,433	47,172	183	32	15	T	ex Eagle Vela-04, NOL Vela-00
New Vision	Atf	1994	164,251	298,033	334	59	16	T	
North Sea	Sgp	2008	59,177	115,325	244	42		T	
Northern Jewel	Atf	1993	164,251	298,033	334	59	15	T	ex New Wisdom-09
Northway	Mhl	1989	79,503	151,910	267	46	14	T	ex Genmar Ariston-05, Crudestar-03, Lioness-96
Pacific Amber	Sgp	1993	28,277	46,878	183	32	14	T	ex Halia-06
Pacific Crystal	Sgp	1993	28,277	46,842	183	32	14	T	ex Hastula-06
Pacific Jade	Sgp	1994	28,277	46,801	183	32	14	T	ex Haustrum-07
Pacific Onyx	Sgp	1988	25,060	40,509	176	32	14	T	ex Astrolabe-94
Pacific Opal	Sgp	1994	28,277	46,851	183	32	14	T	ex Hatasia-07
Pacific Pearl	Sgp	1994	28,277	46,850	183	32	14	T	ex Hadra-07
Pacific Ruby	Iom	1994	28,277	46,878	183	32	14	T	ex Haminea-07
Pacific Tourmaline	Lbr	1989	27,450	45,018	178	30	15	T	ex Hightide-07

Ofer Brothers (Zim). ZIM YOKOHAMA. *Hans Kraijenbosch*

Name	Flag	Year	GRT	DWT	LOA	Bm	Kts	Type	Former names
Pacific Turquoise	Lbr	1989	27,450	45,018	178	30	15	T	ex Highseas-07
Port Arthur	Lbr	1992	25,800	41,490	182	30	14	T	ex Bellus-01
Parkway	Bhs	1990	88,946	152,402	275	50	14	T	ex Genmar Macedon-06, John Young-00
Radiant Jewel	Lbr	1992	156,408	302,419	332	58	15	T	ex Golar Glasgow-01
Raffles Park	Lbr	1992	25,669	41,315	180	31	14	T	ex Bow Trident-01, Petrobulk Stag-94
Rangoon	Sgp	1989	25,740	41,570	181	30	14	T	ex World Sea-04
Savannah	Sgp	1996	28,433	47,172	183	32	15	T	ex Eagle Sagitta-04, NOL Sagitta-00
Silver Jewel	Lbr	1993	149,323	260,995	330	59	15	T	ex Grand Mountain-08, Mitsumine-04
Skyway	Lbr	1991	88,946	155,150	275	50	15	T	ex Genmar Spartiate-06, Bruce Smart-00
Southway	Sgp	1988	79,544	152,412	267	46	14	T	ex Genmar Prometheus-05, Crudesun-03, Bona Liv-97, Golar Liv-93
Starway	Mhl	1991	88,946	155,103	275	48	15	T	ex Genmar Zoe-06, J. Dennis Bonney-00
Sunlight Jewel	Sgp	1993	156,937	302,326	328	57	15	T	Front Tarim-01, Tarim-00
Sunrise Jewel	Lbr	1992	156,408	302,440	332	58	15	T	ex Golar Stirling-01
Westway	Sgp	1988	79,503	151,803	267	46	14	T	ex Genmar Sky-05, Crudesky-03, Barbro-96
White Sea	Lbr	1991	57,082	98,929	243	38	14	T	ex Genmar Trader-06, SCF Trader-01, SKS Trader-95 (conv Obo)

newbuildings: four 114,500 dwt and four 97,000 dwt tankers for 2009-11 delivery.
* managed by Zodiac Maritime Agencies Ltd.

Zim Integrated Shipping Services Ltd/Israel

Funnel: White with blue 'ZIM' below seven gold stars (four above three). **Hull:** White or grey with green boot-topping, or black with white 'ZIM' and red boot-topping. **History:** Founded 1945 as Zim Israel Navigation Co Ltd with 48% government share and 49% owned by Israel Corp (57.3% owned by Ofer Bros). Government share acquired in 2004 and company renamed. **Web:** www.zim.co.il

Name	Flag	Year	GRT	DWT	LOA	Bm	Kts	Type	Former names
Africa Star *	Mlt	1988	18,037	26,152	177	28	19	CC	ex Delmas Capricorne-05, Gluecksburg-04, MSC Quito-02, P&O Nedlloyd Chile-00, CMBT Himalaya-97, CGM Iguacu II-96, Glucksburg-94, Ville de Neptune-92
Andaman Sea	Mlt	1990	37,209	47,230	236	32	21	CC	ex Zim America-07
Asia Star *	Mlt	1994	16,043	20,194	177	28	19	CC	ex Delmas Charcot-04, Indamex New York-03, San Antonio-00, Jolly Avorio-00, San Antonio-99
Colombo Star II *	Cyp	1982	11,731	14,921	153	23	16	CC	ex Fas Port Kelang-03, Colombo Star II-01, Colombo Star I-01, Zim Liverpool-99, Zim Kenya-95, Zim Rotterdam-93, Zim Singapore-92
Jakarta Star II *	Cyp	1983	11,731	14,920	153	23	16	CC	ex Fas Semarang-03, Jakarta Star II-01, Jakarta Star I-01, Zim Salerno-99, City of Salerno-98, Zim Antwerpen-95, Zim Eilat-89
Japan Sea	Isr	1991	37,209	47,230	236	32	21	CC	ex Zim Japan-07
Novorossiysk Star *	Mlt	1999	20,624	25,572	180	28	20	CC	ex Australia Star-06, Kota Sejati-06, Bai Yun He-04
Odessa Star *	Mlt	2000	20,569	25,638	180	28	20	CC	ex Hongkong Star-06, Xiang Yun He-06
Zim Asia	Lbr	1996	41,507	45,850	254	32	21	CC	
Zim Atlantic	Lbr	1996	41,507	45,850	254	32	21	CC	
Zim Barcelona	Isr	2004	53,450	54,740	294	32	24	CC	
Zim Canada	Isr	1990	37,209	47,230	236	32	21	CC	
Zim China	Lbr	1997	41,507	45,850	254	32	21	CC	
Zim Europa	Lbr	1997	41,507	45,850	254	32	21	CC	
Zim Haifa	Isr	2004	54,626	66,938	254	32	24	CC	
Zim Hong Kong	Mlt	1992	37,209	47,230	236	32	21	CC	
Zim Iberia	Lbr	1998	41,507	46,350	254	32	21	CC	
Zim Israel	Mlt	1992	37,209	47,230	236	32	22	CC	
Zim Italia	Isr	1991	37,209	47,230	236	32	21	CC	
Zim Jamaica	Lbr	1997	41,507	45,850	254	32	21	CC	
Zim Korea	Isr	1991	37,209	47,230	236	32	21	CC	
Zim Pacific	Lbr	1996	41,507	45,850	254	32	21	CC	
Zim Qingdao	Lbr	2006	39,906	50,689	261	32	24	CC	
Zim U.S.A.	Isr	1997	41,200	46,250	254	32	21	CC	
Zim Virginia	Isr	2002	53,453	62,740	294	32	24	CC	
Zim Yokohama	Lbr	2007	39,906	52,000	261	32	24	CC	

newbuildings: eight 158,000 grt, ten 108,000 grt, four 91,000 grt and six 18,000 grt container ships for 2009-12 delivery.
* owned by subsidiary Therica Shipping Corp, Hong Kong (China)

Reederei Claus-Peter Offen GmbH & Co   Germany

Funnel: Black with white Maltese Cross on broad blue band edged with narrow white bands, or charterers colours. **Hull:** Light grey, black or red with red boot-topping. **History:** Founded 1971. **Web:** www.offenship.de

Name	Flag	Year	GRT	DWT	LOA	Bm	Kts	Type	Former names
Cap Beaufort *	Lbr	2008	28,616	39,337	222	30	23	CC	
Cap Bianco *	Lbr	2007	28,616	37,053	222	30	23	CC	ex Santa Bianca-07

Name	Flag	Year	GRT	DWT	LOA	Bm	Kts	Type	Former names
Cap Byron *	Lbr	2007	28,616	39,277	222	30	23	CC	ex Santa Bettina-07
Cap Harald	Lbr	2008	41,358	39,750	262	32		CC	
Cap Hamilton	Lbr	2008	41,358	39,750	262	32		CC	
Cap Palliser *	Lbr	2007	22,914	28,220	186	28	21	CC	
Cap Palmerston *	Lbr	2007	22,914	28,187	186	28	21	CC	
Cap Pasley *	Lbr	2007	22,914	21,700	186	28	21	CC	
Cap Portland *	Lbr	2007	22,914	21,700	186	28	21	CC	l/a San Albano
Cap Preston *	Lbr	2007	22,914	21,700	186	28	21	CC	ex San Alvaro-07
CMA CGM Butterfly	Lbr	2008	113,900	120,000	350	43	25	CC	l/a San Albano
CMA CGM Ivanhoe	Lbr	2009	113,900	120,000	350	43	25	CC	ex San Alvaco-07
CMA CGM Lagos *	Lbr	1997	21,531	30,202	182	30	20	CC	ex Canmar Promise-06, Santa Giorgina-03, P&O Nedlloyd Rio Grande-02, l/a Santa Giorgina
CMA CGM Niger *	Lbr	1998	21,583	30,007	183	30	20	CC	ex Santa Fiorenzo-07, P&O Nedlloyd Arica-02, l/a Santa Fiorenzo
CMA CGM Nimba	Deu	1994	21,054	29,744	182	29	20	CC	ex Clan Legionary-08, Santa Margherita-05, P&O Nedlloyd Caribbean-02, P&O Nedlloyd Douala-01, Cielo di Livorno-99, Santa Margherita-94
CMA CGM Nyala *	Lbr	1999	21,583	30,135	183	30	20	CC	ex Santa Fabiola-08, P&O Nedlloyd Singapore-05, l/dn Santa Fabiola
CMA CGM Okume	Lbr	2000	25,294	32,391	207	30	22	CC	ex Santa Alexandra-08, P&O Nedlloyd Abidjan-05, MOL San Paulo-02, P&O Nedlloyd Abidjan-01, Santa Alexandra-00
CMA CGM Orfeo	Lbr	2008	111,249	120,892	350	43	25	CC	
CMA CGM Pelleas	Lbr	2008	111,249	120,853	350	43	25	CC	
CMA CGM Tema	Deu	1996	21,531	30,201	182	30	20	CC	ex Santa Giovanna-06, P&O Nedlloyd Amazonas-01, Santa Giovanna-01, P&O Nedlloyd Amazonas-01, Nedlloyd Amazonas-99, Santa Giovanna-96
CMA CGM Volta	Deu	1998	21,583	30,029	183	30	20	CC	ex Santa Francesca-07, P&O Nedlloyd Sao Paulo-02, l/a Santa Francesca
CPO England **	Lbr	2008	23,353	37,304	184	28	15	T	
CPO Finland **	Lbr	2008	23,353	37,304	184	28	15	T	
CPO France **	Lbr	2008	23,353	37,304	184	28	15	T	
CPO Germany **	Lbr	2008	23,270	37,300	184	28	15	T	
CPO Italy **	Lbr	2008	23,270	37,300	184	28	15	T	
CPO Norway **	Lbr	2008	23,270	37,300	184	28	15	T	
CPO Russia **	Lbr	2008	23,353	37,304	184	28	15	T	
CPO Sweden **	Lbr	2008	23,353	37,304	184	28	15	T	
Delmas Abuja	Deu	1997	21,531	30,252	182	30	20	CC	ex Santa Giulietta-07, P&O Nedlloyd Parana-02, l/a Santa Giulietta
Delmas Bouake *	Lbr	1996	21,531	30,201	182	30	19	CC	ex Clan Tangun-08, Santa Giuliana-05, P&O Nedlloyd Orinoco-01, Nedlloyd Orinoco-99, Santa Giuliana-96

Reederei Claus-Peter Offen. CPO FINLAND. *N. Kemps*

Name	Flag	Year	GRT	DWT	LOA	Bm	Kts	Type	Former names
Ibn Malik	Lbr	1991	21,049	30,007	182	28	19	CC	ex Santa Barbara-07, CCNI Tokyo-07, Santa Barbara I-04, Indfex SCI-02, Santa Barbara I-01, P&O Nedlloyd Bahrain-01, Santa Barbara I-98, Santa Barbara-97, Sea Jade-97, Khaleej Bay-96, Maersk Kanagawa-95, Santa Barbara-94, Puebla-94, Santa Barbara-93
Ibn Qutaibah	Lbr	2008	22,914	28,300	186	28	21	CC	
Ibn Rushd *	Lbr	2008	22,914	28,197	186	28	21	CC	
Maersk Damascus	Deu	2002	45,803	53,081	281	32	25	CC	ex P&O Nedlloyd Palliser-06, I/a Santa Romana
Maersk Decartur	Deu	2002	45,803	53,410	281	32	25	CC	ex P&O Nedlloyd Encounter-06, I/a Santa Rebecca
Maersk Detroit	Deu	2005	54,771	66,821	294	32	25	CC	ex Santa Pelagia-05
Maersk Dieppe	Lbr	2005	54,809	67,310	294	32	25	CC	ex P&O Nedlloyd Doha-05, Santa Placida-04
Maersk Dolores	Deu	2005	54,809	67,255	294	32	25	CC	ex P&O Nedlloyd Delft-05, I/dn Santa Patricia
Maersk Dominica *	Lbr	2002	45,803	53,462	281	32	25	CC	ex Sydney Express-06, P&O Nedlloyd Pegasus-03, I/a Santa Roberta
Maersk Donegal *	Lbr	2005	54,771	67,222	294	32	25	CC	ex P&O Nedlloyd Dublin-05, I/dn Santa Paula
Maersk Douglas	Deu	2005	54,771	66,799	294	32	25	CC	ex Santa Petrissa-05
Maersk Driscoll *	Lbr	2005	54,809	67,310	294	32	25	CC	ex P&O Nedlloyd Dalian-05
Maersk Duffield	Deu	2002	45,803	52,800	281	32	25	CC	ex Columbus New Zealand-06, P&O Nedlloyd Resolution-02, I/a Santa Rosanna
Maersk Dunafare	Deu	2002	45,803	53,452	281	32	25	CC	ex P&O Nedlloyd Botany-05, I/a Santa Ricarda
Maersk Dunedin	Lbr	2005	54,809	67,247	295	32	25	CC	ex P&O Nedlloyd Detroit-05, I/a Santa Pamina
Maersk Durham	Deu	2005	54,809	67,310	294	32	25	CC	ex P&O Nedlloyd Dover-05
Maersk Ipanema	Deu	1995	36,028	45,170	246	32	24	CC	ex P&O Nedlloyd Seattle-05, Chesapeake Bay-98, Santa Ana-95
Maersk Jackson *	Lbr	2006	28,616	39,360	222	30	23	CC	ex Santa Balbina-07
Maersk Jamestown *	Lbr	2006	28,616	39,359	222	30	23	CC	ex Santa Belina-07
Maersk Semarang *	Lbr	2007	94,322	108,448	332	43	25	CC	
Maersk Surabaya	Lbr	2006	94,322	108,351	332	43	25	CC	
MOL Caledon	Deu	2005	58,289	64,519	294	32	25	CC	ex P&O Nedlloyd Livingstone-06
MOL Cullinan *	Lbr	2005	58,289	64,519	294	32	25	CC	ex P&O Nedlloyd Heemskerck-06
MSC Beijing	Lbr	2005	89,954	100,870	325	43	25	CC	
MSC Bruxelles *	Lbr	2005	107,849	110,860	337	46	25	CC	
MSC Busan	Lbr	2005	89,954	104,904	325	43	25	CC	
MSC Charleston *	Lbr	2006	89,954	105,014	325	43	25	CC	ex Santa Leopalda-06
MSC Chicago *	Lbr	2005	107,849	110,852	337	46	25	CC	
MSC Lisbon	Lbr	2007	107,849	110,697	337	46	25	CC	
MSC Marbella	Deu	2002	45,803	53,115	281	32	25	CC	ex Maersk Denton-08, P&O Nedlloyd Mairangi-06, Santa Rufina-02
MSC Roma	Lbr	2006	107,849	110,634	337	46	25	CC	
MSC Shanghai	Lbr	2005	65,483	72,064	275	40	26	CC	I/a Santa Viola
MSC Tokyo *	Lbr	2005	65,483	71,949	275	40	26	CC	I/a Santa Vanessa
MSC Toronto *	Lbr	2006	89,954	100,000	325	43	25	CC	
OOCL Korea	Deu	2001	66,500	67,796	277	40	24	CC	I/a Santa Victoria
OOCL Thailand *	Lbr	2002	65,289	67,644	277	40	24	CC	I/a Santa Virginia
San Alessio	Lbr	2008	22,914	28,142	186	28	21	CC	

Reederei Claus-Peter Offen. MSC SHANGHAI. *Guido van Driessche*

Name	Flag	Year	GRT	DWT	LOA	Bm	Kts	Type	Former names
San Amerigo *	Lbr	2008	22,914	28,186	186	28	21	CC	
San Andres *	Lbr	2008	22,914	28,300	186	28	21	CC	
San Aurelio	Lbr	2008	22,914	28,170	186	28	21	CC	
San Clemente	Lbr	1994	15,778	20,219	167	28	19	CC	ex Canmar Fortune-05, San Clemente-05, Cielo del Chile-03, San Clemente-01, Columbus Bahia-01, San Clemente-99
San Cristobal	Lbr	1995	15,859	20,156	167	28	19	CC	ex Maersk Abidjan-04, San Cristobal-01, Lykes Hawk-00, San Cristobal-99, CGM Saint Exupery-98, Equinox-97, San Cristobal-95
San Felipe	Deu	1996	15,859	20,058	167	28	19	CC	ex Puerto Limon-04, San Felipe-02, Columbus Mexico-01, Lykes Eagle-00, Ivaran Eagle-99, San Felipe-98
San Fernando	Deu	1996	15,859	20,219	167	28	19	CC	ex P&O Nedlloyd Tema-04, San Fernando-02, Lykes Condor-01, Ivaran Condor-99, San Fernando-98
San Francisco	Deu	1996	15,859	20,200	167	28	19	CC	ex Lykes Pilot-06, Maersk Apapa-04, San Francisco-01, Lykes Raven-00, Ivaran Raven-99, San Francisco-98, Contship Brasil-97, Francisco-96, San Francisco-96
San Isidro	Lbr	1993	15,778	20,326	166	28	19	CC	ex YM Fukuoka-06, Maersk Accra-05, YM Fukuoka-05, San Isidro-01, P&O Nedlloyd Lome-00 San Isidro-98
San Lorenzo	Lbr	1993	15,778	20,278	167	28	19	CC	ex YM Fukuoka-05, San Lorenzo-05, Columbus Ohio-02, Altamira-00, San Lorenzo 1-98, San Lorenzo-97
San Vicente	Lbr	1993	15,778	20,278	167	28	19	CC	ex Mercosul Palometa-08, P&O Nedlloyd Zanzibar-01, San Vicente-99, CGM Santos Dumont-98, San Vicente-97
Santa Adriana	Deu	2000	25,294	32,323	207	30	22	CC	ex P&O Nedlloyd Algoa-05, MOL Parana-02, P&O Nedlloyd Algoa-01, I/a Santa Adriana
Santa Alina	Deu	2001	25,294	32,299	207	30	22	CC	ex P&O Nedlloyd Apapa-05, MOL Santos-02, P&O Nedlloyd Apapa-01, I/a Santa Alina
Santa Annabella	Deu	2000	25,294	32,308	207	30	22	CC	ex P&O Nedlloyd Agulhas-05, MOL Paraguay-02, P&O Nedlloyd Agulhas-01, Santa Annabella-00
Santa Arabella *	Lbr	2000	25,294	32,321	207	30	22	CC	ex P&O Nedlloyd Accra-06, MOL Salvador-02, P&O Nedlloyd Accra-01, Santa Arabella-00
Santa Carlotta *	Lbr	2000	37,113	40,018	243	32	23	CC	ex P&O Nedlloyd Olinda-05, I/a Santa Carlotta
Santa Carolina *	Lbr	2000	37,113	40,125	243	32	22	CC	ex P&O Nedlloyd Surat-05, Santa Carolina-01
Santa Catalina	Deu	2001	37,113	40,102	243	32	23	CC	ex P&O Nedlloyd Dejima-05, I/a Santa Catalina
Santa Celina	Deu	2001	37,113	40,018	243	32	23	CC	ex P&O Nedlloyd Chusan-05, Santa Celina-01
Santa Cristina	Deu	2001	37,113	39,300	243	32	23	CC	ex P&O Nedlloyd Bantam-05, I/a Santa Cristina
Santa Elena I *	Lbr	1995	36,028	45,170	246	32	24	CC	ex MSC Johannesburg-07, Santa Elena-04, Maersk Rotterdam-01, New York Senator-98, Santa Elena-95
Santa Federica	Deu	1998	21,583	29,700	182	30	20	CC	ex P&O Nedlloyd Santiago-02, I/a Santa Fredericia

Reederei Claus-Peter Offen. SANTA CARLOTTA. *Phil Kempsey*

Name	Flag	Year	GRT	DWT	LOA	Bm	Kts	Type	Former names
Santa Felicita *	Lbr	1999	21,583	30,135	183	30	20	CC	ex P&O Nedlloyd Seoul-02, I/dn Santa Felicita
Santa Giannina	Lbr	1997	21,531	30,173	182	30	20	CC	ex Cala Palamos-08, P&O Nedlloyd Salsa-05, Santa Giannina-02, P&O Nedlloyd Kingston-02, I/a Santa Giannina
Santa Isabella	Lbr	1986	21,049	30,007	182	29	18	CC	ex Tiger Island-06, Sitc Manila-06, Santa Isabella-04, P&O Nedlloyd Dammam-01, Santa Isabella-99, P&O Nedlloyd Salvador-98, Santa Isabella-97, Nedlloyd van Cloon-97, ScanDutch Helvetia-89, I/a Holsten Sea
Santa Maddalena	Deu	1994	21,054	29,610	182	29	20	CC	ex Delmas Bourgainville-04, P&O Nedlloyd Hawkes Bay-03, P&O Nedlloyd Durban-02, Nedlloyd van Nassau-99, Santa Maddalena-95
Santa Monica	Lbr	1991	21,049	30,007	182	28	18	CC	ex P&O Nedlloyd Samba-05, Santa Monica I-03, P&O Nedlloyd Dubai-00, P&O Nedlloyd van Nes-99, Nedlloyd van Nes-98, Genoa Senator-95, Santa Monica-94
Southampton Express	Lbr	2002	45,803	53,328	281	32	25	CC	ex Maersk Denia-07, P&O Nedlloyd Remuera-06, I/a Santa Rafaela
Tasman Crusader *	Lbr	2007	22,914	28,179	186	28	21	CC	ex San Alfonso-07

newbuildings: ten 165,000 grt, four 158,000 grt, nine 135,000 grt, four 98,400 grt, two 93,750 grt, nine 69,000 grt, ten 50,700 grt container ships, four 180,000 dwt bulk carriers, eight 52,000 dwt tankers for 2009-12 delivery
* managed for MPC Munchmeyer Petersen & Co GmbH qv or ** managed by subsidiary Claus-Peter Offen Tankschiffreederei GmbH & Co KG

Egon Oldendorff OHG   Germany

Funnel: Grey with white 'EO' on broad blue band, or charterers colours. **Hull:** Grey, black or red with red boot-topping. **History:** Founded 1921 as Nordische Dampfer Reederei (Lillenfeld & Oldendorff) GmbH to 1936. Oldendorff Express Lines (formerly CEC) 60% owned from 2006 other 40% Flamar, Belgium. **Web:** www.oldendorff.com

Name	Flag	Year	GRT	DWT	LOA	Bm	Kts	Type	Former names
Albert Oldendorff	Lbr	2004	19,883	31,647	172	27	14	BC	
Alice Oldendorff *	Lbr	2000	28,747	48,000	190	32	14	Bu	
Austin *	Cyp	1995	39,385	75,473	225	32	14	B	ex Raffaele Juliano-07
Beatriz *	Lbr	1993	13,696	22,145	158	25	14	B	ex Dorothea Oldendorff-04
Bernhard Oldendorff	Lbr	1991	43,332	77,548	245	32	14	Bu	ex Yeoman Burn-94
Carl Oldendorff *	Lbr	2002	19,822	31,350	172	27	14	B	
Cathrin Oldendorff *	Lbr	2003	19,883	31,643	172	27	14	B	
Christoffer Oldendorff *	Lbr	1981	37,959	62,732	228	32	14	Bu	ex CSL Innovator-93, Atlantic Huron-88, Pacific Peace-86
Clipper Freeway *	Lbr	1998	18,597	29,227	181	26	14	Co	ex Freeway-07, DS Freeway-07, Mirande-04
Dorthe Oldendorff †	Lbr	1994	13,712	22,059	158	25	14	B	
E. Oldendorff *	Lbr	1983	45,777	78,488	243	32	14	Obo	ex Nobel Fountain-07, Fountain Spirit-04, Teekay Fountain-03, Bona Fountain-99, Hoegh Fountain-92
Eduard Oldendorff *	Lbr	2001	19,882	31,640	172	27	14	B	
Elisabeth Oldendorff **	Lbr	1992	13,696	22,154	158	25	14	B	
Ernst Oldendorff *	Lbr	1997	16,405	26,045	172	25	14	B	ex Jan Hus-98
Fiesta *	Bhs	1997	19,354	29,516	181	26	14	Co	ex DS Fiesta-06, Clipper Fiesta-01
Gertrude Oldendorff *	Lbr	2001	19,882	31,635	172	27	14	B	
Gisela Oldendorff *	Lbr	1997	13,781	20,100	149	23	14	B	
Gitta Oldendorff **	Pan	2005	19,883	32,833	172	27	14	B	
Gretke Oldendorff †	Lbr	1994	13,690	22,050	158	25	14	B	
Harmen Oldendorff *	Lbr	2005	39,568	69,700	225	32	14	B	
Hedwig Oldendorff *	Lbr	1984	90,747	149,863	281	54	13	Obo	ex Behemoth-05, Grouper-04, Algarrobo-02, Nord Atlantic-93, Cast Orca-84
Heinrich Oldendorff *	Lbr	2001	39,893	73,926	225	32	16	B	I/a Elbe River
Henry Oldendorff *	Lbr	1998	16,405	26,031	172	25	14	B	ex Jan Zelivsky-98
Johanna Oldendorff *	Lbr	1998	37,978	69,146	225	32	14	B	ex Sofia III-06, Aifos-03, Ever Victory-02
Lily Oldendorff *	Lbr	2003	19,883	31,350	172	27	14	B	
Lucas Oldendorff *	Lbr	2002	19,882	31,643	172	27	14	B	
Lucy Oldendorff **	Lbr	1992	13,696	22,160	157	25	14	B	ex Kikori Chief-04, Lucy Oldendorff-04
Maria Oldendorff	Lbr	2006	22,698	37,534	178	29	14	B	
Pacific Bangbin **	Pan	1986	12,283	21,649	152	24	14	B	ex Wise King-07, Royal Venture-97, White Coral-93
Pacific Bangcheng **	Pan	1999	15,137	24,383	154	26	14	B	ex Addu Sun-07, Port Star-04
Pacific Bangpu I **	Pan	1985	15,788	26,564	167	26	14	B	ex Addu Moon-07, Superius-04, City Kim-99, Vera Accorde-98
Pacific Bangshen I **	Pan	1984	12,872	21,387	153	24	13	B	ex Shan King-07, Princess Castle-96
Pacific Bangxin **	Pan	1996	14,397	24,034	154	26	13	B	ex Addu Star-07, Glory Island-04,
Pacific Chief *	Atg	1992	15,900	21,763	165	26	16	Co	ex Seaboard Discoverer-08, Tasman Discoverer-07, Henrietta Oldendorff-99, FMG Santiago-99, Henrietta Oldendorff-96, POL Asia-95

Name	Flag	Year	GRT	DWT	LOA	Bm	Kts	Type	Former names
Pacific Faithful *	Lbr	1996	19,354	29,516	181	26	14	Co	ex Christiane Oldendorff-04, Tamaya-99, Christiane Oldendorff-96
Pacific Fantasy *	Lbr	1996	19,354	29,538	181	26	14	Co	ex DS Fantasy-04, Cielo di Spagna-01, Clipper Fantasy-00, Paipote-98, Clipper Fantasy-97, Paipote-97, Clipper Fantasy-96
Pacific Fighter *	Bhs	1998	18,597	29,538	181	26	14	Co	ex Clipper Fighter-04, Dolisle-04
Pacific Freedom *	Lbr	1996	19,354	29,512	181	26	14	Co	ex Ilsabe Oldendorff-05, CSAV Livorno-02, Ilsabe Oldendorff-01, Cielo di Monfalcone-99, Andacollo-98, Ilsabe Oldendorff-97
Regina Oldendorff ‡	Lbr	2006	24,140	37,504	178	29	14	B	
Sophie Oldendorff *	Lbr	2000	41,428	70,034	225	32	14	Bu	
Tasman Chief *	Atg	1992	15,901	21,679	165	26	16	Co	ex Seaboard Adventurer-08, Tasman Adventurer-07, Helga Oldendorff-99, FMG Mexico-99, Helga Oldendorff-96, POL Europe-95
Yeoman Brook §	Lbr	1991	43,332	77,548	245	32	14	Bu	

Also operate a large number of time-chartered vessels and some operated in joint Pool with CSL Group Inc., Canada
* managed by subsidiary Oldendorff Carriers GmbH & Co. KG (formed 2001) and ** managed by Pacific King Shipping Pte Ltd, Singapore.
† managed by Oldendorff Carriers GmbH for Investeringsgruppen Danmark A/S, Denmark or ‡ for Nissen Kaiun KK, Japan
§ on time charter to Foster Yeoman Ltd until 2011.

Reederei "NORD" Klaus E Oldendorff Ltd   Cyprus

Funnel: Grey with white 'N' inside white ring on broad blue band or charterers colours. **Hull:** Dark grey with red boot-topping.
History: Founded 1964 in Germany, relocated to Cyprus in 1987. **Web:** www.rnkeo.com

Name	Flag	Year	GRT	DWT	LOA	Bm	Kts	Type	Former names
Cala Puebla	Cyp	1997	16,264	22,350	179	25	19	CC	ex Nordcoast-05, Safmarine Nahoon-02, DAL East London-02, Nordcoast-01, Alianca Parana-00, Nordcoast-00, CSAV Buenos Aires-99, Nordcoast-97
CMA CGM Aguila	Cyp	1997	24,053	27,100	206	27	20	CC	ex Nordeagle-06, Libra Houston-01, CSAV Seoul-00, Panatlantic-99, Nordeagle-97
CMA CGM Carioca	Cyp	1997	24,053	27,100	206	27	20	CC	ex Nordfalcon-04, CSAV Taipei-01, Panamerican-99, Nordfalcon-97
CMA CGM Colombie	Cyp	1997	24,053	27,100	206	27	20	CC	ex CSAV Livorno-03, Nordhawk-02, Libra Buenos Aires-01, Zim Sao Paulo-99, Panbrasil-98, l/a Nordhawk
CMA CGM Condor	Cyp	1994	14,619	20,255	165	25	19	CC	ex Cala Palamos-04, Nordpartner-01, Cielo del Cile-01, Nordpartner-99, San Miguel-96
CMA CGM Intensity	Iom	2003	25,407	33,900	207	30	22	CC	ex Nordmed-04
Libra Niteroi	Cyp	2003	25,407	33,853	207	30	22	CC	ex Nordatlantic-05, Cala Palos-04, Nordatlantic-03
Libra Patagonia	Cyp	1997	16,252	22,330	179	25	19	CC	ex Nordcloud-03, Niver Austral-99, Nordcloud-98
Nordautumn	Cyp	2008	38,332	45,309	247	32	23	CC	
Nordbaltic	Iom	2003	25,407	33,900	207	30	22	CC	ex CMA CGM Romania-08, Nordbaltic-03
Nordbay	Cyp	2007	62,241	116,104	249	44	15	T	
Nordelbe	Cyp	2001	40,605	75,259	225	32	14	B	

Reederei 'NORD' Klaus E. Oldendorff. NORDMARS. *Hans Kraijenbosch*

Name	Flag	Year	GRT	DWT	LOA	Bm	Kts	Type	Former names
Nordems	Cyp	2001	40,605	75,253	225	32	14	B	
Nordenergy	Cyp	2003	161,306	319,174	333	60	16	T	
Nordmark	Cyp	1998	57,148	89,999	244	42	15	T	
Nordmars	Cyp	2004	42,432	74,999	225	32	14	T	
Nordmerkur	Cyp	2004	42,432	74,999	225	32	14	T	
Nordmosel	Cyp	2001	40,605	75,080	225	32	14	B	
Nordneptun	Cyp	2004	42,432	74,999	225	32	14	T	
Nordpower	Cyp	2003	161,308	319,012	333	60	16	T	
Nordrhine	Cyp	2001	40,605	75,080	225	32	14	B	
Nordriver	Cyp	1997	16,252	22,420	179	25	19	CC	ex Cala Pilar-07, City of Stuttgart-02, Safmarine Inyathi-01, Nordriver-01, Pacific Eagle-01, Nordriver-00, Bogata-99, Nordriver-98
Nordsea	Deu	1996	16,264	22,386	178	25	19	CC	ex CSAV Maya-08, Nordsea-07, Nordseas-06, MOL Sprinter-04, Malacca Star-03, Nordsea-01, Nordseas-01, Pacific Voyager-01, Nordsea-00, Panaustral-98, Nordsea-97
Nordspring	Cyp	2007	38,212	45,230	247	32	23	CC	
Nordstar	Cyp	1998	16,803	23,007	185	25	19	CC	ex P&O Nedlloyd Pampas-02, Nordstar-01, Niver Austral-00, Nordstar-99, CSAV Rio Uruguay-99
Nordstrength	Cyp	1998	57,148	89,999	244	42	15	T	
Nordtrave	Cyp	2001	40,605	75,080	225	32	14	B	
Nordvenus	Lbr	2004	40,000	74,999	225	32	14	T	
Nordwelle	Cyp	2005	27,093	34,600	210	30	22	CC	
Nordweser	Cyp	2001	40,605	75,321	225	32	14	B	
Nordwinter	Cyp	2008	38,332	46,212	247	32	23	CC	
Nordwoge	Cyp	2001	26,611	34,704	210	30	22	CC	
Orange River Bridge	Cyp	2007	38,332	46,321	247	32	23	CC	ex Nordsummer-07
X-Press Khyber	Cyp	1994	16,202	22,450	179	25	19	CC	ex Nordlake-08, YM Okinawa-08, Nordlake-05, CSAV Lonquimay-98, Nordlake-96

newbuildings: four 56,000 dwt bulk carriers for 2010 delivery.
See also Nordcapital Holding GmbH & Cie KG (ER Schiffahrt GmbH & Cie KG)

D Oltmann GmbH & Co
Germany

Funnel: *Mainly in charterers colours.* **Hull:** *Dark grey with red boot-topping.* **History:** *Founded 1871.* **Web:** *www.oltmann.com*

Name	Flag	Year	GRT	DWT	LOA	Bm	Kts	Type	Former names
APL Brazil	Bhs	2004	40,952	55,461	261	32	24	CC	
MSC Bremen	Lbr	2007	54,605	67,033	294	32	25	CC	
MSC England	Bhs	2001	39,812	51,020	258	32	24	CC	ex CMA CGM Vega-07
MSC Ulsan	Bhs	2002	40,108	51,020	258	32	24	CC	
NYK Cosmos	Lbr	2006	40,952	55,483	261	32	24	CC	

newbuildings: three 74,000 grt container ships for 2009-10 delivery.
managed by Bernhard Schulte Shipmanagement (Deutschland) GmbH

Schiffahrts Oltmann Verwaltung GmbH
Germany

Funnel: *Mainly in charterers colours.* **Hull:** *Dark grey with red boot-topping.* **History:** *Founded 1962 as Rederei Gerhard Oltmann KG to 1989.* **Web:** *www.oltship.de*

Name	Flag	Year	GRT	DWT	LOA	Bm	Kts	Type	Former names
CMA CGM Bahia	Atg	2000	25,361	33,937	207	30	22	CC	ex Libra Buenos Aires-06, CMA CGM Chili-02, JPO Aquarius-01
CSAV Yokohama	Deu	2005	25,630	33,742	207	30	22	CC	ex JPO Gemini-05
Hyundai Renaissance	Lbr	2005	35,881	41,743	220	32	22	CC	ex MOL Renaissance-08, JPO Leo-05
JPO Sagittarius **	Lbr	2006	27,100	34,532	210	30	22	CC	
JPO Scorpius **	Lbr	2006	27,100	34,496	210	30	22	CC	
Maersk Dabou *	Lbr	2005	41,359	52,450	264	32	24	CC	ex Seattle Express-07, Maersk Dabou-06, P&O Nedlloyd Cardenas-05, JPO Cancer-05
Maersk Danville *	Lbr	2005	41,359	52,786	264	32	24	CC	ex P&O Nedlloyd Cardigan-05, JPO Capricornus-05
Maersk Dunbar	Lbr	2006	41,359	52,450	264	32	24	CC	ex P&O Nedlloyd Carolinas-06, JPO Libra-05
Maersk Duncan	Lbr	2006	41,359	52,786	264	32	24	CC	ex P&O Nedlloyd Carthago-06, JPO Pisces-05
MOL Dream	Atg	2001	25,361	33,900	207	30	22	CC	ex Trade Rainbow-05, TCL Challenger-02, JPO Aries-01
MSC Caracas	Deu	1998	25,361	33,919	207	30	21	CC	ex Montebello-06, Anika Oltmann-99, Montebello-99, Anika Oltmann-98
Ute Oltmann	Deu	1998	25,359	33,964	207	30	20	CC	ex CP Rangitoto-06, Contship Rangitoto-05, Cielo di San Francisco-05, Ute Oltmann-99

newbuildings: two 50,500 grt, four 42,000 grt container ships and two 57,000 dwt bulk carriers for 2009-10 delivery.
** managed for HCI Capital AG or ** for HCI Hanseatische Schiffstreuhand GmbH.*

Olympic Shipping and Management SA

Greece

Funnel: Orange, large white disc containing blue/yellow pennant flag with five interlocking coloured rings above and below.
Hull: Black with red boot-topping. **History:** Founded 1951 as Olympic Maritime SA to 1992. **Web:** www.onassis.gr

Name	Flag	Year	GRT	DWT	LOA	Bm	Kts	Type	Former names
Calliroe Patronicola	Grc	1985	17,879	29,608	183	23	15	B	
Hawk	Mhl	2000	159,414	306,324	335	58	15	T	
Olympic Faith	Mhl	1991	81,192	147,457	274	45	14	T	
Olympic Flag	Grc	2004	80,591	155,099	274	47	16	T	
Olympic Flair	Grc	1991	81,192	147,396	274	45	14	T	
Olympic Future	Grc	2004	80,591	155,039	274	47	16	T	
Olympic Legacy	Grc	1996	160,129	302,789	332	58	14	T	
Olympic Legend	Grc	2003	160,083	308,500	333	60	15	T	
Olympic Liberty	Grc	2003	160,083	304,992	333	60	15	T	
Olympic Loyalty	Grc	1993	160,129	303,184	332	58	15	T	
Olympic Melody	Grc	1984	17,879	29,640	182	23	14	B	
Olympic Mentor	Grc	1984	17,879	29,693	182	23	14	B	ex Patricia R-88, Calliroe Patronicola-84
Olympic Merit	Grc	1985	17,879	29,611	182	23	14	B	
Olympic Miracle	Pan	1984	17,879	29,670	182	23	14	B	
Olympic Serenity	Grc	1991	52,127	96,733	232	42	13	T	
Olympic Spirit II	Grc	1997	52,197	96,773	232	42	13	T	
Olympic Sponsor	Grc	1994	52,196	96,547	232	42	13	T	

Owned by Alexander S. Onassis Public Benefit Foundation and managed by subsidiary Springfield Shipping Co (Panama) SA, Greece.

Orient Overseas International Ltd

Hong Kong (China)

Orient Overseas Container Line Ltd/Hong Kong (China)

Funnel: Yellow with red and gold flower symbol. **Hull:** Light grey with red 'OOCL', orange with white 'OOCL' or black with red boot-topping. **History:** Parent founded in 1946 as CY Tung Group and OOCL formed in 1969. CY Tung acquired Furness, Withy & Co in 1980, but resold to Rudolf A Oetker in 1990. **Web:** www.oocl.com

Name	Flag	Year	GRT	DWT	LOA	Bm	Kts	Type	Former names
China Act *	Sgp	1995	77,135	151,688	270	43	15	B	
China Fortune *	Sgp	1992	77,096	149,402	270	43	15	B	
China Peace *	Hkg	2005	88,930	174,413	289	45	14	B	
China Progress *	Hkg	2006	88,900	174,400	289	45	14	B	
China Prosperity *	Sgp	1986	83,474	151,013	288	45	14	B	
OOCL Ability †	Pan	1997	16,750	24,346	183	28	19	CC	
OOCL Acclaim †	Pan	1997	16,750	23,850	183	28	18	CC	
OOCL Ambition †	Pan	1997	16,750	23,850	183	28	18	CC	
OOCL America	Hkg	1995	66,047	67,741	276	40	24	CC	
OOCL Antwerp	Pan	2006	66,462	66,940	281	40	25	CC	
OOCL Asia	Hkg	2006	89,097	99,602	323	43	25	CC	
OOCL Atlanta	Hkg	2005	89,097	99,620	323	43	25	CC	
OOCL Australia	Hkg	2006	41,479	52,217	263	32	24	CC	
OOCL Belgium	Hkg	1998	39,174	40,972	245	32	21	CC	
OOCL Britain	Hkg	1996	66,046	67,958	276	40	24	CC	
OOCL Busan	Hkg	2008	40,168	50,567	260	32	23	CC	
OOCL California	Hkg	1995	66,046	67,765	276	40	24	CC	
OOCL Chicago	Hkg	2000	66,677	67,278	277	40	25	CC	
OOCL China	Hkg	1996	66,046	67,625	276	41	24	CC	
OOCL Dubai	Hkg	2006	66,462	66,940	281	40	25	CC	
OOCL Europe	Hkg	2006	89,097	99,618	323	43	25	CC	
OOCL Fair	Hkg	1987	40,980	44,448	241	32	21	CC	ex Oriental Fair-89
OOCL Faith	Hkg	1985	40,980	44,448	241	32	21	CC	ex Veracruz-98, TMM Veracruz-97, Vera Cruz-96, OOCL Faith-96, Oriental Faith-89
OOCL Fidelity	Hkg	1987	40,980	44,477	241	32	21	CC	ex Brooklyn Bridge-91
OOCL Fortune	Hkg	1985	40,978	44,433	241	32	21	CC	ex Oriental Fortune-89
OOCL Freedom	Hkg	1985	40,978	44,452	241	32	21	CC	ex Eagle Malaysia-98, OOCL Freedom-96, Oriental Freedom-89
OOCL Friendship	Hkg	1987	41,664	45,863	241	32	22	CC	ex Anahuac-98, Eagle Anahuac-97, OOCL Friendship-96, Oriental Friendship-89
OOCL Hamburg	Hkg	2004	89,097	99,618	323	43	25	CC	
OOCL Hong Kong	Hkg	1996	66,046	67,637	276	40	24	CC	
OOCL Houston	Hkg	2007	40,168	50,585	260	32	23	CC	
OOCL Italy †	Hkg	2007	66,462	66,940	281	40	25	CC	
OOCL Japan	Hkg	1995	66,046	67,752	276	40	24	CC	
OOCL Kaohsiung †	Hkg	2006	66,462	66,940	281	40	25	CC	
OOCL Kobe	Hkg	2007	40,168	50,554	260	32	23	CC	
OOCL Kuala Lumpur †	Hkg	2007	66,462	66,940	281	40	25	CC	
OOCL Long Beach	Hkg	2003	89,097	99,508	323	43	25	CC	
OOCL Melbourne †	Hkg	2003	34,610	43,093	235	32	22	CC	
OOCL Montreal	Hkg	2003	55,994	47,840	294	32	24	CC	

Orient Overseas International. OOCL ASIA. *Allan Ryszka Onions*

Orient Overseas International. OOCL BUSAN. *Phil Kempsey*

Orient Overseas International. OOCL FORTUNE. *Allan Ryszka Onions*

179

Name	Flag	Year	GRT	DWT	LOA	Bm	Kts	Type	Former names
OOCL Netherlands	Hkg	1997	66,016	67,700	276	40	24	CC	
OOCL Ningbo	Hkg	2004	89,000	99,500	323	43	25	CC	
OOCL Oakland †	Pan	2007	66,462	66,940	281	40	25	CC	
OOCL Osaka †	Pan	2003	34,610	43,093	235	32	22	CC	
OOCL Qingdao	Hkg	2004	89,097	99,600	323	43	25	CC	
OOCL Rotterdam	Hkg	2004	89,097	99,500	323	43	25	CC	
OOCL San Francisco	Hkg	2000	66,677	67,286	277	40	25	CC	
OOCL Shenzhen	Hkg	2003	89,097	99,518	323	43	25	CC	
OOCL Singapore	Hkg	1997	66,086	67,480	276	40	24	CC	
OOCL Southampton	Hkg	2007	89,097	99,678	323	43	25	CC	
OOCL Sydney †	Sgp	2003	34,610	43,093	235	32	22	CC	
OOCL Texas	Hkg	2008	40,168	50,610	260	32	23	CC	
OOCL Tianjin	Hkg	2005	89,097	99,500	323	43	25	CC	
OOCL Tokyo	Hkg	2007	89,097	99,706	323	43	25	CC	
OOCL Vancouver †	Pan	2006	66,462	66,940	281	40	25	CC	
OOCL Xiamen †	Pan	2003	34,610	43,093	235	32	22	CC	
OOCL Yokohama	Hkg	2007	40,168	50,634	260	32	23	CC	
OOCL Zhoushan	Hkg	2006	41,479	52,214	263	32	24	CC	

newbuildings: six 90,700 grt, four 89,000 grt and ten 40,500 grt container ships for 2009-11 delivery.
* owned by subsidiary Chinese Maritime Transport Ltd (formed 1946 and merged with Associated Transport Inc in 2001), Taiwan or † on charter from various Japanese owners or finance houses and managed by Anglo-Eastern Shipmanagement, by Fleet Management Ltd, Hong Kong, by Orient Marine Co Ltd or by Bernhard Schulte Shipmanagement (China) Co Ltd.

Associated Maritime Co (Hong Kong) Ltd/Hong Kong (China)

History: *Formed 1946 jointly by CY Tung as Island Navigation Corp (until 1978) and by Hong Kong Ming Wah Shipping Co. Ltd, Hong Kong (founded 1980 and wholly owned by China Merchants Group).* **Web:** *none found.*

Name	Flag	Year	GRT	DWT	LOA	Bm	Kts	Type	Former names
New Ability *	Lbr	2008	55,898	105,381	229	42	14	T	
New Ace *	Lbr	1987	52,967	88,878	244	40	14	T	ex Atlantic Ace-92
New Activity *	Lbr	2008	55,898	105,342	229	42	14	T	
New Advance *	Lbr	2007	56,172	105,544	229	42	14	T	
New Alliance	Lbr	1998	56,311	106,118	241	42	14	T	
New Ambition *	Lbr	1987	52,967	88,761	244	40	14	T	ex Ambition-91
New Amity	Lbr	1998	56,311	106,120	241	42	14	T	
New Argosy *	Lbr	1987	52,967	88,782	244	40	14	T	ex Atlantic Argosy-92
New Century *	Lbr	2004	156,973	299,031	330	60	14	T	
New Fortuner *	Lbr	1992	78,958	146,041	277	44	14	T	
New Spirit *	Lbr	2005	156,973	298,972	330	60	14	T	
New Valor	Lbr	1992	156,317	281,598	328	57	13	T	
New Venture *	Lbr	1992	156,307	291,640	328	57	13	T	
New Victory *	Lbr	1993	156,307	291,613	328	57	14	T	
New Vitality *	Lbr	1993	153,808	290,691	330	56	15	T	
Pacific Challenger	Hkg	1995	79,755	149,210	270	44	14	B	
Pacific Enterprise	Hkg	1996	79,542	149,363	270	44	14	B	

newbuildings: two 157,000 grt tankers for 2009 delivery.
Owned by OOIL subsidiary Island Navigation Corp International Ltd, Hong Kong (formed 1978 as Golden Peak Maritime Agencies Ltd to 1983) and * managed for Hong Kong Ming Wah Shipping Co Ltd.

Overseas Shipholding Group Inc   USA

Funnel: *Blue with white 'OSG' ('S' having waves in lower part), black top.* **Hull:** *Black with red boot-topping.* **History:** *Formed 1969 Acquired Stelmar Shipping in 2005.* **Web:** *www.osg.com*

Name	Flag	Year	GRT	DWT	LOA	Bm	Kts	Type	Former names
Al Gattara (st) §	Mhl	2007	136,410	106,898	315	50	19	Lng	
Al Gharrafa (st) §	Mhl	2008	136,410	107,000	315	50	19	Lng	
Al Hamla (st) §	Mhl	2008	136,410	106,983	315	50	19	Lng	
Alaskan Explorer †	Usa	2005	110,693	193,049	287	50	15	T	
Alaskan Frontier †	Usa	2004	110,693	193,049	287	50	15	T	
Alaskan Legend †	Usa	2006	110,693	193,048	287	50	15	T	
Alaskan Navigator †	Usa	2005	110,693	193,048	287	50	15	T	
Cabo Hellas *	Mhl	2003	40,038	69,636	228	32	14	T	
Cabo Sounion *	Mhl	2004	40,038	69,636	228	32	14	T	
Overseas Acadia *	Mhl	2008	62,775	113,005	250	44		T	
Overseas Alcesmar	Mhl	2004	30,018	46,215	183	32	14	T	ex Alcesmar-06
Overseas Alcmar	Mhl	2004	30,018	46,245	183	32	14	T	ex Alcmar-06
Overseas Allenmar	Mhl	1988	25,740	41,750	182	30	14	T	ex Allenmar-05, Petrobulk Challenger-01, Osprey Challenger-96, Pacific Challenger-94
Overseas Ambermar	Usa	2002	23,843	35,970	183	27	14	T	ex Ambermar-05
Overseas Andromar	Mhl	2004	30,018	46,195	183	32	14	T	ex Andromar-06
Overseas Ania **	Mhl	1994	53,341	94,847	245	42	14	T	ex Ania-07
Overseas Ann **	Mhl	2001	157,883	309,327	335	58	15	T	
Overseas Antigmar	Mhl	2004	30,018	46,168	183	32	14	T	ex Antigmar-06

Name	Flag	Year	GRT	DWT	LOA	Bm	Kts	Type	Former names
Overseas Ariadmar	Mhl	2004	30,018	46,205	183	32	14	T	ex Ariadmar-06
Overseas Atalmar	Mhl	2004	30,018	46,177	183	32	15	T	ex Atalmar-05
Overseas Athens	Mhl	1987	24,584	39,729	193	32	14	T	ex City University-05, Ocean Challenger-93
Overseas Beryl *	Mhl	1994	53,341	94,797	245	42	14	T	ex Beryl-06
Overseas Camar	Mhl	1988	26,113	45,372	172	32	14	T	ex Camar-05, Petrobulk Cougar-01
Overseas Capemar	Mhl	1988	23,127	37,615	175	30	15	T	ex Capemar-05, Petrobulk Cape-01, Osprey Cape-96, Telaga Ayu-93, Creation-91, l/a Atlantic Chivalry
Overseas Cathy **	Mhl	2004	62,371	112,700	250	44	14	T	
Overseas Chicago (st) †	Usa	1977	44,869	90,638	273	32	16	T	
Overseas Chris **	Mhl	2001	157,883	308,700	335	58	15	T	
Overseas Cleliamar *	Mhl	1993	38,653	68,600	226	32	13	T	ex Cleliamar-05, Double Pride-98, l/a Chemoil Pride
Overseas Colmar	Mhl	1987	24,584	39,729	193	32	14	T	ex Colmar-05, Ocean Conqueror-93
Overseas Diligence (gt) ‡	Usa	1977	22,761	39,959	199	29	14	T	ex Diligence-07, Chevron Louisana-98
Overseas Eliane *	Mhl	1994	53,341	94,813	245	42	14	T	ex Eliane-06
Overseas Equatorial *	Mhl	1997	156,880	273,539	330	58	15	T	
Overseas Ermar	Mhl	1989	22,838	34,999	186	27	14	T	ex Ermar-05, Petrobulk Power-01, Torm Helene-90
Overseas Everglades *	Mhl	2008	62,775	114,000	250	44		T	
Overseas Fran *	Mhl	2001	62,385	112,118	250	44	14	T	
Overseas Fulmar	Mhl	1989	25,368	39,521	182	31	15	T	ex Fulmar-05, Kobe Spirit-93
Overseas Galena Bay ‡	Usa	1982	28,341	50,920	201	32	14	T	ex S/R Galena Bay-06, Chesapeake Trader-01
Overseas Goldmar *	Mhl	2002	40,343	69,684	228	32	14	T	ex Goldmar-05, l/a LMZ Mandi
Overseas Houston ‡	Usa	2007	29,242	46,815	183	32	14	T	
Overseas Integrity (gt) ‡	Usa	1975	22,761	39,847	198	29	14	T	ex Integrity-08, Chevron Oregon-99, Integrity-99, Chevron Oregon-97
Overseas Jacamar	Pan	1999	60,804	104,901	247	42	15	T	ex Jacamar-06
Overseas Jademar *	Mhl	2002	40,343	69,697	228	32	14	T	ex Jademar-05
Overseas Jamar	Mhl	1988	26,113	44,978	172	32	14	T	ex Jamar-05, Petrobulk Jaguar-01
Overseas Josefa Camejo *	Mhl	2001	62,385	112,200	250	44	14	T	
Overseas Joyce	Mhl	1987	48,017	16,141	269	42	14	V	
Overseas Kimolos	Mhl	2008	30,010	51,218	183	32	14	T	
Overseas Limar *	Pan	1996	28,357	46,170	183	32	14	T	ex Limar-05, Osprey Lyra-01
Overseas London *	Mhl	2000	79,751	152,923	269	46	15	T	ex Ottoman Dignity-08
Overseas Long Beach ‡	Usa	2007	29,242	42,994	183	32	14	T	
Overseas Los Angeles ‡	Usa	2007	29,242	46,817	183	32	14	T	l/a Overseas San Francisco
Overseas Luxmar ‡	Usa	1997	28,357	46,162	183	32	14	T	ex Luxmar-05, Petrobulk Pollux-01
Overseas Luzon	Mhl	2006	42,403	74,908	228	32	14	T	ex Amalia Jacob-07
Overseas Maremar **	Usa	1998	28,400	47,225	183	32	15	T	ex Maremar-05, Alam Belia-02
Overseas Mulan *	Mhl	2002	161,233	319,029	333	60	16	T	
Overseas Nedimar	Mhl	1996	28,326	43,999	183	32	14	T	ex Nedimar-05
Overseas New Orleans ‡	Usa	1983	24,816	43,644	201	27	15	T	ex Exxon Yorktown-89, Hunter Armistead-84
Overseas New York ‡	Usa	2008	29,242	46,810	183	32	14	T	
Overseas Newcastle *	Mhl	2001	82,250	164,626	274	50	15	T	ex Besiktas-07

Overseas Shipholding Group. OVERSEAS CAPEMAR. *N. Kemps*

Name	Flag	Year	GRT	DWT	LOA	Bm	Kts	Type	Former names
Overseas Palawan	Mhl	2008	42,010	73,400	229	32		T	
Overseas Pearlmar *	Mhl	2002	40,043	69,697	228	32	14	T	ex Pearlmar-05
Overseas Petromar	Mhl	2001	23,740	35,768	183	27	14	T	ex Petromar-05, I/a Nordafrika
Overseas Philadelphia ‡	Usa	1982	21,446	43,648	201	27	14	T	ex Exxon Princeton-89, Eileen Ingram-84
Overseas Polys *	Mhl	1993	38,653	68,623	226	32	14	T	ex Polys-05, Double Glory-97
Overseas Portland *	Mhl	2001	62,385	112,139	250	44	14	T	
Overseas Primar	Mhl	1988	25,368	39,538	182	31	14	T	ex Primar-05, BP Advocate-93, I/a Onomichi Spirit
Overseas Puget Sound ‡	Usa	1983	27,894	50,860	201	32	14	T	ex Puget Sound-06, S/R Puget Sound-04, Potomac Trader-00
Overseas Rebecca **	Mhl	1994	53,341	94,872	245	42	14	T	ex Rebecca-07
Overseas Regal **	Mhl	1997	164,371	309,966	330	58	16	T	ex Regal Unity-07
Overseas Reginamar	Mhl	2004	42,307	69,999	228	32	14	T	ex Reginamar-05
Overseas Reinemar	Mhl	2004	42,307	70,313	228	32	14	T	ex Reinemar-05
Overseas Reymar *	Mhl	2004	40,038	69,636	228	32	14	T	ex Reymar-05
Overseas Rimar	Mhl	1998	28,357	46,162	183	32	14	T	ex Rimar-05, Petrobulk Sirius-01
Overseas Rosalyn *	Mhl	2003	161,233	317,972	333	60	15	T	
Overseas Rosemar *	Mhl	2002	40,343	69,697	228	32	14	T	ex Rosemar-05
Overseas Rubymar *	Mhl	2002	40,343	69,697	228	32	14	T	ex Rubymar-05
Overseas Sakura	Mhl	2001	159,397	298,641	333	60	15	T	ex Sakura I-06, Berge Sakura-01
Overseas Serifos	Mhl	2008	30,010	51,257	183	32	14	T	
Overseas Shirley *	Mhl	2001	62,385	112,056	250	44	14	T	
Overseas Sifnos	Mhl	2008	30,010	51,225	183	32	14	T	
Overseas Silvermar *	Mhl	2002	40,343	69,609	228	32	14	T	ex Overseas-05, I/a LMZ Zacvi
Overseas Sophie **	Mhl	2003	62,371	112,700	250	44	14	T	
Overseas Sovereign *	Mhl	1996	164,371	309,892	330	58	16	T	ex Sovereign Unity-06
Overseas Takamar	Pan	1998	60,504	103,244	247	42	15	T	ex Takamar-06, P. Alliance-01
Overseas Tanabe *	Mhl	2002	159,383	298,561	333	60	16	T	ex Tanabe-07
Overseas Texas City ‡	Usa	2008	29,242	46,801	183	32	14	T	
Overseas Visayas	Mhl	2006	42,403	74,933	228	32	14	T	ex Carl Jacob-07
Overseas Yellowstone *	Mhl	2008	62,775	112,990	250	44		T	
Overseas Yosemite *	Mhl	2009	62,800	113,000	250	44		T	
Prince									
William Sound † (st)	Usa	1975	64,340	123,936	268	41	17	T	
Raphael *	Mhl	2000	157,883	308,700	335	58	15	T	
Tembek §	Mhl	2007	136,410	106,896	315	50		Lng	
TI Africa *	Mhl	2002	234,006	441,893	380	68	16	T	ex Hellespont Metropolis-04
TI Oceania *	Mhl	2002	234,006	441,585	380	68	16	T	ex Hellespont Fairfax-04

newbuildings: six 73,500 dwt, two 52,000 dwt and three 39,000 dwt tankers for 2009-11 delivery.
owned by OSG Ship Management (GR)Ltd, Greece (formerly Stelmar Tankers Management Ltd to 2005) or * by OSG Ship Management (UK) Ltd (formerly Souter Hamlet Ltd to 1981 and Souter Shipping Ltd to 2001)
** managed by Tanker Management Ltd, UK for Double Hull Tankers Inc, Channel Islands (formerly owned by OSG from 2005 until 2007)
† managed by subsidiary Alaska Tanker Co. LLC (formed jointly with Keystone Shipping Co, USA and BP Shipping Ltd, UK)
‡ managed by OSG Ship Management Inc, USA or § by Bernhard Schulte Shipmanagement (IOM) Ltd.
See also Navion ASA (under Teekay) and Tanker International Pool under CMB (Euronav Luxembourg SA).

Pacific International Lines. KOTA LATIF. *Hans Kraijenbosch*

Name	Flag	Year	GRT	DWT	LOA	Bm	Kts	Type	Former names

Pacific International Lines (Pte) Ltd — Singapore

Funnel: *Red with black 'PIL' on broad white band.* **Hull:** *Black or grey with red boot-topping.* **History:** *Formed 1967.*
Web: *www.pilship.com*

Name	Flag	Year	GRT	DWT	LOA	Bm	Kts	Type	Former names
CSAV Laja *	Sgp	2008	41,482	50,638	261	32	24	CC	ex PST Valour-08
CSAV Lauca *	Sgp	2008	39,906	50,600	261	32	24	CC	
Kota Abadi	Hkg	1984	16,430	21,888	166	27	18	CC	ex Merkur Sea-07, MSC Santiago-00, Merkur Sea-99, CSAV Ranco-98, City of Glasgow-97, Merkur Sea-93, CMB Merkur-91, Nedlloyd Himalaya-90, Merkur Sea-89, Dutch Senator-89, Ville d'Uranus-87, Merkur Sea-86
Kota Ganteng	Hkg	2002	28,676	37,087	227	32	22	CC	
Kota Gemar	Hkg	2002	28,676	37,115	227	32	22	CC	
Kota Gembira	Hkg	2002	28,676	37,114	227	32	22	CC	
Kota Gunawan	Hkg	2003	28,676	37,100	227	32	22	CC	
Kota Kado *	Sgp	2005	31,070	39,916	233	32	22	CC	
Kota Kamil	Sgp	2006	31,070	39,400	233	32	22	CC	
Kota Karim	Sgp	2006	31,070	39,763	233	32	22	CC	
Kota Kaya *	Sgp	2006	31,700	39,400	233	32	22	CC	
Kota Lagu	Sgp	2006	39,906	50,689	261	32	24	CC	
Kota Lahir	Sgp	2006	39,906	52,000	261	32	24	CC	
Kota Laju	Sgp	2007	39,906	52,000	261	32	24	CC	
Kota Lambai	Sgp	2008	39,906	50,596	261	32	24	CC	
Kota Lambang	Sgp	2008	39,906	50,596	261	32	24	CC	
Kota Latif	Sgp	2007	39,906	52,000	261	32	24	CC	
PST Victory *	Sgp	2009	41,482	50,600	261	32	24	CC	

newbuildings: four 76,000 grt, seven more 39,900 grt and seven 21,000 grt container ships for 2009-10 delivery.
* owned by subsidiary PST Management Pte Ltd, Singapore (founded 2006 - www.pacificshippingtrust.com)
See chartered ships with 'Kota' prefix in index. Only larger vessels are listed, combined fleet is 85 mainly Far East container feeder ships.

Papachristidis Ltd — UK

Funnel: *Blue with broad above narrow blue bands, interrupted by blue 'ФВП' within blue ring on white disc.* **Hull:** *White with red boot-topping.* **History:** *Founded 1981 as Papachristidis (UK) Ltd to 1988.* **Web:** *www.hellespont.com*

Name	Flag	Year	GRT	DWT	LOA	Bm	Kts	Type	Former names
Hellespont Pride	Mhl	2006	42,010	73,727	229	32	14	T	
Hellespont Progress	Mhl	2006	42,010	73,727	229	32	14	T	
Hellespont Promise	Mhl	2006	42,010	73,669	229	32	14	T	
Hellespont Prosperity	Mhl	2006	42,010	73,715	229	32	14	T	
Hellespont Protector	Mhl	2006	42,010	73,821	229	32	14	T	
Hellespont Providence	Mhl	2006	42,010	73,784	229	32	14	T	
Hellespont Tatina *	Mhl	1999	56,324	105,535	239	42	14	T	ex Minerva Anna-04, Pine Venture-02
Hellespont Trader	Mhl	1996	79,832	148,435	269	46	15	T	ex Sea Star-05
Hellespont Trinity	Mhl	1996	80,637	148,017	274	48	14	T	ex Marina M-05
Hellespont Triumph	Lbr	1998	81,565	157,406	274	48	14	T	
Hellespont Trooper	Mhl	1996	80,637	147,916	274	48	14	T	ex Spetses-05
Hellespont Trust	Lbr	1999	80,668	147,262	274	48	14	T	

Operated by Hellespont Hammonia GmbH & Co KG, Germany and * managed for Salamon AG, Germany

Papachristidis Ltd . HELLESPONT PROPERITY. *N. Kemps*

Reederei Stefan Patjens GmbH & Co KG   Germany

Funnel: *Charterers colours.* **Hull:** *Various.* **History:** Founded 2000 as *Reederei Stefan Patjens until 2006.*
Web: *www.reederei-patjens.de*

Name	Flag	Year	GRT	DWT	LOA	Bm	Kts	Type	Former names
Maersk Drummond	Lbr	2006	53,453	57,000	294	32	23	CC	I/a Serena
Maersk Drury	Lbr	2006	53,453	57,000	294	32	23	CC	
Maersk Dryden	Lbr	2006	53,453	57,000	294	32	23	CC	I/a Herma
Maersk Dubrovnik	Lbr	2006	53,453	57,000	294	32	23	CC	
Meta	Lbr	2001	32,322	39,300	211	32	22	CC	ex Maersk Perth-06, I/a Meta
OOCL Bangkok	Lbr	2000	32,322	39,300	211	32	22	CC	ex Heike-07, Maersk Pelepas-06, Safmarine Ibhayi-05, Maersk Pelepas-03, Heike-00
OOCL Keelung	Lbr	2000	32,322	39,300	211	32	22	CC	ex Alexandra P-07, Maersk Plymouth-06, Alexandra-00
OOCL Mumbai	Lbr	2001	32,322	39,300	211	32	22	CC	ex Liwia-07, Safmarine Ikapa-06, MSC Canada-03, Liwia-02

newbuildings: 14,000 grt container ship for 2009 delivery.

Dr Peters GmbH & Co KG   Germany

Funnel: *Charterers colours.* **Hull:** *Various former owners or charterers colours.* **History:** *KG investment fund founded in 1960 as Dr Peters GmbH to 1999.* **Web:** *www.drpeters.com*

Name	Flag	Year	GRT	DWT	LOA	Bm	Kts	Type	Former names
Apollo Glory **	Pan	1997	159,422	309,636	333	58	14	T	ex C. Bright-07
Ashna	Mhl	1999	156,417	301,438	330	58	15	T	ex Nordbay-04
Artemis Glory **	Pan	2006	157,844	306,507	332	58	15	T	
Bahamas Spirit ††	Bhs	1996	57,947	107,261	247	42	17	T	ex Sanko Trader-01
Bruno Salamon #	Pan	1998	38,431	73,965	225	32	14	B	ex DS Excellent-01, Ever Excellent-01
Cape Banks †	Deu	1997	21,162	33,540	179	25	14	T	ex Chembulk Hong Kong-02, Cape Banks-97
Cape Bear †	Deu	1997	21,165	33,540	179	25	14	T	ex Chembulk Vancouver-02, Cape Bear-97
Cape Hatteras *	Cyp	1992	10,396	12,854	147	24	17	CC	ex P&O Nedlloyd Inca-05, Cape Hatteras-03, Cala Panama-03, Cape Hatteras-02, Maersk Cebu-00, Cape Hatteras-98, Eagle Dawn-98, Cape Hatteras-95, ACX Iris-95, Cape Hatteras-93
Cape Henry *	Lbr	1992	10,376	12,835	147	24	17	CC	ex Safmarine Athi-02, Cape Henry-02, Avon-98, Halla Liberty-98, Kinabalu-97, Tiger Ocean-96, ACX Aster-95, Ratana Manee-94, TSL Bravo-93, Cape Henry-92
Cape Horn I *	Lbr	1992	10,396	12,854	147	24	17	CC	ex APL Quito-08, MOL Brasilia-07, Cala Porlamar-03, Cape Horn I-02, Otway-99, Maersk Davao-99, Cape Horn I-98, Eagle Star -98, Cape Horn I-97, Maersk La Paz-96, Cape Horn-94, TSL Gallant-94, Cape Horn-92
Cape Norman *	Mhl	1998	17,285	22,148	175	27	20	CC	ex TS Kelang-08, YM Mumbai-07, Cape Norman-05, Hong Kong Star-05, Cape Norman-02, Tiger Breeze-02, Cape Norman-01, Sea-Land Europe-99, Maersk Ankara-99, Cape Norman-98

Reederei Stefan Patjens. META. *Allan Ryszka Onions*

Name	Flag	Year	GRT	DWT	LOA	Bm	Kts	Type	Former names
Cape Race *	Lbr	1993	29,912	35,071	201	32	20	CC	ex MSC Perth-05, Cape Race-03, MSC Argentina-02, Cape Race-01, CSAV Callao-99, Copiapo-98, Jean Bosco-95, Yucatan-94, Jean Bosco-93
Cape Scott *	Lbr	1997	10,197	13,623	151	24	18	CC	ex P&O Nedlloyd Thekwini-06, Cape Scott-02, Independent Leader-99, l/a Cape Scott
Cape Spear *	Lbr	1998	10,925	13,623	151	24	18	CC	ex MSC Coimbra-03, Cape Spear-01
Cape Spencer *	Lbr	1996	10,925	13,623	151	24	18	CC	ex Emirates Karan-08, Cape Spencer-07, TS Hongkong-07, Cape Spencer-03, Fanal Merchant-00, Grafton-99, Cape Spencer-99
Carl Mesem #	Pan	1999	38,431	74,001	225	32	14	B	
Deja Bhum *	Lbr	1996	10,917	13,700	151	24	18	CC	ex Cape Sable-05
DS Performer †	Deu	2000	61,764	109,693	245	42	15	T	ex Peter Maersk-05
DS Power †	Deu	1999	61,764	109,354	245	42	15	T	ex Paula Maersk-05
Eagle Excellence *	Lbr	1995	17,285	22,148	175	27	20	CC	ex Cape Natal-96
Ernst Salamon ‡	Lbr	1999	38,888	74,002	225	32	14	B	ex Far Eastern Queen-01
Eupen §	Lux	1999	23,952	29,121	180	27	16	Lpg	
Ever Shining #	Pan	1999	39,052	74,345	225	32	14	B	
Front Chief †	Bhs	1999	157,863	311,224	334	58	15	T	
Front Commander	Bhs	1999	157,863	311,168	334	58	15	T	
Front Commodore †	Lbr	2000	159,397	298,620	333	60	15	T	ex Stena Commodore-01
Front Crown	Bhs	1999	157,863	311,176	334	58	15	T	ex Front President-99
Front Eagle †	Bhs	2002	160,904	309,064	333	58	15	T	l/a Moseagle
Front Melody †	Lbr	2001	79,525	150,500	272	46	14	T	
Front Symphony †	Lbr	2001	79,525	150,500	272	46	14	T	
Front Tina	Lbr	2000	159,463	298,824	333	60	16	T	
Front Warrior	Bhs	1998	79,669	153,181	269	46	14	T	
Gertrud Salamon ‡	Pan	2000	38,888	74,078	225	32	14	B	ex Far Eastern Media-01
Hyundai Dominion *	Lbr	2001	74,373	60,494	304	40	26	CC	
Hyundai Kingdom *	Lbr	2001	74,373	80,551	304	40	26	CC	
Hyundai National *	Lbr	2001	74,373	60,494	304	40	26	CC	
Hyundai Patriot *	Lbr	2001	74,373	60,551	304	40	26	CC	
Hyundai Republic *	Lbr	2001	74,373	80, 596	304	40	26	CC	
Kiowa Spirit ††	Bhs	1999	62,619	113,334	253	44	14	T	ex Bona Valiant-99
Koa Spirit ††	Bhs	1999	62,619	113,334	253	44	14	T	ex Bona Verity-99
Leo Glory	Pan	2003	160,100	309,233	333	58	15	T	ex Crude Sun-06, Violando-05
Maria Salamon ‡	Pan	2001	38,888	74,117	225	32	14	B	ex Far Eastern Glory-01
Mercury Glory **	Pan	2001	157,831	298,990	332	58	15	T	
Neptune Glory **	Pan	1998	156,716	299,127	332	58	15	T	
Pluto Glory **	Pan	2001	157,831	298,911	332	58	15	T	
Saturn Glory **	Pan	1998	156,397	298,982	332	58	15	T	
Sea Fortune 1	Sgp	2003	159,730	299,097	333	60	15	T	ex Sea Fortune-06
Sanko Venture	Mhl	2002	39,272	70,392	229	32	15	T	ex Stena Venture-07, l/a Sanko Venture
Sunlight Venture	Mhl	2003	39,272	69,910	229	37	15	T	
Titan Glory **	Pan	2000	159,187	308,491	333	58	14	T	
TS Osaka *	Lbr	1997	10,925	13,741	151	24	18	CC	ex Cape Sorrell-03, Independent Concept-99, Cape Sorrell-97
Willi Salamon ‡	Lbr	2000	38,888	74,005	225	32	14	B	ex Far Eastern Harvest-01
Younara Glory **	Pan	2004	161,235	320,051	333	60	14	T	

newbuildings: four 176,000 dwt bulk carriers and two 297,000 dwt tankers for 2009-11 delivery.
*Owned by subsidiary DS-Rendite-Fonds GmbH & Co (formed 2003) or managed by * DS Schiffahrt GmbH & Co KG (formed 2001) with vessels managed by previous owners/operators including ** Northern Marine Management (Deutschland) GmbH, † International Tanker Management Holding Ltd, UAE, †† Teekay Shipping (USA) Inc qv, § Exmar NV, Belgium qv, ‡ EMI Schiffahrts GmbH, # First Steamship (Germany) GmbH.*
Also see managed vessels under Reederei F Laeisz GmbH and Oskar Wehr KG (GmbH & Co)

Polish Ocean Lines (Polskie Linie Oceaniczne)   Poland
Chinese-Polish Joint Stock Shipping Co (Chinsko-Polskie Towarzystwo Okretowe SA)

Funnel: *Cream with cream 'C' and white 'P' on broad red band, narrow black top.* **Hull:** *Light grey with blue 'CHIPOLBROK', green over black boot-topping.* **History:** *Formed jointly by the goverments of China and Poland in 1951.* **Web:** *www.chipolbrok.com.cn or www.chipolbrok.com.pl*

Name	Flag	Year	GRT	DWT	LOA	Bm	Kts	Type	Former names
B. Prus	Cyp	1979	16,869	24,400	171	25	17	Co	ex Concordia Sun-87, Hoegh Sun-84, Costa Mediterranea-83, Concordia Sun-82
Carnival	Mlt	1977	18,772	27,739	171	26	17	Co	ex Cai Lun-91, Willine Tysla-86, Tysla-82
Ceynowa	Mlt	1982	14,056	15,622	157	24	16	C	
Chipolbrok Moon	Hkg	2004	24,167	30,460	200	28	19	Co	
Chipolbrok Sun	Hkg	2004	24,336	30,396	200	28	19	Co	
Chong Ming	Chn	1993	18,177	22,109	170	28	16	Co	
Chopin	Cyp	1988	13,930	18,144	159	23	15	Co	
Hua Tuo	Chn	1983	14,163	15,753	155	23	16	C	

Name	Flag	Year	GRT	DWT	LOA	Bm	Kts	Type	Former names
Jan Dlugosz	Cyp	1984	15,246	15,622	157	25	16	C	
Jia Xing	Chn	1992	18,177	22,109	170	28	16	Co	ex Bao Zheng-92
Leopold Staff	Cyp	2004	24,167	30,469	200	28	19	Co	
Li Bai	Chn	1988	13,843	18,114	159	23	15	Co	
Lu Ban	Chn	1981	14,169	16,152	155	23	16	C	
Lu Xun	Chn	1988	13,843	18,144	159	23	15	Co	
Moniuszko	Mlt	1989	13,938	18,144	159	23	15	Co	
Norwid	Mlt	1998	18,202	22,258	170	28	16	Co	
Pokoj	Cyp	1977	18,846	27,937	171	26	17	Co	ex Terrier-86, Hoegh Carrier-86, Terrier-85, Barber Terrier-84, Terrier-81
Silver Bridge	Mlt	1977	18,846	27,817	171	26	17	Co	ex Ever Happy-06, Da Yu-91, Hoegh Cape-86, Tsu-85, Barber Tsu-84, Tsu-81, Thalatta-77
Szymanowski	Cyp	1991	18,184	22,313	170	28	16	Co	
Taixing	Hkg	1997	18,207	22,271	170	28	16	Co	
Wieniawski	Mlt	1992	18,208	22,130	170	28	16	Co	
Wladyslaw Orkan	Cyp	2003	24,336	30,435	200	28	19	Co	
Yong Xing	Mlt	1998	18,207	22,309	170	28	16	Co	

newbuildings: six 23,000 grt 30,000 dwt general cargo/container for 2009-10 delivery (first to be named Fredro)

Polish Steamship Co (Polska Zegluga Morska)   Poland

Funnel: Black with red band between two narrow white or yellow bands, interrupted by shield with white letters 'PZM' and trident. **Hull:** Black, grey or yellow, some with white 'POLSTEAM', red boot-topping. **History:** Government controlled company founded 1951. **Web:** www.polstream.com

Name	Flag	Year	GRT	DWT	LOA	Bm	Kts	Type	Former names
Alexander 1 **	Mlt	1990	11,572	13,864	149	22	16	Co	ex Alexander-07, Golden Trader-03, Quarry Bay-01, Venus-99, Unisierra-98, Radom-93
Armia Krajowa	Vut	1991	41,266	73,505	229	32	14	B	
Armia Ludowa *	Lbr	1987	21,458	33,640	195	25	15	B	
Bataliony Chlopskie	Lbr	1988	21,460	33,618	195	25	14	B	
Daria	Cyp	1995	25,190	41,260	186	30	14	B	ex Taria-95
Delia	Cyp	1997	25,206	41,185	186	30	14	B	
Diana	Cyp	1997	25,206	41,425	186	30	14	B	
Dorine	Cyp	1998	25,065	41,488	186	30	14	B	
Gardno	Pan	1980	11,632	16,753	159	22	14	B	ex Kopalnia Miechowice-93
General Dabrowski	Pan	1982	23,427	38,591	198	28	15	B	ex Lake Mead-03, General Dabrowski-92
General Grot-Rowecki	Mlt	1985	23,409	38,498	199	28	14	B	
Ignacy Daszynski	Mlt	1988	21,437	33,639	195	25	14	B	
Irma	Cyp	2000	21,387	34,948	200	24	15	B	
Iryda	Cyp	1999	21,387	34,939	200	24	14	B	
Isa	Cyp	1999	21,387	34,939	200	24	14	B	
Isadora	Cyp	1999	21,387	34,948	200	24	14	B	
Isolda	Cyp	1999	21,959	34,949	200	24	14	B	
Jamno	Pan	1980	11,632	16,813	159	22	14	B	ex Kopalnia Gottwald-93
Kaliope	Bhs	1995	11,542	16,888	149	23	14	Tm	ex Fjordnes-97
Kopalnia Borynia	Mlt	1989	8,893	11,899	144	19	14	B	
Kopalnia Halemba	Mlt	1990	8,897	11,715	144	19	14	B	
Kopalnia Rydultowy	Mlt	1990	8,897	11,702	144	19	14	B	
Kujawy	Bhs	2005	24,109	37,965	190	29	14	B	

Polish Ocean (Chinese-Polish JSC). JAN DLUGOSZ. *J. M. Kakebeeke*

Name	Flag	Year	GRT	DWT	LOA	Bm	Kts	Type	Former names
Legiony Polskie	Vut	1991	41,237	73,505	229	32	14	B	
Maciej Rataj	Mlt	1985	21,531	33,750	199	25	15	B	
Magdalena **	Mlt	1988	11,574	13,864	149	22	16	Co	ex Lodz II-00, Pineseas Venture-97, Lodz II-95
Major Hubal	Mlt	1985	21,531	33,725	199	25	15	B	
Mamry II	Pan	1979	11,676	16,653	159	22	15	B	ex Mamry-04, Kopalnia Siemianowice-93
Mazury	Bhs	2005	24,109	38,056	190	29	14	B	
Mitrope	Mlt	1999	11,530	15,718	149	23	13	T	
Nida	Bhs	1993	9,815	13,759	143	21	14	B	ex Nidanes-99, l/a Nida
Nogat	Cyp	1999	11,848	17,064	149	23	13	B	
Odra	Bhs	1992	9,818	13,790	143	21	14	B	ex Odranes-99, l/a Odra
Oksywie	Lbr	1987	21,460	33,580	195	25	14	B	ex Wladyslaw Gomulka-91
Orla	Mlt	1999	11,848	17,064	149	23	14	B	
Orleta Lwowskie	Vut	1991	41,238	73,505	229	32	14	B	
Penelope	Bhs	1996	11,829	15,329	149	23	14	T	
Pilica	Mlt	1999	11,540	17,064	149	23	14	B	
Podhale	Bhs	2005	24,109	38,056	190	29	14	B	
Polska Walczaca	Vut	1992	41,220	73,505	229	32	13	B	
Pomorze Zachodnie	Lbr	1985	16,696	26,696	180	23	14	B	
Powstaniec Listopadowy *	Mlt	1985	21,531	33,767	199	25	14	B	
Powstaniec Styczniowy	Mlt	1986	21,531	33,780	195	25	14	B	
Rega	Bhs	1995	11,542	16,880	149	23	14	C	ex Fossnes-02
Rodlo	Mlt	1985	21,531	33,742	199	25	15	B	
Rolnik	Pan	1975	9,117	14,176	146	21	15	B	
Ros	Mhl	1980	11,676	16,693	159	22	14	B	ex Kopalnia Myslowice-93

Polish Steamship Co.. DORINE. *J. M. Kakebeeke*

Polish Steamship Co. MITROPE. *Guido van Driessche*

Name	Flag	Year	GRT	DWT	LOA	Bm	Kts	Type	Former names
Solidarnosc	Vut	1991	41,252	73,470	229	32	14	B	
Stanislaw Kulczynski	Mlt	1988	21,456	33,627	195	25	14	B	
Szare Szeregi	Vut	1991	41,191	73,505	229	32	14	B	
Szczerin **	Mlt	1987	11,581	13,634	149	20	16	C	
Talty	Pan	1979	11,676	16,728	159	22	14	B	ex Kopalnia Szombierki-93
Uniwersytet Slaski	Mlt	1979	20,357	33,470	198	24	16	B	
Wadag II	Pan	1980	11,632	16,753	159	22	15	B	ex Wadag-04, Kopalnia Siersza-93
Walka Mlodych	Mlt	1978	20,357	33,485	198	24	15	B	
Warmia	Bhs	2006	24,109	38,056	190	29	14	B	
Warta	Bhs	1992	9,815	13,756	144	21	12	B	ex Wartanes-99
Wigry	Pan	1979	11,676	16,653	159	22	14	B	ex Kopalnia Jastrzebie-93
Wisla	Vut	1992	9,815	13,770	143	21	13	B	ex Wislanes-99
Ziemia Chelminska	Lbr	1984	16,699	26,642	180	23	14	B	
Ziemia Cieszynska	Lbr	1992	17,464	26,264	180	23	14	B	ex Lake Carling-03, Ziemia Cieszynska-93
Ziemia Gnieznienska	Lbr	1985	16,696	26,696	180	23	14	B	
Ziemia Gornoslaska	Lbr	1990	17,427	26,209	180	23	14	B	ex Lake Charles-03, Ziemia Gornoslaska-91
Ziemia Lodzka	Lbr	1992	17,458	26,264	180	23	14	B	ex Lake Champlain-03, Ziemia Lodzka-92
Ziemia Suwalska	Lbr	1984	16,696	26,605	180	23	14	B	
Ziemia Tarnowska	Lbr	1985	16,705	26,678	180	23	14	B	
Ziemia Zamojska	Lbr	1984	16,696	26,605	180	23	14	B	

newbuildings: four 80,000 dwt, ten 37,700 dwt, nine 30,000 dwt bulk carriers, eight 17,000 dwt general cargo for 2009-12 delivery.
* owned or managed by Polsteam Oceantramp Ltd (formed 1993) or ** by Euroafrica Linie Zeglugowe (formed 1991 - www.euroafrica.com.pl).

PowerGen plc UK

Funnel: *Red with white 'e-on', black top.* **Hull:** *Black with red boot-topping.* **History:** *Formed 1990.* **Web:** *www.eon-uk.com*

Name	Flag	Year	GRT	DWT	LOA	Bm	Kts	Type	Former names
Lord Hinton	Gbr	1986	14,201	22,447	155	25	12	B	
Sir Charles Parsons	Gbr	1985	14,201	22,530	155	25	12	B	

Owned by subsidiary E.On UK plc (formed 2004) and managed by Meridian Marine Management Ltd.

KG Projex-Schiffahrts GmbH & Co Germany

Funnel: *White lower half and dark blue upper part with white 'PX' between narrow pale blue wavy bands or charterers colours.*
Hull: *Blue with pale blue wavy bands on bows, red boot-topping.* **History:** *Formed 1981.* **Web:** *www.kg-projex.de*

Name	Flag	Year	GRT	DWT	LOA	Bm	Kts	Type	Former names
Chief *	Atg	2001	30,024	36,003	208	32	22	CC	ex CSCL Kelang-08, I/a Chief
Clan Amazonas *	Atg	1996	23,897	30,447	188	30	20	CC	ex Glory-05, Cap Vincent-01, Glory-00, Crowley Americas-99, Glory-99, Pacifico-98
CMA CGM Acaju *	Gbr	1998	23,897	30,416	188	30	21	CC	ex Champion-08, Lykes Falcon-02, CSAV Rimac-00, Mediterraneo-99, Champion-98
CMA CGM Itajai *	Atg	1994	16,915	21,478	168	27	19	CC	ex Triumph-07, Lykes Racer-06, Triumph-04, P&O Nedlloyd Everest-03, Triumph-01, P&O Nedlloyd Lagos-99, Nedlloyd Lagos-98, Nedlloyd Rio-97, I/a Triumph
CSAV Totoral	Atg	2008	32,269	38,636	211	32		CC	ex Penelope-08
CSCL Barcelona *	Atg	2001	30,024	36,019	208	32	22	CC	ex Bonny-01
CSCL Fos	Atg	2001	30,024	35,977	208	32	22	CC	I/a Bosun
CSCL Genoa *	Atg	2001	30,026	36,189	208	32	22	CC	ex Bravo-01
CSCL Jakarta *	Atg	2001	30,024	35,980	208	32	22	CC	I/a Bella
CSCL Napoli *	Atg	2002	30,024	35,971	208	32	22	CC	I/a Mentor
Genoa Senator *	Atg	1997	23,897	30,502	188	30	20	CC	ex Safmarine Letaba-05, Primus-02, CSAV Guayas-99, Primus-99, Sea Parana-99, Primus-97
Harmony *	Atg	1994	16,927	21,480	168	27	19	CC	ex MSC Fado-03, P&O Nedlloyd Beirut-02, DNOL Beirut-99, UB Tiger-98, Beirut-97, Contship Egypt-95, Harmony-94
Hermes	Atg	2006	27,061	34,365	212	30	22	CC	
Maruba Imperator *	Gbr	1997	23,897	30,416	188	30	21	CC	ex Master I-08, P&O Nedlloyd Brunel-06, Master I-03, Master-02, CMA CGM Paris-02, Lykes Kestrel-01, MOL Europe-00, Maersk Miami-99, I/a Master
Maruba Pampero	Atg	2006	27,061	34,393	212	30	22	CC	ex Ulysses-06
Mate	Atg	2004	30,024	36,074	208	32	22	CC	ex Kota Perkasa-07, Mate-04

* managed for Hansa Treuhand Schiffs AG & Co KG

Ray Shipping Israel

Funnel: *Green with large yellow 'R', narrow black top or charterers colours.* **Hull:** *Blue with dark green upperworks, red boot-topping.*
History: *Founded 1993.* **Web:** *www. stamco.gr*

Name	Flag	Year	GRT	DWT	LOA	Bm	Kts	Type	Former names
Amber Arrow	Bhs	2004	57,718	21,120	200	32	20	V	

Ray Shipping. CRYSTAL RAY. *Phil Kempsey*

Ray Shipping. GLOBAL LEADER. *Allan Ryszka Onions*

Ray Shipping. TALIA. *Allan Ryszka Onions*

Name	Flag	Year	GRT	DWT	LOA	Bm	Kts	Type	Former names
Baltic Ace	Bhs	2007	23,498	7,787	147	25	18	V	
Coral Leader	Bhs	2006	41,000	12,164	176	31	19	V	
CSCC Shanghai	Bhs	2008	41,009	12,300	176	31	19	V	
CSCC Tianjin	Iom	2008	41,009	12,300	176	31	19	V	
Crystal Ray	Bhs	2000	57,772	21,400	200	32	20	V	
Danube Highway	Bhs	2006	23,498	7,788	148	25	18	V	
Diamond Ray	Mlt	1979	45,571	17,714	190	32	18	V	ex Honshu I-99, Zama-94, Zama Maru-90
Elbe Highway	Bhs	2005	23,498	7,750	148	25	18	V	
Emerald Leader	Bhs	2008	41,000	12,300	176	31	19	V	
Galaxy Leader	Bhs	2002	48,710	17,127	189	32	20	V	
Garnet Leader	Bhs	2008	57,692	21,020	200	32	20	V	
Gentle Leader	Bhs	2008	57,692	21,122	200	32	20	V	
Global Leader	Bhs	2002	48,710	17,125	199	32	20	V	
Glorious Leader	Bhs	2007	57,692	20,999	200	32	20	V	
Golden Ray II	Lbr	1985	47,343	16,178	190	32	19	V	ex Tepozteco II-02, Nissan Bluebird-94
Goliath Leader	Bhs	2008	57,692	20,958	200	32	20	V	
Graceful Leader	Bhs	2007	57,692	20,986	200	32	20	V	
Guardian Leader	Bhs	2008	57,692	21,182	200	32	20	V	
Hoegh America	Bhs	2003	57,718	21,182	200	32	20	V	ex Hual America-08
Hual Africa	Bhs	2004	57,718	21,214	200	32	20	V	
Istra Ace	Bhs	2007	41,000	12,200	176	31	19	V	
Ivory Arrow	Bhs	2004	57,718	21,300	200	32	20	V	
Jade Arrow	Bhs	1993	47,367	12,271	180	32	18	V	ex Blue Ridge Highway-01
Jasper Arrow	Bhs	2005	57,692	21,040	200	32	20	V	
Lapis Arrow	Bhs	2006	40,500	12,105	176	31	19	V	
Morning Calm	Bhs	2004	57,962	21,005	200	32	20	V	I/a Opal Ray
Morning Champion	Bhs	2005	57,692	21,106	200	32	20	V	
Morning Courier	Bhs	2005	57,692	21,053	200	32	20	V	
Morning Crown	Bhs	2005	57,692	21,052	200	32	20	V	
Morning Menad	Bhs	2007	41,000	12,300	176	31	19	V	
Nordic Ace	Bhs	2007	23,498	7,378	148	25	18	V	
Onyx Arrow	Bhs	2005	57,700	21,000	200	32	20	V	
Pearl Ray	Lbr	1980	45,376	14,837	190	32	18	V	ex San Marcos-01, Oppama-91, Oppama Maru-90
Platinium Ray	Bhs	2000	57,772	21,000	200	32	20	V	
Ruby Ray	Lbr	1978	30,256	10,555	180	28	18	V	ex Lerma-96, Nissan Silvia-84
Sapphire Ray	Pan	1985	38,874	13,019	184	31	18	V	ex Eternal Sailor-01, Hyundai No. 101-96
Seine Highway	Bhs	2007	23,498	8,100	148	25	18	V	
Serenity Ace	Bhs	2008	57,692	21,300	200	32	20	V	
Taipan	Bhs	2006	57,692	21,021	200	32	20	V	
Talia	Bhs	2006	57,700	21,021	200	32	20	V	
Tarifa	Bhs	2007	57,692	21,120	200	32	20	V	
Thames Highway	Bhs	2007	23,498	7,750	148	25	18	V	
Topaz Ray	Pan	1985	38,874	12,595	184	31	18	V	ex Eternal Trader-01, Hyundai No. 102-96
Veracruz I	Pan	1977	30,259	10,535	180	28	18	V	ex Veracruz-02, Guanajuato-01, President-86
Yohjin	Pan	1983	29,933	11,662	164	28	18	V	ex Nosac Yohjin-99, Yohjin-95, I/a Arafura Breeze

newbuilding: 26 vehicle carriers, four 52,000 dwt chemical carriers and two 49,550 grt Lpg tankers for 2008-11 delivery.
Managed by Ray Car Carriers Ltd or Stamco Ship Management Co. Ltd, Greece (formed 1993).
Vessels chartered-out to Hoegh, Kawasaki, NYK, Eukor Car Carriers Inc (under Wallenius-Wilhelmsen) and other operators.

Carsten Rehder Schiffsmakler und Reederei GmbH   Germany

Funnel: Black with white 'CR' on black diamond between narrow red bands on braod white band or charterers colours. **Hull:** Black or green with red boot-topping. **History:** Founded 1903 as Carsten Rehder to 1982 **Web:** www.carstenrehder.de

Name	Flag	Year	GRT	DWT	LOA	Bm	Kts	Type	Former names
Baltic Strait	Lbr	2008	18,102	23,840	182	25	20	CC	
Barents Strait	Lbr	2008	18,102	23,844	183	25	20	CC	
Clou Island	Lbr	2000	17,167	21,331	169	27	20	CC	ex Mira-08, Cala Paestum-07, YM Hakata-04, P&O Nedlloyd Canterbury-03, Mira-02
Clou Ocean	Mhl	1998	10,384	12,184	149	23	19	CC	ex Besire Kalkavan-06
Dover Strait	Mhl	2002	14,241	18,402	159	24	18	CC	ex Cape Serrat-04, MOL Sahara-02, Cape Serrat-02
Marble Strait	Atg	2009	21,018	25,800	180	28	20	CC	
Melbourne Strait	Atg	2008	21,018	25,849	180	28	20	CC	
Mistral Strait	Atg	2009	21,018	25,800	180	28	20	CC	
NileDutch Qingdao	Lbr	2008	21,028	25,826	180	28	20	CC	ex Macao Strait-08

newbuildings: four 57,000 dwt bulk carriers for 2010 delivery.

Name	Flag	Year	GRT	DWT	LOA	Bm	Kts	Type	Former names

Schiffahrtskontor Rendsburg GmbH

Germany

Funnel: *Blue or charterers colours.* **Hull:** *Black or green with red boot-topping.* **History:** *Founded 1971 as Schiffahrtskontor Rendsburg, Peterson, Schluter & Werner.* **Web:** *none found.*

Name	Flag	Year	GRT	DWT	LOA	Bm	Kts	Type	Former names
CMA CGM Accra	Lbr	1997	23,896	30,291	188	30	21	CC	ex Westerburg-07, Tuscany Bridge-07, Westerburg-03, Lykes Achiever-01, Westerburg-98, Maersk La Plata-98, Westerburg-97
CSAV Mexico	Cyp	2002	30,047	35,768	207	32	22	CC	ex Westerland-05, Alianca Hamburgo-03
Maersk Dartmouth	Lbr	2005	54,592	64,660	294	32	23	CC	
Maersk Novazzano	Lbr	1997	23,896	30,600	188	30	21	CC	ex P&O Nedlloyd Horizon-05, Westerems-05, ANL Addax-03, Westerems-02, Lykes Voyager-01, Westerems-98, Maersk Cordoba-98, Westerems-97
MSC Mendosa	Lbr	2007	32,060	39,000	211	32	21	CC	ex Westerdieek-07
Westerdeich	Lbr	1994	15,908	22,343	168	27	19	CC	ex Indamex Liberty-03, Westerdeich-02, Indamex Washington-02, Kota Serika-00, Zim Santos-99, Westerdeich-99, Zim Santos-96, Westerdeich-96, Maersk Rio Grande-96, TSL Gallant-96, Westerdeich-94
Westerhamm	Deu	1998	23,986	30,259	188	30	21	CC	ex Cala Paradiso-08, DAL Karoo-04, Westerhamm-02, Actor-01, Westerhamm-99
Westerhever	Lbr	1994	15,908	22,340	168	27	20	CC	ex P&O Nedlloyd Coleridge-04, Westerhever-03, Maersk Durban-99, Westerhever-98, Maersk Rio Grande-97, CCNI Atacama-96, Westerhever-94
Westermoor	Lbr	2001	30,047	35,653	208	32	22	CC	
Westermuhlen	Lbr	1993	14,961	20,140	167	25	17	CC	ex Cala Pinar del Rio-04, Norasia Chicago-01, CSAV New York-00, Westermuhlen-00, Nedlloyd Singapore-96, Westermuhlen-93
Westertal	Lbr	2006	32,060	38,700	211	32	21	CC	ex CMA CGM Melbourne-08, Westertal-06

managed by Hans Peterson & Soehne GmbH & Co KG (formed 1984) Germany.

Rickmers Reederei GmbH & Cie KG

Germany

Funnel: *Black with houseflag (white 'R' on red over green) on broad white band, or charterers colours.* **Hull:** *Green or black with white 'RICKMERS', red boot-topping or charterer's colours.* **History:** *Founded 1889 as Rickmers Reismuhlen Rhederei & Schiffbau AG, became Reederei Bertram Rickmers GmbH to 1992. Rickmers Linie sold to Hapag Lloyd in 1988 and re-acquired 2000. Acquired CCNI (Deutschland) GmbH (formed 1999) from Compania Chilena de Navegacion Interoceanica in 2004.* **Web:** *www.rickmers.com or www.rickmers-linie.de*

Name	Flag	Year	GRT	DWT	LOA	Bm	Kts	Type	Former names
Anakena ‡	Deu	1996	28,148	44,575	185	32	15	CC	ex CCNI Anakena-08, CSAV Valencia-05, CCNI Anakena-04, I/a Valdemosa
Andre Rickmers	Lux	1998	26,131	30,725	196	30	19	CC	ex Marfret Provence-08, CGM Matisse-98, Andre Rickmers-98
ANL Wangaratta	Lbr	2008	39,906	50,596	260	32	24	CC	
ANL Warrain **	Sgp	2007	39,906	50,629	260	32	24	CC	ex CMA CGM Purple-08
ANL Warringa *	Mhl	2007	39,906	50,629	260	32	24	CC	ex Vicki Rickmers-07
ANL Windarra *	Mhl	2007	39,906	50,769	260	32	24	CC	ex Maja Rickmers-07
ANL Wyong **	Gbr	2008	39,906	52,000	261	32	24	CC	

Schiffs Rendsburg GmbH. WESTERMOOR. *Hans Kraijenbosch*

Name	Flag	Year	GRT	DWT	LOA	Bm	Kts	Type	Former names
Aruni Rickmers §	Deu	2004	21,932	24,219	196	28	22	CC	ex Satha Bhum-07, Moni Rickmers-04
Asta Rickmers §	Mhl	2001	14,278	15,315	159	26	21	CC	ex Hub Racer-01, Asta Rickmers-01
Atalanta ‡	Lbr	1999	28,148	44,593	185	32	15	CC	ex CCNI Arauco-04
Barrier	Mhl	1997	10,743	14,099	163	22	17	CC	ex Mai Rickmers-07, Zim Caribe IV-06, Mai Rickmers-99, Sophie Delmas-98, Mai Rickmers-97
Border	Atg	1993	10,736	14,120	163	22	17	CC	ex Peter Rickmers-07, Zim Mexico III-06, Peter Rickmers-99, Kaiama-99, Peter Rickmers-94
Boundary	Mhl	1993	10,778	14,069	163	22	17	CC	ex Marfret Normandie-08, Maria Rickmers-02, Melbridge Palm-01, Maria Rickmers-98, Karawa-98, Maria Rickmers-97, Karawa-96, Maria Rickmers-95, CCNI Guayas-94, I/a Maria Rickmers
Clan Rickmers **	Lbr	2009	39,906	50,700	260	32	24	CC	
Clipper Emperor §	Mhl	2000	38,878	74,381	225	32	14	B	ex Pacemperor-03
Clipper Monarch §‡	Mhl	2000	38,878	74,381	225	32	14	B	ex Pacmonarch-04
CMA CGM Anapurna	Mhl	2006	21,971	24,069	196	28	23	CC	I/a Jacob Rickmers
CMA CGM Azure ††	Mhl	2007	39,906	50,629	260	32	24	CC	
CMA CGM Buenos Aires	Deu	1998	26,131	30,781	196	30	19	CC	ex Patricia Rickmers-06, Contship Auckland-05, I/a Patricia Rickmers
CMA CGM Everest	Mhl	2006	21,971	24,084	196	28	23	CC	I/a John Rickmers
CMA CGM Jade *	Mhl	2007	41,482	39,906	267	32	24	CC	
CMA CGM Licorne §	Lbr	1998	16,801	23,028	185	25	19	CC	ex Fiona Rickmers-04, Libra Barcelona-03, Fiona Rickmers-02, La Hispaniola-02, Zim Soa Paulo I-01, Paranagua-99, I/a Fiona Rickmers
CMA CGM Onyx *	Sgp	2007	39,906	50,770	267	32	24	CC	
CMA CGM Paulista	Mhl	1997	16,801	23,062	184	25	19	CC	ex Madeleine Rickmers-05, Sagittarius Challenger-01, Madeleine Rickmers-97
CMA CGM Samba	Mhl	1997	10,743	14,191	163	23	17	CC	ex Mabel Rickmers-05, Kribi-98, I/a Mabel Rickmers
CMA CGM St. Laurent §	Mhl	1998	10,752	14,086	163	22	16	CC	ex Laurita-02, Melbridge Pearl-99, Laurita Rickmers-98
CMA CGM St. Martin §	Mhl	1998	10,752	14,040	163	22	16	CC	ex CGM Basse-Terre-01, Lilly Rickmers-98
CSAV Manzanillo	Atg	1996	16,800	22,900	184	25	19	CC	ex Pacific Challenger-01, Christa Rickmers-99, CCNI Arauco-98, Christa Rickmers-96
CSAV Maresias	Mhl	1996	16,801	23,028	185	25	19	CC	ex Delmas Cartier-04, Etha Rickmers-02, CSAV Tokyo-02, Zim Vancouver-01, Etha Rickmers-99, CCNI Antarctico-99, Panamerican-97, CCNI Antartico-96, Etha Rickmers-96
Deike Rickmers	Mhl	1996	16,801	23,100	184	25	19	CC	ex Libra Rio Grande-05, Deike Rickmers-04, P&O Nedlloyd Kowie-03, Deike Rickmers-01, CSAV Genova-00, Deike Rickmers-00, Scorpio Challenger-99, Deike Rickmers-97, Panatlantic-97, I/a Deike Rickmers
Delmas Baudin §‡	Mhl	1997	24,053	28,352	205	27	20	CC	ex CSAV Itajai-04, Johan Rickmers-03, APL Chile-02, Sea Cougar-99, I/a Conti Oakland
Delmas Brazzaville §‡	Lbr	1998	26,131	30,730	196	30	20	CC	ex CSAV Atlanta-06, I/a Clasen Rickmers
Delmas Portugal	Atg	1992	9,601	12,583	150	22	17	CC	ex CMA CGM Karibu-05, Delmas Marula-05, New Orient-04, R.C.Rickmers-99, Nedlloyd Caldera-98, Sea-Land Mexico-95, TSL Bold-94, R.C.Rickmers-92
Denderah Rickmers	Deu	1997	16,801	22,900	184	25	19	CC	ex Norasia Bavaria-05, CSAV Busan-03, Zim Seattle-01, Pictor Challenger-99, Denderah Rickmers-97
Ebba Rickmers **	Lbr	2008	39,906	50,700	260	32	24	CC	
Elisabeth Rickmers †	Atg	1995	16,801	23,190	185	25	19	CC	ex Delmas Joinville-03, Elisabeth Rickmers-03, Pacific Discovery-01, Elisabeth Rickmers-99, CSAV Santos-97, I/a Elisabeth Rickmers
Ernst Rickmers §‡	Mhl	2002	14,278	15,313	159	26	21	CC	ex Turkon America-03, Ernst Rickmers-02
Helene Rickmers †	Mhl	1998	16,801	23,106	184	25	19	CC	ex Lykes Crusader-02, Helene Rickmers-01, CCNI Arica-01, Helene Rickmers-98
Hyundai No. 103	Pan	1986	40,772	12,893	184	31	18	V	
India Rickmers **	Lbr	2008	39,906	50,700	260	32	24	CC	
Ital Fastosa **	Mhl	2006	36,483	42,822	239	32	23	CC	
Ital Festosa **	Mhl	2006	36,483	42,822	239	32	23	CC	
Ital Fiducia	Mhl	2007	36,483	42,822	239	32	23	CC	
Jacky Rickmers §	Deu	2004	21,932	24,200	196	28	22	CC	ex Rithi Bhum-07, Jacky Rickmers-04
Maersk Daesan	Lbr	2005	54,214	68,017	294	32	24	CC	
Maersk Davao	Lbr	2005	54,214	68,187	294	32	24	CC	
Maersk Dhaka	Lbr	2005	54,214	68,187	294	32	24	CC	
Maersk Djibouti **	Lbr	2004	54,214	68,282	294	32	24	CC	

Name	Flag	Year	GRT	DWT	LOA	Bm	Kts	Type	Former names
Maersk Douala §	Lbr	2004	54,214	68,187	294	32	24	CC	
Maersk Durban §	Deu	2004	54,214	68,187	294	32	24	CC	I/dn Jennifer Rickmers
Marie Rickmers §	Lbr	1999	22,817	35,230	171	31	17	CC	ex CCNI Amadeo-07, CCNI Austral-05, CSAV Genova-03, Lykes Challenger-00, I/a Marie Rickmers
Marine Rickmers	Mhl	1998	11,925	14,381	150	23	18	CC	ex P&O Nedlloyd Mahe-05, Marine Rickmers-02, Fanal Mariner-01, Marine Rickmers-99
Maruba Tango ‡	Mhl	1997	24,053	28,366	205	27	20	CC	ex Felicitas Rickmers-05, Sea Jaguar-02, Conti Jacksonville-97
MOL Dedication **	Mhl	2008	39,906	50,629	260	32	24	CC	
MOL Dominance **	Mhl	2008	39,906	50,629	260	32	24	CC	
MOL Unifier	Mhl	1996	16,801	23,045	184	25	19	CC	ex NileDutch President-08, Camilla Rickmers-07, CSAV Livorno-00, Camilla Rickmers-00, CCNI Anakena-98, I/a Camilla Rickmers
MSC Florida	Mhl	2005	51,364	57,000	286	32	25	CC	ex Maya Rickmers-05
Nina Rickmers §	Mhl	2004	21,932	24,279	196	28	23	CC	ex CMA CGM Rio Grande-08, APL Kobe-07, Nina Rickmers-04
Norasia Valparaiso §	Lbr	2002	51,364	58,341	286	32	25	CC	ex Cathrine Rickmers-02
OOCL Achievement §‡	Mhl	2000	14,278	15,299	159	26	21	CC	ex Carla Rickmers-04
OOCL Advance §‡	Mhl	2001	14,278	15,273	159	26	21	CC	ex Jock Rickmers-04, APL Magnolia-01, I/a Jock Rickmers
OOCL Moscow ‡	Mhl	2002	14,290	14,901	159	26	22	CC	ex Sandy Rickmers07, I/a Mirko Rickmers
Paul Rickmers	Lux	1993	10,733	14,191	163	22	17	CC	ex P&O Nedlloyd Amazonas-05, Paul Rickmers-05, MSC Caribbean-03, Paul Rickmers-02, Kamina-97, Zim Argentina-96, Paul Rickmers-94
Pingel Rickmers *	Mhl	2009	39,906	50,600	260	32	24	CC	
Rickmer Rickmers	Atg	1995	16,800	22,900	185	25	19	CC	ex Norasia Sindh-04, Rickmer Rickmers-03, Columbus Hong Kong-02, Sassandra Challenger-01, Rickmer Rickmers-00, CSAV Rosario-98, Rickmer Rickmers-95
Rickmers Chennai #	Cyp	1979	17,128	22,267	178	27	18	C	ex Leon-04, Nacional Vitoria-96, Sonora-94, Gina Luisa-82
Rickmers Dalian	Lbr	2004	23,119	29,900	193	28	19	Co/hl	ex Rickmers Genoa-05
Rickmers Dubai #	Pan	1979	17,128	22,378	178	27	18.	Co/hl	ex Bibi-04
Rickmers Hamburg §†	Mhl	2002	23,119	29,980	193	28	19	Co/hl	
Rickmers Jakarta †	Mhl	2004	23,119	29,750	193	28	19	Co/hl	ex Genoa-03
Rickmers Mumbai #	Pan	1979	17,128	22,229	178	27	19	C	ex Merida-04, Silvia Sofia-87
Rickmers New Orleans	Mhl	2003	23,119	30,095	193	28	19	Co/hl	
Rickmers Seoul	Mhl	2003	23,119	30,151	193	28	19	Co/hl	
Rickmers Singapore	Mhl	2002	23,119	30,018	193	28	19	Co/hl	
Santiago	Mhl	1996	24,046	32,482	174	31	19	CC	ex CCNI Vancouver-07, Togo Star-04, Santiago-02, CCNI Chiloe-00, Maersk Curitiba-98, CCNI Chiloe-96
Saylemoon Rickmers §	Mhl	2003	21,932	24,277	196	28	23	CC	ex CMA CGM Oman-08, Saylemoon Rickmers-07, APL Mumbai-07, Saylemoon Rickmers-04
Sean Rickmers §†	Mhl	1999	16,986	21,184	168	27	20	CC	ex Kindia-04, Indamex Kindia-03, Kindia-02

Reederei Bertram Rickmers . RICKMERS DUBAI. *Guido van Driessche*

Name	Flag	Year	GRT	DWT	LOA	Bm	Kts	Type	Former names
Sophie Rickmers §‡	Lbr	1999	22,817	35,466	171	31	16	Co	ex CCNI Aviles-08, CCNI Antofagasta-05, CSAV Barcelona-03, CCNI Antofagasta-02, CSAV Barcelona-02, CCNI Antofagasta-01, Contship Mexico-01, CCNI Antofagasta-99
Tasman Campaigner §‡	Mhl	2003	16,801	23,063	185	25	19	CC	ex Robert Rickmers-08, E.R. Stettin-03
Tete Rickmers §‡	Mhl	2000	14,278	15,317	158	26	21	CC	
Valbella ‡	Deu	1998	28,148	44,593	185	32	15	Co	
Willi Rickmers §‡	Mhl	1998	26,125	30,738	196	30	19	CC	ex Sea Puma-06, Crowley Lion-01, CSAV Boston-99, I/a Willi Rickmers
Zim Sao Paulo II	Mhl	1997	16,801	22,900	185	25	19	CC	ex Ursula Rickmers-01

newbuildings: eight 135,000 grt, four 91,300 grt, five 88,000 grt, four 41,500 grt, five 32,000 grt, two 16,100 grt and *** two 39,900 grt container ships, four 27,950 dwt, four 24,300 dwt, six 19,000 dwt and four 16,800 dwt general cargo, two 46,800 grt vehicle carriers for 2009-11 delivery.
* owned or managed by Rickmers Shipmanagement (Singapore) Pte Ltd (formed 2006), ** owned by associated Rickmers Maritime, Singapore (formed 2007 – www.rickmers-maritime.com) or § for associated Atlantic Ges. Zur Vermittlung Internationaler Investitionen mbH & Co KG (founded1998 – www.atlantic-fonds.de). † managed by Columbus Shipmanagement GmbH, Germany, †† by Bernhard Schulte Shipmanagement (China) Co Ltd, ‡ by Uniteam Marine Shipping GmbH (formed 1974 as subsidiary of KG Reederei Roth GmbH & Co - www.uniteammarine.com), # owned or managed by Technomar Shipping Inc, Greece.
Also see Nordcapital Holding GmbH (ER Schiffahrt GmbH & Cie KG) and MPC Munchmeyer Petersen & Co GmbH

Rigel Schiffahrts GmbH & Co KG Germany

Funnel: Blue with black 'R' on six-pointed white star on red disc on broad white band. **Hull:** Blue with red boot-topping.
History: Formed 1990. **Web:** www.rigel-hb.com

Name	Flag	Year	GRT	DWT	LOA	Bm	Kts	Type	Former names
Alsterstern	Iom	1994	11,426	17,080	161	23	15	T	
Bro Edgar	Iom	2004	26,634	37,188	186	31	15	T	ex Geestestern-06
Bro Erin	Iom	2004	26,634	37,178	186	31	15	T	ex Huntestern-07
Donaustern	Iom	1995	11,426	17,078	161	23	14	T	
Havelstern	Iom	1994	11,423	17,080	161	23	14	T	
Isarstern	Iom	1995	11,426	17,078	161	23	14	T	
Mekong Star	Iom	2008	23,312	37,500	184	25	14	T	
Orinoco Star	Iom	2009	23,000	37,500	184	25	14	T	
Rheinstern	Iom	1993	11,423	17,080	161	23	14	T	
Rhonestern	iom	2000	14,400	21,871	162	27	15	T	
Themsestern	Iom	2000	14,400	21,871	162	27	15	T	
Travestern	Iom	1993	11,423	17,080	161	23	15	T	
Weichselstern	Iom	1999	14,331	21,950	162	27	15	T	
Wolgastern	Iom	1999	14,331	21,950	162	27	15	T	
Yukon Star	Iom	2009	23,000	37,500	184	25	14	T	
Zambezi Star	Iom	2009	23,000	37,500	184	25	14	T	

Ernst Russ GmbH & Co KG Germany

Funnel: Black with red 'ER' and five pointed star between narrow red bands on broad white band or charterers colours. **Hull:** Black with red boot-topping. **History:** Formed 1893 trading as Ernst Russ to 1992. **Web:** www.ernst-russ.de

Name	Flag	Year	GRT	DWT	LOA	Bm	Kts	Type	Former names
CCNI Magallanes	Lbr	1996	16,800	22,984	184	25	19	CC	ex Mercosul Pescada-07, Sofia Russ-01, CSAV Vancouver-00, Sofia Russ-00, Cielo del Venezuela-99, Sofia Russ-99, CSAV Rungue-98, Sofia Russ-96

Rigel Schiffahrts. RHONESTERN. *Allan Ryszka Onions*

Name	Flag	Year	GRT	DWT	LOA	Bm	Kts	Type	Former names
CSAV San Antonio	Lbr	1996	16,801	23,043	185	25	19	CC	ex Helene Russ-05, WAL Urundi-04, Helene Russ-01, CMA Rotterdam-00, Helene Russ-99, CSAV Rio de Janeiro-98, l/a Helene Russ
Feng	Cyp	1985	12,863	20,333	164	22	13	B	ex Jian Feng Ling-97

Also operates ro-ro vessels in European coastal trades.

Saga Forest Carriers International AS Norway

Funnel: *Black with white outlined dark blue and turquoise 'S' on dark blue above turquoise bands.* **Hull:** *Orange or grey with black 'SAGA', red boot-topping.* **History:** *Pool formed 1991 by NYK with Aaby and Borgestad, who sold to Hesnes Group in 1995. Leif Hoegh & Co joined in 2002.* **Web:** *www.sagafc.com*

Name	Flag	Year	GRT	DWT	LOA	Bm	Kts	Type	Former names
Saga Adventure †	Hkg	2005	29,758	46,627	199	31	15	Boh	
Saga Andorinha §§	Gbr	1998	29,729	47,027	199	31	15	Boh	ex Andorinha-01
Saga Beija-Flor †	Hkg	1997	29,729	47,029	199	31	14	Boh	ex Beija-Flor-03
Saga Crest §	Hkg	1994	29,381	47,069	199	31	15	Boh	
Saga Discovery †	Hkg	2006	29,758	46,618	199	31	15	Boh	
Saga Enterprise ‡	Hkg	2006	29,758	46,550	199	31	15	Boh	
Saga Explorer	Hkg	2006	29,758	46,589	199	31	15	Boh	
Saga Frontier †	Hkg	2007	29,758	46,600	199	31	15	Boh	
Saga Horizon †	Hkg	1995	29,381	47,016	199	31	15	Boh	
Saga Jandaia †	Hkg	1998	29,729	47,016	199	31	15	Boh	ex Jandaia-01
Saga Journey †	Hkg	2007	29,758	46,652	199	31	15	Boh	
Saga Merchant *	Bhs	1977	30,987	44,895	201	31	15	Boh	ex Hoegh Merchant-04, Star Merchant-93, Westwood Merchant-90, Hoegh Merchant-83
Saga Minerva *	Nis	1979	30,995	44,016	201	31	15	Boh	ex Hoegh Minerva-05, Max Oldendorff-03, Hoegh Minerva-01, Star Minerva-89, Hoegh Minerva-87
Saga Miranda *	Nis	1979	30,995	44,016	201	31	15	Boh	ex Hoegh Miranda-05, August Oldendorff-03, Hoegh Mirande-01, Star Miranda-89, Hoegh Mirande-87
Saga Monal **	Bhs	1996	36,463	49,755	200	32	16	Boh	ex Hoegh Monal-04, Saga Challenger-02
Saga Morus **	Bhs	1997	36,463	56,801	200	32	16	Boh	ex Hoegh Morus-04
Saga Navigator †	Hkg	2007	29,758	46,673	199	31	15	Boh	
Saga Odyssey †	Hkg	2008	29,758	46,500	199	31	15	Boh	
Saga Pioneer †	Hkg	2008	29,758	46,627	199	31	15	Boh	
Saga Sky †	Hkg	1996	29,381	47,053	199	31	15	Boh	
Saga Spray **	Hkg	1994	29,381	47,029	199	31	15	Boh	
Saga Tide ‡	Hkg	1991	29,235	57,471	199	31	15	Boh	
Saga Tucano †	Hkg	1998	29,729	47,032	199	31	15	Boh	ex Tucano-01
Saga Viking §	Hkg	2002	29,867	46,500	199	31	14	Boh	
Saga Voyager †	Hkg	2001	29,872	46,882	199	31	14	Boh	
Saga Wave §	Hkg	1991	29,235	47,062	199	31	15	Boh	
Saga Wind †	Hkg	1994	29,381	47,053	199	31	15	Boh	

newbuildings: two 29,750 grt 52,000 dwt open-hatch bulk carriers for 2012 delivery.
* managed by SMT Shipmanagement & Transport Ltd, Cyprus (formed 1990 - www.smt.com.cy), † by Patt Manfield & Co Ltd, Hong Kong or ‡ by Anglo-Eastern Ship Management Ltd, Hong Kong (China). ** owned by Attic Forest AS, Norway (formed 2006) and managed by Patt Manfield & Co Ltd.   § owned by NYK or §§ by Denholm Line Steamers Ltd, UK (formed 1909, parent J&J Denholm Ltd founded 1866).

Saga Forest Carriers. SAGA EXPLORER. *Hans Kraijenbosch*

Samskip HF   Iceland

Ost-West-Handel und Schiffahrt GmbH/Germany

Funnel: White or black with red band. **Hull**: Red, white or blue some with white 'SAMSKIP', red boot-topping. **History**: Founded 1946 as Samband Islenzkra Samvinnufelaga until 1991 and Samband Line to 1994. Ost-West founded 1996 as Ost-West-Handel Bruno Bishoff GmbH until 2000. **Web**: www.samskip.com

Name	Flag	Year	GRT	DWT	LOA	Bm	Kts	Type	Former names
Aurika *	Vct	1979	7,246	8,873	141	20	20	R	ex Erato-05, Athenian Rex-03, Cap Ortegal-96, Royal Lily-89
Baltic Carrier	Bhs	1979	15,834	15,200	169	26	22	R	ex Algeciras Carrier-08, Winter Sun-00, Zenit Sun-87, Winter Sun-84
Baltic Meridian	Vct	1980	10,424	9,852	151	22	22	R	ex Swan Lagoon-03, Pocahontas-93, Isla Plaza-86, Pocahontas-84
Baltic Moon	Vct	1987	10,298	11,022	146	23	18	R	ex Amer Annapurna-08, Arctic Spirit-99, Arctic Universal-97
Baltic Snow **	Mlt	1979	11,243	12,570	144	24	21	R	ex Canadian Star-01, Canadian Reefer-01
Baltic Wave	Vct	1976	10,012	11,092	156	21	24	R	ex Almeda Star-01, Harlech-88, Arran-84, Almeda Star-84
Baltic Wind	Vct	1975	10,012	11,093	156	21	24	R	ex Avelona Star-01, Hornsound-90, Avelona Star-90, Castle Peak-88, Avelona Star84
Crystal Crown	Mlt	1986	12,485	11,330	153	22	18	R	ex Hamburg Trader-04, Reutershagen-93
Crystal Rose	Mlt	1983	9,057	9,339	149	21	19	R	ex Reefer Prince-05, Reefer Princess-97, Lingo-94, Kiwi-87
Electra	Mlt	1985	9,096	11,464	149	22	17	R	ex Elektra-01, Astra-96, Astraia-94, Colombian Reefer-93, Cacilia B-86
Ice Bell	Vct	1976	10,012	11,093	156	21	24	R	ex Avila Star-03, Almeria Star-90, Perth-88, Almeria Star-84
Pietari Bright *	Vct	1979	12,061	12,475	156	23	22	R	ex Antiope-06, Sprinter-02, Tundra Sprinter-91, Hilco Sprinter-88
Pietari Bruin *	Bhs	1980	9,065	12,475	156	23	22	R	ex Amalthia-06, Scamper-02, Scamper Universal-90, Hilco Scamper-81
Pietari Cliff **	Mlt	1985	7,949	10,168	134	20	18	R	ex Baltic Cliff-07, Firenze-02, Bretagne-02, C.R. Dieppe-93, Italian Reefer-88, I/a Extreluz
Pietari Cloud **	Mlt	1985	7,949	10,168	134	20	18	R	ex Baltic Cloud-07, Venizia-02, Brest-02, C.R. Alicante-93, Iberian Reefer-88, I/a Extresol
Pietari Glory **	Vct	1979	10,153	9,996	168	23	21	R	ex Norman Star-04, EW Andes-94, Humboldt Rex No.2-89, Humboldt Rex-89
Santa Marina	Vct	1978	8,507	9,566	150	21	20	R	ex Disko Bay-05, Thistle-93, Paracale-93, Astoria-92, Asama-89, Asama Maru-86

* owned or ** managed by Polaris Maritime Ltd, UK (formed 2005 – www.polaris-maritime.com)

The Sanko Steamship Co Ltd   Japan

Funnel: Light green with two red rings around red disc on broad white band. **Hull**: Light green with white 'SANKO LINE', red boot-topping. **History**: Formed 1934, filed for bankruptcy in 1985 after massive ordering of newbuildings and restructured 1989. **Web**: www.sankoline.co.jp

Name	Flag	Year	GRT	DWT	LOA	Bm	Kts	Type	Former names
Ansac Asia *	Lbr	1998	19,882	33,945	178	28	14	B	
Crystal Mermaid **	Pan	1990	42,465	49,618	224	36	16	Lpg	
Gas Diana ‡	Lbr	2000	46,021	49,999	230	37	16	Lpg	

Sanko Steamship. SANKO ROYAL. *J. M. Kakebeeke*

Name	Flag	Year	GRT	DWT	LOA	Bm	Kts	Type	Former names
Gas Leo	Lbr	1990	44,493	50,357	230	37	16	Lpg	
Gas Scorpio	Lbr	1995	44,546	49,679	230	37	16	Lpg	
Gas Taurus ‡	Lbr	2001	46,021	48,500	230	37	16	Lpg	
Noto Gloria	Lbr	1992	42,286	49,412	224	36		Lpg	
Oval Nova *	Lbr	1993	44,549	50,357	230	37	16	Lpg	
Pacific Century *	Lbr	1991	44,493	50,357	230	37	15	Lpg	
Sanko Ability *	Lbr	2002	50,199	83,657	239	38	14	T	
Sanko Advance *	Lbr	2002	50,199	83,657	239	38	14	T	
Sanko Amity *	Lbr	2002	50,199	84,999	239	38	14	T	
Sanko Blossom *	Pan	2005	56,172	105,699	239	42	14	T	
Sanko Breeze *	Pan	2005	56,172	105,721	239	42	14	T	
Sanko Dynasty *	Pan	1999	57,331	106,644	241	42	14	T	ex Pacific Libra-03
Sanko Eagle *	Lbr	1997	18,108	27,868	169	27	14	B	ex Aqua Crystal-03, Alpha Cosmos-01
Sanko Eternal *	Lbr	1996	18,108	27,917	169	27	14	C	ex Aomori Willow-04
Sanko Falcon *	Lbr	1996	26,058	45,674	186	30	14	B	ex Seagull Hachinohe-04
Sanko Galaxy	Lbr	2005	29,372	52,980	189	32	14	B	
Sanko Glory	Lbr	2005	29,372	52,980	189	32	14	B	
Sanko Harmony *	Lbr	2007	40,865	73,956	229	32		B	
Sanko Heritage *	Lbr	2008	40,865	73,956	229	32		B	
Sanko Independence	Lbr	2008	23,032	22,780	174	28		Lpg	
Sanko Innovator	Lbr	2008	23,032	33,780	174	28		Lpg	
Sanko Jupiter	Lbr	2008	19,883	32,936	177	28		B	
Sanko King	Lbr	2008	31,532	56,260	190	32	14	B	
Sanko Mineral	Lbr	2008	30,360	50,757	190	32		B	
Sanko Oasis *	Pan	1995	81,058	161,192	280	45	14	T	
Sanko Phoenix *	Lbr	1997	27,011	46,610	189	31	14	B	ex Asian Phoenix-05
Sanko Prelude	Hkg	1984	14,147	23,904	160	24	14	B	
Sanko Quality	Lbr	1994	52,498	95,628	247	42	14	T	
Sanko Rally †	Lbr	1994	25,676	42,529	185	31	15	B	
Sanko Rejoice *	Lbr	1994	25,676	42,529	185	31	15	B	
Sanko Reliance *	Lbr	1995	25,676	42,529	185	31	15	B	ex Sanko Robust-06
Sanko Rose *	Lbr	1995	25,676	42,529	185	31	15	B	
Sanko Royal §	Lbr	1995	25,676	42,529	185	31	15	B	
Sanko Sincere	Jpn	1998	29,688	50,655	195	32	15	C	
Sanko Spark *	Hkg	1996	77,211	150,961	274	45	14	B	ex World Spark-04
Sanko Spring	Lbr	1998	29,688	50,655	195	32	15	C	
Sanko Stream	Lbr	1998	29,688	50,655	195	32	15	C	
Sanko Summit	Lbr	1999	29,688	50,655	195	32	15	C	
Sanko Supreme *	Lbr	1999	29,688	50,655	195	32	15	C	
Sanko Titan *	Lbr	2006	30,051	52,514	190	32	15	B	
Sanko Unity	Pan	2000	159,577	298,920	333	60	15	T	

newbuildings: 82,000 dwt, two 60,500 dwt, three 49,900 dwt bulker, 43,700 grt Lpg, two 47,000 dwt, four 19,900 dwt tankers for 2009-11 delivery.
* managed by Sanko Ship Management Co Ltd, Japan, ** for Kumiai Senpaku KK, Japan or † for Sato Steamship KK, Japan.
‡ managed by NYK Shipmanagement Pte Ltd, Singapore or § or by Bernhard Schulte Shipmanagement (India) Pte Ltd for Imabari Senpaku KK.

Saudi Arabian Oil Co   Saudi Arabia

Vela International Marine Ltd/UAE

Funnel: Blue with white square outline containing irregular 10-pointed white star on blue/green background or blue with white 'VELA' below two narrow white bands (top of 'V' merged with lower band). **Hull:** Light grey or dark blue with white 'Vela', red boot-topping.
History: Founded 1933 as California Arabian Standard Oil Co to 1944, then Arabian American Oil Co Ltd to 1988. Wholly government owned since 1980. Vela International subsidiary formed 1990. **Web:** www.saudiaramco.com

Name	Flag	Year	GRT	DWT	LOA	Bm	Kts	Type
Al Bali Star	Lbr	1994	162,181	291,435	333	58	14	T
Albutain Star	Lbr	2008	162,252	319,430	333	60		T
Aldebaran Star	Lbr	2003	60,387	115,999	248	43		T
Almizan Star	Lbr	2008	162,252	319.423	333	60		T
Alnasl Star	Lbr	2005	32,083	49,000	200	32	14	T
Alphard Star	Lbr	1995	159,222	301,858	333	56	14	T
Altair Star	Lbr	2004	32,083	46,000	200	32	14	T
Altarf Star	Lbr	2006	32,083	49,000	200	32	14	T
Alwizan Star	Lbr	2008	160,000	318,000	333	60		T
Aries Star	Lbr	2003	164,292	316,478	333	60	15	T
Capricorn Star	Lbr	2003	164,292	316,507	333	60	15	T
Carina Star	Lbr	1994	159,766	305,668	332	58	14	T
Gemini Star	Lbr	1995	159,222	301,862	333	56	14	T
Hamal Star	Lbr	1994	158,680	301,550	332	58	14	T
Hydra Star	Lbr	1994	159,766	305,846	332	58	14	T
Jahan Star	Lbr	2008	160,000	318,000	333	60		T
Leo Star	Lbr	2002	164,292	316,501	333	60	15	T

Name	Flag	Year	GRT	DWT	LOA	Bm	Kts	Type	Former names
Libra Star	Lbr	1993	162,181	291,435	333	58	14	T	
Markab Star	Lbr	1994	158,680	301,569	332	58	14	T	
Mirfak Star	Lbr	1994	158,680	301,542	332	58	14	T	
Orion Star	Lbr	1994	159,766	305,783	332	58	14	T	
Pherkad Star	Lbr	1995	158,680	301,569	332	58	14	T	
Phoenix Star	Lbr	1993	162,181	291,435	333	58	14	T	
Pisces Star	Lbr	2002	164,292	316,808	333	60	15	T	
Polaris Star	Lbr	1994	158,680	301,591	332	58	14	T	
Shaula Star	Lbr	1994	158,680	301,591	332	58	14	T	
Sirius Star	Lbr	2008	162,252	319,430	333	60		T	
Suhail Star	Lbr	1994	159,222	301,862	333	56	14	T	
Vega Star	Lbr	2008	162,252	318,000	333	60		T	
Zaurak Star	Lbr	2006	32,083	49,000	200	32	14	T	

newbuildings: five 317,000 dwt tankers for 2009-10 delivery.

Reederi Rudolf Schepers GmbH & Co KG   Germany

Funnel: *Black with black 'S' on red diamond on white band, black top.* **Hull:** *Dark blue with red boot-topping.* **History:** *Formed 1994.*
Web: *www.reederei-schepers.com*

Name	Flag	Year	GRT	DWT	LOA	Bm	Kts	Type	Former names
Andrea	Atg	1995	11,964	14,454	150	23	18	CC	ex Bernhard S-08, Sakura-06, Bernhard S-04, MOL Manaus-02, Bernhard S-01
CCNI Cartagena *	Deu	1998	25,624	33,914	207	30	20	CC	ex Heinrich S-06, Zim Singapore I-02, I/a Heinrich S
Christopher	Cyp	2008	16,023	20,073	170	25	19	CC	

Saudi Arabian Oil (Vela International). SIRIUS STAR. *Hans Kraijenbosch*

Reederi Rudolf Schepers GmbH. TORGE S. *J. M. Kakebeeke*

Name	Flag	Year	GRT	DWT	LOA	Bm	Kts	Type	Former names
CMA CGM Brasilia	Deu	2004	25,630	33,390	207	30	21	CC	ex Julius S-04
CMA CGM Cordillera *	Atg	1995	11,964	14,464	150	23	18	CC	ex Inga S-08
CMA CGM Excellence	Atg	2005	35,581	44,135	223	32	22	CC	I/dn Tim S
CMA CGM Maya	Atg	1996	18,166	26,337	179	28	19	CC	ex Calaparana-06, Jan S-04, Helene Delmas-01, SCL Zaandam-00, P&O Nedlloyd Zaandam-99, CMBT Africa-97, Morecombe Bay-97, CMBT Africa-96, I/a Jan S
Constantin S *	Atg	2006	27,227	33,216	200	32	22	CC	
CSAV Paranagua	Atg	2001	35,645	42,211	220	32	22	CC	ex Norasia Everest-06, APL Venezuela-04, I/a Carolina, I/dn Camilla
CSAV Rio Petrohue	Atg	2002	25,630	33,500	207	30	22	CC	ex Safmarine Kei-04, Thea S-02
CSAV Tianjin *	Deu	2005	25,414	33,796	207	30	21	CC	ex Jula S-05
Emirates Norika	Atg	2008	26,435	34,362	209	30	22	CC	
Helene S *	Atg	2006	27,213	32,878	200	32	22	CC	
Jandavid S *	Atg	2003	27,227	33,232	200	32	22	CC	ex CSAV Shenzhen-06, Jandavid S-03
Katrin S	Atg	1995	11,964	14,454	150	23	18	CC	ex CSAV Dominicana-08, CCNI Altamira-08, Katrin S-07, Lykes Commodore-06, MSC Panama-04, Katrin S-03, Santa Paula-97, Katrin S-95
Kerstin S *	Deu	1997	25,361	33,936	207	30	21	CC	ex Valparaiso Express-08, P&O Nedlloyd Pantanal-05, Kerstin S-97
Libra Salvador *	Atg	2002	25,370	33,742	207	30	22	CC	ex NYK Pasion-05, Montemar Salvador-04, NYK Passion-03, Montemar Salvador-03, I/a Harald S
Libra Santos	Atg	2003	35,881	41,850	220	32	22	CC	ex Patricia-04, Amasia-03, I/a Cyrill
Marlene S *	Atg	1995	16,316	23,130	164	28	18	CC	ex Zim Buenos Aires-08, Libra Buenos Aires-99, Marlene S-97
MSC Cristobal	Atg	1997	25,361	33,976	207	30	21	CC	ex Maersk Nantes-07, Michaela S-04, Contship Spirit-03, Michaela S-97
Safmarine Pantanal *	Atg	2006	11,960	14,450	150	23	18	CC	I/a Karin S
Torge S *	Atg	2003	27,227	33,216	200	32	22	CC	ex Maersk Nassau-08, Torge S-04, Superior Container-03
TS Dammam	Atg	2006	35,581	44,053	223	32	22	CC	ex Emirates Wasl-08, Adelheid S-06, Hanjin Pusan-03
TS Pusan	Atg	2008	26,435	34,331	209	30	22	CC	ex Johannes S-08

newbuildings: three 41,500 grt, two * 25,320 dwt and one 17,700 dwt container ships, also two * 57,000 dwt bulk carriers for 2009-10 delivery.
* owned by H. Schepers Bereederungs GmbH & Co KG (www.hschepers.de)

Reederei Karl Schluter GmbH & Co KG   Germany

Funnel: *Blue with blue 'N' on broad white band, plain black or charterers colours.* **Hull:** *Various charterers colours.* **History:** *Formed 1986.* **Web:** www.rks-rd.de

Name	Flag	Year	GRT	DWT	LOA	Bm	Kts	Type	Former names
APL Dallas	Lbr	2008	36,007	42,019	231	32	23	CC	ex MOL Wave-08, APL Dallas-07
APL Minneapolis	Lbr	2008	36,007	42,000	231	32	23	CC	ex MOL Wind-09, APL Minneapolis-08
CMA CGM Respect	Lbr	2006	35,581	44,053	231	32	23	CC	ex Charles Dickens-06
Emirates Kanako	Lbr	2007	35,581	44,023	231	32	23	CC	ex William Shakespeare-07
Federal Mackinac **	Lbr	2004	18,825	27,785	185	24	14	B	
Federal Margaree **	Lbr	2005	18,825	25,781	185	24	14	B	
Federal Mattawa **	Lbr	2005	18,825	27,779	185	24	14	B	
German S	Atg	1990	24,344	31,552	182	31	18	CC	ex MSC Manaus-08, Kota Salam-02, German S-01, City of Haifa-01, CMA Dalian-00, German S-98, German Senator-98
Hermann Hesse	Lbr	2007	18,480	23,716	177	27	20	CC	
Indamex Colorado	Lbr	1995	36,606	45,217	245	32	23	CC	ex Northern Dignity-04, Ville de Gemina-02, Ming Gemina-01, Ville de Gemina-98, Northern Dignity-95
Kota Sabas	Lbr	2007	35,975	42,131	231	32	23	CC	
Laguna	Atg	1997	29,115	40,080	196	32	22	CC	ex Northern Vitality-07, MSC Rio Plata-06, Northern Vitality-02, Ming Trusty-01, Hyundai Trusty-98, I/a Northern Vitality
Maersk Danbury *	Lbr	2005	54,271	66,762	294	32	23	CC	ex Charles Dickens-05
Maersk Davenport *	Lbr	2005	54,271	66,762	294	32	23	CC	ex Ernest Hemingway-05
Maruba Zonda	Lbr	2006	18,480	23,700	177	27	20	CC	I/a Fritz Reuter
Matthias Claudius *	Lbr	2006	18,480	23,685	177	27	20	CC	
MSC Harmony	Atg	1994	19,819	20,252	174	27	18	CC	ex Northern Harmony-07, City of Tunis-05, Northern Harmony-94
MSC Uruguay	Atg	1996	29,115	40,087	196	32	22	CC	ex Northern Virtue-01, Hyundai Majesty-99, Northern Virtue-96

Name	Flag	Year	GRT	DWT	LOA	Bm	Kts	Type	Former names
Northern Fortune	Atg	1991	30,509	30,685	203	31	19	CC	ex Canmar Trader-03, Northern Fortune-02, Zim Ashdod I-01, OOCL Dragon-01, CMA Kawasaki-00, Northern Fortune-98, Zim Ravenna-98, Northern Fortune-97, Zim Brisbane-97, Valencia Senator-95, Northern Fortune-94, A. Abraham-94
Northern Trust	Cyp	1994	35,944	43,025	240	32	21	CC	ex Cosco Bremerhaven-08, Cosco Norfolk-06, Choyang Phoenix-01, Ville de Lyra-97, Northern Trust-94
Northern Valour	Atg	1996	29,115	40,114	196	32	22	CC	ex MSC China-09, Ming Fidelity-00, Hyundai Fidelity-98, Northern Valour-96
Northern Victory	Atg	1997	29,115	40,080	196	32	22	CC	ex MSC Salvador-06, Safmarine Everest-02, CMBT Everest-01, I/a Northern Victory
Theodor Storm	Cyp	2004	28,270	33,282	213	32	23	CC	
Thomas Mann	Lbr	2003	28,270	33,282	213	32	23	CC	

newbuildings: four 41,500 grt and one 30,000 grt container ships for 2009-10 delivery.
* managed for Hansa Hamburg Shipping International GmbH & Co KG. ** chartered to Fednav q.v.

Schoeller Holdings Ltd   Cyprus

Columbia Shipmanagement Ltd/Cyprus

Funnel: Buff or white with blue 'CSM' on broad red band edged with narrow blue bands, *** black with 'S' symbol on broad white band or charterers colours. **Hull:** Green, red or *** black with red boot-topping. **History:** Formed 1978.
Web: www.schoeller-holdings.com

Reederei Karl Schluter. MSC URUGUAY. *Allan Ryszka Onions*

Schoeller Holdings (Columbia). CAPE MANUEL. *Hans Kraijenbosch*

Name	Flag	Year	GRT	DWT	LOA	Bm	Kts	Type	Former names
Astra ***	Mhl	2002	79,525	149,995	272	46	15	T	
Bahia	Deu	2007	41,483	53,125	254	32	21	CC	
Brunhilde Salamon ***	Mhl	2001	39,126	75,940	225	32	14	B	ex Lake Camellia-04
Camberley	Lbr	2006	23,003	26,427	174	28	16	Lpg	
Cape Akrotiri ‡	Cyp	1998	57,148	105,176	244	42	15	T	ex Nordgulf-04
Cape Ancona ‡	Cyp	1998	57,148	105,337	244	42	15	T	ex Nordlight-04
Cape Aspro ‡	Cyp	1998	57,148	105,337	244	42	15	T	ex Nordisle-04
Cape Avila ‡	Cyp	1998	57,148	105,337	244	42	15	T	ex Nordocean-04
Cape Baker ‡	Mhl	2002	84,586	164,487	274	50	15	T	ex Decathlon-03
Cape Balboa ‡	Mhl	2002	84,586	164,236	274	50	15	T	ex Pentathlon-03
Cape Balder ‡	Mhl	2000	81,093	159,998	274	48	15	T	ex Hudson-06, Front Sun-03
Cape Bantry ‡	Mhl	2000	81,093	159,999	274	48	15	T	ex Potomac-06, Front Sky-03
Cape Bari ‡	Mhl	2005	81,076	159,186	274	48	15	T	
Cape Bastia ‡	Mhl	2005	81,076	159,156	274	48	15	T	
Cape Bata ‡	Mhl	2003	81,310	160,289	274	48	15	T	
Cape Bonny ‡	Mhl	2005	81,085	159,152	274	48	15	T	
Cape Bowen ‡	Mhl	2003	81,310	159,988	274	48	15	T	
Cape Brindisi ‡	Mhl	2006	81,076	159,195	274	48	15	T	
Cape Conway	Cyp	1985	17,280	22,312	170	27	17	Co	ex Delmas Touville-02, C.D.Pointe Noire-91, C.R.Pointe Noire-90
Cape Falcon §	Mhl	2003	14,308	16,421	155	25	18	CC	
Cape Faro	Mhl	2006	15,995	20,316	170	25	19	CC	
Cape Fawley	Mhl	2008	15,995	20,358	170	25	19	CC	
Cape Felton	Mhl	2008	15,995	20,351	170	25	19	CC	
Cape Ferrol	Mhl	2008	15,995	20,346	170	25	19	CC	
Cape Flores	Mhl	2005	14,308	16,393	155	25	18	CC	ex TS Ningbo-08, MOL Assurance-07, Cape Flores-05
Cape Forby	Mhl	2006	15,995	20,308	170	25	19	CC	
Cape Fox ‡‡	Mhl	2003	14,308	16,435	155	25	18	CC	ex YM Da Nang-08, TS Yokohama-04, Cape Fox-03
Cape Franklin	Mhl	2006	15,995	20,300	170	25	19	CC	
Cape Fraser	Mhl	2005	14,308	16,403	155	25	18	CC	ex USL Kea-08, Cape Fraser-06
Cape Fresco	Cyp	2004	14,308	16,439	155	25	18	CC	
Cape Fulmar	Mhl	2007	15,995	20,308	170	25	19	CC	
Cape Hastings	Cyp	1994	13,258	17,493	155	23	16	Co	ex Tula-06, Kew Bridge-03, Jolly Ambra-03, Kew Bridge-02, Seaboard Houston-02, Lykes Striker-01, Kew Bridge-00, Zim Houston 1-99, Kew Bridge-98, SEAL Reunion-97, Kapitan N. Petrosyan-94
Cape Hobart	Cyp	1993	13,237	17,546	155	23	16	Co	ex Azteca-07, ANL Progress-03, Melanesian Chief-02, Barnes Bridge-01, Island Chief-00, Chengtu-99, Barnes Bridge-98, SEAL Mauritius-97, Santander-94, Kapitan E. Freyman-93
Cape Howe	Cyp	1992	13.231	17,493	155	23	16	Co	
Cape Hudson	Cyp	1992	13,237	17,491	155	24	16	Co	ex Zapoteca-07, NDS Bengela-03, Waterloo Bridge-03, Nordana Defender-99, Waterloo Bridge-98, Zim Mexico-97, Zim Santos-96, Kapitan N. Kladko-92
Cape Manuel ‡	Cyp	2007	28,007	37,905	222	30	22	CC	
Cape Martin ‡	Cyp	2007	28,007	37,867	222	30	22	CC	
Cape Moreton #	Mhl	1982	16,558	23,706	161	25	16	Co	ex Freya-04, Torm Freya-01, Ove Skou-91
Cape Negro ##	Sgp	1998	17,609	23,752	183	28	19	CC	ex YM Dammam-07, Cape Negro-04, Norasia Malabar-04, Cape Negro-03, Ace Container-03
Cape Norviega ##	Sgp	1998	17,609	24,116	183	28	18	CC	ex Justice Container-03
Cape Preston	Cyp	1983	17,210	22,351	170	27	17	Co	ex Delmas Bougainville-01, C.D.Douala-91, C.R.Douala-90
Cape York	Cyp	1983	17,210	22,351	170	27	17	Co	ex Delmas Durville-02, Griffin Star-98, Australia Current-98, Delmas Joinville-96, C.D.Abidjan-91, C.R.Abidjan-90
CSAV Teno ‡	Cyp	2007	28,007	37,570	222	30	22	CC	
Fedor ***	Mhl	2003	41,397	70,156	228	32	14	T	ex Nidia-04
Golden Isle ‡	Mhl	2001	23,132	30,537	193	28	19	Co	ex Cape Darby-04
Hambisa ††	Mhl	1997	28,027	44,549	183	32	14	T	
Kanpur ##	Lbr	2005	57,243	106,094	244	42	14	T	
King Robert	Mhl	2008	89,510	169,676	291	45		B	ex Golden Sentosa-08
Overseas Meridian ***	Mhl	1997	156,880	300,349	330	58	15	T	ex Meridian Lion-06
Pacific Destiny ‡	Mhl	2002	23,132	30,396	193	28	19	Co	ex Tasman Explorer-08, Cape Denison-06, CCNI Hong Kong-06, Cape Denison-04

Name	Flag	Year	GRT	DWT	LOA	Bm	Kts	Type	Former names
Pacific Dream ‡	Mhl	2002	23,132	30,537	193	28	19	Co	ex Tasman Voyager-08, CCNI Shanghai-06, Cape Don-04
Rickmers Antwerp †	Mhl	2003	23,119	29,912	193	28	19	Co/hl	ex Cape Dart-02
Rickmers Shanghai †	Mhl	2003	23,119	30,095	193	28	19	Co/hl	
Rickmers Tokyo †	Mhl	2002	23,119	29,827	193	28	19	Co/hl	ex Cape Delgardo-02
Salah Al Deen	Mhl	2008	28,007	37,570	222	30	22	CC	ex Cape Magnus-08, l/a King Adam
TS Taichung ‡‡	Mhl	2003	14,308	16,400	155	25	18	CC	ex Cape Frio-05
Vereina	Mhl	2008	16,418	27,112	166	27	14	B	ex Casanna-08
Voyager ***	Mhl	2002	79,525	149,991	272	46	15	T	
YM Subic §	Mhl	2003	14,308	16,584	155	25	18	CC	ex Cape Ferro-05

newbuildings: ten 31,000 dwt and four 19,000 dwt general cargo, four 37,000 grt, four 27,000 grt and ten 18,300 grt container ships, two 114,000 dwt tamkers for 2009-11 delivery.

*Managed by subsidiaries Columbia Shipmanagement Ltd., Cyprus (www.columbia.com.cy) or * by Columbia Shipmanagement (Deutschland) GmbH or ** Columbia Shipmanagement (Singapore) Pte Ltd including ## for Lloyd Fonds AG. † managed by Columbia Shipmanagement (Deutschland) GmbH for Atlantic GmbH & Co KG, Germany (associated with Rickmers Reederei), †† for HCI Hanseatische Capital GmbH (founded 2004 – www. hci.de), ‡ for 40% owned Konig & Cie KG, ‡‡ for Konig subsidiary Marenave Schiffahrts AG (founded 2006 – www.marenave.com), *** for Salamon AG, Germany, § for First Ship Lease Pte Ltd, Bermuda, # for Atlantica Shipping AS, Norway (founded 1997 as joint venture between B Skaugen, AM Nomikos and Egon Oldendorff – www.atlantica-shipping.no) or ## for Foresight Ltd, UK. Also see Kristian Gerhard Jebsens Skipsrederei AS, Knutsen OAS Shipping AS and Rickmers Reederei GmbH & Cie KG.*

Hanse Bereederungs GmbH/Germany

History: *Associate company formed 1976 as Hanse Bereederungs GmbH & Co KG to 2005.* **Web:** *www.hanse-bereederung.de*

Name	Flag	Year	GRT	DWT	LOA	Bm	Kts	Type	Former names
Cape Ann	Cyp	1993	10,859	15,566	158	23	17	Co	ex Ibn Battotah-08, Cape Ann-04, Silver Dawn-03, Maersk Melbourne-98, Silver Dawn-98, Mumbai Bay-97, Silver Dawn-96, Universal Bahana-96
Cape Arago	Cyp	1992	10,837	15,566	158	23	17	Co	ex Silver Sky-03, Maersk Singapore-98, Silver Sky-98, Global Bahana-96
Cape Falster	Mhl	2005	14,308	16,397	156	25	18	CC	
Cape Flint	Mhl	2006	15,995	20,312	170	25	19	CC	
Cape Santiago *	Mhl	2003	14,241	18,402	159	24	18	CC	ex MSC Yaounde-03, Cape Santiago-02
Tiger Pearl	Sgp	1994	17,125	24,136	183	28	20	CC	ex Prosperity Container-03

*managed by Columbia Shipmanagement Ltd., Cyprus or * by Columbia Shipmanagement (Deutschland) GmbH, † by D-S Schiffahrt GmbH or ‡ by First Steamship (Germany) GmbH, all Germany.*

United Product Tanker (UPT) pool

Funnel: *Owners colours.* **Hull:** *Red with white 'UPT'.* **Web:** *www.uptankers.com*

Name	Flag	Year	GRT	DWT	LOA	Bm	Kts	Type	Former names
Cape Bacton	Mhl	2004	25,103	35,156	176	31	14	T	ex Celebes Wind-05, Chabua Amiredjibi-05
Cape Beale ‡	Mhl	2005	25,108	40,327	176	31	14	T	
Cape Beira	Mhl	2005	25,400	40,946	176	31	14	T	ex Sable-05
Cape Benat	Lbr	1998	21,165	33,540	179	25	14	T	
Cape Bilbao	Mhl	2006	25,108	40,000	176	31	14	T	ex Cape Brindsini-06
Cape Bille ‡	Mhl	2003	25,108	35,089	176	31	14	T	
Cape Bird ‡	Mhl	2003	25,108	35,070	176	31	14	T	
Cape Blanc	Lbr	1998	21,165	33,540	179	25	14	T	
Cape Bon ‡	Mhl	2003	25,108	35,089	176	31	14	T	
Cape Bradley	Mhl	2004	25,108	35,159	176	31	14	T	ex J. Shartava-05
Cape Brasilia	Mhl	2006	25,108	40,327	176	32	14	T	

Schoeller Holdings (Columbia). RICKMERS SHANGHAI. *Guido van Driessche*

Name	Flag	Year	GRT	DWT	LOA	Bm	Kts	Type	Former names
Cape Bruny ‡	Mhl	2004	25,108	35,096	176	31	14	T	
Cape Taft	Mhl	2008	42,010	73,711	229	32	14	T	
Cape Talara	Mhl	2008	42,010	73,400	229	32	14	T	
Cape Tallin	Mhl	2008	42,010	73,400	229	32	14	T	
Cape Tampa	Mhl	2009	42,010	73,400	229	32	14	T	
Cape Taura	Mhl	2009	42,010	73,400	229	32	14	T	
Cape Tees	Mhl	2009	42,010	73,400	229	32	14	T	
Cape Texel	Mhl	2009	42,010	73,400	229	32	14	T	
Cape Troy	Mhl	2008	42,010	73,400	229	32	14	T	
Conti Agulhas	Lbr	2008	23,403	37,606	184	27	14	T	
Conti Benguela	Lbr	2008	23,403	37,500	184	27	14	T	
Conti Equator *	Lbr	2008	22,403	37,527	184	27	14	T	
Conti Greenland *	Lbr	2008	22,403	37,606	184	27	14	T	
Conti Guinea *	Lbr	2008	22,403	37,000	184	27	14	T	
Conti Humboldt *	Lbr	2008	22,403	37,000	184	27	14	T	
Mount Adamello ††	Cyp	2004	22,521	40,002	182	27	14	T	
Mount Fuji ††	Cyp	2003	22,515	40,055	182	27	14	T	
Mount Green †	Cyp	2007	22,521	40,055	182	27	14	T	
Mount Karava †	Cyp	2007	22,521	40,020	182	27	14	T	
Mount Hope †	Cyp	2007	22,521	40,009	182	27	14	T	
Mount McKinney ††	Cyp	2004	22,518	39,997	182	27	14	T	
Mount Olympus ††	Cyp	2003	22,515	40,011	182	27	14	T	
Mount Rainier ††	Cyp	2004	22,518	40,012	182	27	14	T	
Mount Robson ††	Cyp	2004	22,518	40,014	182	27	14	T	
Mount Victoria †	Cyp	2007	22,521	40,055	182	27	14	T	
Summit America ††	Cyp	2006	41,021	74,996	229	32	14	T	
Summit Europe ††	Cyp	2006	41,021	74,997	229	32	14	T	

Pool operated by Schoeller Holdings Ltd. Vessels owned/managed by Schoeller Holdings (managed by Columbia Shipmanagement (Deutschland) GmbH) or ‡ for 40% owned Konig & Cie KG, * managed by NSB Niederelbe Schiffahrts GmbH & Co KG for associated Conti Reedere (Conti Holding GmbH & Co KG – www.conti-gruppe.de), † by Hartmann Schiffahrts GmbH & Co KG or †† associated Donnelly Tanker Management Ltd, Cyprus (formed 1995 - www.donnellytanker.com.cy).

The Schulte Group Germany

Funnel: Green with white 'S' on red disc and black top, or charterer's colours. **Hull:** Dark grey with red boot-topping. **History:** Formed 1937. **Web:** www.beschulte.de or www.bs-shipmanagement.com

Name	Flag	Year	GRT	DWT	LOA	Bm	Kts	Type	Former names
Abram Schulte §	Cyp	2004	41,503	72,663	228	32	14	T	l/a Penyu Pulan
Alfred Oldendorff	Lbr	1996	25,074	46,489	190	31	14	B	ex Diamond Halo-04
Angelica Schulte	Lbr	2005	56,163	106,433	243	42	14	T	
Anna Schulte §§	Lbr	2001	26,626	34,717	210	30	22	CC	ex P&O Nedlloyd Andes-05, P&O Nedlloyd Rose-01, l/a Anna Schulte
APL Amman	Lbr	2002	35,589	40,995	232	32	22	CC	ex ANL Emblem-07, CMA CGM Gauguin-03, Arnold Schulte-02
APL Bangkok ‡	Hkg	2006	35,991	42,083	231	32	23	CC	
APL Colorado	Sgp	2009	75,000	79,560	304	40	25	CC	
APL Illinois	Sgp	2009	74,000	79,560	304	40	25	CC	l/dn Dorothea
APL Sharjah	Lbr	2002	35,589	40,995	232	32	22	CC	ex CMA CGM Chardin-07, Friedrich Schulte-02, CMA CGM Gauguin-02, l/a Friedrich Schulte

Schoeller (United Product Tanker). CAPE BENAT. *Allan Ryszka Onions*

Name	Flag	Year	GRT	DWT	LOA	Bm	Kts	Type	Former names
APL Sydney †	Cyp	2006	35,697	41,500	231	32	23	CC	ex Philippa Schulte-06
APL Tennessee	Sgp	2009	74,000	79,560	304	40	25	CC	l/dn Louisa Schulte
APL Texas	Sgp	2009	74,000	79,560	304	40	25	CC	l/dn Charlotte Schulte
APL Washington	Sgp	2009	74,000	79,560	304	40	25	CC	l/dn Astrid Schulte
Auguste Schulte §	Lbr	2002	27,093	34,662	210	30	22	CC	ex CMA CGM Claudel-07, Claudel-02, l/a Alexandria, l/dn Auguste Schulte
Bahama Spirit ***	Vut	1995	26,792	46,606	188	32	14	Bu	ex Freeport Miner-00, San Pietro-99 (conv B-00)
Barnes Bridge ≠	Vct	1982	12,183	16,225	159	21	14	Lpg	ex Tycho Brahe-06
Cala Pinar del Rio †	Atg	1994	14,619	20,275	167	25	17	CC	ex Nordpol-05, Indamex Taj-02, Abidjan Star II-00, Nordpol-99, TNX Mercury-98, Nordpol-98, San Marino-97, Nordpol-94
Canaima *	Ven	1994	18,360	23,267	160	26	16	Lpg	ex Henning Maersk-06
Cap Bisti	Lbr	2001	26,582	34,662	210	30	21	CC	ex Libra Houston-06, Caroline Schulte-02, Thekla Schulte-01
Cap Bizerta **	Cyp	2006	26,671	34,457	210	30	21	CC	ex Margarete Schulte-06
Cap Bon **	Cyp	2006	26.671	34,629	210	30	21	CC	
Cap Breton	Lbr	2001	26,582	33,871	210	30	22	CC	ex Christaine Schulte-07, Elisabeth Schulte-01
Cap Maleas ††	Cyp	2005	18,334	23,679	175	27	20	CC	ex Konrad Schulte-05, l/a Lambert Schulte
Cap Manuel	Lbr	2008	35,991	42,201	231	32	23	CC	l/a Guenther Schulte
Cap Mondego	Lbr	2008	35,991	42,057	231	32	23	CC	ex Georg Schulte-08
Christine O #	Atg	1996	18,070	27,000	175	26	14	B	ex Abbot Point-07, Forest Venture-04
Elise Schulte	Hkg	1999	56,239	106,122	241	42	14	T	ex Ammon-04
Esther Schulte ‡	Cyp	2001	26,582	33,871	210	30	22	CC	ex P&O Nedlloyd Altiplano-05, Esther Schulte-02, l/a Marianne Schulte
Frederike Oldendorff	Lbr	1997	26,586	48,224	189	31	14	B	ex Mercury Trader-03
Green Ace ≠≠	Cyp	2005	18,344	23,579	176	27	20	CC	ex Sea Beta-08, Boomerang 1-06, Sea Beta-06
Henley Bridge ≠	Sgp	1989	19,719	29,171	166	27	16	Lpg	ex BW Munin-08, Berge Munin-07, Cheshire-05
Henrietta Schulte	Lbr	1997	16,281	22,352	179	25	19	CC	ex Cap Rojo-08, Henriette Schulte-05, P&O Nedlloyd Lome-04, FESCO Voyager-02, Henriette Schulte-00, CSAV Brasilia-98, Henriette Schulte-97
Hua Yun He	Lbr	2000	20,624	25,850	180	28	20	CC	
Ibn Al Roomi	Lbr	1999	20,624	25,685	180	28	20	CC	
Imme Oldendorff	Lbr	1999	28,078	48,913	190	32	14	B	ex Royal Chance-03
Johann Schulte	Iom	1997	15,180	17,914	155	23	16	Lpg	
Kadriah II ‡	Mys	1988	18,023	29,998	167	27	14	T	ex Severn-03, Valiant Express-97
Kasper Schulte §	Cyp	2004	41,503	72,718	225	32	14	T	l/a Penyu Hijau
Kew Bridge ≠	Nis	1983	12,240	16,228	159	21	15	Lpg	ex Immanuel Kant-06
Lady Chiara ††	Lbr	1986	16,282	27,325	170	23	15	T	ex Evadia-06, Cielo di Barents-04, Maersk Barents-02, Edzard-97, Maersk Barents-97, Robert Maersk-97
Lambert Schulte †	Sgp	2005	18,334	23,579	175	27	20	CC	ex Cap Agulhas-08, Lambert Schulte-05
Libra Ecuador	Lbr	1997	16,281	22,361	192	25	19	CC	ex Helen Schulte-03, Direct Kiwi-03, Helen Schulte-99, Libra Houston-98, Helen Schulte-97
Louisa Schulte †	Sgp	2008	18.321	23,252	176	27	20	CC	
Ludwig Schulte	Cyp	2008	18,300	23,175	175	27	20	CC	

The Schulte Group. ANNA SCHULTE. *Phil Kempsey*

Name	Flag	Year	GRT	DWT	LOA	Bm	Kts	Type	Former names
Maersk Nairobi	Cyp	2001	26,582	34,717	210	30	22	CC	ex Donata Schulte-06
Maersk Needham *	Sgp	2006	26,671	34,704	210	30	22	CC	ex Hannah Schulte-08
Maersk Norwich *	Sgp	2006	26,671	34,396	210	30	22	CC	
Maersk Noumea	Lbr	2001	26,718	34,717	210	30	21	CC	ex Elisabeth Schulte-06, I/a Esther Schulte
Maersk Rhone	Iom	1999	22,181	35,000	171	27	14	T	ex Rita Maersk-03
Marianne Schulte §§	Lbr	2001	26,718	34,643	210	30	21	CC	ex P&O Nedlloyd Acapulco-05, I/a Marianne Schulte
Maruba Cristina	Lbr	2007	35,991	42,074	231	32	23	CC	ex Cap Moreton-07, I/a Gabriel Schulte
Max Oldebdorff	Lbr	1997	26,586	48,225	189	31	14	B	ex Million Trader-03
May Oldendorff	Lbr	1997	26,040	45,874	188	31	14	B	ex Houyu-03
Montemar Europa ≠≠	Mhl	2003	16,803	22,900	185	25	20	CC	
Nordic Gas *	Sgp	1994	18,360	23,267	160	26	16	Lpg	ex Henriette Maersk-07
NSS Fortune ‡‡	Pan	2003	93,199	184,872	290	47	14	B	
Omega King ‡	Mhl	2004	40,000	75,000	225	32	14	T	ex Everhard Schulte-06
Omega Queen ‡	Hkg	2004	42,432	75,000	225	32	14	T	ex Rudolf Schulte-06
Pacific Horizon ††	Pan	1999	23,458	44,370	182	32	14	T	
Pacific Horizon II *	Pan	2007	25,180	37,981	182	28	14	T	
Pacific Prosperity ‡‡	Pan	1998	90,876	179,385	290	47	14	B	ex Dyna Mercury-02
Pacific Ruby ‡‡	Hkg	1993	147,902	254,095	324	56	15	O	ex Atlantic Ruby-03 (conv T)
Palenque ##	Lbr	1987	23,127	37,574	175	30	15	T	ex Al Soor-94, Atlantic Conquest-90
Phyllis N ‡‡	Lbr	1990	153,347	285,768	328	57	14	T	ex Grand Explorer-08, Neon-04, Argo Elektra-00, Alexita-97, Argo Elektra-93
Renate Schulte	Deu	1994	14,619	20,275	166	25	17	CC	ex CMA CGM Oyapock-08, Karthago-04, Renate Schulte-01, Libra Houston-97, Renate Schulte-96, Europa Express-95, Renate Schulte-94
Ridge	Deu	1995	10,749	14,148	163	22	17	CC	ex Caecilia Schulte-07, CGM Cayenne-02, Caecilia Schulte-99, Atika Delmas-98, CMBT Antarctica-98, Caecilia Schulte-96
Rui Yun He	Lbr	2000	20,569	25,648	180	28	20	CC	ex Karin Schulte-00
Sabrewing ¶¶	Pan	2004	29,647	49,323	186	32	14	T	
Santa Elena ¶	Ven	1986	28,017	50,600	183	32	14	T	ex Sanmar Sentinel-05, Torm Gunhild-96
Sea Alfa ≠≠	Cyp	2005	18,327	23,395	176	27	19	CC	
Sriracha Trader	Tha	1995	28,628	47,629	183	32	14	T	ex Torm Gotland-08
Susanne Schulte §§	Lbr	2001	26,626	34,717	210	30	22	CC	ex P&O Nedlloyd Aconcagua-05, I/a Susanne Schulte
Thekla Schulte §§	Lbr	2001	26,718	34,677	210	30	22	CC	ex P&O Nedlloyd Antisana-05, Thekla Schulte-01, I/a Caroline Schulte
Weser Stahl ***	Cyp	1999	28,564	47,257	192	32	12	Bu	
Wilhelm Schulte	Iom	1997	15,180	17,900	155	23	16	Lpg	

newbuildings: four 40,500 grt, one 36,900 grt container ships, four 18,400 grt Lpg tankers and a 25,000 dwt tanker for 2009-10 delivery.
*Owned or managed by subsidiaries Bernhard Schulte Shipmanagement (Deutschland) GmbH & Co KG (formed 2000 as Reimarus Schiffahrtskantor GmbH to 2006, Hanseatic Shipping (Deutschland) GmbH and Vorsetzen Schiffs GmbH (formed 2000) to 2008), * by Bernhard Schulte Shipmanagement (Singapore) Pte Ltd (Eurasia Marine Services to 2001, Eurasia International (Singapore) Pte Ltd to 2008), ** by Bernhard Schulte Shipmanagement (Bermuda) Ltd Partnership (formed 1978 as Atlantic Marine Ltd to 2007, Dorchester Atlantic Marine Ltd to 2008), † by Bernhard Schulte Shipmanagement (China) Co Ltd (Eurasia Ship Management (Shanghai) Co Ltd to 2008), †† by Bernhard Schulte Shipmanagement Cyprus) Ltd (formed 1972 as Hanseatic Shipping Co to 2008), ‡ by Bernhard Schulte Shipmanagement (Hong Kong) Ltd (formed 1981 and became wholly owned subsidiary in 1988) or ‡‡ by Bernhard Schulte Shipmanagement (India) Pvt Ltd.*
*Managed for *** Algoma Central Corp,Canada, § for HCI Capital AG, Germany, §§ for Commerz Real Fonds, Germany, # for Opielok Reederei GmbH, Germany, ## for Grupo TMM SA de CV, Mexico, ¶ for Goldenport Shipmanagement Ltd, Greece, ¶¶ for Japanese banks, ≠ for MC Shipping Inc, Monaco or ≠≠ for Ship Finance International Ltd, Bermuda.*
Also see Allocean Ltd, Cido Shipping (HK) Co Ltd, ER Schiffahrt GmbH (Nordcapital Holding GmbH), Kristian Gerhard Jebsen Skipsrederi AS, MPC Munchmeyer Petersen & Co GmbH, The National Shipping Company of Saudi Arabia, NileDutch Africa Line and D Oltmann GmbH & Co

Reederei Thomas Schulte GmbH & Co KG   Germany

Funnel: Black with white 'TS' on red diamond on broad green band. **Hull:** Dark green with red boot-topping. **History:** Founded 1985 having previously worked for family company, Bernhard Schulte. **Web:** www.reederei-t-schulte.com

Name	Flag	Year	GRT	DWT	LOA	Bm	Kts	Type	Former names
Annabelle Schulte *	Cyp	2002	27,093	34,638	210	30	22	CC	ex P&O Nedlloyf Barossa Valley-05, P&O Nedlloyd Barossa-02, I/a Kynouria
Antje Schulte	Atg	1997	15,929	22,015	168	27	21	CC	ex Alianca Rotterdam-01, Antje Schulte-00, CGM Mascareignes-99, CGM Santos Dumont II-99, Alianca America-98, CSAV Reloncav-98, Antje Schulte-97
APL Shenzhen	Cyp	2006	35,697	42,141	231	32	23	CC	ex Maria Schulte-06
APL Sokhna	Cyp	2006	35,975	42,164	231	32	23	CC	ex MOL Wonder-08, APL Sokhna-08
Ariake	Cyp	2005	28,592	39,383	222	30	22	CC	I/a Sarah Schulte
Beatrice Schulte	Lbr	2009	39,900	50,500	260	32	24	CC	
Benedict Schulte	Lbr	2009	39,900	50,500	260	32	24	CC	
Benita Schulte	Lbr	2009	39,900	50,500	260	32	24	CC	
Benjamin Schulte	Lbr	2009	39,900	50,500	260	32	24	CC	

Name	Flag	Year	GRT	DWT	LOA	Bm	Kts	Type	Former names
Cap Beatrice ‡	Lbr	2007	28,616	39,462	222	30	23	CC	ex Annina Schulte-07
Cap Capricorn ‡	Lbr	2007	28,616	39,338	222	30	23	CC	ex Valentina Schulte-07
Cap Cleveland ‡	Lbr	2007	28,616	39,339	222	30	23	CC	ex Sofia Schulte-08
CMA CGM Iroko	Deu	1997	15,929	22,015	168	27	21	CC	ex Fabian Schulte-07, Maersk Cabello-98, Fabian Schulte-97
CMA CGM Rose	Lbr	2005	27,779	39,200	222	30	23	CC	ex E.R. Marseille-05
CSAV Itaim ‡	Cyp	2006	35,697	42,106	231	32	23	CC	ex Helena Schulte-06
CSAV Panamby	Cyp	2006	35,697	41,500	231	32	23	CC	I/a Lisa Schulte
CSAV Rotterdam	Cyp	2005	18,334	23,351	176	28	19	CC	I/a Maximilian Schulte, I/dn Laura Schulte
Francisca Schulte	Cyp	1998	15,929	22,020	169	27	21	CC	ex Safmarine Pakistan-06, Francisca Schulte-03, Maersk San Jose-99, I/a Francisca Schulte
Kota Pekarang	Lbr	2005	28,927	39,275	222	30	23	CC	ex E.R. Manchester-05
Kota Pemimpin	Lbr	2005	28,927	39,200	222	30	23	CC	ex E.R. Malta-05
Laura Schulte	Cyp	2004	18,334	23,579	175	27	20	CC	ex Maersk Varna-08, Laura Schulte-04, I/a Maximilian Schulte, I/dn Konrad Schulte
Maersk Nanhai	Cyp	2005	25,406	33,900	207	30	22	CC	ex P&O Nedlloyd Savannah-05, I/a Julia Schulte
Maersk Navia	Cyp	2005	25,406	33,900	207	30	22	CC	ex P&O Nedlloyd Mariana-05, I/a Antonia Schulte
Maersk Neuchatel †	Cyp	2005	25,674	33,651	207	30	22	CC	ex Natalie Schulte-05
Maersk Neustadt †	Lbr	2005	25,674	33,594	207	30	22	CC	ex Isabelle Schulte-05
Marie Schulte †	Atg	2001	16,803	22,900	185	25	20	CC	
Maruba Confidence	Cyp	2000	17,167	21,152	169	27	18	CC	ex Maersk Vienna-07, Direct Eagle-04, Spica-00
NYK Floresta	Cyp	2005	25,406	33,900	208	30	22	CC	ex Victoria Schulte-05
Patricia Schulte *	Cyp	2006	27,779	39,400	222	30	22	CC	
Tatiana Schulte	Cyp	2005	27,779	39,400	222	30	22	CC	

newbuildings: four 50,000 dwt, four 47,000 dwt and two 34,000 dwt container ships, two 115,000 dwt, four 92,500 dwt and two 80,000 dwt bulk carriers for 2010-11 delivery,
* managed by Ocean Shipmanagement GmbH, † for Atlantic. Zur Vermittlung Internationaler Investitionen GmbH & Co or ‡ for Lloyd Fonds AG

Seatrade Groningen BV   Netherlands

Funnel: *Blue with white 'S' and blue 'G' symbol on orange square.* **Hull:** *White with blue 'Seatrade' or charterers name, red boot-topping.* **History:** *Established in 1951 by five captain-owners as NV Scheepvaarts Groningen to 1973. Acquired Dammers & Van der Heide's Shipping & Trading Co BV (formed 1947) in 1989, Triton Schiffahrts GmbH (formed 1994) in 2000 and United Reefers Chartering Ltd (formed 1994 as Global Reefer Trading Ltd to 2002) in 2005. Acquired reefer fleet of Amer Shipping in 2008.*
Web: *www.seatrade.com or www.reedereitriton.de*

Name	Flag	Year	GRT	DWT	LOA	Bm	Kts	Type	Former names
Aconcagua Bay	Pan	1992	9,074	11,581	149	21	19	R	ex United Ice-06, Aconcagua-02
Agulhas Stream *	Ant	1998	9,298	11,048	150	22	20	R	
Atlantic Hope	Pan	1984	7,777	8,494	142	20	18	R	ex Magellan Rex-96
Atlantic Mermaid *	Lbr	1992	9,829	10,464	142	23	19	R	
Atlantic Reefer	Ant	1998	10,991	12,633	145	23	21	R	
Barents Bay §	Vct	1984	7,726	8,549	139	21	17	R	ex Chiricana-00, Juvante-87
Benguela Stream	Nld	1998	9,298	11,016	150	22	20	R	
Boston Bay	Pan	1983	7,741	8,538	139	21	18	R	ex Sun Claudia-06, Levante-98
Bristol Bay §	Pan	1984	7,736	8,556	139	21	17	R	ex Sun Alex-05, Punente-99
Buzzard Bay *	Lbr	1992	10,381	10,621	150	23	20	R	ex French Bay-04, Royal Star-99, Chiquita Honshu-94, Royal Star-92
Cape Passero	Mlt	1991	6,419	6,794	120	19	17	R	
Cape Vincente	Lbr	1991	6,419	6,494	120	19	17	R	
Caribbean Mermaid *	Lbr	1993	9,829	10,464	142	23	19	R	ex Northern Mermaid-04, Caribbean Mermaid-02
Changuinola Bay	Bhs	1988	8,487	9,727	141	21	21	R	ex Sun Rosie-06, Cap Changuinola-00
Cloudy Bay	Mlt	1984	10,325	11,779	152	22	21	R	ex Astro Bright-01, Nordenham-97
Cold Stream	Ant	1994	8,414	10,066	140	22	19	R	I/a Prince of Streams
Comoros Stream †	Nld	2000	11,382	12,906	155	24	21	R	
Condor Bay	Pan	1990	10,405	10,742	150	23	20	R	ex Ivory Nina-03, Ivory Cape-01
Cool Express	Nld	1994	5,471	7,480	126	16	18	R	
Coral Mermaid *	Lbr	1992	9,829	10,461	142	23	19	R	ex Arctic Mermaid-06, Maud-04, Coral Mermaid-01
Discovery Bay	Bhs	1997	8,924	10,100	142	22	21	R	
Eagle Bay *	Ant	1992	10,402	10,621	150	23	20	R	ex Ivory Eagle-03
Eastern Bay †	Pan	1997	8,917	9,662	143	22	19	R	ex Eastern Express-05, I/a Frost Express
Elsebeth †	Nld	1998	10,519	10,327	152	23	21	R	
Elvira †	Nld	2000	10,532	10,309	152	23	21	R	
Emerald †	Nld	2000	10,532	10,346	152	23	21	R	
Esmeralda †	Nld	1999	10,532	10,358	152	23	21	R	
Everest Bay	Lbr	1989	8,739	9,692	141	21	21	R	ex United Cold-06, E.W. Everest-02
Falcon Bay *	Ant	1993	10,374	10,532	150	23	20	R	ex Ivory Falcon-02
Fortuna Bay *	Ant	1993	10,203	11,585	145	22	19	R	ex Fortune Bay-03, Uruguayan Reefer-99
Frio Hellenic §	Pan	1998	9,997	11,070	148	22	21	R	
Fuji Bay	Lbr	1990	9,070	11,540	149	21	17	R	ex Amer Fuji-08

Seatrade Groningen. POLARLIGHT. *Hans Kraijenbosch*

Seatrade Groningen. PRINCE OF SOUNDS. *J. M. Kakebeeke*

Seatrade Groningen. SUMMER PHOENIX. *Allan Ryszka Onions*

Name	Flag	Year	GRT	DWT	LOA	Bm	Kts	Type	Former names
Hawk Bay *	Ant	1992	10,381	10,603	150	23	20	R	ex Roman Bay-04, Roman Star-99, Chiquita Sulu-94
Hope Bay *	Ant	1996	8,396	9,639	143	22	20	R	
Humboldt Bay	Lbr	1990	9,070	11,633	149	21	20	R	ex Amer Whitney-08, Californian Reefer-98, Humboldt Rex-94
Humboldt Rex #	Phl	1998	7,637	9,011	139	21	20	R	
Izumo Bay §	Vct	1984	9,273	10,644	150	21	19	R	ex UB Libra-02, Libra-96, Izumo Reefer-95
Kashima Bay §	Cym	1984	9,273	10,647	150	21	19	R	ex UB Gemini-02, Gemini-96, Kashima Reefer-95
Kasuga Bay §	Cym	1984	9,274	10,647	150	21	19	R	ex Arimao Universal-02, Kasuga Bay-95
Klipper Stream ‡	Nld	1998	9,305	10,936	150	22	21	R	
Koala Bay §§	Lbr	1984	9,057	9,340	149	21	19	R	ex Mulungisi-07, Koala-95
Lake Phoenix *	Lbr	1992	7,303	8,075	134	21	19	R	ex Amber Rose-96
Lombok Strait †	Nld	2002	13,700	13,512	167	25	22	R	ex Leopard Max-02
Luzon Strait †	Nld	2002	13,700	14,413	167	25	22	R	ex Tiger Max-02
Marine Phoenix	Lbr	1994	7,313	7,957	134	21	19	R	ex Amber Lily-97
Mexican Bay *	Pan	1994	10,203	11,575	145	22	20	R	ex Mexican Reefer-06
Nagoya Bay §	Vct	1983	9,755	12,181	150	22	18	R	ex Actric Dawn-00, Cap Frio-95, Oceanic Trader-93, Ocean Pride-92, l/a Ocean Bride
Pacific	Nld	1996	5,918	8,500	134	16	16	R	
Pacific Mermaid *	Pan	1992	9,820	10,466	142	23	19	R	
Pacific Reefer	Ant	1999	10,991	12,625	145	23	21	R	
Pioneer Bay	Pan	1982	7,748	8,678	142	20	17	R	ex Pioneer Express-05, Pioneer Reefer-93, Rehmannia-88, Raffia Universal-86
Polarlight †	Pan	1998	11,417	10,447	154	24	21	R	ex Polarlicht-04
Polarsteam †	Nld	1999	11,417	10,449	154	24	21	R	ex Polarstern-03
Prince of Seas *	Nld	1993	6,363	7,387	120	19	17	R	
Prince of Sounds *	Lbr	1993	7,534	8,053	136	20	19	R	ex Santiago I-04, Santiago-01
Prince of Streams *	Ant	1993	7,533	8,384	137	20	18	R	ex Wilmington-02
Prince of Tides *	Bhs	1993	7,329	5,360	134	21	19	R	
Prince of Waves *	Bhs	1993	7,329	8,039	134	21	19	R	
River Phoenix *	Lbr	1993	7,313	8,044	134	21	19	R	ex Clover Moon-99, Dover Phoenix-97
Royal Klipper ‡	Nld	2000	11,382	12,906	155	24	21	R	ex Equator Stream-00
Royal Reefer §	Vct	1979	9,018	9,125	151	21	20	R	ex African Princess-96, Hawaii-89
Runaway Bay	Bhs	1992	9,070	11,579	149	21	17	R	ex Sun Maria-05, Diamond Reefer-98, Hudson Rex-95
Santa Catharina	Bhs	2000	8,597	9,259	143	22	19	R	
Santa Lucia †	Nld	1999	8,507	9,566	143	22	20	R	l/a Santa Lucia II
Santa Maria †	Ant	1999	8,507	9,566	143	22	20	R	l/a Santa Maria III
Sea Phoenix	Lbr	1992	7,303	8,056	134	21	19	R	ex Amber Cherry-96
Season Trader #	Phl	2000	7,627	9,011	139	21	20	R	
Southern Bay †	Pan	1997	8,879	9,609	143	22	19	R	ex Southern Express-05
Spring Bear	Bhs	1984	12,615	9,472	152	24	19	R	ex Spring Dream-85
Spring Bob	Nld	1984	12,111	10,098	151	24	19	R	ex Spring Blossom-85
Spring Bok	Nld	1984	12,113	10,113	151	24	18	R	ex Spring Bee-02, Spring Bird-84
Spring Deli	Ant	1984	12,783	9,891	152	24	18	R	ex Spring Delight-03
Spring Dragon §	Vct	1984	12,783	9,906	152	24	18	R	ex Spring Dream-98, Spring Desire-89
Spring Panda	Nld	1984	12,111	10,140	151	24	19	R	ex Spring Ballad-85, Spring Blossom-84
Spring Tiger	Nld	1984	12,340	10,110	148	24	19	R	ex Spring Breeze-90
Storm Bay	Vct	1983	10,325	11,720	152	22	21	R	ex Atlantic Dawn-01, Nienburg-95
Summer Phoenix *	Gbr	1993	7,326	8,041	134	21	19	R	ex Spring Phoenix-01, Windward Phoenix-99
Tama Hope	Bhs	1986	6,579	7,690	146	19	18	R	ex Lamitan-93, Tama Hope-92
Tama Star	Bhs	1987	6,579	7,685	146	19	18	R	ex Bulan-93, Tama Star-92
Tasman Bay §	Pan	1989	6,545	7,168	146	19	18	R	ex Kowhai-04
Tasman Mermaid *	Lbr	1993	9,829	10,457	142	23	19	R	ex Antarctic Mermaid-06, Skausund-04, Tasman Mermaid-01
Timor Stream †	Pan	1998	9,307	11,013	150	22	20	R	ex Stream Express-05
Wealth Reefer	Lbr	1986	7,286	7,348	145	20	19	R	ex Kedarnath-08, Virginia Universal-05, Wealth Reefer-96
Whitney Bay	Lbr	1990	8.739	9,692	141	21	21	R	ex United Cool-06, E.W. Whitney-03
Wind Frost	Lbr	1989	9,072	11,622	149	21	19	R	ex Amer Everest-08, Hokkaido Rex-95
Yasaka Bay §	Cym	1983	9,273	10,647	150	21	19	R	ex Pasadena Universal-02, Yasaka Bay-95

newbuildings: eight 15,200 dwt reefer ships for 2010-13 delivery.
In addition to the above, the company also operates about 40 smaller reefer vessels. Owned/managed by subsidiary * Triton Schiffahrts GmbH, Germany (www.reedereitriton.de) or † managed by Triton for MPC Munchmeyer Petersen & Co GmbH qv. § owned by Laskaridis Shipping Co Ltd or ‡ by Jaczon BV, Netherlands (www.jaczon.nl), §§ by Roswell Navigation Corp, Greece or # by Victoria Ship Management Inc, Philippines. Also see vessels chartered from Dole Food Co, Hansa Treuhand Schiffsbeteiligungs AG & Co KG and Thien & Heyenga GmbH

Shell-Royal Dutch Group

UK

Funnel: Yellow with narrow black top. **Hull:** Red, black or grey with red or blue boot-topping. **History:** Formed 1907 jointly by Royal Dutch Petroleum Co (formed 1890) and Shell Transport & Trading Plc (formed 1897). Took control of Mexican Eagle Petroleum Co in 1919. Formed Shell-Mex Ltd in 1921, which merged in 1932 with BP to form Shell-Mex & BP Ltd until separated in 1975. Parent renamed Royal Dutch Shell plc in 2004. **Web:** www.shell.com

Name	Flag	Year	GRT	DWT	LOA	Bm	Kts	Type	Former names
Abadi (st)	Bmu	2002	117,461	72,758	290	46	19	Lng	
Bebatik (st) *	Brn	1972	48,612	51,579	257	35	18	Lng	ex Gadinia-86
Bekalang (st) *	Brn	1973	48,612	51,579	248	35	18	Lng	ex Gadila-86
Bekulan (st) *	Brn	1973	48,612	51,579	248	35	18	Lng	ex Gari-86
Belais (st) *	Brn	1974	48,612	51,579	257	35	18	Lng	ex Gastrana-86
Belanak (st) *	Brn	1975	48,612	51,579	257	35	18	Lng	ex Gouldia-86
Bilis (st) *	Brn	1975	52,708	41,370	248	35	18	Lng	ex Geomitra-86
Bubuk (st) *	Brn	1975	52,708	41,370	248	35	18	Lng	ex Genota-86
Donax **	Sgp	2001	61,764	109,326	245	42	15	T	ex Maersk Prosper-01
Dromus **	Sgp	1999	61,764	110,000	245	42	15	T	ex Maersk Prime-04
Estrella Atlantica §	Arg	1982	17,707	28,750	183	29	15	T	ex Humberto Beghin-95
Estrella Austral §	Arg	1984	28,259	45,718	197	32	14	T	ex Feosa Ambassador 2-88
Estrella Pampeana §	Arg	1981	37,685	57,741	229	32	14	T	ex Zenatia-96, Oak River-88, Salena-81
Ficus	Iom	2001	27,539	44,881	183	32	16	T	I/a Elka Angelique
Fulgur	Iom	2001	27,539	44,787	183	32	16	T	I/a Elka Eleftheria
Fusus	Iom	2001	27,542	44,788	183	32	16	T	ex Elka Nikolas-01
Galea (st)	Sgp	2002	111,459	64,243	290	46	19	Lng	
Galeomma (st)	Sgp	1978	88,581	64,243	290	41	19	Lng	ex Arzew-00, El Paso Arzew-83
Gallina (st)	Sgp	2002	111,459	67,300	290	46	19	Lng	
Gemmata (st)	Sgp	2004	111,459	72,740	290	46	19	Lng	
Helix ‡	Aus	1997	28,810	46,186	183	32	14	T	
LNG Adamawa (st) #	Bmu	2005	115,993	79,586	289	48	19	Lng	
LNG Akwa Ibom (st) #	Bmu	2004	115,993	79,633	289	48	19	Lng	
LNG Bayelsa (st) #	Bmu	2005	114,354	79,822	289	48	19	Lng	
LNG Bonny (st) #	Bmu	1981	85,616	89,654	287	42	20	Lng	ex LNG 559-90, Rhrnania-86
LNG Cross River (st) #	Bmu	2005	115,993	79,591	289	48	19	Lng	
LNG Delta (st) #	Iom	1978	88,936	75,172	289	41	18	Lng	ex Southern-99, El Paso Southern-83
LNG Finima (st) #	Bmu	1984	85,616	71,472	287	42	20	Lng	ex LNG 564-90
LNG Lagos (st) #	Bmu	1976	81,472	68,206	275	42	18	Lng	ex Gastor-91
LNG Port Harcourt (st) #	Bmu	1977	81,472	68,122	275	42	19	Lng	ex Nestor-91
LNG River Niger (st) #	Bmu	2006	115,993	79,541	289	48	19	Lng	
LNG Rivers (st) #	Bmu	2002	114,354	79,866	289	48	19	Lng	
LNG Sokoto (st) #	Bmu	2002	114,354	79,822	289	48	19	Lng	
Northwest Sanderling (st) †	Aus	1989	105,010	66,810	272	47	18	Lng	
Northwest Sandpiper (st) †	Aus	1993	105,010	66,695	272	47	18	Lng	
Northwest Seaeagle (st) †	Bmu	1992	106,283	67,003	272	47	18	Lng	
Northwest Shearwater (st) ††	Bmu	1991	106,283	66,802	272	47	18	Lng	
Northwest Snipe (st) †	Aus	1990	105,010	66,695	272	47	18	Lng	
Northwest Stormpetrel (st) †	Aus	1994	105,010	66,695	272	47	18	Lng	
Ocana ≠	Iom	1999	159,423	300,144	333	60	16	T	ex Front Commerce-04, Stena Commerce-01
Ondina ≠	Iom	2002	156,916	299,157	330	60	16	T	ex Front Stratus-06
Otina ≠	Iom	2002	159,383	298,465	333	60	15	T	ex Hakata-04
Oliva ≠	Iom	2001	158,397	298,530	333	60	15	T	ex Ariake-06, Berge Ariake-01

newbuildings: three 99,000 grt Lng tankers for 2011 delivery.

managed by subsidiary STASCO Ship Management, UK (formerly Shell International Shipping Ltd to 1995) or by STASCO * for Brunei Shell Tankers Sendirian Berhad (formed 1986 jointly with Government of The State of Brunei, Diamond Gas Carriers BV acquiring 25% in 2002), ** for AP Moller Singapore Pte Ltd, Singapore, # for Nigeria LNG Ltd (formed 1989 jointly with Nigerian National Petroleum Corp. (60%), Agip (10%) and Elf(10%)) or ≠ for Frontline Ltd qv.

† operated by Australian LNG Ship Operating Co Pty Ltd (formed 1989 jointly by Shell Co of Australia Ltd and BHP Petroleum Pty Ltd – www.alsoc.com.au) and †† owned by International Gas Transportation Co Ltd (formed jointly with Chevron, BHP, BP and other companies) and managed by BP Shipping Ltd, Bermuda.

‡ owned by Shell Co. of Australia Ltd (founded 1905 as British Imperial Oil Co Ltd to 1937 – www.shell.com.au)

§ owned by Shell Compania Argentina de Petroleo SA (founded 1922 as Diadema Argentina SA de Petroleo to 1960)

Also see vessels under Golar LNG Ltd (Frontline) and Viken Shipping AS.

Solvang ASA

Norway

Funnel: Brown with blue 'CS' on broad white band. **Hull:** Brown with red boot-topping. **History:** Amalgamation of Skibs Solvang (founded 1936) and Clipper Shipping A/S in 1992. **Web:** www.solvangship.com

Name	Flag	Year	GRT	DWT	LOA	Bm	Kts	Type	Former names
Clipper Harald	Nis	1999	10,692	13,779	146	21	17	Lpg	
Clipper Hebe	Nis	2007	13,893	18,110	155	23	17	Lpg	

Name	Flag	Year	GRT	DWT	LOA	Bm	Kts	Type	Former names
Clipper Helen	Nis	2007	13,893	18,110	155	23	17	Lpg	
Clipper Hermes	Nis	2008	13,893	18,880	155	23	17	Lpg	
Clipper Hermod	Nis	2008	13,893	18,110	155	23	17	Lpg	
Clipper Mars	Nis	2008	36,459	43,544	205	32		Lpg	
Clipper Moon	Nis	2003	35,012	44,872	205	32	16	Lpg	
Clipper Neptun	Nis	2008	36,459	43,508	205	32		Lpg	
Clipper Orion	Nis	2008	36,459	43,475	205	32		Lpg	
Clipper Posh	Nis	1983	34,384	46,316	216	32	-	Lpg	ex Nejma-04, Eupen-95, Petrogas II-86, Eupen-84
Clipper Sirius	Nis	2008	42,897	54,048	227	32		Lpg	
Clipper Skagen	Nis	1989	11,822	16,137	158	21	15	Lpg	ex Havkatt-97, Gaz Horizon-94, Sigulda-93
Clipper Sky	Nis	2004	35,158	44,617	205	32	16	Lpg	
Clipper Star	Nis	2003	34,970	44,807	205	32	16	Lpg	
Clipper Sun	Bhs	2008	47,173	58,677	225	37		Lpg	
Clipper Victory	Nis	2009	42,897	54,005	227	32		Lpg	
Clipper Viking	Nis	1998	10,692	13,777	146	21	17	Lpg	

OAO 'Sovcomflot'   Russia

Funnel: *Light blue with blue 'S' symbol on white above dark blue above red narrow bands (some variations).* **Hull:** *Black or red with red boot-topping.* **History:** *Formed 1988 and first former Soviet shipping enterprise with independent capital, but wholly owned within Russian Federation. Merged with Novoship in 2007.* **Web:** *www.sovcomflot.com*

Name	Flag	Year	GRT	DWT	LOA	Bm	Kts	Type	Former names
Aleksey Kosygin	Lbr	2007	87,146	163,545	281	50	15	T	
Anichkov Bridge	Lbr	2003	27,829	47,843	183	32	14	T	
Azov Sea	Lbr	1998	27,526	47,363	182	32	15	T	
Barents Sea	Lbr	1997	27,526	47,431	182	32	15	T	
Bering Sea	Lbr	1998	27,526	47,431	182	32	15	T	
Challenge Passage	Pan	2008	28,823	48,658	180	32	15	T	
East Siberian Sea	Lbr	1998	27,526	47,358	182	32	15	T	
Grand Aniva (st) †	Cyp	2008	122,239	74,044	288	49	19	Lng	
Grand Elena (st) †	Cyp	2007	122,239	74,127	288	49	20	Lng	
Hermitage Bridge	Lbr	2003	28,000	47,842	183	32	14	T	
Kapitan Gotskiy	Rus	2008	49,597	71,228	257	34		T	
Kara Sea	Lbr	1998	27,526	47,343	182	32	15	T	
Laptev Sea	Lbr	1998	27,526	47,314	182	32	15	T	
Ligovsky Prospect	Lbr	2003	62,586	114,639	250	44	15	T	
Liteyny Prospect	Lbr	2003	62,586	104,707	250	44	15	T	ex Stena Contender-07, Liteyny Prospect-04
Moscow Sea	Lbr	1998	27,526	47,363	182	32	15	T	
Narodny Bridge	Lbr	2003	27,829	47,791	183	32	14	T	
Nevskiy Prospect	Lbr	2003	62,586	114,598	250	44	15	T	
Okhotsk Sea	Lbr	1999	27,526	47,363	182	32	15	T	
Okhta Bridge	Lbr	2004	27,829	47,000	182	32	14	T	
Petrodvorets	Lbr	1999	59,731	105,692	248	43	15	T	ex Astro Saturn-01
Petrokrepost	Lbr	1999	59,731	98,039	248	43	15	T	ex Astro Maria-01
Petropavlovsk	Lbr	2002	57,683	106,532	241	42	15	T	
Petrovsk	Lbr	2004	57,683	105,900	241	42	15	T	
Petrozavodsk	Lbr	2003	57,683	106,449	241	42	15	T	

Solvang ASA. CLIPPER ORION. *Allan Ryszka Onions*

Name	Flag	Year	GRT	DWT	LOA	Bm	Kts	Type	Former names
RN Archangelsk **	Cyp	2008	19,986	30,720	176	30		T	ex Archangelsk-08
RN Murmansk **	Cyp	2009	19,994	30,720	176	30		T	
RN Privodino **	Cyp	2009	19,994	30,720	176	30		T	
Romea Champion	Lbr	1992	79,718	154,970	274	44	14	T	ex Tromso Champion-92
SCF Aldan	Lbr	2005	81,076	159,200	274	48	15	T	
SCF Altai	Lbr	2001	81,085	159,169	274	48	15	T	
SCF Amur	Lbr	2007	29,844	47,095	183	32	14	T	
SCF Arctic (st)	Lbr	1969	48,454	40,585	243	34	18	Lng	ex Methane Arctic-06, Arctic Tokyo-93
SCF Baltica	Lbr	2005	65,293	117,153	250	44	15	T	
SCF Byrranga	Lbr	2005	81,076	159,062	274	48	15	T	
SCF Caucasus *	Lbr	2002	81,085	159,173	274	48	15	T	
SCF Khibiny	Lbr	2002	81,085	159,156	274	48	15	T	
SCF Neva	Lbr	2006	29,644	47,125	183	32	14	T	
SCF Pechora	Lbr	2007	29,844	47,218	183	32	14	T	
SCF Polar (st)	Lbr	1969	48,454	40,585	243	34	18	Lng	ex Methane Polar-06, Polar Alaska-94
SCF Sayan	Lbr	2002	81,085	159,184	274	48	15	T	
SCF Tobolsk	Lbr	2006	23,003	26,424	174	28		Lpg	
SCF Tomsk	Lbr	2007	23,003	26,424	174	28		Lpg	
SCF Ural	Lbr	2002	81,085	159,169	274	48	15	T	
SCF Valdai	Lbr	2003	81,085	159,313	274	48	15	T	
SCF Yenisei	Lbr	2007	29,844	47,187	183	32	14	T	
Stena Tiger	Gbr	2004	25,400	40,000	176	31	15	T	ex Olipart-07
Tavrichesky Bridge	Lbr	2006	27,725	46,697	183	32	14	T	
Teatralny Bridge	Lbr	2006	27,725	46,697	183	32	14	T	
TTimofey Guzhenko	Rus	2009	49,597	71,266	257	34		T	ex Shturman Albanov-09
orgovy Bridge	Lbr	2005	27,725	47,363	183	32	14	T	
Tower Bridge	Lbr	2004	27,725	47,363	183	32	14	T	
Transssib Bridge *	Lbr	2008	27,725	46,564	183	32	14	T	
Troitskiy Bridge	Lbr	2003	27,725	41,158	183	32	14	T	
Tropic Brilliance	Lbr	1992	79,718	154,970	274	44	14	T	ex Tromso Brilliance-92
Tuchkov Bridge	Lbr	2004	27,725	47,199	183	32	14	T	
Tverskoy Bridge	Lbr	2007	27,725	46,564	183	32	14	T	
Vasiliy Dinkov	Rus	2008	49,597	71,254	257	34		T	
Victor Konetsky	Lbr	2005	60,434	101,018	247	42		T	
Vladimir Tikhonov	Lbr	2006	87,146	162,397	281	50		T	
Yuri Senkevich	Cyp	2005	60,434	100,971	247	42		T	

newbuildings: five 157-158,000 dwt, four 112,000 dwt, two 70,000 dwt tankers and two 95,800 grt Lng tankers for 2009-11 delivery.
Managed by Unicom Management Services (Cyprus) Ltd (originally formed in 1991 with Acomarit (30%) whose interest was acquired in 1994 - www.unicom-cy.com), by Unicom Management Services (St Peterburg) Ltd or ** by Rosneft Joint Stock Co. † jointly owned with NYK.*

Joint Stock Company Novoship (Novorossiysk Shipping Co)/Russia

Funnel: *Blue with red and black intertwined ropes between narrow diagonal blue bands on broad diagonal white band.* **Hull:** *Black, brown or red with red boot-topping.* **History:** *Formed 1932 and controlled by the Government of The Russian Federation until privatised in 1993. Merged with Sovcomflot in 2007, but operate as separate companies.* **Web:** www.novoship.ru

Adygeya	Lbr	2005	57,177	105,926	244	42	14	T	I/a Four Stream
Aleksandr Pokryshkin	Rus	1987	37,884	67,980	243	32	15	T	
Boris Livanov	Rus	1986	16,502	23,920	185	23	15	B	

OAO 'Sovcomflot'. LIGOVSKY PROSPECT. *Allan Ryszka Onions*

OAO 'Sovcomflot'. SCF VALDAI. *Phil Kempsey*

OAO 'Sovcomflot' (Novoship). NS COMMANDER. *F. de Vries*

OAO 'Sovcomflot' (Novoship). TROGIR. *Tom Walker*

Name	Flag	Year	GRT	DWT	LOA	Bm	Kts	Type	Former names
Elbrus	Mlt	2004	29,327	46,655	183	32	14	T	
Kaluga *	Lbr	2003	62,395	115,707	250	44		T	
Kazan **	Lbr	2003	62,395	115,727	250	44		T	
Krasnodar *	Lbr	2003	62,395	115,605	250	44		T	
Krymsk *	Lbr	2003	62,395	115,605	250	44		T	
Kuban	Lbr	2000	56,076	106,562	243	42	14	T	l/a Moscow Glory
Leonid Sobolyev	Rus	1985	16,502	23,940	184	23	14	B	
Moscow	Lbr	1998	56,076	106,553	243	42	15	T	
Moscow Kremlin	Lbr	1998	56,076	106,521	243	42	15	T	
Moscow River	Lbr	1999	56,075	106,552	243	42	15	T	
Moscow Stars	Lbr	1999	56,076	106,450	243	42	15	T	
Moscow University	Lbr	1999	56,076	106,521	243	42	15	T	
NS Captain *	Lbr	2006	57,248	105,926	244	42	14	T	
NS Century	Lbr	2006	57,248	105,926	244	42	14	T	
NS Challenger	Lbr	2005	57,248	105,926	244	42	14	T	
NS Champion	Lbr	2005	57,248	105,926	244	42	14	T	
NS Clipper	Lbr	2006	57,248	105,926	244	42	14	T	
NS Columbus	Lbr	2007	57,248	105,788	244	42	14	T	
NS Commander *	Lbr	2006	57,248	105,926	244	42	14	T	
NS Concept	Lbr	2005	57,248	105,926	244	42	14	T	
NS Concord	Lbr	2005	57,248	105,926	244	42	14	T	
NS Consul	Lbr	2006	57,248	105,926	244	42	14	T	
NS Corona	Lbr	2006	57,248	105,926	244	42	14	T	
NS Creation	Lbr	2007	57,248	105,000	244	42	14	T	
NS Laguna	Lbr	2007	61,449	115,831	250	44	14	T	
NS Leader	Lbr	2007	61,449	115,857	250	44	15	T	
NS Lion *	Lbr	2007	61,449	115,831	250	44	15	T	
NS Lotus *	Lbr	2008	61,449	115,849	250	44	15	T	
NS Parade *	Lbr	2008	25,400	40,119	176	31	15	T	
NS Point	Lbr	2008	25,400	40,000	176	31	15	T	
NS Power	Lbr	2006	25,467	40,042	176	31	15	T	
NS Pride	Lbr	2006	25,467	40,042	176	31	15	T	
NS Silver	Lbr	2005	27,357	47,197	176	31	14	T	
NS Spirit	Lbr	2006	27,357	46,941	176	31	14	T	
NS Stella	Lbr	2005	27,357	47,197	176	31	14	T	
NS Stream	Lbr	2006	27,357	46,941	176	31	14	T	
Pamir *	Mlt	2004	28,000	46,000	183	32	14	T	
Taganrog	Lbr	1996	26,218	40,713	181	32	14	T	
Taman	Lbr	1996	26,218	40,818	181	32	15	T	
Tambov	Lbr	1996	26,218	40,727	181	32	14	T	
Temryuk	Lbr	1996	26,218	40,584	181	32	14	T	
Tikhoretsk	Lbr	1996	26,218	40,791	181	32	14	T	
Tikhvin	Lbr	1996	26,218	40,727	181	32	15	T	
Timashevsk	Lbr	1996	26,218	40,584	181	32	15	T	
Tomsk	Lbr	1997	26,218	40,703	181	32	15	T	
Trogir	Rus	1995	26,218	40,727	181	32	14	T	
Troitsk	Lbr	1996	26,218	40,816	181	32	15	T	
Tula	Lbr	1997	26,218	40,584	181	32	14	T	
Tver	Lbr	1996	26,218	40,743	181	32	15	T	

newbuildings: six 144,000 dwt and four 112,000 dwt tankers for 2009 delivery.
* managed by subsidiary Novoship (UK) Ltd, UK (formed 1992 - www.novoship.co.uk) ** for Bluewater Engineering BV, Netherlands.

Spar Shipping AS   Norway

Funnel: *White.* **Hull:** *Black with red boot-topping.* **History:** *Formed 1994* **Web:** *www.sparshipping.com*

Name	Flag	Year	GRT	DWT	LOA	Bm	Kts	Type	Former names
Spar Canis *	Nis	2006	32,474	53,565	190	32	14	B	
Spar Cetus	Nis	1998	25,982	45,725	186	30	15	B	ex Golden Protea-02
Spar Draco *	Nis	2006	32,474	53,565	190	32	14	B	
Spar Eight	Nis	1982	22,300	36,227	190	28	14	B	ex Negros Victory-95, Orchid II-91
Spar Emerald	Nis	1987	20,766	34,970	177	30	14	B	ex Mockingbird-97
Spar Garnet *	Nis	1985	18,011	30,686	180	23	14	B	ex Federal Vigra-97, Mary Anne-93
Spar Gemini *	Nis	2007	32,474	53,565	190	32	14	B	
Spar Jade *	Nis	1985	18,011	30,674	180	23	14	B	ex Federal Aalesund-97, Fiona Mary-93
Spar Leo *	Nis	1989	36,074	65,850	226	32	13	B	ex Alianthos-04, CS Elegant-99, Rubin Elegant-94, Young Senator-92
Spar Lupus	Nis	1998	26,400	45,146	186	30	15	B	ex Golden Aloe-02
Spar Lynx *	Nis	2005	32,474	53,565	190	32	14	B	
Spar Lyra *	Nis	2005	32,474	53,565	190	32	14	B	
Spar Neptun *	Nis	1994	36,559	70,101	225	32	15	B	ex Apollon-04, Gran Trader-99
Spar Opal *	Nis	1984	16,861	28,214	178	23	14	B	ex Matane-97, Federal Matane-97, Consensus Atlantic-92, Lake Shidaka-91

Name	Flag	Year	GRT	DWT	LOA	Bm	Kts	Type	Former names
Spar Orion	Nis	1996	26,449	47,639	190	31	14	B	ex Western Orion-01
Spar Ruby *	Nis	1985	16,775	28,259	178	23	14	B	ex Solveig-00, Manila Bellona-98, Liberty Sky-96, Astral Neptune-90
Spar Scorpio *	Nis	2006	32,474	53,565	190	32	14	B	
Spar Sirius	Nis	1996	25,968	45,402	186	30	14	B	ex Western Transporter-01
Spar Taurus *	Nis	2005	32,474	53,565	190	32	14	B	
Spar Topaz	Nis	1987	22,155	38,455	181	31	14	B	ex Azteca 1-96
Spar Two	Pan	1982	22,258	35,971	180	28	14	B	ex Menina Barbara-93
Spar Virgo *	Nis	2005	32,474	53,565	190	32	14	B	

*Vessels owned by Spar Shipholding AS with * management by Fleet Management Ltd, Hong Kong (Noble Group)*

Spliethoff's Bevrachtingskantoor BV   Netherlands

Funnel: *Orange with black 'S' on diagonally quartered white/red/orange/blue flag.* **Hull:** *Brown with white 'spliethoff', green above red boot-topping.* **History:** *Formed 1921.* **Web:** *www.spliethoff.nl*

Name	Flag	Year	GRT	DWT	LOA	Bm	Kts	Type
Damgracht	Nld	2008	13,558	18,000	157	23	17	Co
Danzigergracht	Nld	2009	13,500	18,000	157	23	17	Co
Deltagracht	Nld	2009	13,500	18,000	157	23	17	Co
Diamantgracht	Nld	2009	13,500	18,000	157	23	17	Co
Dijksgracht	Nld	2008	13,558	18,000	157	23	17	Co
Dolfijngracht	Nld	2009	13,500	18,000	157	23	17	Co
Donaugracht	Nld	2009	13,500	18,000	157	23	17	Co
Dynamogracht	Nld	2008	13,500	18,000	157	23	17	Co
Saimaagracht	Nld	2004	18,321	23,660	185	26	19	Co
Sampogracht	Nld	2005	18,321	23,688	185	26	19	Co
Scheldegracht	Nld	2000	16,639	21,250	168	25	19	Co
Schippersgracht	Ant	2000	16,641	21,402	168	25	19	Co
Singelgracht	Nld	2000	16,641	21,402	168	25	19	Co
Slotergracht	Nld	2000	16,641	21,402	168	25	19	Co
Sluisgracht	Nld	2001	16,639	21,250	172	25	19	Co
Snoekgracht	Nld	2000	16,641	21,400	168	25	19	Co
Spaarnegracht	Nld	2000	16,641	21,402	168	25	19	Co
Spiegelgracht	Nld	2000	16,641	21,400	168	25	19	Co
Spuigracht	Nld	2001	16,639	21,349	172	25	19	Co
Stadiongracht	Nld	2000	16,639	21,250	172	25	19	Co
Statengracht	Nld	2004	16,676	21,250	173	26	19	Co
Suomigracht	Nld	2004	18,321	23,660	185	26	19	Co

newbuildings: two 23,700 dwt general cargo vessels on order for 2009-10 delivery.
Also owns Ro-Ro's and smaller vessels operating in coastal trades.

BigLift Shipping BV/Netherlands

Funnel: *Yellow with black 'BigLift'.* **Hull:** *Yellow with blue 'BigLift', red or black boot-topping.* **History:** *Formed 1973 by Nedlloyd Groep NV as Mammoet Shipping BV, joint venture as Mammoet-Hansa AG from 1989, Spliethoff's gained control in 1995, renamed 2000.* **Web:** *www.bigliftshipping.com*

Name	Flag	Year	GRT	DWT	LOA	Bm	Kts	Type
Da Fu **	Pan	1998	14,021	16,957	153	23	15	HL
Da Hua **	Pan	1998	14,021	16,957	153	23	15	HL
Da Qiang **	Pan	1998	14,021	16,957	153	23	15	HL

Spliethoff's Bevrachtingskantor. SLUISGRACHT. *Hans Kraijenbosch*

Name	Flag	Year	GRT	DWT	LOA	Bm	Kts	Type	Former names
Da Zhong **	Pan	1998	14,021	16,957	153	23	15	HL	
Enchanter *	Pan	1998	10,990	16,069	138	23	15	HL	ex Sailer Jupiter-98
Envoyager *	Sgp	1985	15,350	21,183	153	27	15	HL	ex Alps Maru-91
Happy Buccaneer (2)	Nld	1984	16,341	13,740	146	28	15	HL	
Happy Ranger	Nld	1997	10,990	15,065	138	23	16	HL	
Happy River	Nld	1997	10,990	16,516	138	23	16	HL	
Happy Rover	Nld	1997	10,990	15,593	138	23	16	HL	

newbuildings: three 18,700 dwt heavy-lift ships for 2009-10 delivery.
* owned by Pool member Mitsui OSK Lines Ltd (managed by New Asian Shipping Co. Ltd, Hong Kong) qv or ** by Guangzhou Ocean Shipping (COSCO), China.

Star Reefers AS Norway

Funnel: *White with red edged blue 5-pointed star, narrow blue band beneath red top.* **Hull:** *Lilac grey, white or blue with blue waterline over red boot-topping.* **History:** *Founded 1909 as Vestey Brothers, renamed Blue Star Line Ltd in 1911. Blue Star Ship Management Ltd formed 1974. Vestey Group sold container business and Austasia Line subsidiary to P&O in 1998 and the reefers in 2001 to Swan Reefer ASA, which was a 1998 amalgamation of Irgens Larsen (formerly Rederiet Helge R Myhre to 1992 and Kvaerner Shipping AS (formed 1955) to 1995) and Swan Shipping A/S (formed 1989) before being renamed.* **Web:** *www.star-reefers.com*

Name	Flag	Year	GRT	DWT	LOA	Bm	Kts	Type	Former names
Afric Star *	Lbr	1990	11,590	12,683	159	24	18	R	ex Tundra Consumer-04, Del Monte Consumer-00
Almeda Star *	Bhs	1990	11,658	12,714	159	24	20	R	ex Tundra King-05, Del Monte Pride-91
Andalusia Star *	Bhs	1991	11,658	12,714	159	24	20	R	ex Tundra Princess-05, Del Monte Spirit-91
Argentina Star *	Lbr	1992	10,629	10,588	150	23	21	R	ex Polar Argentina-05, Horntide-98, Polar Argentina-98, Gordian-95
Auckland Star *	Bhs	1985	10,691	11,434	151	22	19	R	ex Horncliff-89, Auckland Star-87
Avelona Star *	Bhs	1991	11,658	12,714	159	24	20	R	ex Tundra Queen-05, Del Monte Quality-91
Avila Star *	Lbr	1990	11,590	12,519	159	24	18	R	ex Tundra Trader-04, Del Monte Trader-99
Brasil Star	Lbr	1992	10,629	10,588	150	23	21	R	ex Polar Brasil-05, Hornstream-98, Polar Brasil-98, Numerian-95
Canterbury Star	Lbr	1986	10,291	11,434	151	22	19	R	
Cape Town Star	Bhs	1993	10,614	10,629	150	23	21	R	ex Caribbean Reef-03, Hornbreeze-98, Geestcrest-95, Hornbreeze-95, Caribbean Universal-94
Caribbean Star **	Lbr	1997	11,435	10,362	154	24	20	R	ex Hornsea-00, Caribbean Star-98
Chaiten §	Bhs	1988	13,312	12,838	152	24	18	R	
Chile Star	Lbr	1993	10,629	10,620	150	23	21	R	ex Polar Chile-05, Trajan-96
Colombian Star ‡	Pan	1998	11,733	10,371	154	24	21	R	
Costa Rican Star **	Lbr	1998	11,435	10,350	154	24	21	R	ex Hornwind-02, Costa Rican Star-98
Cote d'Ivoirian Star ‡	Pan	1998	11,733	11,000	154	24	21	R	
Dunedin Star ***	Bmu	1994	8,665	11,793	151	20	22	R	ex Chiquita Joy-06, Joy-00, Chiquita Joy-97
Durban Star	Bhs	1993	10,614	10,629	150	23	20	R	ex Coral Reef-03, Horncloud-98, Geesttide-95, Horncloud-94, Coral Universal-94
Ecuador Star	Lbr	1992	10,629	10,452	150	23	21	R	ex Polar Ecuador-05, Justinian-96
English Star	Bhs	1986	10,291	11,434	151	22	19	R	ex Hornsea-89, English Star-87
Honduras Star	Lbr	1992	10,629	10,593	150	23	21	R	ex Polar Colombia-05, Appian-95
Napier Star ***	Bmu	1994	8,665	11,822	151	20	19	R	ex Chiquita Elke-03, Elke-00, Chiquita Elke-97
Nelson Star ***	Bmu	1993	8,665	11,830	151	20	22	R	ex Chiquita Jean-03, Jean-00, Chiquita Jean-97
Regal Star	Bhs	1993	10,375	10,520	150	23	20	R	ex Tauu-96, Hornstrait-95, Chiquita Tauu-94
Scottish Star	Bhs	1985	10,291	13,058	151	22	19	R	
Solent Star **	Lbr	2001	10,804	9,709	150	23	21	R	
Southampton Star **	Lbr	1999	10,804	9,709	150	23	21	R	
Star Best ‡	Pan	2007	14,030	13,189	163	26	22	R	
Star First ‡	Pan	2006	14,030	13,202	163	26	22	R	
Star Prima ‡	Pan	2006	14,030	13,189	163	26	22	R	
Star Service ‡	Pan	2008	14,030	13,207	163	26	22	R	
Star Stratos ‡	Pan	2007	14,030	13,186	163	26	22	R	
Sun Genius	Bhs	1983	9,417	11,805	146	21	22	R	ex Tudor Star-07, Helene Jacob-96, Saxon Star-94, Helene Jacob-93, Blumenthal-88, Helene Jacob-84
Sun Light	Bhs	1984	9,417	11,660	146	21	22	R	ex Trojan Star-07, Walter Jacob-96, Cap Palmas-94, Walter Jacob-93, Bremerhaven-89, Walter Jacob-84
Swan Chacabuco §	Bhs	1990	13,099	12,974	152	24	18	R	ex Chacabuco-97
Tauranga Star ***	Bmu	1992	7,944	10,963	141	20	20	R	ex Chiquita Frances-02, France-00, Chiquita Frances-98
Timaru Star ***	Bmu	1993	8,665	11,793	151	20	20	R	ex Chiquita Brenda-05, Brenda-00, Chiquita Brenda-97, Chiquita Joy-93
Uruguay Star	Lbr	1993	10,629	10,593	150	23	21	R	ex Polar Uruguay-05, Hadrian-96
Valparaiso Star *	Lbr	1989	8,945	9,867	141	22	20	R	ex Harvester-04, Del Monte Harvester-99
Viking Star **	Bhs	1991	7,239	9,157	138	19	19	R	ex Consensus Reefer-05, Schoener-97, Hornwave-92, Schoener-92

Name	Flag	Year	GRT	DWT	LOA	Bm	Kts	Type	Former names
Wellington Star ***	Bhs	1992	7,944	11,103	141	20	21	R	ex Bothnian Reefer-03

Vessels managed by Star Reefers Poland Sp z.oo, Poland, * by Fleet Management Ltd., Hong Kong (China), ** by Norbulk Shipping UK Ltd, *** by DFM Poland. § chartered from Chartworld Shipping Corp, Greece, ‡ from Nissan Kaiun KK, Japan or † from various other owners.

Starship Constelation Group Monaco

International Andromeda Shipping SAM

Funnel: Grey with 5-pointed yellow star (or colour to match name) superimposed on white 'A'. **Hull:** *Black with red boot-topping.*
History: *Founded 1992.* **Web:** *www.andromeda-shipping.com*

Name	Flag	Year	GRT	DWT	LOA	Bm	Kts	Type	Former names
Blu Star	Lbr	2001	23,682	35,970	183	27	14	T	ex Blue Star-08, British Energy-06, l/a Blue Star
Emerald Star	Nis	2005	23,298	37,270	183	27	14	T	ex Emerald-05
Green Star	Nis	2001	23,682	35,858	183	27	14	T	ex British Enterprise-06, l/a Indigo Star
Scarlet Star	Nis	2005	23,298	37,252	183	27	14	T	
T. C. Gleisner	Nis	2005	23,298	37,269	183	27	14	T	

newbuildings: three 115,000 dwt tankers for 2010-11 delivery (Pink Star, Orange Star and White Star)

Stena AB Sweden

Funnel: *White 'S' on wide red band separated from narrow blue top and black base by narrow white bands.* **Hull:** *Black, grey or blue with 'StenaBulk', red boot-topping or ** red with black 'STENA UGLAND' and nine narrow diagonal stripes (pale blue/yellow/red/white/ dark blue, black above red boot-topping.* **History:** *Founded 1939 as Sten A Olsson Handels A/B to 1963, then Stena Line A/B to 1977. Concordia Maritime AB (formed 1984), jointly owned with Neste, took over Universe Tankships (Delaware) LLC in 1996.* **Web:** *www.stena.com*

Name	Flag	Year	GRT	DWT	LOA	Bm	Kts	Type	Former names
Stena Alexita ‡ (2)	Nor	1998	76,836	127,466	263	46	15	T	
Stena Antarctica **	Cym	2006	61,371	113,500	250	44		T	ex Four Antarctica-06
Stena Atlantica **	Cym	2006	61,371	114,896	250	44		T	ex Four Atlantica-06

Stena AB. STENA ANTARCTICA. *N. Kemps*

Stena AB. STENA PROVENCE. *Hans Kraijenbosch*

Name	Flag	Year	GRT	DWT	LOA	Bm	Kts	Type	Former names
Stena Compass	Bmu	2006	41,589	72,735	229	32	15	T	
Stena Compassion	Bmu	2006	41,589	72,782	229	32	15	T	
Stena Concept †	Bmu	2005	27,357	47,171	183	32	15	T	
Stena Concert †	Bmu	2004	27,463	47,288	183	32	14	T	ex Stena Italica-08
Stena Conqueror †	Ita	2003	27,335	47,323	183	32	14	T	I/a Hellenica
Stena Conquest †	Ita	2003	27,335	47,136	183	32	14	T	ex Hispanica-03
Stena Contest †	Bmu	2005	27,357	47,171	183	32	15	T	
Stena FR8 1 §	Mhl	2007	29,597	46,846	183	32	14	T	ex FR8 Freedom-07
Stena FR8 2 §	Mhl	2007	29,597	46,763	183	32	14	T	ex FR8 Fortitude-07
Stena Natalita (2)	Bhs	2001	62,393	108,073	250	43	14	T	
Stena Paris * (2)	Bmu	2005	36,064	65,125	290	40	14	T	
Stena Performance *	Bmu	2006	36,064	65,125	290	40	14	T	
Stena Perros *	Bmu	2007	36,168	65,086	290	40	14	T	ex Stena Progetra-07
Stena President	Bmu	2007	36,000	66,200	290	40	14	T	
Stena Primorsk *	Lbr	2006	36,064	65,125	290	40	14	T	
Stena Progress *	Bmu	2009	36,064	65,125	290	40	14	T	
Stena Prosperity	Bmu	2009	36,000	65,125	290	40	14	T	
Stena Provence *	Bmu	2006	36,000	65,000	290	40	14	T	
Stena Sirita ‡ (2)	Nor	1999	77,410	127,466	263	46	15	T	

newbuildings: two 65,000 dwt tankers for 2010 delivery (Stena Preference and Stena Premium)
* operated by affiliate Concordia Maritime AB and managed by Northern Marine Management Ltd, UK (www.nmm-stena.com) ** on charter from
Premuda SpA, Italy and managed by Northern Marine Management Ltd or † operated by Northern Marine Management USA LLC. ‡ jointly
owned with Ugland Marine Services AS and managed by Standard Marine Tonsberg AS, Norway.
§ chartered from Navig8 Shipmanagement Pte Ltd, Singapore. Also see Neste Oil Corporation

Stolt-Nielsen Transportation Group Ltd   USA

Funnel: White with large white 'S' on red square, narrow black top. **Hull:** Yellow with black 'STOLT TANKERS', red or pink boot-topping. **History:** Founded 1886 as subsidiary of Stolt-Nielsen SA, Luxembourg (founded 1891), B Stolt-Nielsen & Co to 1931, B Stolt-Nielsen & Sonner A/S to 1961, Jacob Stolt-Nielsen A/S to 1970, Stolt-Nielsen Rederi A/S to 1999, when Stolt Tankers BV was relocated from Norway to Netherlands and Stolt-Nielsen Transportation Group BV to 2007. **Web:** www.stolt-nielsen.com

Name	Flag	Year	GRT	DWT	LOA	Bm	Kts	Type	Former names
Stolt Achievement (me)	Cym	1999	25,427	37,000	177	31	16	T	
Stolt Aquamarine	Cym	1986	23,964	38,746	177	32	15	T	
Stolt Basuto	Sgp	2006	16,442	25,196	159	26	15	T	
Stolt Breland	Nld	2009	25,841	37,141	183	32		T	
Stolt Capability (me)	Lbr	1998	24,625	37,042	177	31	16	T	
Stolt Concept (me)	Cym	1999	24,495	37,236	177	31	16	T	
Stolt Confidence (me)	Cym	1996	24,625	37,015	177	31	16	T	
Stolt Creativity (me)	Cym	1997	24,625	37,271	177	31	16	T	
Stolt Eagle	Lbr	1980	21,043	37,067	177	30	16	T	ex Stolt Ulsan-80
Stolt Efficiency (me)	Cym	1998	24,625	37,271	177	31	16	T	
Stolt Effort (me)	Cym	1999	24,495	37,155	177	31	16	T	
Stolt Emerald	Cym	1986	23,964	38,719	177	32	15	T	
Stolt Excellence	Lbr	1979	20,157	31,379	177	27	16	T	
Stolt Facto	Cym	2008	25,000	44,000	183	32		T	
Stolt Falcon	Lbr	1978	21,043	37,201	174	30	15	T	ex Stolt Seoul-79
Stolt Graceland	Nld	2009	25,841	37,141	183	32		T	
Stolt Helluland	Cym	1990	18,994	31,454	175	30	15	T	
Stolt Hill	Cym	1992	22,620	40,159	176	32	14	T	ex Montana Star-06, Star Sapphire-02
Stolt Innovation (me)	Cym	1996	24,625	37,015	177	31	16	T	
Stolt Inspiration (me)	Cym	1997	24,625	37,205	177	31	16	T	

Stolt-Nielsen Group. STOLT INSPIRATION. *J. M. Kakebeeke*

Name	Flag	Year	GRT	DWT	LOA	Bm	Kts	Type	Former names
Stolt Integrity	Lbr	1977	20,157	32,057	177	27	18	T	
Stolt Invention (me)	Lbr	1998	24,625	37,271	177	31	16	T	
Stolt Island	Nld	2008	25,841	37,141	183	32		T	
Stolt Jade	Cym	1986	23,964	38,746	177	32	15	T	
Stolt Markland	Cym	1991	18,994	31,433	175	30	15	T	
Stolt Mountain	Cym	1994	22,620	40,024	176	32		T	ex Montana Sun-06, Sun Sapphire-02
Stolt Nanami	Cym	2003	11,549	19,932	143	24	14	T	
Stolt Norland	Nld	2009	25,841	37,141	183	32		T	
Stolt Peak	Cym	1991	22,620	40,077	176	32	14	T	ex Montana Blue-06, Blue Sapphire-02
Stolt Perseverance (me)	Cym	2000	25,196	37,059	177	31	16	T	
Stolt Pluto	Cym	2008	26,000	44,000	183	32		T	
Stolt Pondo **	Pan	2007	19,380	33,232	170	27	14	T	
Stolt Pride	Lbr	1976	20,013	31,942	177	27	17	T	
Stolt Protector	Lbr	1983	22,587	39,782	174	32	14	T	ex Stolt Exporter-92, Exporter-88, Atlas Exporter-83
Stolt Sagaland	Cym	2008	25,841	44,044	183	32		T	
Stolt Sapphire *	Lbr	1986	23,964	38,746	177	32	15	T	
Stolt Sea (me)	Cym	1999	14,742	22,198	163	24	15	T	
Stolt Sincerity	Lbr	1976	20,013	31,943	177	27	17	T	
Stolt Sisto	Cym	2008	26,000	44,000	183	32		T	
Stolt Sneland	Cym	2008	25,841	43,000	183	32		T	
Stolt Span (me)	Lbr	1998	14,775	22,273	163	24	15	T	
Stolt Spray (me)	Cym	2000	14,180	22,460	163	24	15	T	
Stolt Stream (me)	Cym	2000	14,180	22,199	163	24	15	T	
Stolt Sun (me)	Cym	2000	14,152	22,460	163	24	15	T	
Stolt Surf (me)	Cym	2000	14,180	22,460	163	24	15	T	
Stolt Topaz	Cym	1986	23,964	38,818	177	32	15	T	
Stolt Valor **	Hkg	2004	15,600	25,100	159	26	15	T	
Stolt Vestland	Cym	1992	19,034	31,494	175	30	15	T	
Stolt Viking (me)	Cym	2001	16,754	26,707	166	27	15	T	ex Isola Blu-05, l/a Isola Verde
Stolt Vinland	Cym	1992	19,034	31,434	175	30	15	T	
Stolt Zulu	Sgp	2006	16,442	25,197	159	26	15	T	

newbuildings: seven 43,000 dwt chemical tankers (Cat class) for 2010-11 delivery.
Managed by Stolt Tankers BV, Netherlands (www.sntg.com).   * owned by NYK Stolt Tankers SA (formed jointly in 2000 with NYK, Japan)
** owned by Central Marine Co. Ltd., Japan (managed by Fleet Management Ltd, Hong Kong).

Suisse-Atlantique Soc de Navigation Maritime SA   Switzerland

Funnel: Black with red diagonal cross and two stars on yellow houseflag interrupting two yellow bands. **Hull:** Black or grey with red boot-topping. **History:** Founded 1941 as Societe de Navigation Maritime Suisse-Atlantique to 1956, then Soc d'Armement Maritime Suisse-Atlantique to 1986. **Web:** none found.

Name	Flag	Year	GRT	DWT	LOA	Bm	Kts	Type	Former names
Celerina	Che	1999	39,161	73,035	225	32	14	B	
Corviglia	Che	1999	39,161	73,035	225	32	14	B	
Engiadina	Che	2002	27,779	40,878	222	30	22	CC	ex Norasia Engiadina-03, Engiadina-02
General Guisan	Che	1999	39,161	73,035	225	32	14	B	
Lausanne	Che	2003	27,779	40,878	222	30	22	CC	
Maersk Juan	Che	2005	28,592	39,384	221	30	23	CC	ex Jaun-05

Stolt-Nielsen Group. STOLT SNELAND. *Hans Kraijenbosch*

Name	Flag	Year	GRT	DWT	LOA	Bm	Kts	Type	Former names
Maersk Jenaz	Che	2005	28,911	39,384	221	30	23	CC	ex Jenaz-05
Nyon	Che	1999	39,161	73,035	225	32	14	B	
Sils	Che	2003	27,779	40,878	221	30	22	CC	ex Norasia Sils-06, Sils-03
Silvaplana	Che	2003	17,951	29,721	171	27	14	B	ex F.D. Clara d'Amato-07, Benedetta d'Amato-06
Silvretta	Che	2003	17,951	29,721	171	27	14	B	ex F.D. Umberto d'Amato-07, Umberto d'Amato-07
St-Cergue	Che	2006	28,911	39,316	221	30	23	CC	

newbuildings: 92,500 dwt bulk carrier for 2009 delivery.

John Swire & Sons Ltd UK

The China Navigation Co Ltd/Hong Kong (China)

Funnel: *Black with diagonally quartered houseflag (white top/bottom, red sides, central vertical blue line).* **Hull:** *Black some with white 'INDOTRANS', red, grey or pink boot-topping.* **History:** *Parent founded 1816 and China Navigation formed 1872. The Bank Line services acquired 2003 (see under Andrew Weir).* **Web:** *www.swire.com or www.cnco.com.hk*

Name	Flag	Year	GRT	DWT	LOA	Bm	Kts	Type	Former names
Erawan	Iom	1982	35,716	64,643	225	32	13	B	ex Camarina-99, Starfest-95, Yamashiro Maru-90
Erradale *	Hkg	1994	82,701	163,554	284	44	15	B	
Pacific Adventurer *	Hkg	1991	18,391	23,737	185	28	18	Co	ex Changsha-05, Pacific Challenger-99
Pacific Celebes	Hkg	1984	30,150	41,600	198	32	16	BC	ex Indotrans Celebes-06, Albert Oldendorff-04, Hoegh Dyke-01
Pacific Discoverer	Hkg	1992	18,391	25,554	185	28	18	Co	ex Tasman Chief-07, Chenan-05, Andes Challenger-99
Pacific Explorer	Hkg	1991	18,391	25,661	185	28	18	Co	ex Chengtu-05, Asian Challenger-99
Pacific Flores	Hkg	1984	30,150	41,600	198	32	16	BC	ex Indotrans Flores-06, Ingrid Oldendorff-04, Hoegh Drake-01
Pacific Java	Hkg	1984	30,150	41,600	198	32	16	BC	ex Indotrans Java-06, Gitta Oldendorff-04, Hoegh Dene-01
Pacific Makassar	Hkg	1984	30,061	41,600	198	32	16	BC	ex Indotrans Makassar-06, Edward Oldendorff-04, Hoegh Duke-01
Pacific Voyager *	Hkg	1991	18,391	23,271	185	28	18	Co	ex Chekiang-05, Atlantic Challenger-99
Tasman Commander	Hkg	1995	18,468	23,586	185	28	19	Co	ex Oceanic Challenger-04, Delmas Joinville-02, Oceanic Challenger-01,
Tasman Endeavour	Hkg	1994	18,451	23,000	185	28	19	Co	ex Caribbean Challenger-03
Tasman Mariner	Hkg	1995	18,468	23,783	185	28	19	Co	ex Delmas Blosseville-04, Tropical Challenger-03, Delmas Blosseville-02, Tropical Challenger-99
Tasman Provider	Hkg	1994	18,451	23,683	185	28	19	Co	ex Meridian Challenger-03, Delmas Forbin-02, Meridian Challenger-00

* owned by Swire Navigation Co Ltd, Hong Kong.

Teekay Corporation Bahamas

Funnel: *White with blue edged red 'TK' symbol, narrow black top.* **Hull:** *Black with red boot-topping.* **History:** *Founded 1984 as Teekay Shipping Co Inc, Canada to 1990, then Western Marine Agencies to 1991. Formed Teekay Shipping (Australia) Pty Ltd in 1998 on acquisition of Caltex Petroleum's Australian Tankships Pty Ltd (formed by 1996 merger of Ampol Ltd (founded 1936 as Australian Motorists Petrol Co Ltd to 1949, formerly Ampol Petroleum Ltd to 1982) and Caltex Tanker Co (Australia) Pty Ltd (formed 1972 as Botany Bay Tanker Co (Australia) Pty Ltd to 1985). Teekay Marine Services GmbH, Germany formed 2003. Acquired Naviera F Tapias SA in 2004, which had been a Spanish subsidiary of AP Moller to 1991 (formed 1988). In 2007 acquired 50% of OMI (founded 1962 as Ogden Marine Inc and spun-off from Ogden Corp in 1984 as OMI Corp, subsidiary being formed in 1998).* **Web:** *www.teekay.com*

Name	Flag	Year	GRT	DWT	LOA	Bm	Kts	Type	Former names
African Spirit	Bhs	2003	79,668	151,736	269	46		T	
Aisha	Bhs	2008	81,732	160,391	274	48		T	ex Apex Spirit-08
Al Areesh (st)	Bhs	2007	99,106	78,520	288	43	20	Lng	
Al Daayen (st)	Bhs	2007	99,106	90,617	288	43		Lng	
Al Huwaila	Bhs	2008	135,848	107,700	315	50		Lng	
Al Kharsaah	Bhs	2008	135,848	107,514	315	50		Lng	
Al Khuwair	Bhs	2008	135,848	107,700	315	50		Lng	
Al Marrouna (st)	Bhs	2007	99,106	90,617	288	43	20	Lng	
Al Shamal	Bhs	2008	135,848	107,500	315	50		Lng	
Algeciras Spirit §	Cni	2000	83,724	160,240	274	48	15	T	ex Nuria Tapias-04
Americas Spirit	Bhs	2003	63,213	111,920	256	45		T	l/dn Limerick Spirit
Arctic Spirit (st)	Bhs	1993	55,174	48,857	239	40	18	Lng	ex Arctic Sun-07
Asian Spirit	Bhs	2004	79,668	151,693	269	46		T	
Ashkini Spirit	Bhs	2003	84,789	165,010	274	50	15	T	ex Ingeborg-07, Aegean Lady-04
Australian Spirit	Bhs	2004	63,213	111,942	256	45		T	
Axel Spirit	Bhs	2004	62,929	115,392	250	44		T	
Barrington	Aus	1989	21,718	33,239	181	27	14	T	ex Australia Sky-96
Basker Spirit *	Bhs	1992	56,020	97,069	241	41	14	T	ex Navion Basker-05, Nordic Yukon-05, Wilma Yukon-01, Wilomi Yukon-96

Name	Flag	Year	GRT	DWT	LOA	Bm	Kts	Type	Former names
Catalunya Spirit (st)	Cni	2003	90,942	72,204	284	43	19	Lng	ex Inigo Tapias-04
Cork Spirit *	Bhs	2007	57,325	105,547	244	42		T	
Donegal Spirit	Bhs	2006	57,325	105,611	244	42		T	
Erik Spirit	Bhs	2005	63,500	114,780	250	44	15	T	
Esther Spirit	Bhs	2004	62,929	115,444	250	44	15	T	
European Spirit	Bhs	2003	79,668	151,848	269	46		T	ex Cork Spirit-03
Everest Spirit	Bhs	2004	62,845	115,048	250	44	14	T	
Falster Spirit	Bhs	1995	52,875	95,317	244	42	14	T	ex Bona Rover-99, Vendonna-96
Fuji Spirit *	Bhs	2003	57,664	106,360	241	42	14	T	
Galicia Spirit	Cni	2004	94,822	76,500	280	43	19	Lng	
Galway Spirit	Bhs	2007	57,325	105,559	244	42		T	
Ganges Spirit	Bhs	2002	81,270	159,452	274	48	15	T	ex Delaware-07
Godavari Spirit	Bhs	2004	81,074	159,106	274	48	15	T	ex Angelica-07, Athenian Glory-04
Goonyella Trader **	Lbr	1996	85,437	170,873	289	45	14	B	
Gotland Spirit	Bhs	1995	52,875	95,370	244	42	14	T	ex Bona Rider-99, Venessa-96
Hamane Spirit *	Bhs	1997	57,463	105,203	245	41	14	T	
Helga Spirit	Bhs	2005	62,929	115,444	250	44	15	T	
Hispania Spirit §§	Cni	2004	94,822	79,363	280	43	19	Lng	ex Fernando Tapias-04
Huelva Spirit §	Cni	2001	83,724	160,383	274	48	15	T	ex Iria Tapias-04
Hugli Spirit	Bhs	2005	29,242	46,889	183	32	14	T	ex Brazos-07, l/a Athenian Splendour
Iron Monarch	Aus	1973	20,145	14,885	179	25		Ro	
Iron Yandi ≠	Aus	1996	82,306	169,963	289	45	14	B	
Iskmati Spirit	Mhl	2003	84,789	165,000	274	50	15	T	ex Arlene-07
Kanata Spirit	Bhs	1999	62,685	113,021	249	44	14	T	
Kareela Spirit	Bhs	1999	62,685	113,021	249	44	14	T	
Kaveri Spirit	Bhs	2004	81,074	159,100	274	48		T	ex Janet-07, Athenian Olympics-04
Kilimanjaro Spirit *	Bhs	2004	62,845	115,048	250	44	14	T	
Kyeema Spirit	Bhs	1999	62,619	113,357	253	44	14	T	l/a Bona Vigour
Leyte Spirit *	Bhs	1992	57,448	98,744	245	41	14	T	
Limerick Spirit	Bhs	2007	57,325	105,547	244	42		T	
Luzon Spirit *	Bhs	1992	57,448	98,629	245	41	14	T	
Madrid Spirit (st)	Cni	2004	90,835	77,213	284	43	19	Lng	ex Ivan Tapias-04
Mahanadi Spirit	Bhs	2000	28,539	47,037	183	32	14	T	ex Guadalupe-07, Alam Bakti-00
Matterhorn Spirit	Bhs	2005	63,694	114,834	254	44	14	T	
Mayon Spirit *	Bhs	1992	57,448	98,507	245	41	14	T	
Narmada Spirit	Bhs	2003	81,074	159,199	274	48		T	ex Adair-07, Athenian Victory-04
Nassau Spirit	Bhs	1998	57,925	107,181	236	42	14	T	ex Avalon Spirit-06, Nassau Spirit-02
Navion Akarita *	Bhs	1991	58,928	107,223	244	42	14	T	ex Nordic Akarita-05, Stena Akarita-02, Akarita-96
Navion Anglia * (2)	Nor	1999	72,449	126,749	265	43	15	T	
Navion Bergen †	Nis	1999	56,207	105,641	239	42	14	T	ex Bergitta-07
Navion Britannia * (2)	Nor	1998	72,110	124,821	265	43	15	T	
Navion Clipper †	Bhs	1993	42,159	78,228	221	38	14	T	ex Polyclipper-98
Navion Europa * (me2)	Nor	1995	73,637	130,596	265	43	15	T	ex Jorunn Knutsen-98
Navion Fennia *	Bhs	1992	50,907	96,058	241	40	14	T	ex Futura-03
Navion Gothenburg †	Bhs	2006	82,647	152,244	274	48		T	ex Roviken-07
Navion Hispania * (2)	Nor	1999	72,132	126,749	265	43	14	T	

Teekay Shipping. NAVION HISPANIA. *Mick Lindsay*

Name	Flag	Year	GRT	DWT	LOA	Bm	Kts	Type	Former names
Navion Marita †	Cym	1999	58,117	103,894	246	42	14	T	ex Nordic Marita-07
Navion Norvegia *	Nor	1995	73,637	130,865	265	43	15	T	ex Hanne Knutsen-98
Navion Oceania * (2)	Nor	1999	72,132	126,749	265	43	14	T	
Navion Oslo †	Bhs	2001	55,796	100,257	238	42	14	T	ex Bertora-08
Navion Savonita †	Nis	1992	58,959	108,153	244	42	15	T	ex Nordic Savonita-07, Stena Savonita-97, Savonita-94
Navion Scandia * (2)	Nor	1998	72,132	126,749	265	43	14	T	
Navion Stavanger †	Bhs	2003	80,691	148,729	277	46	14	T	ex Nordic Stavanger-04, Nordic Liberita-03
Navion Svenita †	Bhs	1997	58,269	106,506	250	42	14	T	ex Nordic Svenita-06, Svenner-98
Navion Torinita ‡	Bhs	1992	58,959	108,683	244	42	14	T	ex Nordic Torinita-05, Torinita-96
Nordic Brasilia †	Bhs	2004	83,119	150,939	275	48		T	l/a Roviken
Nordic Rio †	Bhs	2004	83,120	151,294	277	48	14	T	
Nordic Spirit †	Bhs	2001	83,120	152,292	274	48	15	T	ex Storviken-02
Orana	Bhs	1991	38,844	44,849	200	32	14	Bw	ex Stellar Andes-06
Orkney Spirit	Bhs	1993	55,864	106,233	244	42	14	T	ex Bona Spray-99
Pacific Triangle	Lbr	2000	100,330	184,744	300	50	14	B	
Palmerston	Aus	1990	26,162	36,701	179	32	14	T	ex Ampol TVA-96
Pattani Spirit	Bhs	1988	59,289	106,671	244	42	14	T	ex Namsan Spirit-04
Petroatlantic *	Bhs	2003	54,865	92,968	235	42	14	T	
Petronordic *	Bhs	2002	54,885	92,995	234	42	14	T	
Pinnacle Spirit	Bhs	2008	81,732	160,391	274	48		T	
Pioneer	Aus	1996	17,094	22,140	169	23	15	Bs	ex MRS Pioneer-99
Pioneer Spirit *	Lbr	1993	53,848	96,724	243	42	15	T	ex Pioneer-08
Polar Spirit (st)	Bhs	1993	66,174	48,817	239	40	18	Lng	ex Polar Eagle-08
Poul Spirit *	Bhs	1995	57,463	105,351	245	41	14	T	
Rainier Spirit	Bhs	2005	62,877	114,880	250	44	14	T	
Samar Spirit **	Bhs	1992	57,448	98,640	245	41	14	T	
Saraji Trader	Lbr	1997	85,616	169,907	289	45		B	
Scotia Spirit *	Nis	1993	52,348	95,029	238	42	14	T	ex Navion Scotia-06, Vinga-98
Sebarok Spirit *	Bhs	1993	52,508	95,649	247	42	14	T	
Senang Spirit *	Bhs	1994	52,508	95,649	247	42	14	T	
Sotra Spirit *	Bhs	1995	52,875	95,420	244	42	14	T	ex Bona Robin-99, Ventina-96
SPT Explorer	Bhs	2008	57,657	105,804	241	42	15	T	
SPT Navigator	Bhs	2008	57,657	105,773	241	42	15	T	
Stena Spirit †	Bhs	2001	83,120	152,244	274	48	15	T	ex Erviken-01
Summit Spirit	Bhs	2008	81,732	160,400	274	48		T	
Tangguh Hiri	Bhs	2008	101,957	76,700	282	44		Lng	
Tangguh Sago	Bhs	2009	101,957	76,700	282	44		Lng	
Teesta Spirit	Bhs	2004	29,242	46,921	183	32	14	T	ex Jeanette-07, l/a Athenian Harmony
Teide Spirit §	Pmd	2004	83,594	159,426	274	48	15	T	
Tenerife Spirit §	Cni	2000	83,724	160,373	274	48	15	T	ex Bosco Tapias-04
Toledo Spirit §	Pmd	2005	83,724	159,342	274	48		T	
Torben Spirit *	Bhs	1994	57,486	98,622	245	41	14	T	
Yamuna Spirit	Bhs	2002	81,270	159,435	274	48	15	T	ex Dakota-07

newbuildings: two 102,000 grt Lng tankers, ten 159,000 dwt and four 109,000 dwt tankers for 2009-11 delivery.
Vessels owned by Teekay Shipping (Glasgow) Ltd, UK, by Teekay Shipping (Australia) Pty Ltd, by Teekay Shipping (USA) Inc and Teekay Shipping Spain SL. * owned or managed by Teekay Offshore Loading AS, Norway or by Teekay Navion Offshore Loading Pte Ltd, Singapore
† managed by Petroleo Brasileiro SA, Brazil (www2.petrobras.com.br) or ‡ by Knutsen OAS Shipping AS, Norway.
§ owned by Compania Espanola de Petroleos SA (CEPSA), Spain or # by Getty Maritime (managed by Northern Marine Management Ltd).
§§ managed by Repsol (Gas Natural LNG), Spain. ≠ owned by Teekay Marine Pty Ltd (formed 2001 by Teekay and BHP Billiton Petroleum Pty Ltd, Australia (30%))
In addition, the companies also operate numerous FPSO (floating production and storage offshore) and FSO (floating storage offshore) vessels.
Also see Chevron Corp, ConocoPhillips Inc, USA and DS-Rendite-Fonds GmbH & Co, Germany (under Dr Peters GmbH)

Thien & Heyenga GmbH   Germany

Funnel: Buff with houseflag comprising black over red with white 'T&H' over blue bands or charterers colours. **Hull:** Black, grey, red or blue with red boot-topping. **History:** Formed 1977. **Web:** www.tuh.de

Name	Flag	Year	GRT	DWT	LOA	Bm	Kts	Type	Former names
Glacier Bay *	Atg	1985	8,739	9,746	144	22	17	R	ex Cap Verde-95, Causewaybay-89, Cap Delgado-89
Himalaya Bay *	Lbr	1990	9,070	11,595	149	21	17	R	ex Amer Himalaya-08
Hudson Bay *	Atg	1983	8,052	8,945	140	21	17	R	ex Kiwi-99, Central Reefer-95, Southern Laurel-90, Southern Universal-88
Maersk Rades	Cyp	2007	14,500	18,480	166	25	19	CC	
New Confidence **	Pan	2001	13,764	16,400	155	25	19	CC	l/a Stadt Lubeck
Nova Galicia *	Ant	1983	6,149	6,730	138	19	17	R	ex Sun Princess-96, Sun Field-94
Sable Bay *	Ant	1983	8,739	9,746	144	22	17	R	ex Santorini Rex-96, Cap Valiente-91, Cap Domingo-89
SCI Jyoti **	Atg	2006	27,971	37,929	222	30	21	CC	l/dn Stadt Rostock
SCI Kiran	Atg	2006	27,971	37,938	222	30	21	CC	
Seaboxer	Mlt	1994	16,749	24,024	183	28	19	CC	ex Nantai Venus-99

Name	Flag	Year	GRT	DWT	LOA	Bm	Kts	Type	Former names
Stadt Aachen	Atg	2007	35,573	44,146	223	32	22	CC	
Stadt Coburg	Pan	2009	40,500	53,500	260	32	24	CC	
Stadt Gotha	Atg	2008	15,375	18,299	166	25	19	CC	l/dn Stadt Dresden
Stadt Jena	Atg	2007	15,375	18,279	166	25	19	CC	ex TS Xiamen-08, Stadt Jena-07
Stadt Koln **	Atg	2007	35,375	44,234	223	32	22	CC	
Stadt Marburg	Pan	2009	40,500	53,500	260	32	24	CC	
Stadt Schwerin	Atg	1999	14,241	18,440	159	24	18	CC	ex Melfi Halifax-08, MSC Ireland-04, Jork Venture-02, l/a Armin, l/dn Stadt Schwerin
Stadt Weimar	Atg	2006	27,971	37,934	222	30	21	CC	
Stadt Wismar **	Atg	2006	27,971	37,786	222	30	21	CC	

newbuildings: one further 40,500 grt and one 37,000 grt container ship for 2010 delivery.
* chartered to Seatrade Groningen BV q.v. ** managed for Konig & Cie GmbH & Co KG

A/S Dampskibsselskabet Torm   Denmark

Funnel: *Black with blue 'T' on white band between two red bands.* **Hull:** *Black or grey with red boot-topping.* **History:** *Formed 1889 and 30% owned by Beltest Shipping Co. Ltd., Cyprus. Owns 32% of Dampskibsselskabet 'Norden' A/S, Denmark q.v.. In 2007 acquired 50% of OMI (founded 1962 as Ogden Marine Inc and spun-off from Ogden Corp in 1984 as OMI Corp). In 2008 acquired 50% of FR8, Singapore (formed 2003).* **Web:** *www.torm.dk*

Name	Flag	Year	GRT	DWT	LOA	Bm	Kts	Type	Former names
Bel Taylor	Mhl	1990	43,398	84,040	229	32	14	T	ex Torm Hilde-05, Sitamona-03, Bona Brave-96, Golar Aberdeen-93
Faja De Oro II **	Mex	1995	28,928	47,629	183	32	14	T	ex Torm Alice-05
Gotland Aliya #	Dis	2008	29,283	53,121	183	32	14	T	
Gotland Carolina #	Dis	2006	29,283	53,180	183	32	14	T	
Gotland Sofia #	Dis	2007	29,283	53,187	183	32	14	T	
Potrero del Llano II **	Mex	1999	28,546	47,165	183	32	14	T	ex Torm Agnete-05, Zorca-04
Torm Amazon	Sgp	2002	28,539	47,275	183	32	14	T	ex Amazon-07
Torm Anholt **	Sgp	2004	39,035	74,195	225	32	14	B	
Torm Ann-Marie #	Dis	1997	57,031	99,990	244	42	15	T	
Torm Anna #	Dis	2004	42,432	75,000	225	32	14	T	
Torm Anne **	Sgp	1999	28,932	45,507	180	32	14	T	
Torm Baltic **	Sgp	1997	36,592	69,614	225	32	14	B	ex Navios Minerva-02
Torm Bornholm **	Sgp	2004	40,030	75,912	225	32	14	B	
Torm Camilla †	Dis	2003	30,024	44,990	183	32	14	T	
Torm Carina †	Dis	2003	30,024	46,219	183	32	14	T	
Torm Caroline †	Dis	2002	28,381	46,414	183	32	14	T	
Torm Cecilie †	Nis	2001	28,381	46,414	183	32	14	T	
Torm Charente	Dis	2001	23,740	35,751	183	27	14	T	ex Charente-08
Torm Clara †	Dis	2000	28,381	45,999	183	32	14	T	ex Svart Falk-05, High Svart Falk-03
Torm Emilie †	Dis	2004	42,493	74,999	228	32	16	T	
Torm Estrid	Dis	2004	42,432	74,999	225	32	14	T	
Torm Fox	Dis	2004	23,246	37,000	183	27	14	T	ex Fox-08
Torm Freya	Dis	2003	30,058	46,342	183	32	14	T	
Torm Garonne	Dis	2004	23,346	37,178	183	27	14	T	ex Garonne-08
Torm Gerd	Dis	2002	30,058	46,300	183	32	14	T	
Torm Gertrud	Dis	2002	30,058	46,362	183	32	14	T	
Torm Gudrun	Nis	2000	57,031	99,965	244	42	14	T	
Torm Gunhild	Dis	1999	28,909	45,457	181	32	14	T	

Dampskib. Torm. GOTLAND CAROLINA. *C. Lous*

Name	Flag	Year	GRT	DWT	LOA	Bm	Kts	Type	Former names
Torm Helene	Dis	1997	57,031	99,900	244	42	14	T	
Torm Hellerup	Phl	2008	28,100	45,800	180	32		T	
Torm Helvig	Dis	2005	30,018	46,187	183	32	14	T	
Torm Horizon ***	Dis	2004	29,242	46,955	183	32	14	T	ex Horizon-08, Athenian Horizon-04
Torm Ingeborg	Nis	2003	57,095	99,900	244	42	14	T	
Torm Ismini	Dis	2004	42,432	74,999	228	32	15	T	
Torm Kansas	Dis	2006	29,242	46,922	184	32	14	T	ex Kansas-08
Torm Kristina *	Nis	1999	57,080	105,002	244	42	14	T	
Torm Laura	Dis	2008	29,283	53,160	183	32	14	T	
Torm Loire	Dis	2004	23,200	37,106	183	27	14	T	ex Loire-08
Torm Madison	Dis	2000	23,842	35,833	183	27	14	T	ex Madison-08, Nina-01
Torm Maren	Dis	2008	61,724	109,672	245	42	15	T	
Torm Margit	Nis	2007	61,724	109,672	245	42	15	T	
Torm Margrethe	Dis	2006	61,724	109,637	245	42	15	T	
Torm Marianne	Dis	2008	61,724	109,672	245	42	15	T	
Torm Marie	Dis	2006	61,724	109,637	245	42	15	T	
Torm Marina §	Nis	2007	61,724	109,672	245	42	15	T	
Torm Marta ‡	Nis	1997	36,592	69,638	225	32	14	B	

Dampskib. Torm. TORM ANNA. *Allan Ryszka Onions*

Dampskib. Torm. TORM CARINA. *Allan Ryszka Onions*

Name	Flag	Year	GRT	DWT	LOA	Bm	Kts	Type	Former names
Torm Mary	Dis	2002	30,058	46,634	183	32	14	T	
Torm Mette	Nis	2007	61,724	109,672	245	42		T	
Torm Moselle	Dis	2003	28,567	47,038	183	32	14	T	ex Moselle-08
Torm Neches **	Sgp	2000	28,539	47,052	183	32	14	T	ex Neches-08, Alam Bayu-00
Torm Ohio	Dis	2001	23,235	37,278	183	27	14	T	ex Ohio-08, I/a Borak
Torm Orient	Pan	2008	39,737	76,636	225	32		B	
Torm Ottawa ##	Sgp	2003	42,771	70,296	228	32	15	T	ex Ottawa-08
Torm Platte	Dis	2006	29,242	46,955	183	32	14	T	ex Platte-07
Torm Ragnhild	Dis	2004	40,000	75,000	225	32	14	T	
Torm Republican	Dis	2006	29,242	46,955	183	32	14	T	ex Republican-08
Torm Rhone	Dis	2000	23,740	35,769	183	27		T	ex Rhone-08, Prospero-01
Torm Rosetta	Dis	2003	28,567	47,038	183	32	14	T	ex Rosetta-08
Torm Rotna **	Sgp	2001	40,072	75,971	225	32	14	B	
Torm San Jacinto	Mhl	2002	28,539	47,038	183	32	15	T	ex San Jacinto-08
Torm Saone	Dis	2004	23,246	36,986	183	27	14	T	ex Saone-07
Torm Sara **	Sgp	2003	41,690	72,718	228	32	15	T	ex Penyu Agar-05
Torm Signe **	Sgp	2005	41,503	72,718	228	32	15	T	ex Penyu Siski-05
Torm Sofia **	Sgp	2005	41,503	72,650	228	32	15	T	ex Penyu Daun-05
Torm Tamar ##	Sgp	2003	43,000	70,100	228	32		T	ex Tamar-08
Torm Tevere	Dis	2005	23,246	36,990	183	28	14	T	ex Tevere-08, Tiber-05
Torm Thames	Dis	2005	29,214	47,036	184	32	14	T	ex Thames-08
Torm Thyra	Dis	2003	30,058	46,308	183	32	14	T	
Torm Tina **	Sgp	2001	40,038	75,966	225	32	14	B	
Torm Trinity	Dis	2000	23,842	35,833	183	27	14	T	ex Trinity-08, Snipe-01
Torm Ugland ‡	Nis	2007	42,048	73,706	229	32		T	
Torm Valborg	Nis	2003	57,095	99,900	244	42	14	T	
Torm Venture	Nis	2007	42,048	73,701	229	32		T	
Torm Vita	Dis	2002	30,058	46,308	183	32	14	T	

newbuildings: three 110,000 dwt, nine 51,800 dwt and seven 46,000 dwt tankers for 2008-10 delivery.
* owned by Torm Shipping (Germany) GmbH (formed 2004), ** by Torm Singapore (Pte.) Ltd (formed 1979) or *** by Torm Shipping India Pte Ltd.
† managed by LGR di Navigazione SpA, Italy or ‡ by Thome Ship Management. § owned jointly with TorghattenTrafikkselskap ASA
 # managed for Rederi AB Gotland, Sweden or ## for Tailwinds Pte Ltd, Singapore (Tailwinds AS, Norway)
Company operates about 115 vessels in the Torm LR1, Torm LR2, Torm MR and Torm Handy product tanker pools.

Rederi AB Transatlantic Sweden

Funnel: Yellow with blue 'TA' symbol within blue ring, narrow blue base and top. **Hull:** Grey or white with red boot-topping.
History: Transatlantic (originally founded 1904) was acquired by Bilspedition AB in 1988, which also acquired Cool Carriers (1987), Gorthon (1988), Incotrans (1988), Atlantic Container Line (1988-90) and Swedish Orient (1991). All were later sold, Gorthon Lines AB (formed 1915) to B&N Bylock & Nordsjofrakt AB in 1990, before being spun-off in 1997, acquiring the associated Sea Partner AB management company in 2000, which was renamed Gorthon Fleet Services AB. In 2004 a Gorthon-B&N Transatlantic joint venture was formed and in 2005 B&N Nordsjofrakt merged with Gorthon Lines as Transatlantic. **Web:** www.rabt.se

Finnfighter	Swe	2001	20,851	18,972	179	29	17	Ro	(len)
Nordon	Nld	2002	13,340	16,612	142	22	15	Co	
Transhawk	Gib	2004	13,340	16,558	142	22	15	Co	ex Sandon-08
Transmaple	Swe	1984	13,533	11,491	156	22	15	Ro	ex Maria Gorthon-08
Transoak	Swe	1984	13,525	11,425	156	22	15	Ro	ex Ada Gorthon-08
Transpine	Swe	2002	20,851	18,855	179	29	17	Ro	ex Finnpine-08 (len)
Transwood	Swe	2002	20,851	18,855	179	26	17	Ro	ex Finnwood-08 (len-06)
Viola Gorthon	Swe	1987	18,773	10,917	166	23	20	Ro	

managed by Transatlantic Fleet Services AB (formed 1992). Also operates Ro-Ro vessels on Baltic routes.

Transeste Schiffahrt GmbH Germany

Funnel: Mainly in charterers colours. **Hull:** Black, dark grey, blue or red with red boot-topping. **History:** Formed 1956.
Web: www.transeste.de

CCNI Rimac	Deu	2001	25,703	33,795	208	30	22	CC	ex Wotan-06, MSC Venezuela-03, I/a Wotan
CMA CGM Tunis	Atg	1993	14,953	20,140	167	25	18	CC	ex CMA CGM Venezuela-08, Estetrader-07, City of Oxford-03, Kent Courier-01, Seaboard Toronto-00, Keta-00, Wieland-98, Exporter-97, Red Sea Exporter-95, Wieland-94
CSAV Sao Paulo *	Lbr	2004	35,881	42,300	220	32	22	CC	ex Norasia Andes-06, Anke Ritscher-04
DAL East London *	Lbr	2006	17,360	22,254	179	28	21	CC	ex Helle Ritscher-06
Estebroker *	Atg	1999	25,705	33,843	208	30	22	CC	ex CSAV Trinidad-08, Hanjin Dubai-07, Trade Bravery-05, TPL Merchant-02, Lykes Crusader-01
Jonni Ritscher *	Lbr	2006	17,189	22,243	179	28	21	CC	ex CMA CGM Caribbean-08, Jonni Ritscher-06
MOL Satisfaction *	Atg	1999	25,705	33,750	208	30	22	CC	ex Trade Zale-05, TPL Eagle-02, TMM San Antonio-01, Jan Ritscher-99
Norasia Polaris	Lbr	2004	35,881	42,000	221	32	22	CC	ex Wieland-04
NYK Espirito *	Deu	2001	25,705	33,795	208	30	22	CC	ex Sea Tiger-04, I/a Ulf Ritscher

Name	Flag	Year	GRT	DWT	LOA	Bm	Kts	Type	Former names
Widukind *	Lbr	2006	35,881	42,200	221	32	22	CC	ex SCI Diya-08, Widukind-07, Hera-06

*Managed for owning partner companies Reederei Gerd Ritscher KG (founded 1956 www.ritschership.com) or * Reederei Dietrich Tamke KG (founded 1970), both Germany*

TransPetrol Ltd   Bermuda

Funnel: *Black with white 'tp' above white wave lines.* **Hull:** *Black or brown with red or grey boot-topping.* **History:** *Formed 1979 as TransPetrol Maritime Services NV until 2005.* **Web:** *www.transpetrol.com*

Name	Flag	Year	GRT	DWT	LOA	Bm	Kts	Type	Former names
Advance II *	Sgp	2006	30,032	46,101	183	32	14	T	
Affinity	Sgp	2005	42,661	73,741	228	32	15	T	
Endeavour	Sgp	2004	30,032	46,101	183	32	14	T	
Perseverence	Sgp	2005	42,661	73,788	228	32	15	T	
Progress	Sgp	2009	47,266	82,000	225	37		Lpg	
Promise **	Sgp	1991	58,086	111,587	247	43	14	T	ex Gammatank-00, Apache Spirit-93
Reliance II *	Sgp	2006	30,032	46,101	183	32	14	T	
Resolve	Sgp	2004	30,032	46,048	183	32	14	T	
Tenacity	Sgp	1996	53,371	87,240	228	42	15	T	

newbuildings: one further 82,000 dwt Lpg tanker on order for 2009 delivery.
*Operated by subsidiary TransPetrol Maritime Services Ltd, Belgium and * owned by TransPetrol TMAS, Norway.*
*** managed by International Tanker Management Holding Ltd, UAE.*

TransPetrol. RELIANCE II. *Hans Kraijenbosch*

Trireme Vessel Management. ALBEMARLE ISLAND. *Allan Ryszka Onions*

Trireme Vessel Management NV   Belgium

Funnel: *Dark blue with yellow 'EL' on red disc.* **Hull:** *Orange with red boot-topping.* **History:** *Founded 1988 as Ecuadorian Line Inc NV to 1996.* **Web:** *none found.*

Name	Flag	Year	GRT	DWT	LOA	Bm	Kts	Type	Former names
Albemarle Island	Bhs	1993	14,061	14,160	179	25	21	R	
Arctic Ocean	Bhs	1989	10,829	10,303	151	22	22	R	
Atlantic Ocean	Bhs	1989	10,829	10,285	151	22	22	R	
Baltic Sea	Bhs	1973	6,892	9,072	141	18	22	R	ex Provincia del Guayas-95, Ciudad de Guayaquil-88, Lucky I-84, Lucky-84, Timur Girl-83, Hilco Girl-81, Golar Girl-77
Barrington Island	Bhs	1993	14,061	14,140	179	25	21	R	
Bering Sea	Bhs	1975	9,618	9,744	153	21	21	R	ex Punta Bianca-94 (NE-88)
Celtic Sea	Bhs	1970	9,869	11,902	166	21	22	R	ex Provincia de los Rios-95, Indian Ocean-84, Nippon Reefer-78
Charles Island *	Bhs	1993	14,061	14,140	179	25	21	R	
Coral Sea	Bhs	1976	9,618	9,748	153	21	21	R	ex Punta Verde-94 (NE-88)
Duncan Island *	Bhs	1993	14,061	14,140	179	25	21	R	
Hood Island *	Bhs	1994	14,601	14,140	179	25	21	R	
Indian Ocean	Bhs	1989	10,829	10,313	151	22	22	R	

* on long-term bareboat charter from Dansk Investeringsfond, Denmark.

Tsakos Shipping & Trading SA   Greece

Funnel: *Yellow with red 'T' on broad white band edged with narrow blue bands, narrow black top.* **Hull:** *Black * with white 'TEN', red boot-topping.* **History:** *Formed 1970.* **Web:** *www.tsakoshellas.com or www.tenn.gr*

Name	Flag	Year	GRT	DWT	LOA	Bm	Kts	Type	Former names
Aegeas *	Grc	2007	23,325	39,378	183	27	14	T	
Africa	Bhs	1986	52,518	99,335	247	42	15	T	ex Hawaiian Leader-06, Clare Spirit-03, Bona Ranger-99, Venliza-96, Feliz-93, Beryl-93, l/a Colorado
Afrodite *	Bhs	2005	30,053	52,700	186	32	14	T	ex Western Antarctic-06
Ajax *	Bhs	2005	30,053	52,700	186	32	14	T	ex Western Baltic-06
Alaska *	Grc	2006	85,421	163,250	274	50	15	T	
Andes *	Grc	2003	39,085	68,439	229	32	14	T	
Andromeda *	Grc	2007	23,325	39,378	183	27	14	T	
Antares *	Grc	2006	23,325	36,660	183	27	14	T	
Apollon *	Bhs	2005	30,053	52,700	186	32	14	T	ex Western Pacific-06
Aramis	Lbr	1983	37,895	60,906	228	32	15	T	ex Hydra Mar-98, Caribbean Shoot II-90
Archangel *	Grc	2006	85,421	163,216	274	50	15	T	
Arctic *	Grc	2007	85,431	163,152	274	50	15	T	
Ariadne *	Bhs	2005	30,053	52,700	186	32	14	T	ex Western Icelandic-06
Arion	Grc	2006	23,325	39,478	183	27	14	T	
Aris *	Bhs	2005	30,053	52,700	186	32	14	T	ex Western Atlantic-06
Artemis *	Bhs	2005	30,053	52,700	186	32	14	T	ex Western Arctic-06
Beijing 2008	Lbr	2007	43,158	82,561	229	32	14	B	
Bosporos	Gre	2007	23,310	39,589	183	27	14	T	
Byzantine *	Grc	2007	23,310	39,589	183	27	14	T	
CCNI Mejillones	Pan	1995	18,716	24,370	194	28	20	CC	ex CMA CGM Limon-08, Irenes Logos-06, Ise-02

Tsakos Shipping & Trading. ANDROMEDA. *Hans Kraijenbosch*

Name	Flag	Year	GRT	DWT	LOA	Bm	Kts	Type	Former names
Delphi *	Grc	2004	25,124	37,432	176	31	15	T	
Didimon *	Grc	2004	25,124	37,432	176	31	15	T	ex Dodoni-05
El Junior ‡	Pan	1995	149,896	260,870	335	58	15	T	ex Tohzan-03
Eurochampion 2004 *	Grc	2005	85,431	164,808	274	50	15	T	
Euronike *	Grc	2005	85,431	164,565	274	50	15	T	ex Euroniki-05
Hanjin Elizabeth	Pan	1992	50,792	62,723	290	32	24	CC	ex Hanjin Barcelona-05
Hanjin Irene	Pan	1994	50,792	62,742	290	32	24	CC	ex Hanjin Tokyo-05
Hanjin Sydney	Kor	1987	95,513	188,117	291	48	13	B	ex Westin Nine-89
Hesnes *	Mlt	1990	38,792	68,157	243	32	14	T	
Inca *	Grc	2003	39,085	68,439	229	32	14	T	
Irenes Reliance	Grc	2005	28,592	39,396	222	30	23	CC	
Irenes Remedy	Grc	2005	28,592	39,382	222	30	23	CC	
Izumo Princess *	Grc	2007	55,909	105,374	229	42	14	T	
Kota Segar	Grc	2006	28,592	39,382	222	30	23	CC	
La Esperanza	Pan	1993	158,475	299,700	344	56	14	T	ex Ehm Maersk-03, British Valour-02, Elisabeth Maersk-97
La Madrina *	Grc	1993	158,475	299,700	344	56	14	T	ex Maersk Estelle-04, Estelle Maersk-98
La Paz †	Pan	1995	158,475	299,700	344	56	14	T	ex Evelyn Maersk-03
La Prudencia *	Grc	1992	158,475	298,900	344	56	14	T	ex Maersk Eleo-04, Eleo Maersk-98
London 2012	Lbr	2007	43,158	82,562	229	32	14	B	
Manousos P	Lbr	2008	43,158	82,549	229	32	14	B	
Marathon *	Grc	2003	58,127	107,181	247	42	14	T	
Maya *	Grc	2003	39,085	68,439	229	32	14	T	
Millennium ‡	Pan	1998	156,692	301,171	331	58	15	T	
MSC Brasilia	Pan	1986	35,598	43,270	241	32	21	CC	ex Kobe-02, Hanjin Kobe-02
MSC London	Cyp	1986	36,266	43,270	241	32	21	CC	ex Keelung-03, Hanjin Keelung-02
MSC Rugby	Cyp	1983	31,356	30,941	220	32	22	CC	ex Irenes Myth-08, Global Myth-02, Irenes Myth-97, California Triton-97, Japan Alliance-91
MSC Sardinia	Lbr	1986	36,270	42,880	241	32	22	CC	ex Hong Kong-03, Hanjin Hongkong-03
Neo Energy (st) *	Lbr	2007	100,253	85,602	288	44	19	Lng	
Opal Queen *	Pan	2001	57,920	107,181	247	42	14	T	
Parthenon *	Grc	2003	58,157	107,081	247	42	14	T	
Promitheas *	Grc	2006	66,919	117,055	250	44	15	T	
Propontis *	Grc	2006	66,919	116,610	250	44	15	T	
Proteas *	Grc	2006	66,919	117,055	250	44	15	T	
Sakura Princess *	Grc	2007	55,909	105,385	229	42		T	
SCI Vijay	Cyp	1991	37,410	47,273	236	32	18	CC	ex Australia Bridge-05, Australian Endurance-96
Selecao **	Lbr	2008	41,676	74,296	228	32	15	T	
Silia T *	Grc	2002	84,586	164,286	274	50	15	T	
Socrates **	Lbr	2008	41,676	74,327	228	32	14	T	
Triathlon *	Grc	2002	84,586	164,445	274	50	14	T	
Vergina II *	Cyp	1991	53,569	96,709	247	42	14	T	ex Lark Lake-95
Victory III *	Ven	1990	38,798	68,157	243	32	15	T	ex Ryvingen-95

newbuildings: six 170,000 dwt, two 91,800 dwt, tive 53-55,800 dwt bulk carriers, six 105,400 dwt and four 74,400 dwt tankers and a 51,000 grt container ship for 2009-10 delivery.
 * owned or managed by subsidiaries Tsakos Energy Management Ltd (formed 1993), ** by Tsakos Energy Navigation Ltd (TEN) (formed 1993 as Maritime Investment Fund Ltd to 1996) or # by Entrust Maritime Co Ltd, Greece (formed 1991).
† managed by Wallem Shipmanagement Ltd, Hong Kong or ‡ by Hyundai Merchant Marine Co Ltd.

A/S Uglands Rederi   Norway

Funnel: Yellow with white 'U' on broad red band below black top. **Hull:** Grey, black or orange with black or white 'UGLAND', green or red boot-topping. **History:** Formed 1930. **Web:** www.jjuc.no

Name	Flag	Year	GRT	DWT	LOA	Bm	Kts	Type	Former names
Benarita	Nis	1984	23,594	40,688	183	30	14	B	ex Yuming-91, Sanko Elegance-91
Ellenita	Pan	1984	24,942	42,836	190	30	14	B	ex Golden Topaz-97, Samar Sampaguita-90, Diamond Azalea-89, New Azalea-87, Sanko Azalea-85
Favorita	Nis	2005	30,078	52,292	190	32	14	B	
Fermita	Nis	2001	30,053	52,380	190	32	14	B	
Jorita	Nis	1985	23,981	36,726	179	31	14	B	
Juanita * (2)	Nor	1988	72,129	126,491	260	46	14	T	ex Lisita-89
Livanita	Nis	1997	26,044	45,426	186	30	15	B	
Mattea † (2)	Can	1997	76,216	126,380	272	46	15	T	
Rosita	Nis	2004	30,076	52,292	190	32	14	B	
Senorita	Nor	2008	32,379	58,300	190	32	14	B	
Tamarita	Nis	2001	30,053	52,292	190	32	14	B	
Vinland †	Can	2000	76,567	125,827	272	46	14	T	

newbuildings: seven 43,500 grt 82,200 dwt bulk carriers for 2010-11 delivery.
Owned or managed by subsidiaries Ugland Marine Services AS (formed 1996) and Ugland Shipping A/S (formed 1964)
Managed * for P/R Nordshuttle DA, Norway or † by Canship Ugland Ltd (formed jointly with Canship Ltd). Also see Stena AB and Teekay Corp.

United Arab Shipping Co (SAG)　　　　　　　　　　　　Kuwait

Funnel: *Black, broad white band with red/purple bands above and black/green bands below black 6-spoked wheel containing black crossed anchors on blue centre disc.* **Hull:** *Light grey with black 'UASC', green band over red boot-topping.* **History:** *Founded 1976 as Kuwait Shipping Co (SAK) to 1977. Formed jointly by The Governments of the United Arab Emirates, the States of Bahrain, Kuwait and Qatar, the Kingdom of Saudi Arabia and the Republic of Iraq.* Web: www.uasc.net

Name	Flag	Year	GRT	DWT	LOA	Bm	Kts	Type	Former names
Abu Dhabi	Are	1998	48,154	49,844	277	32	24	CC	
Addiriyah	Sau	1979	20,526	24,272	183	27	17	CC	
Al Bahia	Are	2008	75,579	85,517	306	40	25	CC	
Al Farabi *	Sau	1986	26,464	43,851	178	32		T	
Al Hilal	Pan	2008	75,579	79,030	306	40	25	CC	
Al Ihsa'a	Sau	1983	32,534	35,615	211	32	19	CC	
Al Manakh	Kwt	1983	32,534	35,615	211	32	19	CC	
Al Manamah	Pan	2008	75,579	85,517	306	40	25	CC	
Al Mariyah	Are	1983	32,534	35,615	211	32	19	CC	
Al Mirqab	Kwt	1983	32,534	35,615	211	32	19	CC	
Al Noof	Qat	1998	48,154	49,993	277	32	24	CC	
Al Rawdah	Pan	2008	75,579	85,226	306	40	25	CC	
Al Safat	Kwt	2008	75,579	85,437	306	40	25	CC	
Al Wajba	Qat	1983	32,534	35,615	211	32	19	CC	
Al-Abdali	Kwt	1998	48,154	49,844	277	32	24	CC	
Al-Farahidi	Bhr	1998	48,154	50,004	277	32	24	CC	
Al-Mutanabbi	Bhr	1998	48,154	49,844	277	32	24	CC	
Al-Sabahia	Kwt	1998	48,154	49,848	277	32	24	CC	
Asir	Sau	1998	48,154	49,856	277	32	24	CC	
Deira	Are	1998	48,154	49,993	277	32	24	CC	
Dubai	Are	1982	32,534	35,615	211	32	19	CC	
Fowairet	Qat	1998	48,154	49,993	277	32	24	CC	
Hammurabi	Kwt	1983	32,534	35,615	211	32	19	CC	ex Australian Advance-98, Hammurabi-86
Hatta	Are	2008	75,579	85,614	306	40	25	CC	
Ibn Bassam	Qat	1977	15,125	23,618	175	24	16	C	
Jazan	Pan	2008	75,579	85,463	306	40	25	CC	
Jebel Ali	Are	1979	20,526	24,349	183	27	17	CC	
Khaled Ibn Al Waleed	Are	1983	32,534	35,615	211	32	19	CC	
Mayssan	Bhr	2008	75,579	85,517	306	40	25	CC	
Najran	Sau	1998	48,154	49,993	277	32	24	CC	
Nord Sound *	Pan	2003	28,059	45,975	180	32	14	T	
Qatari Ibn Al Fuja'a	Qat	1983	32,534	35,615	211	32	19	CC	ex Kota Selamat-02, Qatari Ibn Al Fuja'a-00
UACC Al Medina *	Pan	2003	28,059	45,987	180	32	14	T	ex Nord Sea-08
UACC Ibn Al Atheer *	Pan	2003	28,059	45,994	180	32	14	T	ex Pacific Sunshine-08
UACC Ibn Al Haitham *	Mlt	2009	42,010	73,338	229	32	14	T	
UACC Ibn Sina *	Mlt	2008	42,010	73,338	229	32	14	T	

newbuildings: seven other 85,000 dwt container ships on order for 2009 delivery (next Safat and Bahia).
* owned by subsidiary Arabian Chemical Carriers LLC (formed1986, owned jointly with The National Shipping Company of Saudi Arabia until 2007) and managed by Fleet Management Ltd, Hong Kong (Noble Group)

Viken Shipping AS　　　　　　　　　　　　　　　Norway

Funnel: *Cream with narrow blue band on white band on broad red band beneath black top.* **Hull:** *Black, grey or brown, or dark green with red boot-topping.* **History:** *Formed 1993 and de-merged from joint venture with Mowinckel in 2002. Acquired Wallem Group jointly with Clearwater Investments in 2006.* Web: www.vikenship.com

Name	Flag	Year	GRT	DWT	LOA	Bm	Kts	Type	Former names
Algoma Spirit †	Bhs	1986	23,271	34,750	222	23	14	B	ex Sandviken-08, Petka-00
Erviken	Nis	2004	82,647	152,146	275	48	14	T	
Federal Fuji *	Bhs	1986	17,814	29,536	183	23	14	B	
Federal Polaris *	Bhs	1985	17,815	29,536	183	23	14	B	
Inviken *	Bhs	1986	17,313	30,070	189	23	15	B	ex Bar-97
Kronviken	Nis	2006	61,653	113,450	249	44	14	T	
Solviken	Nis	2007	61,653	114,523	249	44	14	T	
Storviken	Nis	2006	82,647	152,013	274	48	14	T	
Tanea **	Iom	2005	62,806	115,340	250	44	15	T	ex Ganstar-05
Torinia **	Iom	2005	62,806	115,340	250	44	15	T	ex Gansky-05
Trochus **	Iom	2006	62,806	115,345	250	44	15	T	l/a Gansea
Utviken *	Bhs	1987	17,191	30,052	189	23	16	B	ex C. Bianco-95, Bijelo Polje-92

managed by subsidiary Wallem Shipmanagement Norway AS (renamed from Viken Ship Management AS in 2006).
On long-term charter to * Fednav Ltd., Canada or to ** Shell-Royal Dutch Group (managed by STASCO Ship Management) qv
† managed by Wallem Shipmanagement Inc, USA.

Name	Flag	Year	GRT	DWT	LOA	Bm	Kts	Type	Former names

F A Vinnen & Co (GmbH & Co) Germany

Funnel: *Black with black 'M' on broad white band, white with blue 'V' or charterers colours.* **Hull:** *Black with red boot-topping.*
History: *Formed 1918 as E C Schramm & Co to 1920.* **Web:** *www.vinnen.com*

Name	Flag	Year	GRT	DWT	LOA	Bm	Kts	Type	Former names
CMA CGM Cartagena *	Lbr	1996	16,800	22,900	185	26	19	CC	ex Merkur Beach-06, Delmas Charcot-03, Merkur Beach-02, MSC Quito-02, Merkur Beach-99, CSAV Rahue-98, I/a Merkur Beach
CMA CGM L'Etoile	Lbr	2005	26,626	34,500	210	30	21	CC	ex E.R. Camargue-05
CMA CGM Ylang	Deu	1997	28,662	39,927	202	31	20	CC	ex Merkur Sky-07, MSC California-05, Merkur Sky-03, MSC Gauteng-02, Merkur Sky-02, MSC Sicily-01, Merkur Sky-99, Zim Piraeus-98, Merkur Sky-98
H&H Tide *	Lbr	1993	9,597	12,575	150	22	17	CC	ex Merkur Bridge-08, Sinar Banda-02, Kota Seri-01, Merkur Bridge-99, New Orient-99, Merkur Bridge-98, Ratana Ganya-97, TSL Bravo-96, Merkur Bridge-93
Merkur Bay	Deu	2002	30,047	35,770	208	32	22	CC	
Merkur Cloud	Lbr	1996	15,929	22,026	168	27	21	CC	ex Kota Molek-07, Merkur Cloud-04, Calapalos-02, I/a Merkur Cloud
Merkur Lake	Lbr	1994	9,600	12,574	150	23	18	CC	ex EWL Suriname-04, Merkur Lake-96, Libra Genova-95, Merkur Lake-95
MOL Heritage	Lbr	1998	15,929	22,026	168	27	21	CC	ex Merkur Tide-08, YM Dubai-07, Merkur Tide-04, Calaparana-03, Merkur Tide-01, Atlantico-01, I/a Merkur Tide
MSC Natal	Lbr	1996	29,181	39,528	203	31	19	CC	ex Merkur Star-06, MSC Oman-03, Merkur Star-02, CMA CGM Seurat-02, Merkur Star-00, Houston Express-98, Merkur Star-96, I/a John Lykes

* managed for Hansa Treuhand Schiffs GmbH & Co KG, Germany qv

H Vogemann GmbH Germany

Funnel: *Red with white 'V', black top.* **Hull:** *Black with red boot-topping.* **History:** *Founded 1886.* **Web:** *www.vogemann.de*

Name	Flag	Year	GRT	DWT	LOA	Bm	Kts	Type	Former names
Bulk Asia *	Lbr	2001	87,590	170,578	289	45	14	B	
Bulk Europe *	Lbr	2001	87,590	169,770	289	45	14	B	
Greta R	Lbr	1989	37,519	68,772	225	32	14	B	ex Achilles-03
Lake Maja	Lbr	1996	15,737	24,518	158	26	14	C	ex Fairy Angel-05
Voge Eva *	Lbr	1997	14,762	23,407	154	26	14	B	ex Clipper Beaufort-07, Sea Amelita-03
Voge Felix *	Lbr	1997	14,599	24,279	157	26	15	B	ex Andros-06, Sea Wisdom-03
Voge Master **	Deu	2006	88,930	174,093	289	45	14	B	ex Avore-07
Voge Paul **	Lbr	1998	14,762	23,494	156	26	15	B	ex Clipper Bounteous-07, Joint Spirit-03, Sea Harvest-98
Voge Prestige **	Lbr	1995	39,283	75,100	225	32	14	B	ex National Prestige-07
Voge Prosperity **	Lbr	1995	39,283	75,100	225	32	14	B	ex National Prosperity-07
Voge Renate *	Lbr	1997	14,762	23,407	154	26	15	B	ex Clipper Breeze-07, Joint Bright-03, Sea Splendor-98
Voge West **	Lbr	1995	38,236	70,728	225	32	14	B	ex Xinshi Hai-08, Brazilian Venture-01
Vogebulker **	Lbr	1999	86,192	169,168	289	45	14	B	ex Heng Shan-04
Vogecarrier *	Lbr	1996	85,706	164,303	289	43	15	B	ex Eurotrader-04, Cherokee-00
Vogerunner	Deu	2009	89,603	176,786	289	45		B	
Vogesailor *	Lbr	1996	86,706	164,188	289	43	15	B	ex Eurosailor-05, Comanche-00
Vogetrader *	Lbr	1996	37,663	72,171	224	32	15	B	ex Far Eastern Progress-01
Vogevoyager	Lbr	1996	37,663	72,105	224	32	15	B	ex Far Eastern Auspice-02

newbuildings: two 38,500 dwt and twelve 33,000 dwt bulk carriers for 2009-11 delivery.
* managed by Wallem GmbH & Co KG (joint venture as Vogemann-Wallem Ltd) or ** by KG Reederei Roth GmbH & Co (founded 1972 as Josef Roth Reederei until 1988 - www.reederei-roth.de)

Vroon BV Netherlands

Funnel: *White with three wavy blue lines at base of blue 'V', narrow blue or black top, * white with blue 'V' symbol inside red square, blue top or † white with blue 'LE', blue top.* **Hull:** *White, grey, black, blue or red with red boot-topping.* **History:** *Formed 1890. Reefer vessels sold to Seatrade in 2005.* **Web:** *www.vroon.nl   www.ivership.com*

Name	Flag	Year	GRT	DWT	LOA	Bm	Kts	Type	Former names
Acadian *	Can	2005	23,356	37,515	183	27	14	T	
Aegean Express	Pan	1997	15,095	18,581	169	27	18	CC	ex YM Bangkok-02, Kuo Ting-01
Arabian Express	Pan	1997	15,095	18,300	169	27	18	CC	ex Kuo Yang-03
Asian Dynasty	Phl	1999	55,719	21,224	200	32	20	V	
Columbian Express	Pan	1986	12,963	20,479	147	25	14	Co	ex ALS Endeavour-01, Columbian Express-98, ALS Strength-97, Kriti Amber-88, ALS Strength-88, Kriti Amber-87
Eurasian Brilliance	Phl	1985	26,746	9,763	159	28	17	V	ex Rubin Crest-94, Dairyu Maru-92

Name	Flag	Year	GRT	DWT	LOA	Bm	Kts	Type	Former names
Eurasian Alliance	Phl	1983	27,013	9,358	159	28	17	V	ex Daishun Maru-94
Eurasian Chariot	Phl	1985	31,923	12,184	172	30	18	V	ex Eurasian Challenge-95, Ocean Cheer-94
Great Eastern *	Mhl	2005	23,356	37,515	183	27	14	T	
Iver Exact *	Nld	2007	29,456	46,575	183	32	14	T	
Iver Example *	Nld	2007	29,456	46,784	183	32	14	T	
Iver Excel *	Nld	1997	29,289	45,750	183	32	14	T	
Iver Experience *	Nld	2000	29,289	45,650	183	32	15	T	
Iver Expert *	Nld	1997	29,289	45,750	183	32	14	T	
Iver Exporter *	Mhl	2000	29,289	45,500	183	32	15	T	
Iver Express *	Nld	2007	29,456	46,825	183	32	14	T	
Iver Progress *	Mhl	2007	23,421	37,412	184	27	14	T	
Iver Prosperity *	Mhl	2007	23,421	37,456	184	27	14	T	
Libra Leader ‡	Pan	1998	57,674	22,734	200	32	19	V	
Merino Express †	Phl	1978	25,756	12,711	176	27	17	Lv	ex Cormo Express-04, Mediterranean Highway-89
New England *	Mhl	2005	23,356	37,515	183	27	14	T	
Nor'easter *	Mhl	2005	23,356	37,515	183	27	14	T	
OOCL Manila ††	Mhl	2001	16,850	21,579	169	27	20	CC	ex Venice Express-08, CP Success-06, Canmar Success-06, Brazilian Express-05
Peruvian Express **	Gib	2007	43,158	82,655	229	32	13	B	
Philippine Express **	Gib	2008	43,158	82,329	229	32	13	B	
Sebring Express	Phl	2009	43,900	14,850	180	30	19	V	
Sepang Express	Phl	2009	43,900	14,850	180	30	19	V	
Silverstone Express	Phl	2009	43,900	14,850	180	30	19	V	
Vega Spirit **	Pan	2001	15,016	22,820	153	25	13	T	ex Iver Spirit-05
Vega Spring **	Pan	2001	15,042	22,780	153	25	14	T	ex Iver Spring-05

newbuildings : eight 92,000 dwt, three 58,000 dwt bulk carriers, two 21,000 grt container ships, one 43,900 grt, four 58,000 grt vehicle carriers for 2009-10 delivery.

Tankers and livestock carriers operated by wholly owned subsidiaries * Iver Ships BV and † Livestock Express respectively.

** managed by Fleet Management Ltd., Hong Kong (www.fleetship.com), ‡ by Hachiuma Steamship Co Ltd or †† by Oceanic Maritime Ltd, UK.

Wagenborg Shipping BV Netherlands

Funnel: Black with two narrow white bands. **Hull:** Light grey with broad red band interrupted by two diagonal white stripes and white 'WAGENBORG', black boot-topping. **History:** Founded 1898 as E Wagenborg's Scheepvaart Expeditiebedrijf NV to 1972 and Wagenborg Scheepvaart BV to 1987. **Web:** www.wagenborg.com

Name	Flag	Year	GRT	DWT	LOA	Bm	Kts	Type	Former names
Amazoneborg	Nld	2007	11,894	17,300	143	22	17	Co	
Americaborg	Nld	2007	11,894	17,300	143	22	17	Co	
Amstelborg *	Nld	2006	11,894	17,300	143	22	17	Co	
Arneborg *	Nld	2006	11,894	17,300	143	22	17	Co	
Asiaborg	Nld	2007	11,894	17,300	143	22	17	Co	
Atlanticborg	Nld	2008	11,894	17,356	143	22	17	Co	
Australiaborg	Nld	2007	11,894	17,300	143	22	17	Co	
Nassauborg	Nld	2005	16,037	17,600	143	22	16	Co	
Oranjeborg	Nld	2004	18,289	15,126	159	26	17	Ro	l/a Finnbirch
Prinsenborg	Nld	2003	16,037	16,740	143	22	16	Co	

Wagenborg Shipping BV. ORANJEBORG. *Hans Kraijenbosch*

Name	Flag	Year	GRT	DWT	LOA	Bm	Kts	Type	Former names
Rhoneborg	Nld	1993	19,573	20,027	174	29	18	CC	ex MSC Java-03, European Express-02, Zim Australia-00, European Express-99, Freshwater Bay-96, European Express-94
Rijnborg	Nld	2007	16,523	18,450	176	24		CC	ex Katharina-08, Rijnborg-07
Tianshan	Nld	2008	11,894	17,300	143	22	17	Co	ex Africaborg-08

* managed for Allocean Maritime Ltd, UK.
The company also operates ro-ro vessels on northern European routes and numerous smaller vessels.

Wallenius Wilhelmsen Logistics   Norway/Sweden

Funnel: *Yellow with yellow 'OW' on broad green band (Wallenius); black with two narrow light blue bands (Wilhelmsen); †† white with USA national flag and 'ARC' houseflag either side of black anchor, narrow black top.* **Hull:** *Green with green 'WALLENIUS' or 'WALLENIUS WILHELMSEN' on white upperworks, green or red boot-topping (Wallenius); red with white lettering, red boot-topping (Wilhelmsen); †† blue with blue 'ARC' on white upperworks, red boot-topping.* **History:** *Wallenius founded 1934. Wilhelmsen founded 1861 as Wilh Wilhelmsen Enterprises A/S to 1985. Wallenius Wilhelmsen merged operations in 1999.* **Web:** *www.walleniuslines.com, www.wallemiusmarine.com, www.wilh-wilhelmsen.com, www.ww-group.com or www.2wglobal.com*

Name	Flag	Year	GRT	DWT	LOA	Bm	Kts	Type	Former names
Aegean Breeze †	Sgp	1983	27,876	12,527	164	28	18	V	
Aida	Swe	2006	60,942	22,564	199	32	19	V	
Aniara	Swe	2008	71,673	30,089	232	32		V	
Arabian Breeze †	Sgp	1983	28,116	12,577	164	28	18	V	
Asian Breeze †	Sgp	1983	27,876	12,562	164	28	18	V	
Atlantic Breeze †	Sgp	1986	41,891	17,176	196	29	18	V	ex Bujin-91
Baltic Breeze †	Sgp	1983	28,116	12,466	164	28	18	V	
Boheme	Swe	1999	67,264	28,360	228	32	20	V	(len-05)
Carmen †	Sgp	1982	50,681	28,566	200	32	19	V	
Courage ††	Usa	1991	52,288	29,213	203	32	19	V	ex Aida-05
Don Carlos	Swe	1997	67,141	28,142	228	32	20	V	(len)
Don Juan	Swe	1995	55,598	22,514	199	32	20	V	
Don Pasquale	Swe	1997	67,141	28,142	228	32	20	V	(len)
Don Quijote	Swe	1998	67,141	28,142	228	32	20	V	(len)
Elektra	Swe	1999	67,264	22,588	228	32	20	V	(len-05)
Falstaff	Swe	1985	51,858	28,529	200	32	20	V	
Faust	Swe	2007	71,583	30,383	228	32		V	
Fedora	Swe	2008	71,583	30,386	228	32		V	
Fidelio	Swe	2008	71,583	30,137	228	32		V	
Figaro †	Sgp	1981	50,681	28,676	200	32	19	V	
Freedom ††	Usa	1997	49,821	19,884	190	32	19	V	ex Takamine-03
Honor ††	Usa	1996	49,821	19,844	190	32	19	V	ex Takasago-05
Independence II ††	Usa	1994	55,598	22,862	199	32	20	V	ex Titus-08
Integrity ††	Usa	1992	52,479	29,152	203	32	20	V	ex Otello-05
Isolde	Swe	1985	51,071	28,396	200	32	19	V	
Liberty ††	Usa	1985	51,858	28,509	200	32	20	V	ex Faust-03
Madame Butterfly	Sgp	1981	50,681	28,689	200	32	19	V	
Manon	Swe	1999	67,264	14,863	228	32	20	V	(len-05)
Medea †	Sgp	1982	50,681	28,566	200	32	19	V	
Mignon	Swe	1999	67,264	28,127	228	32	20	V	(len-05)
Morning Chorus	Sgp	2007	57,536	16,178	200	32	20	V	
Morning Concert	Gbr	2006	57,415	9,306	200	32	20	V	

Wallenius Wilhelmsen. DON PASQUALE. *Allan Ryszka Onions*

Name	Flag	Year	GRT	DWT	LOA	Bm	Kts	Type	Former names
Morning Glory †	Sgp	1978	45,037	15,406	196	32	20	V	ex Aniara-05, Avesta-83
Mosel Ace *	Pan	2000	37,237	12,761	177	31	19	V	
Oberon	Swe	2008	71,673	24,600	232	32		V	
Otello	Swe	2006	60,942	30,134	199	32	19	V	
Pacific Breeze †	Sgp	1986	42,105	17,271	196	29	18	V	
Patriot ††	Usa	1987	47,219	15,680	190	32	18	V	ex Fidelio-03, Skaukar-94, Nosac Skaukar-92
Resolve ††	Usa	1994	49,443	20,082	190	32	19	V	ex Tanabata-03, Nosac Tanabata-96
Rigoletto	Swe	1977	43,487	17,197	192	32	21	V	
Tagus *	Nis	1985	48,357	21,900	195	32	19	V	ex Nosac Express-96
Tai Shan **	Nis	1986	48,676	15,577	190	32	18	V	ex Nosac Tai Shan-96
Taiko	Nis	1984	66,635	43,986	262	32	21	Ro	ex Barber Hector-88
Takara *	Nis	1986	48,547	15,546	190	32	18	V	ex Nosac Takara-96
Takayama	Nis	1983	27,440	10,599	165	28	18	V	ex Nosac Takayama-96, Takayama-86
Talabot †	Sgp	1979	39,884	34,605	229	32	22	Ro	ex Barber Perseus-88
Talisman	Nis	2000	67,140	38,500	241	32	20	Ro	
Tamerlane *	Nis	2001	67,140	38,500	241	32	20	Ro	
Tamesis *	Nis	2000	67,140	39,516	241	32	20	Ro	
Tampa	Nis	1984	66,635	44,013	262	32	21	Ro	ex Barber Tampa-89
Tampere †	Sgp	1979	40,542	35,098	229	32	22	Ro	ex Barber Nara-89
Tancred *	Nis	1987	48,676	15,577	190	32	18	V	ex Nosac Sea-96, Nosac Tancred-89
Tapiola †	Sgp	1978	39,535	33,702	229	32	21	Ro	ex Boogabilla-89
Tarago *	Nis	2000	67,140	39,516	241	32	20	Ro	

Wallenius Wilhelmsen. MEDEA. *David Walker*

Wallenius Wilhelmsen (Eukor). TALISMAN. *Phil Kempsey*

Name	Flag	Year	GRT	DWT	LOA	Bm	Kts	Type	Former names
Taronga	Nis	1996	72,708	48,988	265	32	20	Ro	
Tasco *	Nis	1985	48,393	22,067	195	32	19	V	ex Nosac Explorer-96, Nosac Tasco-89
Tellus †	Nis	1978	47,089	17,406	195	32	19	V	ex Independence-08, Tellus-03, Nosac Ranger-96, Nosac Mascot-88, Nopal Mascot-84
Terrier *	Nis	1982	47,947	17,863	194	32	19	V	ex Nosac Rover-96, Nosac Barbro-89, Nopal Barbro-84
Texas	Nis	1984	66,635	44,080	262	32	21	Ro	ex Barber Texas-89
Tijuca	Nis	2009	75,000	24,600	232	32		V	
Tirranna	Nis	2009	75,000	24,600	232	32		V	
Toba †	Sgp	1979	39,535	34,310	229	32	21	Ro	ex Barber Toba-89
Toledo *	Gbr	2005	61,321	19,628	200	32	20	V	
Tomar *	Nis	2006	61,328	22,144	200	32	20	V	
Tombarra *	Gbr	2006	61,321	19,628	200	32	20	V	
Topeka *	Gbr	2006	61,321	19,600	200	32	20	V	
Toronto *	Gbr	2005	61,321	19,628	200	32	20	V	
Torrens *	Gbr	2004	61,321	14,512	200	32	20	V	
Tortugas *	Gbr	2006	61,321	14,512	200	32	20	V	
Tosca †	Sgp	1978	45,037	15,350	196	32	20	V	
Tourcoing †	Sgp	1978	39,535	33,719	229	32	21	Ro	
Traviata	Swe	1977	43,487	17,197	190	32	19	V	
Trianon **	Nis	1987	49,792	15,536	190	32	18	V	ex Nosac Star-96
Trinidad **	Nis	1987	49,750	15,528	190	32	18	V	ex Nosac Sky-96
Tristan	Swe	1985	51,071	28,536	200	32	19	V	
Turandot	Swe	1995	55,598	22,815	199	32	20	V	
Undine	Swe	2003	67,264	22,616	228	32	20	V	(len-06)

newbuildings: four 61,300 grt, six 68,600 grt and four 77,000 grt vehicle carriers for 2008-12 delivery.
† owned by Wallenius Ship Management Pte. Ltd., Singapore or †† operated by American Roll-on Roll-off Carrier (Interocean American Shipping Corp.) both USA (www.ium.com)
* managed by Wilhelmsen Ship Management AS, (www.wilhelmsen.com), ** by Wilhelmsen Lines Car Carrier Ltd, UK (for Caiano Shipping AS, Norway or Icon Capital Corp, USA) or ‡ by Wallenius Lines (Japan) Ltd. See also Paal Wilson & Co and Dockwise NV

Eukor Car Carriers Inc/South Korea

Funnel: Cream with white curved cross on blue globe or owners colours. **Hull:** Owners colours, some with 'EUKOR' on superstructure. **History:** Founded 2002 by Walleniusrederierna AB (40%), Wilhelmsen ASA (40%), Hyundai Motor Group (10%) and Kia Motor Corp (10%). **Web:** www.eukor.com

Name	Flag	Year	GRT	DWT	LOA	Bm	Kts	Type	Former names
Asian Captain *	Pan	1998	71,383	25,765	229	32	20	V	(len)
Asian Chorus *	Pan	1997	55,729	21,505	200	32	20	V	
Asian Empire *	Pan	1998	71,383	25,765	229	32	20	V	(len)
Asian Grace **	Kor	1996	55,680	21,421	200	32	20	V	
Asian Legend *	Pan	1996	55,680	21,421	200	32	20	V	
Asian Majesty *	Pan	1999	71,383	25,818	229	32	20	V	(len-06)
Asian Parade *	Pan	1996	67,010	21,407	200	32	20	V	(len)
Asian Sun **	Pan	1995	44,891	13,292	185	31	18	V	
Asian Trust	Pan	2000	55,729	15,800	200	32	20	V	
Asian Venture **	Pan	1995	44,891	13,241	185	31	18	V	
Asian Vision	Pan	1997	55,680	21,421	200	32	20	V	
Eternal Clipper	Pan	1980	23,107	10,803	164	25	17	V	ex Hyundai No. 1-96
Eternal Mariner	Pan	1980	23,107	10,758	164	25	17	V	ex Hyundai No. 2-96
Hyundai No. 201 †	Pan	1987	31,367	9,694	174	28	18	V	
Hyundai No. 202 †	Pan	1987	31,367	9,694	174	28	18	V	ex Tongala-99, Hyundai No. 202-97, Nosac Clipper-93, Hyundai No. 202-90
Hyundai No. 203 ‡	Pan	1988	41,353	12,762	184	31	18	V	ex Atlantic Beauty-92, Hyundai No. 203-90
Hyundai No. 206 †	Pan	1987	42,247	12,706	184	31	18	V	ex Oriental Beauty-93, Hyundai No. 206-90
Morning Carol	Pan	2008	57,542	21,044	200	32	20	V	
Morning Celesta	Pan	2008	57,542	20,500	200	32	20	V	
Morning Cello	Sgp	2007	57,542	21,059	200	32	20	V	
Morning Composer	Pan	2008	57,542	21,052	200	32	20	V	
Morning Conductor	Pan	2008	57,542	20,500	200	32	20	V	
Morning Cornet	Sgp	2007	57,542	20,500	200	32	20	V	
Morning Linda	Pan	2008	68,701	28,061	232	32	20	V	
Morning Lisa	Pan	2008	68,701	28,084	232	32		V	
Morning Lucy	Pan	2009	68,701	28,000	232	32		V	
Morning Lynn	Pan	2009	68,701	28,000	232	32		V	
Morning Mermaid †	Pan	1987	42,247	12,706	184	31	19	V	ex Hyundai No. 205-07, Eurasian Beauty-93, Hyundai No. 205-90

newbuildings: four 68,600 grt and four 56,000 grt vehicle carriers for 2009-10 delivery.
Managed mainly by Eukor Car Carriers Inc, South Korea or Eukor Shipowning Singapore Pte Ltd, by Wilhelmsen Shipmanagement Singapore Pte Ltd or Wilhelmsen Ship Management (Korea) Ltd, * by Haeyoung Maritime South Korea or ** chartered from Glovis Logistics, S. Korea.
Over 80 vessels reported operated, including on charter from † Eidseva Rederi ASA, Norway and ‡ from Bergshav Management AS, Norway.
Also see chartered vessels under Cido Shipping, Ray Shipping and Zodiac (Ofer Bros).

Wan Hai Lines Ltd — Taiwan

Funnel: *Blue with large white 'W'.* **Hull:** *Light grey with white outlined 'WAN HAI LINES' in blue and red (A's) lettering, red boot-topping.* **History:** *Founded 1992.* **Web:** *www.wanhai.com.tw*

Name	Flag	Year	GRT	DWT	LOA	Bm	Kts	Type	Former names
Dong Hai Bridge	Sgp	2005	42,579	52,146	269	32	23	CC	ex Wan Hai 502-06
MOL Dynasty	Sgp	2005	42,894	51,300	269	32	23	CC	ex Wan Hai 505-08
Wan Hai 301	Sgp	2001	26,681	30,250	200	32	24	CC	
Wan Hai 302	Sgp	2002	26,681	30,234	200	32	24	CC	
Wan Hai 303	Sgp	2002	26,681	30,500	200	32	24	CC	
Wan Hai 305	Sgp	2002	26,681	30,246	200	32	24	CC	
Wan Hai 306	Sgp	2002	25,836	34,026	197	30	21	CC	
Wan Hai 307	Sgp	2002	25,836	34,026	197	30	21	CC	
Wan Hai 311	Sgp	2005	27,800	32,937	213	32	22	CC	
Wan Hai 312	Sgp	2006	27,800	33,000	213	32	22	CC	
Wan Hai 313	Sgp	2006	27,800	33,000	213	32	22	CC	
Wan Hai 315	Sgp	2006	27,800	33,000	213	32	22	CC	
Wan Hai 316	Sgp	2007	27,800	33,000	213	32	22	CC	
Wan Hai 317	Sgp	2008	27,800	33,000	213	32	22	CC	
Wan Hai 501	Sgp	2005	42,579	52,249	269	32	23	CC	
Wan Hai 503	Sgp	2005	42,579	51,300	269	32	23	CC	
Wan Hai 506	Sgp	2005	42,894	52,146	269	32	23	CC	
Wan Hai 507	Sgp	2007	42,894	52,146	269	32	23	CC	ex Kota Salam-08
Wan Hai 508	Sgp	2007	42,894	52,146	269	32	23	CC	
Wan Hai 509	Sgp	2007	42,894	52,146	269	32	23	CC	
Wan Hai 510	Sgp	2008	42,894	52,146	269	32	23	CC	
Wan Hai 601	Sgp	2007	66,199	67,797	276	40	26	CC	
Wan Hai 602	Sgp	2007	66,199	67,797	276	40	26	CC	
Wan Hai 603	Sgp	2007	66,199	67,797	276	40	26	CC	
Wan Hai 605	Sgp	2008	66,199	67,797	276	40	26	CC	

newbuildings: six 43,400 grt, six 16,700 grt and one 23,560 grt container ships for 2010-12 delivery.
Owned by subsidiary Wan Hai Lines (Singapore) Pte Ltd, Singapore (formed 1997).
Also owns 29 other 12-19,000 grt container ships operating mainly in the Far East.

Warwick & Esplen Ltd — UK

The Hadley Shipping Co Ltd

Funnel: *Yellow with black 'HSC' inside white diamond, black top.* **Hull:** *Black with red boot-topping.* **History:** *Formed 1926.* **Web:**-*www.angloeasterngroup.com*

Name	Flag	Year	GRT	DWT	LOA	Bm	Kts	Type	Former names
Clare	Gbr	2005	40,524	74,759	225	32	13	B	ex Golden Gunn-07
Clymene	Gbr	2006	40,244	73,600	225	32	14	B	ex Ming Mei-06
Cymbeline	Iom	2001	38,299	73,060	225	32	14	B	

managed by Anglo-Eastern (UK) Ltd., UK.

Wan Hai Lines. WAN HAI 508. *J. M. Kakebeeke*

Oskar Wehr KG (GmbH & Co) Germany

Funnel: *Black with blue 'W' in blue ring over two blue bands in centre and towards top of broad yellow band or charterers colours.*
Hull: *Blue or grey with diagonal yellow stripe and blue or red boot-topping.* **History:** *Formed 1945.* **Web:** *www.wehrship.de*

Name	Flag	Year	GRT	DWT	LOA	Bm	Kts	Type	Former names
Callao Express	Mhl	2002	25,703	33,670	208	30	21	CC	ex P&O Nedlloyd Yarra Valley-06, Wehr Oste-03
CCNI Bilboa ‡	Mhl	1997	16,801	23,051	184	25	20	CC	ex P&O Nedlloyd Portbury-06, P&O Nedlloyd Calypso-05, Costa Rica-02, Wehr Koblenz-01, Panamerican-01, CSAV Rio Amazonas-99, I/a Wehr Koblenz
CCNI Fortuna **	Deu	1999	16,802	22,878	184	25	19	CC	ex Wehr Flottbek-08, Alianca Bahia-01, Wehr Flottbek-00
CCNI Hamburgo *	Mhl	1997	16,801	23,021	184	25	19	CC	ex Wehr Altona-08, Lykes Pathfinder-02, Norasia Yantian-01, CSAV Ningpo-00, Kota Sejarah-00, CSAV Rio de la Plata-99, I/a Wehr Altona
CMA CGM Aztec *	Mhl	1998	16,801	22,983	184	25	19	CC	ex Wehr Muden-06, CSAV Hong Kong-06, Wehr Muden-03, TMM Quetzal-01, Wehr Muden-01, CSAV Valencia-00, Crowley Express-00, CSAV Rimac-99, I/a Wehr Muden
CMA CGM Parati †	Mhl	1997	16,801	23,051	184	25	20	CC	ex Delmas Suffren-08, Bremen Senator-06, Wehr Ottensen-04, Indamex Nhava Sheva-02, Wehr Ottensen-01, CSAV Rio Grande-99, Wehr Ottensen-98
CSAV Rio Baker	Mhl	2002	25,630	33,767	207	30	21	CC	ex CCNI Arica-04, Wehr Alster-02
CSAV Rio Maule	Mhl	2002	25,705	33,793	208	30	21	CC	ex Columbus China-04, Wehr Warnow-02
CSAV Rio Puelo	Mhl	2002	25,705	33,795	207	30	21	CC	ex CCNI Aysen-04, I/a Wehr Trave
CSAV Rio Tolten	Mhl	2002	25,703	33,795	208	30	21	CC	ex Wehr Havel-04
Elqui ‡	Mhl	1999	16,177	23,026	184	26	19	CC	I/a Wehr Schulau
Frieda Selmer	Mhl	2004	31,218	55,718	190	32	14	B	
Helene Selmer	Mhl	2005	31,218	55,741	190	32	14	B	
Libra Chile ‡	Mhl	2001	16,802	23,000	185	25	19	CC	I/a Wehr Nienstedten
Maersk Dellys	Mhl	2006	54,193	67,470	294	32	24	CC	ex Wehr Singapore-06
Maersk Derince	Deu	2005	54,193	67,470	294	32	24	CC	ex Wehr Hongkong-06
Mimi Selmer	Mhl	2005	31,500	55,711	190	32	14	B	
MOL Utility **	Deu	1999	16,802	23,028	185	25	19	CC	ex Wehr Rissen-08, Delmas Mascareignes-07, CMA CGM Bourgainville-04, Wehr Rissen-99
NYK Estrela	Mhl	2002	25,624	33,739	208	30	21	CC	ex CSAV Rio Cochamo-05, Wehr Bille-04, CCNI Antartico-03, Wehr Bille-02
Therese Selmer	Mhl	2006	31,500	56,000	190	32	14	B	
Wehr Blankensee ‡	Mhl	1999	16,177	23,021	184	26	19	CC	ex CSAV Montreal-07, Norasia Montreal-01, Illapel-00, I/a Wehr Blankensee
Wehr Elbe ‡	Mhl	2001	25,703	33,795	203	30	22	CC	ex CSAV Callao-08, I/a Wehr Elbe
Wehr Weser ‡	Mhl	2001	25,703	33,795	203	30	22	CC	ex Libra New York-09, I/a Wehr Weser

newbuildings: five 57,000 dwt and six 178,000 dwt bulk carrires for 2009-11 delivery.
* managed for Dr Peters GmbH & Co KG, ** for Hansa Treuhand Schiffs AG, † for Konig & Cie GmbH or ‡ for Lloyd Fonds AG, all Germany.

Andrew Weir & Co Ltd. UK

Andrew Weir Shipping Ltd.

Funnel: *Charterers colours.* **Hull:** *Black with red boot-topping.* **History:** *Founded 1885 as Andrew Weir & Co to 1945, then Andrew Weir Shipping & Trading Co Ltd to 1957. Andrew Weir Shipping founded 1905 as The Bank Line Ltd to 1989.* **Web:** *www.aws.co.uk*

Name	Flag	Year	GRT	DWT	LOA	Bm	Kts	Type	Former names
Boularibank *	Iom	1984	18,663	22,911	174	25	17	Ro	ex Teignbank-06, Nikel-95
Gazellebank *	Iom	1983	18,663	22,911	174	25	17	Ro	ex Foylebank-06, Tiksi-95
Mahinabank *	Iom	1983	18,663	22,911	174	25	17	Ro	ex Speybank-06, Okha-95
Tiger Breeze	Iom	1997	23,734	30,461	188	30	21	CC	ex MOL Callao-07, City of London-04, CGM Caravelle-01, City of London-98
Tikeibank *	Iom	1983	18,663	22,911	174	25	17	Ro	ex Arunbank-06, Bratsk-95

* on charter to The China Navigation Co Ltd (John Swire & Sons Ltd), who acquired The Bank Line services in 2003.
Also operates large roll-on, roll-off vessels on charter to UK Government and in European trades.

Westfal-Larsen & Co AS Norway

Funnel: *Yellow with two narrow black bands, narrow black top.* **Hull:** *Dark blue or red with red boot-topping.* **History:** *Formed 1905.*
Web: *www.wlco.no*

Name	Flag	Year	GRT	DWT	LOA	Bm	Kts	Type	Former names
Fossanger *	Nis	1988	22,637	40,264	171	32	14	T	ex Northern Wolf-89, Fort Wolf-88
Mauranger	Lbr	1995	25,707	41,109	180	31	14	T	ex Bow Tribute-01
Moldanger	Lbr	1997	25,707	40,845	180	31	14	T	ex Bow Triton-01
Ravnanger	Nis	2000	28,246	46,541	183	32	14	T	ex Minerva Joanna-07
Risanger	Nis	2000	28,246	46,270	183	32	14	T	ex Minerva Julie-07

Name	Flag	Year	GRT	DWT	LOA	Bm	Kts	Type	Former names

Managed by Westfal-Larsen Management AS (formed 1996), * managed for Fratelli D'Amato SpA, Italy.

Star Shipping Pool/Norway

Funnel: *Yellow with two blue stars on white panel with blue top and bottom edges.* **Hull:** *Blue or grey with red or blue boot-topping.*
History: *Formed 1970 by A/S Billabong (40%), Olsen and Westfal-Larsen (each 30%) until 1988, then Billabong and Westfal-Larsen (each 50%) or their subsidiaries.* **Web:** *www.starshipping.com*

Name	Flag	Year	GRT	DWT	LOA	Bm	Kts	Type	Former names
Heranger *	Sgp	1995	37,150	44,251	199	31	16	Boh	ex Star Heranger-08
Hosanger *	Sgp	1995	37,150	44,251	199	31	16	Boh	ex Star Hosanger-08
Oshimana *	Sgp	2003	36,324	48,661	199	32	16	Boh	ex Star Oshimana-08
Providana *	Sgp	2007	39,258	54,694	213	32		Boh	
Star Alabama †	Nis	1985	20,916	30,204	169	27	15	Boh	ex Hawaiian Rainbow-92
Star Altanger *	Sgp	1986	20,125	30,382	169	27	15	Boh	ex Northern Dawn-96, Star New York-91, New York Rainbow-89
Star America †	Nis	1985	20,929	30,168	169	27	15	Boh	ex Canadian Rainbow-91, Star Canadian-90, Canadian Rainbow-89
Star Atlantic †	Nis	1986	20,125	30,402	165	26	15	Boh	ex Hoegh Mistral-03, Star Atlantic-03, Hoegh Mistral-03, Star Texas-90, Texas Rainbow-89
Star Austanger *	Nis	1985	20,915	30,173	169	27	15	Boh	ex Anthony Rainbow-92
Star Canopus ‡	Grc	2002	25,388	45,635	180	31	14	B	ex Star Mizuho-07
Star Capella ‡	Grc	2001	25,388	45,601	180	31	14	B	
Star Derby †	Nis	1979	27,104	43,700	183	31	15	Boh	ex Star Carrier-85
Star Dieppe †	Nis	1977	27,104	43,082	183	31	15	Boh	ex Star Shiraz-79, Star Dieppe-77
Star Dover †	Nis	1977	27,911	43,082	183	31	15	Boh	ex Star Estahan-79, Star Dover-77
Star Eagle †	Nis	1981	24,479	39,749	180	29	15	Boh	
Star Evviva †	Nis	1982	24,479	39,718	180	29	15	Boh	
Star Florida †	Nis	1985	25,345	40,790	187	29	15	Boh	
Star Fraser †	Nis	1985	25,345	40,840	187	29	15	Boh	
Star Fuji †	Nis	1985	25,345	40,850	187	29	15	Boh	
Star Geiranger	Nis	1986	27,972	43,131	200	29	15	Boh	
Star Gran †	Nis	1986	27,192	43,759	198	29	16	Boh	ex Triton-86
Star Grindanger	Nis	1986	27,972	43,131	201	29	15	Boh	
Star Grip †	Nis	1986	27,192	43,712	198	29	16	Boh	
Star Hansa †	Nis	1996	32,749	46,580	198	31	16	Boh	
Star Hardanger *	Sgp	1995	34,364	44,251	199	31	16	Boh	
Star Harmonia †	Nis	1998	32,749	46,604	198	31	16	Boh	
Star Herdla †	Nis	1994	32,744	47,942	198	31	16	Boh	
Star Hidra †	Nis	1994	32,749	46,547	198	31	16	Boh	
Star Hoyanger *	Sgp	1995	34,363	44,251	199	31	16	Boh	
Star Ikebana *	Sgp	1999	30,840	39,751	185	31	16	Boh	
Star Indiana *	Sgp	2000	30,745	39,760	185	31	16	Boh	
Star Inventana *	Sgp	2000	30,745	39,789	185	31	16	Boh	
Star Isfjord †	Nis	2000	29,898	41,749	185	31	16	Boh	
Star Ismene †	Nis	1999	28,898	41,777	185	31	16	Boh	
Star Isoldana *	Sgp	2000	30,745	39,465	185	31	16	Boh	
Star Istind †	Nis	1999	29,898	41,749	185	31	16	Boh	
Star Japan †	Nis	2004	32,844	46,387	198	31	16	Boh	
Star Java †	Nis	2006	32,879	46,387	198	31	16	Boh	

Andrew Weir & Co. BOULARIBANK. *Hans Kraijenbosch*

Name	Flag	Year	GRT	DWT	LOA	Bm	Kts	Type	Former names
Star Juventus †	Nis	2004	32,844	44,837	198	31	16	Boh	
Star Langanger *	Sgp	1986	29,275	41,425	195	32	14	Boh	ex Hawthorn Hill-89, Geliga-86
Star Leikanger *	Sgp	1986	29,275	41,409	195	32	14	Boh	ex Maritime Wisdom-89, Wisteria Hill-87, Gemar-86
Star Okiana *	Sgp	2003	36,324	48,661	199	32	16	Boh	
Star Optimana *	Sgp	2003	36,324	48,661	199	32	16	Boh	
Star Osakana *	Sgp	2004	36,324	48,661	199	32	16	Boh	
Star Polaris ‡	Grc	1996	26,897	43,775	190	31	14	B	
Star Pollux ‡	Grc	1996	26,922	43,769	190	31	14	B	
Star Siranger *	Sgp	1991	11,878	17,012	149	23	14	Boh	ex T.S.Adventure-93

*newbuildings: six 46,600 dwt tankers, four 48,800 dwt and three 54,000 dwt open-hatch bulk carriers for 2009-10 delivery.
Owned by Westfal-Larsen or * subsidiary Masterbulk Pte. Ltd., Singapore (formed 1995 – www.masterbulk.com.sg) or † by Greig Shipping Group AS (formed 1981 as Billabong Ship Management A/S & Co to 1991, A/S Billabong to 2002 and Greig Billabong AS to 2006 – www.greig.no), both Norway. Also operates chartered vessels including ‡ owned by Rethymnis & Kulukundis Ltd, UK (www.randk.co.uk) subsidiary Pegasus Maritime Enterprises Inc, Greece.*

Anders Wilhelmsen & Co AS   Norway

Funnel: *Black with white 'W' on red over black divided diamond between two narrow red bands on broad white band.* **Hull:** *Grey or red with red boot-topping.* **History:** *Formed 1939 as A Wilhelmsen to 1964 and sometime 47% owner of Euronav. OHT formed 2005.* **Web:** *www.wilhelmsen.com or www.oht.no*

Name	Flag	Year	GRT	DWT	LOA	Bm	Kts	Type	Former names
Heavylift Ancora **	Nis	1989	38,722	54,000	223	45	15	HLs	ex Ancora-08, Songa Ancora-08, Ancora-05, Leon Spirit-04, Borja Tapias-04 (conv T/sht-08)
Heavylift Eagle *	Nis	1981	31,021	31,809	199	42	14	HLs	ex Willift Eagle-08, Willift Lady-06, Lucky Lady-06, Albe-94, World Cliff-90, Cliff-84, World Cliff-83 (conv T/sht-06)
Heavylift Falcon *	Nis	1981	31,027	31,908	199	42	14	HLs	ex Willift Falcon-08, Nilos-08, Nile-95, World Zeal-90 (conv T/sht-07)
Heavylift Hawk *	Nis	1989	38,722	54,000	223	45	15	HLs	ex Hawk-08, Hawker-08, Front Transporter-07, Genmar Transporter-04, Crude Transporter-03, Nord-Jahre Transporter-00, Jahre Transporter-93 (conv T/sht-08)
Wilana	Nis	1997	79,494	149,706	270	45	15	T	
Wilmina	Nis	1997	79,388	149,775	270	45	15	T	

*Managed by Wilhelmsen Marine Services AS and * operated by Offshore Heavy Transport AS, Norway (** managed by Aquaship Ltd, Latvia)*

Reederei Gebruder Winter GmbH & Co KG   Germany

Funnel: *Mainly charterers colours.* **Hull:** *Grey, blue or red with red boot-topping.* **History:** *Founded in 1900 and shipowners since 1970 as Schiffahrtskontor Reederei Gebruder Winter to 1999.* **Web:** *www.winter-ship.de*

Name	Flag	Year	GRT	DWT	LOA	Bm	Kts	Type	Former names
Adelaide Express	Deu	1998	23,297	30,241	188	30	21	CC	ex Classica-06, Safmarine Mtata-05, Maersk Dakar-04, Classica-02, Libra Buenos Aires-02, Classica-01, CMA Djakarta-00, Jolly Ocra-99, Classica-98
Cap Serrat	Deu	1998	23,897	30,258	188	30	21	CC	ex Columba-08, Safmarine Gonubie-08, Libra Houston-02, TMM Veracruz-01, APL Atlantic-00, Columba-99, Maersk Genoa-98, I/a Columba
Cassandra B	Atg	2008	18,263	23,978	182	25		CC	ex Convent-08
Clipper	Atg	2008	18,199	23,831	182	25		CC	
Commodore	Atg	2001	30,047	35,770	208	32	22	CC	ex MSC Andes-02, Commodore-01
Concord	Atg	1994	14,968	20,088	167	25	19	CC	ex Cala Piedad-07, Concord-03, Mercosul Pintado-03, Safmarine Emonti-02, Egoli Star I-01, Concord-99, Libra Santos-99, DG Concord-97, Concord-97, Victoria Bay-95, Concord-94
Courier	Atg	1995	14,860	20,140	167	26	19	CC	ex Indamex Ganges-02, Libra Miami-00, Libra Buenos Aires-97, CSAV Rahue-96, Velma Lykes-95, I/a Courier
Maersk Pecem	Atg	2004	30,051	35,770	208	32	22	CC	ex Commander-04
Rothorn *	Atg	1996	12,029	14,587	157	24	18	CC	ex MOL Amazonas-02, Guatamala-01, Rothorn-98
USL Kiwi	Atg	1996	12,029	14,643	157	24	18	CC	ex Shion-06, Caravelle-04, Cala Porlamar-04, Pellini-02, Caravelle-01, UB Puma-97, Caravelle-96
Weisshorn *	Atg	1996	12,029	14,643	157	24	19	CC	ex MSC Ghana-04, Weisshorn-02, DAL East London-01, Weisshorn-00, P&O Nedlloyd Maurttius-99, Weisshorn-98

*newbuildings: four 18,100 grt and one 37,000 grt container ships for 2008-10 delivery.
* managed for Contal Shipping Ltd, Switzerland (formed 1975 - www.contal.ch)*

Reederei Hermann Wulff

Germany

Funnel: *Yellow with green 'W' on white diamond, black top or charterers colours* **Hull:** *Black or green with red boot-topping.*
History: *Formed 1960 by fifth generation of seafaring family.* **Web:** *www.reederei-wulff.de*

Name	Flag	Year	GRT	DWT	LOA	Bm	Kts	Type	Former names
Al Khor	Lbr	2009	75,604	85,622	304	40		CC	ex Ilse Wulff-09
Ibn Abdoun	Lbr	2002	32,284	39,350	211	32	22	CC	ex CMA CGM Seagull-05, P&O Nedlloyd Dammam-03, Antje-Helen Wulff-02
Ibn Asakir	Lbr	1999	32,322	39,128	211	32	22	CC	ex CSAV Rio Maipo-07, NYK Prosperity-04, Weserwolf-03, Columbia Bridge-01, Weserwolf-00
Ibn Khaldoun	Lbr	1999	32,221	39,340	211	32	21	CC	ex Aramac-05, Elbwolf-02, Ipex Equality-01, Elbwolf-99
Ibn Khallikan *	Deu	2006	32,322	39,340	211	32	22	CC	ex OOCL Energy-08, Hermann Wulff-06
Kollmar	Lbr	1993	16,233	21,540	182	25	20	CC	ex Ilse Wulff-06, Nigeria Star-03, Ilse Wulff-01, Direct Kookaburra-01, Isle Wulff-99, Maersk Pretoria-99, Maersk Pireaus-98, TSL Unity-98, Ilse Wulff-95, Contship Rotterdam-94, Ilse-93
Manuela	Lbr	1993	16,233	21,540	182	25	20	CC	ex Inaba-06, Hermann-04, P&O Nedlloyd Cotonou-03, Hermann-02, Direct Kea-01, MSC Cali-99, Hermann-99, Maersk Aarhus-98, Hermann-98, Sea Harmony-97, Hermann-96, CCNI Angol-96, Hermann-95, Contship New York-95, Hermann-93, Deppe Europe-93, Hermann-93

Anders Wilhelmsen. HEAVYLIFT FALCON. *C. Lous*

Reederei Gebruder Winter. CLIPPER. *J. M. Kakebeeke*

Name	Flag	Year	GRT	DWT	LOA	Bm	Kts	Type	Former names
MSC Firenze	Deu	2006	51,350	58,260	292	32	24	CC	ex Maersk Duesseldorf-08, Hijaz-08, Maersk Diadem-06, Viktoria Wulff-06
MSC Siena	Deu	2006	52,701	58,281	292	32	24	CC	ex Maersk Diadema-08, Charlotte Wulff-06

newbuildings: two 92,300 dwt bulk carriers for 2010 delivery.
* managed for Ship Invest Emissionshaus AG, Germany.

Yangming Marine Transport Corp   Taiwan

Funnel: Black with yellow band on broad red band interupted by white square containing blue 'Y' on white 'M' symbol within red outline. **Hull:** Black with white 'YANG MING LINE', red boot-topping. **History:** Government controlled and formed 1973.
Web: www.yml.com.tw

Name	Flag	Year	GRT	DWT	LOA	Bm	Kts	Type	Former names
Giuseppe Rizzo	Lbr	2004	41,205	77,684	225	32	14	B	
Medi Taipei	Lbr	2003	39,727	76,633	225	32	14	B	
YM America	Lbr	1992	46,728	46,785	276	32	21	CC	ex Ming America-04
YM Asia	Lbr	1991	46,728	46,772	276	32	21	CC	ex Ming Asia-04
YM Bamboo	Lbr	2001	64,005	68,615	275	40	26	CC	ex Bamboo Bridge-06, Jupiter Bridge-05, Ming Bamboo-02
YM Cosmos	Pan	2001	64,254	68,413	275	40	25	CC	ex Ming Cosmos-05
YM Cultivation	Twn	1996	35,905	69,163	225	32	14	B	ex Ming Cultivation-04, Bel Best-02
YM Cypress	Lbr	2001	64,254	68,303	275	40	25	CC	ex Cypress Bridge-06, Mercury Bridge-05, Ming Cypress-02
YM Earth **	Pan	2003	17,153	22,078	171	28	19	CC	ex Ming Earth-04
YM East	Twn	1995	46,697	45,995	276	32	21	CC	ex Ming East-05, Maersk Long Beach-96, Ming East-95
YM Efficency	Lbr	2009	42,741	52,773	269	32	24	CC	
YM Elixir	Lbr	2008	42,741	51,870	269	32	24	CC	
YM Enhancer	Lbr	2008	42,741	52,773	269	32	24	CC	
YM Eminence	Lbr	2009	42,741	52,773	269	32	24	CC	
YM Equality	Lbr	1996	36,559	70,252	225	32	14	B	ex Krabi Navee-06, Bel Ace-03
YM Europe	Twn	1992	46,728	46,772	276	32	21	CC	ex Ming Europe-04
YM Fortune	Lbr	1983	29,872	30,669	210	32	23	CC	ex Kota Permas-04, Med Taichung-03, Maersk Dubai-96, Ming Fortune-94
YM Fountain	Lbr	2004	64,254	68,615	275	40	26	CC	
YM Glory	Lbr	1980	29,873	31,208	210	32	20	CC	ex Glory Bridge-06, Ocean Gulf-04, Gulf Bridge-03, Ming Glory-98
YM Great	Pan	2004	66,332	67,270	279	40	26	CC	
YM Green	Lbr	2001	64,254	68,413	275	40	26	CC	ex Ming Green-05
YM March **	Pan	2004	66,332	67,270	279	40	25	CC	I/a Ming March
YM New Jersey **	Pan	2006	54,828	65,123	294	32	23	CC	
YM North	Lbr	1995	46,697	45,995	276	32	21	CC	ex Ming North-05
YM Orchid	Pan	2000	64,254	68,303	275	40	26	CC	ex Ming Orchid-05
YM Pine	Lbr	2001	64,005	68,615	275	40	26	CC	ex Pine Bridge-06, Venus Bridge-05, Ming Pine-02
YM Plum	Pan	2000	64,254	68,413	275	40	26	CC	ex Ming Plum-05
YM Prominence	Lbr	1987	40,436	40,845	270	32	20	CC	ex Ming Prominence-04
YM Prosperity	Lbr	1988	40,415	40,845	270	32	20	CC	ex Med Taipei-04, Ville d'Hydra-95, Ming Prosperity-94

Yangming Marine. YM UNITY. *Hans Kraijenbosch*

Name	Flag	Year	GRT	DWT	LOA	Bm	Kts	Type	Former names
YM Rightness	Lbr	2004	41,400	77,684	225	32	14	B	
YM South	Twn	1995	46,697	45,995	276	32	21	CC	ex Ming South-05
YM Success	Lbr	2004	64,254	68,615	275	40	25	CC	
YM Sun	Lbr	1980	29,873	31,265	210	32	20	CC	ex Ocean Genius-04, Sun River-01, Ming Sun-98
YM Uberty	Lbr	2008	90,507	103,614	333	43	25	CC	
YM Ultimate	Lbr	2007	90,389	101,411	333	43	25	CC	
YM Unison	Lbr	2006	90,389	101,030	333	43	25	CC	
YM Unity	Lbr	2006	90,389	101,411	333	43	25	CC	
YM Upward	Lbr	2008	90,507	101,000	333	43	25	CC	
YM Utmost	Lbr	2006	90,389	101,411	333	43	25	CC	
YM Utopia	Lbr	2008	90,507	103,614	333	43	25	CC	
YM Virtue	Lbr	2003	39,749	73,840	225	32	14	B	ex Ming Virtue-05
YM Wealth	Lbr	2004	64,254	68,615	275	40	26	CC	
YM West	Lbr	1995	46,697	45,995	276	32	21	CC	ex Ming West-05, Maersk Singapore-96, Ming West-95
YM Zenith	Lbr	1996	46,697	45,995	276	32	21	CC	ex Ming Zenith-04

newbuildings: eight 90,000 grt, four 74,900 grt, seven 42,800-47,500 grt container ships and two 81,000 dwt bulk carriers for 2009-12 delivery.
* owned by YML Shipping Enterprise Corp Ltd, Taiwan (formed 1999) or ** chartered from various owners.
Also owns 15 feeder container ships (15-16,500 grt) operating mainly in the Far East and manages five tankers owned by associated Government controlled Chinese Petroleum Corp (formed 1959 - wwwcpc.com.tw).
See other chartered ships with 'YM' prefix in index.

Reederei Horst Zeppenfeld GmbH & Co KG   Germany

Funnel: *Cream with black top.* **Hull:** *Black with red boot-topping.* **History:** *Founded 1971.* **Web:** *www.zeppenfeld.com*

Name	Flag	Year	GRT	DWT	LOA	Bm	Kts	Type	Former names
Alioth *	Sgp	2006	16,162	17,219	161	25	19	CC	
Mizar	Lbr	2005	16,162	17,350	161	25	19	CC	
USL Condor *	Sgp	2008	16,162	17,350	161	25	19	CC	ex Algol-06

* owned by associated Reederei Navylloyd AG, Switzerland (founded 1981)

Vroon BV. IVER EXAMPLE. *Hans Kraijenbosch*

INDEX

Royal Caribbean. NAVIGATOR OF THE SEAS. Phil Kempsey

Name	No.	Name	No.	Name	No.	Name	No.
Astor	26	Auk Arrow	100	Banastar	106	Berge Summit	44
Astor	33	Aurelia	43	Banda Sea	96	Berge Sword	44
Astra	201	Aurika	196	Bandaisan *	133	Bergen Arrow	100
Astral Ace	131	Aurora	12	Bangkok Express	156	Bergen Max	74
Astrea	48	Aurora	43	Baniyas	106	Bering Sea	210
Astro Altair	34	Austin	175	Bantry	106	Bering Sea	170
Astro Antares	34	Austin Angol	143	Barbet Arrow	99	Bering Sea	226
Astro Arcturus	34	Australiaborg	230	Barcelona Express	88	Berlin Express	88
Astro Caesar	34	Australian Spirit	219	Barents Bay	206	Bernhard Oldendorff	175
Astro Callisto	34	Australis	48	Barents Sea	210	Bet Commander	74
Astro Canopus	34	Austria	72	Barents Sea	169	Bet Fighter	74
Astro Capella	34	Authentic	112	Barents Strait	190	Bet Intruder	74
Astro Capricorn	34	Autumn Wind	152	Bargara	47	Bet Prince	74
Astro Carina	34	Avalon	43	Barkald	106	Bet Scouter	74
Astro Cassiopeia	34	Avelona Star	215	Barmbek1	84	Betis	54
Astro Castor	34	Avila Star	215	Barnes Bridge	204	Betty Knutsen	106
Astro Centaurus	34	Avoca	47	Barrier	192	Bijin	149
Astro Challenge	34	Avocet Arrow	99	Barrington Island	226	Bilbao Knutsen	107
Astro Chloe	34	Axel Maersk	134	Barrington	219	Bilis	209
Astro Chorus	34	Axel Spirit	219	Barsam	97	Bing He	50
Astro Corona	34	Axios	113	Baru	106	Bing N	46
Astro Cygnus	34	Azamara Journey	22	Basker Spirit	219	Bio Bio	144
Astro Leon	34	Azamara Quest	22	Bataliony Chlopskie	186	Black Marlin	68
Astro Libra	34	Azim	97	Batavia	170	Black Prince	20
Astro Luna	34	Azov Sea	210	Bauhinia Bridge	103	Black Sea	170
Astro Lupus	34	Azul Cielo	131	Bauta	106	Black Watch	20
Astro Lyra	34	Azul Fortuna	131	Bavaria Express	166	Blandine Delmas	59
Astro Patroclus	34	Azura	12	Bay Bridge	103	Bleu de France	22
Astro Pegasus	34	B. Prus	185	Bay Ranger	74	Blu Star	216
Astro Perseus	34	Babitonga	109	BBC Amazon	40	Blue Diamond	165
Astro Phaethon	34	Baco-Liner 1	36	BBC Elbe	40	Blue Giant	92
Astro Phoenix	34	Baco-Liner 2	36	BBC Ems	40	Blue Hawk	149
Astro Plato	34	Baco-Liner 3	36	BBC Leer	40	Blue Marlin	68
Astro Polaris	34	Bahama Spirit	204	BBC Mississippi	41	Blue Master	115
Astro Pythia	34	Bahamas Spirit	184	BBC Ostfriesland	41	Blue Monarch	18
Astro Saturn	34	Bahia Blanca	164	BBC Rheiderland	41	Bodega Sea	162
Astro Sculptor	35	Bahia Castillo	164	BBC Weser	41	Boheme	231
Astro Sirius	35	Bahia Grande	164	Beagle Sea	162	Bonanza	107
Astro Taurus	35	Bahia Laura	164	Beatrice Schulte	205	Bonita	47
Asuka II	18	Bahia	201	Beatriz	175	Bonn Express	88
Atagosan Maru	131	Bahia	54	Beaufort Sea	170	Border	192
Atalandi	127	Bai An Hai	52	Bebatik	209	Boris Livanov	211
Atalanta	192	Bakkedal	105	Bebedouro	36	Borkum	41
Athena	13	Balder	105	Beech Galaxy	54	Bosporos	226
Athens Highway	103	Balgarka	145	Beijing 2008	226	Bossclip Trader	55
Athens Star	49	Bali Sea	96	Bekalang	209	Boston Bay	206
Athinea	48	Balkan	107	Bekulan	209	Botany Sea	162
Atlantic Blue	53	Balkan	145	Bel Taylor	222	Boularibank	235
Atlantic Breeze	231	Ballangen	106	Belaia	37	Boundary	192
Atlantic Breeze	53	Ballina	72	Belais	209	Bourgogne	60
Atlantic Cartier	82	Balmoral	20	Belanak	209	Bow Americas	162
Atlantic Companion	82	Baltic Ace	190	Belgian Reefer	152	Bow Architect	162
Atlantic Compass	82	Baltic Advance	96	Belgica	71	Bow Atlantic	162
Atlantic Concert	82	Baltic Ambition	96	Belisland	37	Bow Cape	162
Atlantic Conveyor	82	Baltic Breeze	231	Bellavia	67	Bow Cardinal	162
Atlantic Crown	53	Baltic Captain I	96	Bellona	149	Bow Cecil	162
Atlantic Diana	53	Baltic Carrier	196	Belo Horizonte	54	Bow Cedar	162
Atlantic Eagle	53	Baltic Champion	96	Beluga Constellation	37	Bow Century	162
Atlantic Frontier	53	Baltic Chief I	96	Beluga Constitution	37	Bow Chain	162
Atlantic Gemini	53	Baltic Commander I	96	Beluga Generation	37	Bow Cheetah	162
Atlantic Grace	53	Baltic Commodore	96	Beluga Graduation	37	Bow Clipper	162
Atlantic Hawk	113	Baltic Faith	96	Beluga Gratification	37	Bow Eagle	162
Atlantic Hero	133	Baltic Favour	96	Beluga Gravitation	37	Bow Europe	162
Atlantic Highway	103	Baltic Force	97	Beluga Indication	37	Bow Fagus	162
Atlantic Hope	206	Baltic Freedom	97	Beluga Intonation	37	Bow Faith	162
Atlantic Hope	53	Baltic Front	97	Beluga Participation	37	Bow Favour	162
Atlantic Leo	53	Baltic Highway	103	Beluga Persuasion	37	Bow Fertility	162
Atlantic Liberty	133	Baltic Leader	149	Beluga Profession	37	Bow Fighter	162
Atlantic Mermaid	206	Baltic Mariner	97	Beluga Promotion	37	Bow Firda	162
Atlantic Ocean	226	Baltic Marshall	97	Benarita	227	Bow Flora	162
Atlantic Olive	53	Baltic Merchant	97	Benedict Schulte	205	Bow Flower	162
Atlantic Prosperity	133	Baltic Meridian	196	Benguela Stream	206	Bow Fortune	162
Atlantic Reefer	206	Baltic Monarch	97	Benita Schulte	205	Bow Fraternity	162
Atlantic Rose	53	Baltic Moon	196	Benjamin Schulte	205	Bow Hector	162
Atlantic Spirit	131	Baltic Sea	169	Berge Arzew	44	Bow Heron	162
Atlantic Spirit	96	Baltic Sea	226	Berge Atlantic	44	Bow Hunter	162
Atlantic Star	54	Baltic Sky I	97	Berge Bonde	44	Bow Kiso	162
Atlantic Trader	42	Baltic Snow	196	Berge Commander	44	Bow Leopard	162
Atlanticborg	230	Baltic Soul	97	Berge Danuta	44	Bow Lion	163
Atlantik Frigo	152	Baltic Strait	190	Berge Frost	44	Bow Maasslot	163
Atlas Amelia	39	Baltic Sun II	97	Berge Nantong	44	Bow Maasstroom	163
Atlas Highway	103	Baltic Wave	97	Berge Ningbo	44	Bow Oceanic	163
Atlxco	131	Baltic Wave	196	Berge Pacific	44	Bow Octavia	163
Attar	99	Baltic Wind	97	Berge Racine	44	Bow Olivia	163
Auckland Star	215	Baltic Wind	196	Berge Shan	44	Bow Omaria	163
Auguste Schulte	204	Banasol	106	Berge Stahl	44	Bow Ophelia	163

Name	No.	Name	No.	Name	No.	Name	No.
Bow Orania	163	British Tenacity	40				
Bow Orelia	163	British Trader	40				
Bow Pacifico	163	British Tranquility	40				
Bow Panther	163	British Unity	40				
Bow Peace	163	British Vine	40				
Bow Pioneer	163	British Willow	40				
Bow Power	163	Britta Maersk	134				
Bow Pride	163	Bro Agnes	41				
Bow Prima	163	Bro Albert	41				
Bow Prosper	163	Bro Alexandre	41				
Bow Puma	163	Bro Alma	41				
Bow Rio	54	Bro Anna	41				
Bow Saga	163	Bro Anton	41				
Bow Santos	163	Bro Arthur	41				
Bow Sea	163	Bro Atland	41				
Bow Sirius	163	Bro Axel	41				
Bow Sky	163	Bro Caroline	41				
Bow Spring	163	Bro Catherine	41				
Bow Star	163	Bro Cecile	41				
Bow Summer	163	Bro Charlotte	41				
Bow Sun	163	Bro Deliverer	41				
Bow Viking	163	Bro Designer	41				
Braemar	20	Bro Developer	41				
Brasil Star	215	Bro Distributor	41				
Bravery Ace	131	Bro Edgar	194				
Brazil Star	166	Bro Edward	41				
Brazilian Reefer	152	Bro Elizabeth	41				
Braztrans I	62	Bro Ellen	42				
Bregen	38	Bro Elliot	42				
Bremen	26	Bro Erin	194				
Bremen Bridge	103	Bro Etienne	42				
Bremen Express	88	Bro Premium	42				
Bremen Max	74	Bro Priority	42				
Brigit Maersk	134	Bro Promotion	42				
Brilliance of the Seas	21	Bro Provider	42				
Brilliant Ace	131	Bro Sincero	42				
Brilliant Jewel	170	Broadgate	166				
Brisbane	47	Brother Glory	166				
Bristol Bay	206	Brugge Max	74				
Britain Star	62	Brugge Venture	60				
Britanis	48	Brunhilde Salamon	201				
British Chivalry	39	Bruno Salamon	184				
British Commerce	39	Brussels	60				
British Confidence	39	Bubuk	209				
British Cormorant	39	Buccleuch	166				
British Councillor	39	Bujin	149				
British Courage	39	Bulduri	110				
British Courtesy	39	Bulk Asia	229				
British Curlew	39	Bulk Avenir	37				
British Cygnet	39	Bulk Europe	229				
British Diamond	39	Bunga Bidara	128				
British Eagle	39	Bunga Delima	128				
British Emerald	39	Bunga Kantan Dua	128				
British Emissary	39	Bunga Kantan Satu	128				
British Ensign	39	Bunga Kantan Tiga	128				
British Envoy	39	Bunga Kasturi	129				
British Esteem	39	Bunga Kasturi Dua	129				
British Explorer	39	Bunga Kasturi Empat	129				
British Falcon	39	Bunga Kasturi Enam	128				
British Fidelity	39	Bunga Kasturi Lima	128				
British Gannet	39	Bunga Kasturi Tiga	128				
British Harmony	39	Bunga Kekaras	129				
British Hawthorn	39	Bunga Kelana 3	129				
British Hazel	39	Bunga Kelana 4	129				
British Holly	39	Bunga Kelana 5	129				
British Innovator	39	Bunga Kelana 6	129				
British Integrity	39	Bunga Kelana 7	130				
British Kestrel	39	Bunga Kelana 8	130				
British Laurel	39	Bunga Kelana 9	130				
British Liberty	39	Bunga Kelana Dua	129				
British Loyalty	39	Bunga Kelana Satu	129				
British Mallard	39	Bunga Kenanga	130				
British Merchant	39	Bunga Kenari	128				
British Merlin	39	Bunga Kerayong	130				
British Oak	39	Bunga Melati 3	128				
British Osprey	39	Bunga Melati 4	128				
British Pioneer	39	Bunga Melati 5	128				
British Pride	39	Bunga Melati 6	128				
British Progress	39	Bunga Melati 7	128				
British Purpose	40	Bunga Melati Dua	128				
British Robin	40	Bunga Melati Satu	128				
British Ruby	40	Bunga Pelangi Dua	128				
British Sapphire	40	Bunga Raya Dua	128				
British Security	40	Bunga Raya Satu	128				
British Serenity	40	Bunga Saga 9	128				
British Swift	40	Bunga Seroja Dua	128				

Claes Maersk	134
Clan Amazonas	188
Clan Challenger	42
Clan Rickmers	192
Clara Maersk	134
Clare	234
Clelia II	29
Clementine Maersk	134
Clifford Castle	144
Clifford Maersk	134
Clifton Bridge	104
Clipper Adventurer	26
Clipper Emperor	192
Clipper Freeway	175
Clipper Gemini	92
Clipper Glory	55
Clipper Grace	55
Clipper Harald	209
Clipper Hebe	209
Clipper Helen	210
Clipper Hermes	210
Clipper Hermod	210
Clipper Lagoon	56
Clipper Lake	55
Clipper Lancaster	55
Clipper Lancelot	55
Clipper Lasco	55
Clipper Mars	210
Clipper Melody	55
Clipper Mercury	56
Clipper Mermaid	56
Clipper Monarch	192
Clipper Moon	210
Clipper Morning	56
Clipper Neptun	210
Clipper Odysse	26
Clipper Orion	210
Clipper Posh	210
Clipper Sirius	210
Clipper Skagen	210
Clipper Sky	210
Clipper Star	210
Clipper Sterling	55
Clipper Sun	210
Clipper Talent	56
Clipper Tango	56
Clipper Target	55
Clipper Tarpon	56
Clipper Taurus	56
Clipper Tenacious	55
Clipper Terminus	56
Clipper Terra	56
Clipper Texan	55
Clipper Tivoli	55
Clipper Trust	55
Clipper Tsuji	56
Clipper Valour	55
Clipper Valour	56
Clipper Victory	210
Clipper Viking	210
Clipper	237
Clou Island	190
Clou Ocean	190
Cloudy Bay	206
Clover Ace	131
Club Med 2	30
Clymene	234
CMA CGM Acaju	188
CMA CGM Accra	191
CMA CGM Aegean	153
CMA CGM Aguila	176
CMA CGM Alabama	158
CMA CGM Alcazar	57
CMA CGM Amber	57
CMA CGM America	37
CMA CGM Anapurna	192
CMA CGM Andromeda	57
CMA CGM Anemone	153
CMA CGM Aristote	57
CMA CGM Auckland	143
CMA CGM Aztec	235
CMA CGM Azure	192
CMA CGM Bahia	177
CMA CGM Baudelaire	158
CMA CGM Beirut	87
CMA CGM Bellini	57
CMA CGM Berlioz	57
CMA CGM Bizet	57
CMA CGM Blue Whale	57
CMA CGM Brasilia	199
CMA CGM Buenos Aires	192
CMA CGM Butterfly	172
CMA CGM Camellia	57
CMA CGM Capella	158
CMA CGM Capri	57
CMA CGM Carioca	176
CMA CGM Carmen	154
CMA CGM Cartagena	229
CMA CGM Castilla	33
CMA CGM Chateau d'If	57
CMA CGM Chopin	57
CMA CGM Colombie	176
CMA CGM Comoe	143
CMA CGM Condor	176
CMA CGM Copernic	109
CMA CGM Coral	57
CMA CGM Cordillera	199
CMA CGM Corfu	42
CMA CGM Cortes	33
CMA CGM Courage	95
CMA CGM Debussy	57
CMA CGM Dolphin	57
CMA CGM Don Carlos	154
CMA CGM Don Giovanni	154
CMA CGM Ebony	143
CMA CGM Eiffel	57
CMA CGM Elbe	66
CMA CGM Esmeraldas	59
CMA CGM Esperanza	158
CMA CGM Everest	192
CMA CGM Excellence	199
CMA CGM Fidelio	57
CMA CGM Florida	57
CMA CGM Force	95
CMA CGM Fort St. Georges	57
CMA CGM Fort St. Louis	57
CMA CGM Fort St. Pierre	57
CMA CGM Fort Ste. Marie	57
CMA CGM Fortuna *	158
CMA CGM Galaxy	158
CMA CGM Galilee	32
CMA CGM Gardenia	57
CMA CGM Georgia	57
CMA CGM Herodote	57
CMA CGM Homere	57
CMA CGM Hugo	158
CMA CGM Hydra	158
CMA CGM Iguacu	143
CMA CGM Impala	57
CMA CGM Intensity	176
CMA CGM Iroko	206
CMA CGM Itajai	188
CMA CGM Ivanhoe	172
CMA CGM Jade	192
CMA CGM Jaguar	154
CMA CGM Jamaica	159
CMA CGM Junior S	57
CMA CGM Kailas	57
CMA CGM Kalamata	66
CMA CGM Kingfish	57
CMA CGM Kingston	154
CMA CGM Komodo	66
CMA CGM L'Astrolabe	154
CMA CGM L'Etoile	229
CMA CGM La Boussole	154
CMA CGM La Tour	57
CMA CGM La Traviata	57
CMA CGM Lagos	172
CMA CGM Lavender	154
CMA CGM Licorne	192
CMA CGM Lilac	57
CMA CGM Lotus	66
CMA CGM Lys	57
CMA CGM Maasai	97
CMA CGM Manet	57
CMA CGM Marlin	57
CMA CGM Matisse	57
CMA CGM Maya	57
CMA CGM Medea	57
CMA CGM Mimosa	154
CMA CGM Montenegro	102
CMA CGM Mozart	57
CMA CGM Musca	159
CMA CGM Nabucco	57
CMA CGM New Jersey	57
CMA CGM Newtonl	84
CMA CGM Niger	172
CMA CGM Nilgai	154
CMA CGM Nimba	172
CMA CGM Norma	57
CMA CGM North Africa 1	57
CMA CGM North Africa 2	57
CMA CGM Nyala	172
CMA CGM Oceano	57
CMA CGM Okapi	57
CMA CGM Okume	57
CMA CGM Onyx	192
CMA CGM Orca	57
CMA CGM Orchid	32
CMA CGM Orfeo	172
CMA CGM Oryx	67
CMA CGM Otello	57
CMA CGM Pacifico	159
CMA CGM Parati	235
CMA CGM Parsifal	154
CMA CGM Passiflore	66
CMA CGM Paulista	192
CMA CGM Pelleas	172
CMA CGM Platon	57
CMA CGM Potomac	57
CMA CGM Puccini	57
CMA CGM Puget	57
CMA CGM Qingdao	157
CMA CGM Ravel	58
CMA CGM Respect	58
CMA CGM Rigoletto	58
CMA CGM Rose	206
CMA CGM Rossini	58
CMA CGM Samba	192
CMA CGM Sambhar	37
CMA CGM Sapphire	167
CMA CGM Scala	58
CMA CGM Simba	58
CMA CGM St. Laurent	192
CMA CGM St. Martin	192
CMA CGM Straus	58
CMA CGM Swordfish	58
CMA CGM Tarpon	58
CMA CGM Tema	172
CMA CGM Thalassa	159
CMA CGM Togo	143
CMA CGM Tosca	58
CMA CGM Tulip	32
CMA CGM Tunis	224
CMA CGM Utrillo	58
CMA CGM Vanille	66
CMA CGM Vela	159
CMA CGM Verdi *	57
CMA CGM Verlaine	159
CMA CGM Vernet	159
CMA CGM Violet	58
CMA CGM Virginia	58
CMA CGM Vivaldi	58
CMA CGM Volta	172
CMA CGM Voltaire	159
CMA CGM Wagner	58
CMA CGM White Shark	58
CMA CGM Yantian	154
CMA CGM Ylang	229
CMB Biwa	59
Cold Stream	206
Colin Jacob	99
Colombian Star	215
Colombo Express	88
Colombo Star II	171
Colorado Highway	104
Colorado Voyager	50
Columbia Leader	149
Columbian Express	229
Columbine Maersk	134
Combi Dock I	92
Combi Dock III	92
Comet Ace	131
Commodore	237
Comoros Stream	206
Concord Bridge	104
Concord	237
Condor	33
Condor Arrow	100
Condor Bay	206
Conquistador	47
Constantia	74
Constantin S	199
Constitution Spirit	62
Conti Agulhas	203
Conti Asia	159
Conti Barcelona	159
Conti Benguela	203
Conti Emden	118
Conti Equator	203
Conti Esperance	159
Conti Germany	159
Conti Greenland	203
Conti Guinea	203
Conti Harmony	97
Conti Hong Kong	159
Conti Humboldt	203
Conti Jork	159
Conti Salome	159
Conti Shanghai	37
Conti Singa	37
Conti Sydney	159
Conti Valencia	159
Continental Highway	104
Continental Spirit	62
Cool Express	206
Cooper River Bridge	104
Copacabana	165
Copenhagen Express	88
Coral	16
Coral Highway	104
Coral Leader	190
Coral Mermaid	206
Coral Princess	12
Coral Sea	170
Coral Sea	226
Cordelia	32
Corinthian II	28
Cork Spirit	220
Cormorant Arrow	100
Cornelia Maersk	134
Cornelius Maersk	134
Coronado	47
Corviglia	218
Cosco Africa	50
Cosco America	50
Cosco Antwerp	51
Cosco Asia	51
Cosco Atlantic	51
Cosco Beijing	63
Cosco Brisbane	118
Cosco China	154
Cosco Chiwan	118
Cosco Dalian	51
Cosco Dammam	107
Cosco Europe	51
Cosco Felixstowe	51
Cosco Germany	154
Cosco Guangzhou	63
Cosco Hamburg	51
Cosco Hellas	63
Cosco Hong Kong	51
Cosco Indian Ocean	51
Cosco Karachi	92
Cosco Lianyungang	118
Cosco Long Beach	154
Cosco Melbourne	107
Cosco Napoli	154
Cosco Ningbo	63
Cosco Oceania	51
Cosco Pacific	51
Cosco Panama	118
Cosco Qingdao	51
Cosco Rotterdam	51
Cosco Seattle	154
Cosco Shanghai	51
Cosco Shekou	118
Cosco Shenzen	154
Cosco Singapore	51
Cosco Sydney	107
Cosco Tianjin	51
Cosco Vancouver	154
Cosco Xiamen	51
Cosco Yantian	63
Cosco Yokohama	154
Cosmic Jewel	170
Cosmic	112
Cosmos Ace	131
Cosmos Venture	131
Cospearl Lake	52
Costa Allegre	9
Costa Atlantica	9
Costa Classica	9
Costa Concordia	9
Costa Deliziosa	9
Costa Europa	9
Costa Fortuna	9
Costa Luminosa	9
Costa Magica	9
Costa Marina	9
Costa Mediterranea	9
Costa Pacifica	9
Costa Rican Star	215
Costa Romantica	9
Costa Serena	9
Costa Victoria	9
Cote d'Ivoirian Star	215
Cotinga Arrow	99
Cotswold	167
Countess	18
Courage	231
Courageous Ace	131
Courcheville	60
Courier	237
Cozumel Cement	99
CPO England	172
CPO Finland	172
CPO France	172
CPO Germany	172
CPO Italy	172
CPO Norway	172
CPO Russia	172
CPO Sweden	172
Crane Arrow	100
Cristal	16
Crown Emerald	152
Crown Garnet	152
Crown Jade	152
Crown Opal	152
Crown Princess	12
Crown Ruby	152
Crown Sapphire	152
Crown Topaz	152
Crystal Ace	131
Crystal Crown	196
Crystal Mermaid	196
Crystal Ray	190
Crystal Rose	196
Crystal Serenity	18
Crystal Symphony	18
CSAV Appennini	109
CSAV Cantabrian	157
CSAV Chicago	71
CSAV Hamburgo	42
CSAV Itaim	206
CSAV Itajai	69
CSAV Jura	109
CSAV Laja	183
CSAV Lauca	183
CSAV Lonquen	143
CSAV Lonquimay	143
CSAV Manzanillo	192
CSAV Maresias	192
CSAV Mexico	191
CSAV Moema	69
CSAV New York	42
CSAV Panamby	206
CSAV Paranagua	199
CSAV Pyrennes	109
CSAV Rahue	157
CSAV Ranquil	157
CSAV Rauten	157
CSAV Renaico	157
CSAV Rio Aysen	167
CSAV Rio Baker	235
CSAV Rio Grande	167
CSAV Rio Imperial	167
CSAV Rio Lontue	92
CSAV Rio Maule	235
CSAV Rio Nevado	167
CSAV Rio Petrohue	199
CSAV Rio Puelo	235
CSAV Rio Rapel	32
CSAV Rio Tolten	235
CSAV Romeral	118
CSAV Rotterdam	206
CSAV Rungue	118
CSAV Rupanco	157
CSAV San Antonio	195
CSAV Santos	92
CSAV Sao Paulo	224
CSAV Teno	201
CSAV Tianjin	199
CSAV Totoral	188
CSAV Tubul	108
CSAV Venezuela I	84
CSAV Yokohama	177
CSCC Shanghai	190
CSCC Tianjin	190
CSCL Africa	52
CSCL Asia	52
CSCL Barcelona	188
CSCL Chiwan	52
CSCL Dalian	52
CSCL Europe	66
CSCL Felixstowe	52
CSCL Fos	188
CSCL Fuzhou	154
CSCL Genoa	188
CSCL Hamburg	52
CSCL Jakarta	188
CSCL Kobe	154
CSCL Le Havre	66
CSCL Long Beach	66
CSCL Los Angeles	154
CSCL Melbourne	52
CSCL Montevideo	52
CSCL Napoli	188
CSCL New York	52
CSCL Ningbo	52
CSCL Panama	52
CSCL Pusan	66
CSCL Qingdao	52
CSCL Rotterdam	52
CSCL San Jose	52
CSCL Santiago	52
CSCL Sao Paulo	52
CSCL Seattle I	84
CSCL Sydney	52
CSCL Tianjin	52
CSCL Vancouver	53
CSCL Zeebrbrugge	53
CSK Beilun	61
Cumbria	167
Cygnus Reefer	152
Cygnus Voyager	79
Cymbeline	234
Cypress Pass	38
Da Fu	214
Da He	51
Da Hua	214
Da Qiang	214
Da Zhong	215
Daewoo Brave	93
Daewoo Challenge	93
Daffodil	97
Dafnis	165

Name	No.	Name	No.	Name	No.	Name	No.	Name	No.	Name	No.
Mount Fuji	203	MSC Carouge	160	MSC India	122	MSC Mia Summer	124	MSC Sola	126	Navion Hispania	220
Mount Green	203	MSC Catania	168	MSC Ines	122	MSC Michaela	124	MSC Sophie	126	Navion Marita	221
Mount Hope	203	MSC Charleston	173	MSC Ingrid	122	MSC Michele	124	MSC Soraya	126	Navion Norvegia	221
Mount Karava	203	MSC Chelsea	120	MSC Iris	122	MSC Mira	155	MSC Splendida	18	Navion Oceania	221
Mount McKinney	203	MSC Chiara	120	MSC Ivana	122	MSC Mirella	124	MSC Stefania	126	Navion Oslo	221
Mount Olympus	203	MSC Chicago	173	MSC Jade	122	MSC Monica	124	MSC Stella	126	Navion Savonita	221
Mount Rainier	203	MSC Chile	110	MSC Japan	63	MSC Monterey	161	MSC Sudan	64	Navion Scandia	221
Mount Robson	203	MSC Chitra	120	MSC Jasmine	122	MSC Musica	18	MSC Suez	126	Navion Stavanger	221
Mount Victoria	203	MSC Christina	120	MSC Jeanne	122	MSC Namibia	64	MSC Sukaiyna	126	Navion Svenita	221
Mozu Arrow	101	MSC Clorinda	120	MSC Jemima	122	MSC Natal	229	MSC Susanna	126	Navion Torinita	221
MS Simon	49	MSC Colombia	168	MSC Jenny	122	MSC Natalia	124	MSC Sweden	126	Navix Azalea	133
MS Sophie	49	MSC Cordoba	160	MSC Jessica	122	MSC Nederland	125	MSC Tampa	65	Naxihe	51
MSC Acapulco	32	MSC Corinna	120	MSC Jilhan	122	MSC Nerissa	125	MSC Tanzania	110	Naxos	39
MSC Accra	119	MSC Corsica	120	MSC Joanna	122	MSC New York	37	MSC Tasmania	126	NCC Abha	144
MSC Adele	119	MSC Cristiana	120	MSC Jordan	122	MSC Nicole	125	MSC Texas	161	NCC Arar	144
MSC Adriana	119	MSC Cristobal	199	MSC Judith	122	MSC Nikita	125	MSC Tia	126	NCC Asir	144
MSC Africa	119	MSC Dalton	143	MSC Katherine Ann	122	MSC Nilgun	125	MSC Tina	126	NCC Baha	144
MSC Agata	119	MSC Damla	120	MSC Kenya	110	MSC Noa	125	MSC Toba	64	NCC Dammam	144
MSC Alabama	63	MSC Daniela	120	MSC Kerry	122	MSC Normandie	125	MSC Togo	64	NCC Haiel	144
MSC Alessia	160	MSC Dartford	143	MSC Kim	122	MSC Nuria	125	MSC Tokyo	173	NCC Hijaz	144
MSC Alexa	119	MSC Darwin	168	MSC Kiwi	33	MSC Olga	125	MSC Tomoko	126	NCC Jubail	144
MSC Alexandra	119	MSC Davos	69	MSC Korea	64	MSC Opera	18	MSC Toronto	173	NCC Mekka	144
MSC Almeria	143	MSC Debra	120	MSC Krittika	166	MSC Orchestra	18	MSC Turchia	69	NCC Najd	144
MSC Alpana	119	MSC Deila *	120	MSC Krystal	122	MSC Oriane	125	MSC Tuscany	64	NCC Qassim	144
MSC Alyssa	119	MSC Denisse	120	MSC Kyoto	64	MSC Ornella	125	MSC Uganda	110	NCC Rabigh	144
MSC America	119	MSC Didem	120	MSC Lana	122	MSC Oslo	125	MSC Ukraine	126	NCC Riyad	144
MSC Amsterdam	32	MSC Diego	120	MSC Lara	122	MSC Palermo	110	MSC Ulsan	177	NCC Sudair	144
MSC Amy	119	MSC Don Giovanni	120	MSC Laura	122	MSC Pamela	125	MSC Uruguay	199	NCC Tabuk	144
MSC Anafi	119	MSC Donata	120	MSC Lauren	122	MSC Paola	125	MSC Valencia	71	NCC Tihama	144
MSC Anahita	119	MSC Dymphna	120	MSC Laurence	122	MSC Parana	65	MSC Vanessa	126	NDS Prodigy	148
MSC Anastasia	119	MSC Eagle	66	MSC Lausanne	161	MSC Paris	71	MSC Venezia	126	Nedlloyd Adriana	137
MSC Ancona	119	MSC Edith	120	MSC Lea	122	MSC Patricia	125	MSC Venezuela	168	Nedlloyd Africa	143
MSC Andalucia II	165	MSC Edna	120	MSC Leanne	123	MSC Peggy	125	MSC Venice	64	Nedlloyd America	143
MSC Angela	119	MSC Egypt	69	MSC Leigh	123	MSC Perle	125	MSC Veronique	126	Nedlloyd Asia	143
MSC Aniello	119	MSC Ela	120	MSC Leila	123	MSC Peru	65	MSC Vienna	157	Nedlloyd Barentsz	137
MSC Annamaria	119	MSC Elena	120	MSC Levina	123	MSC Pilar	125	MSC Vittoria	126	Nedlloyd de Liefde	137
MSC Annick	119	MSC Eleni	120	MSC Lieselotte	123	MSC Pina	125	MSC Viviana	126	Nedlloyd Drake	137
MSC Ans	119	MSC Eleonora	121	MSC Linzie	123	MSC Pioneer	125	MSC Volos	127	Nedlloyd Europa	143
MSC Antonia	119	MSC Eliana	121	MSC Lirica	18	MSC Poesia	18	MSC Voyager	127	Nedlloyd Evita	143
MSC Antwerp	63	MSC Eloise	121	MSC Lisa	123	MSC Poh Lin	125	MSC Washington	64	Nedlloyd Honshu	143
MSC Arabia	119	MSC Emma	121	MSC Lisbon	173	MSC Prague	157	MSC Wellington	118	Nedlloyd Hudson	137
MSC Armonia	18	MSC Endurance	121	MSC London	227	MSC Prospect	33	MSC Xian	155	Nedlloyd Juliana	137
MSC Asli	119	MSC England	177	MSC Lorena	123	MSC Provider	33	MSC Yokohama	64	Nedlloyd Marita	137
MSC Astrid	119	MSC Erminia	121	MSC Loretta	123	MSC Rachele	125	MSC Zanzibar	127	Nedlloyd Maxima	143
MSC Asya	119	MSC Esthi	121	MSC Lucia	123	MSC Rafaela	125	MSC Zurich	33	Nedlloyd Mercator	137
MSC Atlantic	119	MSC Eugenia	121	MSC Lucy	123	MSC Rania	125	MSC Antares	155	Nedlloyd Oceania	143
MSC Augusta	119	MSC Everest	137	MSC Ludovica	123	MSC Rebecca	125	Mulberry	98	Nedlloyd Tasman	137
MSC Aurelie	119	MSC Eyra	121	MSC Lugano	123	MSC Regina	125	Myrto	49	Nedlloyd Teslin	143
MSC Aurora	119	MSC Fabienne	121	MSC Luisa	123	MSC Rhone	125	Mystic	47	Nedlloyd Valentina	137
MSC Austria	63	MSC Fantasia	18	MSC Madeleine	123	MSC Rimini	126	Nada V	149	Nele Maersk	137
MSC Ayala	119	MSC Favolosa	18	MSC Maeva	123	MSC Rita	126	Nadezhda	114	Nelson Star	215
MSC Baleares	119	MSC Federica	121	MSC Magali	123	MSC Roberta	126	Naesborg	67	Neo Energy	227
MSC Bali	119	MSC Fiammetta	121	MSC Magnifica	18	MSC Roma	173	Nagoya Bay	208	Neptune Ace	132
MSC Baltic	66	MSC Finland	121	MSC Mahima	166	MSC Romania II	64	Najran	228	Neptune Glory	185
MSC Banu	119	MSC Firenze	239	MSC Malacca	140	MSC Ronit	126	Nakskov Maersk	137	Neptune Voyager	50
MSC Barbara	120	MSC Flaminia	160	MSC Malaga	161	MSC Rosa M	126	Nala Delmas	59	Neste	147
MSC Basel	110	MSC Florentina	121	MSC Malaysia	143	MSC Rosaria	126	Namur	60	Netsanet	75
MSC Beatrice	120	MSC Floriana	121	MSC Malin	123	MSC Rossella	126	Nancy Knutsen	107	Nevskiy Prospect	210
MSC Beijing	173	MSC Florida	193	MSC Malta	69	MSC Rugby	227	Nandu Arrow	101	New Ability	180
MSC Belem	33	MSC France	69	MSC Mandraki	64	MSC Sabrina	126	Napier Star	215	New Ace	180
MSC Belgium	120	MSC Francesca	121	MSC Mandy	123	MSC Salerno	143	Nara	170	New Activity	180
MSC Belize	87	MSC Freedom	121	MSC Manila	123	MSC Samantha	126	Narmada Spirit	220	New Advance	180
MSC Benedetta	120	MSC Gabriella	121	MSC Manu	123	MSC Sandra	126	Narodny Bridge	210	New Alliance	180
MSC Bengal	155	MSC Gemma	155	MSC Mara	123	MSC Santhya	126	Nashwan	144	New Ambition	180
MSC Bilboa	71	MSC Geneva	160	MSC Marathon	66	MSC Sarah	126	Nassau Spirit	220	New Amity	180
MSC Black Sea	165	MSC Germany	63	MSC Marbella	173	MSC Sardinia	227	Nassauborg	230	New Argosy	180
MSC Borneo	120	MSC Gianna	121	MSC Maria	123	MSC Sariska	126	Natalie Bolten	39	New Brisk	132
MSC Boston	37	MSC Gina	121	MSC Maria Elena	123	MSC Scandinavia	87	Nataly	114	New Century	180
MSC Brasilia	227	MSC Giorgia	121	MSC Maria Laura	123	MSC Scotland	126	National Geographic Endeavour	29	New Confidence *	221
MSC Bremen	177	MSC Giovanna	121	MSC Maria Pia	123	MSC Seine	126	New Delhi Express	90
MSC Brianna	120	MSC Giulia	121	MSC Marianna	123	MSC Selin	126	National Geographic Explorer	29	New Dynamic	147
MSC Brooke	120	MSC Grace	121	MSC Marina	123	MSC Sena	126	New England	230
MSC Bruxelles	173	MSC Greece	33	MSC Marta	124	MSC Seoul	126	National Geographic Polaris	29	New Fortuner	180
MSC Bulgaria	120	MSC Hailey	121	MSC Martina	124	MSC Serena	126	New Nada	149
MSC Busan	173	MSC Hanne	121	MSC Marylena	124	MSC Shanghai	173	Nautic	97	New Orleans Express	90
MSC Caitlin	120	MSC Harmony	199	MSC Matilde	124	MSC Shannon	126	Nautica	18	New Spirit	180
MSC Calcutta	120	MSC Heidi	122	MSC Maureen	124	MSC Shaula	126	Navigator of the Seas	22	New Valor	180
MSC Camille	120	MSC Himalaya	122	MSC Maya	124	MSC Sheila	126	Navigo	42	New Venture	180
MSC Canberra	120	MSC Hina	122	MSC Mediterranean	124	MSC Shenzen	143	Navion Akarita	220	New Victory	180
MSC Candice	120	MSC Hobart	155	MSC Mee May	124	MSC Sicily	64	Navion Anglia	220	New Vision	170
MSC Caracas	177	MSC Hong Kong	143	MSC Mekong	124	MSC Siena	239	Navion Bergen	220	New Vitality	180
MSC Carina	120	MSC Ibiza	122	MSC Melissa	124	MSC Sierra	64	Navion Britannia	220	New York Express	64
MSC Carla	120	MSC Ilaria	122	MSC Mendosa	191	MSC Silvana	126	Navion Clipper	220	New York Star	49
MSC Carmen	120	MSC Ilona	161	MSC Meraviglia	18	MSC Sindy	126	Navion Europa	220	Newcastle Max	75
MSC Carol	120	MSC Imma	122	MSC Messina	168	MSC Sinfonia	18	Navion Fennia	220	Newforest	168
MSC Carolina	120	MSC Immacolata	122	MSC Mexico	64	MSC Socotra	126	Navion Gothenburg	220	Newport Bridge	104

255

Name	Pg	Name	Pg	Name	Pg	Name	Pg	Name	Pg	Name	Pg
TS Pusan	199	Vega Star	198	Walka Mlodych	188	WilliamBritish Beech	39	Yacht Express	68	York Castle	145
TS Qingdao	43	Vega Trader	134	Waltz	93	Williamsburg Bridge	105	Yamato	105	Yorktown Express	92
TS Shenzhen	70	Vega Voyager	50	Wan Hai 301	234	Wilmina	237	Yamatogawa	105	Younara Glory	185
TS Singapore	70	Vega	34	Wan Hai 302	234	Wind Frost	208	Yamuna Spirit	221	Yu He	52
TS Taichung	202	Velopoula	74	Wan Hai 303	234	Wind Spirit	8	Yangtze River	143	Yuan He	52
TS Taipei	70	Venice Bridge	105	Wan Hai 305	234	Wind Star	8	Yasaka Bay	208	Yue He	52
TS Xingang	43	Venice	48	Wan Hai 306	234	Wind Surf	8	Yeoman Bank	79	Yufusan	134
Tsing Ma Bridge	105	Ventura	12	Wan Hai 307	234	Windfield	101	Yeoman Bontrup	79	Yuguhe	52
Tsingtao Express	91	Ventura	48	Wan Hai 311	234	Windsor Castle	145	Yeoman Bridge	79	Yukon Star	194
Tsunomine	133	Veracruz Express	92	Wan Hai 312	234	Windsor Knutsen	107	Yeoman Brook	176	Yuri Senkevich	211
Tsuru Arrow	99	Veracruz I	190	Wan Hai 313	234	Wisla	188	YM America	239	Yuriy Arshenevskiy	115
Tsurumi	152	Vereina	202	Wan Hai 315	234	Wisteria Ace	133	YM Anping	161	Yuriy Dolorukiy	115
Tuchal	99	Vergina II	227	Wan Hai 316	234	Wladyslaw Orkan	186	YM Asia	239	Zaandam	11
Tuchkov Bridge	211	Verila	146	Wan Hai 317	234	Wolgastern	194	YM Bamboo	239	Zagros	99
Tula	213	Verrazano Bridge	105	Wan Hai 501	234	World Lake	46	YM Colombo	155	Zambezi Star	194
Turama	30	Vesteralen	16	Wan Hai 503	234	World Lion	46	YM Cosmos	239	Zanis Griva	111
Turandot	233	Vibeke	38	Wan Hai 506	234	World Luck	46	YM Cultivation	239	Zapolyarye	115
Turid Knutsen	107	Viborg	116	Wan Hai 507	234	World Spirit	133	YM Cypress	239	Zaurak Star	198
Turin Express	32	Victor Konetsky	211	Wan Hai 508	234	Wren Arrow	101	YM Earth	239	Zaven	99
Tver	213	Victoria Bridge	105	Wan Hai 509	234	Wugang Asia	169	YM East	239	Zeinat 2	49
Tverskoy Bridge	211	Victorius	75	Wan Hai 510	234	Wugang Atlantic	169	YM Efficency	239	Zenith	22
Tzarevetz	146	Victory	56	Wan Hai 601	234	Wugang Orient	169	YM Elixir	239	Zenith Leader	169
UACC Al Medina	228	Victory Ace	133	Wan Hai 602	234	Wybelsum	41	YM Eminence	239	Zetland	169
UACC Ibn Al Atheer	228	Victory III	227	Wan Hai 603	234	Xanadu	48	YM Enhancer	239	Zhen He	52
UACC Ibn Al Haitham	228	Victory	92	Wan Hai 605	234	Xanadu	72	YM Equality	239	Zhong He	52
UACC Ibn Sina	228	Vidzeme	111	Wanhe	51	Xiang He	51	YM Europe	239	Zhuang He	52
UBC Santa Marta	93	Vigdis Knutsen	107	Warbah	109	Xibohe	51	YM Fortune	239	Ziemia Chelminska	188
UBC Stavanger	93	Viking Star	215	Warmia	188	Xin Bei Lun	53	YM Fountain	239	Ziemia Cieszynska	188
UBC Tampico	93	Viktor Tkachyov	115	Warnow Beluga	43	Xin Beijing	53	YM Glory	239	Ziemia Gnieznienska	188
UBC Tokyo	93	Ville d'Aquarius	59	Warnow Dolphin	43	Xin Chang Sha	53	YM Great	239	Ziemia Gornoslaska	188
Ubud	46	Ville d'Orion	59	Warnow Porpoise	43	Xin Chang Shu	53	YM Green	239	Ziemia Lodzka	188
Ugale	111	Ville de Mars	59	Warnow Vaquita	43	Xin Chi Wan	53	YM Hamburg	169	Ziemia Suwalska	188
Umiak I	79	Ville de Taurus	161	Warta	188	Xin Chong Qing	53	YM Hiroshima	87	Ziemia Tarnowska	188
Umm Bab	35	Vincent Thomas Bridge	105	Washington Express	92	Xin Da Lian	53	YM Ibiza	161	Ziemia Zamojska	188
Undine	233	Vine	169	Washington Highway	105	Xin Dan Dong	53	YM Kaohsiung	169	Zim Asia	171
Universal Brave	48	Vinland	227	Washington Senator	161	Xin Fang Cheng	53	YM March	239	Zim Atlantic	171
Universal Crown	96	Vinni	38	Washington Voyager	50	Xin Fei Zhou	53	YM Mersin	70	Zim Barcelona	171
Universal Hope	96	Viola Gorthon	224	Washusan	134	Xin Fu Zhou	53	YM Milano	66	Zim Beijing	155
Universal Peace	96	Violetta	70	Waterford	169	Xin Hai Kou	53	YM Moji	169	Zim California	166
Universal Prime	48	Vipava	70	Waterman N	47	Xin Hong Kong	53	YM New Jersey	239	Zim Canada	171
Universal Queen	96	Virana	37	Wealth Reefer	208	Xin Huang Pu	53	YM Ningbo	67	Zim China	171
Universal Spirit	133	Virginia Bridge	105	Weaver Arrow	101	Xin Jin Zhou	53	YM North	239	Zim Europa	171
Uniwersytet Slaski	188	Virgo Leader	152	WEC Vermeer	107	Xin Lian Yun Gang	53	YM Orchid	239	Zim Genova	166
Ural	46	Visea	99	Wehr Blankensee	235	Xin Los Angeles	53	YM Osaka	70	Zim Haifa	171
Urals Princess	99	Vision of the Seas	22	Wehr Elbe	235	Xin Mei Zhou	53	YM Pine	239	Zim Hong Kong	171
Urals Star	99	Vision Star	28	Wehr Weser	235	Xin Nan Sha	53	YM Plum	239	Zim Iberia	171
Ursula Delmas	59	Vistamar	28	Weichselstern	194	Xin Nan Tong	53	YM Portland	70	Zim India	169
Uruguay Star	215	Vitosha	146	Weisshorn	237	Xin Ning Bo	53	YM Prominence	239	Zim Israel	171
USL Condor	240	VL Malibu	237	Wellington Express	92	Xin Ou Zhou	53	YM Prosperity	239	Zim Italia	171
USL Kiwi	237	Vladimir Tikhonov	211	Wellington Star	216	Xin Pu Dong	53	YM Rightness	240	Zim Jamaica	171
Usma	111	Vliet Trader	43	Weser Stahl	205	Xin Qin Huang Dao	53	YM Seattle	66	Zim Kingston I	86
Ute Oltmann	177	Vobster	99	Westerdam	11	Xin Qing Dao	53	YM Shanghai	169	Zim Korea	171
Utopia Ace	133	VOC Gallant	92	Westerdeich	191	Xin Quan Zhou	53	YM Singapore	66	Zim Livorno	166
Utviken	228	Voge Eva	229	Westerhamm	191	Xin Ri Zhou	53	YM South	240	Zim Mediterranean	166
Uzava	111	Voge Felix	229	Westerhever	191	Xin Shan Tou	53	YM Subic	202	Zim New York	65
Vaafi	99	Voge Master	229	Westermoor	191	Xin Shanghai	53	YM Success	240	Zim Pacific	171
Valbella	194	Voge Paul	229	Westermuhlen	191	Xin She Kou	53	YM Sun	240	Zim Panama	169
Valbella	70	Voge Prestige	229	Western Highway	105	Xin Su Zhou	53	YM Taichung	67	Zim Piraeus	65
Valdivia	70	Voge Prosperity	229	Western Wave	39	Xin Tai Cang	53	YM Tianjin	161	Zim Pusan	169
Valencia Bridge	105	Voge Renate	229	Westertal	191	Xin Tian Jin	53	YM Uberty	240	Zim Qingdao	171
Valencia Carrier	67	Voge West	229	Westfalia Express	169	Xin Wei Hai	53	YM Ultimate	240	Zim Rio Grande	66
Valencia Express	91	Vogebulker	229	Westfield	101	Xin Wu Han	53	YM Unison	240	Zim Santos	86
Valentina	70	Vogecarrier	229	Westmed II	65	Xin Xia Men	53	YM Unity	240	Zim Sao Paulo II	194
Valerie	61	Vogerunner	229	Westway	171	Xin Ya Zhou	53	YM Upward	240	Zim Savannah	156
Valparaiso Star	215	Vogesailor	229	White Sea	171	Xin Yan Tai	53	YM Utmost	240	Zim Shanghai	65
Valpolicella	145	Vogetrader	229	Whitney Bay	208	Xin Yan Tian	53	YM Utopia	240	Zim Shekou	166
Van Dyck	145	Vogevoyager	229	Widukind	225	Xin Yang Pu	53	YM Vancouver	66	Zim Shenzhen	169
Vancouver Bridge	105	Vola 1	146	Wieniawski	186	Xin Yang Shan	53	YM Virtue	240	Zim U.S.A.	171
Varden	129	Volans Leader	152	Wigry	188	Xin Yang Zhou	53	YM Wealth	240	Zim Virginia	171
Varzuga	115	Volendam	11	Wilana	237	Xin Ying Kou	53	YM West	240	Zim Xiamen	169
Vasiliy Dinkov	211	Voyager	202	Wild Cosmos	153	Xin Zhan Jiang	53	YM Yantian	66	Zim Yokohama	171
Vecchio Bridge	105	Voyager of the Seas	22	Wild Heather	153	Xin Zhang Zhou	53	YM Zenith	240	Zoja I	111
Vecht Trader	43	Vulturnus	145	Wild Jasmine	153	Xinsheng Hai	52	Yohjin	190	Zoja II	111
Veendam	11	Wadag II	188	Wild Lotus	153	Xinyuan Hai	38	Yohteisan	134	Zuiderdam	11
Vega III	38	Wafrah	109	Wild Peony	153	Xpedition	22	Yong Xing	186	Zuma	48
Vega Leader	152	Wafrah	144	Wilhelm Schulte	205	Ya He	51	Yordan Lutibrodski	146		
Vega Spirit	230	Waikiki	48	Willi Rickmers	194			Yordanka Nikolova	146		
Vega Spring	230			Willi Salamon	185			York	169		